Contributions to Finance and Accounting

The book series 'Contributions to Finance and Accounting' features the latest research from research areas like financial management, investment, capital markets, financial institutions, FinTech and financial innovation, accounting methods and standards, reporting, and corporate governance, among others. Books published in this series are primarily monographs and edited volumes that present new research results, both theoretical and empirical, on a clearly defined topic. All books are published in print and digital formats and disseminated globally. This book series is indexed in Scopus.

Duncan Smith

Money Laundering, Terrorist Financing and Virtual Assets

Cases and Materials

Springer

Duncan Smith
Oberanven, Luxembourg

ISSN 2730-6038 ISSN 2730-6046 (electronic)
Contributions to Finance and Accounting
ISBN 978-3-031-59841-8 ISBN 978-3-031-59842-5 (eBook)
https://doi.org/10.1007/978-3-031-59842-5

This Springer imprint is published by the registered company Springer Nature Switzerland AG
The registered company address is: Gewerbestrasse 11, 6330 Cham, Switzerland

Foreword

The quantity of money laundering, as with corruption and other economic crimes, is difficult to estimate with accuracy. However, academics and practitioners agree on the following distinctive features of money laundering.

The first is that it involves significant amounts of money. A study by the United Nations on Drugs and Crime estimates the volume in a range between 2.7% and 5% of global GDP.

The underlying criminal activities behind these estimates are diverse and dynamic. A recent study by Transcrime describes ten such activities, including traditional crimes, such as drug and human trafficking, counterfeiting, gambling, and tobacco smuggling. But there are more and new trends, such as trade mis-invoicing, illicit mining, cybercrime, environmental crime, antiques smuggling, and the use of crypto-currencies for illicit payments and transactions. The criminal organizations behind these illicit activities are adaptable in nature and tend to conduct such activities simultaneously, shifting focus according to profit margins, demand for goods, and other considerations.

The second consensus is that criminal organizations prioritize enjoying the proceeds of their criminal enterprise. They invest significant efforts in schemes to legitimize illicit gains avoiding detection and sanctions. Criminal organizations are constantly perfecting methods to ensure the transformation of illicit resources into legal assets. Sectors of choice to invest the proceeds of crime are wide and varied: construction, finance, the hospitality industry—hotels, bars, restaurants—and art, as well as those sectors where informality is significant.

The third consensus is the high risk for the stability of political systems and well-functioning markets. As the UNODC points out, organized crime and weak and failing states have a symbiotic relationship and "the more the State is absent or deficient in the provision of legal employment and public goods, the more communities are susceptible to becoming dependent on and supporters of criminal organizations." The European Commission notes how organized crime funnels illicit funds into the legal economy, not only to maximize profit, but also to "facilitate and conceal ongoing illicit activities, launder illicit proceeds, perpetrate fraud, exert control . . ., or strategically influence local politics and public administration."

The financial sector and banks are at the crossroads of these issues. Not only because they are the first line of defense in protecting the legal economy from illicit funds, but also because the world is financially integrated. Therefore, illicit financial flows are not only domestic but also global. As the IMF argues, weak AML/CFT frameworks facilitate legitimizing illicit funds and may have a macroeconomic impact.

Hence the importance of international standards to ensure countries understand the specific risks in their jurisdictions, adopt necessary measures, and cooperate with other jurisdictions to prevent and prosecute money laundering and its predicate offenses.

This book is an excellent contribution to the discussion. It provides the needed conceptual framework to understand the multifaceted nature of money laundering. Along with the traditional schemes, it also provides an insight into current trends in illicit activities—such as crypto-currency schemes and NFTs. This is combined with an interesting list of recent cases from different jurisdictions, which covers some of the most significant ones in terms of volume and impact, and those involving crypto-currencies.

Duncan Smith's book provides a great blend of theory and practice, providing a better understanding of the complex phenomena of money laundering, the centrality of the banking sector, and the tools we need to strengthen the AML/CFT framework.

Washington, DC Roberto de Michele

Acknowledgments

This book adds to my earlier economic crime books (both published by Springer):

(i) Promoting Integrity in the Work of International Organisations: Minimising Fraud and Corruption in Projects
(ii) Fraud and Corruption: Cases and Materials

This one covers different (but in many cases, related) white-collar crimes. I hope practitioners and students can use the book to improve current (and even find new, alternative) ways to deter, prevent, detect, and resolve them.

As always, I am very grateful to my family (daughters Kirsty, Ella, and Laura and wife Joanne) for their love, help, and support, especially during and after the serious medical issues that have affected the family—any proceeds that I receive are passed to Headway, the excellent brain injury charity based in the UK.

The suggestion of Rev. Jim Cox to add to and publish my handwritten notes after my serious cycling accident in 2017 (resulting in book #1 above) remains a notable turning point in my recovery leading to these previously unimagined publications—I am forever grateful for his friendship and suggestion.

Having recently taken (early) retirement, I am grateful for the suggestions of former EIB colleagues Andrea Perin and Valerie Hakmann-Pare, as well for the review/input of Robert Schofield and suggestions of Declan O'Hannrachain.

The errors are mine and mine alone—major parts of the text are reproduced from public sources, so please check for updates for corrections/developments. As far as I am aware, the information is correct as at January 1, 2024.

Contents

Abbreviations and Acronyms

AML	Anti-money laundering
AMLA	Anti-Money Laundering Authority (Europe)
AUSTRAC	Australian Transaction Reports and Analysis Centre
BMP	Best market practice
CDPP	Commonwealth Director of Public Prosecutions (Australia)
CPS	Crown Prosecution Service (UK)
DoJ	Department of Justice (US)
EC	European Commission
EBA	European Banking Authority
EIB	European Investment Bank
EU	European Union
FATF	Financial Action Task Force
FBI	Federal Bureau of Investigation (US)
FCA	Financial Conduct Authority (UK)
FINCEN	Financial Crimes Enforcement Network (US)
FIU	Financial Intelligence Unit
IFA	Institute of Financial Accountants (UK)
IMF	International Monetary Fund
IRS	Inland Revenue Service (US)
KYC	Know-Your-Customer
LLC	Limited Liability Company
MAS	Monetary Authority of Singapore
ML	Money laundering
MSB	Money Service Business
OECD	Organisation for Economic Co-operation and Development
OCCRP	Organised Crime and Reporting Project
OFSI	Office of Financial Sanctions Implementation (UK)
OFAC	Office of Foreign Assets Control (US)
OLAF	Office contre la Lutte Anti-Fraud (Europe)
OPBAS	Office for Professional Body AML Supervision (UK)

PNF	Parquet National Financier, French prosecutor of financial crime (France)
PBS	Professional Body Supervisors
POCA	Proceeds of Crime Act
RBA	Risk-based approach
SAR	Suspicious Activity Report
SEC	Securities and Exchange Commission (US)
SFO	Serious Fraud Office (UK)
TF	Terrorist financing
UN	United Nations
UNODC	United Nations Office on Drugs and Crime
VAT	Value added tax
VA	Virtual assets
VASP	Virtual Assets Service Provider
WEF	World Economic Forum

Part I
Introduction and Background

Chapter 1
Introduction

1.1 What Is Money Laundering?

Once criminals have illicitly obtained large quantities of funds by fraud, corruption, selling drugs or other (usually economic) crime, they seek to "launder" the funds to confuse and mislead the authorities to "clean" it, thus making it less traceable and identifiable as the proceeds of criminality and the funds more usable for their own benefit. While laundering the assets/money means passing them through complex and, if possible international, financial processes, the clean funds can then be used in apparently legitimate business or personal transactions.

As seen later, the benefits of money laundering extend not just to those smuggling (and being paid for) drugs but more widely to other criminals such as fraudsters and organized crime gangs who use national and international processes to mask the money's origin.

1.2 Which International Institutions are Endeavouring to Combat Money Laundering?

i. **United Nations (UN)**

The UN is the formal body by which all nation states agree and monitor internationally binding objectives. The UN Office on Drugs and Crime (UNODC) stated in "Questions, Answers and Facts about Money Laundering":[1]

A: . . . enterprise criminals of every sort, from drug traffickers to stock fraudsters to corporate embezzlers and commodity smugglers, must launder money for two

[1] https://www.imolin.org/imolin/gpml.html#:~:text=The%201988%20UN%20Convention%20against,are%20fully%20implementing%20its%20measures

D. Smith, *Money Laundering, Terrorist Financing and Virtual Assets*, Contributions to Finance and Accounting, https://doi.org/10.1007/978-3-031-59842-5_1

reasons. The first is that the money trail itself can become evidence; the second is that the money can be the target of investigation and seizure. The operational principles of money laundering are as follows: first, moving the funds from direct association with the crime; second, disguising the trail to foil pursuit; and, third, making the money available to the criminal once again with its origins hidden from view.

Q: How much money is laundered every year and how much is recovered by law enforcement?

A: Estimates have ranged as high as $300 billion to $500 billion a year. Law enforcement authorities recover about $500 million in a good year . . .

Q: What are the consequences of money laundering activities for national economies?

A: Money laundering undermines international efforts towards free and competitive markets, and the development of national economies:

It distorts the functioning of markets: money laundering transactions can increase the demand for cash, create exchange rate volatility and generate unfair competition.

It damages credibility and therefore the stability of financial markets: bank collapses related to organized crime activities can have a domino effect on the financial system of individual countries or regions.

Small States are particularly vulnerable to money laundering. The economic power generated by outlaw activities provides criminal organizations with leverage on small economies. The absence of appropriate controls, or of the capacity to enforce them, provides de facto impunity to criminals . . . [which in turn undermines a country's rule of law and effective government.]

Q: What should the international community do?

A: The members of the international community have agreed to comply with the existing international instruments currently governing money laundering by the year 2003.[2] Of particular importance is adherence to the provisions of the 1988 United Nations Convention against Illicit Traffic in Narcotic Drugs and Psychotropic Substances. But the international community needs to continue to question the way banks are defined. Should they be chartered by Governments in order to tighten controls? How should they be regulated? Should we allow companies to be formed in places where they have no apparent purpose connected with normal commercial activities, or whose owners may conceal their identity? An emphasis must be placed on systemic reforms, rather than specific tinkering with the odd regulation. The harmonization of regulatory regimes covering financial havens, trusts, shell companies and banks should be a main goal.

Q: What can the UN Global Programme against Money Laundering (GPML) do to help?

[2] Although this text is more than 20 years old, it is as relevant now as it was then—funds obtained by criminals are laundered to mask their origins and reduce the risk of seizure by law enforcement.

A: Developing countries, and those with economies in transition, are in particular need of technical assistance and training. Local law enforcement cannot crack down on complex financial crimes unless they know the tricks of the money launderer. The UN Global Programme against Money Laundering is ready to provide expert training, assistance, public awareness and research tools on the art of financial investigations, prosecutions, best banking practices and financial regulations for government, business, law enforcement and judicial professionals.

(ii) **Financial Action Task Force (FATF)**

FATF is the global money laundering and terrorist financing watchdog. It sets international standards that aim to prevent these illegal activities and the harm they cause to society.[3]

FATF has primary responsibility for developing worldwide standards for AML/CFT. It works closely with other organizations, including the IMF, the World Bank, the United Nations, and FATF-style regional bodies (FSRBs).

To help national governments set up effective AML/CFT regimes, the FATF issues recommendations covering the criminal justice system, the financial sector, certain non-financial businesses and professions, transparency, and mechanisms of international cooperation. Together with the FSRBs, the IMF and World Bank, the FATF monitors countries' compliance with these recommendations.[4]

FATF states that money laundering is:

... the processing of ... criminal proceeds to disguise their illegal origin. This process is of critical importance, as it enables the criminal to enjoy these profits without jeopardising their source.

Illegal arms sales, smuggling, and the activities of organised crime, including for example drug trafficking and prostitution rings, can generate huge amounts of proceeds. Embezzlement, insider trading, bribery and computer fraud schemes can also produce large profits and create the incentive to "legitimise" the ill-gotten gains through money laundering.

When a criminal activity generates substantial profits, the individual or group involved must find a way to control the funds without attracting attention to the underlying activity or the persons involved. Criminals do this by disguising the sources, changing the form, or moving the funds to a place where they are less likely to attract attention.[5]

[3] https://www.fatf-gafi.org/en/home—it should be noted that FATF also include the financing of the proliferation of weapons of mass destruction as a third pillar of concern.

[4] https://www.imf.org/en/About/Factsheets/Sheets/2023/Fight-against-money-laundering-and-terrorism-financing

[5] In response to mounting concern over money laundering, the Financial Action Task Force on money laundering (FATF) was established by the G-7 Summit in Paris in 1989 to develop a co-ordinated international response. One of the first tasks of the FATF was to develop Recommendations, 40 in all, which set out the measures national governments should take to implement effective anti-money laundering programmes.

In Frequently Asked Questions, FATF also provides further explanation about the importance of money laundering:

Money laundering is a threat to the good functioning of a financial system; however, it can also be the Achilles heel of criminal activity.

In law enforcement investigations into organised criminal activity, it is often the connections made through financial transaction records that allow hidden assets to be located and that establish the identity of the criminals and the criminal organisation responsible.

When criminal funds are derived from robbery, extortion, embezzlement or fraud, a money laundering investigation is frequently the only way to locate the stolen funds and restore them to the victims.

Most importantly, however, targeting the money laundering aspect of criminal activity and depriving the criminal of his ill-gotten gains means hitting him where he is vulnerable. Without a usable profit, the criminal activity will not continue.[6]

(iii) **Organisation for Economic Co-operation and Development (OECD)**

The OECD is an international organisation that works to shape policies that foster prosperity and equality with 60 years of experience. They work together with governments, policy makers and citizens to establish evidence-based international standards and to find solutions to a range of social, economic and environmental challenges.

It has raised major concerns about money laundering and has published: Money Laundering and Terrorist Financing Awareness Handbook for Tax Examiners and Tax Auditors in 2009 (which has been updated since). The OECD notes:

Financial crimes, including tax evasion, money laundering, and terrorist financing undermine jurisdictions' political and economic interests and pose a serious threat to national security. Tax crime is a key source of dirty money and as such, tax authorities have a central role to play in identifying and reporting money laundering and terrorist financing. The purpose of this handbook is to raise the awareness level of tax examiners, auditors, and investigators, of their role in combatting these illegal activities by:

- Describing the nature of money laundering and terrorist financing activities so that tax examiners and auditors can better assist criminal investigators in countering these crimes;
- Providing guidance in identifying money laundering and terrorist financing during the conduct of normal tax audits;
- Describing the resources and tools that are available for effective detection and deterrence.[7]

---

[6] https://www.fatf-gafi.org/en/pages/frequently-asked-questions.html#tabs-36503a8663-item-6ff811783c-tab

[7] The website notes that: The OECD Handbook is designed so that tax administrations can adapt it to their domestic context, taking into account the varying roles that tax administrations have in

(iv) **World Economic Forum (WEF)**

The WEF, which convenes regular meetings on global economic performance and policy, is concerned about the impact of money laundering in the global economy and states:

> Money laundering is big business, so big, that to handle the movement of enormous sums of money, fraudsters are increasingly turning to Trade-Based Money Laundering (TBML). In developing countries, TBML and associated tax evasion contributed to . . . [significant] losses between 2008 and 2017. Tackling TBML is complicated by cross-jurisdiction trade, multinational companies, and globalized trade pathways.

(v) **European Investment Bank (EIB)**

EIB Group is the banking arm of the European Union (EU), owned by the EU member states, that provides financing for infrastructure and commercial investment in line with EU policies, inside the EU and across the world. It has published an Anti-Money Laundering and Combatting the Financing of Terrorism Policy. ("AML-CFT Policy").[8] It contains the key principles for anti-money laundering and combating financing of terrorism applicable to EIB Group activities and is in line with the principles of relevant EU legislation as amended and supplemented from time to time,[9] best banking practice and applicable market standards.

Para 2.3 on page 2 defines money laundering ("ML") as follows:

ML[10] is intentionally engaging in:

a) the conversion or transfer of property, knowing that such property is derived from criminal activity or from an act of participation in such activity, for the purpose of concealing or disguising the illicit origin of the property or of assisting any person who is involved in the commission of such an activity to evade the legal consequences of that person's action;
b) the concealment or disguise of the true nature, source, location, disposition, movement, rights with respect to, or ownership of, property, knowing that such property is derived from criminal activity or from an act of participation in such an activity;

---

relation to reporting unusual or suspicious transactions, receiving suspicious transaction reports and investigating money laundering offences https://www.oecd.org/tax/crime/money-laundering-awareness-handbook.htm

[8] https://www.eib.org/en/publications/eib-group-anti-money-laundering-and-combatting-the-financing-of-terrorism-policy

[9] Directive (EU) 2018/843 of the European Parliament and of the Council of 30 May 2018 amending Directive (EU) 2015/849 on the prevention of the use of the financial system for the purposes of money laundering or terrorist financing, and amending Directives 2009/138/EC and 2013/36/EU.

[10] See also the definitions in Art. 1 (3) and (4) Anti-Money Laundering Directive (AMLD).

c) the acquisition, possession or use of property, knowing, at the time of receipt, that such property was derived from criminal activity or from an act of participation in such an activity;
d) the participation in, association to commit, attempts to commit and aiding, abetting, facilitating and counselling the commission of any of the actions referred to in foregoing points.

ML shall be regarded as such even where the activities which generated the property to be laundered were carried out in any country/jurisdiction.[11]

The policy covers a range of measures to prevent it such as risk management, counterparty due diligence, reporting obligations, data management and training.

(vi) **World Bank**

The World Bank, the international public bank with 189 member countries, works to alleviate global poverty and build shared prosperity, notes in a section about Financial Market Integrity on its website[12] that:

Our Financial Integrity unit helps countries build capacity to pursue the 'dirty money' that flows through the global financial system, imposing a significant cost on national security, economic opportunity, and the rule of law in developing countries. As criminals gain new abilities to move funds across borders without detection, we are working to bolster the capacity of societies to uncover, prosecute, and prevent such movements in the future, as well as to restitute official funds stolen in corruption back to public coffers.

What We Do

The Financial Integrity team provides client countries with tools for increasing transparency and for preventing and pursuing illicit financial flows (IFF) to reinforce the integrity of the financial system. Our technical assistance in anti-money laundering/countering the financing of terrorism (AML/CFT) offers innovative avenues for fighting crime and addressing the intersections of IFF and development—including as it pertains to human security, corruption, financial inclusion, and the ease of doing business.

The Financial Integrity group also houses the Stolen Asset Recovery Initiative (StAR), a partnership between the World Bank Group and the United Nations Office on Drugs and Crime (UNODC). StAR was founded to support international efforts to end safe havens for corrupt funds, working with developing countries and financial centers to prevent the laundering of the proceeds of corruption, and to facilitate more systematic and timely return of stolen assets for public use.

Technical Assistance

[11] See definition in Art. 1 (3) AML Directive.

[12] https://www.worldbank.org/en/topic/financialmarketintegrity

A key part of the World Bank's remit is to improve the performance of countries across the world in managing economic flows, and in addressing weaknesses that undermine countries' economic effectiveness. In the area of money laundering, the World Bank lists a number of its practical tools and training activities in this area:[13]

1.3 What Is Terrorist Financing?

While money laundering covers a multitude of sins, terrorist financing is specifically defined in a number of agreements/conventions and by a range of international organisations.

The Terrorist Financing Convention,[14] agreed in 1999 by 132 signatories from across the globe and which became effective in 2002, defines terrorist financing. Article 2(1)(a) and (b) of the Terrorist Financing Convention, states:

Any person commits an offence within the meaning of this Convention if that person by any means, directly or indirectly, unlawfully and wilfully provides or collects funds with the intention that they should be used or in the knowledge that they are to be used, in full or in part, in order to carry out . . .:

a) An act which constitutes an offence within the scope of and as defined in one of the treaties listed in the annex;[15] or
b) Any other act intended to cause death or serious bodily injury to a civilian, or to any other person not taking an active part in the hostilities in a situation of armed conflict, when the purpose of such act, by its nature or context, is to intimidate a population, or to compel a government or an international organization to do or to abstain from doing any act.[16]

---

[13] For example, by:

- Supporting assessments around the risks and impacts of money laundering and terrorist financing in their jurisdictions.
- Implementing a risk based-approach to AML/CFT on the basis of the above assessment, and developing counter-measures.
- Reviewing the effectiveness of laws, regulations and institutional frameworks and recommending improvements.
- Building capacity for systematic data collection on proceeds of crimes and associated financial flows.

[14] Officially named: the International Convention for the Suppression of the Financing of Terrorism, https://treaties.un.org/doc/db/terrorism/english-18-11.pdf; https://en.wikipedia.org/wiki/Terrorist_Financing_Convention

[15] For further detail of the "acts", see Para 15 of FATF's Guidance, which notes that there are a significant number of them set out in the nine Conventions listed in Annex 1 of the *Terrorist Financing Convention*.

[16] See Para 13 of FATF's Guidance on Criminalising Terrorist Financing (Recommendation 5): https://www.fatf-gafi.org/content/dam/fatf-gafi/guidance/Guidance-Criminalising-Terrorist-Financing.pdf.coredownload.inline.pdf

In attempting to identify who would be covered under this definition, the OECD's Handbook for Tax Examiners and Auditors[17] states:

Terrorist organisations vary widely, ranging from large, state-like organisations to small, decentralised groups and self-directed networks. Terrorist attacks have also been committed by individuals who have found inspiration in radicalised environments or through self-radicalisation.

These "lone actors" also need to fund their activities and they may present particular challenges in terms of identifying observable indicators.

Lone actor terrorists tend to be divided into two main classes: those who are inspired by radical ideas promoted by terrorist organisations, usually located abroad; and those who are radicalised based on a trigger within the environment in which they live (e.g. anti-government). The lone actor terrorist seeks to take the entire process into his or her own hands, from financing him or herself to undertaking the attack.

Terrorists' financing requirements reflect this diversity, varying greatly between organisations. Financing is required not just to fund specific terrorist operations, but also to meet the broader organisational costs of developing and maintaining a terrorist organisation and to create an enabling environment necessary to sustain its activities.

Those who engage in acts of terror require funds to support those activities. From everyday living expenses such as food and shelter, to travelling, training and equipment, to the acts themselves, funds must be raised. These funds may originate from third parties (financiers and supporters) or from their own assets or income, and from legal or illegal sources. Lone actors may self-fund their activities from legitimate sources (e.g. wages or income, savings, credit cards) or illicit means (e.g. crime, terrorist financiers or operators) or receive financial support from others (e.g. family, friends, public benefits, charities etc.).

The direct costs of mounting individual attacks have been low relative to the damage they may yield. However, maintaining a terrorist network or even a specific cell to provide for recruitment, planning, and procurement between attacks represents a significant drain on resources.

Significant infrastructure is required to sustain international terrorist networks and promote their goals over time. Organisations require significant funds to create and maintain an infrastructure of organisational support, to sustain an ideology of terrorism through propaganda, and to finance the ostensibly legitimate activities needed to provide a veil of legitimacy for terrorist organisations.

[17] https://www.oecd.org/tax/crime/money-laundering-and-terrorist-financing-awareness-handbook-for-tax-examiners-and-tax-auditors.pdf

1.4 How Do International Institutions Address Terrorist Financing?

(i) FATF

The FATF Recommendations[18] note that, as a result of "... diverse legal, administrative and operational frameworks and different financial systems" that different countries have, FATF has produced and adopted official Recommendations which "set an international standard, which countries should implement through measures adapted to their particular circumstances".

The FATF Recommendations were adopted on 16 February 2012 and have been regularly updated since, with the most recent update in February 2023. They use a risk-based approach which emphasizes the need for countries to identify and understand the money laundering and terrorist financing risks they are exposed to and thereby ensures they prioritise resources to mitigate risks in the highest risk areas.

In particular, FATF state:[19]

Combatting terrorist financing has been a priority for the FATF since 2001. However, in 2015, the scope and nature of terrorist threats globally intensified considerably, with terrorist attacks in many cities across the world, and the terrorist threat posed by the so-called Islamic State of Iraq and the Levant (ISIL/Da'esh), and by Al-Qaeda and their affiliated terrorist organisations.

Since then, the terrorism threats have continued to evolve, from large terrorist organisations, to returning terrorist fighters and right-wing extremists. Funds flow cross-border to providing resources for nationally designated organisations, and many jurisdictions continue to suffer from persistent attacks from small cells and radicalised lone actors, drawing inspiration from a range of dangerous ideologies.

The FATF plays a central role in global efforts in combatting terrorist financing, through its role in setting global standards to combat terrorist financing, assisting jurisdictions in implementing financial provisions of the United Nations Security Council resolutions on terrorism, and evaluating countries' ability to prevent, detect, investigate and prosecute the financing of terrorism. Yet many countries have not yet implemented the FATF Standards effectively. They do not understand the nature of terrorist financing risks they face, nor have effective means to combat them.

The FATF Strategy on Combating Terrorist Financing sets out the broad objectives for FATF's work in this area. Under this strategy, the FATF, in close collaboration with the regional FATF-style regional bodies and other partners such as the UN, the FATF has completed work to support countries around the world in combatting terrorist financing.

---

[18] https://www.fatf-gafi.org/en/publications/fatfrecommendations/documents/fatf-recommendations.html

[19] https://www.fatf-gafi.org/en/topics/Terrorist-Financing.html

FATF has also published a number of relevant documents, including:

- Ethnically or Racially Motivated Terrorism Financing;[20]
- Terrorist Financing Risk Assessment Guidance;[21] and
- Risk of terrorist abuse in non-profit organisations.[22]

(ii) **OECD**

OECD first launched the Handbook for Tax Examiners and Tax Auditors[23] in 2009 as a practical tool to assist tax authorities in identifying money laundering during the course of audits. The handbook has more recently been revised to include new material to increase the detection and reporting of terrorist financing. In particular the OECD notes:

> Financial crimes, including tax evasion, money laundering, and terrorist financing undermine jurisdictions' political and economic interests and pose a serious threat to national security. Tax crime is a key source of dirty money and as such, tax authorities have a central role to play in identifying and reporting money laundering and terrorist financing. The purpose of this handbook is to raise the awareness level of tax examiners, auditors, and investigators, of their role in combatting these illegal activities . . .

(iii) **EIB**

EIB's policy defines Terrorist Financing ("TF") as:

> . . . the provision or collection of funds, by any means, directly or indirectly, with the intention that they be used, or in the knowledge that they are to be used (in full or in part) to commit or to contribute to the commission of any of the offences referred to . . .[24]

EIB monitors the projects it finances to ensure that the funds are applied for the particular purpose. In particular, under the procurement[25] and other applicable policies (such as the Covenant of Integrity which bidders must sign), there are a

[20] https://www.fatf-gafi.org/en/publications/Methodsandtrends/Ethnically-racially-motivated-terrorism-financing.html

[21] https://www.fatf-gafi.org/en/publications/Methodsandtrends/Terrorist-financing-risk-assessment-guidance.html

[22] https://www.fatf-gafi.org/en/publications/Methodsandtrends/Risk-terrorist-abuse-non-profits.html

[23] https://www.oecd.org/tax/crime/money-laundering-awareness-handbook.htm

[24] In Articles 3 to 10 of Directive (EU) 2017/541 of 15 March 2017 on combatting terrorism.
Where TF concerns any of the offences laid down in articles 3, 4 and 9 of Directive (EU) 2017/541

[25] See EIB's Guide to Procurement: https://www.eib.org/en/publications/guide-to-procurement

number of possibilities for EIB staff to access the project site(s) and review the progress of the project under the Finance Contract signed by both parties (the Borrower and EIB) when the loan is approved. Any suspected breach, such as fraud, corruption, collusion or coercion can be investigated by EIB and those found to be involved can be sanctioned.

Chapter 2
Definitions of Money Laundering in Different Jurisdictions

Although many jurisdictions seek to meet international standards, the actual definition of money laundering contained in national legislation can vary. Below we look at a number of jurisdictions (UK, US, EU Member States, Australia and Singapore but no doubt there are others that are relevant too, such as China, Japan, Canada, Brazil, South Africa, the Caribbean and elsewhere). As a result of the differences in the offence (and likely punishment if convicted), it is possible that criminals "shop around", not just for the best financial and other locations in which to launder the funds but also to minimize the risk of being identified, investigated, prosecuted and convicted.

Generally:[1]

> Money laundering is the process of illegally concealing the origin of money, obtained from illicit activities such as drug trafficking, corruption, embezzlement or gambling, by converting it into a legitimate source. It is a crime in many jurisdictions with varying definitions. It is usually a key operation of organized crime.
>
> In United States law, money laundering is the practice of engaging in financial transactions to conceal the identity, source, or destination of illegally gained money. In United Kingdom law, the common law definition is wider. The act is defined as "taking any action with property of any form which is either wholly or in part the proceeds of a crime that will disguise the fact that that property is the proceeds of a crime or obscure the beneficial ownership of said property".
>
> In the past, the term "money laundering" was applied only to financial transactions related to organized crime. Today its definition is often expanded by government and international regulators such as the US Office of the Comptroller of the Currency to mean "any financial transaction which generates an asset or a value as the result of an illegal act," which may involve actions such as tax evasion or false accounting. In the UK, it does not need to involve money, but any economic

[1] See Wikipedia: https://en.wikipedia.org/wiki/Money_laundering

D. Smith, *Money Laundering, Terrorist Financing and Virtual Assets*, Contributions to Finance and Accounting, https://doi.org/10.1007/978-3-031-59842-5_2

good. Courts involve money laundering committed by private individuals, drug dealers, businesses, corrupt officials, members of criminal organizations such as the Mafia, and even states.

(i) United Kingdom

In the UK, the Proceeds of Crime Act 2002 (POCA) aims to prevent criminals from money laundering by making activities such as concealment and conversion of criminal property as criminal offences. It also provides some tools to freeze and recover illegally obtained assets. The sentence for an offence can be, whilst dependent on the nature, severity and circumstances of the crime, up to 14 years in prison and include financial penalties.[2]

The Crown Prosecution Service or CPS note that:[3]

Money laundering is defined in the POCA as *"the process by which the proceeds of crime are converted into assets which appear to have a legitimate origin, so that they can be retained permanently or recycled into further criminal enterprises"*. Money laundering can be broken down into two categories:

- Those who commit offences and then launder the proceeds of those criminal offences. The criminal offences are referred to as "predicate offences".
- Those whose only criminal involvement is to launder the proceeds of crime committed by others.

The UK also uses regulations to try to prevent the financial system being used to launder money and finance terrorists. For example, under the UK Money Laundering Regulations 2007 (reg 3), relevant persons including finance institutions (like banks and building societies) must undertake due diligence of a customer, such as to identify and verify the identity of the customer and any beneficial owner, whilst also seeking to establish the purpose and intended nature of the business relationship.[4]

A Fact Sheet providing an Overview of POCA 2002 has been prepared by the Home Office (the government department responsible for the legislation) and is available.[5] It includes important summaries about: (i) confiscation; (ii) civil recovery and cash seizure; (iii) revenue functions (taxation); (iv) money laundering;

---

[2] See: https://sanctionscanner.com/blog/anti-money-laundering-regulations-in-the-united-kingdom-uk-210#:~:text=Proceeds%20of%20Crime%20Act%20(POCA)&text=Its%20primary%20aim%20is%20to,offenses%20under%20the%202,002%20POCA

[3] https://www.cps.gov.uk/legal-guidance/money-laundering-offences

[4] https://www.lexisnexis.co.uk/legal/glossary/money-laundering

[5] https://assets.publishing.service.gov.uk/media/5a7d7b6740f0b64fe6c23fae/Fact_Sheet_-_Overview_of_POCA__2_.pdf

(v) production, disclosure and unexplained wealth orders; and (vi) national and international cooperation.

The British **Institute of Financial Accountants** (IFA) state:[6]

The definition of money laundering is broad. Money laundering is a process whereby criminals:

- retain, disguise and conceal the proceeds of their crimes;
- raise, consolidate or retain funds for use in financing terrorism.

. . . the [offences created by the] Proceeds of Crime Act 2002 (POCA) . . . include . . . facilitating any handling or possession of criminal property.

Criminal property (defined in POCA) constitutes or represents a person's benefit from criminal conduct where the alleged offender knows or suspects that the property in question represents such a benefit. Criminal property may take any form, including money or money's worth, securities, tangible property and intangible property.

Money laundering can be carried out in any part of the world and can range from a single act involving one person to complex set ups involving various individuals. There are no materiality or deminimis exceptions in relation to money laundering.

To put the problem of money laundering in the UK into context:[7]

The scale of [international] money laundering is difficult to assess . . . [but] . . .
The top five countries in terms of value of money laundered are [estimated to be] . . .:

US – £216.5bn.
UK – £88bn.
France – £54.5bn.
Germany – £51.3bn.
Canada – £25.6bn.

(ii) United States of America

As noted by the Department of Justice or DoJ, the US definition is:[8]

Section 1956(a) defines three types of criminal conduct: domestic money laundering transactions (§ 1956(a)(1)); international money laundering transactions

[6]https://www.ifa.org.uk/technical-resources/aml#:~:text=In%20UK%20law%20money%20laundering,or%20possession%20of%20criminal%20property

[7]An article written by Evie Lee (dated May 2022, updated in April 2023) for CPD: https://cpdonline.co.uk/knowledge-base/business/money-laundering/

[8]https://www.justice.gov/archives/jm/criminal-resource-manual-2101-money-laundering-overview

(§ 1956(a)(2)); and undercover "sting" money laundering transactions (§ 1956(a)(3)). *See* this Manual at 2182.[9]

To be criminally culpable under 18 U.S.C. § 1956(a)(1), a defendant must conduct or attempt to conduct a financial transaction, knowing that the property involved in the financial transaction represents the proceeds of some unlawful activity, with one of the four specific intents discussed below, and the property must *in fact* be derived from a specified unlawful activity.

The actual source of the funds must be one of the specified forms of criminal activity identified by the statute, in 18 U.S.C. § 1956(c)(7), or those incorporated by reference from the RICO statute (18 U.S.C. § 1961(1)). Section 1956(c)(7)(B) includes in the list of specified unlawful activity certain offenses against a *foreign* nation. Thus, proceeds of certain crimes committed in another country may constitute proceeds of a specified unlawful activity for purposes of the money laundering statutes.

(iii) European Union

There are a series of EU Directives attempting to prevent the misuse of the financial system and to improve cooperation between EU Member States in the fight against money laundering. In particular:[10]

---

[9] § 1956 Laundering of monetary instruments

a. A. Whoever, knowing that the property involved in a financial transaction represents the proceeds of some form of unlawful activity, conducts or attempts to conduct such a financial transaction which in fact involves the proceeds of specified unlawful activity --

   A. (i) with the intent to promote the carrying on of specified unlawful activity; or (ii) with intent to engage in conduct constituting a violation of section 7201 or 7206 of the Internal Revenue Code of 1986; or
   B. knowing that the transaction is designed in whole or in part -- (i) to conceal or disguise the nature, the location, the source, the ownership, or the control of the proceeds of specified unlawful activity; or (ii) to avoid a transaction reporting requirement under State or Federal law,

shall be sentenced to a fine of not more than $500,000 or twice the value of the property involved in the transaction, whichever is greater, or imprisonment for not more than twenty years, or both.

Also, it is noted that: "To combat this criminal activity, (the use of offshore accounts by criminals to hide money because they offer greater privacy, less regulation, and reduced taxation), Congress passed the Bank Secrecy Act of 1970, which requires banks to report any financial transactions of $10,000.01 or more. Congress followed up this Act sixteen years later with the Money Laundering Control Act of 1986, which rendered money laundering a federal crime. In 2001, Congress passed the USA Patriot Act, which expanded the scope of reporting responsibilities and included more types of financial institutions in an effort to combat the financing of terrorist activities" at https://www.law.cornell.edu/wex/money_laundering

[10] https://eur-lex.europa.eu/EN/legal-content/glossary/money-laundering.html#:~:text=Its%20measures%20are%20governed%20by,and%20the%20financing%20of%20terrorism

[The EU's] measures are governed by the Treaty on the Functioning of the European Union (TFEU):

- under Title VII (approximation of laws for the internal market): with the creation of the internal market, rules were implemented throughout the EU in order to effectively prevent money laundering and the financing of terrorism. Financial movements are regulated to ensure that transactions can be fully traced and monitored. Financial and certain non-financial operators must also identify their clients (including beneficial owners of companies and trusts), monitor transactions and report any suspicions of money laundering to Financial Intelligence Units;
- under Title V (police and judicial cooperation in criminal matters): focuses on defining offences and on strengthening mutual assistance.

EU financial crime rules are mostly based on international standards adopted by the Financial Action Task Force.

Directive (EU) 2018/843 – the EU's Fifth Anti-Money Laundering Directive, which amends the Fourth Anti-Money Laundering Directive (Directive (EU) 2015/849) – aims to combat money laundering and the financing of terrorism by preventing the financial market from being misused for these purposes.

Directive (EU) 2018/1673 aims to criminalise money laundering when it is intentional and with the knowledge that the property came from criminal activity. It defines criminal offences and sanctions in the area of money laundering and allows Member States to criminalise money laundering where the offender suspected or ought to have known that the property came from criminal activity. This directive translates into EU law the Council of Europe Convention on Laundering, Search, Seizure and Confiscation of the Proceeds from Crime and on the Financing of Terrorism - the Warsaw Convention, and recommendations issued by the FATF in relation to the criminalisation of money laundering and terrorist financing. It complements and reinforces the application of Anti-Money Laundering Directive by ensuring a robust law enforcement and judicial response to the laundering of illicit money.[11]

In Directive 2018/1673, money laundering is defined as:

the following conduct, when committed intentionally, is punishable as a criminal offence:

(a)	the conversion or transfer of property, knowing that such property is derived from criminal activity, for the purpose of concealing or disguising the illicit origin of the property or of assisting any person who is involved in the commission of such an activity to evade the legal consequences of that person's action;

(continued)

[11] https://home-affairs.ec.europa.eu/policies/internal-security/organised-crime-and-human-trafficking/money-laundering_en

(b)	the concealment or disguise of the true nature, source, location, disposition, movement, rights with respect to, or ownership of, property, knowing that such property is derived from criminal activity;
(c)	the acquisition, possession or use of property, knowing at the time of receipt, that such property was derived from criminal activity.

In 2020, the European Commission adopted an EU action plan on preventing money laundering and terrorist financing, which includes measures it will take to better enforce, supervise and coordinate the relevant EU rules.[12] At the same time, it published a method to identify high-risk non-EU countries with deficient anti-money laundering and countering terrorist financing regimes that pose significant threats to the EU's financial system.[13]

(iv) Singapore

The Corruption, Drug Trafficking and Other Serious Crimes (Confiscation of Benefits) Act 1992 (CDSA) defines the offence as:[14]

54.—(1) Any person who —

a) conceals or disguises any property which is, or in whole or in part, directly or indirectly, represents, the person's benefits from criminal conduct;
b) converts or transfers that property or removes it from the jurisdiction; or.
c) acquires, possesses or uses that property, shall be guilty of an offence.

(2) Any person who, knowing or having reasonable grounds to believe that any property is, or in whole or in part, directly or indirectly, represents, another person's benefits from criminal conduct —

a) conceals or disguises that property; or
b) converts or transfers that property or removes it from the jurisdiction, shall be guilty of an offence.

An article entitled Anti-Money Laundering (AML) in Singapore: Complete Guide (2023) states:[15]

---

[12] https://finance.ec.europa.eu/publications/action-plan-comprehensive-union-policy-preventing-money-laundering-and-terrorism-financing_en

[13] EUR-Lex, a website facilitating access to EU law: https://eur-lex.europa.eu/EN/legal-content/glossary/money-laundering.html#:~:text=Money%20laundering%20is%20the%20process,of%20their%20property%20or%20income

[14] https://sso.agc.gov.sg/Act/CDTOSCCBA1992?ProvIds=P16-#pr54-

[15] Article written by Oraz Kereibayev, https://sumsub.com/blog/anti-money-laundering-aml-in-singapore-complete-guide-2023/

Singapore has a robust and open economy, with reasonable taxes and a well-qualified labor market. The city-state focuses on doing business internationally, which has appealed to companies from all over the world.

Thus, it's no surprise that the World Bank ranks the country as the second best in the world for business. However, Singapore's open economy can attract financial criminals who intend to conceal the source of their income through money laundering or fund terrorism. To mitigate this risk, Singapore has established several governmental authorities and a robust AML regulatory framework.

Since 2016, Singapore has taken a number of considerable actions to strengthen its AML framework. This has generated a positive response from international organizations such as the Financial Action Task Force (FATF), which stated in its latest review that Singapore is steadily developing its AML regulatory framework and sufficiently ensuring that companies implement them.

Businesses planning to launch in Singapore need to comply with all the relevant regulations and guidelines. To simplify the process, we at Sumsub have prepared this article to explain how companies can stay compliant…

AML regulations in Singapore apply to financial institutions as well as certain designated business, including but not limited to:

- Banks
- Casinos
- Exchange companies
- Brokers
- Financial advisers
- Real estate agents
- Dealers of precious metals
- Payment service providers

The following types of transactions fall under AML regulations:

- Money transfers (both domestic and international)
- E-money issuance
- Account issuance
- Money exchange
- Virtual assets …

The Monetary Authority of Singapore (MAS) is Singapore's central bank and integrated financial regulator. Its focus is regulating and licensing financial institutions, such as banks, crypto-related businesses, and brokers. The MAS also publishes guidelines for other types of financial institutions such as insurance companies …

The MAS is not the only financial regulator in Singapore. Facilities such as casinos are overseen by the Casino Regulatory Authority of Singapore. Meanwhile, real estate agencies have to comply with Council for Estate Agencies regulations …

The main AML regulation in Singapore is the Corruption, Drug Trafficking, and Other Serious Crimes Act 1992 (CDSA) . . .[16]

Also:

The key legislation . . . is the CDSA . . . which expands the scope of money laundering offences to include non-drug related activities. According to the CDSA, the laundering of proceeds from 10 types of drug dealing offences in the First Schedule and serious crimes specified in the Second Schedule, (collectively, "criminal conduct") constitutes a money laundering offence.[17]

The Monetary Authority of Singapore (MAS) provides the following overview of money laundering:[18]

. . . MAS is firmly committed to safeguarding Singapore as a clean and trusted financial centre . . . Singapore is an active member of the Financial Action Task Force (FATF), the global standard setting and oversight body for AML/CFT. As co-chair of its Policy Development Group, Singapore collaborates closely with fellow AML/CFT policy makers and supervisors to develop international standards. We are also a founding member of the Asia / Pacific Group on Money Laundering . . .

The requirements and expectations on financial institutions are set out in MAS' AML/CFT Notices, Guidelines, and other Guidance issued by MAS.[19]

---

[16]Some other important AML regulations include:
- MAS Notice 626
- MAS Notice 1014
- MAS Notice 824
- MAS Notice PSN01
- MAS Notice PSN02

[17]https://singaporelegaladvice.com/law-articles/anti-money-laundering-laws-and-you/#:~:text=Money%20laundering%20(ML)%20is%20defined,originated%20from%20a%20legitimate%20source

[18]https://www.mas.gov.sg/regulation/anti-money-laundering

[19]Financial institutions should also refer to:

- AML/CFT announcements and media releases for information on high-risk jurisdictions.
- AML/CFT Guidance Papers issued by international bodies, including the FATF.

Financial institutions must also comply with the various Regulations made pursuant to section 192, read with sections 15(1)(b) and 219(d), of the Financial Services and Markets Act 2022 to discharge or facilitate the discharge of Singapore's obligations by virtue of decisions of the Security Council of the United Nations. They must also comply with obligations to combat terrorism financing such as those found in the Terrorism (Suppression of Financing) Act 2002 . . .

Under the Financial Services and Markets Act 2022, a financial institution that fails or refuses to comply with any requirements in the applicable AML/CFT Notice is guilty of an offence and is liable on conviction to a fine not exceeding $1 million for each offence. In the case of a continuing offence, such a financial institution will be subject to a further fine of $100,000 for every day or part of the day during which the offence continues after conviction.

(v) Australia

In Australia, the investigation and prosecution of suspected money laundering offences will take place as follows:[20]

The Commonwealth Department of Public Prosecutions (CDPP), Australia's federal prosecution service, prosecutes money laundering offences at the Commonwealth level. The Australian Transaction Reports and Analysis Centre, the Australian Federal Police and the Australian Border Force act as partner agencies to the CDPP in prosecuting money laundering offences. The Australian Federal Police also leads the Criminal Assets Confiscation Taskforce that, as stated on its website, collaborates with other agencies to 'identify, investigate and litigate appropriate asset confiscation matters at the Commonwealth level'.

State- and territory-based public prosecution services and local police departments enforce and prosecute offences at their respective levels. However, it is unlikely that a prosecution under a state or territory law for money laundering would be pursued if one has already been brought at the federal level. At the state and territory levels, police focus is on the investigation of predicate offences and money laundering prosecution only in simple cases where offenders may be caught in possession of cash ...

Both natural and legal persons can be prosecuted for money laundering offences ....

The relevant division of the Criminal Code Act 1995 (Cth) (the Criminal Code) creates multiple offences that cover a wide range of criminal activity. The offences are based on a person dealing with money or property that is proceeds of crime, or will be (or is at risk of becoming) an instrument of crime. Broadly, the elements of the offence are:

- the existence of money or property;
- a dealing (physical conduct such as receiving, possessing, concealing or disposing of the money or property, importing or exporting it, or engaging in banking transactions) in money or property being unlawful because the proceeds are proceeds of crime, or the proceeds are at risk of being used in the commission of or to facilitate a crime; and
- the person believed that the money or property was the proceeds of a crime, or was reckless or negligent about that fact.

Generally, a person commits an offence of money laundering if they deal with money or other property that is, or is reasonably suspected of being, the proceeds of crime and one of the following states of mind is present:

[20] https://www.lexology.com/library/detail.aspx?g=a4e6caa8-0ed7-44ae-9006-2403b70d5b54#:~:text=Both%20natural%20and%20legal%20persons%20can%20be%20prosecuted%20for%20money%20laundering%20offences.&text=What%20constitutes%20money%20laundering%3F,wide%20range%20of%20criminal%20activity

- intentionality: the money or property is, and is believed to be, proceeds of crime, or the person intends that the money or property will become an instrument of crime;
- recklessness: the money or property is proceeds of crime, or there is a risk that it will become an instrument of crime, and the person is reckless to this fact; or
- negligence: the money or property is proceeds of crime, or there is a risk that it will become an instrument of crime, and the person is negligent as to this fact.

An offence under section 400.9 of the Criminal Code does not require the element of intention, recklessness or negligence be present. Rather, the offence is established where it is reasonable to suspect that money or property was the proceeds of crime.

'Proceeds of crime' means any money or other property wholly or partly derived or realised, directly or indirectly, by any person from the commission of an offence against a law of Australia or a foreign country that may be dealt with as an indictable offence (even if it may, in some circumstances, be dealt with as a summary offence). Money or other property is an instrument of crime if it is used (or used to facilitate) in the commission of an offence against such a law.

Offences contained in the Anti-Money Laundering and Counter-Terrorism Financing Act 2006 (the AML/CTF Act) are also used in prosecuting money laundering offences.

The offences at a state and territory level differ according to areas such as relevant predicate offences, the intent of the defendant and penalties attached to the offences.

Financial institutions generally cannot be prosecuted for their customers' money laundering crimes (unless the elements of the offence can otherwise be established). However, crimes committed by customers may cause financial institutions to contravene a regulatory offence under the AML/CTF Act should the offending conduct not be appropriately identified and managed (eg, by failing to report a suspicious matter) . . . .

Under the POC [Proceeds of Crime] Act, a freezing order can be made by a magistrate against an account with a financial institution if:

- there are reasonable grounds to suspect that the balance of the account is proceeds of a particular offence, or it is wholly or partly an instrument of a serious offence; and
- there is a risk that the account's balance will be reduced so that a person will not be deprived of all or some of such proceeds or such an instrument.

The POC Act also enables forfeiture orders to be made under which property must be surrendered to the government if certain offences have been committed.

Both the freezing and forfeiture orders are part of the POC Act's implementation of a confiscation scheme, which outlines processes relating to confiscation that also include restraining orders (prohibiting disposal of or dealing with property) and pecuniary penalty orders (requiring payment of amounts based on benefits derived from committing offences). The POC Act also has provisions that outline ways in which information can be gathered, such as examining any person about the affairs of people covered by the examination orders and requiring financial institutions to provide information and documents relating to accounts and transactions.

Similar legislation has been enacted in the states and territories of Australia that relates to making such orders and confiscation of profits and other proceeds of crime.

Money laundering in Australia can therefore be investigated and prosecuted as criminal offences, as noted above. The Australian Federal Police would undertake the investigation and, once sufficient evidence is obtained, a prosecution will be led by the CDPP,[21] Australia's federal prosecutors.

The Australian Transaction Reports and Analysis Centre (AUSTRAC) is Australia's Financial Intelligence Unit and AML regulator.[22] Australia's Anti-Money Laundering and Counter-Terrorism Financing Act 2006 provides the structure for regulation of financial, gambling, remittance and bullion sectors which provide designated services, as listed in the Act.

Currently, there is reform of Australia's AML/CTF regime—consultations are on-going and there may be changes in it to "ensure it is fit-for-purpose" and it "responds to the evolving threat environment and meets international standards set…" by FATF.

[21] Commonwealth Director of Public Prosecutions at: https://www.cdpp.gov.au

[22] www.ag.gov.au

Chapter 3
More on Money Laundering

3.1 Three Stages of Money Laundering

There are generally considered to be three stages of money laundering allowing the laundered funds to be released into the financial system. These three stages are:

- Placement;
- Layering; and
- Integration/extraction.

These stages are sometimes undertaken by the criminals themselves or they can use professionals such as real estate agents, lawyers, accountants, other professionals and a network of individuals, entities and corporations to do so.[1]

The OECD notes the following about the money laundering process[2]:

> One of the primary needs of tax fraudsters and of those involved in a wide range of criminal activities is to disguise the illicit source of money. This is done by converting the "dirty money" and "washing" it into a form that will be difficult to retrace to its origins. For instance, this could be done by placing the "dirty money" in bank accounts, real estate, stocks, insurance premiums and other assets in the hope that these assets can be used later on without arousing suspicion. Whether the crime is a tax crime, trafficking in narcotics, illegal sales of weapons, corruption or any of a vast range of criminal activities, they all share a basic money laundering process. The process that money launderers use to legitimise the appearance of their illicit proceeds is globally known to take place in three stages: placement, layering and integration.

---

[1] See also FATF's report entitled "Professional Money Laundering" dated July 2018: https://www.fatf-gafi.org/content/dam/fatf-gafi/reports/Professional-Money-Laundering.pdf

[2] https://www.oecd.org/tax/crime/money-laundering-and-terrorist-financing-awareness-handbook-for-tax-examiners-and-tax-auditors.pdf

D. Smith, *Money Laundering, Terrorist Financing and Virtual Assets*, Contributions to Finance and Accounting, https://doi.org/10.1007/978-3-031-59842-5_3

The integration stage may be further divided into two parts: justification and investment. The crime of money laundering is committed at each stage of the process, and it is not necessary for the illicit funds to go through all three stages.

Placement

The goal in this stage is to deposit criminal proceeds, generally cash, into the financial system (usually bank accounts) at home and/or abroad. For this purpose, cash could be switched into other valuables like trade goods, diamonds, gold bars or cheques. Cash can be exchanged into other currencies, in larger denominations and/or split up in smaller sums which allow easy transportation by cash couriers. Cash or other valuables can be transported abroad, away from the country where the crime was committed, to the country of residence of the criminal or a specific country where cash can be easily deposited or invested.

Transportation (of physical assets) can take place by such means as car, plane, train (passengers or cargo) or boats.

Furthermore, cash can be transferred by using an underground banking system. For all of these acts, criminals can use third parties, i.e. either individuals or corporations. Money derived from fraud, such as tax fraud or investment fraud, could also be held in a bank account and therefore, exchanged electronically. Goods from theft can be exchanged for other valuables. Cryptocurrencies are a new asset class for money laundering as they can be transacted anonymously anywhere in the world using the internet. As criminal proceeds no longer solely take the form of cash or money in a bank account, tax examiners and tax auditors should be aware that new and more efficient placement methods may be used.

Layering

The goal in this stage is the concealment of the criminal origin of the proceeds. Money can be transferred and split frequently between bank accounts, countries, individuals and/or corporations, thus distancing it from its criminal origin. Money can also be withdrawn in cash from one location and deposited into bank accounts at a different location. It is common to use bank accounts in countries with strict banking secrecy laws and to nominate offshore corporations as the bank account holders. Cryptocurrencies with an illicit source (e.g. on the dark web) can be sent to a mixing service to conceal the criminal origin.

Integration: justification

The goal in this stage is to create an apparent legal origin for the criminal proceeds. This can be done by:

- Doing business with yourself (e.g. falsifying sources of income, capital gains and/or loans)
- Disguising the ownership of assets
- Using the criminal proceeds in transactions with third parties

The money launderer creates an apparent legal origin of the money by fabricating transactions which are supported by falsified and fabricated documents such as invoices, reports, contracts, agreements, bookkeeping entries, and deeds as well as false statements, both written or spoken. Common justification methods used include:

- Fabricating a loan ...
- Fabricating a rise in net worth (e.g. buying and selling real estate and other items, fabricating casino winnings, lottery prizes, inheritance, etc.)
- Disguising the ownership of assets and interest in businesses (e.g. through the use of relatives, foreign legal entities, nominees, etc.)
- Price-manipulating (e.g. over- and under-invoicing)
- Manipulating turnover/sales by commingling illicit and legal sources of income

Integration: investment

The goal in this final stage is to use criminal proceeds for personal benefit. Cash, electronic money and cryptocurrencies can be used for:

- Safekeeping: e.g. cash on hand, cryptocurrencies in a wallet
- Consumption: e.g. day to day expenditures, lavish lifestyle, jewellery, vehicles, yachts, art
- Investing: e.g. bank accounts, real estate, stocks, securities, receivables, funding of legitimate and illicit business activities, repayment of loans

Criminals may want to display their wealth and wealthy lifestyle by acquiring "badges of wealth" such as luxury homes, vehicles, boats, jewellery, etc. Criminals will seek to launder the proceeds from their crimes to pay for these in order to avoid detection by the tax or law enforcement authorities.

Extending beyond a review of previous procedures/processes and the traditional uses of money laundering by criminals especially organised crime groups, the OECD also warns about more modern, current trends:[3]

The traditional methods of money laundering have centred on the use of cash-based businesses and this remains an important area. However, criminals will continue to seek out innovative methods to exploit weaknesses in the financial systems and to try to keep ahead of the investigators. Real estate, loans and trade based money laundering are known methods for criminals to launder the proceeds of crime. These will be described in detail at a later stage.

More recent trends include:

- Cryptocurrencies have, in a relatively short period of time, developed into a new payment method and as a means to store value. Financial transaction systems that are based on blockchain technology promise faster, cheaper and anonymous transactions. The speed and global availability of cryptocurrencies, coupled with the limited regulations, the disaggregation of established financial intermediaries and the potential to hide the true identity of the owners, make them an attractive method for criminals.

[3] Page 19.

- Funnel accounts refer to one or more bank accounts used for illegal funds deposited at one geographical location that gives criminals immediate access to the money via withdrawals in a different geographic location.
- Offshore bank accounts of foreign legal entities continue to be used to make it difficult to track money flows. Overly complex transactions or opaque ownership structures, including sequential or layered legal entities or trusts in multiple jurisdictions, including financial centres, persist. The purpose of these activities is to hide the origin of the funds and their beneficial owners.
- Professional enablers and intermediaries (e.g. attorneys, accountants, trust and company services providers, notaries, estate agents, etc.) traditionally planned and created structures, based on their clients' needs, whether for legitimate or criminal reasons. Their participation usually stops once the entities are formed and accounts opened. Over time, some professional enablers move beyond just establishing money laundering or tax evasion vehicles to actively managing their criminal clients' illicit funds and providing money laundering as a service.
- Third Party Money Laundering Groups form part of an arrangement whereby a criminal organisation makes use of a third party for the laundering of its criminally derived proceeds. The Third Party Money Laundering Group may establish complex and/or durable means of "processing" its clients' illicit funds, without exposure to or knowledge of the clients' predicate offences. The criminal organisation pays a fee or commission but otherwise does not have to deal with the efforts and risk associated with the money laundering activities, allowing it to focus on its criminal activities.

3.2 Risks Arising from Money Laundering

Finance Sector: As noted in an article published by the International Monetary Fund (IMF) recently,[4] money laundering poses a risk to the stability of the financial sector. To minimise the risk and resolve issues, curbing cross-border illicit proceeds demands a united global effort and innovative approaches. In particular, the article notes that:

> Cross-border financial crime is here to stay. While people everywhere enjoy the convenience of a globally connected financial system, criminals exploit this intricate network to move illicit funds across borders and evade capture. As these criminals protect their ill-gotten wealth derived from tax evasion, corruption, and drug trafficking, among others, financial crimes thrive. No financial institution or country is immune. Money laundering scandals caused bank collapses and shocked countries. Ultimately, society pays the cost through an

[4] In an article by Pierre Bardin, Antoine Bouveret, Grace Jackson and Maksym Markevych dated September 4, 2023: https://www.imf.org/en/Blogs/Articles/2023/09/04/money-laundering-poses-a-risk-to-financial-sector-stability

erosion of trust in the integrity of the financial system, often leading taxpayers to subsidize failing banks and limiting customer access to credit.

Banks, as gatekeepers to the financial system, battle unceasingly against money laundering and terrorist financing. But national anti-money laundering efforts focus primarily on domestic risks, and as a result they often lag. Bank regulators also play a crucial role, but often don't make the best use of limited resources, and divergent approaches hamper effective global collaboration.

IMF staff partnered with eight Nordic and Baltic countries—Denmark, Estonia, Finland, Iceland, Latvia, Lithuania, Norway, and Sweden—in a first-of-its-kind anti-money laundering technical assistance project.[5] Our findings reveal that combatting money laundering is beyond the capacity of any single nation—and that countries must innovate together to find a solution.

Tracking criminal proceeds

IMF staff is constantly expanding the toolkit to help Fund members focus on cross-border illicit flows. Using machine learning technologies and data analysis, we scrutinize financial movements, gaining insights into the global landscape and identifying indicators of potential macro-critical money laundering scenarios. Our analysis features in the annual health checks of IMF member economies (e.g., Singapore 2022 Article IV consultation[6]) and under the Financial Sector Assessment Program[7] (e.g., UK 2022 FSAP[8]).

Collaborating with the Nordic-Baltic countries, we used these tools to improve countries' understanding of unusual financial flows warranting scrutiny. These tools enhance countries' ability to screen potential illicit financial flows and focus on emerging threats. Collaboration also allows countries to identify and connect seemingly disconnected cross-border money laundering and terrorism financing threats.

3.3 FATF Threat Assessment

In FATF's Global Money Laundering & Terrorist Financing Threat Assessment (dated July 2010), Annex C is entitled "Crime and Terrorism – Harm Framework" which states:

---

[5] https://www.imf.org/en/Publications/CR/Issues/2023/09/01/Nordic-Baltic-Regional-Report-Technical-Assistance-Report-Nordic-Baltic-Technical-538762?cid=bl-com-1EUREA2023003

[6] https://www.imf.org/en/Publications/CR/Issues/2022/07/20/Singapore-2022-Article-IV-Consultation-Press-Release-Staff-Report-and-Statement-by-the-521048

[7] https://www.imf.org/en/Publications/fssa

[8] https://www.imf.org/en/Publications/CR/Issues/2022/02/22/United-Kingdom-Financial-Sector-Assessment-Program-Financial-System-Stability-Assessment-513442

The harms of crime and terrorism are significant and can be seen as occurring at three levels – individual and local, community and regional and national and international.

At the individual and local level, the use of commodities or services controlled by criminals has a negative impact on individuals in terms of health, personal wealth and quality of life. Damage caused to individuals includes the effect of these undesirable behaviours on others, i.e., young people drawn into crime by easy money, power or sense of affiliation. There is also a direct negative impact on those that are personally living criminal lifestyles, as they face a higher risk of physical violence.

Terrorism has also developed to seriously threaten the safety of individuals. In recent decades, both criminals and terrorists have committed and sponsored kidnapping, and used violence and intimidation to coerce innocent individuals into facilitating crime and to achieve political or military goals.

At the community and regional level, there is damage to the reputations of areas in which illegal activity is prevalent and financial losses to legitimate businesses due to being the victims of crime and terrorism. In addition, terrorist attacks also devastate the local areas that are targeted. The long-term effect of these activities serves to undermine public confidence in law enforcement and the wider criminal justice system.

Finally, at the national and international level, the global reach of organised crime and terrorism has weakened economies, corrupted governments and caused or exacerbated the failure of states.

Jurisdictions that contain or suffer from organised crime and terrorism may also suffer from the reputational and financial impact on their institutions and economies. The prevalence of extremist views associated with terrorism can also damage social fabric.

The Annex also includes a chart which sets out the harms as they apply to crime and terrorism and cross references them to the type of harm. These harms relate predominantly to predicate criminal activity or terrorism, rather than the subsequent money laundering and financing of terrorism. However, as these are a facilitator of these activities, in many cases it will be difficult to extract the harms completely.

3.4 Links to Fraud, Corruption and Other Economic Crime

The **IMF** notes the problems and risks with the links between financial and economic crime on the one side and money laundering/terrorist financing on the other:

The IMF is concerned about the consequences of money laundering, terrorism financing, and proliferation financing (providing funds or financial services for nuclear, chemical, or biological weapons), as well as related crimes that undermine the financial sector and the broader economy. These crimes can make countries less stable, which in turn, can weaken law and order, governance, regulatory effectiveness, foreign investments, and international capital flows.

Money laundering and terrorism financing activity in one country can have serious adverse effects across borders and even globally. Countries with weak or ineffective controls are especially attractive for money launderers and financiers of terrorism. These criminals seek to conceal their criminal activities by exploiting the complexity of the global financial system, the differences between national laws, and the speed at which money can cross borders…

OECD: The Link between corruption & money laundering

A regional OECD seminar also noted the links between economic crime and money laundering: the OECD's Anti-Corruption Network for Eastern Europe and Central Asia (ACN)[9] held a seminar entitled "Investigation and Prosecution of Corruption: Financial Investigations and Links with Money Laundering".[10] The seminar brought together investigators and prosecutors (from ACN countries), as well as national authorities in charge of investigating and prosecuting corruption-related and money laundering offences, as well as representatives of Financial Investigation Units (FIUs) and other responsible public bodies dealing with corruption and money-laundering.

In particular, the participants appreciated the opportunity for investigators/ prosecutors to meet with the FIUs, to learn about predicate offences and typologies of money-laundering/corruption, the links to organised crime and new types of crime, such as electronic fraud, to discuss how law-enforcement and anti-money laundering specialists support each other by using analytical tools/financial analysis and methods for tracing assets.

[9] ACN was established in 1998 to support its members in their fight against corruption by providing a regional forum for promotion of anti corruption activities, exchange of information, elaboration of best practices and donor coordination. ACN is open for countries in Central, Eastern and South Eastern Europe, Caucasus and Central Asia. The OECD and EU members, international organisations, multilateral development banks, civil society and business associations also participate in its activities. The ACN Secretariat is based at the OECD Anti-Corruption Division. The Secretariat is guided by the ACN Steering Group and reports to the OECD Working Group on Bribery: https://www.oecd.org/corruption/acn/48916988.pdf

[10] The seminar was held in June 2011 in Kyiv, Ukraine.

Chapter 4
Common Money Laundering Schemes and Red Flags or Warnings of It

4.1 Common Schemes

There are many different and varied ways to launder money. A number of methods can be used and some finance industries are particularly vulnerable, such as:

- banks and banking institutions (both deposits and loans)
- insurance companies
- markets such as for stocks, shares and derivatives
- money brokers and foreign exchange bureaus
- e-commerce
- casinos and other places of high value gambling and
- the buying and selling of property, etc.

This is before considering using the more criminally-oriented, such as:

- people using fake identities
- transactions between international networks of corporate entities and
- professionals whose job is to clean the tainted funds.

The following are seven common ways used to launder funds:[1]

Criminals use many different tactics to conceal the origin of illegal funds. While it would be nearly impossible to write an exhaustive list, here are some of the most common money laundering schemes.

Smurfing or structuring

This money laundering scheme is when a criminal splits up a large amount of money into smaller chunks to avoid their transactions appearing suspicious. Financial

[1] According to Linkurious, a company that "provides the next generation of data visualization and analytics solutions powered by graph technology. We help teams of analysts and investigators swiftly and accurately find insights otherwise hidden in complex connected data so they can make more informed decisions, faster": https://linkurious.com/aml-investigation-solution/

D. Smith, *Money Laundering, Terrorist Financing and Virtual Assets*, Contributions to Finance and Accounting, https://doi.org/10.1007/978-3-031-59842-5_4

institutions are obligated to report transactions above $10,000, so depositing a large amount of criminal proceeds simply isn't an option. By enlisting the help of associates, friends, or relatives, sometimes in several countries, a criminal can have those individuals deposit smaller amounts into their accounts and then have that money wired to his own account.

Round tripping

This is when funds are sent on a "trip" to various accounts, individuals, shell companies, countries with low regulatory standards, etc. before being sent back to their owner with a shiny veneer of legitimacy. The idea is to create a complicated path that's hard to follow. It's easy for analysts and investigators to miss a step in this complex journey of criminal funds, making them difficult to trace back to their original source.

Shell companies

Shell companies exist only on paper and have no real operations or assets. Money launderers will layer the money through a series of shell company transactions to disguise its criminal origins. For example, a shell company may "buy" a service from another shell company owned by the same criminal network. Or dirty money might be sent through shell companies as "payments" for fictitious goods and services. Shell companies make it extremely difficult for authorities to trace the true source of the money. Many criminals register shell companies in countries with lax regulations and strict privacy laws to better hide their activities.

Money laundering through cryptocurrency

For a long time, cash was king for criminal activity, but that's no longer the case. Virtual currencies like Bitcoin are not regulated in a uniform way, making them an easy vehicle to launder criminal proceeds. Certain types of cryptocurrency also allow for a great deal of anonymity. This money laundering scheme has emerged recently, and regulators and financial institutions are now trying to keep up.

Trade-based money laundering

This scheme takes advantage of the complexity of international laws and regulations. A money launderer may manipulate invoices or the value of goods in order to move money around and give it the appearance of being legitimate. Moving funds through different countries, with the involvement of several individuals or businesses, makes it easier for criminals to evade standard AML checks.

Gambling

Since lots of cash moves through casinos, both online and offline, it can be a natural place for illicit money to be laundered. Both the layering and placement steps of the money laundering process are relatively easy at a casino. With two accomplices sitting at the same table, one can lose on purpose, quietly transferring money to the other.

Reselling assets

Cash can easily be made to look legitimate through reselling assets. Criminals may purchase big-ticket items with cash, and then quickly resell those items to have money they are able to actually use in their bank account. Real estate is one of the most common vehicles for this type of money laundering, but luxury cars and other such items are popular placements for illicit funds.

World Economic Forum

While not providing red flags, the WEF has identified the following examples as methods used by trade based money laundering (TBML) fraudsters of which to be aware:

- Invoicing scams

  Mispricing, also called trade misinvoicing, is a common technique used in TBML. Goods invoices are deliberately misrepresented in terms of value, type, or volume. The technique involves over or under-invoicing and can also use a system of multiple-invoicing, also known as split-invoicing.
- Phantom shipments

  Some TBML scams use phantom shipments—shipments of goods that don't occur, or that don't exist. Fake documentation is generated as if the goods will be shipped. Foreign remittances are received by the exporters as part of import/export collusion. The whole process looks legitimate, money is exchanged, but no actual goods are shipped.
- Over or under-shipment

  This is allegedly the most common form of transactions used to facilitate TBML across borders. The seller ships more/less than the invoiced quantity or quality of goods thereby misrepresenting the true value of goods in the documents. The effect is similar to over/under invoicing.

  The trick in the mechanisms used in TBML fraud is that they look legitimate. By appearing as real-world transactions and ticking the regulatory boxes, they can more easily go under the radar. Whatever mechanism is used to move money or hide funds, the ultimate outcome is to overcome structures put in place to prevent this type of fraud. Regulations and other structures attempt to prevent this type of sophisticated and highly obfuscated activity. However, some contradictions in these attempts may be thwarting the wider handling of TBML.

4.2 Red Flags of Money Laundering

There are a number of other publications that identify possible red flags (or warnings) that money laundering may be occurring:

(1) FATF's Recommendations

FATF's Recommendations[2] are a key list of measures to be adopted in order to combat money laundering and terrorist financing. If an entity, especially in the finance sector, is involved in a transaction that doesn't meet domestic rules and the international standards, regulators and investigators may negatively infer red flags:

The FATF Recommendations set out a comprehensive and consistent framework of measures which countries should implement in order to combat money laundering and terrorist financing, as well as the financing of proliferation of weapons of mass destruction. Countries have diverse legal, administrative and operational frameworks and different financial systems, and so cannot all take identical measures to counter these threats.

The FATF Recommendations, therefore, set an international standard, which countries should implement through measures adapted to their particular circumstances. The FATF Standards comprise the Recommendations themselves and their Interpretive Notes, together with the applicable definitions in the Glossary.

(2) FATF's Virtual Assets Red Flag Indicators of Money Laundering and Terrorist Financing[3] (dated September 2020)

The following is a list of red flags for virtual assets published by FATF:

Virtual assets use innovative technology to swiftly transfer value around the world and have many potential benefits, including making payments faster and cheaper. But the anonymity associated with them also attracts criminals, who have used virtual assets to launder proceeds from a range of offences such as the drugs trade, illegal arms smuggling, fraud, tax evasion, cyber attacks, sanctions evasion, child exploitation and human trafficking.

In response, the FATF report will help national authorities detect whether virtual assets are being used for criminal activity. Based on more than 100 case studies collected by members of the FATF Global Network, it highlights the most important red flag indicators that could suggest criminal behaviour. Key indicators in this report focus on:

Technological features that increase anonymity - such as the use of peer-to-peer exchanges websites, mixing or tumbling services or anonymity-enhanced cryptocurrencies

- Geographical risks—criminals can exploit countries with weak, or absent, national measures for virtual assets

[2] https://www.fatf-gafi.org/en/publications/fatfrecommendations/documents/fatf-recommendations.html

[3] https://www.fatf-gafi.org/content/fatf-gafi/en/publications/Methodsandtrends/Virtual-assets-red-flag-indicators.html

- Transaction patterns—that are irregular, unusual or uncommon which can suggest criminal activity
- Transaction size—if the amount and frequency has no logical business explanation
- Sender or recipient profiles—unusual behaviour can suggest criminal activity
- Source of funds or wealth—which can relate to criminal activity

This report will help virtual asset service providers, financial institutions, and designated non-financial businesses and professions, and other reporting entities detect and report suspicious transactions. It will also provide useful information for financial intelligence units, law enforcement agencies, prosecutors and regulators to analyse suspicious transaction reports or monitor compliance with anti-money laundering and counter-terrorist financing controls.

This report complements the RBA [Risk Based Approach] for Virtual Assets & Virtual Asset Service Providers[4] (June 2019) which explains how to understand the money laundering and terrorist financing risks of virtual assets, how to licence and register the sector, actions sectors need to take to know information about their customers, how to store this information securely, and how to detect and report suspicious transactions.

(3) Finance Sector

The following is a list of red flags published for the finance sector on an analyst company website:[5]

One of the keys to detecting money laundering schemes is identifying specific red flags that may indicate suspicious behavior. Here are some of the common red flags to look out for:

Unusual transaction patterns

Transactions that deviate from a customer's typical behavior warrant further investigation. Such transactions may include unusually large amounts or deposits of multiple smaller amounts that were likely structured to avoid reporting requirements.

Large amounts of cash or wire transfers

Transactions involving large sums of cash, particularly if they are structurally designed to avoid reporting requirements, are often associated with money laundering schemes.

Transactions from countries with weak AML laws

Transactions involving high-risk countries with weak anti-money laundering laws or a significant presence of criminal activity certainly don't systematically indicate suspicious activity. However, transactions from such countries warrant extra scrutiny to be sure no criminal activity is going on.

Transactions involving high-risk industries or products

[4] Risk Based Approach.

[5] Linkurious at: https://linkurious.com

Certain industries and products have a higher risk of being used for money laundering, such as the jewellery and precious metals industry, the art market, and the gambling industry. Transactions involving these industries or products should be closely monitored to flag any suspicious activity.

Frequent and unexplained changes to accounts or beneficiaries

Multiple changes to account information or beneficiaries, especially rapid or frequent changes, along with inconsistent or incomplete information warrant closer examination.

By flagging these warning signs early on and taking the necessary steps to investigate them, financial institutions and other organizations can take proactive measures to mitigate risk and prevent money laundering.

The following is another list of red flags for the finance sector:[6]

The growing complexity, diversity and interconnectedness of the financial system is creating new opportunities for criminals. As a result, the anti-money laundering (AML) red flags firms [that compliance teams] ... AML red flags are common warning signs alerting firms and law enforcement to a suspicious transaction that may involve money laundering... Here are ... 10 AML red flag indicators:[7]

1. Secretive new clients who avoid personal contact

   Firms should have Know Your Customer (KYC) and customer due diligence (CDD) procedures in place when onboarding new clients. If a customer refuses to answer questions about themselves, firms should consider whether this is suspicious, especially if they have criminal associations, or know an unusual amount about the money laundering process.
2. Unusual transactions

   Customers trying to launder funds may carry out unusual transactions. Firms should look out for activity that is inconsistent with their expected behavior, such as large cash payments, unexplained payments from a third party, or use of multiple or foreign accounts. These are all AML red flags.
3. Unusual source of funds

   Transactions involving large amounts of cash or private funding could indicate money laundering, and if cash deposits or complex crypto assets are involved, identifying the source can be difficult.
4. Transaction has unusual features

   The size, nature or frequency of transactions, or repetitive instructions involving common features, are all AML red flags. Firms should be particularly alert if a transaction appears unusual for the customer's profile, or if there is unexplained urgency.
5. Geographic concerns

[6] Published by Comply Advantage at: https://complyadvantage.com/insights/aml-red-flags/

[7] The list was published 23 September 2022, updated 26 July 2023.

If a firm is not local to the customer, why are they using it? Unexplained connections with—and movement of money between—jurisdictions should also raise suspicions.

6. Politically exposed persons

   Individuals—and their family and associates—in high positions are more vulnerable to corruption and could pose a higher risk of money laundering for quid-pro-quo favors or kickbacks. While no standardized global definition exists, PEPs typically include heads of state, senior politicians or government officials, judicial or military officials, senior executives of state-owned corporations, or important political party officials.

7. Ultimate beneficial ownership is unclear

   Ultimate beneficial owners are the people who ultimately own or manage a company. Complex ownership structures, or the use of shell companies, could be an attempt to disguise criminal activities and carry out financial crime.

8. Jurisdiction risk

   Some countries or jurisdictions have high levels of corruption, unstable governments, or are known as money laundering havens. They could also have inadequate AML/CFT regulatory and judicial frameworks, or be subject to economic sanctions. Transactions that involve these countries should be carefully monitored as AML red flags.

9. Sanctions exposure

   It is important that firms review relevant international sanctions lists to ensure that customers are not sanctioned themselves, or involved, or transacting with, a sanctioned entity. As Russia's invasion of Ukraine has demonstrated, sanctions lists are subject to change at short notice. This means firms need to ensure they have a real-time plan for managing rapid changes.

10. Adverse media

    Additional checks may also be needed if the customer is a subject of negative news media in any part of the world, as this could increase AML risk. Firms should ensure their adverse media screening is appropriately aligned with common predicate offenses.

(4) <u>Legal Sector</u>

The UK Law Society, the governing body for solicitors in Britain, notes the following "Common Warning Signs" of possible money laundering for lawyers it regulates:

Unusual and secretive clients

It's important that you make fully informed and risk-based decisions on new clients and new types of business from both new and existing clients.

To help assess the risk posed by new clients, you should try to understand why they chose your firm. For example:\

- why is a client who lives far from your firm contacting you in relation to a retainer which has no geographic connection to your firm?

- why is a client instructing you in a field or type of work you have not practised in before?
- why are foreign nationals, who are overseas residents, instructing your firm when you have no connection or profile within that country?

Your practice should have customer due diligence (CDD) procedures in place to identify clients.

If a client refuses to answer questions or give you information about themselves, you should consider whether this is suspicious.

Unusual transactions

Clients trying to launder funds will often try to carry out unusual transactions. The transaction may be unusual for:

- your firm
- your understanding of a client in their position
- the type of retainer they're undertaking

This may not be enough to give rise to a suspicion of money laundering, but it's a warning sign that needs to be followed up.

Unusual source of funds

Regulation 28 of the (UK) Money Laundering, Terrorist Financing and Transfer of Funds (Information on the Payer) Regulations 2017 (MLR 2017) requires scrutiny of transactions to make sure that they're consistent with your knowledge of the client.

Large amounts of cash or private funding, even if held in a bank account, may be a warning sign of money laundering.

You should consider how the client is able to have this amount of private funding and whether it's consistent with what you know about them. You may even ask for documentary evidence to support their account, for example:

- bank statements
- recently filed business accounts
- documents confirming the source, such as a sale of a house or shares

Where cash is involved, identifying the source of funds becomes more challenging. For example, a bank statement showing a large withdrawal might not refer to the cash you're trying to identify.

Equally, a bank statement showing a large cash deposit does not provide you with information about its origin.

In these situations, you should ask yourself:

- is this consistent with what I know about the client?
- does the information make me suspect there is criminal property involved?

Third-party funding

Third-party funding is a normal feature of many conveyancing transactions and other retainers. However, it can also be a way to layer criminal property.

You should consider why the funds are coming from the third party:

- is it a gift or a loan, and if so, what practical or legal consequences are there?
- how can the third party afford to provide this money?
- have the funds come from someone else because your client is on the sanctions list and cannot access a bank account of their own?

If you have a third-party funder, you should consider the risk of money laundering and whether you should conduct any checks on them and the source of funds.

Sudden changes in instructions

In challenging economic times and a fast-paced global economy, transactions can fall through and your client's instructions may change without warning.

Ask yourself whether there's a reasonable explanation for any changes to the retainer, for example the company goes bankrupt or a couple buying a home decide to divorce.

Where there is no clear explanation, particularly if there are other warning signs, you should ask questions such as:

- is this sudden urgency a ploy to ensure that you do not ask too many questions or to encourage you to pay out funds before you realise that the cheque they gave you was fraudulent?
- does the sudden settlement of litigation or falling through of a property or company deal mean that the initial instructions were just a ploy to get money into your client account?

Sham litigation is just one of the methods in which sudden changes of instructions feature.

HM Treasury's[8] national risk assessment of money laundering and terrorist financing specifies the following services as most likely to be abused by money launderers:

- trust and company formation
- conveyancing
- the operation of a client account

To reduce risks when operating in these areas, you must make sure you:

- comply with the anti-money laundering guidance for the legal sector
- pay attention to warning signs that could signal the presence of money laundering.

You should also apply appropriate levels of CDD [due diligence] and enhanced due diligence before providing these services.

Trust and company formation

According to the national risk assessment, money laundering investigations often see the use of trusts and companies as vehicles to hide beneficial ownership.

[8] The Treasury is the UK Government's Ministry of Finance.

Service providers who offer, for example, the replacement of nominee directors or registered offices, are most at risk.

If a client engages you to create and/or manage an entity without seeking legal advice beyond the routine aspects of formation, you should consider whether they're attempting to add a layer of legitimacy to their activities through your involvement.

Warning signs include:

- secretive or suspicious behaviour by the client
- formation of a shell company in an offshore jurisdiction without a legitimate commercial purpose
- interposition of an entity in a transaction without any clear need
- unnecessarily complex corporate structures

You should pay special attention where trust and company services:

- are provided in conjunction with the other services identified as high risk
- involve high-risk jurisdictions

Conveyancing

Firms that facilitate property transactions should ensure the higher money laundering risks in conveyancing are:

- reflected explicitly in their internal risk assessment
- mitigated through comprehensive and effective CDD

Warning signs include:

- rapid succession of transactions relating to the same property
- use of cash or third-party intermediaries without adequate commercial explanation
- use of overseas trusts or companies to conceal property ownership
- unexpected early repayments, for example of a mortgage

  The national risk assessment says that special attention should be paid to transactions involving 'super-prime' residential property in London and Edinburgh.

Commercial property takes longer to move and is therefore subject to a lower risk rating.

However, it can be purchased to set up a network of opaque company structures or to create cash-intensive businesses involving money laundering or predicate offences.

Client accounts

The national risk assessment views the rapid and often large-scale movement of funds through client accounts as a money laundering risk.

You must comply with the SRA Accounts Rules, which:

- prohibit the use of the client account as a banking facility
- require all monies in the account to be linked to an underlying transaction or retainer

Warning signs include:

- instructions to act as a bank or escrow agent, or pay bills unrelated to the matter
- instructions to return overpayments to a client or a third party
- instructions to pay out funds at intervals
- transactions aborted for no clear reasons

The presence of cash in a transaction can act as a warning sign.

The national risk assessment says that the use of cash has declined, but it remains a popular means of payment. Firms should adopt a cash policy in response to the risks posed by cash.

You should pay special attention to cash transactions. You should not accept cash payments above the limit specified in your company's cash policy . . .

Preventing money laundering

[As a solicitor or an informed party in the transaction] You can reduce the chance of money laundering occurring and protect yourself from regulatory or law enforcement action with a few key steps:

- stay alert to warning signs
- ask questions
- document the answers you're given
- follow your firm's internal reporting procedures and consider whether you need to make a suspicious activity report

It's also good practice to have a cash acceptance policy to:

- mitigate insurance risks
- reduce risk to your staff when they carry large amounts of cash to the bank
- provide a clear signal to clients that you will not accept being used for money laundering

You should also:

- be careful who you give your account details to
- request that all funds are transferred electronically to help provide an audit trail
- ask your accounts staff to monitor your bank statements for any cash payments into your client account
- match cash payments to retainers and review the retainer in light of the risks posed by the cash payment
- encourage your fee earners to ask questions about the client and the purpose and nature of the retainer, including the source of funds
- consider whether the explanations for the existence of large amounts of cash or private funding are credible and, if not, consider your obligations under the UK's Proceeds of Crime Act 2002.

(5) Updating for New Schemes

There is continuous pressure on commercial enterprises and institutions to continuously update the lists of money laundering red flags that are used, as criminals constantly re-invent and develop new ways to launder and hide the funds they have gained through criminal means. Consequently, new schemes and processes are continually being developed.

Financial institutions, and many others, are required to monitor transactions, the available background data and previous/current patterns (eg. of the people and entities involved), in order to identify (and stop themselves being involved in) new money laundering schemes as and when they emerge.

This is important not just to keep their own involvement in a transaction legitimate and lawful but also to ensure that national (potentially international) standards are not broken, which can result in:

- Closer scrutiny by their national regulator which can lead to disciplinary proceedings;
- A criminal investigation on the transaction as part of a wider review; and even
- A criminal prosecution and conviction for their role (and the red flags that may have been overlooked) in facilitating the transaction or series of transactions.

These negative possibilities are all possible (depending on the size and importance of the entity involved, even highly likely) and they don't include any additional negative publicity (on social media, TV, radio and in the general and specialist press) that previous cases have demonstrated will be likely to result, including the loss of other clients in the short or medium term who do not want to be associated with the allegations made against the institution concerned.

Chapter 5
Other Possible Corporate Controls

5.1 Internal Controls

Many corporate entities have internal policies and procedures to restrict the ability of an individual staff member from engaging in economic crime for or on behalf of the firm and to ensure that the company's operations and trading is legitimate.

Indeed, a range of preventive and other measures can be taken, including:

- Training of operational teams so that they know what to do/not do, why and how to do it;
- Undertaking due diligence on new clients and monitoring of existing ones;
- Providing advice to operational teams;
- Producing relevant policies such as a Code of Conduct and an AML/CFT company policy;
- Use of IT support to enhance due diligence reviews and searches on sanctions, blacklists and name screening;
- Regulatory and FIU liaison; and
- Production of Suspicious Activity Reports (SARs).

(i) Code of Conduct

One key factor in how a company operates is that companies should have a Code of Conduct applicable to all staff, including senior management, which would include behaviours that were unacceptable including to prohibit staff (and prevent them) from engaging in fraud, cheating, economic crimes or paying bribes to others on behalf of the company by using corporate funds. In some firms, there may even be a particular Code of Conduct for senior management, such as the Chief Compliance Officer, Chief Financial Officer and Chief Operating Officer, President and Board of Directors.

(ii) Preventive Measures

a. Due Diligence—a company would normally take certain measures to conduct background checks, review and verify the available information and

D. Smith, *Money Laundering, Terrorist Financing and Virtual Assets*, Contributions to Finance and Accounting, https://doi.org/10.1007/978-3-031-59842-5_5

documents about a new partner, client or customer, including looking at important factors such as their assets and liabilities, in order to minimise the risk that the partner is going to cheat, defraud, or cause other damage to them. This may be a simple exercise if the company is small; equally it can be a larger, longer-term project if the client's complex corporate structure(s) and international operations needs to be reviewed.

Once approved, a client's situation should be regularly monitored with further checks/reviews in case of significant changes to their assets, liabilities, trading situation or a dramatic change to the risk profile they represent.

A company can also undertake Customer Due Diligence (CCD) to assess the risks in a transaction. This CDD can be enhanced or simplified depending on the size of the company/nature of the client and other circumstances. In cases where a client's funds are sourced in high-risk or lightly regulated countries or other risks (such as whether related businesses are susceptible to money laundering or countries with a high risk of terrorist financing are involved) are identified, enhanced due diligence would become necessary with greater detail, history etc. required before the client can be accepted and the transaction undertaken.

One of the purposes of the review would be to identify whether there are any politically-exposed persons (PEPs) involved, a category identified by FATF. PEPs are considered to be senior people in prominent public positions as well as their family and close associates and it would be important to identify the PEPs sources of wealth and funds. More rigorous monitoring of their account may also result.

b. Know Your Customer (KYC)—this tends to be a standard process in the financial and other sectors. It is the process used to verify a client's identity and know the client's investment knowledge and financial profile.

   Additional problems may arise (leading to wider and more detailed due diligence becoming necessary) if a client is introduced by an intermediary, agent or other third party.

   Once the initial KYC review is complete, there would normally be an ongoing monitoring to ensure continued and relevant up-to-date information is available.

These KYC and CCD checks would normally be allocated to a team of compliance professional; in some cases, where the background or context of the client is identified to be of higher risk in due diligence and KYC, enhanced CCD checks will need to be undertaken. Similarly if the risks are low, a simplified CCD process may be appropriate.

KYC can also benefit significantly from access to Company and Ultimate Beneficial Ownership registers. However, in a recent case, the Court of Justice of the EU (ECJ) ruled in favour of privacy and data protection of the ultimate beneficial owners (UBO) of corporate entities, whose fundamental rights were infringed by one of the provisions of the EU secondary law.[1]

5.2 Other Controls

(i) Company Records & Accounts

Corporate accounting records are prepared by the company, usually with the assistance of an external accounting firm. They are a written record that explains the business activities and the financial performance. These accounts largely an external-facing document, used to reflect the company's financial situation (usually including a balance sheet—what assets it owns, the debts it owes and is owed—and a profit and loss account—the company profit or loss taking into account the running costs and it sales) at the end of the financial year for use by interested third parties such as partners, existing and possible future shareholders/investors, banks, etc.[2]

Under domestic legislation, apart from the preparation of yearly accounts, relevant accounting and other documents are likely to be legally required to be retained. For one reason, the regulators and law enforcement would like, if necessary, to be able to inspect original documents and establish an evidence trail in a suspicious transaction. The availability of records created for a particular customer or client before and after a particular transaction can assist greatly in the detection and investigation of economic crime more generally, and money laundering and terrorist financing in particular.

Such requirements may even deter a criminal from seeking to engage in a course of conduct in a particular country, especially if they know that every call or discussion, every instruction, the flow of funds and the customer's explana-

[1] Judgment—22/11/2022—Luxembourg Business Registers Case C-37/20 (Joined Cases C-37/20, C-601/20). See also an article entitled Privacy and Data Protection vs public access to entrepreneurs' personal data. Score 2:0 – How did the ECJ balance the rights to privacy and data protection against transparency of Ultimate Beneficial Owners registries in *WM and Sovim SA v Luxembourg Business Registers*? by Magdalena Brewczynska dated 15 December 2022 in the European Law Blog at: https://europeanlawblog.eu/2022/12/15/privacy-and-data-protection-vs-public-access-to-entrepreneurs-personal-data-score-20/

[2] The Companies Act 2006 in the UK requires the directors to ensure that the company's annual accounts provide a true and fair view; the Sarbanes-Oxley Act 2002 (ref: Pub. L. 107-204 or 116 Stat. 745) in the USA was passed to improve the accuracy and reliability of corporate disclosures following major corporate scandals such as Enron and WorldCom; the Corporations Act 2001 in Australia regulates business entities; and the Singapore Companies Act 1967 (as amended by the Companies, Business Trusts and Other Bodies (Miscellaneous Amendments) Act 2023 in Singapore.

tion thereof and the other relevant information provided are recorded regularly and would be available to law enforcement for inspection.

The FATF Recommendation 11 (see below) provides a minimum time for banks and financial institutions to retain records—at least five years after the date of the transaction and five years after the relationship has ended.

(ii) External Requirements

There are a number of other controls imposed on companies, including Reporting Obligations.

In particular, finance institutions are required to monitor the transactions which they conduct on behalf of their clients. This monitoring includes an obligation to report any suspicious transactions to a national Financial Intelligence Unit (FIU). The reports that result and are submitted by the institutions are known as Suspicious Activity Reports (SARs).

Given that the submission of such reports goes against data privacy and banking secrecy, they are usually governed by domestic legislation. Further discussion of the FIUs will follow below.

(iii) National Limits imposed by legislation

When large payments are made across borders, there may be national limits imposed by domestic legislation to large cash payments.[3]

In the UK, consumers can make cash payments without any limits.

The traders, however, need to register themselves with tax authorities as 'High Value Dealers' if accepting cash payments in excess of € 10,000. Exclusions apply.[4]

In the US, the IRS state that a person must file Form 8300 if they receive cash of more than US$10,000 from the same payer or agent:

- In one lump sum.
- In two or more related payments within 24 h. For example, a 24-h period is 11 a.m. Tuesday to 11 a.m. Wednesday.
- As part of a single transaction or two or more related transactions within a 12 month period.[5]

There is no single EU-wide standardised upper limit for cash payments in the EU but it is very likely that this will come: in the fight against money laundering and terrorist financing, the European Parliament and the Council of Ministers have

[3] https://cellpointdigital.com/articles/blog/cross-border-payments-the-issues-and-challenges# and https://stripe.com/en-gb-lu/resources/more/cross-border-payments-explained

[4] https://www.evz.de/en/shopping-internet/cash-payment-limitations.html#:~:text=United-Kingdom,cash-payments-without-any-limits

[5] https://www.irs.gov/newsroom/understand-how-to-report-large-cash-transactions#:~:text=A-person-must-file-Form,related-payments-within-24-hours

agreed on a standardised upper limit of EUR10,000. The law still needs to be formally adopted. Member states that already have lower cash limits can retain them.[6]

In Singapore, it is necessary to file a Cash Transaction Report ("**CTR**") with the Suspicious Transaction Reporting Office ("**STRO**") for cash and cash equivalent transactions exceeding S$20,000.[7]

In Australia: Under the Currency (Restrictions on the Use of Cash) Bill 2019, Clause 12 would create a criminal offences for entities that:

- make or accept a payment in cash where the cash is A$10,000 or more or
- make or accept a series of payments for a supply or gift where the total amount of cash is A$10,000 or more.[8]

[6] Report dated January 2024: https://www.evz.de/en/shopping-internet/cash-payment-limitations.html#:~:text=In-the-fight*against-money,upper-limit-of-10%2C000-euros

[7] https://acd.mlaw.gov.sg/transaction-based-requirements/#:~:text=File-Cash-Transaction-Report-("CTR,to-e%2Dfile-your-CTR

[8] https://www.aph.gov.au/Parliamentary_Business/Bills_Legislation/bd/bd1920a/20bd089#:~:text=Cash-includes-both-physical-and-digital-currency.&text=Clause-12-creates-criminal-offences,cash-is-%2410%2C000-or-more

Chapter 6
More on Terrorist Financing

UNODC defines terrorist financing as:[1]

> . . . the raising of money involving the solicitation, collection or provision of funds, with the intention that it may be used to support terrorist acts, terrorists or terrorist organisations. Whether they are part of large terrorist organisations which control territory, or members of small terrorist cells, terrorists need money. Their funds may originate from legitimate sources, or from criminal activities. A lack of funds limits their ability to prepare and carry out attacks, and to develop as an organisation.

The UN Office of Drugs and Crime (UNODC) provides training courses to professionals as part of a comprehensive program entitled Countering Financing of Terrorism to build capacity in analysis, investigation, disruption and inter-agency cooperation to support national efforts to combat the financing of terrorism.[2]

The funding of terrorist causes can be undertaken in two ways:

- the financing of the long term terrorist movement; or
- the shorter term funding of specific terrorist attacks.

These different methods can lead to different approaches to obtain, collect and disguise the use of the funds. Such differences are extrapolated and become even more distinct when the terrorist organisation actually controls land, rather than merely conducting operations inside it, such as ISIS.

[1] https://www.unodc.org/centralasia/en/news/countering-terrorism-financing-is-in-focus-of-the-unodc-training-course-for-tajik-authorities.html#:~:text=The-Programme-on-Countering-Financing,country%27s-national-capacity-to-counter

[2] https://www.unodc.org/centralasia/en/news/countering-terrorism-financing-is-in-focus-of-the-unodc-training-course-for-tajik-authorities.html#:~:text=The-Programme-on-Countering-Financing,country%27s-national-capacity-to-counter. In 2021–2022, UNODC trained over 70 specialists-practitioners of law enforcement agencies and supervisory authorities on combating terrorism financing.

D. Smith, *Money Laundering, Terrorist Financing and Virtual Assets*, Contributions to Finance and Accounting, https://doi.org/10.1007/978-3-031-59842-5_6

There are other differences between money laundering and terrorist financing:

- the funds involved in money laundering are usually significant. The launderers who handle the proceeds of serious crime are dealing with very large quantities indeed (as noted by the quotes above) but terrorists can operate (and unfortunately can still be successful) on a very limited budget. This poses significant difficulties to those institutions that are trying to disrupt the flow of funds to terrorists whereas suspicious systems (especially those processing large sums) that the launderers use can be detected and stopped.
- The nature of terrorism and the lack of agreement internationally about what and who a terrorist is compares unfavourably to the general global agreement that criminals are identifiable, should be apprehended and prevented for benefitting financially from the crimes they have committed. There are also possible political elements to be taken into account: free speech or restricted for good reason? Legitimate protest or life-endangering crime? Freedom fighter or terrorist?
- The extension of terrorism and the financing of terrorism into wider society can develop and involve others in certain circumstances (especially involving others in the same regional/national, ethnic or religious group) whereas the money laundering that criminals undertake (and indeed the crimes giving rise to the funds that need laundering) is unlikely to involve others except than the victims.

FATF has worked to counter the threats of financing of terrorism:[3]

Combatting terrorist financing has been a priority for the FATF since 2001. However, in 2015, the scope and nature of terrorist threats globally intensified considerably, with terrorist attacks in many cities across the world, and the terrorist threat posed by the so-called Islamic State of Iraq and the Levant (ISIL/Da'esh), and by Al-Qaeda and their affiliated terrorist organisations.

Since then, the terrorism threats have continued to evolve, from large terrorist organisations, to returning terrorist fighters and right-wing extremists. Funds flow cross-border to providing resources for nationally designated organisations, and many jurisdictions continue to suffer from persistent attacks from small cells and radicalised lone actors, drawing inspiration from a range of dangerous ideologies.

The FATF plays a central role in global efforts in combatting terrorist financing, through its role in setting global standards to combat terrorist financing, assisting jurisdictions in implementing financial provisions of the United Nations Security Council resolutions on terrorism, and evaluating countries' ability to prevent, detect, investigate and prosecute the financing of terrorism. Yet many countries have not yet implemented the FATF Standards effectively. They do not understand the nature of terrorist financing risks they face, nor have effective means to combat them.

[3]https://www.fatf-gafi.org/en/topics/Terrorist-Financing.html

The FATF Strategy on Combating Terrorist Financing sets out the broad objectives for FATF's work in this area. Under this strategy, the FATF, in close collaboration with the regional FATF-style regional bodies and other partners such as the UN, the FATF has completed work to support countries around the world in combatting terrorist financing.

FATF also publishes a number of useful guides including:

- *Ethnically or Racially Motivated Terrorism Financing:* This report aims to increase the understanding of terrorist financing risks related to extreme right wing actors. It encourages countries to continue to develop their understanding of this increasingly transnational criminal activity, including by considering ethnically or racially motivated terrorism financing in their national risk assessments;[4]
- *Terrorist Financing Risk Assessment Guidance*: This guidance aims to assist practitioners, and particularly those in lower capacity countries, in assessing terrorist financing risk, by providing good approaches, relevant information sources and practical examples based on country experience;[5] and
- *Risk of terrorist abuse in non-profit organisations:* Terrorist organisations need funds, material, personnel and public influence to carry out their illegal activities. Non-profit organisations NPO rely on the same capabilities to further their legitimate and good causes. This typologies report examines in detail, how and where NPOs are at risk of terrorist abuse and provides a number of red flag indicators to help all stakeholders identify and investigate possible cases of abuse.[6]

The OECD Handbook for Tax Examiners and Tax Auditors[7] that was mentioned earlier also includes financing of terrorism. They note that "financial crimes, including tax evasion, money laundering, and terrorist financing undermine jurisdictions' political and economic interests and pose a serious threat to national security. Tax crime is a key source of dirty money and as such, tax authorities have a central role to play in identifying and reporting money laundering and terrorist financing". The purpose of OECD's handbook is to: "raise the awareness level of tax examiners, auditors, and investigators, of their role in combatting these illegal activities". The handbook covers areas such as: Real Estate, Cash, Loans and Professional Service Providers.

---

[4]https://www.fatf-gafi.org/en/publications/Methodsandtrends/Ethnically-racially-motivated-terrorism-financing.html

[5]https://www.fatf-gafi.org/en/publications/Methodsandtrends/Terrorist-financing-risk-assessment-guidance.html

[6]https://www.fatf-gafi.org/en/publications/Methodsandtrends/Risk-terrorist-abuse-non-profits.html

[7]https://www.oecd.org/ctp/crime/money-laundering-awareness-handbook-for-tax-examiners-and-tax-auditors.pdf. The Handbook notes that the members of OECD are: Australia, Austria, Belgium, Canada, Czech Republic, Denmark, Finland, France Germany, Greece, Hungary, Iceland, Ireland, Italy, Japan, Korea, Luxembourg, Mexico, the Netherlands, New Zealand, Norway, Poland, Portugal, the Slovak Republic, Spain Sweden, Switzerland, Turkey, UK and USA.

UNODC has a Global Legal Assistance Programme and programs against money laundering and terrorism. Throught them, UNODC provides assistance with ratification and implementation of the UN instruments (against drugs, organized crime, corruption and terrorism). In particular, UNODC works to assist with upgrading essential legislation in support of countries ratifying the UN Conventions against:

- Transnational Organized Crime;
- Corruption; and
- Anti-terrorism instruments including the latest convention against terrorism financing and nuclear terrorism.[8]

In 2017, the WEF noted a report produced by the Institute for Economics & Peace had identified that:[9]

The number of terrorism deaths globally declined for the second consecutive year . . . But in developed nations, deaths increased, and terrorism has spread to more countries. In part, this reflects the changing dynamics of terrorism as witnessed in the developed world, from high intensity sophisticated attacks to more low-tech, low-cost and lone actor attacks. Such a shift in tactics mimics the evolutions in terrorism funding and highlights the need to consider longer-term strategies to inhibit the rise of terrorism.

In 2016, ISIL was the world's wealthiest terrorist group. Its estimated annual revenue, according to the Global Terrorism Index, peaked at US$2billion in 2015, which is the equivalent to the GDP of some small nations. However, as the loss of its self-proclaimed caliphate has shown, the group's strategy of self-funding in controlled territory has left them susceptible to any action that impinges on its territory. During the last year, ISIL's funding structure has caved following major territorial losses in Iraq and Syria, as half of its funds were sourced from oil smuggling. ISIL was producing up to 75,000 barrels per day and generating revenues of US$1.3 million per day.

[8] https://www.unodc.org/centralasia/en/terrorism-prevention.html

[9] https://www.weforum.org/agenda/2017/11/terror-attacks-are-increasingly-self-funded-how-can-we-stop-them/

Chapter 7
New frontiers: i) Cryptocurrency, ii) Decentralised Finance (DeFi), & iii) Non-Fungible Tokens (NFT)

7.1 Cryptocurrency

Cryptocurrency is generally defined as: A digital currency designed to work as a medium of exchange through a computer network that is not reliant on any central authority, such as a government or bank, to uphold or maintain it.[2] It is a decentralized system for verifying that the parties to a transaction have the money they claim to have, eliminating the need for traditional intermediaries, such as banks, when funds are being transferred between two entities . . .

According to Jan Lansky, a cryptocurrency is a system that meets six conditions:[38]

1. The system does not require a central authority; its state is maintained through distributed consensus.
2. The system keeps an overview of cryptocurrency units and their ownership.
3. The system defines whether new cryptocurrency units can be created. If new cryptocurrency units can be created, the system defines the circumstances of their origin and how to determine the ownership of these new units.
4. Ownership of cryptocurrency units can be proved exclusively cryptographically.
5. The system allows transactions to be performed in which ownership of the cryptographic units is changed. A transaction statement can only be issued by an entity proving the current ownership of these units.
6. If two different instructions for changing the ownership of the same cryptographic units are simultaneously entered, the system performs at most one of them.[1]

[1] https://en.wikipedia.org/wiki/Cryptocurrency

D. Smith, *Money Laundering, Terrorist Financing and Virtual Assets*, Contributions to Finance and Accounting, https://doi.org/10.1007/978-3-031-59842-5_7

A general perception that assets held remotely (even anonymously) in a digital cryptocurrency are neither subject to (i) regulation or supervision by national regulators; nor (ii) investigation or prosecution by national law enforcement or prosecutors; so that criminal offences like fraud, corruption, cheating and misrepresentations affecting such assets are much less likely to be investigated and prosecuted in national courts, especially if lengthy and detailed but virtual transactions need to be explained to a jury.

However, this may not necessarily be the case as regulators and law enforcement come to a greater understanding of the virtual systems and how they can be manipulated. UNODC have adopted the following objectives:[2]

- Increased institutional efficiency and effectiveness in the prevention, disruption, investigation, prosecution and adjudication of cybercrime, in line with human-rights principles;
- Increased knowledge and sensitize society to reduce cybercrime risks;
- Strengthened national and international communication and cooperation between government, law enforcement and the private sector to enhance prevention, disruption and investigation of cybercrime; and
- Adoption of effective regulatory frameworks leading to a sustainable and long-term response to counter cybercrime according to international standards.

a. UK

The National Crime Agency (NCA) note that:

> Cyber crime continues to rise in scale and complexity, affecting essential services, businesses and private individuals alike. Cyber crime costs the UK billions of pounds, causes untold damage and threatens national security.[3]

The NCA acknowledge that cyber crime is a global threat and the suspects and their technical infrastructure are often based overseas, making collaboration with other international law enforcement necessary. The NCA:

> ... focus on critical cyber incidents as well as longer-term activity against the criminals and the services on which they depend. We work closely with UK police, regional organised crime units, and partners in international law enforcement such as Europol, the FBI and the US Secret Service to share intelligence and coordinate action. We have also developed close and effective partnerships with private industry to share information and technical expertise.

The UK has also developed the National Cyber Security Centre (NCSC), as a part of the Government Communications Headquarters (GCHQ), an intelligence and security organisation. They support British organisations in the public and private

---

[2] https://www.unodc.org/unodc/en/cybercrime/home.html

[3] https://www.nationalcrimeagency.gov.uk/what-we-do/crime-threats/cyber-crime?highlight=WyJyYW5zb20iXQ==

sectors and if an incident occurs, NCSC provide "effective incident response to minimise harm to the UK, help with recovery, and learn lessons for the future."[4]

b. USA

The Market Integrity and Major Frauds (MIMF) Unit of the US Department of Justice recently stated the following:[5]

> MIMF is a national leader in prosecuting fraud and market manipulation involving cryptocurrency. Since 2019, the Unit has charged cryptocurrency fraud cases involving over $2 billion in intended financial losses to investors from around the world. Prosecutors use blockchain data analytics and traditional law enforcement techniques to identify and prosecute complex cryptocurrency investment schemes; price and market manipulation involving cryptocurrencies; unregistered cryptocurrency exchanges involved in fraud schemes; and insider trading schemes affecting cryptocurrency markets. Prosecutors in the Unit frequently work in parallel with the U.S. Securities and Exchange Commission and the Commodity Futures Trading Commission.

In particular, they claim that in the 6 months to June 2022, the Unit charged 8 defendants in relation to financial losses of more than US$ 2bn and US$ 56 mn in funds recovered.

The FBI state the following about the cyber threat:[6]

> Malicious cyber activity threatens the public's safety and our national and economic security. The FBI's cyber strategy is to impose risk and consequences on cyber adversaries. Our goal is to change the behavior of criminals and nation-states who believe they can compromise U.S. networks, steal financial and intellectual property, and put critical infrastructure at risk without facing risk themselves. To do this, we use our unique mix of authorities, capabilities, and partnerships to impose consequences against our cyber adversaries.
>
> The FBI is the lead federal agency for investigating cyber attacks and intrusions. We collect and share intelligence and engage with victims while working to unmask those committing malicious cyber activities, wherever they are …
>
> A Complex, Global Concern
>
> Our adversaries look to exploit gaps in our intelligence and information security networks. The FBI is committed to working with our federal counterparts, our foreign partners, and the private sector to close those gaps.
>
> These partnerships allow us to defend networks, attribute malicious activity, sanction bad behavior, and take the fight to our adversaries overseas. The FBI fosters this team approach through unique hubs where government, industry, and

[4] https://www.ncsc.gov.uk/section/about-ncsc/what-we-do

[5] https://www.justice.gov/criminal/criminal-fraud/crypto-enforcement

[6] https://www.fbi.gov/investigate/cyber

academia form long-term trusted relationships to combine efforts against cyber threats.

Within government, that hub is the National Cyber Investigative Joint Task Force (NCIJTF). The FBI leads this task force of more than 30 co-located agencies from the Intelligence Community and law enforcement. The NCIJTF is organized around mission centers based on key cyber threat areas and led by senior executives from partner agencies. Through these mission centers, operations and intelligence are integrated for maximum impact against U.S. adversaries.

c. UN Office of Drugs and Crime (UNODC)

The UNODC refers to a concept known as UNODC—SHERLOC: Sharing Electronic Resources and Laws on Crime—The SHERLOC portal is an initiative to facilitate the dissemination of information regarding the implementation of the United Nations Convention against Transnational Organized Crime, the three Protocols thereto and the international legal framework against terrorism.[7]UNODC has also published a number of relevant reports including: Women in Cyber Newsletter,[8] UNODC Cyber Crunch Newsletter[9] and Darknet Cybercrime Threats to Southeast Asia (English)[10] and has a Cryptocurrencies E-Learning course.[11]

d. Blockchain

Blockchain.com (formerly **Blockchain.info**) is a cryptocurrency financial services company. The company began as a Bitcoin blockchain explorer in 2011[12] and later created a cryptocurrency wallet that accounted for more than a quarter of bitcoin transactions between 2012 and 2020. It also operates a cryptocurrency exchange and provides institutional markets lending business and data, charts, and analytics.[13]A cryptocurrency exchange helps to convert digital assets in money and money into the digital assets, working like a stockbroker, allowing its users to buy, sell, and trade cryptocurrencies.

[7] https://sherloc.unodc.org/cld/en/st/home.html

[8] https://www.unodc.org/documents/Cybercrime/tools-and-resources/women_in_cyber_newsletter_march_2023.pdf

[9] https://www.unodc.org/documents/Cybercrime/tools-and-resources/unodc_cyber_crunch_newsletter_issue01_sep2022.pdf

[10] https://www.unodc.org/roseap/uploads/archive/documents/darknet/index.html

[11] https://www.unodc.org/unodc/en/cybercrime/tools-and-resources

[12] Ben Reeves started it in 2011, launching a website that could be used to track bitcoin transactions and allowing bitcoin users to see the details of public cryptocurrency transactions if they have the identifying hash code for the transaction.

[13] https://en.wikipedia.org/wiki/Blockchain.com#cite_note-McMillan201403-8

7.2 Decentralised Finance (DeFi)

This concept provides financial instruments without having to rely on intermediaries like brokers, exchanges or banks. The rules that consumers use when accessing capital and financial services from centralised financial institutions like banks and brokerages in the U.S. are defined by the Federal Reserve and Securities and Exchange Commission (SEC). DeFi challenges this centralized financial system by empowering individuals with unregulated peer-to-peer transactions.

Components of DeFi are cryptocurrencies, blockchain technology, and software that allow people to transact financially with each other. However, DeFi is still in its infancy, and may be vulnerable to hacks and thefts because of programming and weak testing before applications are launched.[14]

7.3 Non Fungible Token (NFT)

NFTs are unique cryptographic tokens that are used to certify ownership and authenticity.[15] They can be sold or traded and are stored on blockchain. The NFT is a distinct token that cannot be replicated, copied or divided and can represent real-world assets like artwork and real estate.

As a result of the development of the concept of digital ownership, there has been some confusion and frustration.[16] Indeed, NFTs have drawn criticism for the use in art scams and been compared to a Ponzi scheme. During their peak, the three biggest NFT platforms were Ethereum, Solana, and Cardano.

The market in NFT grew rapidly in 2020, tripling to US$250 million. In 2021, interest in NFTs increased after a number of high-profile sales and art auctions. However, in May 2022 *The Wall Street Journal* reported that the NFT market was "collapsing" in part because of interest rate rises but also the WSJ said "NFTs are among the most speculative."[17]

---

[14] https://www.investopedia.com/decentralized-finance-defi-5113835#:~:text=Decentralized-finance%2C-or-DeFi%2C-uses,transact-financially-with-each-other

[15] https://en.wikipedia.org/wiki/Non-fungible_token

[16] https://www.kraken.com/learn/what-are-non-fungible-tokens-nft#

[17] Paul Vigna's article dated May 3, 2022: "NFT Sales Are Flatlining". *The Wall Street Journal.*

Chapter 8
Supervision & Regulation; Investigation & Prosecution

A. **Supervision & Regulation**

Supervision of money laundering and terrorist financing is governed by a number of different organisations, nationally and internationally. The following are particular international regulatory and supervisory authorities with an important role to play in this regard.

a) **FATF**[1]
   See above the description and purpose of FATF. FATF are active in updating material and publishing the materials in support of states attempting to combat money laundering.
b) **Egmont Group of Financial Intelligence Units**[2]
   The Egmont Group was set up in 1995 to facilitate cooperation between FIUs—the Egmont Group provides a discussion forum for FIUs to review and improve national AML programmes.
c) **Moneyval**[3]
   Moneyval is the abbreviated name of the Committee of Experts on the Evaluation of Anti-Money Laundering Measures and the Financing of Terrorism. It is a monitoring body of the Council of Europe, with 47 member

[1] https://www.fatf-gafi.org/en/the-fatf.html

[2] As a global organization, the Egmont Group facilitates and prompts the exchange of information, knowledge, and cooperation amongst member FIUs. Access the Egmont Group core documents including the Charter and Principles for Information Exchange Between Financial Intelligence Units. The Egmont Group provides FIUs with a platform to securely exchange expertise and financial intelligence to combat money laundering, terrorist financing, and associated predicate crimes: https://egmontgroup.org/

[3] A full list of their competencies and tasks are listed on their website: https://www.coe.int/en/web/moneyval

D. Smith, *Money Laundering, Terrorist Financing and Virtual Assets*, Contributions to Finance and Accounting, https://doi.org/10.1007/978-3-031-59842-5_8

states, reporting directly to the Committee of Ministers of the Council of Europe.[4]

Moneyval seeks to assess national compliance with the principal international standards to counter money laundering and the financing of terrorism and the effectiveness of the implementation, as well as making recommendations to national authorities for necessary improvements to their systems.

d) **Wolfsberg Group**[5]

Wolfsberg Group is a group of 12 global commercial banks (including HSBC, Barclays, Sociate Generale, Santander, Goldman Sachs, Deutsche Bank, JP Morgan Chase and UBS) aiming to develop frameworks, standards and guidance for the management of financial crime risks.

This includes the Correspondent Banking Due Diligence Questionnaire (CBDDQ)[6] which has been revised and updated periodically. The Group also works towards promoting engagement between public and private sectors in combatting illicit financial activity. The group also works as an advocate for the finance industry with international standard setters, national law enforcement, financial intelligence units, supervisors and regulators seeking to prevent the misuse of the global financial system.

e) **European Banking Authority**

The European Banking Authority (EBA):[7]

> ... is an independent EU Authority which works to ensure effective and consistent prudential regulation and supervision across the European banking sector. Its overall objectives are to maintain financial stability in the EU and to safeguard the integrity, efficiency and orderly functioning of the banking sector.
>
> The main task of the EBA is to contribute to the creation of the European Single Rulebook in banking whose objective is to provide a single set of harmonised prudential rules for financial institutions throughout the EU. The Authority also plays an important role in promoting convergence of supervisory practices and is mandated to assess risks and vulnerabilities in the EU banking sector.

In particular, the EBA attempts to ensure:

> ... the integrity, transparency and orderly functioning of financial markets. As part of this mandate, the EBA works to prevent the use of the financial system for the purposes of money laundering and terrorist financing (ML/TF).

---

[4] https://en.wikipedia.org/wiki/Moneyval

[5] https://wolfsberg-group.org

[6] https://wolfsberg-group.org/about/#working-groups

[7] https://www.eba.europa.eu/homepage and https://en.wikipedia.org/wiki/European_Banking_Authority

The EBA recently launched a new database (called EuReCA) for anti-money laundering and counter-terrorist financing (AML/CFT). This system will track CFT/AML weaknesses[8] and:

> ... will be central to coordinating efforts by competent authorities and the EBA to prevent and counter money laundering and terrorist financing (ML/TF) risks in the European Union.
>
> EuReCA will contain information on material weaknesses in individual financial institutions in the EU that competent authorities have identified. Competent authorities will also be reporting the measures they have imposed on financial institutions to rectify those material weaknesses.
>
> Examples of material weaknesses include the lack of adequate AML/CFT policies and procedures including the absence of transaction monitoring at the group level and the absence of policies and procedures for high-risk customers, which increase the ML/TF risk associated with the financial institution. EuReCA also includes internal audit findings identified by a prudential authority during an on-site inspection about which the management body of the senior management appeared to have been informed and decided not to remediate.

f) **Others**

Beyond the banking sector, there are a number of other organisations working internationally to coordinate their members interests and assist to combat money laundering and terrorist financing. Organisations such as the International Association of Insurance Supervisors (IAIS)[9] working in the insurance sector and International Association of Securities Commissions (OICV-IOSCO)[10] have published guidance for their members.

B. Examples of National & Regional Supervisory/Regulatory Authorities

1) UK

i. UK Law Society

The UK Law Society has published a Suspicious Activity Reports Guide (dated August 2023) which explains:

> ... when and how to make a suspicious activity report (SAR), what to include, how to request a defence against money laundering (DAML) and what happens if you fail to report suspicious activity to the National Crime Agency (NCA).
>
> A suspicious activity report (SAR) is a disclosure made to the National Crime Agency (NCA) about known or suspected:

---

[8] The link is: https://www.eba.europa.eu The legal basis for the EuReCA database is set out in article 9(a)(1) and (3) of the EBA Regulation. It will contain information on "material weaknesses" in individual financial institutions policies, procedures and governance making them vulnerable.

[9] https://www.iaisweb.org

[10] https://www.iosco.org

- money laundering – under part 7 of the Proceeds of Crime Act 2002 (POCA)
- terrorist financing – under part 3 of the Terrorism Act 2000 (TACT)

This guide explains how to report suspicious activity to the NCA. It assumes that the person making the SAR is a money laundering reporting officer (MLRO) or their deputy. . .

Identifying money laundering

Before making a SAR, you need to be clear about who you're reporting and why. You should consider:

- why you're suspicious
- what transaction you're involved in
- whether the client is a suspect or a victim . . .

When to make a SAR

Regulated sector—If you're an MLRO working in the regulated sector, you must make a SAR if you know or suspect, or have reasonable grounds for knowing or suspecting, that a person is engaged in money laundering.

Non-regulated sector—If you're an MLRO working in the non-regulated sector, you must make a SAR if you know or suspect that money laundering is taking place.

Forming a suspicion

You'll need to decide whether you've formed a suspicion before you're obliged to make a SAR.

The threshold for suspicion is low. The leading test comes from R v Da Silva [2006] EWCA Crim 1654.

You have a reportable suspicion if you think there's a possibility, which is more than fanciful, that the relevant facts exist. In Da Silva, it was noted that "a vague feeling of unease would not suffice".

Once you've formed your suspicion, it's good practice to document the basis for your reasons. This will help to defeat any allegations of reporting in bad faith . . .

A detailed SAR helps the NCA to quickly identify whether your client is a person of interest and to fill intelligence gaps on, for example, new aliases . . .

ii. **UK Financial Conduct Authority (FCA)**[11]

The FCA regulate financial services firms and financial markets in the UK. The Office for Professional Body Anti-Money Laundering Supervision (OPBAS) was established to strengthen the UK's AML supervisory regime, supervising the 25 professional body supervisors (PBSs) in the legal and accountancy sectors:[12]

[11] https://www.fca.org.uk/

[12] https://www.fca.org.uk/about/how-we-operate/who-work-with/opbas

OPBAS is housed within the FCA and our key objectives are to reduce the harm of money laundering and terrorist financing by:

1. ensuring a robust and consistently high standard of supervision by the PBSs overseeing the legal and accountancy sectors
2. facilitating collaboration and information and intelligence sharing between PBSs, statutory supervisors and law enforcement agencies

The OPBAS Regulations 2017 give us powers to ensure that PBSs meet the standards required by the Money Laundering Regulations 2017 (MLRs).

The FCA states:[13]

The Money Laundering and Terrorist Financing (Amendment) Regulations 2019 sets out the amendments to the Money Laundering, Terrorist Financing and Transfer of Funds (Information on the Payer) Regulations 2017 (MLRs).

Following consultation, changes to the Financial Crime Guide which reflect amendments to the MLRs are now in effect (from 1 October 2020).

The Proceeds of Crime Act 2002 requires you to submit a Suspicious Activity Report to the National Crime Agency if you know or suspect that a person is engaged in, or attempting, money laundering.

The MLRs (as amended) apply to banks, building societies and credit unions. They also apply to other firms undertaking certain financial activities (see Schedule 2 of the regulations). These will normally include investment managers and stockbrokers, e-money institutions, payment institutions, consumer credit firms offering lending services, financial advisors, investment firms, asset managers and those providing safety deposit services.

These regulations require you to apply risk-based customer due diligence measures and take other steps to prevent your services from being used for money laundering or terrorist financing.

Businesses carrying out certain crypto asset activities also need to comply with the MLRs in relation to those activities from 10 January 2020, and to register with us during 2020.

We require all authorised firms subject to the Money Laundering Regulations to meet additional but complementary regulatory obligation to apply policies and procedures to minimise their money laundering risk. Your internal controls effectively monitor and manage your firm's compliance with anti-money-laundering (AML) policies and procedures. These controls need to be appropriate to the size of your firm, the products you offer, the parts of the world where you do business and types of customers who use your services.

We also require that firms:

- give overall responsibility for anti money-laundering systems and controls to a director or senior manager. They should know about the money-laundering

[13] https://www.fca.org.uk/firms/financial-crime/money-laundering-terrorist-financing

risks to your firm and make sure steps are taken to mitigate those risks effectively

- appoint a Money Laundering Reporting Officer (MLRO), who is a focus for the firm's AML activity. The MLRO supervises the firm's compliance with its AML obligations. If you are a sole trader with no employees you are not subject to this requirement

Central to meeting your AML obligations is a risk assessment of your firm's business, as it will help you develop effective and proportionate prevention procedures. As the risks change over time, your risk assessment will need to be kept up-to-date. Once these procedures are in place, you will need to make sure that your employees understand and comply with them. You will also need to keep monitoring the procedures to ensure that they continue to be appropriate for your business as it develops, and that they work well.

We have provided examples of good and poor practice in our Financial Crime: A Guide for Firms to help you in benchmarking your existing systems or creating new ones. The Joint Money Laundering Steering Group has also produced guidance to help you meet your AML obligations.

Brokers and insurers

Although mortgage brokers, general insurers and general insurance brokers are not subject to our AML rules and the Money Laundering Regulations, they still need systems and controls to prevent financial crime. They are also subject to the Proceeds of Crime Act 2002.

Without these controls (e.g. no process for reporting knowledge or suspicions of money laundering) they will be at risk of committing money-laundering offences. Therefore, many mortgage and insurance brokers choose to implement controls like those adopted by firms subject to the Money Laundering Regulations and our AML rules.

The risk-based approach to anti-money laundering

The risk-based approach means a focus on outputs. Firms that apply a risk-based approach to anti-money laundering (AML) will focus AML resources where they will have the biggest impact.

Firms must have in place policies and procedures in relation to customer due diligence and monitoring, among others, but neither the law nor our rules prescribe in detail how firms have to do this. Firms' practices will vary depending on the nature of the money-laundering risks they face and the type of products they sell. For example, a large retail bank with many customers will likely need to develop or purchase customer monitoring software, but a smaller organisation may be able to monitor its customers using a low-tech solution.

Firms applying a risk-based approach need to be proactive in seeking out information about money-laundering trends and threats from external sources, such as law enforcement, as well as relying on their own experiences and observations. This allows firms to effectively review and revise their use of AML tools to fit the specific risks that they face.

iii. UK – Finance Intelligence Unit (FIU)

The UK Financial Intelligence Unit states:[14]

The UK Financial Intelligence Unit (UKFIU) has national responsibility for receiving, analysing and disseminating intelligence submitted through the Suspicious Activity Reports (SARs) regime, to share with law enforcement agencies at home and internationally. The UKFIU sits at the heart of the regime, providing the gateway to reporters and a repository of data to inform law enforcement.

Preventing and disrupting organised crime and terrorist finance

Illicit finance and money laundering underpin and enable most forms of organised crime. This activity allows criminals to further their operations and conceal their assets which impacts the national security of the United Kingdom.

The UKFIU's work with SARs plays a critical role in alerting law enforcement to potential instances of money laundering and terrorist financing. SARs are a vital source of intelligence, not only on economic crime but on a wide range of criminal activity. They are instrumental in, and have helped with, identifying fraud victims, sex offenders, murder suspects, missing persons, people traffickers, fugitives and terrorist financing.

The UKFIU is housed within the National Crime Agency's National Economic Crime Centre (NECC).

Suspicious Activity Reports

Suspicious Activity Reports (SARs) alert law enforcement to potential money laundering or terrorist financing. SARs are made by financial institutions and professionals such as solicitors, accountants and estate agents. They can also be submitted by private individuals where they have suspicion or knowledge of money laundering or terrorist financing.

2) USA

There have been a number of high profile money laundering-related cases in the USA over the years including Al Capone. Indeed, Jeffrey Robinson[15] claims that it has been a major part of the criminal landscape and that political crises like Watergate and Irangate were essentially money laundering exercises.

i. US FBI

Amongst a range of crimes including economic crime, the Federal Bureau of Investigation (FBI) investigates Money Laundering:[16]

---

[14] https://nationalcrimeagency.gov.uk/what-we-do/crime-threats/money-laundering-and-illicit-finance/ukfiu

[15] In his 1997 book: The Laundrymen: Inside Money Laundering, the World's Third Largest Business.

[16] https://www.fbi.gov/investigate/white-collar-crime

Money laundering is turning "dirty" money "clean" by making it look like money from crimes actually came from legitimate sources.

Money laundering allows criminals to:

- hide and accumulate wealth
- avoid prosecution
- avoid taxes
- increase profits through reinvestment
- fund further criminal activity

The FBI focuses its efforts on money laundering facilitation—targeting professional money launderers, key facilitators, gatekeepers, and complicit financial institutions, among others.

Criminals who engage in money laundering derive their proceeds through:

- Complex financial crimes
- Health care fraud
- Human trafficking
- International and domestic public corruption
- Narcotics trafficking
- Terrorism

Criminals use a number of tools to launder money, including:

- Financial institutions
- International trade
- Precious metals
- Real estate
- Third party service providers
- Virtual currency

ii. <u>US Financial Crimes Enforcement Network (FINCEN)</u>

FINCEN state:[17]

The mission of the Financial Crimes Enforcement Network is to safeguard the financial system from illicit use, combat money laundering and its related crimes including terrorism, and promote national security through the strategic use of financial authorities and the collection, analysis, and dissemination of financial intelligence—FinCEN Supports Local, State, Federal, and International Law Enforcement Investigations.

Statute 31 U.S.C. 310 establishes FinCEN[18] as a bureau within the Treasury Department and describes FinCEN's duties and powers to include:

[17] https://www.fincen.gov/about/mission

[18] https://www.fincen.gov/resources/fincens-legal-authorities

- Maintaining a government-wide data access service with a range of financial transactions information
- Analyzing and disseminating information in support of law enforcement investigatory professionals at the Federal, State, Local, and International levels
- Determining emerging trends and methods in money laundering and other financial crimes
- Serving as the Financial Intelligence Unit of the United States
- Carrying out other delegated regulatory responsibilities

iii. US Department of Justice Money Laundering and Asset Recovery Section (DoJ MLARS)

MLARS state the following on their website:[19]

The Money Laundering and Asset Recovery Section (MLARS) leads the Department's asset forfeiture and anti-money laundering enforcement efforts. MLARS provides leadership by: (1) prosecuting and coordinating complex, sensitive, multi-district, and international money laundering and asset forfeiture investigations and cases; (2) providing legal and policy assistance and training to federal, state, and local prosecutors and law enforcement personnel, as well as to foreign governments; (3) assisting Departmental and interagency policymakers by developing and reviewing legislative, regulatory, and policy initiatives; and (4) managing the Department's Asset Forfeiture Program, including distributing forfeited funds and properties to appropriate domestic and foreign law enforcement agencies and to community groups within the United States, as well as adjudicating petitions for remission or mitigation of forfeited assets. To this effect, MLARS is comprised of seven units and associated teams.

3) Europe

Member States such as Luxembourg need to ensure their domestic systems are as money-laundering and terrorist financing proof as possible. Hence their National Risk Assessment of Money Laundering and Terrorist Financing assessment report (dated 15th September 2020).[20]

However, in general the European Member States rely on the coordination of the European Union to ensure what they are doing collectively is consistent. In March 2023, the European Parliament welcomed "new EU measures against money laundering and terrorist financing"[21] that are being put in place to close gaps in the EU's existing structure:

[19] https://www.justice.gov/criminal/criminal-mlars

[20] https://mj.gouvernement.lu/dam-assets/dossiers/blanchiment/en-nra-import-version-2982022.pdf

[21] https://www.europarl.europa.eu/news/en/press-room/20230327IPR78511/new-eu-measures-against-money-laundering-and-terrorist-financing

MEPs approved stricter rules to close existing gaps in combating money laundering, terrorist financing and evasion of sanctions in the EU.

On Tuesday, MEPs from the Economic and Monetary Affairs and Civil Liberties, Justice and Home Affairs committees adopted their position on three pieces of draft legislation on the financing provisions of EU Anti-Money Laundering and Countering the Financing of Terrorism (AML/CFT) policy. The package consists of:

- the EU "single rulebook"—regulation—with provisions on conducting due diligence on customers, transparency of beneficial owners and the use of anonymous instruments, such as crypto-assets, and new entities, such as crowdfunding platforms. It also includes provisions on so-called "golden" passports and visas. The text was adopted with 99 votes to 8 and 6 abstentions.
- The 6th Anti-Money Laundering—directive—containing national provisions on supervision and Financial Intelligence Units, as well as on access for competent authorities to necessary and reliable information, e.g. beneficial ownership registers and assets stored in free zones. The text was adopted with 107 votes to 5 and 0 abstentions.
- The regulation establishing the European Anti-Money Laundering Authority (AMLA) with supervisory and investigative powers to ensure compliance with AML/CFT requirements. The text was adopted with 102 votes to 11 and 2 abstentions . . .

Prevention of money laundering and terrorist financing

According to the adopted texts, entities, such as banks, assets and crypto assets managers, real and virtual estate agents and high-level professional football clubs, will be required to verify their customers' identity, what they own and who controls the company. They will also have to establish detailed types of risk of money laundering and terrorist financing in their sector of activity, and transmit the relevant information to a central register.

To restrict transactions in cash and crypto assets, MEPs want to cap payments that can be accepted by persons providing goods or services. They set limits up to €7000 for cash payments and €1000 for crypto-asset transfers, where the customer cannot be identified. Given the manifest risk of misuse by criminals, MEPs want to ban any citizenship by investments schemes ("golden passports") and impose strong AML controls on residence by investment schemes ("golden visas").

Financial Intelligence Units

Each member state should establish a financial intelligence unit (FIU) to prevent, report and combat money laundering and terrorist financing. FIUs should share information with each other and with competent authorities as well as cooperate with AMLA, Europol, Eurojust and the European Public Prosecutor's office.

Information on beneficial ownership

To detect money laundering schemes and freeze assets in time, national FIUs and other competent authorities should be able to access information on beneficial ownership, bank accounts, land or real estate registers. As certain commodities are attractive for criminals, MEPs also want member states to aggregate information on ownership of goods such as yachts, planes and cars worth over €200,000 or goods stored in free zones.

MEPs agreed that beneficial ownership means having 15% plus one share, or voting rights, or other direct or indirect ownership interest, or 5% plus one share in the extractive industry or a company exposed to a higher risk of money laundering or terrorist financing.

Beneficial owners' registers

Information on beneficial ownership held in national central registers should be available digitally, in an EU official language plus English, and include current and historical information for a defined period. The entity in charge of the central register will have the right to request from corporate and legal entities any information necessary to identify and verify their beneficial owners.

This information will have to be up to date and available to FIUs, AMLA, competent authorities, self-regulatory bodies and obliged entities. Not providing accurate and adequate data to registers will be sanctioned. Entities in charge of central registers should be able to employ an adequate technology to carry out verifications.

Access to information

Following the latest Court of Justice ruling, MEPs decided that persons with legitimate interest, such as journalists, reporters, any other medias, civil society organisations, higher education institutions, should be able to access the register, including the interconnected central registers. Their access right will be valid for at least two and a half years. Member states will automatically renew access but also revoke it or suspend if it is abused.

The legitimate interest should apply without any discrimination based on nationality, country of residence or of establishment.

AMLA to ensure consistent enforcement

The new AMLA [the EU's Anti-Money Laundering Authority] would monitor risks and threats within and outside the EU and directly supervise specific credit and financial institutions, classifying them according to their risk level. Initially, it would be tasked with supervising 40 entities with the highest residual risk profile and present in at least two member states. At a minimum, one entity from each member state would be chosen.

To fulfil its duties, AMLA could mandate companies and people to hand over documents and other information, conduct on-site visits with judicial authorisation, and impose sanctions of 500,000 €– two million euros, or 0.5–1% of annual turnover, for material breaches—and up to 10% of the total annual turnover of the obliged entity in the preceding business year.

In their position on the draft law, MEPs wish to extend the agency's competence to drawing up lists of high-risk non-EU countries. MEPs also want to give AMLA the powers to mediate between national financial supervisors and settle disputes, supervise and investigate the national implementation of the single AML rulebook, ensure stronger oversight of the supervisors in the non-financial sector and receive whistleblower complaints . . .

It is notable that the proposed new EU Money Laundering Authority (AMLA) will promote a more consistent enforcement, will monitor compliance as well as risks and threats within and outside the EU, and directly supervise specific high-risk credit and financial institutions. It will also be able to impose sanctions (in particular, large fines) for material breaches. The EU has not yet decided on the seat of the authority.[22]

The European Parliament's approval was based on the European Commission presenting in July 2021 an package of legislation to strengthen the EU's anti-money laundering ("AML") and countering the financing of terrorism ("CFT") rules ("AML Package").[23]

The package consisted of four pieces of legislation.

- The EU "single rulebook" regulation provides guidelines for completing customer due diligence, disclosing the identities of beneficial owners, using anonymous instruments like crypto-assets, and introducing new entities such as crowdfunding platforms. It also includes clauses on "golden" passports and visas.
- The 6th Anti-Money Laundering directive includes national provisions on oversight, Financial Intelligence Units ("FIUs"), and information sharing requirements which will provide competent authorities with access to reliable information, such as beneficial ownership registrations and assets kept in free zones.
- The regulation establishing the European Anti-Money Laundering Authority ("AMLA") with supervisory and investigative powers, to ensure compliance with AML/CFT requirements.
- Amendment of the EU Transfer of Funds regulation on the information accompanying the transfers of funds and certain crypto-assets, in order to make it possible to trace respective transfers . . .

The EU Transfer of Funds Regulation (TFR)

As well as being part of the AML proposal, the EU TFR is also part of a wider crypto-asset regulatory framework including the Markets in Crypto-assets ("MiCA") regulation. The TFR regulates the EU's 'Travel Rule'. It aims to harmonize the rules for crypto-assets and their service providers across the EU. Amongst others, Crypto Asset Service Providers (CASPs) transacting crypto-assets on behalf of their clients are required to accompany transfers of crypto-assets with information on their originator and beneficiary. It will apply to all crypto-asset transfers, regardless of the amount. Every CASP is required to collect and transmit information on originators and beneficiaries (including intermediaries) . . .

[22] https://www.gleisslutz.com/en/Another_step_in_the_EUs_fight_against_money_laundering_and_terrorist_financing.html

[23] https://www.ey.com/en_mt/articles/the-eu-aml-package%2D%2D-where-is-it-in-the-legislative-process-

The original timeline for the AMLA regulation suggested that the Authority would be established at the beginning of 2023. However, it appears the EU Parliament is already behind schedule, with further disruptions to the legislative process expected due to the change in presidency later this year and the EU Parliament elections in 2024.

The final proposal, TFR, will apply from January 2025. MiCA will generally enter into force in July 2023, however, the provisions concerning Stablecoins will enter into force in July 2024.

4) Singapore

Monetary Authority of Singapore (MAS)

The Monetary Authority of Singapore (MAS) is responsible for payment compliance and for pursuing allegations involving money laundering within the country's financial institutions:[24]

AML legislation in Singapore

The primary law in Singapore relating to money laundering is the Corruption, Drug Trafficking and Other Serious Crimes (Confiscation of Benefits) Act (CDSA). Sections 43, 44, 46, and 47 of the CDSA cover the prevention of money laundering and its criminalization. With respect to terrorist financing, Singapore passed the Terrorism Suppression of Financing Act in 2002.

In 2019, the government passed the Payment Services Act (PSA), which took effect in January 2020. The Act supersedes two prior laws and details regulatory expectations for payment service providers.

AML regulators in Singapore

The PSA designates the Monetary Authority of Singapore (MAS) as responsible for payment compliance. The MAS is also responsible for pursuing allegations involving money laundering within the country's financial institutions. MAS documented its approach to enforcement in an Enforcement Monograph. The agency also publishes a report detailing its enforcement activity every 18 months.

MAS recently increased its scrutiny of shell companies as a means of uncovering money laundering schemes. The MAS anti-money laundering unit employs approximately 30 investigators. In fact, Singapore's authorities played an instrumental role in the investigation of the 1Malaysia Development Berhad (1MDB)[25] scandal, which included pursuing the arrest of Jho Low for his role in the scheme, as well as the investigation of entities connected to illegal activity, including money laundering.

Additional agency bodies, including the Council for Estate Agents, and the Casino Regulatory Authority of Singapore, handle investigations in their respective industries.

[24] https://www.dowjones.com/professional/risk/glossary/anti-money-laundering/singapore/#:~:text=AML-regulators-in-Singapore,within-0the-country%27s-financial-institutions

[25] See case description later.

The Suspicious Transaction Reporting Office (STRO) is the country's intelligence unit. In that role, it receives suspicious transaction reports (STRs), cash movement reports (CMRs), and cash transaction reports (CTRs) as a means of uncovering money laundering schemes.

Also, the context of Singapore is important to appreciate:[26]

- Singapore, home to 5.45 million people, is the world's third-largest offshore financial hub after Switzerland and Hong Kong. It is also where many global elites park their assets. The value of assets managed in Singapore has surged over the last few years to over C$5.4 trillion, nearly 80 per cent from foreign sources. (For context, the country's GDP is about C$640 billion.) In recent years, there has been a flood of cross-border wealth flowing in from China, as that country's elites are feeling squeezed by new Chinese government policies and anxious about regional tensions.
- Singapore has seen a high number of money laundering cases in recent years, with 240 convictions and C$1.2 billion in assets seized between 2020 and 2022.

Implications

Challenges to 'zero tolerance.' The city-state has long touted its zero-tolerance approach to money laundering, and this year, the government introduced stricter regulations to reinforce this approach. The regulations include a law that allows banks to share information about high-risk clients with one another and a mandate requiring property developers to conduct greater due diligence and report suspicious transactions. But this latest case exposes other gaps in the city-state's regulatory framework. In response to this latest case, the Singaporean government announced the formation of an inter-ministerial committee to bolster the country's anti-money laundering regime.

Chinese investors will face closer scrutiny. *Bloomberg* reported that Singaporean banks are strengthening their client-review procedures, and some have closed the accounts of Chinese clients who hold multiple passports. At least two of the 10 individuals arrested in August in Singapore were wanted in China on the same charges.

The scandal has been politically damaging for the ruling People's Action Party (PAP), which will undergo a rare leadership transition in 2024. The PAP, led by Singaporean Prime Minister Lee Hsien Loong, was already under fire for events that are quite unusual in light of Singapore's history and traditions—a corruption investigation into its transport minister, the resignation of its parliament speaker due to an extramarital affair, and the investigation of two senior ministers for allegedly renting out state-owned bungalows.

5) Australia

[26] See the full text of the note prepared by the Asia Pacific Foundation of Canada at: https://www.asiapacific.ca/publication/massive-money-laundering-case-rocks-singapore#:~:text=Singapore-has-seen-a-high,seized-between-2020-and-2022

The Attorney-General's Department announced that it was seeking to modernise Australia's anti-money laundering and counter-terrorism financing regime and launched a public consultation on proposed reforms in April 2023:[27]

The Australian Government is committed to protecting the integrity of the Australian financial system and improving Australia's AML/CTF regime to ensure it is fit-for-purpose, responds to the evolving threat environment, and meets international standards set by the Financial Action Task Force (FATF), the global financial crime watchdog and standard-setter.

The Australian Institute of Criminology estimates that serious and organised crime cost the Australian community up to A$60.1 billion in 2020–21, with illicit financing at the centre of most crime types.[1] It directly impacts the safety and wellbeing of Australian communities, and exploits and distorts legitimate markets and economic activity. The AML/CTF regime is a central part of Australia's efforts to prevent criminals from enjoying the profits of their illegal activity and stopping funds from falling into the hands of terrorist organisations.

No legitimate business wants to wittingly, or unwittingly, assist the laundering of money that aids the commissioning of serious crimes including terrorism, child abuse and the illicit drug trade. The purpose of the AML/CTF regime is to assist businesses to identify these risks in the course of providing their services. In doing so, the AML/CTF regime sets out a range of measures to protect regulated entities that are at the front line in preventing serious financial crimes. These obligations build resilience against misuse by criminals within regulated sectors and require the reporting of certain transactions to government for use as financial intelligence to combat money laundering, terrorism financing and other serious financial crime. These reports are vital in understanding and stopping the flow of illicit funds into, out of and within Australia . . .

The Australian Government is committed to consulting with industry in the consideration of the reforms proposed in this paper. Consultation on the first consultation paper, Modernising Australia's anti-money laundering and counter-terrorism financing regime, closed on 16 June 2023. This paper was the first step in developing reforms to the Act. A second consultation paper, informed by industry submissions on this paper, will be released later in 2023. We will continue to engage with industry on the proposed reforms . . .

Domestic regulation

The AML/CTF Act provides the means to help deter, detect and disrupt money laundering and terrorism financing. It also provides financial intelligence to revenue and law enforcement agencies.

The AML/CTF Act implements a risk-based approach to regulation.

The AML/CTF Act sets out general principles and obligations. Details of how these obligations are to be carried out are set out in the Anti-Money Laundering and Counter-Terrorism Financing Rules Instrument 2007 (No. 1) (AML/CTF Rules).

---

[27] https://www.ag.gov.au/crime/anti-money-laundering-and-counter-terrorism-financing#:~:text=The-Australian-Transaction-Reports-and,regulator-and-financial-intelligence-unit

Businesses must meet the minimum obligations set out in the AML/CTF Act and AML/CTF Rules. Beyond that, each business must assess the risks of potential money laundering or terrorism financing when providing a designated service to a customer.

At this point, the Australian Transaction Reports and Analysis Centre (AUSTRAC) is Australia's AML/CTF regulator and Financial Intelligence Unit.

C. **Criminal Investigation & Prosecution**

As noted above, cases of conduct which are criminal in nature can also be investigated; if sufficient evidence can be obtained, a prosecution of those involved in the criminality (not only of the person/people responsible for the underlying criminal activity but also of those who assisted in laundering the proceeds) can result.

In the UK, these cases would largely be coordinated by the National Crime Agency (NCA) with the involvement of the Crown Prosecution Service in any legal proceedings or by the Serious Fraud Office. In the US, the FBI would undertake the investigation with criminal (and/or linked civil) proceedings being brought by the Department of Justice.

However, in many cases money laundering is not the only criminality to occur so charges covering the laundering are included with the overall charges (in the indictment etc.) along with charges for the predicate offences (e.g., robbery, fraud, corruption, etc.). In America, the inclusion of additional criminal charges increases the potential sentence of a successful prosecution and therefore this increases the chances of a partial plea by the suspect.

1) **UK**

In the UK, the Proceeds of Crime Act 2002 (POCA) aims to prevent criminals from money laundering by making activities such as concealment and conversion of criminal property as criminal offences. It also provides some tools to freeze and recover illegally obtained assets.

The sentence for an offence can be, whilst dependent on the nature, severity and circumstances of the crime, up to 14 years in prison and include financial penalties.[28]

The UK also uses regulations to try to prevent their financial system being used to launder money and finance terrorists. For example, under the UK Money Laundering Regulations 2007 (reg 3), relevant persons including finance institutions (like banks and building societies) must undertake due diligence of a customer, such as to identify and verify the identity of the customer and any beneficial owner, whilst also seeking to establish the purpose and intended nature of the business relationship.[29]

---

[28] See: https://sanctionscanner.com/blog/anti-money-laundering-regulations-in-the-united-kingdom-uk-210#:~:text=Proceeds-of-Crime-Act-(POCA)&text=Its-primary-aim-is-tooffenses-under-the-2002-POCA

[29] https://www.lexisnexis.co.uk/legal/glossary/money-laundering

A Fact Sheet providing an Overview of POCA 2002 has been prepared by the Home Office (the government department responsible for the legislation) and is available.[30] It includes important summaries about: (i) confeiscation; (ii) civil recovery and cash seizure; (iii) revenue functions (taxation); (iv) money laundering; (v) production, disclosure and unexplained wealth orders; and (vi) national and international cooperation.

The UK's **Crown Prosecution Service** notes the following about money laundering in the Proceeds of Crime Act 2002:[31]

Money laundering offences are found in Part 7 of Proceeds of Crime Act 2002 ('POCA').

Money laundering describes offences concerning the possession, concealment, conversion, transfer or making of arrangements relating to the proceeds of crime. This is not limited to money or cash...

Money laundering is defined ... as "the process by which the proceeds of crime are converted into assets which appear to have a legitimate origin, so that they can be retained permanently or recycled into further criminal enterprises".

Money laundering can be broken down into two categories:

- Those who commit offences and then launder the proceeds of those criminal offences. The criminal offences are referred to as "predicate offences".
- Those whose only criminal involvement is to launder the proceeds of crime committed by others ...

Criminal Property

The [prosecution] has to prove that the laundered proceeds are "criminal property". Section 340 of POCA sets out that property is criminal property if:

- It constitutes a person's benefit from criminal conduct or it represents such a benefit (in whole or part and whether directly or indirectly), and
- The alleged offender knows or suspects that it constitutes or represents such a benefit ...

Criminal Conduct

For the purposes of POCA 'criminal conduct' is conduct which:

- Constitutes an offence in any part of the UK, or
- Would constitute an offence in any part of the UK if it occurred there.

Offences

There are two main types of money laundering prosecution. There are:

[30] https://assets.publishing.service.gov.uk/media/5a7d7b6740f0b64fe6c23fae/Fact_Sheet_-_Overview_of_POCA__2_.pdf

[31] https://www.cps.gov.uk/legal-guidance/money-laundering-offences#:~:text=Money-laundering-offences-are-found,limited-to-money-or-cash

- "Mixed" cases in which money laundering can be charged or included on an indictment in which the underlying predicate offence is included. These are:
  - "Own proceeds" or "self-laundering", where the defendant in a money laundering case may also be the author of the predicate crime; or
  - Laundering by a person or persons other than the author of the predicate offence.
- Cases where money laundering is the sole charge capable of proof or the most appropriate charge.

A conviction for committing money laundering offences in the UK can result in sentences including up to 14 years imprisonment, fines and confiscation orders.[32] Each case is, of course, different with the facts and circumstances varying, so the sentencing judge will arrive at an individual sentence. However, key factors in the sentence include the culpability of the individual and others, whether there has been the abuse of a position of power, trust or responsibility and the amounts and length of time involved.

In addition:

> Money laundering is an integral component of much serious criminality. To complete the assessment of harm [resulting from the offending], the court should take into account the level of harm associated with the underlying offence to determine whether it warrants upward adjustment . . .[33]

2) **USA**

(i) Financial Crimes Enforcement Network (FINCEN)

FINCEN state:[34]

> The mission of the Financial Crimes Enforcement Network is to safeguard the financial system from illicit use, combat money laundering and its related crimes including terrorism, and promote national security through the strategic use of financial authorities and the collection, analysis, and dissemination of financial intelligence - FinCEN Supports Local, State, Federal, and International Law Enforcement Investigations.

Statute 31 U.S.C. 310 establishes FinCEN[35] as a bureau within the Treasury Department and describes FinCEN's duties and powers to include:

- Maintaining a government-wide data access service with a range of financial transactions information

[32] Under the Proceeds of Crime Act 2002, offences such as concealing, disguising, converting, transferring and removing criminal property are punishable with a maximum of 14 years imprisonment, see the section on money laundering in www.sentencingcouncil.org.uk

[33] www.sentencingcouncil.org.uk

[34] https://www.fincen.gov/about/mission

[35] https://www.fincen.gov/resources/fincens-legal-authorities

- Analyzing and disseminating information in support of law enforcement investigatory professionals at the Federal, State, Local, and International levels
- Determining emerging trends and methods in money laundering and other financial crimes
- Serving as the Financial Intelligence Unit of the United States
- Carrying out other delegated regulatory responsibilities

(ii) Federal Bureau of Investigation (FBI)

The FBI[36] would investigate economic crimes in America (fraud, corruption, money laundering, etc.) and focus on analyzing intelligence and solving regional, national, and/or international cases. The FBI works closely with partner law enforcement and regulatory agencies

- the Securities and Exchange Commission
- the Internal Revenue Service
- the U.S. Postal Inspection Service
- the Commodity Futures Trading Commission
- the Treasury Department's Financial Crimes Enforcement Network

(iii) Department of Justice's Money Laundering and Asset Recovery Section (DoJ MLARS)

MLARS state the following on their website:[37]

> The Money Laundering and Asset Recovery Section (MLARS) leads the Department's asset forfeiture and anti-money laundering enforcement efforts. MLARS provides leadership by: (1) prosecuting and coordinating complex, sensitive, multi-district, and international money laundering and asset forfeiture investigations and cases; (2) providing legal and policy assistance and training to federal, state, and local prosecutors and law enforcement personnel, as well as to foreign governments; (3) assisting Departmental and interagency policymakers by developing and reviewing legislative, regulatory, and policy initiatives; and (4) managing the Department's Asset Forfeiture Program, including distributing forfeited funds and properties to appropriate domestic and foreign law enforcement agencies and to community groups within the United States, as well as adjudicating petitions for remission or mitigation of forfeited assets. To this effect, MLARS is comprised of seven units and associated teams.

Sentence: There is no minimum sentence in the USA but guidelines for sentencing can be very high—anyone convicted of money laundering could be harshly sentenced, such as up to 20 years of imprisonment and fines of US$500,000 or twice the value of the property (which ever is greater).

---

[36] https://www.fbi.gov/investigate/white-collar-crime

[37] https://www.justice.gov/criminal/criminal-mlars

The factors to be taken into account by a US judge include: (i) the extent to which the individual is responsible; (ii) their knowledge and involvement in the overall circumstances; (iii) whether the individual already has a criminal record; (iv) whether they plead guilty or are found guilty by a jury.[38]

3) **Europe**

(i) **European Union (EU)**

As noted above, in March 2023, a press release by the European Parliament welcomed new EU measures against money laundering and terrorist financing[39] that are being put in place to close gaps in the EU's existing structure.

It is notable that the proposed new EU authority (AMLA) will promote a more consistent enforcement, will monitor compliance as well as new risks and developing threats within and outside the EU, and directly supervise specific high-risk credit and financial institutions. It will also be able to impose sanctions (in particular, large fines) for material breaches. The EU has not yet decided on the seat of the authority.[40]

(ii) **European Public Prosecutor's Office (EPPO)**

The European Public Prosecutor's Office (EPPO)[41] is an independent public prosecution office of the European Union that is responsible for investigating, prosecuting and bringing to judgment crimes against the financial interests of the EU. These crimes include several types of fraud, money laundering and corruption, etc.

The EPPO undertakes investigations, prosecutions and exercises the functions of prosecutor in the competent courts of the participating Member States[42] until the case has been finally resolved. The EPPO works with OLAF,[43] Eurojust,[44] Europol,[45] European Court of Auditors,[46] European Investment Bank (EIB)[47] and the European Investment Fund (EIF).[48] The EPPO also works with other European

[38] There is further discussion of the consequences of a conviction for money laundering by Federal Criminal Practice Group of Price Benowitz LLP at www.whitecollarattorney.net; www.ussc.gov, etc.

[39] https://www.europarl.europa.eu/news/en/press-room/20230327IPR78511/new-eu-measures-against-money-laundering-and-terrorist-financing

[40] https://www.gleisslutz.com/en/Another_step_in_the_EUs_fight_against_money_laundering_and_terrorist_financing.html

[41] https://www.eppo.europa.eu/en

[42] 22 EU countries joined the EPPO and participate in the enhanced cooperation. These are: Austria, Belgium, Bulgaria, Croatia, Cyprus, Czechia, Estonia, Finland, France, Germany, Greece, Italy, Latvia, Lithuania, Luxembourg, Malta, Netherlands, Portugal, Romania, Slovakia, Slovenia, Spain.

[43] https://anti-fraud.ec.europa.eu/index_en

[44] https://www.eurojust.europa.eu

[45] https://www.europol.europa.eu

[46] https://www.eca.europa.eu/en

[47] https://www.eib.org/en/

[48] https://www.eif.org/index

agencies and authorities of non-participating EU Member States and non-EU states (third countries) as well as international organisations such as the Council of Europe, Interpol, etc.

In addition, as a result of the EU Directives noted earlier, there are many similarities between jurisdictions such as France and German:

France:

The national prosecuting authority for money laundering is, since 2013, Procurer de la Republic Financier (or prosecutor for financial crime, PNF) and will also look at a number of predicate offences such as corruption or tax fraud. An investigation is led by the gendarmerie (or police) and supervised by the PNF or the local prosecutor.

For individuals, the sentence for a conviction of money laundering is five years imprisonment with a fine of up to EUR 375,000. In a situation with aggregated money laundering, the sentence is a maximum ten years imprisonment and a fine of EUR 750,000.[49]

French courts have extraterritorial jurisdiction over money laundering in a number of circumstances, including: (i) if a French national undertakes conduct abroad and the conduct is punishable under the law of the other country; or (ii) if the offence (s) are committed abroad against a French national. If an individual is convicted of a criminal offence, a court can order the confiscation of an asset as part of the penalty where it is the result of the criminal offence.

Germany:

The Federal Financial Criminal Police in cooperation with the State Offices of Criminal Investigation and regional state prosecutors are responsible for investigating and prosecuting criminial offences of money laundering.

For individuals, the conviction for a money laundering offence may result in a sentence of up to five years. This would increase to ten years if the crime is organised or commercial. Confiscation orders can also be issued in respect of the proceeds of crime which have been obtained by or used for the criminal offence which led to a conviction.

German criminal law will only apply extraterritorially to money laundering offences if, for example (i) the victim is German and the offence is also prosecutable in the other country; or (ii) the offender is German.[50]

Italy:

Public prosecutors are the main body responsible for investigating and prosecuting money laundering offences (as well as any other offences). They are assisted by the police forces (which include the state police, the Carabinieri and the financial police, the Guardia di Finanza) are responsible for investigating money laundering.[51] In a recent case, Italian police arrested 33 people in a new crackdown on a network of

---

[49] www.iclg.com

[50] Also www.iclg.com

[51] https://www.lexology.com/library/detail.aspx?g=ac5b198b-e2f7-41b4-889b-f0acc8c1f151

Chinese money brokers who allegedly laundered over 50 million euro ($52.5 million) from drug trafficking groups, including the 'Ndrangheta mafia.[52]

Confiscation of the relevant money or goods is compulsory in the event of conviction of individuals for the offence of money laundering and conviction of corporations in relation to the money laundering offences committed by their managers or employees.

If confiscation of the specific money or goods is not possible, Italian law provides for confiscation 'for equivalent', namely the confiscation of different money or goods of the same value.

At a pretrial stage, during the investigations, prosecutors can request the judge to grant seizure of the 'profit' or 'price' of a money laundering offence, even for an 'equivalent amount', according to case law. Such a request is usually granted.

Italian criminal law, which is generally also applicable to money laundering offences, provides that Italian courts have jurisdiction on all offences committed within Italian territory; namely, when at least part of the prohibited conduct (e.g., the decision to launder money in a foreign territory) takes place in Italy and regardless of the offender's nationality (or corporate offender's main seat) or the offender's residence (article 6 of the Italian Criminal Code—ICC).

With regard to money laundering offences committed outside Italian territory, Italian law provides for extraterritorial jurisdiction only to a limited extent, where stringent requirements are fulfilled (e.g., the presence in Italy of the suspect and particular request of proceedings by the Minister of Justice (articles 9 to 10 of the ICC)).

For convictions, individuals face imprisonment of 4–12 years and fines of 5000 € - 25,000 €[53] and the confiscation of the relevant money/goods.

Additional punishments are also applicable to individuals, such as disqualification from holding public office, disqualification from practising a profession or art and temporary disqualification from managing corporations or enterprises (article 28 et seq of the ICC).[54]

4) **Singapore**

The Singapore Police Force investigate allegations of criminal money laundering and can take custody of physical items such as cash, electronic devices or personal belonging such as jewels under the Criminal Procedure Code, whilst they can issue an order to freeze funds in a financial institution until the there is a criminal conviction or an acquittal.[55]

---

[52] https://www.reuters.com/world/italy-police-take-down-chinese-shadow-network-laundering-mafia-cash-2023-10-04/ . See also: Joint action in Germany and Italy against money laundering via rental of luxury cars - https://www.eurojust.europa.eu/news/joint-action-germany-and-italy-against-money-laundering-rental-luxury-cars

[53] imprisonment of 2–8 years and fines of 5000 € - 25,000 € for the crime of self-money laundering.

[54] https://www.lexology.com/library/detail.aspx?g=ac5b198b-e2f7-41b4-889b-f0acc8c1f151

[55] See www.straitstimes.com

Individuals convicted of money laundering in Singapore may be sentenced with imprisonment for up to 10 years, a fine of up to S$ 500,000 or both.[56]

5) **Australia**

In Australia, the investigation and prosecution of suspected money laundering offences will take place as follows:[57]

The Commonwealth Department of Public Prosecutions (CDPP), Australia's federal prosecution service, prosecutes money laundering offences at the Commonwealth level. The Australian Transaction Reports and Analysis Centre, the Australian Federal Police and the Australian Border Force act as partner agencies to the CDPP in prosecuting money laundering offences. The Australian Federal Police also leads the Criminal Assets Confiscation Taskforce that, as stated on its website, collaborates with other agencies to 'identify, investigate and litigate appropriate asset confiscation matters at the Commonwealth level'.

State- and territory-based public prosecution services and local police departments enforce and prosecute offences at their respective levels. However, it is unlikely that a prosecution under a state or territory law for money laundering would be pursued if one has already been brought at the federal level. At the state and territory levels, police focus is on the investigation of predicate offences and money laundering prosecution only in simple cases where offenders may be caught in possession of cash …

Both natural and legal persons can be prosecuted for money laundering offences ….

The relevant division of the Criminal Code Act 1995 (Cth) (the Criminal Code) creates multiple offences that cover a wide range of criminal activity. The offences are based on a person dealing with money or property that is proceeds of crime, or will be (or is at risk of becoming) an instrument of crime. Broadly, the elements of the offence are:

- the existence of money or property;
- a dealing (physical conduct such as receiving, possessing, concealing or disposing of the money or property, importing or exporting it, or engaging in banking transactions) in money or property being unlawful because the proceeds are proceeds of crime, or the proceeds are at risk of being used in the commission of or to facilitate a crime; and
- the person believed that the money or property was the proceeds of a crime, or was reckless or negligent about that fact.

[56]Under section 54 of the Corruption, Drug Trafficking and Other Serious Crimes Act 1992 (CDSA).

[57]https://www.lexology.com/library/detail.aspx?g=a4e6caa8-0ed7-44ae-9006-2403b70d5b54#:~:text=Both-natural-and-legal-persons-can-be-prosecuted-for-money-laundering-offences.&text=What-constitutes-money-laundering%3F,wide-range-of-criminal-activity

Generally, a person commits an offence of money laundering if they deal with money or other property that is, or is reasonably suspected of being, the proceeds of crime and one of the following states of mind is present:

- intentionality: the money or property is, and is believed to be, proceeds of crime, or the person intends that the money or property will become an instrument of crime;
- recklessness: the money or property is proceeds of crime, or there is a risk that it will become an instrument of crime, and the person is reckless to this fact; or
- negligence: the money or property is proceeds of crime, or there is a risk that it will become an instrument of crime, and the person is negligent as to this fact.

An offence under section 400.9 of the Criminal Code does not require the element of intention, recklessness or negligence be present. Rather, the offence is established where it is reasonable to suspect that money or property was the proceeds of crime.

'Proceeds of crime' means any money or other property wholly or partly derived or realised, directly or indirectly, by any person from the commission of an offence against a law of Australia or a foreign country that may be dealt with as an indictable offence (even if it may, in some circumstances, be dealt with as a summary offence). Money or other property is an instrument of crime if it is used (or used to facilitate) in the commission of an offence against such a law.

Offences contained in the Anti-Money Laundering and Counter-Terrorism Financing Act 2006 (Cth) (the AML/CTF Act) are also used in prosecuting money laundering offences.

The offences at a state and territory level differ according to areas such as relevant predicate offences, the intent of the defendant and penalties attached to the offences.

Financial institutions generally cannot be prosecuted for their customers' money laundering crimes (unless the elements of the offence can otherwise be established). However, crimes committed by customers may cause financial institutions to contravene a regulatory offence under the AML/CTF Act should the offending conduct not be appropriately identified and managed (eg, by failing to report a suspicious matter)....

Under the POC Act, a freezing order can be made by a magistrate against an account with a financial institution if:

- there are reasonable grounds to suspect that the balance of the account is proceeds of a particular offence, or it is wholly or partly an instrument of a serious offence; and
- there is a risk that the account's balance will be reduced so that a person will not be deprived of all or some of such proceeds or such an instrument.

The POC Act also enables forfeiture orders to be made under which property must be surrendered to the government if certain offences have been committed.

Both the freezing and forfeiture orders are part of the POC Act's implementation of a confiscation scheme, which outlines processes relating to confiscation that also include restraining orders (prohibiting disposal of or dealing with property) and pecuniary penalty orders (requiring payment of amounts based on benefits derived from committing offences). The POC Act also has provisions that outline ways in which information can be gathered, such as examining any person about the affairs of people covered by the examination orders and requiring financial institutions to provide information and documents relating to accounts and transactions.

Similar legislation has been enacted in the states and territories of Australia that relates to making such orders and confiscation of profits and other proceeds of crime.

Money laundering in Australia can therefore be investigated and prosecuted as criminal offences, as noted above. The Australian Federal Police would undertake the investigation and, once sufficient evidence is obtained, a prosecution will be lead by the CDPP, Australia's federal prosecutors.

The Australian Transaction Reports and Analysis Centre (AUSTRAC) is Australia's Financial Intelligence Unit and AML regulator.[58] Australia's Anti-Money Laundering and Counter-Terrorism Financing Act 2006 provides the structure for regulation of financial, gambling, remittance and bullion sectors which provide designated services, as listed in the Act.

Law enforcement also have powers to "follow the money" and to seek to freeze and confiscate assets. The Australian POC provides for them to be able to freeze bank accounts and seek forfeiture of the funds/assets if offences have been committed and they are found to be the proceeds of crime.

There is also a degree of extraterritorial application based on the offender's nationality or being the proceeds of a crime or conduct in Australia.

Sentences: Significant sentences can be imposed in cases where a suspect is criminally convicted—the length of possible imprisonment ranges from 6 months to life along with monetary penalties. In each case, the outcome will depend primarily on: (i) the value of the money and property involved; and (ii) the defendant's state of mind (intentionally, recklessly or negligently).[59]

Currently, there is a process of reform of Australia's AML/CTF regime ongoing—there may be changes in it to "ensure it is fit-for-purpose" and it "responds to the evolving threat environment and meets international standards set . . ." by FATF. In particular, the Attorney-General's Department announced that it was seeking to modernise Australia's anti-money laundering and counter-terrorism financing regime and launched a public consultation on proposed reforms in April 2023:[60]

The Australian Government is committed to protecting the integrity of the Australian financial system and improving Australia's AML/CTF regime to ensure it is fit-for-purpose, responds to the evolving threat environment, and meets international standards set by the Financial Action Task Force (FATF), the global financial crime watchdog and standard-setter.

[58] www.ag.gov.au

[59] www.lexology.com

[60] https://www.ag.gov.au/crime/anti-money-laundering-and-counter-terrorism-financing#:~:text=The-Australian-Transaction-Reports-and,regulator-and-financial-intelligence-unit

The Australian Institute of Criminology estimates that serious and organised crime cost the Australian community up to A$60.1 billion in 2020–21, with illicit financing at the centre of most crime types.[1] It directly impacts the safety and wellbeing of Australian communities, and exploits and distorts legitimate markets and economic activity. The AML/CTF regime is a central part of Australia's efforts to prevent criminals from enjoying the profits of their illegal activity and stopping funds from falling into the hands of terrorist organisations.

No legitimate business wants to wittingly, or unwittingly, assist the laundering of money that aids the commissioning of serious crimes including terrorism, child abuse and the illicit drug trade. The purpose of the AML/CTF regime is to assist businesses to identify these risks in the course of providing their services. In doing so, the AML/CTF regime sets out a range of measures to protect regulated entities that are at the front line in preventing serious financial crimes. These obligations build resilience against misuse by criminals within regulated sectors and require the reporting of certain transactions to government for use as financial intelligence to combat money laundering, terrorism financing and other serious financial crime. These reports are vital in understanding and stopping the flow of illicit funds into, out of and within Australia.

The AML/CTF regime represents a significant partnership between government and industry.

The Australian Government is committed to consulting with industry in the consideration of the reforms proposed in this paper. Consultation on the first consultation paper, Modernising Australia's anti-money laundering and counter-terrorism financing regime, closed on 16 June 2023. This paper was the first step in developing reforms to the Act. A second consultation paper, informed by industry submissions on this paper, will be released later in 2023. We will continue to engage with industry on the proposed reforms, including on sector-specific issues as required.

Domestic regulation

The AML/CTF Act provides the means to help deter, detect and disrupt money laundering and terrorism financing. It also provides financial intelligence to revenue and law enforcement agencies.

The AML/CTF Act implements a risk-based approach to regulation.

The AML/CTF Act sets out general principles and obligations. Details of how these obligations are to be carried out are set out in the Anti-Money Laundering and Counter-Terrorism Financing Rules Instrument 2007 (No. 1) (AML/CTF Rules).

Businesses must meet the minimum obligations set out in the AML/CTF Act and AML/CTF Rules. Beyond that, each business must assess the risks of potential money laundering or terrorism financing when providing a designated service to a customer.

The Australian Transaction Reports and Analysis Centre (AUSTRAC) is currently Australia's AML/CTF regulator and financial intelligence unit.

Part II
Cases

Chapter 9
UK and Scandinavian Cases

1. **Entities based in the UK**[1]

   i. **Standard Chartered**[2]

On 6 August 2012, the New York Department of Financial Services (DFS), led by Benjamin Lawsky, accused Standard Chartered of hiding $250 billion in transactions involving Iran, labelling it a "rogue institution". The bank was ordered to appear and defend its actions, or risk losing its license to operate in the state of New York. The DFS said it had documents showing a cover up of transactions allegedly used to fund terrorist groups in the Middle East.[50]

On 14 August 2012, Lawsky announced that the DFS and Standard Chartered reached a settlement that allows the bank to keep its licence to operate in New York. According to the terms of the settlement, the bank agreed to pay a $340 million fine.[51]

The bank agreed to install a monitor to oversee the bank's money laundering controls for at least 2 years, and appoint "permanent officials who will audit the bank's internal procedures to prevent offshore money laundering".[51] The monitor will report directly to the DFS.[52] Lawsky's statement said "the parties have agreed that the conduct at issue involved transactions of at least $250bn."[53] The bank issued a statement confirming that a settlement with the DFS had been reached and that "a formal agreement containing the detailed terms of the settlement is expected to be concluded shortly".[53]

Other US agencies—including the Federal Reserve, the Federal Bureau of Investigation, the Treasury Department, and the Justice Department—had also

[1]Listed on FCA's website (https://www.fca.org.uk/firms/financial-crime/money-laundering-terrorist-financing) and recent SFO Cases (https://www.sfo.gov.uk/our-cases/)

[2]https://www.dfs.ny.gov/reports_and_publications/press_releases/pr1209213 . See also: https://en.wikipedia.org/wiki/Standard_Chartered; https://www.sc.com/en/

D. Smith, *Money Laundering, Terrorist Financing and Virtual Assets*, Contributions to Finance and Accounting, https://doi.org/10.1007/978-3-031-59842-5_9

begun investigations into the laundering allegations and were reportedly taken off guard by the speed of the settlement.[51]

The Treasury stated that its own investigation of Standard Chartered will continue.[54] Several financial analysts predicted that, due to its strong financial position, the bank would be able to easily cover the $900 million fine without having to raise extra capital.[54]

On 6 August 2014, Lawsky was reported to be preparing a new action against Standard Chartered over computer system breakdowns and was "discussing a potential settlement".[55]

On 19 August 2014, the bank was fined $300 million by the New York Department of Financial Services for breach of money-laundering compliance related to potentially high-risk transactions involving Standard Chartered clients in Hong Kong and the UAE. The bank issued a statement accepting responsibility and regretting the deficiencies, at the same time noting the ruling would not jeopardize its U.S. licenses.[56][57]

In April 2019, it was reported that Standard Chartered may have to pay approximately $1 billion to settle its ongoing investigations in the US and UK. Earlier in February the company had set aside $900 million towards resolution of violations of U.S. sanctions and forex trading regulations. The company also faces a penalty of roughly $134 million from the United Kingdom's Financial Conduct Authority related to historical financial crime controls which takes the amount to over $1 billion.

ii. **Coutts**[3]

In March 2012 Coutts was fined £8.75 m for breaches of money laundering rules after "serious" and "systemic" problems in handling the affairs of "politically exposed persons", customers entrusted with a prominent public function, requiring money-laundering checks. The Financial Services Authority (FSA) fined Coutts because of an "unacceptable risk" that the bank could have been handling the proceeds of crime for a 3-year period up to November 2010 after failing to properly deal with "politically exposed" customers.

Following an industry-wide review in 2010, the FSA found that Coutts was not conducting robust-enough checks on such high-risk customers and was not monitoring relationships with them properly. The FSA reviewed a sample of 103 high-risk customer files, and identified deficiencies in 73 of them.[48] The FSA's acting director of enforcement and financial crime, Tracey McDermott, said that "Coutts's failings were significant, widespread and unacceptable. Its conduct fell well below the standards we expect and the size of the financial penalty demonstrates how seriously we view its failures".

Coutts's bonus system rewarded bankers for opening accounts, providing an incentive to bring in new business without too much scrutiny, and the bank's anti-money laundering team, required to identify high-risk customers, failed to identify

[3]https://en.wikipedia.org/wiki/Coutts

enough "politically exposed persons".[48] In two cases reviewed by the FSA, bankers did not conduct appropriate checks on the customers, and failed to identify serious criminal allegations against them. There were five cases where sources had provided "adverse intelligence" such as allegations of criminal activity, but all the accounts had been approved by Coutts.

A spokesperson for Coutts said that there was no evidence that money laundering took place as a result of its deficient controls, and said that "We recognise our systems weren't totally adequate in the past and we've taken steps to improve these". Coutts would have been fined £12.5 m if it had not agreed to settle at an early stage in the investigation.

iii. **EFG**[4]

The Monetary Authority takes disciplinary action against EFG Bank AG, Hong Kong Branch for contraventions of Anti-Money Laundering and Counter-Terrorist Financing Ordinance (15 Aug 2023)

The Hong Kong Monetary Authority (HKMA) announced today (15 August) that it had completed an investigation and disciplinary proceedings for EFG Bank AG, Hong Kong Branch (EFGHK) under the Anti-Money Laundering and Counter-Terrorist Financing Ordinance (Chapter 615 of the Laws of Hong Kong) (AMLO) (Note 1). The Monetary Authority (MA) has imposed a pecuniary penalty of HK$16,000,000 against EFGHK for contraventions of the AMLO.

The disciplinary action (Note 2) follows an on-site examination and further investigation by the HKMA on EFGHK's systems and controls for compliance with the AMLO. The investigation identified control deficiencies in respect of conducting customer due diligence (CDD) on customers transferred from another financial institution during the period from 21 February 2016 to 16 January 2018, as well as on-boarding CDD and on-going CDD measures on some other customers during the period from 1 April 2012 to 31 October 2018. In addition, during the period from 1 April 2012 to 31 October 2018, EFGHK failed to establish and maintain effective procedures for carrying out its duties under the AMLO in relation to CDD and on-going monitoring of business relationships with customers.

In deciding the disciplinary action, the MA has taken into account all relevant circumstances and factors, including the following:

(a)	the seriousness of the investigation findings;
(b)	the need to send a clear deterrent message to EFGHK and the industry about the importance of effective controls and procedures to address the risks of money laundering and terrorist financing;
(c)	EFGHK has taken remedial and enhancement measures to address the deficiencies identified by the HKMA; and
(d)	EFGHK has no previous disciplinary record in relation to the AMLO and cooperated with the HKMA during the investigation and enforcement proceedings.

[4] https://www.hkma.gov.hk/eng/news-and-media/press-releases/2023/08/20230815-6/

Ms Carmen Chu, Executive Director (Enforcement and AML) of the HKMA, said, "CDD and continuous monitoring of business relationships with customers are crucial measures for Authorized Institutions (AIs) to protect accounts from being abused for financial crime and safeguard banking system integrity. AIs are key stakeholders in the anti-money laundering and counter-terrorist financing ecosystem and should uphold the international standards incorporated in the AMLO as well as the relevant guidelines and circulars issued by the HKMA in their conduct of business. . ."

Notes:

1.	Prior to 1 March 2018, the short title of Chapter 615 of the Laws of Hong Kong was the Anti-Money Laundering and Counter-Terrorist Financing (Financial Institutions) Ordinance.
2.	The disciplinary action is taken under section 21 of the AMLO. The AMLO imposes customer due diligence and record-keeping requirements on specified financial institutions, including Authorized Institutions, and designated non-financial businesses and professions. As regards Authorized Institutions, the MA is the relevant authority under the AMLO.

AND

FCA fines EFG Private Bank £4.2 m for failures in its anti-money laundering controls[5]

Press Release First published: 24/04/2013 Last updated: 29/11/2021

The Financial Conduct Authority (FCA) has fined EFG Private Bank Ltd (EFG) £4.2 million for failing to take reasonable care to establish and maintain effective anti-money laundering (AML) controls for high risk customers. The failings were serious and lasted for more than 3 years.

EFG is the UK private banking subsidiary of the EFGI Group, a global private banking group, based in Switzerland. EFG provides private banking and wealth management services to high net worth individuals including some from overseas jurisdictions recognised as presenting a higher risk of money laundering and/or bribery and corruption. At the end of 2011 around 400 of EFG's 3342 customer accounts were deemed by the firm to present a higher risk of money laundering or reputational risk, and of these 94 were held by politically exposed persons (PEPs).

As part of a thematic review of how UK banks were managing money laundering risk in higher risk situations, the Financial Services Authority (FSA) visited EFG in January 2011. That visit and further investigation caused serious concern to the FSA. The investigation found that EFG had not fully put its AML policies into practice. Of particular concern was that 17 of 36 reviewed customer files, opened between December 2007 and January 2011, contained customer due diligence that highlighted significant money laundering risks, but insufficient records of how the bank's senior management had mitigated those risks.

[5] https://www.fca.org.uk/news/press-releases/fca-fines-efg-private-bank-£42m-failures-its-anti-money-laundering-controls#:~:text=The%20Financial%20Conduct%20Authority%20(FCA,for%20more%20than%20three%20years

Of these 17 files, the FSA found that the risks highlighted in 13 files related to allegations of criminal activity or that the customer had been charged with criminal offences including corruption and money laundering.

For example in one account, EFG's due diligence highlighted that a prospective client had acquired their wealth through their father, about whom there were allegations of links with organised crime, money-laundering and murder. However there was insufficient information on file to explain how the bank concluded that this risk was acceptable or how it was mitigating the risks.

EFG also failed to appropriately monitor its higher risk accounts. Of the 99 PEP and other high risk customer files reviewed by the FSA, 83 raised serious concerns about EFG's monitoring of the relationship.

As a result of these failures, EFG breached FSA Principle 3, requiring it to take reasonable care to organise and control its affairs responsibly and effectively.

Tracey McDermott, head of enforcement and financial crime, said:

"One of the FCA's objectives is to protect and enhance the integrity of the UK financial system. This includes ensuring money in the UK system is clean.

"Banks are the first line of defence to make sure that proceeds of crime do not find their way into the UK. In this case while EFG's policies looked good on paper, in practice it manifestly failed to ensure that it was addressing its AML risks. Its poor implementation of its agreed policies risked the bank handling the proceeds of crime. These failures merited a strong penalty from the FCA.

"Firms that accept business from high risk customers must have systems, controls and practices to manage that risk. The FCA will continue to focus on high risk customers and business."

EFG settled at an early stage of the investigation and qualified for a 30% discount on its fine. Without the discount the fine would have been £6 million.

Notes for editors

1. The Final Notice for EFG Private Bank Ltd.
2. On 22 June 2011, the FSA published its findings from a thematic review, which focused on how banks manage money laundering risk in higher risk situations. The FSA published a Policy Statement PS11/15 Financial crime: a guide for firms on 9 December 2011. This contains guidance on steps firms can take to reduce their financial crime risk, including in their dealings with high risk and PEP customers.
3. EFG breached Principle 3 of the FCA's Principles for Businesses. Principle 3 is set out in the FCA Handbook and states: a firm must take reasonable care to organise and control its affairs responsibly and effectively, with adequate risk management systems.
4. The FSA fined Coutts and Habib Bank AG Zurich for similar AML failings.
5. On the 1 April 2013 the Financial Conduct Authority (FCA) became responsible for the conduct supervision of all regulated financial firms and the prudential supervision of those not supervised by the Prudential Regulation Authority (PRA).

6. The FCA has an overarching strategic objective of ensuring the relevant markets function well. To support this it has three operational objectives: to secure an appropriate degree of protection for consumers; to protect and enhance the integrity of the UK financial system; and to promote effective competition in the interests of consumers
7. You can find more information about the FCA, as well as how it is different to the PRA.

iv. **Habib Bank AG Zurich**[6]

Habib Bank Limited (Urdu: حبیب بینک محدود) abbreviated as **HBL**, is a Pakistani multinational bank based at Habib Bank Plaza, Karachi, Pakistan. . .

DFS Investigation

In September 2017, HBL agreed to pay a fine of $225 million in an out-of-court settlement with the New York State Department of Financial Services (DFS) against 53 separate violations allegedly committed between 2007 and 2017.[25][26]

Following this, HBL shares surged 5%, to Rs.160.58 per share, amid investor relief that the fine was not larger than $225 million.[27] The penalty, however, is the largest ever imposed upon a Pakistani financial institution. HBL had already agreed to surrender its licence to operate a branch in New York that had been operational since 1978.[25]

The DFS had earlier sought up to $630 m in penalties from HBL for failing to comply with state and federal laws at its only U.S. branch.[28] According to The Nation, compliance issues dated back to 2015 when the DFS told Karachi-listed Habib Bank (HBL) to institute a series of reforms about the bank's policies for preventing illicit money transfers. In a December 2015 statement, the DFS identified issues in the bank's anti-money laundering compliance.[29]

Habib also allegedly cleared transactions to a cybercriminal wanted by the US Federal Bureau of Investigation and a Chinese weapons manufacturer that was subject to US sanctions. Since Habib's New York operations were used to clear dollar-denominated transactions, the bank is required to follow US "know your customer" rules and sanctions law.[30]

Allegations of terror financing

On 28 September 2022, a New York district court passed an order under the Justice Against Sponsors of Terrorism Act placing secondary liability on Habib Bank Limited as a party that "aids and abets, by knowingly providing substantial assistance, or who conspires with the person who committed such an act of international terrorism". The plaintiff claimed that between 2010 and 2019, the bank had aided and abetted Al-Qaeda terrorism and had participated in a conspiracy to launch attacks in Afghanistan that killed or injured 370 people. In response, HBL released a statement claiming the accusations were "meritless" and that the bank was fiercely and thoroughly contesting them.[31][7]

[6] https://en.wikipedia.org/wiki/Habib_Bank_Limited

[7] See HBL press release in response: **HBL faces liability in terror financing case in US, bank says will 'vigorously' contest allegations** dated September 29, 2022

v. Guaranty Trust Bank (UK) Ltd[8]

FCA fines Guaranty Trust Bank (UK) Limited £7.6 million for further failures in its anti-money laundering systems and controls

Press Release dated 10/01/2023 (Last updated: 10/01/2023)

The Financial Conduct Authority (FCA) has fined Guaranty Trust Bank (UK) Limited (GT Bank) £7,671,800 for serious weaknesses in its anti-money laundering (AML) systems and controls between October 2014 and July 2019.

During the relevant period, GT Bank failed to undertake adequate customer risk assessments, often not assessing or documenting the money laundering risks posed by its customers.

The bank also failed to monitor customer transactions and business relationships to the required standard.

These weaknesses were repeatedly highlighted to GT Bank by internal and external sources, including the FCA, but despite this, GT Bank failed to take appropriate action to fix them.

From early 2018 GT Bank stopped taking on new customers. Later that year GT Bank agreed to wider voluntary restrictions on business, given the FCA's ongoing concerns. Requirements remained in place until the middle of 2021 when they were lifted after the bank completed a remediation plan, checked by an independent third party.

GT Bank's conduct is particularly egregious as this is not the first time that the bank has faced enforcement action in relation to its AML controls, with the FCA fining GT Bank £525,000 in August 2013 for serious and systemic failings.

The FCA requires firms to have in place effective AML controls to mitigate the risk of individuals and organisations using financial institutions to circumvent restrictions designed to prevent them benefitting from assets obtained by illegal means.

Mark Steward, Executive Director of Enforcement and Market Oversight at the FCA, said:

'GT Bank should have acted quickly to put in place adequate AML controls following its fine in 2013 but it failed to do so. GT Bank did not develop a plan that was capable of addressing its AML weaknesses, exposing it and the broader market to financial crime risks for a prolonged period.'

'Firms must protect themselves and those dealing with them from financial crime risks, especially money laundering. The FCA is determined to ensure the market for financial services is safe, clean and trusted with robust systems and controls in place to stymie financial crime. The FCA will continue to take action when these standards are not met.'

---

[8] https://www.fca.org.uk/news/press-releases/fca-fines-guaranty-trust-bank-uk-limited-ps76-million-further-failures-its-anti-money-laundering; also https://en.wikipedia.org/wiki/Guaranty_Trust_Holding_Company_PLC

GT Bank has not disputed the FCA's findings and agreed to settle, which means it has qualified for a 30% discount. Without this discount, the financial penalty would have been £10,959,700.

Notes to Editors

1. GT Bank is a wholly owned subsidiary of Guaranty Trust Bank Nigeria Limited, which is a wholly owned subsidiary of Guaranty Trust Bank Holding Company Plc., a Nigerian multinational financial services institution that provides a range of banking services across Africa and the United Kingdom. Guaranty Trust Bank Holding Company Plc is a public limited company, listed on both the London and Nigerian stock exchanges.
2. Final Notice for GT Bank.
3. On 8 August 2013, the FCA issued a Final Notice and imposed a financial penalty of £525,000 on GT Bank for failing to maintain adequate AML systems and controls between 19 May 2008 and 19 July 2010.
4. In early 2018, GT Bank suspended onboarding of new customers. In May 2018 a Skilled Person report was produced which highlighted significant deficiencies regarding GT Bank's AML systems and controls. GT Bank then agreed to the voluntary imposition of wider requirements on its business on 13 November 2018.
5. Following improvements made to its AML systems and controls, requirements were lifted after GT Bank completed a remediation plan, which was verified by a Skilled Person.
6. Reducing and preventing financial crime is a key part of the FCA's 3-year strategy to prevent serious harm and set higher standards in financial markets.
7. Find out more information about the FCA.

vi. **Miranda**

SFO secures over $7 million from convicted Brazilian money launderer, 17 March, 2023.[9]

Today, the SFO recovered over $7,699,204 from convicted money launderer, Mario Ildeu de Miranda, after its investigation revealed he had channelled criminal proceeds through multiple international bank accounts using several different company names.

This is the largest ever amount seized by the SFO from a single bank account.

Mr. Miranda, 71, was convicted of 37 counts of money laundering in Brazil in 2019 as part of 'Operation Car Wash', in which Brazilian authorities uncovered extensive and systemic bribery centred around state-owned oil company Petrobras. Mr. Miranda, a former executive at Petrobras, was sentenced to over 6 years in prison and ordered to pay $24,750,000 in Brazil.

[9] https://www.sfo.gov.uk/2023/03/17/sfo-secures-over-7-million-from-convicted-brazilian-money-launderer/

In August 2020, the SFO froze a UK bank account that contained over $7,699,204 following a report that these funds were linked to Mr. Miranda.

The SFO's investigation subsequently uncovered that these funds had been transferred out of Mr. Miranda's main Swiss bank account and channelled through other banks in Switzerland, Malta, Portugal, the UAE and the Bahamas before being deposited in London—where the SFO froze the account.

The investigation also exposed how Mr Miranda spent suspected proceeds of crime to fund his extravagant lifestyle. This included over $1 million on hotels and casinos in Las Vegas, as well as $95,000 on a new luxury car.

Mr. Miranda remains the subject of two ongoing investigations into corruption in Brazil.

Lisa Osofsky, Director of the Serious Fraud Office (SFO), said: "Over 2 years, we unpicked a complex web of transactions across the world – exposing Mr Miranda's attempt to conceal criminal proceeds and ensuring that the UK cannot be used as a hiding place for criminal assets."

AND

SFO's largest forfeiture as court seizes more than $7 million By Bianca Castro, 21 March 2023.[10]

A convicted money launderer must forfeit more than $7 million after a Serious Fraud Office investigation uncovered a UK bank account connected to his 'unlawful conduct'.

Mario Ildeu de Miranda, 71, was convicted of 37 counts of money laundering in Brazil. Miranda, a former executive at Petrobras, a Brazilian-owned oil company, was sentenced to 4 years 10 months and 10 days imprisonment. He was also ordered to pay $24,750,000 in Brazil following an investigation into bribery and corruption in relation to a contract between Petrobras and construction giant the Odebrecht Group.

Miranda was said to be one of the 'financial operators' who received $24,749,975 from Odebrecht and made onward transfers of $11,500,500 to Petrobras employees.

A subsequent investigation by the Serious Fraud Office uncovered a UK bank account which contained almost $7,700,000. The SFO found the funds had been transferred out of Miranda's main Swiss bank account and channelled through other banks. The money in the frozen account was found to have come from multiple sources including banks in the Bahamas, Switzerland, Malta and Portugal. Other financial transactions between the 'frozen account' also came from accounts in the UAE and Paris.

District Judge Clarke, sitting at Westminster Magistrates Court, said today: 'It is clear to me that the money which was paid into the account from [Odebrecht] was money from a bribe. This would be an offence here in the UK.

'Perhaps more importantly, this money is as a result of a bribe and the treatment of that money thereafter has clearly been treated in Brazil as money laundering. That

[10] https://www.lawgazette.co.uk/news/sfos-largest-forfeiture-as-court-seizes-more-than-7-million/5115501.article

is what the respondent has been convicted of. The money was illegitimate as it came from unlawful conduct.'

The judge added: 'I am satisfied on the balance of probabilities that the money derives from unlawful conduct, namely money laundering and satisfies the dual criminality test and therefore is recoverable property.

The judge said Miranda 'ought to be in a position to explain' the money and 'if there is an innocent explanation' but had not 'satisfactorily' done so.

She ordered the forfeiture of $7,699,204.09 and £698,635.98, subject to orders of costs.

It is the largest ever amount seized by the SFO from a single bank account.

Lisa Osofsky, director of the SFO, said: 'Over 2 years, we unpicked a complex web of transactions across the world, exposing Mr. Miranda's attempt to conceal criminal proceeds and ensuring that the UK cannot be used as a hiding place for criminal assets.'

vii. **Shahenshah and Ullah: Afren**

Ex-Afren CEO & COO convicted of fraud and money laundering over $300 million oil business deal (24 October, 2018)[11]

Today, Osman Shahenshah and Shahid Ullah were found guilty of fraud and money laundering offences from which they personally received more than $17 m and laundered $45 m by deceiving the Afren Board into agreeing a $300 m business deal.

Following a shareholder revolt which objected to their £6.6 m and £3.8 m salary packages and faced with the possibility of lower remuneration in future, the two hatched a fraudulent scheme to secretly increase their pay.

Shahenshah and Ullah created a side deal with one of Afren's Nigerian oil partners that would allow them to benefit from payments Afren would make.

The men recommended a transaction to the Afren Board, who then approved payments of hundreds of millions of dollars without knowing that Shahenshah and Ullah stood to personally benefit.

The transaction was claimed to be necessary to maintain the business partnership, but the fact that Shahenshah and Ullah stood to benefit personally remained hidden.

Lisa Osofsky, Director of the Serious Fraud Office said:

"Greed motivated this crime. Osman Shahenshah and Shahid Ullah failed in their duties as company directors, abused their positions and lied to their board.

"Instead of acting in their company's best interests, they used Afren like a personal bank account to fund an illicit deal, with no regard for the consequences.

[11] https://www.sfo.gov.uk/2018/10/24/ex-afren-ceo-coo-convicted-of-fraud-and-money-laundering-over-300-million-oil-business-deal/; see also an article by Richard Cassin (October 24, 2018) entitled UK Enforcement: Former Oil Execs convicted of $45million kickback scheme at https://fcpablog.com/2018/10/24/uk-enforcement-former-oil-execs-convicted-of-45-million-kick/

"Fraud corrodes confidence, undermines trust and damages the reputation of the UK at home and abroad. It is our mission to bring those committing this crime to justice."

The criminal investigation into the former CEO and COO of the collapsed oil and gas exploration company began in June 2015 following a self-report by the company, with the defendants charged with four offences in September last year.

Shahenshah and Ullah recommended that the Afren Board agree to a $300 m payment to Oriental Energy Resources Ltd, the company's oil field partner in Nigeria. Unknown to the Afren board, Shahenshah and Ullah had struck a side deal with Oriental which led to 15% of the $300 m was then paid out to a Caribbean shell company controlled by the defendants. The men then used the $45 m to purchase luxury properties in Mustique and the British Virgin Islands. A smaller portion of the $45 m laundered was split between Oriental employees and a close network of Afren staff dubbed 'The A Team'.

The two men were found not guilty on a separate charge relating to a management buyout of another of Afren's business partners ...

Osman Shahenshah and Shahid Ullah sentenced to 30 years for Afren fraud and money laundering (29 October, 2018)[12]

Today, Osman Shahenshah and Shahid Ullah received a total of 30 years for fraud and money laundering offences they had committed whilst they were CEO and Chief Operating Officer of Afren Plc.

The men were found guilty at trial earlier this month for a scheme they created to profit from business deals Afren made with its Nigerian oil partners, without the knowledge of Afren's board of directors.

Shahenshah and Ullah laundered more than $45 m from a $300 m deal they recommended to Afren, using their illicit proceeds to purchase luxury properties in the Caribbean.

Sentencing Shahenshah, His Honour Judge Gledhill QC said:

"You believed that you were above the law, you believed that you were so clever that no one would ever discover your offending."

Lisa Osofsky, Director of the Serious Fraud Office said:

"The significant sentences reflect the seriousness of this fraud. Shahenshah and Ullah violated their duties and their employees, the board of directors and shareholders paid the price.

"They abused their positions to line their own pockets and it is satisfying that they have been brought to justice.

"I would like to thank our international partners in the US Department of Justice, who greatly assisted with our investigation."

[12]https://www.sfo.gov.uk/2018/10/29/osman-shahenshah-shahid-ullah-sentenced-to-30-years-for-afren-fraud-money-laundering/

Shahenshah and Ullah hatched their scheme to secretly increase their income when faced with the possibility of lower remuneration in the future after shareholders rejected their £6.6 m and £3.8 m salary packages in 2013.

Shahenshah and Ullah recommended that the Afren Board agree to a $300 m payment to Oriental Energy Resources Ltd, the company's oil field partner in Nigeria. Unknown to the Afren board, Shahenshah and Ullah had struck a side deal with Oriental which led to 15% of the $300 m being paid out to a Caribbean shell company controlled by the defendants.

The men then used the $45 m to purchase luxury properties in Mustique and the British Virgin Islands. A smaller portion of the $45 m laundered was split between Oriental employees and a close network of Afren staff dubbed 'The A Team'.

In March 2018, following an investigation by the Insolvency Service, both Shahenshah and Ullah were banned by the courts from being company directors for 14 years for failing to declare to the Afren board their vested interests in a number of high-value transactions they had recommended.

The SFO's criminal investigation into the actions of the former CEO and COO of the collapsed oil and gas exploration company began in June 2015 following a self-report by the company's administrators, with the defendants charged with four offences in September last year.

Notes to Editors

1. Osman Shahenshah, former co-founder and Chief Executive Officer of Afren received 6 years jail for one count of fraud, contrary to section 1 of the Fraud Act 2006; 6 years concurrent for one count of money laundering, contrary to section 329 of the Proceeds of Crime Act 2002; and 4 years concurrent for one count of money laundering, contrary to section 328 of the Proceeds of Crime Act 2002.
2. Shahid Ullah, former Chief Operating Officer of Afren received 5 years jail for one count of fraud, contrary to section 1 of the Fraud Act 2006; 5 years concurrent for one count of money laundering, contrary to section 329 of the Proceeds of Crime Act 2002; and 4 years concurrent for one count of money laundering, contrary to section 328 of the Proceeds of Crime Act 2002.
3. Osman Shahenshah and Shahid Ullah were both convicted of the following offences, relating to misconduct between 1st May 2013 and 29th July 2014:
   a. One count of fraud by abuse of position, contrary to sections 1 and 4 of the Fraud Act 2006.
   b. One count of money laundering, contrary to section 328 of the Proceeds of Crime Act 2002.
   c. One count of money laundering, contrary to section 329 of the Proceeds of Crime Act 2002.
4. Osman Shahenshah and Shahid Ullah were found not guilty of the following offence, relating to misconduct between 1st May 2013 and 29th July 2014:
   a. One count of fraud by abuse of position, contrary to sections 1 and 4 of the Fraud Act 2006.

5. Afren Plc was an oil and gas exploration and production company, founded in 2004. The company is now in administration.
6. Further information can be found on the Afren case page on our website.

AND

SFO secures £5.45 m confiscation order against ex-Afren CEO and COO (31 July, 2020)[13]

The SFO has today secured confiscation orders totalling £5,450,000 against the former Chief Executive Officer and Chief Operating Officer of Afren. Former CEO Osman Shahenshah was ordered to pay £2,935,000 and former COO Shahid Ullah was ordered to pay £2,515,000.

After deceiving the board of Afren into a $300 m deal from which they personally stood to gain over $17 m, Shahenshah and Ullah were each found guilty of one count of fraud and two counts of money laundering in October 2018. The two men hatched the scheme following a shareholder revolt which objected to their £6.6 m and £3.8 m salary packages and threatened the possibility of lower remuneration in future. Seeking to maintain their high rate of pay, they created a side deal with one of Afren's Nigerian oil partners whereby 15% of Afren's payment to the company would be paid out to a Bermudan shell company controlled by Shahenshah and Ullah.

Lisa Osofsky, Director of the Serious Fraud Office, said:

"These men reacted to shareholder concerns about their high remuneration by defrauding the very company that paid them. Their selfish actions showed cynical disregard for the law, their colleagues and common decency.

"Our pursuit of fraudsters does not stop at conviction, and I'm delighted that our Proceeds of Crime team have been able to identify considerable criminal gains from these men."

Having secretly put this deal in place, the two men recommended to the Afren board a $300 m payment to the Nigerian oil partners. When this payment was made, Shahenshah and Ullah, along with some staff at the Nigerian partner and a close network of Afren staff dubbed 'The A Team', received $45 m from the deal. The two men used this money to purchase luxury properties in Mustique and the British Virgin Islands.

Notes to Editors:

Osman Shahenshah and Shahid Ullah were convicted on 24 October 2018 and sentenced on 29 October 2018.

Osman Shahenshah, former co-founder and Chief Executive Officer of Afren, received 6 years' imprisonment for one count of fraud, contrary to section 1 of the Fraud Act 2006; 6 years' concurrent for one count of money laundering, contrary to

[13] https://www.sfo.gov.uk/2020/07/31/sfo-secures-5-45m-confiscation-order-against-ex-afren-ceo-and-coo/

section 329 of the Proceeds of Crime Act 2002; and 4 years' concurrent for one count of money laundering, contrary to section 328 of the Proceeds of Crime Act 2002.

Shahid Ullah, former Chief Operating Officer of Afren, received 5 years' imprisonment for one count of fraud, contrary to section 1 of the Fraud Act 2006; 5 years' concurrent for one count of money laundering, contrary to section 329 of the Proceeds of Crime Act 2002; and 4 years' concurrent for one count of money laundering, contrary to section 328 of the Proceeds of Crime Act 2002.

Osman Shahenshah and Shahid Ullah were found not guilty of the following offence, relating to misconduct between 1st May 2013 and 29th July 2014: One count of fraud by abuse of position, contrary to sections 1 and 4 of the Fraud Act 2006.

Afren Plc was an oil and gas exploration and production company, founded in 2004. The company is now in administration.

Scandinavian Cases

i. Danske Bank[14]

The **Danske Bank money laundering scandal** arose in 2017–2018, when it became known that around €800 billion of suspicious transactions had flowed from Estonian, Russian, Latvian and other sources through the Estonia-based bank branch of Denmark-based Danske Bank from 2007 to 2015.[1][2][3] It has been described as possibly the largest money laundering scandal ever in Europe,[4] and as possibly the largest in world history.[5] It includes incoming funds from Estonia (23%), Russia (23%), Latvia (12%), Cyprus (9%), UK (4%) and others (30%, more than 150 countries each of which account for a smaller part than the UK). Outgoing funds were distributed between Estonia (15%), Latvia (14%), China (7%), Switzerland (6%), Turkey (6%) and others (52%).

Financial Supervision

Danske Bank, headquartered in Copenhagen, is the largest bank in Denmark. The bank's local branch in Estonia, which was acquired by Danske Bank as part of a merger with Finnish Sampo Bank in 2007, was used for the activities.[3][6] It was under the jurisdiction of both the Financial Supervisory Authority of Denmark (due to the location of the headquarters) and the Financial Supervisory Authority of Estonia (due to the location of the branch), and both have blamed the other side for deficiencies.[7][8] The Danish and the Estonian supervisory authorities later released a joint press release on collaborating and sharing information on the case.[9] Both were allegedly criticized in a draft prepared by the European Banking Authority, an EU banking watchdog controlled by the national financial supervisory authorities of EU members states. However, the EBA closed its investigation early and did not publish the findings—a decision that itself caused criticism.[8][10]

[14] https://en.wikipedia.org/wiki/Danske_Bank_money_laundering_scandaland

Events

In 2012, the Estonian Financial Supervision Authority came out with a critical report on the Danske Bank's activities. One of Russian whistleblower Sergei Magnitsky's stolen Hermitage Capital Management subsidiaries, *Diron Trade LLP* which had a Great Britain postal box, assisted in $5.8 billion in money laundering transfers between Swedbank's Baltic subsidiaries and Danske Bank during 6 months in 2010 and 2011 according to SVT.[11] During that time, Aivars Bergers, a board member of Latvia's leading pro-Russian party *Harmony* and one of its largest financiers, received EUR 270,000 from *Diron Trade LLP* and *Murova Systems LLP*, a company which has a Great Britain postal box and is associated with the Azerbaijani Laundromat in which $2.9 billion was money laundered through Danske Bank's Estonia branch.[11][12][13] In 2013, the first whistleblower disclosed that Danske's branch in Tallinn was knowingly dealing with funds from the family of the Russian President Vladimir Putin (his cousin Igor Putin) and the Russian security service (FSB). The claims were not properly looked into and hence did not catch enough attention.[14] The local Estonian branch of Danske Bank, after being acquired in 2007, still used its own IT-system and many documents were written in Estonian or Russian. Despite these differences in systems and language, the Danske Bank did not implement changes that would make it easier to control for the headquarters in Denmark.[14] In a 2018 report released by Bruun & Hjejle, a law firm retained by Danske Bank, the bank claimed to have had believed for a "long time" that the high risks represented by non-resident customers were mitigated by proper Anti-Money-Laundering procedures. It had become clear that the AML procedures were not sufficient after being tipped off by an internal whistleblower.[15] The whistleblower was later identified as Howard Wilkinson, former head of trading for Danske Bank in Estonia, Latvia & Lithuania.[16]

According to the Danish FSA, non-resident portfolios from Russia in 2012 made up 35% of the profits of the local branch. The overall percentage of Russian clients in the branch was 8%. Some of these transaction have been linked to the Russian Government and were done via shell companies that were registered in the United Kingdom, Cyprus and New Zealand, as well as other banks in Latvia and Moldova. The second highest amount of non-resident portfolios were from the United Kingdom. Another significant non-resident portfolio has been linked to the President of Azerbaijan and his family.

In 2013, US bank JPMorgan Chase halted its services to the Estonian branch of the bank, suspecting it was laundering large amounts of Russian money. Other banks continued providing services into 2015.

In 2014, The Estonian Financial Supervision Authority found "large-scale, long-lasting systemic violations of anti-money laundering rules" in the Estonian branch of Danske Bank and notified the Danish authorities on the findings. According to the Estonian Financial Supervision Authority, the activities decreased after they requested the bank to target the violations.

According to the Danish FSA, a critical report sent by the Estonian FSA was discussed at the bank's board meeting on October 7, 2014. The conclusions of the report were "toned down" in the minuted discussions of the Executive Board. According to the report, during a meeting in June 2014, the bank's board members "were interested in the branch's earnings, while the minutes have not recorded any comments on the significant AML challenges."

A former executive of the Estonian branch of Danske Bank was found dead on September 25, 2019. Estonian police discovered the body of Aivar Rehe, who was in charge of the branch from 2007 until 2015, during a search operation after his disappearance that began 2 days earlier. Rehe was a key witness in the ongoing criminal investigation. The cause of his death has been reported as suicide.

Results

Ten former employees in the local branch of the bank were arrested by Estonian authorities in December 2018,[22] and the bank was required by the Estonian government to close its Estonian branch in 2019.

The CEO Thomas Borgen resigned in 2018 following the scandal. Danish authorities charged him in May 2019 with neglecting his responsibilities.[24] At the same time, Danish prosecutors charged Henrik Ramlau-Hansen, the bank's former finance director, with failing to prevent the suspicious transactions. The Danish Parliament increased penalties for money laundering eight-fold, making them some of the toughest in Europe.

All charges against Danske bankers (Thomas Borgen, Henrik Ramlau-Hansen, and Lars Morch) were dropped in April 2021. Thomas Borgen was also acquitted in a civil lawsuit related to the Danske money laundering scandal in November 2022.

The value of Danske Bank shares was halved in 2018. The bank has said it will donate 1.5 billion kroner (c. US$225 million) to a charity. It expects to pay fines of several billion dollars to financial regulators in Denmark, the U.S. and other European countries.

In December 2022, Danske Bank pled guilty and agreed to a $2 billion fine in a case from the United States Department of Justice.

AND

Danske Bank Pleads Guilty to Fraud on U.S. Banks in Multi-Billion Dollar Scheme to Access the U.S. Financial System[15] (December 13, 2022)

Largest Bank in Denmark Agrees to Forfeit $2 Billion

Danske Bank A/S (Danske Bank), a global financial institution headquartered in Denmark, pleaded guilty today and agreed to forfeit $2 billion to resolve the United States' investigation into Danske Bank's fraud on U.S. banks.

According to court documents, Danske Bank defrauded U.S. banks regarding Danske Bank Estonia's customers and anti-money laundering controls to facilitate access to the U.S. financial system for Danske Bank Estonia's high-risk customers, who resided outside of Estonia – including in Russia. The Justice Department will

[15] https://www.justice.gov/opa/pr/danske-bank-pleads-guilty-fraud-us-banks-multi-billion-dollar-scheme-access-us-financial

credit nearly $850 million in payments that Danske Bank makes to resolve related parallel investigations by other domestic and foreign authorities.

"Today's guilty plea by Danske Bank and two-billion-dollar penalty demonstrate that the Department of Justice will fiercely guard the integrity of the U.S. financial system from tainted foreign money – Russian or otherwise," said Deputy Attorney General Lisa O. Monaco. "Whether you are a U.S. or foreign bank, if you use the U.S. financial system, you must comply with our laws. We expect companies to invest in robust compliance programs – including at newly acquired or far-flung subsidiaries – and to step up and own up to misconduct when it occurs. Failure to do so may well be a one-way ticket to a multi-billion-dollar guilty plea."

"Danske Bank lied to U.S. banks about its deficient anti-money laundering systems, inadequate transaction monitoring capabilities, and its high-risk, offshore customer base in order to gain unlawful access to the U.S. financial system," said Assistant Attorney General Kenneth A. Polite, Jr. of the Justice Department's Criminal Division. "Today, Danske Bank accepted responsibility for defrauding U.S. financial institutions and funneling billions of dollars in suspicious and criminal transactions through the United States. As part of its guilty plea, Danske Bank will forfeit over $2 billion and implement significant changes to its compliance program and AML controls. This coordinated resolution with the Securities and Exchange Commission (SEC) and Danish authorities sends a clear message that the Department of Justice stands ready to work with our partners around the world to investigate corporate wrongdoing and hold bad actors accountable for their criminal conduct."

"For years, Danske Bank lied and deceived U.S. banks to pump billions of dollars of suspicious and criminal funds through the U.S. financial system," said U.-S. Attorney Damian Williams for the Southern District of New York. "In doing so, Danske Bank, the largest bank in Denmark, deliberately disregarded U.S. law of which it is well aware, facilitated the laundering of criminal and suspicious proceeds through the United States, and placed the U.S. financial network at risk, all in the name of its bottom line. The bank is now being held to account. For its years-long criminal conduct, today Danske Bank pleaded guilty to conspiring to commit bank fraud, will forfeit over $2 billion, and will implement and maintain a revamped compliance program and AML controls. Banks and other financial institutions around the world should heed this message: If you want to use the U.S. financial system, you must play by the rules. If you don't, we will hold you accountable."

"Danske Bank's guilty plea for defrauding U.S. banks should serve as a stark warning to others that we will uncover the truth and deliver accountability," said FBI Deputy Director Paul Abbate. "The FBI, working with international partners, will vigorously investigate any institution, wherever based, which is engaged in manipulating U.S. financial systems to enable money laundering. The FBI remains committed to safeguarding our national and economic security from threats which could cause harm to American institutions."

According to admissions and court documents, between 2008 and 2016, Danske Bank offered banking services through its branch in Estonia, Danske Bank Estonia. Danske Bank Estonia had a lucrative business line serving non-resident customers known as the NRP. Danske Bank Estonia attracted NRP customers by ensuring that they could transfer large amounts of money through Danske Bank Estonia with little, if any, oversight. Danske Bank Estonia employees conspired with NRP customers to shield the true nature of their transactions, including by using shell companies that obscured actual ownership of the funds. Access to the U.S. financial system via the U.S. banks was critical to Danske Bank and its NRP customers, who relied on access to U.S. banks to process U.S. dollar transactions. Danske Bank Estonia processed $160 billion through U.S. banks on behalf of the NRP.

U.S. banks required Danske Bank and Danske Bank Estonia to provide information to open and maintain accounts, including information related to anti-money laundering (AML) controls, transaction monitoring, and customers. Danske Bank knew that the U.S. banks expected honest, complete, and accurate responses and that the U.S. banks would not maintain, or open, U.S. dollar accounts for Danske Bank Estonia without the required information.

By at least February 2014, as a result of internal audits, information from regulators, and an internal whistleblower, Danske Bank knew that some NRP customers were engaged in highly suspicious and potentially criminal transactions, including transactions through U.S. banks. Danske Bank also knew that Danske Bank Estonia's anti-money laundering program and procedures did not meet Danske Bank's standards and were not appropriate to meet the risks associated with the NRP. Instead of providing the U.S. banks with truthful information, Danske Bank lied about the state of Danske Bank Estonia's AML compliance program, transaction monitoring capabilities, and information regarding Danske Bank Estonia's customers and their risk profile.

Today, Danske Bank pleaded guilty to one count of conspiracy to commit bank fraud. Under the terms of the plea agreement, the company has agreed to criminal forfeiture of $2.059 billion. Danske Bank will also enter into separate criminal or civil resolutions with domestic and foreign authorities and the department will credit approximately $850 million in payments the bank makes to the SEC and the Danish authorities.

The department reached its resolution with Danske Bank based on a number of factors, including the nature, seriousness, and pervasiveness of the offense conduct. This included a bank fraud conspiracy in which Danske Bank misled U.S. banks in order to maintain and in one case open U.S. dollar accounts through which Danske Bank processed $160 billion for its non-resident customers; the bank's failure to voluntarily and timely disclose the conduct to the department; the state of Danske Bank's compliance program and the progress of its remediation; the bank's resolutions with other domestic and foreign authorities, including the imposition of an independent expert by Danish authorities; and the bank's continued cooperation with the department's ongoing investigation. Danske Bank received full credit for cooperation and remediation because it provided full cooperation with the investigation and demonstrated recognition and affirmative acceptance of responsibility for its criminal conduct, including by, among other things, providing substantial information from its internal investigation, voluntarily and expediently producing a significant amount of documents located outside the United States in ways that did not implicate foreign data privacy laws, making foreign witnesses available for interviews, collecting and producing voluminous evidence and information including with translations where necessary, and providing detailed analysis of complex, cross-border transactions. Danske Bank has also enhanced and committed to continue improving its compliance programs and has agreed to the appointment of an independent expert selected by its regulator.

Additionally, the SEC announced a separate settlement with Danske Bank today in connection with a related, parallel proceeding. Under the terms of that resolution, Danske Bank agreed to pay approximately $413 million, which includes a civil monetary penalty of $178.6 million, as well as disgorgement that will be credited to any such payments made to the Danish authorities or the department in connection with Danske Bank's guilty plea.

The FBI is investigating the case . . . .

The department appreciates the significant assistance provided by the SEC and the authorities in Denmark. The department further appreciates the assistance provided by authorities in Estonia in response to multiple Mutual Legal Assistance requests.

MLARS' Bank Integrity Unit investigates and prosecutes complex, multi-district, and international criminal cases involving financial institutions. The unit's prosecutions focus on banks and other financial institutions, including their officers, managers, and employees, whose actions threaten the integrity of the individual institution or the wider financial system.

Updated December 13, 2022

ii. **Swedbank**

Settlement Agreement between the U.S. Department of the Treasury's Office of Foreign Assets Control and Swedbank AS (Latvia) (June 20, 2023)[16]

The U.S. Department of the Treasury's Office of Foreign Assets Control (OFAC) today announced a settlement with Swedbank AS (Latvia) ("Swedbank Latvia"), a subsidiary of Swedbank AB (publ), headquartered in Stockholm, Sweden. Swedbank Latvia has agreed to remit $3,430,900 to settle its potential civil liability for 386 apparent violations of OFAC's Crimea sanctions. Throughout 2015 and 2016, a customer of Swedbank Latvia used Swedbank Latvia's e-banking platform from an internet protocol address in Crimea to send payments to persons in Crimea through U.S. correspondent banks. The settlement amount reflects OFAC's determination that Swedbank Latvia's apparent violations were not voluntarily self-disclosed and were non-egregious.

For further details on the OFAC settlement, see the OFAC Enforcement Notice: https://ofac.treasury.gov/media/931911/download?inline which provides greater detail, including on:

[16]https://ofac.treasury.gov/recent-actions/20230620_33#:~:text=Swedbank%20Latvia%20has%20agreed%20to,violations%20of%20OFAC%27 s%20Crimea%20sanctions

- the Conduct Leading to Apparent Violations;
- Penalty Calculations and General Factors Analysis (including 3 aggravating factors and 3 mitigating factors); and
- Compliance Considerations.[17]

Swedbank reaches agreement with OFAC (June 19, 2023)[18]

Swedbank has now reached a final agreement with the US Treasury's Office for Foreign Assets Control (OFAC) regarding the bank's historical shortcomings. OFAC has concluded that the transactions, which were disclosed by the bank to the authority, constitute a violation of applicable regulations.

Swedbank has agreed to remit SEK 37 million regarding the settlement relating to violation of OFAC regulations. The settlement concerns transactions that were conducted by Swedbank in Latvia in 2015–2016.

The transactions, which Swedbank reported to OFAC in March 2020, consisted of salary payments and payments that were associated with the operation of a vessel whose owner and operator were located in Crimea, that were subject to US economic sanctions. In total, the settlement involves 386 transactions with a total value of USD 3.3 million.

"Swedbank takes the historical shortcomings seriously, and has learned from them in the comprehensive work that has been performed to strengthen internal governance and control" says Tomas Hedberg, Head of Special Task Force and Deputy President and CEO, Swedbank.

The bank made a provision of SEK 40 million regarding the agreement with OFAC, in March.

The investigations by the US Department of Justice (DoJ), US Securities and Exchange Commission (SEC), and Department of Financial Services in New York (DFS) are ongoing. Swedbank is holding separate discussions with these agencies through our US legal advisors. These investigations are at different stages.

At this time, the bank cannot assess the extent of potential financial consequences, nor when the investigations will be completed.

---

[17] "... This case demonstrates the importance of implementing and maintaining effective risk-based sanctions controls, especially for sophisticated financial institutions operating in proximity to high-risk regions... In addition, this case illustrates the importance of undertaking reasonable efforts to investigate red flags. Ignoring or failing to heed such warnings can cause apparent violations to multiply quickly. Rather than dismissing such concerns and relying on unsubstantiated assurances, financial institutions and other persons made aware of such issues, should diligently work to identify risks that may exist. Here the bank's own KYC information supported the concerns of its correspondent bank, yet I went ignored..."

[18] https://www.swedbank.com/newsroom/press-releases.details.3D1A880222F404B3.html

AND

Former Swedbank Chief Acquitted Over AML Disclosures report by Koos Couvée (January 25, 2023)[19]

A Swedish court on Wednesday cleared Swedbank's former chief executive Birgitte Bonnesen of deceiving investors in 2018 and 2019 amid allegations that the lender's affiliate in Estonia handled large volumes of suspicious funds.

Following weeks of hearings described in the local press as Sweden's "trial of the century," a panel of two judges at Stockholm District Court found Bonnesen, 66, not guilty of fraud nor market manipulation after reviewing statements she made to the press about Swedbank Estonia's anti-money laundering program.

Bonnesen's comments on the affiliate at times appeared "somewhat misleading" but did not rise to the level of fraudulent misrepresentation, the judges ruled. "The statements have either been correct, and/or too general to reach the [standard of] criminal liability."

The judges further ruled that Bonnesen, who has consistently denied wrongdoing in the year since Swedish prosecutors filed criminal charges against her, could not be held liable for any headlines chosen by news outlets that may have misrepresented her position.

Bonnesen was also cleared Wednesday of disclosing insider information by telling shareholders near the end of her 3-year tenure in February 2019 that Swedish broadcaster *SVT* would soon report that Swedbank Estonia handled thousands of payments tied to the scandal-plagued, now-defunct Danske Bank Estonia.

Swedbank's share values plunged in the days after the program aired.

The case against Bonnesen, who led Swedbank during the most turbulent period in the lender's 203-year history, marked the first prosecution of a senior executive of any Nordic or Baltic lender involved in any one of a series of high-profile money laundering schemes that have come to light in Estonia, Latvia and Lithuania over the past 6 years.

Prosecutors alleged that Bonnesen committed fraud and market manipulation on four separate occasions in late 2018 and again in early 2019 by intentionally or negligently making misleading statements about Swedbank Estonia in claiming that the affiliate did not have any significant current or historic AML-related deficiencies.

One of those statements occurred in October 2018, when Bonnesen told *Svenska Dagbladet* that a confidential, in-house assessment of Swedbank's exposure to suspicious clients of Danske Bank Estonia, which had just then admitted to handling more than €200 billion in potentially illicit funds, showed "nothing" in the way of warning signs.

[19] https://www.moneylaundering.com/news/former-swedbank-chief-acquitted-over-aml-disclosures/; https://www.occrp.org/en/daily/17272-swedbank-ex-ceo-cleared-of-money-laundering-cover-up; https://www.amlintelligence.com/2023/01/swedish-court-finds-former-swedbank-ceo-not-guilty-of-fraud/

Prosecutors alleged that Bonnesen, who led Swedbank's Baltic portfolio from 2011 to 2014, already knew by that point that hundreds of opaque entities had moved billions of dollars through corporate accounts in Estonia over nearly a decade.

But the judges ruled Wednesday that Bonnesen made her comments to *Svenska Dagbladet* and other news outlets in the present tense and spoke too generally to meet the criminal threshold.

They also ruled that her subsequent claim to the Swedish newspaper that Swedbank never served the customers of Danske Bank named by *SVT* was accurate.

Accountability

The Swedish Financial Supervisory Authority fined Swedbank a record €360 million in March 2020 for systemically and egregiously violating AML requirements in Estonia and Latvia, as well as back home in Sweden. Swedbank also failed to cooperate fully with regulators at home and in the Baltics during their investigation, the FSA noted.

Wednesday's decision to acquit Bonnesen stands in contrast to the findings of a Swedbank-commissioned internal review by global law firm Clifford Chance that the lender published in the days following the fine.

Clifford Chance concluded that "certain disclosures" Bonnesen made during the relevant period concerning Swedbank's historic and current AML controls—and also about the lender's exposure to clients and transactions tied to Danske Bank—"-were either inaccurate or failed on multiple occasions to provide sufficient clarity and context."

The law firm found that Swedbank Estonia handled €21 billion of suspicious payments from 2014 to 2019, while Swedbank Latvia and Swedbank Lithuania together processed around €15.5 billion of potentially illicit funds.

Prosecutors did not charge Bonnesen for any AML violations that occurred on her watch at Swedbank. Still, her acquittal will do little to counter the view that pursuing criminal liability against senior executives for compliance-related failures is a nonstarter.

"It sends a very underwhelming message to AML professionals who spend long hours monitoring transactions and flagging suspicious activity," Samantha Sheen, former AML director for ACAMS, told moneylaundering.com. "They'll conclude that it doesn't matter how hard you try, people at the top are never held accountable."

Board members forced Bonnesen to resign in March 2019 as the pressure reached the boiling point at Swedbank, which is still the target of a criminal investigation in Estonia for alleged violations that occurred from 2014 to 2016.

Several other former senior employees of Swedbank Estonia also reportedly face the prospect of AML-related criminal charges in the Baltic nation, as do 19 former employees of Danske Bank Estonia.

In April 2021, Danish prosecutors dropped money laundering charges against Danske Bank's former chief executive Thomas Borgen, former financial executive Henrik Ramlau-Hansen and former business banking director Lars Stensgaard Morch.

Eight executives of ABLV, which collapsed in February 2018 after U.S. officials accused the lender of enabling illicit finance on a massive scale, face trial this year for allegedly helping clients from Russia and other former Soviet states launder vast sums.

Bonnesen's attorney did not respond to a request for comment.

AND

... On 20 February 2019 Swedish broadcaster SVT revealed that Swedbank is under investigation for alleged link in money laundering scandal by Estonian authorities due to suspicious transactions through Danske Bank which is being investigated in Denmark, Estonia, Britain, France and the United States. Estonian authorities confirmed findings by SVT. At least 40 billion Swedish crowns (£3.3 billion) had been transferred between accounts at Swedbank and Danske in the Baltics between 2007 and 2015, SVT's Uppdrag Granskning investigative programme reported. Chief executive Birgitte Bonnesen was fired in March 2019 during the money laundering scandal and her severance pay was cancelled. The bank's chairman Lars Idermark resigned the following month. Swedbank was subsequently fined a record SKr4bn ($380 m) by Swedish and Estonian regulators ...[20]

iii. **Skandinaviska Enskilda Banken AB**[21] (SEB) (OCCRP article)

Sweden's SEB bank has to pay a SEK1 billion (US$107 million) administrative fine for failing to provide adequate anti-money laundering (AML) measures in its subsidiaries in Baltic countries, Swedish financial watchdog announced last week.

The bank was involved in a massive money laundering scandal that first engulfed Denmark's largest lender, Danske Bank, whose Estonian branch was found to have processed suspicious transactions worth billions of dollars. Some of the funds allegedly belonged to Russian money launderers.

Sweden's Financial Inspection started probing SEB in 2015 in coordination with authorities in Estonia, Latvia and Lithuania. The investigation was wrapped up in 2019 and showed that "SEB's subsidiary banks in the Baltics have been exposed to an elevated risk of money laundering."

Investigators concluded that "customers with a higher risk of money laundering," had made a "substantial portion of the subsidiary banks' business volumes and transactions," a statement from the Financial Inspection said.

Therefore, the "bank has had deficiencies in identifying and managing the risk of money laundering associated with some of their non-resident customers and resident customers with non-resident owners," according to FI.

"The bank has done too little, too late," the FI's Director General, Erik Thedéen said.

SEB bank said it will now analyse the country's financial watchdog's decision.

---

[20] https://en.wikipedia.org/wiki/Swedbank

[21] https://www.occrp.org/en/daily/12651-swedish-seb-bank-fined-for-poor-anti-money-laundering-measures

"We always strive to adhere to current regulations and our high internal standards, and we continuously develop the bank's abilities to prevent, detect and report suspected money laundering and other types of financial crime," SEB's President and CEO Johan Torgeby said reacting to FI's sanctions.

That work, he added, "is of highest priority and will never end, not least since crime constantly finds new ways."

iv. **Troika Laundromat**[22]

Troika laundromat or **ŪkioLeaks**[1] is a money laundering scheme organized by Russia's former largest investment bank – Troika Dialog. This scheme allowed allowed the flow of some $4.8 billion of funds from Russian companies and figures into Europe and the US between 2003 and early 2013. It was discovered by the Organized Crime and Corruption Reporting Project (OCCRP) with 21 media partners from Europe, North America, and South Korea in 2019.[2][3][4][5]

Investigation

The scheme was discovered in a large set of transactions and other documents collected by OCCRP[2] and 20 media partners[6] including 15 min.lt.[2] The findings draw on a massive—possibly the largest ever—leak of bank records, emails and contracts. Investigative journalists sifted through 1.3 million bank transactions between 233,000 companies and individuals, with a total value over US$470 billion, dated between 2006 and 2012.[6]

Erich Rebasso

Between December 2006 and February 2008, Erich Rebasso, an Austrian lawyer used 150 individual transactions to send almost US$96 million to laundromat accounts at Ukio Bankas, a Lithuanian bank.[7]

In 2008, Rebasso sent a letter to the main Vienna headquarters of the Federal Criminal Police, the country's top law enforcement agency. In his five-page letter he confess that he has been used for criminal purposes and is willing to submit the matter to the required criminal review.[7]

Rebasso's confessional letter had little effect. While police looked into the matter, it was 2 years later when they informed him that they had stopped the proceedings because they believed any potential crime had happened outside their jurisdiction and been committed by foreigners.[7]

In 2012, Rebasso was ambushed and killed by 2 men.[7][8]

Sergei Magnitsky

More than $130 million was transferred through the Troika Laundromat by companies involved in the fraud that Magnitsky uncovered.[6][9]

Sergei Magnitsky was detained in 2009 and passed away in custody after informing the authorities of the crime.[6][9]

[22] https://en.wikipedia.org/wiki/Troika_laundromat

Scheme

A Russian investment bank named Troika Dialog was established in the 1990s. In 2012, it was acquired by state-owned Sberbank. At least 75 companies were registered in tax haven British Virgin Islands by Troika Dialog. They were additionally incorporated under shell corporations in different tax heavens.[6][10]

In total, over $4.3 billion[11] was paid into Troika network, however the value of transactions between the companies managed by Troika Dialog was an estimated $8.8bn, suggesting money was spun around for a number of cycles before exiting.[12]

In order to protect themselves, the organizers of this system used the identities of poor people[2] such as Armenian workers in Mocsow[6] as unwitting signatories in the secretive offshore companies that ran the system.[2] Those shell companies did operations with fake paperwork.[6]

The laundromat let oligarchs and politicians to secretly buy from state-owned companies, to buy real-estates both in Russia and abroad, to buy yachts, to hire music superstars for private parties etc.[2]

Connection with European banks

At least 35 of total shell corporations had accounts in Lithuanian defunct bank—Ukio Bankas.[6][13][11]

Austria's Raiffeisen and Germany's Commerzbank have neglected AML obligations during handling the Troika's money.[6][11][14]

Ruben Vardanyan

Ruben Vardanyan was the head of Troika Dialog at the time. He′s a former adviser to Vladimir Putin and has close ties to him.[15] Vardanyan has been listed by *Forbes* magazine as one of the richest persons in Russia.[3] He supposedly provided a loan to a business that was a part of the plan, according to one document that bears his signature, but the OCCRP claims there is no "definitive evidence" that he was aware of the fraud.[16]

According to Vardanyan, who was mentioned by the OCCRP, his bank didn't do anything improper and ran similarly to other investment banks at the time. However, he said that he "couldn't possibly know" about every transaction that his bank carried out on behalf of customers.[16] However, the data, which is being scrutinized by government prosecutors in Lithuania, raises concerns about the bank's transfers being only lightly inspected. Data shows that shell company named Quantus sent nearly $500,000 to pay Vardanyan's credit card bills. Other than that, his wife and mother-in-law received 935,000 euros and 900,000 euros respectively . . .[15]

v. **Sergei Magnitski**[23]

Sergei Leonidovich Magnitsky (. . . 8 April 1972–16 November 2009) was a Russian tax adviser responsible for exposing corruption and misconduct by

[23] https://en.wikipedia.org/wiki/Sergei_Magnitsky

Russian government officials while representing client Hermitage Capital Management.[1] His arrest in 2008 and subsequent death after 11 months in police custody generated international attention and triggered both official and unofficial inquiries into allegations of fraud, theft and human rights violations in Russia.[2][3][4] His posthumous trial was the first in the Russian Federation.

Magnitsky alleged there had been large-scale theft from the Russian state, sanctioned and carried out by Russian officials. He was arrested and eventually died in prison 7 days before the expiration of the 1-year term during which he could be legally held without trial.[5][6] In total, Magnitsky served 358 days in Moscow's Butyrka prison. He developed gall stones, pancreatitis, and a blocked gall bladder, and was denied medical care. A human rights council set up by the Kremlin found that he had been physically assaulted shortly before his death.[7][8] His case became an international *cause célèbre*.[9]

The United States Congress and President Barack Obama enacted the Magnitsky Act at the end of 2012, barring those Russian officials believed to be involved in Magnitsky's death from entering the United States or using its banking system. In response, Russia condemned the Act and claimed Magnitsky was guilty of crimes.[10] Nearly a dozen other nations, as well as the European Union, have subsequently implemented or considered Magnitsky legislation.

In early January 2013, the *Financial Times* wrote that "the Magnitsky case is egregious, well documented and encapsulates the darker side of Putinism".[11]

Background

Magnitsky was an auditor at the Moscow law firm Firestone Duncan, working for its owner, Jamison Firestone.[12] He worked with Firestone Duncan client Hermitage Capital Management, an investment advisory firm accused of tax evasion and tax fraud by the Russian Interior Ministry.[13]

Over the years of its operation Hermitage had, on a number of occasions, supplied to the press information related to corporate and governmental misconduct and corruption within state-owned Russian enterprises.[14] Hermitage's company co-founder, American Bill Browder, was expelled from Russia in November 2005 as a purported national threat; Browder arrived in Moscow, was told his visa had been annulled, and was deported the next day.[9] Browder has said that he represented a threat only "to corrupt politicians and bureaucrats" in Russia, and believed that he was removed to leave his company open for exploitation.[2]

On 4 June 2007, Hermitage's Moscow office was raided by about 20 Ministry of Interior officers. The offices of Firestone Duncan were also raided. The officers had a search warrant alleging that Kamaya, a company administered by Hermitage, had underpaid its taxes. This was highly irregular, as the Russian tax authorities had just confirmed in writing that this company had overpaid its tax. In both cases, the search warrants permitted the seizure of materials related only to Kamaya. But, in both cases the officers illegally seized all the corporate, tax documents and seals for any company that had paid a large amount of Russian taxes, including documents and seals for many of Hermitage's Russian companies.[15] In October 2007, Browder received word that one of the firms maintained in Moscow had a trial against it for an alleged unpaid debt of hundreds of millions of dollars. According to Browder, this was the first time he had heard of this court case and he did not know the lawyers who represented his company in court.[9] Magnitsky was assigned to investigate the case.

Exposing the scandal

In his investigation, auditor Magnitsky came to believe that the police had given the materials taken during the police raids to organized criminals, who used them to take over three of Hermitage's Russian companies and who fraudulently reclaimed $230 m (£140 m) of the taxes previously paid by Hermitage.[5][16] He also claimed police had accused Hermitage of tax evasion solely to justify the police raids, so they could take the materials needed to hijack the Hermitage companies and effect the tax refund fraud. Magnitsky's testimony implicated police, the judiciary, tax officials, bankers, and the Russian mafia.[5] In spite of the initial dismissal of his claims, Magnitsky's core allegation that Hermitage had not committed fraud—but had been victimized by it—was eventually validated. A sawmill foreman pleaded guilty in the matter to "fraud by prior collusion", though the foreman would maintain that police were not part of the plan.[16] Before then, however, Magnitsky became the subject of investigation by one of the policemen against whom he had testified as involved in the fraud. According to Browder, Magnitsky was "the 'go-to guy' in Moscow on courts, taxes, fines, anything to do with civil law."[9]

According to Magnitsky's investigation, the documents that had been taken by the Russian police in June 2007 were used to forge a change in ownership of Hermitage.[9] The thieves used the forged contracts to claim Hermitage owed $1 billion (~$1.37 billion in 2022) to shell companies. Unknown to Hermitage, those claims were later authenticated by judges. In every instance, lawyers hired by the thieves to represent Hermitage pleaded guilty on the company's behalf and agreed to the claims, thereby obtaining penalties for debts that did not exist; all while Hermitage officials were unaware of these court proceedings.[9]

The new owner, based in Tatarstan, turned out to be Viktor Markelov, a convicted murderer released 2 years into his sentence.[9] The company's fake debt was used to make the companies look unprofitable in order to justify a refund of $230 million in tax that the companies had paid when they had been under Hermitage's control. The refund was issued on Christmas Eve 2007 and was the largest tax rebate in Russian history.[9]

Hermitage contacted the Russian government with the findings of its investigation. The money, which was not Hermitage's, belonged to the Russian state. Rather than opening a case against the police and the thieves, the Russian authorities opened a criminal case against Magnitsky...[9]

International reactions

In late 2010, international attention to the matter intensified, with the European Parliament calling for 60 officials believed to be connected to Magnitsky's death to be banned from entering the European Union, and the Parliament of Canada resolving to deny visas to and freeze the Canadian assets of allegedly involved officials.[citation needed] The EU Parliament also urged members to freeze assets of officials, while similar measures were under consideration in the United States.[42][43] In October 2010, US Senator John McCain co-sponsored the Justice for Sergei Magnitsky Act, which would forbid entry to the US to 60 individuals named in court documents related to the Magnitsky case. McCain said the law would help to "identify those responsible for the death of this Russian patriot, to make their names famous for the whole world to know, and then to hold them accountable for their crimes."[44] The law is considered analogous to the Foreign Corrupt Practices Act of 1977 in the precedent it hopes to create.[45] In July 2011, the US stated that dozens of Russian officials were barred from entering the United States due to their involvement in the death of Magnitsky...[46]

vi. **Why does Scandinavia have so many money laundering scandals?**[24] Article by Jesse van Genugten (FCPA Blog, December 13, 2019)

A trove of money laundering scandals erupted in Northern Europe this year, tying major financial institutions from all three Scandinavian countries to alleged bribery schemes, attempts to evade U.S. sanctions, and serious regulatory failures. As the Northern European financial landscape is rapidly engulfed by investigations led by authorities in both the United States and the respective home countries, it begs the question: were these Scandinavian banks uniquely susceptible to be used as conduits for money laundering and bribery or, to the contrary, is the active enforcement simply exposing the possibility of widespread vulnerability in global financial institutions?

Just last week, on November 29, the Norwegian government announced that it had begun investigating DNB ASA, an entity in which it holds a 34.3% stake, for its role in channeling illicit funds to Namibian officials as bribes in exchange for increased fishing quotas in the country's territorial waters. It is the third major bank in Norway, Sweden, and Denmark to face serious questions regarding the institutions' handling of funds.

Danske Bank, the largest bank in Denmark, admitted earlier this year that its Estonian subsidiary helped thousands of its customers launder tens of billions of euros as it ignored warnings about the suspicious nature of the transactions.

Likewise, authorities allege that Swedbank, which is headquartered in Stockholm, Sweden, helped to launder as much as $23 billion since the start of the decade. News reports indicate that most of those illicit funds came from Russian sources.

The Danske Bank and Swedbank investigations began when authorities dove deeper into money laundering allegations stemming from the activities of the banks' Estonian subsidiaries, but the scope of both investigations have since expanded substantially. The Swedbank investigation now includes alleged links to Sergei Magnitsky, a Russian lawyer who died in custody after investigating tax fraud, and to deposed Ukrainian President Viktor Yanukovych.

[24]See the FCPA Blog article at: https://fcpablog.com/2019/12/13/why-does-scandinavia-have-so-many-money-laundering-scandals/

Further complicating matters, Swedish state broadcasters reported last week that Skandinaviska Enskilda Banken AB (SEB) is also suspected of enabling the laundering of around $50 million linked to the Magnitsky case through its Swedish and Baltic accounts. SEB may yet be the latest Scandinavian bank dragged into the morass.

For Danske Bank and Swedbank, its chief executives could not weather the storm: both were ousted as a result of the brooding scandal. That said, given the extensive cooperation DNB ASA has offered the Norwegian authorities, it is not immediately clear its own chief executive will suffer the same fate.

Perhaps both as a precautionary and reactionary measure, the Nordic region's six major banks founded a customer checking center in July, a joint Know-Your-Customer (KYC) registry to combat financial crimes and centralize compliance efforts. In addition to the four banks discussed above, the coalition includes Handelsbanken (Sweden), and Nordea (Finland).

Notably, the Nordic KYC platform is not unique. There were, for example, recent launches of Afreximbank's Mansa platform to monitor customer data for counterparties in Africa and CordaKYC to serve as a consolidated blockchain platform for nearly 40 institutions in 19 countries.

These multilateral efforts of course indicate that Scandinavian banks are not the only entities that seek to face head-on the vexing issue of conducting customer due diligence.

I turn back to my original question: What made the Scandinavian banks so attractive for money laundering purposes? I do not seek to profess the answer. But my first instinct is to note that the problem is not unique to Scandinavia. Shedding daylight on the illicit practices does not mean the banks discussed above are outliers. Rather, the rapid exposure of the illegal activities in the Scandinavian financial institutions, both alleged and proven, indicates that substantial steps are being taken to eradicate money laundering in the region. Surely, then, we must hope that other regions will follow suit with similar enforcement actions — as the problem certainly persists in other places as well.

Chapter 10
Other Money Laundering Cases

1. **Deutsche Bank**[1]

Deutsche Bank AG . . . is a German multinational investment bank and financial services company headquartered in Frankfurt, Germany, and dual-listed on the Frankfurt Stock Exchange and the New York Stock Exchange. Founded in 1870, the bank grew through multiple acquisitions . . .

As of 2018, the bank's network spanned 58 countries with a large presence in Europe, the Americas, and Asia.[4] It is a component of the DAX stock market index and is often referred to as the largest German banking institution, even though the Sparkassen-Finanzgruppe comes well ahead in terms of combined assets.

Deutsche Bank has been designated a global systemically important bank by the Financial Stability Board since 2011. [5] It has been designated as a Significant Institution since the entry into force of European Banking Supervision in late 2014, and as a consequence is directly supervised by the European Central Bank.[6][7]

According to a 2020 article in the *New Yorker*, Deutsche Bank had long had an "abject" reputation among major banks, as it has been involved in major scandals across different issue areas . . .[5]

Libor scandal, 2015

On 23 April 2015, Deutsche Bank agreed to a combined US$2.5 billion in fines—a US$2.175 billion fine by American regulators, and a 227 million euros penalty by British authorities—for its involvement in the Libor scandal uncovered in June 2012. It was one of several banks colluding to fix interest rates used to price hundreds of trillions of dollars of loans and contracts worldwide, including mortgages and student loans.[134][135] Deutsche Bank also pleaded guilty to wire fraud, acknowledging that at least 29 employees had engaged in illegal activity. It was required to

[1] https://en.wikipedia.org/wiki/Deutsche_Bank

D. Smith, *Money Laundering, Terrorist Financing and Virtual Assets*, Contributions to Finance and Accounting, https://doi.org/10.1007/978-3-031-59842-5_10

dismiss all employees who were involved with the fraudulent transactions . . .[134] [13 5] The fine represented a record for interest rate related cases, eclipsing a $1.5 billion Libor related fine to UBS, and the then-record $450 million fine assessed to Barclays earlier in the case.[135][134] The size of the fine reflected the breadth of wrongdoing at Deutsche Bank, the bank's poor oversight of traders, and its failure to take action when it uncovered signs of abuse internally.[134]

U.S. sanctions violations, 2015

On 5 November 2015, Deutsche Bank was ordered to pay US$258 million (237.2 million euros) in penalties imposed by the New York State Department of Financial Services (NYDFS) and the United States Federal Reserve Bank after the bank was caught doing business with Burma, Libya, Sudan, Iran, and Syria, which were under US sanctions at the time. According to the US federal authorities, Deutsche Bank handled 27,200 US dollar clearing transactions valued at more than US$10.86 billion (9.98 billion euros) to help evade US sanctions between early 1999 until 2006 which were done on behalf of Iranian, Libyan, Syrian, Burmese, and Sudanese financial institutions and other entities subject to US sanctions, including entities on the Specially Designated Nationals by the Office of Foreign Assets Control.[136][137]

In response to the penalties, the bank will pay US$200 million (184 million euros) to the NYDFS while the rest (US$58 million; 53.3 million euros) will go to the Federal Reserve. In addition to the payment, the bank will install an independent monitor, fire six employees who were involved in the incident, and ban three other employees from any work involving the bank's US-based operations . . . [138]

Russian money-laundering operations

In January 2017, the bank was fined $425 million by the New York State Department of Financial Services (DFS)[142] and £163 million by the UK Financial Conduct Authority[143] regarding accusations of laundering $10 billion out of Russia.[144][145][146]

In the decade preceding the Russian mirror-trading scheme, Deutsche Bank was informed of substantial and widespread compliance concerns. The offsetting trades in this instance lacked economic purpose and could have been used to facilitate money laundering or other illegal activity.[147] On 30 January 2017, the NYSDFS (New York State Department of Financial Services) fined Deutsche Bank $425 million for violating New York's anti-money laundering laws. There was a "mirror trading" scheme involved. Deutsche Bank's Moscow, London, and New York branches laundered $10 billion out of Russia.[148]

The Global Laundromat scandal revealed Deutsche Bank's involvement in a vast money-laundering operation over the period 2010–2014. The operation may have involved as much as $80 billion. In 2019, *The Guardian* reported that a confidential internal report at Deutsche Bank showed that the bank could face fines, legal action, and even possible prosecution of senior management over the bank's role in the money laundering.[149]

In 2020, it was reported that Deutsche Bank was pursuing an expansion of its Russia operations.[150]

In the wake of Russia's 2022 invasion of Ukraine, Deutsche Bank refused to close down its Russia business. At the same time, other banks and major businesses were exiting Russia.[151]

In June 2023, the bank notified customers that it could no longer guarantee them access to the shares they hold on the basis of depositary receipts issued prior to February 2022. He explained this by the shortage of shares in the Russian depository. The bank also warned that it would be able to return the funds for the share significantly below the market price.[152]

AND

Deutsche Bank Agrees to Pay over $130 Million to Resolve Foreign Corrupt Practices Act and Fraud Case[2] (January 8, 2021)

Deutsche Bank Aktiengesellschaft (Deutsche Bank or the Company) has agreed to pay more than $130 million to resolve the government's investigation into violations of the Foreign Corrupt Practices Act (FCPA) and a separate investigation into a commodities fraud scheme.

The resolution includes criminal penalties of US$85,186,206, criminal disgorgement of $681,480, victim compensation payments of $1,223,738, and $43,329,622 to be paid to the U.S. Securities & Exchange Commission in a coordinated resolution.

Deutsche Bank is a multi-national financial services company headquartered in Frankfurt, Germany. The charges arise out of a scheme to conceal corrupt payments and bribes made to third-party intermediaries by falsely recording them on Deutsche Bank's books and records, as well as related internal accounting control violations, and a separate scheme to engage in fraudulent and manipulative commodities trading practices involving publicly-traded precious metals futures contracts.

Deutsche Bank entered into a three-year deferred prosecution agreement (DPA) with the Criminal Division's Fraud Section and Money Laundering and Asset Recovery Section (MLARS) and with the U.S. Attorney's Office for the Eastern District of New York. The criminal information was filed today in the Eastern District of New York charging Deutsche Bank with one count of conspiracy to violate the books and records and internal accounting controls provisions of the FCPA and one count of conspiracy to commit wire fraud affecting a financial institution in relation to the commodities conduct.

"Deutsche Bank engaged in a seven-year course of conduct, during which it failed to implement a system of internal accounting controls regarding the use of company funds and falsified its books and records to conceal corrupt and improper payments," said Acting Deputy Assistant Attorney General Robert Zink of the Justice Department's Criminal Division. "Separately, Deutsche Bank traders on three continents sought to manipulate our public financial markets through fraud for five years. This resolution exemplifies the department's commitment to help ensure that publicly traded companies devise and implement appropriate and proper

[2] https://www.justice.gov/opa/pr/deutsche-bank-agrees-pay-over-130-million-resolve-foreign-corrupt-practices-act-and-fraud

systems of internal accounting controls and maintain accurate and truthful corporate documentation. It also stands as an example of the department's efforts to police the public U.S. markets so that all may continue to trust, and rely upon, the integrity of our public financial systems."

"Deutsche Bank engaged in a criminal scheme to conceal payments to so-called consultants worldwide who served as conduits for bribes to foreign officials and others so that they could unfairly obtain and retain lucrative business projects," stated Acting U.S. Attorney Seth D. DuCharme of the Eastern District of New York. "This office will continue to hold responsible financial institutions that operate in the United States and engage in practices to facilitate criminal activity in order to increase their bottom line."

"The U.S. Postal Inspection Service takes pride in investigating complex fraud and corruption cases that impact American investors," said Inspector in Charge Delany De Léon-Colón of the U.S. Postal Inspection Service's Criminal Investigations Group. "This type of deceptive activity can cause immeasurable economic losses to competitive markets around the world. The combined efforts of our partners at the FBI and Department of Justice helped to bring today's significant action which illustrates our efforts to protect the United States and the international marketplace."

The FCPA Case

According to admissions and court documents, between 2009 and 2016, Deutsche Bank, acting through its employees and agents, including managing directors and high-level regional executives, knowingly and willfully conspired to maintain false books, records, and accounts to conceal, among other things, payments to a business development consultant (BDC) who was acting as a proxy for a foreign official and payments to a BDC that were actually bribes paid to a decisionmaker for a client in order to obtain lucrative business for the bank. In some instances, Deutsche Bank made payments to BDCs that were not supported by invoices or evidence of any services provided. In other cases, Deutsche Bank employees created or helped BDC's create false justifications for payments.

In relation to a Saudi BDC, Deutsche Bank admitted that its employees conspired to contract with a company owned by the wife of a client decisionmaker to facilitate bribe payments of over $1 million to the decisionmaker. Deutsche Bank approved the BDC relationship despite Deutsche Bank employees knowing about the relationship between the Saudi BDC and the decisionmaker, and approved the corrupt payments despite Deutsche Bank employees openly discussing the need to pay the Saudi BDC in order to incentivize her husband to continue to do business with Deutsche Bank. In requesting approval of one payment, Deutsche Bank employees cautioned that the "client and [the Saudi BDC] are intimately linked and ... any cessation of payment to the [the Saudi BDC] will certainly prompt a significant outflow of [business]" from the client.

Deutsche Bank also contracted with an Abu Dhabi BDC to obtain a lucrative transaction, despite Deutsche Bank employees knowing that the Abu Dhabi BDC lacked qualifications as a BDC, other than his family relationship with the client decisionmaker, and that the Abu Dhabi BDC was in fact acting as proxy for the client decisionmaker. Deutsche Bank paid the Abu Dhabi BDC over $3 million without invoices.

By agreeing to misrepresent the purpose of payments to BDCs and falsely characterizing payments to others as payments to BDCs, Deutsche Bank employees conspired to falsify Deutsche Bank's books, records, and accounts, in violation of the FCPA. Additionally, Deutsche Bank employees knowingly and willfully conspired to fail to implement internal accounting controls in violation of the FCPA by, among other things, failing to conduct meaningful due diligence regarding BDCs, making payments to certain BDCs who were not under contract with Deutsche Bank at the time, and making payments to certain BDCs without invoices or adequate documentation of the services purportedly performed.

Deutsche Bank will pay a total criminal penalty of $79,561,206 in relation to the FCPA scheme. In a related matter with the U.S. Securities & Exchange Commission, Deutsche Bank will also pay $43,329,622 in disgorgement and prejudgment interest.

The Commodities Fraud Case

According to admissions and court documents, between 2008 and 2013, Deutsche Bank precious metals traders engaged in a scheme to defraud other traders on the New York Mercantile Exchange Inc. and Commodity Exchange Inc., which are commodities exchanges operated by the CME Group Inc. On numerous occasions, traders on Deutsche Bank's precious metals desk in New York, Singapore, and London placed orders to buy and sell precious metals futures contracts with the intent to cancel those orders before execution, including in an attempt to profit by deceiving other market participants through injecting false and misleading information concerning the existence of genuine supply and demand for precious metals futures contracts.

On Sept. 25, 2020, a Chicago federal jury found two former Deutsche Bank precious metals traders, James Vorley, 42, of the United Kingdom, and Cedric Chanu, 40, of France and the United Arab Emirates, guilty of wire fraud affecting a financial institution for their respective roles in the commodities scheme. A third former Deutsche Bank trader, David Liew, 35, of Singapore, pleaded guilty on June 1, 2017, to conspiracy to commit wire fraud affecting a financial institution and spoofing. A fourth former Deutsche Bank trader, Edward Bases, 58, of New Canaan, Connecticut, was charged in a third superseding indictment on Nov. 12, 2020, and awaits trial on fraud and conspiracy charges. An indictment is merely an allegation and all defendants are presumed innocent until proven guilty beyond a reasonable doubt in a court of law.

Deutsche Bank has agreed to pay a total criminal amount of $7,530,218 in relation to the commodities scheme. This amount includes criminal disgorgement of $681,480, victim compensation payments of $1,223,738, and a criminal penalty of $5,625,000, which will be fully credited against Deutsche Bank's payment of a civil monetary penalty of $30 million to the U.S. Commodity Futures Trading Commission in January 2018 in connection with substantially the same commodities conduct.

The department reached this resolution with Deutsche Bank based on a number of factors, including the Company's failure to voluntarily disclose the conduct to the department and the nature and seriousness of the offense, which included corrupt payments, willful violations of the FCPA accounting provisions, and commodities trading violations in three countries. Deutsche Bank received full credit for its cooperation with the department's investigations and for its significant remediation. Penalties associated with both the FCPA and wire fraud conspiracies reflect a discount of 25% off the middle of the otherwise-applicable U.S. Sentencing Guidelines fine range, to account for Deutsche Bank's 2015 resolution in connection with its manipulation of the London Interbank Offered Rate . . .

The Fraud Section is responsible for investigating and prosecuting all FCPA matters. Additional information about the Justice Department's FCPA enforcement efforts can be found at www.justice.gov/criminal-fraud/foreign-corrupt-practices-act.

MLARS's Bank Integrity Unit investigates and prosecutes banks and other financial institutions, including their officers, managers, and employees, whose actions threaten the integrity of the individual institution or the wider financial system . . .

Updated January 27, 2021

N.B. there are also links to (1) the Deferred Prosecution Agreement (63 pages) & (2) the Information containing the charges (25 pages)

2. **ING**[3]

The **ING Group** (Dutch: *ING Groep*) is a Dutch multinational banking and financial servicescorporation headquartered in Amsterdam. Its primary businesses are retail banking, direct banking, commercial banking, investment banking, wholesale banking, private banking, asset management, and insurance services. With total assets of US$967.8 billion,[2] it is one of the biggest banks in the world, and consistently ranks among the top 30 largest banks globally.

ING is the Dutch member of the Inter-Alpha Group of Banks, a co-operative consortium of 11 prominent European banks.[4] Since the creation in 2012, ING Bank is a member in the list of global systemically important banks. It has been designated as a Significant Institution since the entry into force of European Banking Supervision in late 2014, and as a consequence is directly supervised by the European Central Bank.[5][6]

In 2020, ING had 53.2 million clients in more than 40 countries.[7] The company is a component of the Euro Stoxx 50 stock market index.[8] The long-term debt for the company as of December 2019 is 150 billion euros.[9]

ING is an abbreviation for *Internationale Nederlanden Groep* (lit. 'International Netherlands Group'). The orange lion on ING's logo alludes to the group's Dutch origins . . .[10]

[3] https://en.wikipedia.org/wiki/ING_Group

Money laundering case
In September 2018, ING agreed to pay 775 million euros to end a money laundering probe.[84]

In September 2020, FinCEN Files disclosed that ING in Poland helped Russian and Ukrainian clients to launder huge amounts of money out of Russia . . .[85]
AND

Netherlands Public Prosecution Service press report:[4]
ING pays 775 million due to serious shortcomings in money laundering prevention (04-09-2018)

ING Bank N.V. (ING) in Amsterdam has accepted and paid a settlement of EUR 775,000,000 offered by the Netherlands Public Prosecution Service (Openbaar Ministerie, hereinafter referred to as NPPS). The NPPS has accused ING in the Netherlands of having violated the Anti-Money Laundering and Counter Terrorism Financing Act (Wet ter voorkoming van witwassen en financieren van terrorisme, hereinafter referred to as the AML/CTF Act) for many years and on a structural basis. This took place in such a way that the bank is also accused of culpable money laundering: the bank failed to prevent bank accounts held by ING clients in the Netherlands between 2010 and 2016 from being used to launder hundreds of millions of euros.

ING is an internationally operating bank. ING's banking services in the Netherlands are provided by the business unit ING Bank Netherlands (hereinafter referred to as ING NL). According to the NPPS, ING NL did not properly fulfil its role as gatekeeper of our financial system, as outlined in the AML/CTF Act. The AML/CTF Act is a law that seeks to prevent financial crime such as money laundering and terrorism financing, as far as possible. Under the AML/CTF Act, gatekeepers are required to conduct client due diligence and report unusual transactions to the Financial Intelligence Unit (hereinafter referred to as FIU).

The criminal investigation revealed that ING NL was seriously deficient in this respect. As a result, clients were able to use accounts held with ING NL for criminal activities for many years, virtually undisturbed. According to the NPPS, ING NL should have seen that certain cash flows through bank accounts held by ING NL clients were possibly the result of crime. In that respect, the bank wrongly took insufficient action. For this reason, the NPPS accuses the bank of not only violating the AML/CTF Act, but also of culpable money laundering.

Structural lack of attention for AML/CTF Act compliance

The investigation by the Dutch Fiscal Information and Investigation Service (*Fiscale inlichtingen- en opsporingsdienst*, hereinafter referred to as FIOD) started at the beginning of 2016. The reason was that companies or individuals that had come under suspicion in several criminal investigations held accounts with ING NL,

[4] https://www.prosecutionservice.nl/latest/news/2018/09/04/ing-pays-775-million-due-to-serious-shortcomings-in-money-laundering-prevention#:~:text=ING%20pays%20775%20million%20due%20to%20serious%20shortcomings%20in%20money%20laundering%20prevention,-News%20item%20%7C%2004&text=ING%20Bank%20N.V.%20(ING)%20in,hereinafter%20referred%20to%20as%20NPPS).

leading to suspicions that ING NL was not sufficiently investigating clients, was insufficiently monitoring bank accounts and did not report unusual transactions, or reported them too late.

Over the course of this investigation, the suspicion arose that ING NL's behaviour with regard to these specific clients was not just an isolated incident, but the result of structural shortcomings at ING NL in implementing the policy to prevent financial economic crime. The absence or insufficient conducting of client due diligence led to ING NL's acceptance of clients without sufficiently investigating the risks associated with those clients. Clients were also classified in the wrong client segments. Client relationships and bank accounts were not sufficiently monitored and, when necessary, not terminated by the bank in a timely manner. The compliance department was understaffed and inadequately trained. Partly due to the limited personnel capacity, the system for monitoring transactions was set up by the bank in such a way that only a limited number of money laundering signals were generated. Only the proverbial tip of the iceberg was investigated. In short, the bank did not sufficiently recognise the risks of money laundering. If an unusual transaction was nevertheless recognised, it was regularly not reported to the FIU, or was reported too late.

Money laundering

The criminal investigation revealed that the risks run by the bank actually materialised. ING NL missed potential signals of money laundering. The investigation looked into four cases. These cases revealed that ING NL clients were able to misuse the bank accounts they held with ING NL.

For example, an international telecom provider transferred bribes worth tens of millions of dollars via its bank accounts with ING NL to a company which was owned by the daughter of the then president of Uzbekistan. ING NL reported the unusual transactions to the FIU far too late. In addition, ING NL did not sufficiently investigate the identity of the actual owner of the company.

According to the NPPS, a women's underwear trader was also able to launder approximately EUR 150,000,000 through its bank accounts held with ING NL. It should have been clear to the bank that the monetary flows had little to do with the lingerie trade and were therefore unusual. The NPPS has accused the suspects in this case of laundering hundreds of millions of euros of criminal money. Here, too, the bank did not conduct sufficient client due diligence and the company was classified in the wrong segment. The monitoring system did generate alerts regarding unusual monetary flows, but these were wrongfully and almost without further investigation set aside by the bank as 'not unusual'.

Another case concerns a one-man business in building materials with no address in the Netherlands. The company had a business account with ING NL to which 15 mobile ATMs were linked. Contrary to ING's rules, these mobile ATMs were placed and used by the one-man business in Suriname. They were allegedly to be used for purchases. Investigations have shown that the one-man business actually acted as a currency exchange office. A total amount of EUR 9,000,000 was transferred to the one-man business' bank accounts with ING NL, even though no building materials were purchased for that amount. In reality, debit cards were used in the mobile ATMs in Suriname in exchange for cash. ING NL carried out almost no client due diligence and the company's transactions were not properly monitored.

A case was also investigated in which, over a year, more than EUR 500,000 was deposited in cash into the ING bank accounts of two connected companies. These companies were apparently involved in the import of and trade in fruit and vegetables from South America. This was probably a front for money laundering. Only one of the cash deposits was flagged by the bank as potential money laundering. In addition, ING NL was far too late in reporting an unusual transaction to the FIU.

According to the NPPS, ING NL should and could have also recognised that the funds that were held in ING's accounts in these cases probably originated from crime. It failed to do so, and even when ING NL did recognise the fact, it failed to respond adequately. That is why the NPPS has accused ING NL of being guilty of the crime of culpable money laundering.

Cases are illustrative

According to the NPPS, the cases described above serve as examples. The NPPS has access to multiple indications that the AML/CTF Act has been violated, as well as signals of culpable money laundering. These signals stem from other criminal investigations or from media reports. These signals were not investigated in detail, but confirm the picture of ING NL falling short in complying with the AML/CTF Act, as a result of which the bank was unable to prevent criminal money from being laundered, in spite of the fact that, in its role as gatekeeper, the bank should have made efforts to prevent this from happening.

ING NL was warned on multiple occasions by the Dutch Central Bank (*De Nederlandsche Bank N.V.*, hereinafter referred to as DNB). DNB also took formal measures. Certainly from 2010 onwards, ING NL was aware of the weaknesses in the implementation of its policy but failed to address them adequately. Enhancement programmes were in place, but were not carried out with enough vigour by ING NL. For instance, although ING NL did look at solutions for individual incidents, the structural problems in the monitoring system were not sufficiently recognised and addressed. In consultation with DNB and the FIOD, the NPPS decided to approach the bank's conduct as criminal activity.

For a detailed description of the offenses, including criminal offenses, see the statement of facts (pdf, 315 kB).

Natural persons

The criminal investigation brought to light the fact that one of the main reasons for the shortcomings was the insufficient attention paid by ING NL to compliance risk management (business over compliance). The responsibility for compliance with the AML/CTF Act rests with three different divisions of the bank. None of these divisions oversaw the whole picture. This in part explains why senior management was not fully aware of the seriousness of the shortcomings, and their persistence. The NPPS has therefore attributed the offenses to the organisation as a whole. Many individual persons are responsible for part of the culpable behaviour. The offences are therefore not individually attributable to specific persons, not even the management at ING NL. The Supreme Court (*Hoge Raad*) sets a high bar for prosecuting individuals for directing criminal offences. In this case, not only must awareness be proven, but also that those persons consciously instigated criminal offences or deliberately failed to stop them. The ING NL investigation did not demonstrate that this was the case.

Appropriate settlement

The NPPS sees the payment of a total of EUR 775,000,000 as an appropriate and effective settlement. This amount consists of a fine of EUR 675,000,000 and a disgorgement of EUR 100,000,000. In addition, the bank will enact compliance measures.

According to the NPPS, the facts in this case are extremely serious. As a systemic bank, ING Bank N.V. bears a great responsibility, a responsibility that goes beyond clients or shareholders. It shares responsibility for the reliability of our financial system and can and should make an important contribution to its integrity. Service providers such as banks must protect society against abuse of the financial system for laundering criminal funds or financing terrorism. ING NL can therefore specifically be expected to demonstrate corporate social responsibility and to maintain high integrity principles.

The investigation revealed that ING NL has seriously betrayed the trust placed in the bank. The serious shortcomings in implementing the policy have resulted in some clients who were engaged in criminal activities being able to use bank accounts held with ING NL for years, virtually undisturbed. To determine the fine, the NPPS considered the seriousness of the facts and the nature of the accused. In addition, the fact that the accused cooperated with the investigation and already during the course of the investigation elaborated and started to implement a far-reaching remediation and enhancement programme was taken into account. This programme is subject to intense monitoring by DNB. The NPPS considers the fine of EUR 675,000,000 to be appropriate. It is a fine that deals a tangible blow to the accused and does justice to the shocked legal system.

In addition, EUR 100,000,000 is being disgorged. This is the amount that ING NL has wrongfully earned through savings accumulated over a period of years on expenditure for personnel whose task was to ensure implementation of the compliance policy.

The settlement will also have an impact on the future, as ING NL has acknowledged that there have been serious shortcomings, and the bank has taken a significant number of measures to put its house in order. DNB will ensure that the remediation measures are carried out properly. For the NPPS, the introduction of an adjusted compliance policy at ING NL and the supervision of that policy by DNB were decisive factors in offering this settlement.

Documents

- **Transaction Settlement agreement**
  Decree, order or decision | 04-09-2018
- **Statement of facts ING**

For a detailed description of the offenses, including criminal offenses, see the statement of facts.

- Decree, order or decision | 04-09-2018

3. **Rabobank**[5]

Rabobank (Dutch pronunciation: [ˈraːboːbɑŋk]; full name: *Coöperatieve Rabobank U.A.*) is a Dutch multinational banking and financial services company headquartered in Utrecht, Netherlands. The group comprises 89 local Dutch Rabobanks (2019), a central organisation (Rabobank Nederland), and many specialised international offices and subsidiaries. Food and agribusinessconstitute the primary international focus of the Rabobank Group.[2] Rabobank is the second-largest bank in the Netherlands in terms of total assets.[3]

In terms of Tier 1 capital, the organisation is among the 50 largest financial institutions in the world. As of 2022, total assets amount to 628 billion euros with a net profit of 2.7 billion euros.[1]

Rabobank has been designated as a Significant Institution since the entry into force of European Banking Supervision in late 2014, and as a consequence is directly supervised by the European Central Bank.[4][5]

AND

Rabobank NA Pleads Guilty, Agrees to Pay Over $360 Million (February 7, 2018)[6]

As a Result of Rabobank's Bank Secrecy Act and Anti-Money Laundering Failures it Processed over $360 Million in Illicit Funds and then Conspired with its Executives in an Attempt to Conceal These Ongoing Failures From its Regulator

Rabobank National Association (Rabobank), a Roseville, California subsidiary of the Netherlands-based Coöperatieve Rabobank U.A., appeared today before U.-S. Magistrate Judge Jill L. Burkhardt and pleaded guilty to a felony conspiracy charge for impairing, impeding and obstructing its primary regulator, the Department of the Treasury's Office of the Comptroller of the Currency (the OCC) by concealing deficiencies in its anti-money laundering (AML) program and for obstructing the OCC's examination of Rabobank. Rabobank will forfeit $368,701,259 as a result of allowing illicit funds to be processed through the bank without adequate Bank Secrecy Act (BSA) or AML review . . .

At today's hearing, Rabobank pleaded guilty to conspiracy to defraud the United States and to corruptly obstruct an examination of a financial institution. In pleading guilty, Rabobank admitted to conspiring with several former executives to defraud the United States by unlawfully impeding the OCC's ability to regulate the bank, and to obstruct an examination by the OCC of its operations throughout California, including its Calexico and Tecate bank branches. Rabobank admitted that its deficient AML program allowed hundreds of millions of dollars in untraceable cash, sourced from Mexico and elsewhere, to be deposited into its rural bank branches in Imperial County, and transferred via wire transfers, checks, and cash transactions, without proper notification to federal regulators as required by law. Knowing these

[5] https://en.wikipedia.org/wiki/Rabobank

[6] https://www.justice.gov/opa/pr/rabobank-na-pleads-guilty-agrees-pay-over-360-million

failures, during the OCC's 2012 examination of Rabobank's BSA/AML compliance program, Rabobank executives actively sought to hide and minimize the deficiencies in its AML program in an effort to deceive the regulators as to its true state in hopes of avoiding regulatory sanctions that had previously been imposed on Rabobank in 2006 and 2008 for nearly identical failures.

Rabobank's guilty plea comes less than 2 months after a former Rabobank vice president, George Martin, entered into a deferred prosecution agreement with the United States for his role in aiding and abetting Rabobank's failure to maintain an AML program that met BSA requirements. Martin admitted his conduct in federal court in San Diego on Dec. 14, 2017. As part of its guilty plea, Rabobank agreed to cooperate with the United States' continuing investigation.

"When Rabobank learned that substantial numbers of its customers' transactions were indicative of international narcotics trafficking, organized crime, and money laundering activities, it chose to look the other way and to cover up deficiencies in its anti-money laundering program," said Acting Assistant Attorney General Cronan. "Worse still, Rabobank took steps to obstruct an examination by its regulator into those same deficiencies. The integrity of our financial system depends on prompt reporting by banks and other financial institutions of suspicious, potentially criminal transactions, and on these entities' truthfulness and transparency with their regulators. Rabobank's guilty plea today and forfeiture of more than $360 million is a warning to financial institutions that there are significant consequences for banks that engage in obstructive conduct in an effort to hide their anti-money laundering program failures from their regulators."

"Rabobank had an obligation to shine light on suspected drug traffickers, money launderers and organized crime," said U.S. Attorney Braverman.

"Instead, this bank deliberately allowed hundreds of millions of dollars of suspicious cash transactions and wire transfers to flow through its branches and took measures to hide this activity from regulators. We will vigorously protect the integrity of the banking system, and we will not allow the financial institutions in our communities to play any role in facilitating international money laundering or financing transnational criminal organizations."

"It is the responsibility of Homeland Security Investigations to monitor and investigate activity which exploits the global infrastructure, to include financial systems," said Special Agent in Charge Shaw. "This complex investigation revealed, and Rabobank admits, that Rabobank was aware of the extreme risk that it was processing hundreds of millions of dollars related to transnational crime and international money laundering—activity which plagues the Southwest Border. This plea and significant forfeiture send a strong message to financial institutions that this activity will not be tolerated."

"Today, Rabobank is being held accountable for its illegal actions involving the movement of more than $360 million through the U.S. financial system on behalf of high risk customers," said Special Agent in Charge Rowe. "In today's environment of increasingly sophisticated financial markets, it's critical that global institutions follow U.S. law and abide by our anti-money laundering regulations. The IRS is proud to share its world-renowned financial investigative expertise in this and other complex financial investigations."

The BSA requires financial institutions to implement and maintain an AML compliance program reasonably designed, among other things: (i) to detect suspicious activity indicative of money laundering and other crimes and (ii) to assure and monitor compliance with the BSA's recordkeeping and reporting requirements, including to report to the U.S. Department of the Treasury any suspicious transactions (through the filing "suspicious activity reports" or "SARs") indicative of a possible violation of the law. In its plea agreement, Rabobank admitted knowing that between 2009 and 2012 its BSA/AML program failed in significant ways. Some of these BSA/AML program failures resulted from policies and procedures at Rabobank that precluded and suppressed investigations into suspicious transactions that occurred at its branches, by its accountholders, or by individuals conducting transactions on behalf of its accountholders that had various indications of being involved in, derived from, or promoting illegal conduct.

According to court documents, Rabobank received regular alerts of transactions by "High-Risk" customers, or through accounts deemed to be "High-Risk," and that had been the subject of prior SARs filed by Rabobank. These High-Risk customers and accounts included those controlled and managed by Mexican businesses, non-resident aliens, and U.S.-based accountholders who transacted hundreds of millions of dollars in untraceable cash, sourced from Mexico and elsewhere, into and through Rabobank accounts.

According to court documents, Rabobank also created and implemented policies and procedures to prevent adequate investigations into these suspicious transactions, customers, and accounts. Among those policies and procedures was Rabobank's "Verified List"—a policy that effectively resulted in Rabobank executing an end-run the BSA/AML and SAR requirements. In particular, Rabobank instructed its employees that if a customer was on the "Verified List," no further review of that customer's transactions was necessary -- even if the transactions generated an internal alert, or the customer's activity had changed dramatically from when it was "verified." Rabobank's BSA/AML staff were further instructed to aggressively increase the number of bank accounts on the Verified List, as evidenced by the fact that in 2009, Rabobank had less than 10 "verified" customers, but by 2012, as a result of its defective BSA/AML policies and procedures, it had more than 1,000 "verified" customers.

Additionally, Rabobank admitted failing to monitor and conduct adequate investigations into these transactions and submit SARs to the Financial Crimes Enforcement Network (FinCEN), as required by the BSA. Rabobank's border branches, including those located in Calexico and Tecate in Imperial County, California, were heavily dependent on cash deposits from Mexico. Rabobank knew that millions of dollars in cash deposits at these branches were likely tied to illicit conduct. In particular, the Calexico branch, located about two blocks from the U.S.-Mexico border, was the "highest performing" branch in the Imperial Valley region due to the cash deposits from Mexico. Throughout the relevant time period, Rabobank continued this practice of soliciting cash-intensive customers from Mexico and elsewhere, all the while employing the foregoing inadequate BSA/AML policies and procedures to address the obvious, known "High Risks" associated with these accounts, transactions, and transactors.

When the OCC began conducting its periodic examination of Rabobank in 2012, Rabobank, acting through three of its executives, agreed to, among other things, knowingly obstruct the OCC's examination. Rabobank responded to the OCC's February 2013 initial report of examination with false and misleading information about the state of Rabobank's BSA/AML program. Rabobank also made false and misleading statements to the OCC regarding the existence of reports developed by a third-party consultant, which detailed the deficiencies and resulting ineffectiveness of Rabobank's BSA/AML program.

To further conceal the inadequate nature of its BSA/AML program and to avoid "others contradicting our findings" and statements to the OCC, Rabobank demoted or terminated two RNA employees who were raising questions about the adequacy of Rabobank's BSA/AML program . . .

Updated April 13, 2018

Attachments

Information [PDF, 989 KB]

Plea Agreement [PDF, 3 MB]

4. **Wirecard**[7]

Wirecard AG is an insolvent[4] German payment processor and financial services provider whose former CEO, COO, two board members, and other executives have been arrested or otherwise implicated in criminal proceedings.[5] In June 2020, the company announced that 1.9 billion euros in cash was missing. It owed 3.2 billion euros in debt. In November 2020, the company was dismantled after it sold the assets of its main business unit to Santander Bank for 100 million euros. Other assets, including its North American, UK and Brazilian units had been previously sold at nondisclosed prices.[6] The company offered electronic payment transaction services and risk management, and issued and processed physical and virtual cards. As of 2017, the company was listed on the Frankfurt Stock Exchange, and was a part of the DAX stock index from September 2018 to August 2020.

The company is at the center of an international financial scandal. Allegations of accounting malpractices had trailed the company since the early days of its incorporation, reaching a peak in 2019 after the *Financial Times* published a series of investigations along with whistleblowercomplaints and internal documents. On 25 June 2020, Wirecard filed for insolvency following revelations that an amount of 1.9 billion euros was "missing".[7][8] Long-time CEO Markus Braunsubsequently resigned and was later arrested. Former COO Jan Marsalek disappeared, after being

[7] https://en.wikipedia.org/wiki/Wirecard See also FCPA Blog articles: Germany triggers international manhunt for missing Wirecard executive by Harry Cassin (August 13, 2020) and Site Visits: Sometimes the best due diligence is done on foot by George Porter (July 24, 2023).

fired from his position and board seat, and remains a fugitive wanted by the German police. He has been on Europe's Most Wanted list since 2020.[9]

On 25 August 2020, the court-appointed insolvency administrator issued a statement that "under the preliminary insolvency administration, it has since been possible to stabilize the ongoing business and create a basis for its continuation." The statement mentioned how "far-reaching cuts are therefore necessary in order to make any kind of continuation possible" and announced the impending layoff of around 730 employees, in addition to all members of the management board.[10]

In March 2022, Munich public prosecutors charged former CEO, Markus Braun, with fraud, breach of trust and accounting manipulation. If found guilty on all these charges, he could face up to 15 years in prison.[11] Braun was held in the Stadelheim prison as a pre-trial custody until the trial began . . .[12]

Scandal and insolvency

Beginning in April 2015, the *Financial Times* blog FT Alphaville wrote a series of blog posts that questioned Wirecard's business model and criticised the company's accounting practices.[31]

In February 2016, the 101-page "Zatarra Report"[32] appeared, documenting alleged fraud and money laundering at Wirecard. It was co-written by British short sellers Fraser Perring of Viceroy Research and Matthew Earl of ShadowFall, who sent the report to the German financial agency Bafin. On the urging of Wirecard, Bafin and Bavarian prosecutors then initiated criminal investigations against Perring and other short sellers for market manipulation. The cases were dropped in March 2020.[33] In February 2017, the German *Manager Magazin*published a lengthy article about Wirecard in which it alleged misleading reporting practices.[13]

On 30 January 2019, Wirecard shares plunged after the *Financial Times* reported that a senior executive was suspected of "falsification of accounts" and "money laundering" and round-tripping in the company's Asia-Pacific operations.[34] Wirecard issued a statement calling the report "false, inaccurate, misleading and defamatory".[35] Wirecard also announced a lawsuit against the *Financial Times* for "unethical reporting" and a lawsuit for market manipulation.[36][37]

The public prosecutor's office Munich I in February 2019 launched criminal investigations against *Financial Times* journalist Dan McCrumbecause of alleged violations of the German Securities Trading Act (*Wertpapierhandelsgesetz, WpHG*).[38] The German Federal Financial Supervisory Authority BaFin banned short selling Wirecard shares on 18 February 2019 until 18 April 2019. According to BaFin, the measure was not meant to take sides in the controversy between Wirecard and the *Financial Times*.[39] On 15 October 2019, the *Financial Times*published documents which it claimed to be Wirecard's internal accounting spreadsheets.[40]

In 2019, the accounting firm KPMG was hired by Wirecard for an independent audit to address the mentioned allegations. In March 2020, Wirecard claimed that KPMG concluded that no discrepancy was determined during the audit.[41] However, on 28 April 2020 the auditor KPMG announced that it had not received sufficient documentation to address all allegations of accounting irregularities, with Wirecard shares tumbling 26%.[42] London Based Hedge-Fund TCI and others shortsellers like Armin S. filed criminal complaints against Wirecard.[43][44] On 5 June, Wirecard's headquarters were searched by police as part of a criminal investigation into potentially misleading statements to investors by CEO Markus Braun and three other board members regarding the audit.[45] The company then reported on 18 June 2020 that 1.9 billion euros was missing in cash from the company's accounts, this following an audit by Ernst & Young.[46] Braun resigned as CEO the following day, to be replaced by James Freis.[47] Over two days, the company's stock fell 72%.[48] On 22 June 2020, Braun was arrested by German police under accusations of "inflating Wirecard AG's sales volume with fake income".[49] On 11 September 2020, Freis announced in an email that he had stepped down from the CEO position, after 85 days, with immediate effect.[50]

In January 2020, Wirecard announced that a contract extension would be offered to chief executive Markus Braun.[51][52] At the same time, its long-time chairman stepped aside. In April, an auditor found questionable accounting practices. According to auditing firm Ernst & Young, a trustee of Wirecard tried to "deceive the auditor", resulting in the bank processor being unable to release the share results for 2019. In a statement, Wirecard announced that it was "working intensively together with the auditor towards a clarification of the situation".[53]

In June 2020, it was revealed that 1.9 billion euros was "missing". As a result, Wirecard's share value decreased by over 72%, and its CEO, Markus Braun, resigned.[54] Wirecard appointed James Freis to the position on an interim basis. Freis had only joined the company the evening before. A few days later, the management board stated that the 1.9 billion euros amount likely did not exist.[55] Two banks in the Philippines who were allegedly holding the money said that they did not have the sum and never did.[56] The firm's Moodys credit rating was demoted to B3 on 19 June 2020, before this rating was removed entirely 3 days later.[57]

A criminal investigation began on 22 June 2020;[1] Wirecard's recently resigned CEO, Markus Braun, was arrested the same day.[58] On 25 June, Wirecard filed for bankruptcy, citing "over-indebtedness".[59] On 25 August 2020, the firm's administration axed the contracts of its chief executive manager as well as two additional managers. Furthermore, 730 company staff were also cut.[60] In September 2020, the German parliament announced that it would organize an inquiry in order to fully investigate the reasons why the government failed to prevent the corporate fraud.[61]

The UK Financial Conduct Authority froze the activities of Wirecard's British subsidiary, Wirecard Card Solutions Limited, between 26 June 2020 and 30 June 2020, after which Wirecard UK operations were allowed to resume, albeit with restrictions.[62][63] Singapore's central bank, the Monetary Authority of Singapore (MAS), announced in September 2020 that it has directed Wirecard's Singapore branch to stop their payment services there, and return all funds owed, in light of the company's insolvent business and inability to continue providing payment services in Singapore.[64]

A report published in June 2020 by the interdisciplinary journalism laboratory Citizen Lab at the University of Toronto stated that persons and organisations publicly critical of Wirecard had been the target of sustained hacking and phishing attempts by a hackers-for-hire group dubbed Dark Basin. According to the report, some of the critical entities, which included hedge funds, short sellers, investigators, and journalists, were "targeted almost daily for months, and continued to receive messages for years". The report linked the attacks "with high confidence" to the Indian company *BellTroX InfoTech* which has a history of other hacking-for-hire operations.[65][66] U.S. prosecutors in New York and the FBI reportedly started an investigation into the hacker-for-hire allegations.[67] Wirecard denied any wrongdoing.[65]

On 20 May 2021, Pav Gill, Wirecard's senior legal counsel based in Singapore who looked after all legal aspects of Wirecard's business and operations in the Asia-Pacific region, revealed himself to be the whistleblower who provided the material exposing the fraud to the Financial Times.

During June 2023, Singapore's State Court sentenced James Wardhana, Wirecard's international finance manager to 21 months and Chai Ai Lim, Wirecard Asia's Head of Finance, to 10 months of imprisonment.[68]

5. **Klyuyev v [EU] Council** in the European Court of Justice (ECJ)[8]

The General Court annulled the freezing of funds of seven members of the former Ukranian ruling class, including Viktor Yanukovych, the former President of Ukraine.[9]

The General Court of the EU annulled the financial sanctions imposed upon Ukrainian Member of Parliament Serhiy Klyuyev by the Council of the EU.[10] In its decision, the court noted that the European Council, introducing sanctions, should have checked grounds for accusations against those named and if there were grounds for "doubting the authenticity of evidence," which Ukraine provided the EU.[14]

6. **US Bancorp**[10]

U.S. Bancorp (stylized as **us bancorp**) is an American bank holding company based in Minneapolis, Minnesota, and incorporated in Delaware.[4] It is the parent company of **U.S. Bank** National Association, and is the fifth largest banking institution in the United States.[5] The company provides banking, investment, mortgage, trust, and payment services products to individuals, businesses, governmental entities, and other financial institutions. As of 2019, it had 3106 branches and 4842 automated teller machines, primarily in the Western and Midwestern United States.[2] In 2023 it

[8]https://en.wikipedia.org/wiki/Serhiy_Klyuyev & https://curia.europa.eu/juris/liste.jsf?language=en&num=T-731/15

[9]The ruling of the ECJ General Court was reported in the ECJ's Press Release 93/2019 of 11 July 2019. See also https://curia.europa.eu/jcms/upload/docs/application/pdf/2019-07/cp190093en.pdf . Also the ECHR case: S and Marper v UK: https://justice.org.uk/s-marper-v-uk-2008/ and https://en.wikipedia.org/wiki/S_and_Marper_v_United_Kingdom

[10]https://en.wikipedia.org/wiki/U.S._Bancorp

ranked 149th on the Fortune 500,[6] and it is considered a systemically important bank by the Financial Stability Board. The company also owns Elavon, a processor of credit card transactions for merchants, and Elan Financial Services, a credit card issuer that issues credit card products on behalf of small credit unions and banks across the U.S.[7]

U.S. Bancorp operates under the second-oldest continuous national charter, originally Charter #24, granted in 1863 following the passage of the National Bank Act. Earlier charters have expired as banks were closed or acquired, raising U.S. Bank's charter number from #24 to #2. The oldest national charter, originally granted to the First National Bank of Philadelphia, is held by Wells Fargo, which was obtained upon its merger with Wachovia . . .[8]

In February 2018, the bank was charged by the Department of Justice with failing to implement measures preventing illegal activities, including one case of abetting.[167] U.S. Bancorp agreed to pay $613 million in fines and implement measures to improve the monitoring of its customer transactions.[167] In September 2018, $505 million was distributed to customers of an illegal payday loan business whose suspicious activities US Bancorp had failed to report.[168]

AND

Criminal Charges Against U.S. Bancorp For Violations Of The Bank Secrecy Act (US DoJ press report, February 15, 2018)[11]

Charges to Be Deferred For Two Years Under an Agreement Requiring U.-S. Bancorp to Admit Its Conduct and Pay Penalty of $528 Million

Geoffrey S. Berman, the United States Attorney for the Southern District of New York, announced criminal charges against U.S. Bancorp ("USB") consisting of two felony violations of the Bank Secrecy Act ("BSA") by its subsidiary, U.S. Bank National Association (the "Bank"), the fifth largest bank in the United States, for willfully failing to have an adequate anti-money laundering program ("AML") and willfully failing to file a suspicious activity report ("SAR"). The case is assigned to United States District Judge Lewis A. Kaplan.

Mr. Berman also announced an agreement (the "Agreement") under which USB agreed to accept responsibility for its conduct by stipulating to the accuracy of an extensive Statement of Facts, pay a $528 million penalty, and continue reforms of its BSA/AML compliance program. Assuming USB's continued compliance with the Agreement, the Government has agreed to defer prosecution for a period of two years, after which time the Government will seek to dismiss the charges. The Agreement is pending review by the Court. The penalty shall be collected through the Bank's forfeiture to the United States of $453 million in a civil forfeiture action also filed today, with the remaining $75 million satisfied by the Bank's payment of a civil money penalty assessed by the Office of the Comptroller of the Currency (the "OCC").

[11] https://www.justice.gov/usao-sdny/pr/manhattan-us-attorney-announces-criminal-charges-against-us-bancorp-violations-bank

U.S. Attorney Geoffrey S. Berman stated: "U.S. Bank's AML program was highly inadequate. The Bank operated the program 'on the cheap' by restricting headcount and other compliance resources, and then imposed hard caps on the number of transactions subject to AML review in order to create the appearance that the program was operating properly. The Bank also concealed its wrongful approach from the OCC. As a result, U.S Bank failed to detect and investigate large numbers of suspicious transactions. With today's resolution, the Bank has accepted responsibility for its criminal conduct and committed to completing the reform of its AML program."

The OCC, the Financial Crimes Enforcement Network ("FinCEN"), and the Board of Governors of the Federal Reserve System ("FRB") have also reached agreements with the Bank to resolve related regulatory actions. For purposes of its action, which was also filed today, FinCEN is represented by this Office's Civil Division. FinCEN's agreement with the Bank requires the Bank to pay an additional $70 million for civil violations of the BSA, and it includes further admissions by the Bank, including that the Bank filed more than 5000 currency transaction reports with incomplete and inaccurate information, which impeded law enforcement's ability to identify and track potentially unlawful behavior. FinCEN's agreement with the Bank is pending review by the Court.

According to the documents filed today in Manhattan federal court:

USB's Failure to Maintain an Adequate AML Program

From 2009 and continuing until 2014, USB willfully failed to establish, implement, and maintain an adequate AML program. Among other things, USB capped the number of alerts generated by its transaction monitoring systems, basing the number of such alerts on staffing levels and resources, rather than setting thresholds for such alerts that corresponded to a transaction's level of risk. The Bank deliberately concealed this from the OCC, the Bank's primary regulator.

USB was well aware that these practices were improper, were resulting in the Bank missing substantial numbers of suspicious transactions, and were placing the Bank at risk of regulatory action. Bank documentation from as early as 2005 acknowledged that alert limits were based on staffing levels and, as a result, a risk item for the bank. For example, in a December 1, 2009,F memo from the Bank's then AML Officer (the "AMLO") to the then Chief Compliance Officer (the "CCO"), the AMLO explained that while the Bank was experiencing significant increases in SAR volumes, the Bank's staff was "stretched dangerously thin" and warned that a "regulator could very easily argue that this testing should lead to an increase in the number of queries worked." The Bank conducted below-threshold testing ("BTT"), which consisted of investigating a limited number of transactions that fell outside alert limits to see if thresholds should be adjusted so that more alerts would be investigated. The Bank's BTT regularly found that SARs should have been filed on more than 25%, and as much as 80%, of the tested transactions. Rather than increase resources and lower thresholds to detect such suspicious activity, as repeatedly requested by the responsible AML employees, the Bank instead decided to stop conducting BTT altogether.

An OCC examiner assigned to the Bank repeatedly warned USB officials, including the AMLO, of the impropriety of managing the Bank's monitoring programs based on the size of its staff and other resources. Knowing that the OCC would find USB's resource-driven alert limits to be improper, Bank officials, including the CCO, deliberately concealed these practices from the OCC. For example, a Bank employee deliberately excluded references to resource limitations from the minutes of an internal Bank meeting for fear that the OCC would disapprove of the Bank's practices, and in order to protect himself and his supervisor from adverse consequences. Indeed, the AMLO described USB's AML program to another senior manager as an effort to use "smoke and mirrors" to "pull the wool over the eyes" of the OCC.

USB also failed to monitor Western Union ("WU") transactions involving non-customers of the Bank that took place at Bank branches. The Bank processed WU transactions involving non-customers even though they would not be subject to the Bank's transaction monitoring systems. Even when Bank employees flagged specific non-customer transactions raising AML-related concerns, the transactions went uninvestigated. It was not until July 1, 2014, that the Bank implemented a new policy that prohibited WU transactions by non-customers.

In the course of this investigation, the Bank analyzed the impact of its deficient monitoring practices. For just the six months prior to taking steps to remedy the practices, the Bank's analysis resulted in the generation of an additional 24,179 alerts and the filing of 2,121 SARs.

USB's Failure to Timely File Suspicious Activity Reports Relating to Scott Tucker

From October 2011 through November 2013, the Bank willfully failed to timely report suspicious banking activities of Scott Tucker, its longtime customer, despite being on notice that Tucker had been using the Bank to launder proceeds from an illegal and fraudulent payday lending scheme using a series of sham bank accounts opened under the name of companies nominally owned by various Native American tribes (the "Tribal Companies"). From 2008 through 2012, Tucker's companies extended approximately five million loans to customers across the country, while generating more than $2 billion in revenues and hundreds of millions of dollars in profits. Most of this money flowed through accounts that Tucker maintained at the Bank.

USB employees responsible for servicing Tucker's ongoing account activity disregarded numerous red flags that Tucker was using the tribes to conceal his ownership of the accounts. For example, Tucker spent large sums of monies from accounts in the names of Tribal Companies on personal items, including tens of millions of dollars on a vacation home in Aspen and on Tucker's professional Ferrari racing team. USB also received subpoenas from regulators investigating Tucker's businesses. In September 2011, after news organizations published reports examining Tucker's history and questionable business practices, the Bank reviewed Tucker's accounts, and an AML investigator reported to supervisors, among other things, that "it looks as though Mr. Tucker is quite the slippery individual" who "really does hide behind a bunch of shell companies." Based on its findings, the

Bank closed the accounts in the names of the Tribal Companies but failed to file a SAR.

The Bank also left open Tucker's non-tribal accounts and opened new ones, allowing over $176 million more from his illegal payday business to flow into the Bank. Despite also learning of an April 2012 Federal Trade Commission lawsuit against Tucker and the Tribal Companies, the Bank did not file a SAR regarding Tucker until served with a subpoena by this Office in November 2013.

On October 13, 2017, Tucker was convicted in the United States District Court for the Southern District of New York of various offenses arising from his payday lending scheme. The Government intends to recommend that the amounts forfeited by USB be distributed to victims of Tucker's scheme, consistent with the applicable Department of Justice regulations, through the ongoing remission process…

Updated February 15, 2018

Attachments

U.S. v. US Bank Stip and Settlement [PDF, 953 KB]

U.S. v. US Bank Complaint [PDF, 346 KB]

U.S. v. US Bank DPA [PDF, 7 MB]

U.S. v. US Bank Forfeiture Complaint [PDF, 2 MB]

7. **Barclays**

Barclays Agrees to Pay $2 Billion in Civil Penalties to Resolve Claims for Fraud in the Sale of Residential Mortgage-Backed Securities (March 29, 2018)[12]

Two Former Barclays Executives Agree to Pay $2 Million to Resolve Claims Brought Against Them Individually

The United States has reached agreement with Barclays Capital, Inc. and several of its affiliates (together, Barclays) to settle a civil action filed in December 2016 in which the United States sought civil penalties for alleged conduct related to Barclays' underwriting and issuance of residential mortgage-backed securities (RMBS) between 2005 and 2007. Barclays will pay the United States two billion dollars ($2,000,000,000) in civil penalties in exchange for dismissal of the Amended Complaint.

Following a 3-year investigation, the complaint in the action, United States v. Barclays Capital, Inc., alleged that Barclays caused billions of dollars in losses to investors by engaging in a fraudulent scheme to sell 36 RMBS deals, and that it misled investors about the quality of the mortgage loans backing those deals. It alleged violations of the Financial Institutions Reform, Recovery, and Enforcement Act of 1989 (FIRREA), based on mail fraud, wire fraud, bank fraud, and other misconduct.

Agreement has also been reached with the two former Barclays executives who were named as defendants in the suit: Paul K. Menefee, of Austin, Texas, who served as Barclays' head banker on its subprime RMBS securitizations, and John T. Carroll,

[12] https://www.justice.gov/opa/pr/barclays-agrees-pay-2-billion-civil-penalties-resolve-claims-fraud-sale-residential-mortgage

of Port Washington, New York, who served as Barclays' head trader for subprime loan acquisitions. In exchange for dismissal of the claims against them, Menefee and Carroll agree to pay the United States the combined sum of two million dollars ($2,000,000) in civil penalties.

The settlement was announced by Richard P. Donoghue, United States Attorney for the Eastern District of New York, and Laura S. Wertheimer, Inspector General, of the Federal Housing Finance Agency Office of the Inspector General (FHFA-OIG).

"This settlement reflects the ongoing commitment of the Department of Justice, and this Office, to hold banks and other entities and individuals accountable for their fraudulent conduct," stated United States Attorney Donoghue. "The substantial penalty Barclays and its executives have agreed to pay is an important step in recognizing the harm that was caused to the national economy and to investors in RMBS."

"The actions of Barclays and the two individual defendants resulted in enormous losses to the investors who purchased the Residential Mortgage-Backed Securities backed by defective loans," stated FHFA-OIG Inspector General Wertheimer. "Today's settlement holds accountable those who waste, steal or abuse funds in connection with FHFA or any of the entities it regulates. We are proud to have partnered with the U.S. Department of Justice and the U.S Attorney's Office for the Eastern District of New York on this matter."

The scheme alleged in the complaint involved 36 RMBS deals in which over $31 billion worth of subprime and Alt-A mortgage loans were securitized, more than half of which loans defaulted. The complaint alleged that in publicly filed offering documents and in direct communications with investors and rating agencies, Barclays systematically and intentionally misrepresented key characteristics of the loans it included in these RMBS deals. In general, the borrowers whose loans backed these deals were significantly less creditworthy than Barclays represented, and these loans defaulted at exceptionally high rates early in the life of the deals. In addition, as alleged in the complaint, the mortgaged properties were systematically worth less than what Barclays represented to investors. These are allegations only, which the Defendants dispute, and there has been no trial or adjudication or judicial finding of any issue of fact or law . . .

The press release from the Eastern District of New York orignially announcing the filing of the suit can be found here.

Updated March 29, 2018

Attachments

barclays_first_amended_complaint_final_as_filed [PDF, 984 KB]

barclays_settlement_agreement_fully_executed_w_annex_and_appx_3.29.1 8 [PDF, 414 KB]

8. **Mashreq Bank**

Issue 1 (2018)

DFS (Department of Financial Services) FINES MASHREQBANK AND ITS NEW YORK BRANCH $40 MILLION FOR VIOLATIONS OF NEW YORK

ANTI-MONEY LAUNDERING AND RECORDKEEPING LAWS[13] (October 10, 2018)

DFS Examinations Found Multiple Deficiencies in the Bank's Compliance with Anti-Money Laundering Laws and Office of Foreign Asset Controls Regulations

Bank Must Hire Third-Party Consultant to Address Compliance Deficiencies and Review Transaction Clearing Activity

Financial Services Superintendent Maria T. Vullo today announced that the Department of Financial Services has fined United Arab Emirates-based Mashreqbank PSC and its New York branch $40 million for violations of U.S. Bank Secrecy Act (BSA) and Anti-Money Laundering (AML) laws in the New York branch's U.S. dollar clearing operations. Under a consent order announced today Mashreqbank must also immediately hire a third-party compliance consultant to oversee and address deficiencies in the branch's compliance function, including compliance with BSA/AML requirements, federal sanctions laws and New York law and regulations. The bank must also hire a third party "lookback consultant" to conduct a review of the branch's transaction clearing activity for April 2016 to September 2016, along with other remedial actions. The consent order stems from examinations by DFS and the Federal Reserve Bank of New York (FRBNY).

"Mashreqbank failed to fully comply with critical New York and federal banking laws aimed at combating international money laundering, terrorist financing and other related threats by failing to provide adequate oversight of transactions by customers in high-risk regions," **said Superintendent Vullo**.

"DFS appreciates Mashreqbank's strong cooperation in resolving this matter. By this consent order, the bank is being held accountable for ensuring vigilance against money laundering and other illicit activity to ensure that our financial system remains safe and sound."

Mashreqbank is the oldest and largest private bank in the UAE, and its New York branch is its only one located in the United States. The New York branch offers correspondent banking and trade finance services and provides U.S. dollar clearing services to clients located in Southeast Asia, the Middle East and Northern Africa—regions that present a high risk in connection with financial transactions. The branch engaged in a substantial amount of U.S. dollar clearing activity for foreign customers in high risk jurisdictions. For example, in 2016, the branch cleared more than 1.2 million U.S. Dollar transactions with an aggregate value of over $367 billion. In 2017, the branch cleared well over 1 million U.S. Dollar transactions with an aggregate value exceeding $350 billion.

DFS acknowledges Mashreqbank's strong cooperation in this matter, including demonstrating a commitment to remediating the shortcomings identified, and to building an effective and sustainable BSA/AML and OFAC compliance infrastructure. Among other factors, DFS has given substantial weight to the laudable conduct of Mashreqbank described in the Consent Order in agreeing to the terms and

[13] https://www.dfs.ny.gov/reports_and_publications/press_releases/pr1810101

remedies of the consent order, including the amount of the civil monetary penalty imposed.

DFS conducted a safety and soundness examination of the New York branch's operations in 2016, finding that the branch had been unable to meet its commitments to improve its compliance function sufficiently. Following this examination, DFS examiners issued the branch a low overall score, whereas two years earlier the New York branch had received a satisfactory score on its safety and soundness examination. This downgrade was the result mainly of deficiencies in the New York branch's Bank Secrecy Act and Anti-Money Laundering ("BSA/AML") program, as well as certain defects identified in its program and policies designed to comply fully with OFAC regulations. At the time of the 2016 Examination, the branch's BSA/AML and OFAC policies lacked detail, nuance or complexity, doing little more than citing standard language from applicable regulations.

Subsequently, in November and December of 2017, DFS examiners, along with examiners from FRBNY, conducted a joint examination. Examiners found that records regarding specific alerts and dispositions continued to lack detailed information, making it difficult for examiners to assess the adequacy of investigations conducted by compliance staff. Rationales for closing alerts also failed to include essential information.

Further, the examination found that each transaction monitoring alert would be reviewed only once by a single reviewer, who would then determine whether the alert should be closed or escalated, but without adequate quality assurance reviews. The branch's OFAC program also suffered from certain deficiencies in important aspects of its recordkeeping. The branch maintained inadequate documentation concerning its dispositions of OFAC alerts and cases, with branch compliance staff failing to properly substantiate its rationales for waiving specific alerts and cases.

The joint examination also found that the bank's Head Office failed to provide sufficient oversight of a third-party auditor hired to conduct the branch's 2017 AML/BSA audit and to evaluate the branch's remedial work. The 2017 examination detailed additional deficiencies and assigned the New York branch another low score for the second consecutive examination cycle, which followed the branch's earlier failures to fully remediate compliance issues.

Under the consent order announced today, Mashreqbank must also submit to DFS the following:

- A written revised BSA/AML compliance program for the New York branch acceptable to DFS;
- A written program to reasonably ensure the identification and timely, accurate, and complete reporting by the New York branch of all known or suspected violations of law or suspicious transactions to law enforcement and supervisory authorities, as required by applicable suspicious activity reporting laws and regulations;
- A written enhanced customer due diligence program acceptable to DFS;

- A written plan to enhance oversight, by the management of the bank and the New York branch, of the branch's compliance with BSA/AML requirements, New York State laws and regulations, and the regulations issued by OFAC.

Mashreqbank must engage an independent third-party consultant, chosen by DFS to oversee and address deficiencies in the branch's compliance function, including compliance with BSA/AML requirements, federal sanctions laws, and New York law and regulations.

A copy of the consent order can be found here.

AND

Mashreq New York Branch Announces Settlement with the New York State Department of Financial Services[14] (09/11/2021)

Mashreq has reached settlements with the New York Department of Financial Services ("DFS"), the Office of Foreign Assets Control of the United States Department of the Treasury ("OFAC"), and the Federal Reserve Board and the Federal Reserve Bank of New York (the "Federal Reserve"). These settlements pertain to alleged conduct which involved USD transactions that primarily took place over a decade ago. Mashreq is committed to complying with all laws and regulations governing our industry and fully cooperated with these government regulators on this matter. The terms of these settlements are as follows:

- The Bank will pay a penalty of USD 100 million to DFS. DFS determined that the Bank's OFAC compliance program is adequate, with sufficient controls in place, and therefore did not require the Bank to engage in any further remediation. DFS also recognized the Bank's continued cooperation and demonstrated commitment to building an effective and sustainable compliance program.
- The OFAC settlement does not include any fine or subsequent action, in part due to OFAC's acknowledgement of the Bank's substantial cooperation and extensive remediation of its sanctions compliance program, among other factors.
- The Federal Reserve settlement does not include any fine and acknowledges Mashreq's commitment to compliance with U.S. law and enhancing its OFAC compliance program. The settlement requires Mashreq to submit an acceptable program to ensure compliance with OFAC regulations, in addition to conducting, on an annual basis, a risk-focused sampling of USD payments and engaging an independent third party to conduct a review of its OFAC policies and procedures. Following the Reserve Bank's approval of Mashreq's OFAC compliance program, Mashreq is to complete a global OFAC risk assessment.

The core conduct here was stopped by Mashreq in 2009 ... Mashreq has since dedicated significant resources to strengthening its compliance policies and procedures to ensure it is conducting its business in accordance with all applicable laws and regulations in the regions in which Mashreq operates.

Issue 2 (2021)

[14] https://www.mashreqbank.com/en/uae/news/2021/november/mashreq-ny-fin-services-settlement/

The U.S. Department of the Treasury's Office of Foreign Assets Control Issues Finding of Violation to Mashreqbank psc [15] (11/09/2021)

The U.S. Department of the Treasury's Office of Foreign Assets Control (OFAC) today announced the issuance of a Finding of Violation ("FOV") to Mashreqbank psc ("Mashreq"), a financial institution headquartered in the United Arab Emirates with a branch in London, United Kingdom. Between January 4, 2005 and February 6, 2009, Mashreq's London branch processed 1760 outgoing payments totaling $4,085,427,520 through financial institutions in the United States in violation of OFAC's now-repealed Sudan sanctions program, which prohibited the exportation, directly or indirectly, of services to Sudan. This FOV is part of a global settlement between Mashreq, the New York State Department of Financial Services and the Federal Reserve Board of Governors.

For more information, please visit the following web notice.

AND

… $100 MILLION PENALTY ON MASHREQBANK FOR VIOLATIONS OF SANCTIONS LAWS[16]

Acting Superintendent of Financial Services Adrienne A. Harris announced today that Mashreqbank, PSC ("Mashreqbank" or the "Bank") has agreed to pay $100 million in penalties pursuant to a Consent Order entered into with the New York State Department of Financial Services ("DFS" or the "Department"). The Consent Order resolves the Department's investigation in illegal and non-transparent payments related to the Sudan that Mashreqbank processed through financial institutions in New York State, including Mashreqbank's own New York Branch, between 2005 and 2014. DFS found that such transactions were in violation of U.S. sanctions laws.

"The sanctions regulations exist to protect the national security of the United States, and Mashreq's actions to circumvent those regulations were illegal and dangerous and will not be tolerated in an institution that has enjoyed the benefits of doing business in New York," **said Acting Superintendent Harris.** "The Department remains committed to taking action against financial institutions that behave in ways that are designed to subvert those regulations."

In 1997, the United States imposed sanctions against the Sudan due to its government's "continued support for international terrorism; ongoing efforts to destabilize neighboring governments; and the prevalence of human rights violations, including slavery and the denial of religious freedom. . . ." (See E.O. 13067). These sanctions rules generally required financial institutions operating in the United States to refrain from conducting business with the Sudan, the Sudanese government and any Sudanese Specially Designated Nationals.

The Department's investigation found that Mashreqbank instructed its employees to avoid populating certain fields in the payment messages sent between banks so as to conceal the prohibited Sudanese element of these transactions, thus bypassing the sanction filters of other banks which might otherwise trigger an alert or freeze the

---

[15] https://ofac.treasury.gov/recent-actions/20211109

[16] https://www.dfs.ny.gov/reports_and_publications/press_releases/pr202111091

transaction. This resulted in Mashreqbank processing prohibited payments totaling over $4 billion between 2005 and 2009.

In 2009, a Swiss bank used by Mashreqbank to process these transactions rejected a Sudan-related U.S. dollar-denominated transaction. The next day, news broke that the Swiss bank was being investigated by the New York County District Attorney's Office for violating economic sanctions rules.

As a result, Mashreqbank closed all U.S. dollar accounts held by Sudanese banks with Mashreqbank. The Bank, however, did not disclose these prohibited transactions to the Department, as required by regulation, until 2015.

Indeed, despite having ample notice of the prohibited nature of the Sudan-related transitions by 2009, the Department also found that, between 2010 and 2014, Mashreqbank's New York Branch processed additional Sudan-related, prohibited payments, totaling approximately $2.5 million.

Under the settlement reached today, in addition to payment of a $100 million penalty, Mashreqbank will be required to report on the status and sustainability of the Bank's U.S. Department of the Treasury Office of Foreign Assets Control ("OFAC") compliance program.

DFS acknowledges the Bank's substantial cooperation with the investigation and its ongoing remedial efforts.

The Department coordinated its investigation into Mashreqbank with OFAC and the Federal Reserve Board, each of which has reached their own settlements with the Bank.

Read a copy of the consent order on the DFS website.

9. **Gazprombank Switzerland**

Swiss regulator sanctions Gazprombank Switzerland for 'serious AML breaches' Article by Richard Cassin dated February 2, 2018 [17]

Switzerland's top financial regulator sanctioned the local unit of Russia's Gazprombank after an anti-money laundering investigation triggered by the Panama Papers.

The Swiss Financial Market Supervisory Authority or FINMA said Thursday that Gazprombank (Switzerland) Ltd. is barred from taking on new private clients after being "in serious breach of its anti-money laundering due diligence requirements" from 2006 to 2016.

FINMA said it opened investigations into 30 banks following the release in 2016 of the Panama Papers. It did in-depth investigations into around 20 banks.

The Panama Papers are more than 10 million records from the Mossack Fonseca law firm. The **leaked documents** published by the International Consortium of Investigative Journalists (ICIJ) name than 200,000 anonymous offshore companies the firm formed for clients around the globe.

[17] FCPA Blog article at https://fcpablog.com/2018/02/02/swiss-regulator-sanctions-gazprombank-switzerland-for-seriou/

Gazprombank Switzerland showed "serious shortcomings in the prevention of money laundering," FINMA said.

The bank "failed to carry out adequate economic background clarifications" when accepting new clients and opening new accounts.

FINMA also said Gazprombank Switzerland "failed to keep appropriate records of the transactions and relationships, and frequently did not validate the documentation it obtained."

In addition to the ban on new private clients, FINMA ordered Gazprombank Switzerland to set up a new risk committee.

Gazprombank is controlled by the Russia state-controlled oil firm, Gazprom.

FINMA said it has now concluded its investigations related to the Panama Papers.

* * *

Here's FINMA's full February 1, 2016 **statement**:

The Swiss Financial Market Supervisory Authority FINMA has identified serious shortcomings in anti-money laundering processes regarding private clients at Gazprombank (Switzerland) Ltd. The bank failed to carry out adequate economic background clarifications into business relationships and transactions with increased money laundering risks. FINMA has banned Gazprombank from accepting new private clients until further notice.

In 2016, based on information from the Panama Papers, FINMA launched an investigation into more than 30 Swiss banks. As part of this review, it opened enforcement proceedings against Gazprombank (Switzerland) Ltd. (Gazprombank Switzerland) in relation to potential breaches of anti-money laundering rules. Gazprombank Switzerland focuses primarily on corporate clients and, in particular, on trade finance and commercial lending. In its enforcement proceedings, FINMA examined the manner in which the bank had exercised its anti-money laundering due diligence requirements for a number of business relationships involving private clients and politically exposed persons using offshore companies.

Inadequate clarification

FINMA's investigation, which was completed in January 2018, found that Gazprombank Switzerland was in serious breach of its anti-money laundering due diligence requirements in the period from 2006 to 2016. In many cases, the bank's risk categorisation of its business relationships was found to be incorrect or was carried out too late. It failed to clarify the background of business relationships and transactions with the necessary depth and attention to detail. The bank also failed to keep appropriate records of the transactions and relationships, and frequently did not validate the documentation it obtained. The bank also failed in some instances to report suspicious business relationships to the Money Laundering Reporting Office Switzerland (MROS) within an appropriate timeframe. The bank's organisation and risk management and control functions have therefore shown serious shortcomings in the prevention of money laundering.

Many of these breaches relate to relationships that were initiated by the bank's predecessor institution (Russian Commercial Bank Ltd) prior to 2009. The bank has taken various measures to improve its organization, risk management and control functions. Nevertheless, the bank has been instructed to review and, to the extent necessary, modify its anti-money laundering processes. FINMA will closely monitor the implementation of these measures and those initiated by the bank itself, and has appointed an external auditor to supervise the process.

FINMA bans private client business

In view of the shortcomings identified in the bank's anti-money laundering control system, FINMA has banned Gazprombank Switzerland from expanding its activities with private individuals. No new relationships with private clients may be accepted and existing relationships must be strictly monitored. Gazprombank Switzerland must also establish from among its Board of Directors a Risk Committee with a majority of independent members.

Conclusion of FINMA's investigations relating to the Panama Papers

Following revelations from the Panama Papers, FINMA carried out investigations at more than 30 Swiss banks, focusing on their implementation of anti-money laundering regulations. In-depth investigations were carried out at around 20 banks. Where necessary, FINMA required banks to take action to improve their anti-money laundering processes. The conclusion of FINMA's proceedings against Gazprombank Switzerland also marks the conclusion of FINMA's activities linked with the Panama Papers.

Money laundering prevention: key priority for FINMA

The prevention of money laundering is a key priority for FINMA. Over recent years, FINMA has issued on average more than ten enforcement rulings a year imposing sanctions relating to money laundering and has taken a range of measures, including the dissolution of a bank, a licence withdrawal from a fiduciary company and the disgorgement of illegally generated profits. FINMA has also enforced changes to governance structures at supervised institutions and set strict limits on certain new business activities. In the past years, FINMA has issued industry bans against eight bank managers following serious breaches of due diligence requirements. Between 2016 and 2017 FINMA launched enforcement proceedings against seven bank managers.

10. **Sergei Roldugin**[18]

Sergei Pavlovich Roldugin ... is a Russian cellist and businessman, based in St Petersburg. He is a close friend of Vladimir Putin. He has been implicated in several money laundering and offshore wealth schemes for Russian elites. Following the Russian invasion of Ukraine in 2022, the European Union sanctioned Roldugin.[3]

Early life

Roldugin was born in Sakhalin where his father, a military man, was stationed. While he was young, his parents moved to Riga, Latvia, where he studied and

[18] https://en.wikipedia.org/wiki/Sergei_Roldugin

became fluent in Latvian at Latvian School.[4] He has relatives in Riga where his parents are buried.[4]

During his mandatory enlistment with the Soviet Army at a base in Leningrad, he went AWOLfrom the base and met Vladimir Putin using the phone number that his older brother the KGB agent Evgeny Roldugin, who had attended KGB school with Putin, gave to Sergei.[5]

Career

He was awarded the 1980 Prague Spring International Music Festival Competition's 3rd prize. In 1984 Roldugin was appointed the Kirov Opera Theatre Orchestra's principal cellist. He subsequently held a professorship at the Saint Petersburg Conservatory, where he served as the institution's rector from 2002-05. The Mariinsky Theatre Orchestra's Guest Conductor, he has been named a People's Artist of Russia.

Since the 1990s, Roldugin has been engaged in the oil and media business.[6] He is known for having initiated the renovation of the decayed Alexis Palace as a music school and for having performed at the ruins of Palmyra a month after the site was reconquered from the ISIL.[7]Roldugin plays the *Stuart* cello made by Antonio Stradivari in 1732; the instrument cost him $12 million.[8]

Relationship with Vladimir Putin

Sergei Roldugin is a godfather to Maria Vorontsova (b. 1985), Vladimir Putin's older daughter.[9][10][11] He has been friends with Putin since the late 1970s.[9][12] In March 2016 *The Guardian* described Roldugin as "Putin's best friend". It was Roldugin who introduced Putin to Lyudmila, his future wife.[13]

In connection with the Panama Papers, the Organized Crime and Corruption Reporting Project described Roldugin as the "secret caretaker" of Putin's hidden wealth through his participation in transactions with Mossack Fonseca and Dietrich, Baumgartner & Partner, who are Swiss lawyers in Zurich, to various offshore companies including Panama registered International Media Overseas, British Virgin Islands (BVI)registered Sonnette Overseas, Sunbarn Ltd and Sandalwood Continental, and the BVI registered Ove Financial Corp.[10][14][15][16][17][18][19]

Wealth

In 2008 under Sergey Skvortsov's leadership, Troika Dialog spearheaded the alliance of AvtoVAZ-Renault-Nissan and the partnership among KAMAZ OJSC, Daimler AG Concern and Rostec.[20][21][22][23] In early April 2008, Rubin Vandaryan stated that Troika Dialog through Avtoinvest and Kamaz-Capital had the controlling stake in KamAZ.[24] Since March 2008 through a deal with the Republic of Tatarstan, Troika Dialog was the nominal owner of AvtoVAZ and KamAZ for the beneficial owner Sergei Roldugin.[24][25][26][27]

Roldugin has maintained close financial ties with the Cyprus-based RCB Bank which is a subsidiary of VTB Bank, Yuri Kovalchuk of Rossiya Bank, Oleg Gordin who owns Sandalwood Continental as the legal representative of Roldugin through

Roldugin's sole ownership of International Media Overseas and is a St Petersburg businessman with Rossiya Bank, Aleksander Plekhov who owns Sunbarn Ltd as the legal representative of Roldugin through Roldugin's sole ownership of Sonnette Overseas and is a St Petersburg businessman with Rossiya Bank, Yevgeny Malov who is a partner of Gennady Timchenko and one of the founders of the oil trader Gunvor, the Rotenberg family (Arkady, Igor, and Boris), Suleyman Kerimov, Alexei Mordashov, and other Russian oligarchs.[15][16][28][29][30][31]

Established by Mikhail Lesin in the early 1990s, Video International (VI) is one of Russia's largest television advertising firms which Roldugin has a large stake through the Cyprus-based Med Media Network which is solely owned by Roldugin's International Media Overseas.[12][16][32] In 2003, Roman Abramovich, who is the beneficial owner of Sara Trust Settlement which, through its ownership of several shell companies, owned both Finoto Holdings and Grosora Holdings which were established in early 2003, gained a 25% stake in Video International through his beneficial ownership of two firms Finoto Holdings and Grosora holdings which each gained an 12.5% stake in Video International for only $130,000 for each stake and was well below the fair market value of each stake in Video International.[33] On 10 September 2003, Yuri Zapol, who is a friend of Mikhail Lesin, owned a 41.5% stake in Video International and sold a 25% stake in Video International to Abramovich for only 8 million rubles.[34] Vladimir Milov, who is an active opposition figure, has been declared a "foreign agent" by Russian authorities, and is a former deputy energy minister during President Putin's first term, stated, "This package was clearly worth much more, by many orders of magnitude."[33] In 2004, Abramovich received $1.8 million in dividends from his 25% stake in Video International.[34] Later, in 2010, Abramovich sold his Video International stake of 12.5% held by Finoto Holdings for $20 million to Med Media Network, which is nominally owned by Sergei Roldugin, and sold his Video International stake of 12.5% held by Grosora Holdings for $20 million to Namiral Trading Ltd, which was later associated with Alexander Plekhov (Russian: Александр Плехов) who often acts in Rodulgin's interests.[34][33] Plekhov's firms the Cyprus registered Namiral Trading Ltd and the British Virgin Islands registered Norma Group Ltd own a combined stake of 20% in Video International and have accounts with Gazprombank in Zurich, Switzerland, which often supports the interests of Rossiya Bank through the Swiss law firm Dietrich, Baumgartner & Partners which is located in Zurich as well.[35][36][37][38]

In March 2019, Roldugin was implicated in a nearly $9 billion global money laundering scheme allegedly constructed by Sberbank CIB(formerly known as "Troika Dialog"), in which Roldugin received $69 million.[39] The money laundering scheme is known as **ŪkioLeaks**[40] or the **Troika Laundromat**.[41][42]

2016 United States elections hacking

According to Andrei Soldatov, the 3 April 2016 release of the Panama Papers, which is known in Russia as OffshoreGate (Russian: "Офшоргейта"), and, in particular, information about Roldugin's nearly $2 billion in assets, which are closely associated with Vladimir Putin's assets, directly led to a *quid pro quo* or a tit for tat with

Putin ordering hacks of Hillary Clinton, her party and others to support Donald Trump's 2016 Presidential campaign and his party.[43][44][45][46][47][48][49][50][a][b] Dmitri Alperovitch, one of the founders of CrowdStrike, stated, "They ([hackers]) cast a wide net without knowing in advance what the benefit might be," and Andrei Soldatov said, "It was a series of tactical operations. At each moment, the people who were doing this [hacking] were filled with excitement over how well it was going, and that success pushed them to go even further."[46]

Sanctions
After Russia's 2022 invasion of Ukraine, the European Union and the United Kingdom sanctioned Roldugin in March.[3][54]

Then in June 2022, the US sanctioned him pursuant to Executive Order 14024,[55] and others like Severstal chairman Alexey Mordashov,[56] Yury Slyusar, president of United Aircraft Corporation; Vitaly Savelyev, Russia's transport minister; Maksim Reshetnikov, the country's minister of economic development; Irek Envarovich Faizullin, the minister of construction, housing, and utilities; Dmitry Yuryevich Grigorenko, the deputy prime minister and chief of the government staff; and Maria Zakharova, the spokesperson of the Russian Foreign Ministry.[55]

Early in March 2023, four Gazprombank Switzerland employees in Zurich were put on trial for the help provided to Roldugin to evade money laundering laws, prior to 2016 and found guilty . . .[57][58]

11. **Haiti Telco & Duperval**

Former Haitian Government Official Sentenced to Nine Years in Prison for Role in Scheme to Launder Bribes (May 21, 2012)[19]

WASHINGTON—Jean Rene Duperval, a former director of international relations for Telecommunications D'Haiti S.A.M. (Haiti Teleco), a Haitian state-owned telecommunications company, was sentenced today to nine years in prison for his role in a scheme to launder bribes paid to him by two Miami-based telecommunications companies.

The sentence was announced by Assistant Attorney General Lanny A. Breuer of the Justice Department's Criminal Division; U.S. Attorney for the Southern District of Florida Wifredo A. Ferrer; and Special Agent in Charge Jose A. Gonzalez of Internal Revenue Service-Criminal Investigation (IRS-CI), Miami Field Office.

Duperval, 45, of Miramar, Fla., was sentenced by U.S. District Judge Jose E. Martinez in the Southern District of Florida. Judge Martinez also ordered Duperval to forfeit $497,331.

---

[19] https://www.justice.gov/opa/pr/former-haitian-government-official-sentenced-nine-years-prison-role-scheme-launder-bribes . See also FCPA Blog articles: https://fcpablog.com/2012/03/13/duperval-convicted-in-haiti-telco-trial/ and https://fcpablog.com/2012/05/22/duperval-jailed-for-nine-years/

Duperval was convicted in March 2012 of two counts of conspiracy to commit money laundering and 19 counts of money laundering. He has been in custody since his conviction.

"Mr. Duperval took bribes in exchange for giving companies an unfair and illegal advantage in the marketplace, and then tried to hide these illicit transactions behind the cloak of shell corporations and fake invoices," said Assistant Attorney General Breuer. "Just as we prosecute corrupt businesspeople under the FCPA, we will hold accountable corrupt foreign officials when they seek to launder the proceeds of that bribery through the U.S. financial system. Today's nine-year prison sentence sends a strong message to foreign officials and others who would facilitate foreign corruption that they will face serious consequences."

"Duperval's money laundering scheme was an attempt to conceal the payment of bribes to foreign officials to obtain an unfair business advantage in the marketplace," said U.S. Attorney Ferrer. "Today's sentence, however, helps level the playing field for all legitimate businesses that honestly compete in the marketplace for foreign or domestic business."

"IRS Criminal Investigation continues to expand its international efforts to aggressively investigate those individuals who engage in money laundering and bribery schemes," said IRS-CI Special Agent in Charge Gonzalez. "Individuals involved in corrupt international endeavors, as uncovered in this case, will get caught and this sentencing should serve as a strong warning to those considering similar conduct."

Duperval was the director of international relations for Haiti Teleco, the sole provider of land line telephone service in Haiti. According to the evidence presented at trial, two Miami-based telecommunications companies had a series of contracts with Haiti Teleco that allowed the companies' customers to place telephone calls to Haiti.

Duperval was convicted for participating in a scheme to commit money laundering from 2003 to 2006, during which time the telecommunications companies collectively paid approximately $500,000 to two shell companies to funnel the bribes to Duperval.

The purpose of these bribes, according to the evidence presented at trial, was to obtain various business advantages from Duperval, including the issuance of preferred telecommunications rates, a continued telecommunications connection with Haiti and the continuation of a particularly favorable contract with Haiti Teleco. To conceal the bribe payments, Duperval instructed the companies to forward the payments to the shell companies. To support these payments, the companies and their executives created false documents claiming that the payments were for "consulting services" or for "international minutes from USA to Haiti." No actual services were performed. The funds were then disbursed from the shell companies for the benefit of Duperval and his family. To conceal the nature of these funds, Duperval falsely characterized these payments as "commissions" and "payroll."

Duperval was the seventh defendant involved in the corruption scheme to be sentenced, which includes the following individuals:

- On April 27, 2009, Antonio Perez, a former controller at one of the Miami-based telecommunications companies, pleaded guilty to one count of conspiracy to violate the Foreign Corrupt Practices Act (FCPA) and money laundering. On Jan. 12, 2010, he was sentenced to 24 months in prison.
- On May 15, 2009, Juan Diaz, the president of J.D. Locator Services, pleaded guilty to one count of conspiracy to violate the FCPA and money laundering. He admitted to receiving more than $1 million in bribe money from telecommunications companies. On July 30, 2010, he was sentenced to 57 months in prison, which he is currently serving.
- On Feb. 19, 2010, Jean Fourcand, the president and director of Fourcand Enterprises Inc., pleaded guilty to one count of money laundering for receiving and transmitting bribe monies in the scheme. On May 5, 2010, he was sentenced to six months in prison, which he is currently serving.
- On March 12, 2010, Robert Antoine, a former director of international affairs for Haiti Teleco, pleaded guilty to one count of conspiracy to commit money laundering. He admitted to receiving more than $1 million in bribes from Miami-based telecommunications companies. On June 2, 2010, he was sentenced to 48 months in prison, which he is currently serving.
- On Aug. 4, 2011, Joel Esquenazi and Carlos Rodriguez, who were the former president and vice-president, respectively, of one of the telecommunications companies, were convicted by a federal jury of one count of conspiracy to violate the FCPA and wire fraud, seven counts of FCPA violations, one count of money laundering conspiracy and 12 counts of money laundering. On Oct. 25, 2011, Esquenazi was sentenced to 15 years in prison, the longest sentence ever imposed in a case involving the FCPA. On the same day, Rodriguez was sentenced to 84 months in prison for his role in the bribery scheme. Both are currently serving their sentences.

In a second superseding indictment, Washington Vasconez Cruz, Amadeus Richers and Cecilia Zurita were charged in a related scheme to commit foreign bribery and money laundering from December 2001 through January 2006. The defendants are fugitives. An indictment is merely an accusation, and defendants are presumed innocent until and unless proven guilty beyond a reasonable doubt...

Updated September 15, 2014

AND

The World Bank's Stolen Asset Recovery (StAR) Initiative:
Jean Rene Duperval (Haiti Teleco)[20]—Last Update: August 16, 2023
Case Summary

As part of his sentencing, Mr. Duperval was ordered to forfeit $497,331 in proceeds of crime. (Source: U.S. v. Esquenazi, et al, Case No. 1:09-cr-21010-MGC (S.D. Fla.), Superseding Indictment filed July 12, 2011; Order of Forfeiture, May 21, 2012.)

[20] https://star.worldbank.org/asset-recovery-watch-database/jean-rene-duperval-haiti-teleco

According to the US Government's Forfeiture motion, "The evidence at trial also showed that he laundered the $497,331 in the United States through the bank accounts of two South Florida companies, Crossover Records and Telecom Consulting Services, owned by his siblings." (Source: US v. Duperval, Case No. 1:09-cr-21010 (S.D.Fla.), United States' Motion for Entry of Forfeiture Money Judgment at Sentencing and Incorporated Memorandum of Law, filed May 18, 2012.)

Disposition of Criminal Case(s)

According to a US Department of Justice Press Release, in May 2012, "Jean Rene Duperval, a former director of international relations for Telecommunications D'Haiti S.A.M. (Haiti Teleco), a Haitian state-owned telecommunications company, was sentenced today to nine years in prison for his role in a scheme to launder bribes paid to him by two Miami-based telecommunications companies." (Source: US Department of Justice press release, "Former Haitian Government Official Sentenced to Nine Years in Prison for Role in Scheme to Launder Bribes," May 21, 2012.)

UNCAC Offenses Implicated

Article 16. Bribery of foreign public officials and officials of public international organizations
Article 23. Laundering of proceeds of crime ...

12. **Vladimir Luca Filat**[21]

Vladimir Filat (born 6 May 1969), commonly referred to as **Vlad Filat** ... is a Moldovan businessman and politician, founder of Liberal Democratic Party of Moldova. He was the Prime Minister of Moldova from 25 September 2009 to 25 April 2013. He also was appointed as the Interim President of Moldova for a brief period of time in 2010.[1] Following his conviction on charges of accepting bribes, Filat was released from jail in December 2019, 6 years earlier than his initial sentence.

Education and early career

Vlad is the second child of Maria and Vasile Filat and was born on May 6, 1969, in Lăpuşna, a commune in the Moldavian SSR. Alongside his two sisters (Ala and Valentina) and brother Ion, Vlad grew up in a part of Lăpuşna called "Talcioc". In 1986, he graduated from high school in his hometown. Between 1986 and 1987, he worked at the school radio station until he was called up for military service. He carried out his compulsory military service in the Soviet Army (May 8, 1987–August 15, 1989), in Simferopol and Sevastopol. He served in the KGB's Border Troops, holding the rank of private first class and being decorated by his KGB superiors.[2]

From 1989 to 1990, he studied at the Cooperation College (*Kooperativny technikum*) of Chişinău, going on to study law at the University of Iaşi

[21] https://en.wikipedia.org/wiki/Vlad_Filat . See also FCPA Blog report: https://fcpablog.com/tag/vlad-luca-filat/

(1990–1994). As a student, he was the leader of the "League of students from Bessarabia in Romania", an organization formed by Moldovan students in Romania. In Iaşi, among his classmates was Alexandru Tănase. While he was a student in Iaşi, he met his wife Sanda in the autumn of 1991; they dated for only three months before they married.

Between 1994 and 1998, Vlad Filat initiated and conducted more business in Romania. He was general director of "RoMold Trading SRL" in Iaşi (1994–1997) and the president of the Administrative Council of "Dosoftei" company in Iaşi (1997–1998).

Early political activity

Filat was a member of the Democratic Party of Moldova (PDM) from 1997, when the party was founded, until 2007. Having returned to Moldova for good in 1998, he was appointed general director of the Department of Privatization and State Property Administration from the Ministry of Economy and Reform of the Government of the Republic of Moldova (1998—1999).

He was a State minister in the Ion Sturza cabinet of Alliance for Democracy and Reforms from 12 March 1999, to 12 November 1999. In 2000, Filat was elected Vice-President of the Democratic Party (PDM). In the 2005 parliamentary election, he became a member of the Moldovan Parliament. Until March 2009, he was Vice-President of the Parliamentary Commission for Security, Public Order, and Defense. He was also a member of the EU-Moldova Parliamentary Cooperation Committee.

He ran for Mayor of Chişinău in the 2007 local election and won 8.32% of the vote, in fourth place. Soon after the local election, in September 2007, he left the Democratic Party after ten years of political activity inside the party. Filat has been the President of the Liberal Democratic Party of Moldova since December 2007.

Moldovan parliamentary election, 2009

Main articles: Moldovan parliamentary election, April 2009 and Moldovan parliamentary election, July 2009

In the April 2009 parliamentary election, his party won 15 seats and in the July 2009 parliamentary election PLDM became the second party in the country with 18 seats and the first party within the Alliance For European Integration (AIE).

Alliance for European Integration

Main article: Alliance for European Integration

After the July 2009 parliamentary election, alongside Mihai Ghimpu, Marian Lupu, and Serafim Urechean, Vlad Filat signed the Alliance For European Integration (AIE) in a press-conference on August 8, 2009. Towards the end of August 2009, he became the candidate of the Alliance For European Integration (AIE) for the position of Prime Minister of Moldova.

Prime Minister

The Constitutional Court of Moldova confirmed earlier on September 17, 2009 the legitimacy of Mihai Ghimpu's position as Acting President of Moldova, which gave him the right to nominate a prime minister. On the same day, Ghimpu signed a decree nominating Filat for the office of prime minister. Earlier on September 17, the parliament approved a new government structure; according to the draft structure, the number of ministries remains unchanged at 16 but their names and responsibilities have been changed.[3]

The Alliance for European Integration gave a vote of confidence to the new government headed by PM Vladimir Filat at a plenary meeting on September 25, 2009.

On March 8, 2013 Filat was dismissed by motion of censure following charges of corruption, abuse of power and influence peddling.[4] In spite of this, President Nicolae Timofti decreed that members of the government should continue to exert their public duties until a new government were to be formed.[5]

Subsequently, on April 10, 2013 the President nominated Vlad Filat as a candidate for Prime Minister, authorizing him with the mission of forming a new government. However, on April 22, 2013, the Constitutional Court ruled that this decree is unconstitutional, stating that a Prime Minister ousted by vote of no confidence following suspicions of corruption cannot further perform this duty and that the President has the constitutional obligation to appoint in the interim capacity a member of the government whose integrity was not affected.[6]

The President appointed Iurie Leancă as Acting Prime Minister on April 25, 2013.

Arrest and accusations of corruption

Filat was stripped of his immunity and handcuffed in parliament on October 15, 2015.[7] He was investigated for the 2014 Moldovan bank fraud scandal and accused of having taken bribes of about $250 million from Ilan Shor, who was chairman of the board at Savings Bank from April to November 28, 2014.

Filat has denied wrongdoing and said the allegations against him are politically motivated.[8]

On June 27, 2016, Vlad Filat was sentenced to 9 years in prison.[9]

in February 2019, Filat's son was ordered to pay nearly half a million pounds after an investigation by the National Crime Agency found that he had paid £390,000 up front for a lavish apartment in the Knightsbridge area of London and £200,000 for a Bentley Bentayga. With no registered income in the UK, three bank accounts belonging to his son were frozen under Criminal Finances Act 2017 . . .[10]

13. Mahmoud Thiam

Former Guinean Minister of Mines Convicted of Receiving and Laundering $8.5 Million in Bribes from China International Fund and China Sonangol US DoJ press report, May 4, 2017[22]

[22] https://www.justice.gov/opa/pr/former-guinean-minister-mines-convicted-receiving-and-laundering-85-million-bribes-china . See also FCPA Blog report: U.S. jails former Guinea mining minister for laundering China bribes by Richard L. Cassin (dated August 28, 2017) at: https://fcpablog.com/2017/08/28/us-jails-former-guinea-mining-minister-for-laundering-china/

A former Minister of Mines and Geology of the Republic of Guinea, has been convicted by a federal jury for his role in a scheme to launder bribes paid to him by executives of China Sonangol International Ltd. (China Sonangol) and China International Fund, SA (CIF). The jury reached its verdict yesterday after five hours of deliberations, following a seven-day trial.

Acting Assistant Attorney General Kenneth Blanco of the Justice Department's Criminal Division, Acting U.S. Attorney Joon Kim for the Southern District of New York, Assistant Director Stephen Richardson of the FBI's Criminal Investigative Division and Assistant Director in Charge William F. Sweeney Jr. of the FBI's New York Field Office announced the conviction.

Mahmoud Thiam, 50, of New York, was convicted of one count of transacting in criminally derived property and one count of money laundering. According to the charges, the funds that were laundered were proceeds derived through violations of Guinean bribery laws.

"As a high-level Minister in Guinea, Thiam sold out his country and then used U.S. banks and real estate to hide millions in bribes paid to him by a Chinese conglomerate," said Acting Assistant Attorney General Blanco. "Corruption is a global disease that undermines the rule of law everywhere. The Justice Department is committed to investigating and prosecuting those who commit these crimes and use the U.S. financial system and free marketplace to conceal and benefit from their crimes."

"As a New York federal jury has now found, Thiam abused his official government position to enrich himself at the expense of one of Africa's poorest countries," said Acting U.S. Attorney Kim. "Thiam laundered the proceeds of his bribery scheme into the United States to fund his lavish lifestyle, buying a multi-million dollar estate in Dutchess County, and paying for private schools for his children. Thanks to the work of the FBI, Thiam's scheme was exposed and he was swiftly convicted."

"This conviction showcases the FBI's commitment to combatting corruption domestically and abroad," said Assistant Director Stephen Richardson. "Thiam's misuse of his official position for personal gain violated federal law and the trust of the Guinean people. I applaud the excellent work that our employees put into this case and thank all of our partners who helped bring Thiam to justice."

"The conviction of Thiam demonstrates that no one who violates public office is above the law when they are involved in corruption," said Assistant Director in Charge Sweeney. "The FBI's International Corruption Squads were established to take on foreign corruption cases like this that use money laundering and lies to deceive the trust in public office."

According to evidence presented at trial, China Sonangol, CIF and their subsidiaries signed a series of agreements with Guinea that gave them lucrative mining rights in Guinea, and Thiam influenced the Guinean government's decision to enter into those agreements while serving as Guinea's Minister of Mines and Geology from 2009 to 2010.

The evidence showed that Thiam participated in a scheme to launder money from 2009 to 2011, during which time China Sonangol and CIF paid him $8,500,000 to a bank account in Hong Kong. Thiam then transferred approximately $3,900,000 to the United States through bank accounts and other means, and used the money to pay for luxury goods and other expenses, according to trial evidence. To conceal the bribe payments, Thiam falsely claimed to banks in Hong Kong and the United States that he was employed as a consultant and that the money was income from the sale of land which he earned before he was a minister, according to the evidence.

The purpose of the bribes, according to the evidence presented at trial, was to obtain substantial rights and interests in natural resources in Guinea, including the right to be the first and strategic shareholder with Guinea of a national mining company into which Guinea had to, among other things, transfer all of its stakes in various mining projects and future mining permits or concessions that the government decided to develop on its own. China Sonangol and CIF, through their subsidiaries, also obtained exclusive and valuable rights to conduct business operations in a broad range of sectors of the Guinean economy, including mining, according to the trial evidence.

Thiam was detained pending trial and is still in the custody of the U.S. Marshals. Sentencing is scheduled for Aug. 11, 2017 . . .

Updated October 3, 2017

AND

Former Guinean Minister of Mines Sentenced to Seven Years in Prison for Receiving and Laundering $8.5 Million in Bribes From China International Fund and China Sonangol[23] (August 25, 2017)

A former Minister of Mines and Geology of the Republic of Guinea was sentenced today to seven years in prison, and three years of supervised release, for laundering bribes paid to him by executives of China Sonangol International Ltd. (China Sonangol) and China International Fund, SA (CIF). . .

Mahmoud Thiam, 50, of New York, New York, was sentenced by U.S. District Judge Denise L. Cote of the Southern District of New York. Thiam was convicted on May 3, after a seven-day trial of one count of transacting in criminally derived property and one count of money laundering.

"Mahmoud Thiam engaged in a corrupt scheme to benefit himself at the expense of the people of Guinea," said Acting Assistant Attorney General Blanco. "Corruption is a cancer on society that destabilizes institutions, inhibits fair and free competition, and imposes significant burdens on ordinary law-abiding people just trying to live their everyday lives. Today's sentence sends a strong message to corrupt individuals like Thiam that if they attempt to use the U.S. financial system to hide their bribe money they will be investigated, held accountable, and punished."

"As a unanimous jury found at trial, Thiam abused his position as Guinea's Minister of Mines to take millions in bribes from a Chinese conglomerate, and then launder that money through the American financial system," said Acting

[23] https://www.justice.gov/opa/pr/former-guinean-minister-mines-sentenced-seven-years-prison-receiving-and-laundering-85

U.S. Attorney Kim. “Enriching himself at the expense of one Africa’s poorest countries, Thiam used some of the Chinese bribe money to pay his children’s Manhattan private school tuition and to buy a $3.75 million estate in Dutchess County. Today’s sentence shows that if you send your crime proceeds to New York, whether from drug dealing, tax evasion or international bribery, you may very well find yourself at the front end of long federal prison term.”

"Thiam abused his official position, but the outcome shows that no one is above the law," said Assistant Director Stephen E. Richardson. "The FBI will not stand by while individuals attempt to live by their own rules and use the United States as a safe haven for their ill-gotten gains. I would like to applaud the dedicated investigators and prosecutors who have worked to hold those who have committed these crimes accountable for their illegal actions.”

“Today’s sentencing should remind the public that no matter who you are, or how much money you have, you’re not immune from prosecution. The FBI will continue to use all resources at our disposal to uncover crimes of this nature and expose them for what they really are,” said Assistant Director in Charge Sweeney

According to evidence presented at trial, China Sonangol, CIF and their subsidiaries signed a series of agreements with Guinea that gave them lucrative mining rights in Guinea. In exchange for bribes paid by executives of China Sonangol and CIF, Thiam used his position as Minister of Mines to influence the Guinean government’s decision to enter into those agreements while serving as Guinea’s Minister of Mines and Geology from 2009 to 2010. The evidence further showed that Thiam participated in a scheme to launder the bribe payments from 2009 to 2011, during which time China Sonangol and CIF paid him $8.5 million through a bank account in Hong Kong. Thiam then transferred approximately $3.9 million to bank accounts in the U.S. and used the money to pay for luxury goods and other expenses. To conceal the bribe payments, Thiam falsely claimed to banks in Hong Kong and the U.S. that he was employed as a consultant and that the money was income from the sale of land that he earned before he was a minister.

The trial evidence showed that the purpose of the bribes was to obtain substantial rights and interests in natural resources in Guinea, including the right to be the first and strategic shareholder with Guinea of a national mining company into which Guinea had to, among other things, transfer all of its stakes in various mining projects and future mining permits or concessions that the government decided to develop on its own. China Sonangol and CIF, through their subsidiaries, also obtained exclusive and valuable rights to conduct business operations in a broad range of sectors of the Guinean economy, including mining. . .

Updated November 8, 2017

14. **Jianxing Chen**

Leader of International Money Laundering Network Sentenced for Laundering Millions of Dollars in Drug Proceeds[24] (US DoJ press report, September 12, 2023)

A foreign national was sentenced today to 10 years in prison and ordered to forfeit $6 million for conspiracy to commit money laundering after laundering millions of dollars of drug proceeds on behalf of international drug trafficking organizations.

According to court documents, from at least 2014 to 2020, **Jianxing Chen**, 42, of Belize City, Belize, led and controlled a network of couriers who transported cash generated by the sale of cocaine throughout the United States—including Chicago, Houston, Los Angeles, New York, and Atlanta—from those locations to New York City. From there, the cash was laundered through a variety of methods until it, or its equivalent value, was remitted to drug trafficking organizations in Latin America, including Mexico. Chen received "contracts" to transport and launder this money through co-conspirators who were prosecuted and convicted based on the same superseding indictment.

Chen coordinated the laundering of multimillion dollar quantities of drug proceeds from Latin American drug trafficking organizations, including organizations based in Mexico, into the hands of Chinese nationals, who subsequently engaged in a sophisticated scheme to covertly launder the drug money into mainland China, largely circumventing the U.S. financial system.

Chen pleaded guilty on May 23. In October 2021, co-defendant Xizhi Li was sentenced to 15 years in prison for leading the conspiracy to launder tens of millions of dollars for foreign drug trafficking organizations. Li signed a consent order of forfeiture for $10,000,000 to the United States pursuant to his plea . . .

The Justice Department's Office of International Affairs provided valuable assistance in securing the extradition of Chen from Peru. The United States also thanks Peruvian law enforcement authorities for their assistance and collaboration . . .

This effort is part of an Organized Crime Drug Enforcement Task Forces (OCDETF) operation. OCDETF identifies, disrupts, and dismantles the highest-level criminal organizations that threaten the United States using a prosecutor-led, intelligence-driven, multi-agency approach. . .

Updated September 12, 2023

15. **Commonwealth Bank**[25]

The **Commonwealth Bank of Australia (CBA)**, or **CommBank**, is an Australian multinational bank with businesses across New Zealand, Asia, the United States, and the United Kingdom. It provides a variety of financial services, including retail, business and institutional banking, funds management, superannuation, insurance, investment, and broking services. The Commonwealth Bank is the largest Australian

[24] https://www.justice.gov/opa/pr/leader-international-money-laundering-network-sentenced-laundering-millions-dollars-drug

[25] https://en.wikipedia.org/wiki/Commonwealth_Bank

listed company on the Australian Securities Exchange as of August 2015, with brands including Bankwest, Colonial First State Investments, ASB Bank (New Zealand), Commonwealth Securities (CommSec) and Commonwealth Insurance (CommInsure).[3] Its former constituent parts were the **Commonwealth Trading Bank of Australia**, the **Commonwealth Savings Bank of Australia**, and the **Commonwealth Development Bank**.

Founded in 1911 by the Australian Government and fully privatised in 1996, the Commonwealth Bank is one of the "big four" Australian banks, with the National Australia Bank (NAB), ANZ and Westpac. The bank was listed on the Australian Stock Exchange on 12 Sep 1991 ...[4]

In 2018, findings from the Royal Commission into Misconduct in the Banking, Superannuation and Financial Services Industry have indicated a negative culture within the bank, amid allegations of fraud, deception, and money laundering, among various other crimes.[6]

In 2022, the Commonwealth Bank hold the 49th position in the "Top 1000 World Banks"....

Money laundering scandal

In August 2017, the financial intelligence agency Australian Transaction Reports and Analysis Centre (AUSTRAC) launched civil proceedings in the Federal Court of Australia, alleging that CBA had breached money laundering and terrorism financing laws on 53,700 occasions. The breaches related to the bank's use of intelligent deposit machines (IDMs) between November 2012 and September 2015—the bank claimed that a programming error allowed depositors to instantly credit cash deposits to their accounts, whilst failing to report amounts over $10,000 to AUSTRAC, and not enforcing any limits to the number of transactions ...[57]

AND

AUSTRAC and CBA agree $700m penalty[26], 4 June 2018

An agreement has been reached today between AUSTRAC and the Commonwealth Bank of Australia (CBA) for a $700 million penalty to resolve Federal Court proceedings relating to serious breaches of anti-money laundering and counter-terrorism financing (AML/CTF) laws.

The parties will jointly approach the Federal Court seeking orders to this effect. It is anticipated that a hearing on penalty will be scheduled in the coming months.

If agreed by the Federal Court this will represent the largest ever civil penalty in Australian corporate history.

AUSTRAC's enforcement action against CBA followed exhaustive investigations into CBA's AML/CTF compliance and risk management practices, particularly in relation to its Intelligent Deposit Machines (IDMs).

These investigations, undertaken in partnership with the Australian Federal Police, NSW Police Force and Western Australia Police, identified that CBA's IDMs were being used to launder the illicit proceeds of crime.

[26] https://www.austrac.gov.au/news-and-media/media-release/austrac-and-cba-agree-700m-penalty

In reaching today's agreement, CBA has admitted it contravened the Anti-Money Laundering and Counter-Terrorism Financing Act 2006 (AML/CTF Act) on 53,750 occasions.

In summary, CBA accepted that:

- it failed to carry out an appropriate assessment of the money laundering and terrorism financing (ML/TF) risks of its IDMs prior to October 2017
- it failed to complete the introduction of appropriate controls to mitigate and manage the ML/TF risks of IDMs prior to April 2018
- it failed to provide 53,506 threshold transaction reports to AUSTRAC on time for cash transactions of $10,000 or more through IDMs from November 2012 to September 2015, having a total value of about $625 million
- for a period of three years, it did not comply with the requirements of its AML/CTF program relating to monitoring transactions on 778,370 accounts
- it failed to report suspicious matters on time, or at all, involving transactions in the tens of millions of dollars
- even after it became aware of suspected money laundering or structuring on CBA accounts, it did not monitor its customers to mitigate and manage ML/TF risk, including the ongoing ML/TF risks of doing business with those customers.

AUSTRAC's CEO, Nicole Rose PSM said this outcome sends a strong message to industry that serious non-compliance with the AML/CTF Act will not be tolerated.

"As we have seen in this case, criminals will exploit poor business practices to launder the proceeds of their crimes," Ms Rose said.

"This has real impacts on the everyday lives of Australians and puts the community at risk by increasing opportunities for terrorists to support attacks here and overseas, and enabling organised crime groups to peddle drugs to our families and friends.

"We know that businesses are the first line of defence in protecting the community and our financial system from criminal abuse, and it is critical for AML/CTF compliance and risk management to be embedded in business strategy and practices.

"I hope this result alerts the financial sector to the consequences of poor compliance, and reinforces that businesses need to take their obligations seriously."

Ms Rose added that AUSTRAC's focus is to work collaboratively with and support industry to deter criminal activity and welcomed CBA's decision to commence work on a Program of Action to address their AML/CTF compliance failings.

"We will continue to work collaboratively with CBA as it progresses this work and I am encouraged by the manner in which CBA has handled these negotiations.

"We want compliance to be voluntary, and even taken on with enthusiasm, however we will not shy away from using our enforcement powers where necessary. In the end our role is about protecting the community and we take this role seriously."

15. **1MDB & Jho Low (Singapore)**[27]

Low Taek Jho[a] (born 4 November 1981),[1] often called **Jho Low**, is a Malaysian businessman and international fugitive, wanted by authorities in connection with the 1Malaysia Development Berhad scandal (1MDB scandal).[3][4][5] He has been named the mastermind of the massive fraud, which prosecutors allege was a scheme to siphon US$4.5 billion from 1MDB into Low's personal accounts.[6][7][8][9][10] He is the beneficiary of numerous discretionary trust assets said by the US government to originate from payments out of the Malaysian 1MDB fund. Low has maintained his innocence and contends that Malaysian authorities are engaging in a campaign of harassment and political persecution due to his prior support of former Prime Minister Najib Razak,[11] whose part in the 1MDB scandal had led to Najib being convicted on seven counts of abuse of power, money laundering and criminal breach of trust.[12][13]

Early life

Low was born to a wealthy Malaysian Chinese family. He is of Teochew descent and he grew up in George Town, on Penang Island. His family has traditionally maintained a low profile. His grandfather Low Meng Tak was a businessman born in Guangdong in China.[14] Meng Tak had interests in iron-ore mining and liquor distilleries in Thailand in the 1960s and 1970s, and in real estate in Thailand, Malaysia, and Hong Kong.[14] Low's father Tan Sri Larry Low Hock Peng founded investment holding company MWE Holdings.[15][16]

Low was the youngest of three children. He attended Chung Ling High School and The International School of Penang (Uplands) before being sent to the elite Harrow School in London.[15] The school boasts notable alumni, including former British Prime Minister Winston Churchill and the first Prime Minister of India, Jawaharlal Nehru.[17] He took this opportunity to rub shoulders with students from powerful families, including royals from the Middle East and Brunei.[18] In London, he developed a "close relationship" with Riza Aziz, the stepson of former Malaysian Prime Minister Najib Razak.[19][20] Low then enrolled in the undergraduate program of the University of Pennsylvania's Wharton School, where he continued to develop connections with Malaysians as well as Kuwaiti and Jordanian interests and began managing money for his friends and family.[21][18][22] He graduated from Wharton in 2005.[23][24]

Low can speak Malay, English, Cantonese, Hokkien, and Teochew.[15]

Business dealings and wealth

Although earlier in his career Low had often claimed to be investing and making purchases on behalf of other investors or "friends" to maintain a low profile about his family's wealth, in 2015 Low said that his family had considerable independent means.[21][18] While a 2015 *New York Times* article suggested that his family was of

[27] https://en.wikipedia.org/wiki/Jho_Low . See also 1MDB at: https://en.wikipedia.org/wiki/1Malaysia_Development_Berhad_scandal

"somewhat deflated affluence,"[21] a 2014 *Wall Street Journal* profile had called him a "scion."[25]

Career

Low's first major deal was the Kuwait Finance House's 2006 purchase for US$87 million of a luxury high-rise apartment building in Kuala Lumpur.[14] According to *The New York Times*, "By 2007, Low had formed an investment group that included a Malaysian prince, a Kuwaiti sheikh and a friend from the United Arab Emirates who went on to become ambassador to the United States and Mexico, and is now one of the most powerful right hand persons for the Crown Prince of Abu Dhabi."[21] By 2010, Low had consolidated his fortune into Jynwel Capital, of which Low was the principal steward.[14]

As steward of Jynwel, Low cultivated relationships with some of the world's largest and most reputable sovereign wealth funds, including Abu Dhabi's Mubadala Development Co and the Kuwait Investment Authority.[26] Jynwel is connected with deals including the acquisition of New York's Park Lane Hotel for US$660 million in 2013 with The Witkoff Group and Mubadala; the takeover of Coastal Energy in 2014 for US$2.2 billion; and the buyout of EMI's music publishing business in 2012 for US$2.2 billion with the Blackstone Group, Sony Corporation and Mubadala.[27] Low was the architect for Jynwel Capital's unsuccessful US$2.2 billion bid to buy Reebok from Adidas AG in October 2014.[28]

Low supported Aziz in the establishment of Red Granite Pictures, a Hollywood production company responsible for films including *Wolf of Wall Street* and *Dumb and Dumber To*.[29] Recovery of the rights in both movies was the subject of actions for recovery by the US Government in 2013 and 2016.[30] The claims were settled in August 2018, with the settlement stipulating that the payment should not be construed as "an admission of wrongdoing or liability on the part of Red Granite".[31]

In 2019, US authorities pursuing Low described him as a financial intermediary, which allowed him to use his connections to high net worth individuals and international institutions to launder the money stolen through manipulation of the 1Malaysia Development Berhad.[32]

Najib Razak became Prime Minister of Malaysia in 2009. Soon, he became president of the board of advisers for 1Malaysia Development Berhad (1MDB), a Malaysian sovereign wealth fund. Although Low never received an official position, he admits that he occasionally "consulted" with 1MDB, and was involved in a number of transactions connecting his own interests with those of 1MDB, which he claimed were "arms-length and legally sound."[21][33]

The *Wall Street Journal* has reported that a $33.5 million condominium in Manhattan was owned by a shell company under control of Low's family trust, and then was sold and transferred to a shell company controlled by Razak's stepson.[34] Another home in Beverly Hills, "known as the pyramid house for a gold pyramid in its garden", was owned by a shell company controlled by the Low family trust, and was sold and transferred to Razak's stepson by transferring shares of the shell company to him.[34]

In October 2016, Interpol published a red notice at Singapore's request to locate and arrest Low in an investigation related to 1MDB fund flows within its jurisdiction.[35] The request for assistance to provisionally arrest Low was sent to the Hong Kong Department of Justice in April 2016, according to a representative for Singapore's police, but the request was rejected by the Hong Kong authorities.[36]

After the Malaysian general election in 2018, new Prime Minister Mahathir Mohamad re-opened the extensive investigations into the 1MDB matter and, despite prior findings by former Malaysian Attorney General Mohamed Apandi Ali and the Malaysian Anti-Corruption Commission that no crime had been committed, issued arrest warrants against Low.[37] The filing of these charges leading to the arrest warrant were described by a spokesperson for Low as "political reprisal" by the Mahathir regime which was described as having a disregard for the rule of law.[*neutrality is disputed*][38] In light of the warrants, some consider him a fugitive as he has reportedly been sought by the Malaysian authorities in connection with the 1MDB matter, notwithstanding that Low agreed to assist with the probe.[*neutrality is disputed*][39][40]

According to *South China Morning Post* reports, Low is still involved in affairs of his Hong Kongcompanies. He signed documents for private equity firm Jynwel Capital and non-profit group Jynwel Charitable Foundation in July 2018,[41] even though Malaysian authorities were looking to arrest him in connection with the 1MDB scandal which he has stated as politically motivated.[42] He was alleged to have been in discussions with the Malaysian government on a potential deal, but the Malaysian government and he did not come to a deal.[43]

Low allegedly purchased a US$325,000 white Ferrari as a wedding gift for Kim Kardashian in 2011.[44] The Department of Justice (DoJ) was reported to have sought restitution from other famous celebrities who had received gifts from Low, among them Leonardo DiCaprio, who has since returned Picasso and Basquiat paintings; and Miranda Kerr who returned diamond jewellery with a market value of US$8 million.[44][45][46]

Low invested $100 million for production of *The Wolf of Wall Street*, which was subsequently nominated for the Oscars. Leonardo DiCaprio specially thanked Low for his involvement during one of the awards ceremonies.[47] Red Granite, a productions company that was backed by Low, threw a lavish party in Cannes, France, complete with a performance by Kanye West.

In June 2017, the US Government, in proceedings brought against certain assets in the Central District of California, sought return of millions worth of assets derived from the Malaysian 1MDB wealth fund. On 1 November 2018, Low and two ex-Goldman Sachs bankers, Tim Leissner and Roger Ng Chong Hwa, were indicted by the United States Department of Justice in connection with the 1MDB allegations.[48][49]

On 31 October 2019, Low entered into a global, comprehensive settlement with the US government forever resolving all civil, criminal, and administrative proceedings concerning asset forfeiture claims against various Low-linked assets.[50][51] The settlement did not resolve the government's underlying money laundering and bribery charges and is not otherwise tied to the ongoing U.S. criminal case against him.[52]

In 2019, Low was accused of a connection to the Burning Sun scandal through his friendship with Korean musician Psy; Low, Psy and others denied the allegations.[53][54] The case was closed for lack of evidence.[55][56]

On June 11, 2021, the U. S. Department of Justice announced charges related to violation of United States federal law.[57] "Low Taek Jho, 39, also known as Jho Low, and Prakazrel "Pras" Michel, 48, are alleged to have conspired with Elliott Broidy "related to their" ... engaging in undisclosed lobbying campaigns at the direction of Low and the Vice Minister of Public Security for the People's Republic of China".[57]

Citizenship

Low, born in Malaysia and granted Malaysian citizenship at birth, has reportedly possessed numerous passports obtained by economic citizenship.[58] Low is presumed to have used these passports, from Caribbean and Mediterranean nations, to evade arrest.[58]

Malaysia does not recognize dual citizenship,[59] and in June 2018, Malaysian immigration authorities revoked Low's Malaysian passport on the basis that having more than one passport is a criminal offence in Malaysia.[60]

In 2019, it was reported that Low had been granted a Cypriot passport years earlier, under a Cypriot citizenship investment scheme,[61] "within two days after investing in some property" in Cyprus.[62] At the time, Low had not yet been criminally charged for the 1MDB scandal, but was already under investigation.[63] Low's Cypriot passport came to light after the Cyprus Papers revealed that the Cypriot government, under the presidency of Nicos Anastasiades, had granted citizenship to Cambodian elites, bringing scrutiny to the investment scheme.[64]

Career as a fugitive

Low is believed to be residing in China where he secretly travels extensively through major cities. In November 2020, Al-Jazeera reported that Low was currently living in Macau, in "a house owned by a senior member of the Chinese Communist Party."[65] He has managed to travel freely despite the Malaysian police submitting an Interpol red notice, saying these actions are politically motivated.[66][67][68] The Chinese government has denied harboring Low despite being filmed at Disneyland Shanghai on Christmas Eve 2019 on a witness's cellphone.[69][70]

In May 2023, Malaysian Prime Minister Anwar Ibrahim said that his government was collaborating with many countries to expedite Low's extradition back to Malaysia.[71]

Politics

Electioneering in Malaysia

Consistent with his personal connections to the Najib Razak family, Low supported and funded the Prime Minister with 1MDB cash during the 2013 elections.[18] He organised a free pro-government concert in his home state of Penang featuring American musicians Busta Rhymes and Ludacris,[33] which was criticised by the local opposition government as unfair electioneering even though Low's close friend claimed the concert was for charity.[33][21]

Lobbying activities in the United States

According to a 6 May 2019 United States Department of Justice's indictment, Low was allegedly involved in a conspiracy to gain access to, and potentially influence, Barack Obama's 2012 campaign without disclosing the foreign origins of the money funneled to Obama's Super PAC.[72] The indictment against Low revealed that he directed the transfer of US$21.6 million from foreign entities to former Fugees rapper Pras in 2012 for funneling into the US election.[73]

Low was also helped by former Justice Department employee Higginbotham, who pleaded guilty to a charge in November 2018, to set up bank accounts for a lobbying campaign against the US investigations into the 1MDB scandal.[74][75] In response, a spokesman for Low stated that "Mr. Low has never made any campaign contribution directly or indirectly in the United States."[76]

The FBI has considered whether a donation of $100,000 to Trump Victory in 2017 originated with Low.[77][78][79]:340 The Wall Street Journal reported that $75 million was offered to Elliott Broidy, a businessman and a Republican fundraiser, and his wife if the Justice Department ended its probe into 1MDB.[80][79]:392

In June 2021, Low was charged by a federal grand jury for running a back-channel campaign to get the Trump administration to drop an investigation of Low and the 1MDB investment company.[81][82]

Social life

Low once lived a high-profile social life before becoming an international fugitive.[83][84] Low's lavish lifestyle was purportedly funded by money pilfered from the 1MDB fund . . .[85]

Philanthropy

Low has contributed money to various charities.[92] However, much, if not all, of his charitable giving occurred after the 1MDB scandal began to unfold, and thus critics claim that the money provided to various charities was stolen from 1MDB and that Low's charitable giving is simply part of a public relations strategy to burnish Low's tarnished image . . .[93][92][94]

AND

Najib Razak/Singapore[28]

Mohammad Najib bin Tun Haji Abdul Razak . . . is a Malaysian politician who served as the sixth Prime Minister of Malaysia from 2009 to 2018. In 2020, he was convicted of corruption in the 1Malaysia Development Berhad scandal,[3] one of the largest money-laundering and embezzlement scandals in history.[4][5] He is the son of former prime minister Abdul Razak Hussein. Najib Razak was the chairman of the Barisan Nasional (BN) coalition from April 2009 to May 2018 and the

[28] https://en.wikipedia.org/wiki/Najib_Razak

president of the United Malays National Organisation (UMNO) from November 2008 to May 2018,[6][7][8] which had maintained control of Malaysia's government with a parliamentary majority for more than sixty years until the coalition's defeat in the 2018 general election.

Najib was elected to the Parliament of Malaysia in 1976, at the age of 23, replacing his deceased father in the Pahang-based seat of Pekan. In the same year, he was appointed the head of UMNO Youth's Pekan branch and became a member of the youth wing's Executive Council. In the early years of his political career, Najib took on a deputy minister role in 1976, and between 1982 and 1986, he was the Menteri Besar of Pahang. Thereafter, until 2009, he was rotated throughout the Cabinet of Malaysia, taking on various ministerial portfolios in defence, education, culture, youth and sports, and finally finance. Between 1993 and 2009, Najib was a vice-president of UMNO.[9]

Najib's tenure as prime minister, between 2009 and 2018, was marked by economic liberalisation measures, such as cuts to government subsidies, loosening of restrictions on foreign investment, and reductions in preferential measures for ethnic Malays in business. After the 2013 election, his government pursued a number of its critics on sedition charges, the imprisonment of opposition leader Anwar Ibrahim following a conviction for sodomy and the implementation of a Goods and Services Tax (GST). He also led the country through the Malaysia Airlines Flight 370 disaster and a dispute with North Korea following the assassination of Kim Jong-nam. In 2015, Najib became implicated in a major corruption scandal involving state investment firm 1Malaysia Development Berhad (1MDB) which led to rallies calling for his resignation, spearheaded by the grassroots movement Bersih.[10][11][12] These protests culminated in the Malaysian Citizens' Declaration by Mahathir Mohamad, Pakatan Harapan and NGOs which sought to oust Najib.[13][14]

Najib's response to the corruption accusations was to tighten his grip on power by replacing then-deputy prime minister Muhyiddin Yassin, suspending two newspapers and pushing through parliament a controversial National Security Council Bill that provides the prime minister with unprecedented powers.[15][16] Najib's various subsidy cuts have contributed to soaring living costs,[17] while fluctuating oil prices and the fallout from the 1MDB scandal led to a depreciation of the Malaysian currency.[18][19] These ended with BN's loss in the 2018 general elections, the results of which Najib then accepted and promised to help facilitate a smooth transition of power.[20]

On 3 July 2018, Najib was arrested by the Malaysian Anti-Corruption Commission (MACC), which investigated how RM42 million (US$10.6 million) went from SRC International, a company related to 1MDB, into Najib's bank account.[21] In the process, the police seized a number of fashion accessories worth $273 million while searching through his properties.[22] Najib was subsequently charged and convicted by the High Court on abuse of power, money launderingand criminal breach of trust, becoming the first Prime Minister of Malaysia to be convicted of corruption,[23][24] and was sentenced to 12 years' imprisonment and fined RM210 million.[25][26]The sentence was upheld by the Federal Court on 23 August 2022.[27] He is currently serving his sentence in Kajang Prison . . .[28]

1Malaysia Development Berhad scandal

On 2 July 2015, *The Wall Street Journal* ran an exposé alleging that MYR 2.672 billion (US$700 million) had been channelled from 1MDB into Najib's personal bank accounts, triggering widespread calls for his resignation.[143][144][145] Najib denied any wrongdoing and announced plans to sue the newspaper for libel[146] but eventually failed to do so.[147] On 6 July 2015, amid the 1MDB scandal, the ringgit fell to 3.8050 against the US dollar, the first time it slid beyond the 3.80 currency peg, which was lifted in 2005.[148] To back up the allegations, on 7 July 2015, *The Wall Street Journal* released a batch of partially redacted documents that purportedly show how nearly US$700 million (RM2.6 billion) was moved from 1MDB into Najib's personal bank accounts. These documents relate to transactions in March 2013, December 2014 and February 2015.[149]

The multi-agency task force investigating these allegations reported on 10 July 2015 that Najib's bank accounts at AmBank Islamic were closed before *The Wall Street Journal* reported the transfers of billions of ringgit to those accounts, thereby confirming that Najib had two accounts at that bank. The task force also confirmed that the six accounts it had just frozen did not belong to Najib but did not name the holders of those accounts[150] Najib's handling of the corruption scandal was criticised by, among others, former Prime Minister Mahathir Mohamad and then Deputy Prime Minister Muhyiddin Yassin. During Najib's mid-term Cabinet reshuffle on 28 July 2015, Najib dropped Muhyiddin from his position as Deputy Prime Minister, as well as other Ministers who had been critical of his leadership. Najib stated that the reason for this was to create a more "unified team".[151]

On 1 August 2015, Najib addressed UMNO delegates in Seremban and in a clear reference to the Sarawak Report, the London-based whistleblower site founded and operated by journalist Clare Rewcastle Brown, demanded that "white people" stay out of Malaysia's affairs and stressed that he valued loyalty above all, and not smart people.[152]

On 3 August 2015, the Malaysian Anti-Corruption Commission stated that the RM 2.6 billion that had been banked into Najib's personal account came from donors, not 1MDB,[153] but did not elaborate on who the donors were or why the funds were transferred, nor why this explanation had taken so long to emerge since the allegations were first made on 2 July 2015.[154][155] Umno Kuantan division chief Wan Adnan Wan Mamat later claimed that the RM 2.6 billion was from Saudi Arabia as thanks for fighting ISIS. He further claimed that the Muslim community in the Philippines as well as southern Thailand had also received similar donations, and that since the donations were made to Najib personally as opposed to UMNO, the funds were deposited into Najib's personal accounts.[156]

The scandal took a dramatic twist on 28 August 2015 when a member of Najib's own party, Anina Saaduddin, UMNO's Langkawi Wanita (women's) representative, filed a civil suit against him alleging a breach of duties as trustee and that he defrauded party members by failing to disclose receipt of the donated funds, and account for their use. This suit was filed in the Kuala Lumpur High Court and also named party Executive Secretary Abdul Rauf Yusof. Expressing fear that Najib would wield influence to remove any member of UMNO "for the sole purpose of avoiding liability" the court was also petitioned for an injunction to restrain UMNO, its Supreme Council, state liaison body, divisions and branches from removing the nominal plaintiff as a party member pending the determination of the suit. The plaintiff also sought repayment amounting to US$650 million, the amount allegedly deposited by Najib to a Singapore bank, an account of all monies that he had received in the form of donations, details of all monies in the AmPrivate Banking Account No 2112022009694 allegedly belonging to Najib, along with damages, costs, and other reliefs.[157]

On 21 September 2015, the New York Times reported that US investigators were investigating allegations of corruption involving Najib as well as people close to him. In particular, investigators focused on properties in the United States that were purchased in recent years by shell companies owned by Najib's stepson Riza Aziz or connected to a close family friend, as well as a $681 million payment made to what is believed to be Najib's personal bank account.[158]

The claimed MYR 2.6 billion "donation" into Najib's personal accounts led the opposition to table a no-confidence motion against Najib, on 18 October 2015.[159]

On 26 January 2016, Malaysia's Attorney General Mohamed Apandi Ali announced that the investigation into the $681 million payment into Najib's personal bank account had been closed. The Anti-Corruption Commission investigating the gift, led by Apandi, concluded that no laws had been broken and that the gift did not amount to graft. Apandi was appointed attorney general by Najib in August 2015 after the previous attorney general, Abdul Gani Patail, was abruptly dismissed by Najib. Although Bernama, Malaysia's state-run news service, reported that Abdul Gani was removed for health reasons, many speculated that his dismissal was related to the 1MDB corruption investigation.[160] The Attorney General then said that the [Saudi Royal Family] was the source of the $681 million gift,[161] although doubts remained as the Saudi ministries of foreign affairs and finance had no information on the purported gift.[162]

Najib was reported to have returned $620 million to the Saudi royal family in 2013, but no explanation was given as to the reason for the investment or what happened to the $61 million Najib did not return.[163] Najib hailed the results of the investigation and reiterated his denial of any wrongdoing.

On 28 March 2016, the Australian television programme *Four Corners* in an episode called *State of Fear: Murder and Money in Malaysia*,[164] aired new allegations about the large sums of money that have flowed into the bank accounts of Najib Razak.

On 30 March 2016, the Wall Street Journal, Time and several other news agencies reported that Prime Minister Najib Razak and his wife, Rosmah Mansor had spent $15 million on luxury goods and extravagant travel expenses.[165] During Najib Razak's golf diplomacy with U.S. President Barack Obama on 24 December 2014, Malaysian investigation documents show that Rosmah Mansor had purchased items amounting to $130,625 at a Chanel store in Honolulu, Hawaii. The allegation was confirmed when a store employee at the Chanel store in the upscale Ala Moana Center recalled Najib's wife shopping there just before 25 December 2014.[166]

In April 2016, Mohd Nazifuddin Najib, the son of Najib, has been named in the Panama Papers.[167]

In July 2016, the United States Department of Justice launched a civil lawsuit[168] to seize American assets worth over US$1 billion (4.1 billion MYR) allegedly obtained from US$3.5 billion (14.38 billion MYR) of misappropriated 1MDB funds. Within the civil lawsuit, a government official of high rank who had control over 1MDB was referred to as "Malaysian Official 1", and mentioned over 30 times. "Malaysian Official 1" was alleged to have received around US$681 million (2.797 billion MYR) of stolen 1MDB money via Falcon Bank, Singapore on 21 and 25 March 2013, of which US$650 million (2.0 billion MYR) was sent back to Falcon Bank on 30 August 2013.[169] In September 2016, Najib was identified as "Malaysian Official 1" by Abdul Rahman Dahlan, Minister in the Prime Minister's Department and the Barisan Nasional strategic communications director. Dahlan also claimed that Najib was not named because he was "not part of this investigation".[170][171]

On 15 June 2017, The United States Department of Justice followed up on its July 2016 lawsuit by issuing a civil action in rem to forfeit assets involved in and traceable to an international conspiracy to launder money misappropriated from 1Malaysia Development Berhad ("a strategic investment and development company wholly-owned by the government of Malaysia"). The writ provided detailed justifications for seeing to forfeit specific items and property located in the United States and abroad, including in the United Kingdom and Switzerland.[172] [173]

As a consequence of the 15 June 2017 writ, on 28 February 2018 Indonesian authorities seized the luxury yacht linked to the 1MDB investigations in waters off Bali, on behalf of the FBI.[174] Additionally, on 7 March 2018 in Californian courts, the producers of the 'Wolf of Wall Street' film agreed to pay $60m to settle Justice Department claims it financed the movie with money siphoned from 1MDB.[175]

In a speech in December 2017, US attorney general Jeff Sessions said of the scandal: "This is kleptocracy at its worst."[176][177]

Subsequent arrest, legal proceedings and conviction

On 3 July 2018 after the 14th Malaysian general election, Najib was arrested by the Malaysian Anti-Corruption Commission (MACC) as part of investigations into how RM42 million (US$10.6 million) went from SRC International into Najib's bank account.[178][179][180] The following day, Najib was indicted in the High Court in Kuala Lumpur on three counts of criminal breach of trust and one count of abuse of power in connection with SRC International funds totalling RM42 million.[181][182][183] He was granted bail at RM1 million after pleading not guilty with his trial set for 18 February 2019.[184]

On 8 August 2018, Najib was charged with three further counts of money laundering as part of the MACC's investigation into the 1MDB scandal. Najib has denied making three transfers totaling RM42 from SRC International into his bank accounts.[185][186][187]

On 10 September 2018, Najib posted a copy of the letter that purportedly came from Prince Saud Abdulaziz Al-Saud of Saudi Arabia on his Facebook account, as a proof of the alleged financial donation of US$100mil (RM304.5mil) given to him in 2011.[188][189] He said he decided to reveal the documents in a bid to clear his name of various accusations and slander, and would continue to do so on his social media accounts.[190][191]

On 19 September 2018, Najib was arrested following two hours of questioning by the MACC, believed to be in relation to the RM2.6 billion donation he received in year 2013. Najib was charged on 20 September 2018 at the Sessions Court in Jalan Duta.[192][193][194] However, he pleaded not guilty and was released on bail after his court appearance.[195] On 21 September, he made a brief appearance at the Sessions Court registry to sign his bail at RM3.5 million for 25 counts of money laundering and abuse of power charges in relation to 1MDB. He has posted RM1 million for his bail, while the remaining RM2.5 million will be settled in instalments by the following week.[196][197] In August 2019, during his second trial, Najib faces four charges of abuse of power and 21 charges of money laundering for receiving illegal transfers of RM 2.3 billion between 2011 and 2014.

On 28 July 2020, the High Court convicted Najib guilty on all seven counts of abuse of power, money laundering and criminal breach of trustin relation to the SRC International case, becoming the first Prime Minister of Malaysia to be convicted of corruption.[23] High Court judge Mohamad Nazlan bin Mohamad Ghazali has delivered the verdict regarding the misappropriation of RM42 million (US$10 million) from SRC International, a former subsidiary of 1MDB.[198] In total, Najib faces 42 charges, of which 35 in another four trials are yet to be decided on.[199]

On the day of his conviction, Najib was sentenced to 12 years' imprisonment and a fine of RM210 million (for the first charge). He was also given six concurrent sentences of 10 years' imprisonment for the other six charges. If he fails to pay the fine, he will be serving another five years in prison. He would be appealing against the verdict of the High Court.[25][26] The High Court granted a stay of execution of the conviction with an increased bail of RM 2 million with reporting to the police on the first and the fifth day of every month.[200]

Appeal

Najib's appeal hearing in front of the Court of Appeal of Malaysia began on 5 April 2021.[201] On 8 December 2021, the Court of Appeal of Malaysia dismissed Najib's appeal, therefore upholding both his conviction and 12-year sentence. Judge Abdul Karim Abdul Jalil has also condemned Najib's actions as a "national embarrassment".[202] Najib's lawyer stated that his client, who remained outside prison on bail, would further appeal to the Federal Court of Malaysia against his conviction and sentence.[203] On 16 August 2022, Malaysia's supreme court rejected Najib's appeal for a retrial, stating that the case had no evidence of bias. The Federal Court indicated that it would hear a final appeal by Razak in the SRC corruption case from 18 August 2022.[204][205]

On 23 August 2022, when the Federal Court was finishing hearing the appeal, Najib's counsel made an application to recuse the Chief JusticeTengku Maimun.[206]

This application was dismissed[207] and the Federal Court upheld the Court of Appeal's conviction,[208] handing down its full judgment here. Upon the dissolution of Parliament on 10 October 2022, Najib's Pekan parliamentary seat was automatically vacated, and as he has been convicted of a crime, he is no longer eligible to stand in general elections.

Najib is the first Malaysian former prime minister to be convicted and jailed for corruption.[209] Rumours that he would receive special treatment during his sentence were denied by officials . . .[210][211]

16. **Isabel De Santos (Angola)**[29]

Isabel dos Santos . . . is an Angolan businesswoman, the eldest child of Angola's former President José Eduardo dos Santos, who ruled the country as a dictator from 1979 to 2017.[5] Once considered Africa's richest woman according to *Forbes* magazine, with a net worth exceeding US$2 billion, she was dropped from the magazine's list in January 2021 after the freezing of her assets in Angola, Portugal and the Netherlands.[6] She owes $340 million to the Portuguese company PT Ventures.[7]

In 2013 *Forbes* described how dos Santos acquired her wealth by taking stakes in companies doing business in Angola, suggesting that her wealth came almost entirely from her family's power and connections.[8][9] Since 2018, the Angolan government has been trying to prosecute Isabel dos Santos for corruption that may have led to Angola's ongoing recession.[10] On 30 December 2019, the Luanda Provincial Court ordered to freeze dos Santos's Angolan bank accounts and to seize her stake in local companies, including Unitel (Angola) and Banco de Fomento Angola.[11] Two weeks later, the Angolan Government announced it prepared the legal battle to confiscate dos Santos's assets in Portugal,[12] a process that in operation in the form of letters rogatory sent to Portugal to stop the transfer of funds from Portuguese Commercial Bank to a Russian bank.[*which?*][13] As of January 2020, she was under investigation in Portugal and has since taken on the United Arab Emirates as her official country of residence.[14][15][16] In December 2021, the US State Department barred Dos Santos and her immediate family from entering the United States, citing "significant corruption by misappropriating public funds for her personal benefit".[17][18][19] On 18 November 2022, Interpol issued a warrant for her arrest.[20] In December 2023 her assets were frozen following a hearing at the High Court in London.[21]

Family and education

Isabel dos Santos was born in Baku, Azerbaijan Soviet Socialist Republic,[22] the eldest daughter of Angola's longtime President José Eduardo dos Santos (1942–2022) and his first wife, the Russian-born Tatiana Kukanova, whom he met while studying in the then Soviet republic of Azerbaijan.[23][24][25] Her father's parents came from São Tomé and Príncipe.[26][27] She attended an all girls boarding

[29] https://en.wikipedia.org/wiki/Isabel_dos_Santos

school in Kent, Cobham Hall School, and St Paul's Girls' School in London.[28] She studied electrical engineering[29] at King's Collegein London.[30][failed verification] There she met her husband from Zaire (now Democratic Republic of the Congo), Sindika Dokolo,[31] a son of a millionaire from Kinshasa and his Danish wife.[32] In October 2020, her husband, Sindika Dokolo, died in a diving accident in Dubai at the age of 48.[33]

Isabel dos Santos is a citizen of both Russia and Angola.[34]

Career

In the early 90s, dos Santos started working as a project manager engineer for Urbana 2000, a subsidiary of Jembas Group, that had won a contract to clean and disinfect Luanda.[35] Thereafter, she set up a trucking business. The widespread use of walkie-talkie technology paved the way for a subsequent foray into telecoms.[4] In 1997, she started her first business, opening the Miami Beach Club, one of the first night clubs and beach restaurants on Luanda Island.[36] In 1997, dos Santos entered the international business world, creating companies and holdings in Angola but mostly abroad, making substantial investments in high-profile enterprises, especially in Portugal.[37][38] As of 2014, holdings of dos Santos included:[39][40]

- Trans Africa Investment Services, a Gibraltar-based vehicle founded together with her mother for the diamond business
- Unitel International Holdings B.V.: change of name of Kento and Jadeium, based in Amsterdam, company vehicle for dos Santos' investment in telecommunications
- Santoro Finance: company vehicle for dos Santos' investment in Banco BPI based in Lisbon
- Esperaza Holding B.V.: based in Amsterdam, energy and oil
- Condis: a retail business based in Luanda

In June 2016, her father appointed her as chair of Sonangol, the Angolan state oil company.[41] In November 2017, João Lourenço, the new Angolan President, fired her just two months after being sworn into office in the wake of similar appointments of children of the president to key posts.[42]

On 30 December 2019, the Luanda Provincial Court ordered the preventive seizure of the personal bank accounts of dos Santos, her husband, Sindika Dokolo, and Mário Filipe Moreira Leite da Silva. According to the Attorney General's office, the three businesspeople entered into deals with the Angolan state through the companies Sodiam, a public diamond sales company, and Sonangol, the state oil company. With these deals, the Angolan state suffered a loss of $1.14 billion.[43] The court produced a document showing that the assets and many others owned by dos Santos had been acquired using funds from two state-owned companies.[44] In January 2020, the Portuguese Attorney-General's Office opened an investigation into a number of her operations after Ana Gomes, a Portuguese Member of the European Parliament laid charges against her.[14] Following the seizure, she assumed the UAE as her official country of residence.[15][16] In January 2021, Forbes removed her from the list of the richest people in Africa, since her assets in Angola and Portugal had been frozen.[6]

Investments in Portugal

Since 2008 dos Santos has had interests in key Portuguese sectors, such as telecommunications, media, retail, finance and the energy. In 2012 dos Santos made a series of acquisitions in ZON Multimédia, a telecommunications and media company providing mobile and fixed telephony, cable television, satellite television and internet. From an initial small stake in the company, she became the biggest shareholder, with 28.8% in 2012. The acquisitions were made via holding companies Jadeium and Kento, later Netherlands-based Unitel International Holdings BV.[45][46][47][48][49][50][51][52][53][54]

In 2010, she bought a 20% stake at Banco Português de Investimento through Santoro Holding .[55][56] She has other major stakes with the Angolan state oil company Sonangol through their mutual European Law holding, based in the Netherlands, named Esperanza Holding, in Portuguese Galp Energia.[57] Dos Santos is a founding member and board member of Banco BIC Português,[58] which recently acquired Banco Português de Negócios, a nationalized bank.

In December 2012, dos Santos announced the invitation for a merger of ZON with Sonaecom, approved in March 2013 by the General Assembly.[50] Since her investments in Portugal were in listed companies they were subject to official supervision of the Portuguese Securities Market Commission (Comissão do Mercado de Valores Mobiliários, CMVM, in Portuguese).[59]

On 27 August 2013, after the green light from the Competition Authority, the merger of the two companies was formalized with the transfer to ZOPT, a special purpose vehicle created to advance the operation, which became the owner of more 50% of the capital of the new group, the shares that dos Santos and Sonaecom hold on Zon and Optimus respectively. There was a capital increase of ZOPT through contribution in kind from 50 to 716 million euros, while Sonaecom subscribed 358 million shares of the company, by delivering 81.8% of its stake in Optimus. The Angolan businesswoman, on her turn, subscribed exactly the same number of shares of ZOPT, through her holdings Kento and UnitelInternational, delivering 28.8% of the stake in ZON.[60][61][62][63] With this transfer of shareholdings in Optimus and Zon, Sonaecom and dos Santos became holders of over 50% stake in the merged company: Zon Optimus SGPS. On this occasion, a new strategy for the company was announced by dos Santos, with a multimarket vision.[64][65] On 1 October 2013, dos Santos attended the first General Assembly of Zon Optimus.[66]

In November 2014, dos Santos launched a takeover bid for Portugal Telecom, SGPS, S.A., valuing the firm's shares at 1.35 euros a share, in what was seen as a rival bid to a previous 7 billion euros offer from Altice, though the offer made by Altice was on PT Portugal, not on PT SGPS.[67] On 1 December 2014, she formally registered her offer at the Portuguese Securities Market Commission.[68]

In January 2017 Unitel, led by dos Santos, purchased 2% of Banco Fomento de Angola (BFA) from BPI for 28 million euros and controlled 51.9% of the bank's capital.[69] In December 2016 the National Bank of Angola (BNA), the sector regulator, had approved this operation. In February 2017 dos Santos sold her position in Banco BPI, following the takeover bid launched by CaixaBank. From her ownership from 2009 to 2017 she won more than 80 million euros in capital gain, not only from the sale of the 18.5% holding on BPI, but also from the dividends from 2008 and 2009, worth around 12.6 million euros.[70]

Investments in Angola

In April 2011, dos Santos with 51% control of Condis, signed a joint partnership with the Portuguese Sonae group for the development and operation of a retail trading company in Angola. The entry in Angola by the Portuguese group led by Paulo de Azevedo was to be performed by the Continente (Angola), which planned to open the first supermarket by 2013 in Angola.[71]

She created Unitel (Angola) in partnership with Portugal Telecom, after a tender process she considered fair.[4] As of 2013, she had acquired the mobile operator T+ in Cape Verde also through Unitel International Holding, a platform for Unitel investments where Portugal telecom has no presence, and gained the license to establish the second telecom operator in São Tomé and Príncipe.[72][73][74] In May 2013, dos Santos announced during a visit to São Tomé and Príncipe that Unitel would invest in education in the country to train engineers, managers and other technicians and also focus on job creation.[75]

By 2015, dos Santos owned a share of satellite-TV operator ZAP, which had in December 2013 acquired the rights to distribute *Forbes* in a number of Portuguese-speaking countries, namely Portugal, Angola, and Mozambique. It had been announced that most of the content would be produced by a local team, complemented by content for the North American edition, therefore potentially allowing influence on *Forbes*content. It was initially planned that the first edition of the Portuguese language *Forbes* would be published during the second quarter of 2014.[76]

In October 2022, Angolan President President João Lourenço issued a decision to nationalise the Angolan operator Unitel, ending her links with the operator.[77]

Prosecution, 2018–present

Since 2018, the Angolan government has been trying to prosecute Isabel dos Santos for corruption which may have led to Angola's recession.[10] On 30 December 2019, the Luanda Provincial Court ordered to freeze dos Santos's Angolan bank accounts and to seize her stake in local companies, including Unitel (Angola) and Banco de Fomento Angola.[11]/ In January 2019, the Angolan Government announced it prepared the legal battle to confiscate dos Santos's assets in Portugal,[12]/ and sent letters rogatory to Portugal to stop the transfer of funds from Portuguese Commercial Bank to a Russian bank.[13] As of January 2020, she was under investigation in Portugal and has since assumed the United Arab Emirates as her official country of residence.[14][15][16] In December 2021, the US State Department barred Dos Santos and her immediate family from entering the United States, citing "significant corruption by misappropriating public funds for her personal benefit".[17][18][19] On 18 November 2022, Interpol issued a warrant for her arrest.[20] She currently lives in Dubai, and has made at least one trip to Qatar.[78]

Luanda Leaks, 2020

On 19 January 2020 the International Consortium of Investigative Journalists (ICIJ) published a detailed report on how dos Santos amassed her wealth over the years. The report, based on information provided by corruption watchdog The Platform to Protect Whistleblowers in Africa—which it called *Luanda Leaks*—said she "made a fortune at the expense of the Angolan people".[79] The night of 22 January, three days after the leaks, her personal wealth manager and private banking director Nuno Ribeiro da Cunha was found dead in the garage of his house . . .[80]

NB. The cases above are examples—there are many other money laundering or terrorist financing cases reported by law enforcement (eg. in press and annual reports), such as UK FIU SARs 2022[30]*, US FINCEN,*[31] *AUSTRAC,*[32] *and Commission de Surveillance due Secteur Financier (CSSF) in Luxembourg.*[33] *Indeed, the re-distribution of funds can include elements of money laundering in many frauds or other economic crimes, such as those undertaken by Madoff*[34] *or allegedly by Mmobuosi.*[35]

---

[30]https://nationalcrimeagency.gov.uk/who-we-are/publications/632-2022-sars-annual-report-1/file

[31]https://www.fincen.gov/annual-report

[32]https://www.austrac.gov.au/about-us/corporate-information-and-governance/annual-reports

[33]For example, https://www.cssf.lu/wp-content/uploads/CSSF_RA_2020_EN.pdf

[34]https://en.wikipedia.org/wiki/Madoff_investment_scandal

[35]https://www.sec.gov/news/press-release/2023-254

Chapter 11
Terrorist Financing Cases

Lafarge (Syria): Lafarge Pleads Guilty to Conspiring to Provide Material Support to Foreign Terrorist Organizations[1] (DoJ report, October 18, 2022)

In Justice Department's First Corporate Material Support for Terrorism Prosecution, Lafarge S.A. and its Syrian Subsidiary Admit Revenue-Sharing Agreement with ISIS and Agree to Pay $778 Million in Fines and Forfeiture.

A global building materials manufacturer and its subsidiary pleaded guilty today to a one-count criminal information charging them with conspiring to provide material support and resources in Northern Syria from 2013 to 2014 to the Islamic State of Iraq and al-Sham (ISIS) and the al-Nusrah Front (ANF), both U.S.-designated foreign terrorist organizations. Immediately following the defendants' guilty pleas this morning, U.S. District Judge William F. Kuntz II sentenced the defendants to terms of probation and to pay financial penalties, including criminal fines and forfeiture, totaling $777.78 million.

According to court documents, Lafarge S.A., headquartered in Paris, France, and Lafarge Cement Syria (LCS) S.A., headquartered in Damascus, Syria, schemed to pay ISIS and ANF in exchange for permission to operate a cement plant in Syria from 2013 to 2014, which enabled LCS to obtain approximately $70.3 million in revenue.

"The terrorism crimes to which Lafarge and its subsidiary have pleaded guilty are a vivid reminder of how corporate crime can intersect with national security," said Deputy Attorney General Lisa O. Monaco. "The defendants partnered with ISIS, one of the most brutal terrorist organizations the world has ever known, to enhance profits and increase market share—all while ISIS engaged in a notorious campaign of violence during the Syrian civil war. This case sends the clear message to all companies, but especially those operating in high-risk environments, to invest in

[1] https://www.justice.gov/opa/pr/lafarge-pleads-guilty-conspiring-provide-material-support-foreign-terrorist-organizations . See also https://en.wikipedia.org/wiki/Lafarge_scandal

D. Smith, *Money Laundering, Terrorist Financing and Virtual Assets*, Contributions to Finance and Accounting, https://doi.org/10.1007/978-3-031-59842-5_11

robust compliance programs, pay vigilant attention to national security compliance risks, and conduct careful due diligence in mergers and acquisitions."

"The defendants routed nearly six million dollars in illicit payments to two of the world's most notorious terrorist organizations—ISIS and al-Nusrah Front in Syria—at a time those groups were brutalizing innocent civilians in Syria and actively plotting to harm Americans," said Assistant Attorney General Matthew G. Olsen of the Justice Department's National Security Division. "There is simply no justification for a multi-national corporation authorizing payments to designated terrorist organizations."

From approximately May 2010 to September 2014, Lafarge, through LCS, operated a cement plant in the Jalabiyeh region of Northern Syria (the Jalabiyeh Cement Plant) that Lafarge had constructed at a cost of approximately $680 million. After the start of the Syrian Civil War in 2011, Lafarge and LCS negotiated agreements to pay armed factions in the Civil War to protect LCS employees, to ensure continued operation of the Jalabiyeh Cement Plant, and to obtain economic advantage over their competitors in the Syrian cement market.

As Lafarge executives made clear in contemporaneous emails, their motives were primarily economic. LCS executives purchased raw materials needed to manufacture cement from ISIS-controlled suppliers; paid monthly "donations" to armed groups, including ISIS and ANF, so that employees, customers and suppliers could traverse checkpoints controlled by the armed groups on roads around the Jalabiyeh Cement Plant; and eventually agreed to make payments to ISIS based on the volume of cement that LCS sold to its customers, which Lafarge and LCS executives likened to paying "taxes."

Lafarge and LCS executives intentionally structured their agreements with ISIS to compensate the terrorist organization based on the amount of cement that LCS was able to sell—effectively, a revenue-sharing agreement—to incentivize the terrorist group to act in LCS's economic interest.

As a condition of entering into this revenue-sharing agreement, Lafarge and LCS executives sought ISIS's assistance to impose costs on competitors selling Turkish cement imported into northern Syria, which was often sold more cheaply than cement produced at the Jalabiyeh Cement Plant. LCS executives made clear to the intermediaries negotiating with ISIS that, in exchange for LCS paying ISIS 750 Syrian Pounds per each ton of cement that it sold, they expected ISIS to take action against its competitors, either by stopping the sale of competing imported Turkish cement in the areas under ISIS's control, or by imposing taxes on competing cement that would allow LCS to raise the prices at which it sold cement.

"In the midst of a civil war, Lafarge made the unthinkable choice to put money into the hands of ISIS, one of the world's most barbaric terrorist organizations, so that it could continue selling cement," said U.S. Attorney Breon Peace for the Eastern District of New York. "Lafarge did this not merely in exchange for permission to operate its cement plant—which would have been bad enough—but also to leverage its relationship with ISIS for economic advantage, seeking ISIS's assistance to hurt Lafarge's competition in exchange for a cut of Lafarge's sales. Today, Lafarge has admitted and taken responsibility for its staggering crime. Never before has a corporation been charged with providing material support and resources to foreign terrorist organizations. This unprecedented charge and resolution reflect the extraordinary crimes committed and demonstrates that corporations that take actions in contravention of our national security interests in violation of the law will be held to account."

"This guilty plea is a result of extraordinary collaboration among the FBI, the Department of Justice, and our international partners," said FBI Deputy Director Paul Abbate. "The result demonstrates to anyone who would seek to contribute to ISIS's terrorist activities, that the FBI will relentlessly pursue, and hold them accountable, regardless of where, or how, they attempt to hide."

From August 2013 through October 2014, Lafarge and LCS paid ISIS and ANF, through intermediaries, the equivalent of approximately $5.92 million, consisting of fixed monthly "donation" payments to ISIS and ANF, payments to ISIS-controlled suppliers to purchase raw materials, and variable payments based on the amount of cement LCS sold. Lafarge and LCS also paid the equivalent of approximately $1.11 million to the third-party intermediaries for negotiating with and making payments to ISIS and ANF on Lafarge's and LCS's behalf. In addition, when LCS eventually evacuated the Jalabiyeh Cement Plant in September 2014, ISIS took possession of cement that LCS had produced in furtherance of the conspiracy, and ISIS sold the cement at prices that would have yielded ISIS approximately $3.21 million. As a result of the scheme, LCS obtained approximately $70.30 million in total sales revenue from August 2013 through 2014. The gains to all participants in the conspiracy, including LCS, the intermediaries and the terrorist groups, totaled approximately $80.54 million.

Lafarge and LCS executives actively concealed their scheme to provide material support to ISIS and ANF. For example:

- Lafarge and LCS executives required intermediaries to create business entities with names not obviously linked to the intermediaries and created invoices with false descriptions of services rendered for an intermediary to submit to LCS.
- LCS executives structured the revenue-sharing payments to ISIS so that LCS's customers would pay ISIS the amounts owed under LCS's agreement with ISIS, while LCS discounted the prices it charged to the customers to reimburse them. To ensure that LCS's customers did not underpay ISIS, LCS agreed to provide ISIS with periodic sales reports, which ISIS could use to verify that LCS's customers were paying the amounts owed under the terms of LCS's agreement with ISIS.
- To further conceal the arrangements, Lafarge and LCS executives attempted to require ISIS not to include the name "Lafarge" on the documents memorializing and implementing their agreements.
- Many of the Lafarge and LCS executives involved in the scheme used personal email addresses, rather than their corporate email addresses, to carry out of the conspiracy.
- In October 2014, as a condition of paying an intermediary for having negotiated with ISIS and other armed groups, Lafarge and LCS executives required the

intermediary to sign an agreement terminating his agreement to provide services to LCS. Critically, the Lafarge and LCS executives backdated the termination agreement to Aug. 18, 2014, a date shortly after the United Nations Security Council had issued a resolution calling on member states to prohibit doing business with ISIS and ANF, to falsely suggest that he had not been negotiating with ISIS on behalf of LCS after the U.N. resolution.

Lafarge was eventually acquired by a competitor (the Successor Company) in a transaction that closed on July 10, 2015. Lafarge executives did not disclose LCS's payments to ISIS and ANF to the Successor Company during pre-acquisition diligence meetings, and the Successor Company conducted neither pre- nor post-acquisition due diligence of LCS's operations in Syria, which had terminated by the time the transaction closed. Lafarge, LCS and the Successor Company also did not self-report the conduct or fully cooperate in the investigation.

Lafarge and its subsidiary pleaded guilty to conspiring to provide material support to designated foreign terrorist organizations and admitted to negotiating with and paying armed groups and terrorists, negotiating revenue-sharing agreements with ISIS to seek economic advantage, and concealing their payments, falsified records, and backdated contracts.

The FBI's New York Joint Terrorism Task Force is investigating the case. The Justice Department's Office of International Affairs provided critical assistance in this case. The Department also appreciates the significant cooperation and assistance provided by the French, Moroccan and Lebanese authorities . . .

Updated October 18, 2022

AND

Lafarge Pleads Guilty to Financing ISIS, Agrees to Pay $778 M Fine (article by Henry Pope, 20 October 2022)[2]

Lafarge, the world's largest cement manufacturer, pleaded guilty in a U.S. court Tuesday to conspiring to finance terrorist organizations, including the Islamic State, in exchange for preferential treatment for its Syria-based operations.

The French cement company subsequently agreed to pay US$778 million in fines and forfeitures to the American government, as penance for financing ISIS and the al-Nusrah Front (ANF) via its cement plant operations in war-torn Syria.

Lafarge, a division of Holcim Group, a Swiss multinational building company, operated a cement plant in the Jalabiyeh region of northern Syria between 2010 and 2014 that had cost approximately $680 million to develop, according to the U.-S. Department of Justice (DOJ).

At the outbreak of Syrian Civil War in 2011, executives at the cement manufacturing company negotiated clandestine agreements, wherein they paid armed factions to protect their employees and receive preferential treatment, out of economic self-interest.

[2] https://www.occrp.org/en/daily/16923-lafarge-pleads-guilty-to-financing-isis-agrees-to-pay-778m-fine

Raw materials were purchased from ISIS-controlled suppliers and monthly taxes were paid so that, in exchange, Lafarge personnel could traverse checkpoints controlled by the armed groups around its Jalabiyeh Cement Plant.

From August 2013 to October 2014, for instance, $5.92 million was paid to terrorist groups in the form of monthly "donations". And in September 2014, when the French company abandoned the plant, ISIS swooped in and sold the remaining cement, valued at $3.21 million.

"In the midst of a civil war, Lafarge made the unthinkable choice to put money into the hands of ISIS, one of the world's most barbaric terrorist organizations, so that it could continue selling cement," said U.S. Attorney Breon Peace for the Eastern District of New York.

Assistant Attorney General Matthew G. Olsen, meanwhile, noted how the funds supplied by the French cement manufacturer to ISIS and ANF allowed the world's most notorious terrorist organizations to brutalize innocent civilians across Syria.

The amounts paid in these tributes were reportedly structured according to the quantities of cement that the company could sell, as part of a revenue-sharing agreement that encouraged the terrorist groups to act in Lavarge's economic interests.

"Lafarge did this not merely in exchange for permission to operate its cement plant—which would have been bad enough—but also to leverage its relationship with ISIS for economic advantage, seeking ISIS's assistance to hurt Lafarge's competition in exchange for a cut of Lafarge's sales," Peace said.

The company's executives petitioned ISIS to impose costs on its competitors who sold Turkish cement imported into northern Syria, a product that otherwise would have been cheaper than the cement produced at the Jalabiyeh Cement Plant, the DOJ noted.

This included cases where ISIS outright stopped the sale of imported Turkish cement in areas that were under the control of the terrorist group.

Part of Lafarge's guilty plea included admissions that it falsified records and backdated contracts with its terrorist partners, as part of its clandestine arrangements to avoid accountability.

For example, company executives asked ISIS not to include the Lafarge name on any documents that would otherwise incriminate them. They also used their personal email addresses, in lieu of their corporate ones, to carry out the conspiracy, the DOJ said.

All in all, the French cement company made $70.30 million in profits from their business dealings with the terrorist groups from August 2013 through 2014.

Eric Olsen, the company's first chief executive following the merger with Holcim, stepped down in 2017 after the payments originally came to light.

An April 2017 statement from the board concluded that Olsen "was not responsible for, nor thought to be aware of, any wrongdoings," as part of the company's internal review.

However, the board did acknowledge that "a number of measures taken to continue safe operations at the Syrian plant were unacceptable, and significant errors of judgement were made that contravened the applicable code of conduct."

Lafarge has similarly had its name dragged through the mud in the French legal system, following a 2016 criminal complaint filed by the Paris-based Sherpa, a watchdog NGO that reports on corporate crime.

Following Sherpa's 2018 submission of a legal memorandum into Lafarge's actions, the company was charged in French court with crimes against humanity.

Anna Kiefer, the group's advocacy and litigation director, recounted how the original ruling found the cement company guilty of financing the Islamic State, but that these actions did not represent an intent to commit crimes against humanity.

The Supreme Court, however, intervened to reverse the ruling on Lafarge's intent, stating that its executives must've known that ISIS planned to use the company's money to fund acts of terror in Syria and across the globe.

This decision, Kiefer wrote, set "a ground-breaking precedent on corporate complicity in crimes against humanity."

As another chapter in this legal saga comes to a close, U.S. Deputy Attorney General Lisa O. Monaco remarked that the case "sends the clear message to all companies, but especially those operating in high-risk environments, to invest in robust compliance programs, pay vigilant attention to national security compliance risks, and conduct careful due diligence in mergers and acquisitions."

"The terrorism crimes to which Lafarge and its subsidiary have pleaded guilty," Monaco added, "are a vivid reminder of how corporate crime can intersect with national security."

Chapter 12
Violating Economic Sanctions

i) **ING Bank**

ING Bank N.V. Agrees to Forfeit $619 Million for Illegal Transactions with Cuban and Iranian Entities (US DoJ press report, June 12, 2012)[1]

WASHINGTON—ING Bank N.V., a financial institution headquartered in Amsterdam, has agreed to forfeit $619 million to the Justice Department and the New York County District Attorney's Office for conspiring to violate the International Emergency Economic Powers Act (IEEPA) and the Trading with the Enemy Act (TWEA) and for violating New York state laws by illegally moving billions of dollars through the U.S. financial system on behalf of sanctioned Cuban and Iranian entities. The bank has also entered into a parallel settlement agreement with the Treasury Department's Office of Foreign Assets Control (OFAC) . . .

A criminal information was filed today in federal court in the District of Columbia charging ING Bank N.V. with one count of knowingly and willfully conspiring to violate the IEEPA and TWEA. ING Bank waived the federal indictment, agreed to the filing of the information and has accepted responsibility for its criminal conduct and that of its employees. ING Bank agreed to forfeit $619 million as part of the deferred prosecution agreements reached with the Justice Department and the New York County District Attorney's Office.

According to court documents, starting in the early 1990s and continuing until 2007, ING Bank violated U.S. and New York state laws by moving more than $2 billion illegally through the U.S. financial system—via more than 20,000 transactions—on behalf of Cuban and Iranian entities subject to U.S. economic sanctions. ING Bank knowingly and willfully engaged in this criminal conduct,

[1] https://www.justice.gov/opa/pr/ing-bank-nv-agrees-forfeit-619-million-illegal-transactions-cuban-and-iranian-entities-0 . See also the article: More than Sanctions: Criminally Prosecute Big Banks for Money Laundering article by Allison Haugen, dated May 2015 in the International Affairs Review at: https://www.iar-gwu.org/blog/2015/05/19/more-than-sanctions-criminally-prosecute-big-banks-for-money-laundering

D. Smith, *Money Laundering, Terrorist Financing and Virtual Assets*, Contributions to Finance and Accounting, https://doi.org/10.1007/978-3-031-59842-5_12

which caused unaffiliated U.S. financial institutions to process transactions that otherwise should have been rejected, blocked or stopped for investigation under regulations by OFAC relating to transactions involving sanctioned countries and parties.

"The fine announced today is the largest ever against a bank in connection with an investigation into U.S. sanctions violations and related offenses and underscores the national security implications of ING Bank's criminal conduct. For more than a decade, ING Bank helped provide state sponsors of terror and other sanctioned entities with access to the U.S. financial system, allowing them to move billions of dollars through U.S. banks for illicit purchases and other activities," said Assistant Attorney General Monaco. "I applaud the agents, analysts and prosecutors who for years pursued this case."

"Banks that try to skirt U.S. sanctions laws undermine the integrity of our financial system and threaten our national security," said U.S. Attorney Machen. "When banks place their loyalty to sanctioned clients above their obligation to follow the law, we will hold them accountable. On more than 20,000 occasions, ING intentionally manipulated financial and trade transactions to remove references to Iran, Cuba and other sanctioned countries and entities. Today's $619 million forfeiture—the largest ever—holds ING accountable for its wrongdoing."

"For years, ING Bank blatantly violated U.S. laws governing transactions involving Cuba and Iran, and then used shell companies and other deceptive measures to cover up its criminal conduct," said Assistant Attorney General Breuer. "Today's resolution reflects a strong collaboration among federal and state law enforcement partners to hold ING accountable."

"Investigations of financial institutions, businesses and individuals who violate U.S. sanctions by misusing banks in New York are vitally important to national security and the integrity of our banking system," said New York County District Attorney Vance. "These cases give teeth to sanctions enforcement, send a strong message about the need for transparency in international banking and ultimately contribute to the fight against money laundering and terror financing. I thank our federal partners for their cooperation and assistance in pursuing this investigation."

"Today, ING Bank was held accountable for their illegal actions involving the movement of more than $2 billion through the U.S. financial system on behalf of Cuban and Iranian entities subject to U.S. economic sanctions," said FBI Assistant Director in Charge McJunkin. "Investigations of this type are complicated and demand significant time and dedication from agents, analysts and prosecutors. In this case, their steadfast tenacity brought this case through to today's result, and we will continue to pursue these matters in diligent fashion."

"In today's environment of increasingly sophisticated financial markets, it's critical that global institutions follow U.S. law, including sanctions against other countries," said IRS Criminal Investigation Chief Weber. "The IRS is proud to share its world-renowned financial investigative expertise in this and other complex financial investigations. Creating new strategies and models of cooperation among our law enforcement partners to ensure international financial compliance is a top-priority of the IRS."

"Our sanctions laws reflect core U.S. national security and foreign policy interests and OFAC polices them aggressively. Today's historic settlement should serve as a clear warning to anyone who would consider profiting by evading U.S. sanctions," said OFAC Director Szubin. "We commend our federal and state colleagues for their work on this important investigation."

The Scheme

According to court documents, ING Bank committed its criminal conduct by, among other things, processing payments for ING Bank's Cuban banking operations through its branch in Curaçao on behalf of Cuban customers without reference to the payments' origin, and by providing U.S. dollar trade finance services to sanctioned entities through misleading payment messages, shell companies and the misuse of ING Bank's internal suspense account.

Furthermore, ING Bank eliminated payment data that would have revealed the involvement of sanctioned countries and entities, including Cuba and Iran; advised sanctioned clients on how to conceal their involvement in U.S. dollar transactions; fabricated ING Bank endorsement stamps for two Cuban banks to fraudulently process U.S. dollar travelers' checks; and threatened to punish certain employees if they failed to take specified steps to remove references to sanctioned entities in payment messages.

According to court documents, this conduct occurred in various business units in ING Bank's wholesale banking division and in locations around the world with the knowledge, approval and encouragement of senior corporate managers and legal and compliance departments. Over the years, several ING Bank employees raised concerns to management about the bank's sanctions violations. However, no action was taken.

For decades, the United States has employed sanctions and embargoes on Iran and Cuba. Financial transactions conducted by wire on behalf of Iranian or Cuban financial institutions have been subject to these U.S. sanctions. The TWEA prohibits U.S. persons from engaging in financial transactions involving or benefiting Cuba or Cuban nationals and prohibits attempts to evade or avoid these restrictions. IEEPA makes it a crime to willfully attempt to commit, conspire to commit, or aid and abet in the commission of any violations of the Iranian Transaction Regulations, which prohibit the exportation of any services from the United States to Iran and any attempts to evade or avoid these restrictions. IEEPA and TWEA regulations are administered by OFAC.

The Investigation

The Justice Department's investigation into ING Bank arose out of ongoing investigations into the illegal export of goods from the United States to sanctioned countries, including Iran. For instance, ING processed payments on behalf of one customer, Aviation Services International B.V. (ASI), a Dutch aviation company which was the subject of a U.S. Commerce Department-initiated criminal investigation, through the United States for trade services relating to the procurement by ASI of dual-use U.S. aviation parts for ASI's Iranian clients. The ING Bank investigation also resulted in part from a criminal referral from OFAC, which was conducting its own probe of ING Bank.

ING Bank's forfeiture of $309.5 million to the United States and $309.5 million to the New York County District Attorney's Office will settle forfeiture claims by the Department of Justice and the state of New York. In light of the bank's remedial actions to date and its willingness to acknowledge responsibility for its actions, the Department will recommend the dismissal of the information in 18 months, provided ING Bank fully cooperates with, and abides by, the terms of the deferred prosecution agreement.

OFAC's settlement agreement with ING deems the bank's obligations to pay a civil settlement amount of $619 million to be satisfied by its payment of an equal amount to the Justice Department and the state of New York. OFAC's settlement agreement further requires the bank to conduct a review of its policies and procedures and their implementation, taking a risk-based sampling of U.S. dollar payments, to ensure that its OFAC compliance program is functioning effectively to detect, correct and report apparent sanctions violations to OFAC.

The case was prosecuted by Trial Attorney Jonathan C. Poling of the Justice Department's National Security Division; Assistant U.S. Attorneys Ann H. Petalas and George P. Varghese, of the National Security Section of the U.S. Attorney's Office for the District of Columbia; and Trial Attorney Matthew Klecka of the Criminal Division's Asset Forfeiture and Money Laundering Section.

The case was investigated by the FBI's Washington Field Office and the IRS-Criminal Investigation's Washington Field Division, with assistance from the Treasury Department's OFAC and the Commerce Department's Bureau of Industry and Security.

The Department of Justice expressed its gratitude to Executive Assistant District Attorney, Chief of Investigation Division Adam Kaufmann; and Assistant District Attorneys Sally Pritchard and Garrett Lynch of the New York County District Attorney's Office, Major Economic Crimes Bureau.

Updated September 15, 2014

ii) **BNP Paribas Bank** (US DoJ press report)[2]

BNP Paribas S.A. (BNPP), a global financial institution headquartered in Paris, was sentenced today for conspiring to violate the International Emergency Economic Powers Act (IEEPA) and the Trading with the Enemy Act (TWEA) by processing billions of dollars of transactions through the U.S. financial system on behalf of Sudanese, Iranian and Cuban entities subject to U.S. economic sanctions. BNPP was

[2] https://www.justice.gov/opa/pr/bnp-paribas-sentenced-conspiring-violate-international-emergency-economic-powers-act-and#:~:text="BNPP%2C-the-world%27s-fourth-largest,%2C"-said-U.S.-Attorney-Bharara

sentenced to a five-year term of probation, and ordered to forfeit $8,833,600,000 to the United States and to pay a $140,000,000 fine. Today's sentencing is the first time a financial institution has been convicted and sentenced for violations of U.-S. economic sanctions, and the total financial penalty—including the forfeiture and criminal fine—is the largest financial penalty ever imposed in a criminal case ...

"BNP Paribas flouted U.S. sanctions laws to an unprecedented extreme, concealed its tracks, and then chose not to fully cooperate with U.S. law enforcement, leading to a criminal guilty plea and nearly $9 billion penalty" said Assistant Attorney General Caldwell. "BNPP deliberately disregarded the law and provided rogue nations, and Sudan in particular, with vital access to the global financial system, helping that country's lawless government to harbor and support terrorists and to persecute its own people. Today's sentence demonstrates that financial institutions will be punished severely but appropriately for violating sanctions laws and risking our national security interests."

"BNPP, the world's fourth largest bank, has now been sentenced to pay a record penalty of almost $9 billion for sanctions violations that unlawfully opened the U.S. financial markets to Sudan, Iran, and Cuba," said U.S. Attorney Bharara. "BNPP provided access to billions of dollars to these sanctioned countries, and did so deliberately and secretly, in ways designed to evade detection by the U.-S. authorities. The sentence imposed today is appropriate for BNPP's years-long and wide-ranging criminal conduct."

"The sentencing of BNP Paribas Bank and the $9 Billion monetary penalty should sound the alarm to international financial institutions thinking of perpetrating these crimes," said Chief Weber. "The ability of IRS-CI and our partners to expose blatant violations of U.S. embargos and sanctions has changed the way financial matters are handled worldwide. We will continue to use our financial expertise to uncover these types of violations, as well as methodical and deliberate actions to conceal prohibited transactions from U.S. regulators and law enforcement."

In connection with its guilty plea on July 9, 2014, BNPP admitted that from at least 2004 through 2012, it knowingly and willfully moved over $8.8 billion through the U.S. financial system on behalf of Sudanese, Iranian and Cuban sanctioned entities, in violation of U.S. economic sanctions. The majority of illegal payments were made on behalf of sanctioned entities in Sudan, which was subject to U.-S. embargo based on the Sudanese government's role in facilitating terrorism and committing human rights abuses. BNPP processed approximately $6.4 billion through the United States on behalf of Sudanese sanctioned entities from July 2006 through June 2007, including approximately $4 billion on behalf of a financial institution owned by the government of Sudan, even as internal emails showed BNPP employees expressing concern about the bank's assisting the Sudanese government in light of its role in supporting international terrorism and committing human rights abuses during the same time period. Indeed, in March 2007, a senior compliance officer at BNPP wrote to other high-level BNPP compliance and legal employees reminding them that certain Sudanese banks with which BNPP dealt "play a pivotal part in the support of the Sudanese government which ... has hosted Osama Bin Laden and refuses the United Nations intervention in Darfur."

Similarly, from October 2004 through early 2010, BNPP knowingly and willfully processed approximately $1.74 billion on behalf of Cuban sanctioned entities. BNPP admitted that it continued to do U.S. dollar business with Cuba long after it was clear that such business was illegal. BNPP further admitted that its conduct with regard to the Cuban embargo was both "cavalier" and "criminal."

BNPP also engaged in more than $650 million of transactions involving entities tied to Iran, and this conduct continued into 2012—nearly two years after the bank had commenced an internal investigation into its sanctions compliance and pledged to cooperate with the government. The illicit Iranian transactions included transactions for a petroleum company based in Dubai that was effectively a front for an Iranian petroleum company and an Iranian oil company.

In accepting BNPP's guilty plea, Judge Schofield stated that BNPP's actions "not only flouted U.S. foreign policy but also provided support to governments that threaten both our regional and national security and, in the case of Sudan, a government that has committed flagrant human rights abuses and has known links to terrorism." Judge Schofield further stated that the forfeiture of over $8 billion will "surely have a deterrent effect on others that may be tempted to engage in similar conduct, all of whom should be aware that no financial institution is immune from the rule of law."

The Justice Department is exploring ways to use the forfeited funds to compensate individuals who may have been harmed by the sanctioned regimes of Sudan, Iran and Cuba. As a preliminary step in this process, the Justice Department is inviting such individuals or their representatives to provide information describing the nature and value of the harm they suffered. Beginning today (May 1, 2015), interested persons can learn more about this process and submit their information at www.usvbnpp.com, or call 888-272-5632 (within North America) or 317-324-0382 (internationally).

In addition to its federal criminal conviction, BNPP pleaded guilty in New York State Supreme Court to falsifying business records and conspiring to falsify business records. BNPP also agreed to a cease and desist order and to pay a civil monetary penalty of $508 million to the Board of Governors of the Federal Reserve System. The New York State Department of Financial Services announced that BNPP agreed to, among other things, terminate or separate from the bank 13 employees, including the Group Chief Operating Officer and other senior executives; suspend U.S. dollar clearing operations through its New York Branch and other affiliates for one year for business lines on which the misconduct centered; extend for two years a monitorship put in place in 2013; and pay a monetary penalty of $2.24 billion. In satisfying its criminal forfeiture penalty, BNPP will receive credit for payments it made in connection with its resolution of these related state and regulatory matters. The Treasury Department's Office of Foreign Assets Control also levied a fine of $963 million, which will be satisfied by payments made to the Justice Department . . .

Updated May 1, 2015

Chapter 13
Virtual Assets

1. **Qakbot** (NCA Press report,[1] dated 29 **August 2023)**

Qakbot: cyber crime service taken out in international operation (August 2023)

An international operation involving the National Crime Agency has led to the takedown of Qakbot malware, which facilitated ransomware attacks and caused millions of pounds worth of damage worldwide.

Qakbot malware (also known as 'Qbot' and 'Pinkslipbot') infected more than 700,000 computers globally, including in the UK, via spam emails.

The operation, led by the FBI and DoJ, saw the seizure of Qakbot's infrastructure in the US and across Europe on Saturday [26 August], with the NCA ensuring UK servers were taken offline.

US authorities also seized around 8.6 million dollars-worth of illicit cryptocurrency profits.

The administrators behind Qakbot offered access to it for a fee and it was a go-to service for cyber criminals for at least 16 years.

It was used by the criminal groups behind the notorious Conti, ProLock, Egregor, REvil, MegaCortex, and Black Basta ransomware strains to steal personal data, including banking credentials, from victims.

Will Lyne, Head of Cyber Intelligence at the NCA, said: "This investigation has taken out a prolific malware that caused significant damage to victims in the UK and around the world.

"Qakbot was a key enabler within the cyber crime ecosystem, facilitating ransomware attacks and other serious threats.

"The NCA is focused on disrupting the highest harm cyber criminals by targeting the tools and services that underpin their offending.

[1] https://www.nationalcrimeagency.gov.uk/news/qakbot-cyber-crime-service-taken-out-in-international-operation

D. Smith, *Money Laundering, Terrorist Financing and Virtual Assets*, Contributions to Finance and Accounting, https://doi.org/10.1007/978-3-031-59842-5_13

"This activity demonstrates how, working alongside international partners, we are having an impact on those key enablers and the ransomware business model."

The NCSC's Ransomware Hub offers a range of information and guidance aimed at helping organisations defend against ransomware.

AND

Identification and Disruption of QakBot Infrastructure[2] (report dated August 30, 2023)

The Cybersecurity and Infrastructure Security Agency (CISA) and Federal Bureau of Investigation (FBI) are releasing this joint Cybersecurity Advisory (CSA) to disseminate QakBot infrastructure indicators of compromise (IOCs) identified through FBI investigations as of August 2023. On August 25, FBI and international partners executed a coordinated operation to disrupt QakBot infrastructure worldwide. Disruption operations targeting QakBot infrastructure resulted in the botnet takeover, which severed the connection between victim computers and QakBot command and control (C2) servers. The FBI is working closely with industry partners to share information about the malware to maximize detection, remediation, and prevention measures for network defenders.

CISA and FBI encourage organizations to implement the recommendations in the Mitigations section to reduce the likelihood of QakBot-related activity and promote identification of QakBot-facilitated ransomware and malware infections. **Note:** The disruption of QakBot infrastructure does not mitigate other previously installed malware or ransomware on victim computers. If potential compromise is detected, administrators should apply the incident response recommendations included in this CSA and report key findings to a local FBI Field Office or CISA at cisa.gov/report.

2. **Bitzlato**

Founder and Majority Owner of Cryptocurrency Exchange Charged with Processing Over $700 Million of Illicit Funds (US DoJ note dated January 18, 2023)[3]

The founder and majority owner of a cryptocurrency exchange, Bitzlato Ltd (Bitzlato), was arrested last night in Miami for his alleged operation of a money transmitting business that transported and transmitted illicit funds and that failed to meet U.S. regulatory safeguards, including anti-money laundering requirements.

Anatoly Legkodymov, 40, a Russian national who resides in Shenzhen, People's Republic of China, is scheduled to be arraigned this afternoon in the U.S. District Court for the Southern District of Florida. French authorities and the U.-S. Department of the Treasury's Financial Crimes Enforcement Network (FinCEN) are taking concurrent enforcement actions.

"Today the Department of Justice dealt a significant blow to the cryptocrime ecosystem," said Deputy Attorney General Lisa O. Monaco. "Overnight, the

[2] https://www.cisa.gov/news-events/cybersecurity-advisories/aa23-242a

[3] https://www.justice.gov/opa/pr/founder-and-majority-owner-cryptocurrency-exchange-charged-processing-over-700-million

Department worked with key partners here and abroad to disrupt Bitzlato, the China-based money laundering engine that fueled a high-tech axis of cryptocrime, and to arrest its founder, Russian national Anatoly Legkodymov. Today's actions send the clear message: whether you break our laws from China or Europe—or abuse our financial system from a tropical island—you can expect to answer for your crimes inside a United States courtroom."

"As alleged, the defendant helped operate a cryptocurrency exchange that failed to implement required anti-money laundering safeguards and enabled criminals to profit from their wrongdoing, including ransomware and drug trafficking," said Assistant Attorney General Kenneth A. Polite, Jr. of the Justice Department's Criminal Division. "The National Cryptocurrency Enforcement Team's tremendous efforts to disrupt Bitzlato and arrest the defendant demonstrate that we will continue to work with our partners—both foreign and domestic—to combat cryptocurrency-fueled crimes, even if they transcend international borders."

According to court documents, Legkodymov is a senior executive and the majority shareholder of Bitzlato, a Hong Kong-registered cryptocurrency exchange that operates globally. Bitzlato has marketed itself as requiring minimal identification from its users, specifying that "neither selfies nor passports [are] required." On occasions when Bitzlato did direct users to submit identifying information, it repeatedly allowed them to provide information belonging to "straw man" registrants.

"Institutions that trade in cryptocurrency are not above the law and their owners are not beyond our reach," said U.S. Attorney Breon Peace for the Eastern District of New York. "As alleged, Bitzlato sold itself to criminals as a no-questions-asked cryptocurrency exchange, and reaped hundreds of millions of dollars' worth of deposits as a result. The defendant is now paying the price for the malign role that his company played in the cryptocurrency ecosystem."

As a result of these deficient know-your-customer (KYC) procedures, Bitzlato allegedly became a haven for criminal proceeds and funds intended for use in criminal activity. Bitzlato's largest counterparty in cryptocurrency transactions was Hydra Market (Hydra), an anonymous, illicit online marketplace for narcotics, stolen financial information, fraudulent identification documents, and money laundering services that was the largest and longest running darknet market in the world. Hydra users exchanged more than $700 million in cryptocurrency with Bitzlato, either directly or through intermediaries, until Hydra was shuttered by U.S. and German law enforcement in April 2022. Bitzlato also received more than $15 million in ransomware proceeds.

"The FBI will continue to pursue actors who attempt to mask their criminal activity behind keyboards and use means such as cryptocurrency to evade law enforcement," said Associate Deputy Director Brian Turner of the FBI. "We, along with our federal and international partners, will work relentlessly to disrupt and dismantle these types of criminal enterprises. Today's arrest should serve as a reminder the FBI will impose risk and consequences upon those who engage in these activities."

"As alleged today, Legkodymov knowingly allowed Bitzlato to become a perceived safe haven for funds used for and resulting from a variety of criminal activities," said Assistant Director in Charge Michael J. Driscoll of the FBI New York Field Office. "The FBI and our partners remain steadfast in our commitment to keeping cryptocurrency markets—as with any financial market—free from illicit activity. Today's action should serve as an example of this commitment as Legkodymov will now face the consequences of his actions in our criminal justice system."

As alleged in the complaint, Bitzlato's customers routinely used the company's customer service portal to request support for transactions with Hydra, which Bitzlato often provided, and admitted in chats with Bitzlato personnel that they were trading under assumed identities. Moreover, Legkodymov and Bitzlato's other managers were aware that Bitzlato's accounts were rife with illicit activity and that many of its users were registered under others' identities. For instance, on May 29, 2019, Legkodymov used Bitzlato's internal chat system to write to a colleague that Bitzlato's users were "known to be crooks," using others' identity documents to register their accounts. Legkodymov was repeatedly warned by colleagues that Bitzlato's customer base consisted of "addicts who buy drugs at [] Hydra" and "drug traffickers," with one senior executive even stressing that Bitzlato should combat drug dealers only "nominally," to avoid hurting the company's bottom line. An internal spreadsheet saved in Bitzlato's shared management folder encapsulated the company's view of itself: "Positives: No KYC . . . Negatives: Dirty money . . . ."

As alleged in the complaint, although Bitzlato claimed not to accept users from the United States, it did substantial business with U.S.-based customers, and its customer service representatives repeatedly advised users that they could transfer funds from U.S. financial institutions. Moreover, Legkodymov—who himself administered Bitzlato from Miami in 2022 and 2023—received reports reflecting substantial traffic to Bitzlato's website from U.S.-based Internet Protocol addresses, including over 250 million such visits in July 2022.

Legkodymov is charged with conducting an unlicensed money transmitting business. If convicted, he faces a maximum penalty of 5 years in prison.

Concurrent with the arrest announced today, French authorities, working with Europol and partners in Spain, Portugal, and Cyprus, dismantled Bitzlato's digital infrastructure, seized Bitzlato's cryptocurrency, and took other enforcement actions.

In addition, the Treasury Department's FinCEN announced an Order pursuant to section 9714(a) of the Combating Russian Money Laundering Act, as amended, identifying Bitzlato as a "primary money laundering concern" in connection to Russian illicit finance. The order imposes a special measure prohibiting certain transmittals of funds involving Bitzlato by any covered financial institution.

National Cryptocurrency Enforcement Team (NCET) Trial Attorneys Alexander Mindlin, Scott Meisler, and Matthew Blackwood of the Justice Department's Criminal Division and Assistant U.S. Attorney Artie McConnell for the Eastern District of New York are prosecuting the case, with assistance from Paralegal Specialist Mary Clare McMahon.

The Justice Department investigated this case in close coordination with French law enforcement authorities and the Treasury Department's FinCEN, both of which took separate enforcement actions today under their respective authorities. The Justice Department's Office of International Affairs and the FBI's Legal Attaché in France provided critical assistance in this case, with significant support from the department's Cyber Operations International Liaison. The NCET and U.-S. Attorney's Office for the Eastern District of New York also extend their appreciation to the Cyber Division of the Paris Prosecution Office and to France's Gendarmerie Nationale Cyberspace Command (Cyber Crime Investigation Unit / C3N). Assistance was also provided by the Customs and Border Protection, the Transportation Safety Administration, and the New York City Police Department. EUROPOL and Dutch and Belgian authorities have contributed to the overall investigation with respect to operational expertise, coordination, and information-sharing.

The NCET was established to combat the growing illicit use of cryptocurrencies and digital assets. Under the Criminal Division, the NCET conducts and supports investigations into individuals and entities that enable the use of digital assets to commit and facilitate a variety of crimes, with a particular focus on virtual currency exchanges, mixing and tumbling services, and infrastructure providers. The NCET also sets strategic priorities regarding digital asset technologies, identifies areas for increased investigative and prosecutorial focus, and leads the department's efforts to collaborate with domestic and foreign government agencies as well as the private sector to aggressively investigate and prosecute crimes involving cryptocurrency and digital assets.

A criminal complaint is merely an allegation. All defendants are presumed innocent until proven guilty beyond a reasonable doubt in a court of law.

Updated January 18, 2023

Attachment

Complaint [PDF, 837 KB]

AND

Bitzlato: senior management arrested[4]

Platform infrastructure shut down in France for allegedly laundering criminal assets, with six people targeted in Cyprus, Spain, Portugal and the USA

An operation led by French and US authorities, and strongly supported by Europol, has targeted the crypto exchange platform Bitzlato. The globally operating Hong Kong-registered cryptocurrency exchange is suspected of facilitating the laundering of large amounts of criminal proceeds and converting them into roubles. Law enforcement authorities took down the digital infrastructure of the service, based in France, and interrogated leading members of the platform's management. The operation also involved law enforcement and judicial authorities from Belgium, Cyprus, Portugal, Spain and the Netherlands.

[4] https://www.europol.europa.eu/media-press/newsroom/news/bitzlato-senior-management-arrested

Almost half of all Bitzlato transactions linked to criminal activities

Targeting crucial crime facilitators such as crypto exchanges is becoming a key priority in the battle against cybercrime. Bitzlato allowed the rapid conversion of various crypto-assets such as bitcoin, ethereum, litecoin, bitcoin cash, dash, dogecoin and USDT into Russian roubles. It is estimated that the crypto exchange platform has received a total of assets worth EUR 2.1 billion (BTC 119000).

While the conversions of crypto-assets into fiat currencies is not illegal, investigations into the cybercriminal operators indicated that large volumes of criminal assets were going through the platform. The analysis indicated that about 46% of the assets exchanged through Bitzlato, worth roughly EUR 1 billion, had links to criminal activities.

Cryptanalysis uncovered that the majority of suspicious transactions are linked to entities sanctioned by the Office of Foreign Assets Control (OFAC), with others linked to cyber scams, money laundering, ransomware and child abuse material. For example, investigations showed that 1.5 million BTC transactions have been made directly between Bitzlato users and the Hydramarket, taken down in April 2022.

This exchange platform, available both in Russian and English language, rented dedicated servers from a hosting company in France. The coordinated action of the judicial and law enforcement authorities from the different involved countries led to the takedown of the platform, seizures of present financial assets, and further technical analysis.

Overall results

- 5 individuals arrested so far (1 in Cyprus, 3 in Spain and 1 in the US);
- 1 individual questioned in Portugal;
- The main administrator arrested in the US;
- CEO, Financial director and Marketing director arrested in Spain;
- 8 house searches (4 in Spain, 1 in Cyprus, 2 in Portugal, 1 in US);
- Takedown of the digital infrastructure of the service, enabling further analysis and investigation;
- Seizures include crypto wallets worth about EUR 18 million in cryptocurrency at the time of writing, vehicles and electronic equipment;
- 100+ accounts at other crypto exchange frozen, involving a total of EUR 50 million.

Cryptoanalysis and international coordination to uncover links

During the first phases of the investigative activities, Europol facilitated the information exchange, provided analytical support linking available data to various criminal cases within and outside the EU, and supported the investigation through the analysis of millions of cryptocurrency transactions.

On the action day, Europol deployed 13 of its experts on the spot (10 in France, 1 in Cyprus, 1 in Spain and 1 in Portugal) and supported the deployment of national investigators in other countries taking part in the operational activities. Europol supported the law enforcement authorities involved with coordination related to cryptocurrency analysis, cross checking of operational information against Europol's databases, and operational analysis. At this moment, already over 3500 bitcoin addresses and over a 1000 Bitzlato user details showed links with various criminal cases reported in Europol's systems. Analysis of this data and other related cases is expected to trigger further investigative activities.

Law enforcement authorities involved

- Cyprus: Cyprus Police
- Belgium: Federal Police (Federale Politie/Police Fédérale)
- France: National Gendarmerie (Gendarmerie Nationale)
- United States: Federal Bureau of Investigation
- Spain: Civil Guard (Guardia Civil)
- Netherlands: National Police (Politie) and the Fiscal Information and Investigation Service (FIOD)
- Portugal: Judicial Police (Policia Judiciaria)

3. **FTX & Sam Bankman-Fried**[5]

The bankruptcy of FTX, a Bahamas-based cryptocurrency exchange, began in November 2022. The collapse of FTX, caused by a spike in customer withdrawals that exposed an $8 billion hole in FTX's accounts,[1] served as the impetus for its bankruptcy. Prior to its collapse, FTX was the third-largest cryptocurrency exchange by volume and had over one million users.

On 2 November 2022, *CoinDesk* published an article stating that Alameda Research, a trading firm affiliated with FTX and owned by FTX chief executive Sam Bankman-Fried, held a significant amount of FTX's exchange token, FTT.[2][3] The article triggered a spike in withdrawals from FTX, but eventually customers became unable to retrieve the money they had deposited in the exchange.[4] On 11 November, FTX, Alameda Research, and over 100 affiliated entities filed for bankruptcy. Bankman-Fried resigned as FTX CEO and was replaced by John J. Ray III.[5][6]

The collapse of FTX has had a wide impact on cryptocurrency markets, with comparisons made to the Enron scandal and Madoff investment scandal, and was described by federal prosecutors as "one of the biggest financial frauds in American history."[7][8] Following the bankruptcy, the Securities Commission of the Bahamas froze the assets of one of FTX's subsidiaries.[9] Bankman-Fried's net worth, estimated at $16 billion prior to the collapse, was reported as having been wiped out,[10] and several institutional investors of FTX wrote off their investment stakes in the company.[11][12] Some $473 million in funds were later taken from FTX in an "unauthorized transaction".[13] The collapse of FTX has resulted in a ripple effect across cryptocurrency markets, with the price of Bitcoin falling to its lowest level in two years.[14]

In late 2022 and early 2023, key executives from FTX and Alameda, such as Caroline Ellison, Gary Wang and Nishad Singh pleaded guilty to defrauding FTX

[5] https://en.wikipedia.org/wiki/Bankruptcy_of_FTX; see also FCPA Blog article by Harry Cassin dated 3 July 2023 entitled: Former FTX GC-Chief Compliance Officer helped insiders divert billions, complaint alleges at https://fcpablog.com/2023/07/03/former-ftx-gc-chief-compliance-officer-helped-insiders-divert-billions-complaint-alleges/

customers and related charges.[15] In October 2023, all three testified that it was Bankman-Fried that directed them to commit fraud.[16] On 2 November 2023, Sam Bankman-Fried was convicted of defrauding customers of FTX and lenders of Alameda Research.[17]

Background

Sam Bankman-Fried co-founded Alameda Research, a cryptocurrency trading firm, in 2017.[18] In 2019, Bankman-Fried had the idea of starting a cryptocurrency exchange to help bring in revenue to fund Alameda's activities, and founded FTX.[19] Bankman-Fried was the CEO of both companies until he formally stepped down from his position at Alameda in October 2021, promoting traders Caroline Ellison and Sam Trabucco to co-CEOs.[20] Ellison was reported to have a romantic involvement with Bankman-Fried.[21] As of August 2021, Bankman-Fried still owned 90% of Alameda.[18]

The close relationship and potential conflicts of interest between Alameda and FTX drew scrutiny from the rest of the cryptocurrency industry.[22][19] Alameda was once the largest trader on FTX, bringing liquidity to the exchange.[22] Between 1 June 2022 and 22 July 2022, Alameda's known wallets were the largest stablecoin depositors and sources of liquidity to all of FTX's known wallet addresses, accounting for 10% of Tether transfers and 30% of USD Coin transfers on the exchange.[22] According to John J. Ray III, Alameda had a "secret exemption" from FTX's auto-liquidation protocol.[23][24]

Alameda Research suffered a series of losses in May and June 2022, which anonymous sources told *The Wall Street Journal* resulted in FTX lending the trading firm more than half of its customer funds, a decision that the sources said FTX CEO Sam Bankman-Fried described as a 'poor judgment call'.[25][26] This was explicitly forbidden by FTX's terms-of-service.[27] On 12 November 2022, *The Wall Street Journal* reported that anonymous sources had said that Alameda CEO Caroline Ellison said that she, Bankman-Fried, Gary Wang, and Nishad Singh were aware of that decision.[28] The same was reported on *The New York Times* on 14 November 2022.[29] FTX used software to conceal the misuse of customer funds.[23][24]

Timeline

***CoinDesk* article**

In the days leading up to the crisis, *CoinDesk* reported that Alameda Research held a significant amount of FTT, and that these FTT holdings made up a considerable portion of their assets.[30] *CoinDesk* reported that there were $5.1 billion worth of FTT tokens in circulation, and that Alameda's balance sheet held $3.66 billion of "unlocked FTT", $2.16 billion of "FTT collateral", and $292 million of "locked FTT".[30] Following months of arguments and disagreements between Changpeng Zhao, the CEO of Binance, and Bankman-Fried, tensions between the two had intensified days before the crisis.[31] Zhao's firm Binance had obtained $2.1 billion in Binance USD and FTT coins in 2021, following a deal in which FTX bought back an equity stake held by Binance in FTX, and in early November 2022 it had 23 million FTT tokens, worth about $529 million at the time.[32]

Binance divestment and proposed acquisition

On 7 November 2022, Zhao announced that Binance had intended to sell its holdings in FTT.[33][32] The sale of Binance's holdings in FTT, compounded with the low trading volume of FTT and the enmity between Zhao and Bankman-Fried, resulted in the price of the token plummeting.[34][35][36] Binance had received FTT from FTX in 2021 during a transaction in which FTX bought back Binance's equity stake in FTX.[37] Zhao cited "recent revelations that came to light" as the motivation for selling FTT.[37] *Bloomberg* and *TechCrunch* reported that any sale by Binance would likely have an outsized impact on FTT's price, given the token's low trading volume.[38][39]The announcement by Zhao of the pending sale and disputes between Zhao and Bankman-Fried on Twitter led to a decline in the price of FTT and other cryptocurrencies,[40] resulting in $6 billion of customer withdrawals from FTX.[41] FTX became unable to meet the demand for further withdrawals, and on 8 November, Bankman-Fried and Zhao jointly announced Binance had entered into a non-binding agreement to purchase FTX to ensure that customers could recover their assets in a timely manner.[42][43] The deal did not include the sale of FTX.US.[42]Zhao announced on Twitter that the company would complete due diligence soon, adding that all crypto exchanges should avoid using tokens as collateral.[44][45] He also wrote that he expected FTT to be "highly volatile in the coming days as things develop". On the day of that announcement, FTT lost 80 percent of its value.[46]

Binance acquisition dropped

On 9 November, Bloomberg called the acquisition of FTX by Binance "unlikely" due to the poor state of FTX's finances.[47] Bloomberg also reported that the United States Securities and Exchange Commission and Commodity Futures Trading Commission were investigating the nature of FTX's connections to Bankman-Fried's other holdings and its handling of client funds.[48] Later that day, the *Wall Street Journal*reported that Binance would not move forward with the deal to acquire FTX.[49] Binance cited FTX's reported mishandling of customer funds and pending investigations of FTX as the reasons for not pursuing the deal.[50] Bankman-Fried said in a Slack message that FTX had learned through the press about Binance's concerns and decision.[51]

Collapse and further rescue attempts

On 9 November, FTX's website said that it was not processing withdrawals at that time.[41] Bankman-Fried said that although the firm's assets were worth more than its clients' deposits, it would need funds from outside to meet demand for withdrawals due to a lack of liquidity.[52][53]Bankman-Fried stated on 9 November that FTX.US, as a separate company, was "not currently impacted" by the crisis.[54]

On 10 November, *Axios* reported that FTX approached Kraken for a potential rescue deal.[55] Bankman-Fried made several statements on 10 November, taking responsibility for FTX's failure and indicating that FTX was attempting to raise $10 billion in emergency financing to remain solvent.[56][57][58] Bankman-Fried also announced that Alameda Research would cease trading and end operations.[59] FTX's in-house legal and compliance teams had, for the most part, resigned by 10 November.[60][61] Anonymous sources cited by the *Wall Street Journal* on

10 November said that Alameda Research owed FTX some $10 billion, as FTX had lent funds placed on the exchange for trading to Alameda so that Alameda could make investments with the money.[62]

Though Bankman-Fried said that FTX.US customers did not have reason to worry on Twitter on 10 November, employees began attempting to sell assets belonging to the firm on the same day.[63] These assets include stock-clearing company Embed Financial Technologies and the naming rights to FTX Arena.[63] Disagreements emerged between remaining executives, with Bankman-Fried and FTX COO Constance Wang resisting urges from Ryne Miller, a member of FTX US's legal team, to end trading on the exchanges.[64] Bankman-Fried continued to seek funding even as Miller informed other executives that he believed there was a "0%" chance of securing further investment.[64] Miller and other executives asked Bankman-Fried to cede control of FTX US to them, which he resisted.[64] On 11 November, Bankman-Fried announced that he had filed FTX US for bankruptcy along with FTX and Alameda.[65] Bankman-Fried continued to seek capital for FTX after the bankruptcy, and claimed without evidence that a potential backer had emerged soon after the filing.[64]

On 12 November, anonymous sources cited by the *Wall Street Journal* said Alameda CEO Caroline Ellison disclosed to other Alameda employees that she, Sam Bankman-Fried, Gary Wang, and Nishad Singh knew that client deposits were transferred from FTX to Alameda.[66]An anonymous source cited by the *New York Times* on 14 November said the same.[67] Anonymous sources cited by the *Wall Street Journal*said the funds were used in part to pay back loans Alameda had taken to make investments.[66] On 10 November, the Securities Commission of the Bahamas froze the assets of one of FTX's subsidiaries, FTX Digital Markets Ltd, "and related parties", and provisionally appointed an attorney as liquidator.[68][69] Japan's Financial Services Agency ordered FTX Japan to suspend some operations.[70][71] The company's Australian subsidiary was placed under administration.[70]

On the same day, a team running the FTX Future Fund, a charitable group bankrolled by Bankman-Fried, announced their collective resignations.[72] Future Fund had committed $160 million in charitable grants and investments by 1 September of that year.[73]

Bankruptcy

On 11 November, FTX, FTX US, Alameda Research, and more than 100 affiliates filed for bankruptcy in Delaware.[74][72][75] Anonymous sources cited by the *New York Times* said that the exchange owes as much as $8 billion.[72] The crypto lender BlockFi, which was affiliated with FTX, announced on 10 November that it was suspending operations as a result of FTX's collapse.[72] Bankman-Fried resigned as CEO and was replaced by John J. Ray III, a corporate restructuring specialist who previously oversaw the liquidation of Enron.[74][75][76] As of 12 November, Bankman-Fried told Reuters that he was still in the Bahamas,[77] though other high-ranking FTX employees had begun leaving for Hong Kong, the location of the company's former headquarters, or other locations.[78] Authorities in the Bahamas, including the Royal Bahamas Police Force, questioned Bankman-Fried on 12 November.[79] Despite FTX's bankruptcy, Bankman-Fried continued to attempt to raise money for the firm during the weekend of 12 and 13 November.[80]

Unauthorized transactions

Late on 11 November, some $473 million in funds were removed from FTX through what Ryne Miller, FTX US's general counsel, characterized as "unauthorized transactions".[81] Miller further announced that FTX and FTX US intended to move remaining funds denominated in cryptocurrency to offline "cold storage".[81] The funds taken from FTX were mostly stablecoins such as Tether, and were quickly exchanged for Ether, a method used by cryptocurrency thieves to thwart attempts to retrieve stolen funds.[82] A person speaking on behalf of FTX in a Telegram chat referred to the "unauthorized transactions" as a "hack" and encouraged users to delete FTX mobile apps as they were compromised.[78] Kraken has since announced its assistance in identifying the perpetrator.[83] On 14 November, Kraken's chief security officer said on Twitter that the firm knew "the identity" of a user who paid transaction fees associated with moving the stolen money through their Kraken account.[84] In an interview with Kelsey Piper published 16 November by *Vox*, Bankman-Fried blamed an "ex-employee" or malware on a device owned by an ex-employee for the theft.[85]

Between $1 billion and $2 billion in customer funds reportedly could not be accounted for as of 12 November.[86] The *Financial Times* reported that FTX's balance sheet shortly before the bankruptcy showed $9 billion in liabilities against $900 million in liquid assets, $5 billion in "less liquid" assets, and $3.2 billion in illiquid private equity investments.[87] American columnist Matt Levine described that among its less liquid assets that "[FTX] relied on to be able to pay out customer balances" were two tokens that "it had just made up", referring to the FTX Token and Serum, a separate cryptocurrency accounted for in the balance sheet.[88]

Contagion fears and impact on cryptocurrency markets

Cryptocurrencies experienced swings and declines in value as news of FTX's collapse first emerged in early November: Tether dropped below its peg price of $1.00 to $0.97[89] and Bitcoin sank to its lowest price in 2 years.[75] Share prices for publicly traded cryptocurrency companies declined.[90] The price of Solana, which was affiliated with Bankman-Fried, declined as well.[91] The crisis at FTX has inspired an increase in withdrawals from other exchanges.[92] A decline in the value of Cronos, the token of exchange Crypto.com, triggered fears of the potential for a collapse similar to that of FTX and spurred withdrawals from the platform.[93] CEO Kris Marszalek provided assurances that the firm was liquid and that it did not use Cronos in a manner similar to the way FTX used FTT.[93] Bloomberg reported that the collapse of FTX exacerbated institutional skepticism of cryptocurrencies as an asset class.[94]

BlockFi, a cryptocurrency lender, filed for Chapter 11 bankruptcy protection on 28 November; the firm had earlier begun preventing withdrawals.[95][96] The company disclosed "significant exposure" to FTX on 14 November.[96] Another cryptocurrency lender, Genesis, a subsidiary of Digital Currency Group, halted withdrawals on 16 November.[97] This halt caused Gemini, an exchange owned by the Winklevoss twins, to cease allowing redemptions for clients using a service provided through a partnership with Genesis.[98] Another Digital Currency Group subsidiary, Grayscale, saw the value of its flagship offering, the publicly traded Grayscale Bitcoin Trust, decline by 20% over the two weeks preceding 17 November.[99] Grayscale Bitcoin Trust was trading at a discounted price, 42% below the value of its Bitcoin, as of 14 November.[100]

Bankruptcy of Silvergate Bank

Silvergate Bank covered colossal losses on the bankruptcy of FTX. On 9 March 2023 Silvergate Bank announced it would wind down its operations and undergo liquidation, in turn creating a domino effect of chain insolvencies.[101][102] On 12 March 2023, Signature Bank, who catered to operators such as Binance and Celsius Network, collapsed after being closed by the New York State Department of Financial Services after being designated a systemic risk following a run.[103] After Silicon Valley Bank‘s collapse, Signature Bank's collapse was the third largest in United States history.[104]

Investigations

Lawsuits and legal involvement

Following the collapse of FTX, the Royal Bahamas Police Force launched a criminal investigation into the company.[105][27]

Anonymous sources cited by Bloomberg said that the office of the United States Attorney for the Southern District of New York had begun an investigation into FTX's collapse as of 14 November.[28]

The United States House Committee on Financial Services plans to conduct hearings in December on the collapse of FTX, and committee leaders said they would seek testimony from Bankman-Fried.[106]

On 15 November 2022, a class-action lawsuit was filed in Miami against Bankman-Fried and several celebrities, including American football quarterback Tom Brady and comedian Larry David, alleging the company engaged in deceptive practices; they are seeking damages.[107]The lawsuit also named Gisele Bündchen, Steph Curry, Shaquille O'Neal, Udonis Haslem, David Ortiz, Trevor Lawrence, Shohei Ohtani, Naomi Osaka, and Kevin O'Leary.[108]

On 21 December 2022, both Caroline Ellison (former CEO of Alameda) and Gary Wang (former Chief Technology Officer of FTX) pled guilty to fraud and other charges and were cooperating with federal investigators in criminal case against Sam Bankman-Fried. In the signed agreements Ellison and Wang agreed to "cooperate fully" and "truthfully and completely disclose all information concerning all matters".[109]On 3 January 2023, Bankman-Fried pled not guilty to fraud and other charges. His trial began in October 2023.[110] On 2 November 2023, Bankman-Fried was found guilty of all charges...[17]

AND

Bankman-Fried Charged in an Eight-Count Indictment with Fraud, Money Laundering, and Campaign Finance Offenses[6]

Damian Williams, the United States Attorney for the Southern District of New York, Merrick B. Garland, the United States Attorney General, and Michael J. Driscoll, the Assistant Director in Charge of the New York Field Office of the Federal Bureau of Investigation ("FBI"), announced today the unsealing of an Indictment charging SAMUEL BANKMAN-FRIED, a/k/a "SBF," with conspiracy to commit wire fraud, wire fraud, conspiracy to commit commodities fraud, conspiracy to commit securities fraud, conspiracy to commit money laundering, and conspiracy to defraud the Federal Election Commission and commit campaign finance violations. The charges in the Indictment arise from an alleged wide-ranging scheme by the defendant to misappropriate billions of dollars of customer funds deposited with FTX, the international cryptocurrency exchange founded by the defendant, and mislead investors and lenders to FTX and to Alameda Research, the cryptocurrency hedge fund also founded by the defendant. BANKMAN-FRIED was arrested yesterday in the Bahamas on these charges and will be presented before a Bahamian magistrate judge today.

U.S. Attorney Damian Williams said: "One month ago, FTX collapsed, causing billions of dollars in losses to its customers, lenders, and investors. Now, a federal grand jury in New York has indicted the former founder and chief executive officer of FTX and charged him with crimes related to the phenomenal downfall of that one-time cryptocurrency exchange, including fraud on customers, investors, lenders, and our campaign finance system. As today's charges make clear, this was not a case of mismanagement or poor oversight, but of intentional fraud, plain and simple."

Attorney General Merrick B. Garland said: "The Justice Department has filed charges alleging that Samuel Bankman-Fried perpetrated a range of offenses in a global scheme to deceive and defraud customers and lenders of FTX and Alameda, the defendant's crypto hedge fund, as well as a conspiracy to defraud the United States government. We allege that the defendant conspired to defraud customers by misappropriating their deposits; to defraud lenders; to commit securities fraud and money laundering; and to violate campaign finance laws. As this indictment demonstrates, the U.S. Department of Justice will aggressively investigate and prosecute alleged criminal wrongdoing in the financial system and violations of federal elections laws. We will continue to work to ensure U.S. capital markets operate honestly and with the integrity that investors, lenders, and the American people are entitled to."

FBI Assistant Director Michael J. Driscoll said: "As the indictment today alleges, Bankman-Fried knowingly defrauded the customers of FTX.com through the misappropriation of the customer deposits to pay expenses and debts of a different company he also owned as well as make other investments. If you deceive and

[6] https://www.justice.gov/usao-sdny/pr/united-states-attorney-announces-charges-against-ftx-founder-samuel-bankman-fried

defraud your customers, the FBI will be persistent in our efforts to bring you to justice."

As alleged in the Indictment unsealed in Manhattan federal court and court filings:[1]

SAMUEL BANKMAN-FRIED was the founder and chief executive officer of FTX, an international cryptocurrency exchange. Since 2019, the defendant and his co-conspirators perpetrated a scheme to defraud customers of FTX by misappropriating billions of dollars of those customers' funds. As alleged, the defendant used billions of dollars of FTX customer funds for his personal use, to make investments and millions of dollars of political contributions to federal political candidates and committees, and to repay billions of dollars in loans owed by Alameda Research, a cryptocurrency hedge fund also founded by the defendant. BANKMAN-FRIED also allegedly defrauded lenders to Alameda Research and equity investors in FTX by concealing his misuse of customer deposits in financial information that was provided to them.

SAMUEL BANKMAN-FRIED and his co-conspirators made millions of dollars in political contributions funded by Alameda Research to federal political candidates and committees in advance of the 2022 election. To conceal the fact that those contributions were paid for using funds from a corporation and to evade contribution limits and reporting requirements, BANKMAN-FRIED caused contributions to be reported in the names of co-conspirators rather than in the name of the true source of the funds.

* * *

SAMUEL BANKMAN-FRIED, 30, of Stanford, California, is charged with two counts of wire fraud conspiracy, two counts of wire fraud, and one count of conspiracy to commit money laundering, each of which carries a maximum sentence of 20 years. He is also charged with conspiracy to commit commodities fraud, conspiracy to commit securities fraud, and conspiracy to defraud the United States and commit campaign finance violations, each of which carries a maximum sentence of 5 years.

The statutory maximum sentences are prescribed by Congress and are provided here for informational purposes only, as any sentencing of the defendant will be determined by a judge.

Mr. Williams praised the investigative work of the FBI. He also expressed appreciation for the assistance of the Justice Department's Office of International Affairs, National Cryptocurrency Enforcement Team, Public Integrity Section, and the Drug Enforcement Administration, as well as that of the Securities and Exchange Commission and the Commodity Futures Trading Commission, both of which separately initiated civil proceedings against the defendant today. Mr. Williams further thanked the Bahamas Office of the Attorney-General & Ministry of Legal Affairs as well as the Royal Bahamas Police Force for their assistance.

This case is being handled by the Office's Securities and Commodities Fraud Task Force. Assistant U.S. Attorneys Nicolas Roos and Danielle Sassoon are in charge of the prosecution. The Money Laundering and Transnational Criminal

Enterprises Unit and Assistant U.S. Attorneys Samuel Raymond and Thane Rehn also contributed to the investigation.

The allegations in the Indictment are merely accusations, and the defendant is presumed innocent unless and until proven guilty.

AND

... **The Conviction Of Samuel Bankman-Fried**[7] (November 2, 2023)

"Sam Bankman-Fried perpetrated one of the biggest financial frauds in American history—a multibillion-dollar scheme designed to make him the King of Crypto—but while the cryptocurrency industry might be new and the players like Sam Bankman-Fried might be new, this kind of corruption is as old as time. This case has always been about lying, cheating, and stealing, and we have no patience for it.

When I became U.S. Attorney, I promised we would be relentless in rooting out corruption in our financial markets. This is what relentless looks like. This case moved at lightning speed—that was not a coincidence, that was a choice. This case is also a warning to every fraudster who thinks they're untouchable, that their crimes are too complex for us to catch, that they are too powerful to prosecute, or that they are clever enough to talk their way out of it if caught. Those folks should think again, and cut it out. And if they don't, I promise we'll have enough handcuffs for all of them.

This verdict would not have been possible without the amazing work by the career prosecutors from my Office and the FBI agents who have given their all for this case. We have pushed them hard, and they have delivered every step of the way. They are the best of the best, and I am grateful for them.

This case has received a tremendous amount of attention, and I understand why that is, but the women and men of the Southern District of New York consistently deliver outstanding public service on behalf of the American people—without fear or favor and often without any public recognition. They do it because they believe in the rule of law, because they love this country, and because they are patriots. I am proud to serve with them."

* * *

Bankman-Fried, 31, of Stanford, California, was convicted of two counts of wire fraud conspiracy, two counts of wire fraud, and one count of conspiracy to commit money laundering, each of which carries a maximum sentence of 20 years in prison. He was also convicted of conspiracy to commit commodities fraud and conspiracy to commit securities fraud, each of which carries a maximum sentence of five years in prison.

The statutory maximum sentences are prescribed by Congress and are provided here for informational purposes only, as any sentencing of the defendant will be determined by a judge.

[7] https://www.justice.gov/usao-sdny/pr/statement-us-attorney-damian-williams-conviction-samuel-bankman-fried#:~:text=Bankman%2DFried%2C%2031%2C%20of,of%2020%20 years%20in%20prison

Updated November 2, 2023
AND
… **Statement on Guilty Verdict in Jury Trial of Sam Bankman-Fried**[8] (November 2, 2023)

The Justice Department issued the following statement from Attorney General Merrick B. Garland on today's jury conviction in the trial of Sam Bankman-Fried:

"Sam Bankman-Fried thought that he was above the law. Today's verdict proves he was wrong. This case should send a clear message to anyone who tries to hide their crimes behind a shiny new thing they claim no one else is smart enough to understand: the Justice Department will hold you accountable. I am grateful to the U.S. Attorney's Office for the Southern District of New York and the FBI for their outstanding work in bringing Mr. Bankman-Fried to justice."

4. **OneCoin**[9]

N.B. not to be confused with the Onecoin issued by Chinese company Xunlei.

OneCoin is a fraudulent cryptocurrency scheme[1][2] conducted by offshore companies OneCoin Ltd, based in Bulgaria and[3] registered in Dubai, and OneLife Network Ltd (registered in Belize), both founded by Ruja Ignatova in concert with Sebastian Greenwood.[4] OneCoin is considered a Ponzi scheme due to its organisational structure of paying early investors using money obtained from newer ones. It was also a pyramid scheme due to the recruiting of investors without providing any actual product.[5] The company secretly conducted database entry scam simulating transactions not registered by an actual blockchain, and with no mining behind the apparent cryptocurrency release and circulation. Many of those characters central to OneCoin had been previously involved in similar and different other schemes and business malpractices separate from each other.[6] OneCoin was described by *The Times* as "one of the biggest scams in history".[7]

US prosecutors have alleged the scheme brought in approximately $4 billion worldwide.[8] In China, law enforcement recovered 1.7 billion yuan (US$267.5 million) while prosecuting 98 people.[9]Ignatova disappeared in 2017 near the time a secret US warrant was filed for her arrest and her brother, Konstantin Ignatov, took her position. Most of the leaders have now disappeared or been arrested, though Ignatova has escaped arrest.[10] Greenwood was arrested in 2018,[11] as was Konstantin Ignatov in March 2019.[12] In November 2019, Ignatov pleaded guilty to charges of money laundering and fraud. The total maximum sentence for the charges is 90 years in prison.[13] In 2022 Greenwood pleaded guilty, and in 2023 was sentenced to 20 years for wire fraud and money laundering.[14]

Concept

OneCoin was launched in late 2014. It was not a decentralized cryptocurrency but rather a centralized pyramid scheme hosted on OneCoin Ltd's servers which was

---

[8] https://www.justice.gov/opa/pr/attorney-general-merrick-b-garland-statement-guilty-verdict-jury-trial-sam-bankman-fried

[9] https://en.wikipedia.org/wiki/OneCoin

marketed as a cryptocurrency. The scheme was set up by Ruja Ignatova with Sebastian Greenwood acting as the lead distributor in the pyramid.[15]

According to OneCoin, its main business was selling educational material for cryptocurrency trading: investors could buy "educational packages" costing anywhere from 100 euros to 118,000 euros,[16] or—according to one industry blog—225,500 euros.[17] According to a suitfiled by former investors, much of the content in those packages was plagiarized from various free sources, including Wikipedia.[18][*better source needed*] Investors also received "tokens" that could be assigned to mine OneCoins.[19] Mining was said to be taking place at two sites in Bulgaria and one in Hong Kong.[20]

In typical OneCoin recruiting meetings, recruiters would focus on cryptocurrency investment, and the "educational material" was barely mentioned.[21][22][*better source needed*]

The only way to exchange OneCoins for other currencies was the *OneCoin Exchange* ("xcoinx"), an internal marketplace for members who had invested more than a set amount. OneCoins could be exchanged for euros, which were placed in a "virtual wallet", from which they could request a wire transfer. The marketplace had daily selling limits based on which package the seller had invested in, greatly limiting the amount of OneCoins which could be exchanged by the scam's victims.[*citation needed*] As lead distributor, 5% of all OneCoin sales went to Greenwood, who made over US$300 million.[15]

On 1 March 2016, without notice, OneCoin issued an internal notice that the marketplace would be closed for two weeks for maintenance, explaining that this was necessary due to the "high number of miners" and for "better integration with blockchain".[23] On 15 March 2016, the market re-opened.[*citation needed*] It was shut down again without notice in January 2017, though individuals affiliated with the company continued to accept funds.[24][10]

Legal issues and criticism

2015

On 30 September 2015, Bulgaria's Financial Supervision Commission (FSC) issued a warning of potential risks in new cryptocurrencies, citing OneCoin as an example.[25] After the warning, OneCoin ceased all activity in Bulgaria and started to use banks in foreign countries to handle wire transfers from participants.[26]

2016

In February 2016, the British newspaper *Daily Mirror* wrote that OneCoin / OneLife is a get-rich-quick scheme scam and a cult, calling it "virtually worthless".[27]

The company and the scheme is on the observation lists of many authorities; among them are authorities in Bulgaria, Finland,[16][28][29] Sweden,[30] Norway[31] and Latvia.[32] Authorities in many countries have warned of potential risks involved in businesses like OneCoin and undertaken prosecutions against persons linked to OneCoin, including CEO Ruja Ignatova and her brother Konstantin Ignatov.[12]

In March 2016, the Direct Selling Association in Norway warned against OneCoin, comparing it to a pyramid scheme.[4]

In December 2016, the Italian Antitrust Authority (Autorità Garante della Concorrenza e del Mercato) "adopted an interim injunction against the company One Network Services Ltd, active in the promotion and dissemination of cryptocurrency OneCoin", and its representatives in Italy, describing their activities as an "illegal pyramid sales system" (*"sistema di vendita piramidale vietato dalla legge"*), and ordering them to cease promoting and selling OneCoin in Italy[33] On 27 February 2017, after concluding their investigation, AGCM banned all activity on OneCoin until further notice.[34]

In December 2016, the Hungarian Central Bank issued a warning that OneCoin is a pyramid scheme,[35] and in China that same year several members and investors of OneCoin were arrested and US$30.8 million worth of assets seized.[36]

2017

In March 2017, the Croatian National Bank (HNB) advised the public to "exercise a high degree of caution" in decisions involving OneCoin, noted that OneCoin operations are not supervised by the HNB, and warned that possible losses will be fully borne by the investors.[37]

On 23 April 2017, Indian police arrested 18 people in Navi Mumbai for organizing a OneCoin recruitment event. The police attended the event undercover to judge the accusations before they decided to act. Further investigation was begun with the intent of revealing the higher levels of the pyramid.[38][39] In May, the investigation recovered Rs 24.57 crores ($3.32 million USD) in nine bank accounts. A further Rs 75 crores ($10.12 million USD) were transferred out before authorities were able to seize it.[40] Early in the month of May, two more people were arrested and a further Rs 24 crores ($3.24 million USD) were seized from bank accounts. A special investigation team of 15 individuals including 4 assistant police inspectors was formed under Senior Police Inspector Shivaji Awate with the stated goal of following the money trail and possibly lead to further arrests.[41]

On 27 April 2017, Germany's Federal Financial Supervisory Authority (BaFin) issued cease and desist orders to Onecoin Ltd, Dubai, and OneLife Network Ltd, Belize.[42] The Authority concluded that trading in OneCoins was fraudulent "own funds" trading.[42]

On 28 April 2017, Bank of Thailand issued a warning against OneCoin, stating it was an illegal digital currency and that it should not be used in trade.[43]

On 29 May 2017, International Financial Services Commission of Belize (IFSC) issued a warning about OneLife Network Ltd conducting trading business without license or permission from *IFSC* or any other authority. OneLife Network Ltd was directed to cease and desist from carrying on with the illegal trading business.[44]

On 16 June 2017, the CEO of OneCoin Ltd claimed OneCoin was licensed by the Vietnamese government, that it was legally permissible to use them as a digital currency and that it was the first cryptocurrency in Asia officially licensed by any government.[45] On 20 June 2017, Vietnam's Ministry of Planning and Investment (MPI) issued a statement that the document which OneCoin used as proof was forged. They stated that the document was against the MPI regulations and that the person who supposedly signed the document was not in the position claimed by the document at the time when the document was created. MPI warned individuals and enterprises to be vigilant if they encounter the document during business.[46][45]

On 10 July 2017, Ruja Ignatova, the CEO, was charged in India with duping investors as a part of the Indian investigation.[6]

2018

On 17 and 18 January 2018, Bulgarian police raided OneCoin's office in Sofia at the request of the prosecutor's office in Bielefeld, Germany. German police and Europol took part in the bust and the investigation. Also 14 other companies, tied to OneCoin, were investigated and 50 witnesses were questioned. OneCoin's servers and other material evidence were seized.[47]

On 3 May 2018, the Central Bank of Samoa (CBS) banned all foreign exchange transactions related to OneCoin and OneLife.[48] The bank had earlier in March issued a warning about OneCoin.[49] CBS describes OneCoin as a very-high-risk pyramid scheme.

Ruja Ignatova's collaborator and OneCoin's co-founder Sebastian Karl Greenwood (age 46–47) was arrested in Thailand in July 2018. He was imprisoned in Thailand pending extradition to the United States. Greenwood is a father of four and a citizen of Sweden and the UK.[14][50][11] Greenwood used money from Onecoin to buy international real estate, expensive clothing and watches, and to make a SKr 6,500,000 down-payment on a Sunseeker yacht.[50]

2019

Ruja Ignatova's brother Konstantin Ignatov was arrested in March 2019.[12] In a plea deal made on 4 October (made public 12 November), he pleaded guilty to fraud and money laundering in connection with the scheme.[51]

On 21 November 2019 the New York Federal Court found lawyer Mark Scott guilty of money laundering and bank fraud for his role in routing US$400 m out of the US.[52]

On 24 November 2019 the BBC published a detailed investigation of OneCoin and Ignatova titled "Cryptoqueen: How this woman scammed the world, then vanished". The reporters believe that Ignatova resides in Frankfurt under a false identity.[53]

2020

In 2020 the FinCEN Files showed that BNY Mellon flagged to FinCEN $137 m of transactions related to OneCoin.[*citation needed*]

2021

The company OneCoin, Ruja Ignatova and Gilbert Armenta have been found in default at an ongoing trial in the US.[54]

2022

In May 2022, Europol added Ignatova to their "Europe's Most Wanted" list, offering a 5000 € reward for information leading to her arrest.[55][56] On June 30, the Federal Bureau of Investigation added Ignatova to the FBI Ten Most Wanted Fugitives list, offering a reward of up to $100,000 for information leading to her arrest.[57]

In December, Greenwood pleaded guilty to wire fraud and money laundering in the a US federal court.[14]

2023

In March 2023, OneCoin's former legal and compliance officer Irina Dilkinska was caught and extradited from Bulgaria to the United States.[58]

Frank Schneider, former intelligence officer of Luxembourg and advisor to Ignatova, has absconded.[59] Journalists speculate that Ignatova might have been murdered.[59]

In September 2023, Greenwood was sentenced to a 20-year federal prison term (minus 5-years already served) by a New York Federal court . . .[14][60][50]

AND

Co-Founder Of Multibillion-Dollar Cryptocurrency Scheme "OneCoin" Sentenced To 20 Years In Prison (DoJ press notice)[10]

OneCoin Was a Fraudulent Cryptocurrency Marketed and Sold to Millions of Victims Around the World, Resulting in Billions of Dollars in Losses.

Damian Williams, the United States Attorney for the Southern District of New York, announced today that KARL SEBASTIAN GREENWOOD, who co-founded OneCoin with RUJA IGNATOVA, a/k/a "the Cryptoqueen," was sentenced to 20 years in prison for his orchestration of the massive OneCoin fraud scheme. OneCoin, which began operations in 2014 and was based in Sofia, Bulgaria, marketed and sold a fraudulent cryptocurrency by the same name through a global multi-level-marketing ("MLM") network. As a result of misrepresentations that GREENWOOD, IGNATOVA, and others made about OneCoin, millions of victims invested over $4 billion worldwide in the fraudulent cryptocurrency. Today's sentence was imposed by U.S. District Judge Edgardo Ramos. IGNATOVA, who was added to the Federal Bureau of Investigation's ("FBI") Top Ten Most Wanted List in June 2022, remains at large.

U.S. Attorney Damian Williams said: "As a founder and leader of OneCoin, Karl Sebastian Greenwood operated one of the largest fraud schemes ever perpetrated. Greenwood and his co-conspirators, including fugitive Ruja Ignatova, conned unsuspecting victims out of billions of dollars with promises of a 'financial revolution' and claims that OneCoin would be the 'Bitcoin killer.' In fact, OneCoins were entirely worthless, and investors were left with nothing, while Greenwood lined his own pockets with over $300 million. We hope this lengthy sentence resonates in the financial sector and deters anyone who may be tempted to lie to investors and exploit the cryptocurrency ecosystem through fraud."

According to public court filings and statements made in Court:

GREENWOOD and IGNATOVA co-founded OneCoin Ltd ("OneCoin") in 2014. OneCoin was based in Sofia, Bulgaria. OneCoin marketed and sold a fraudulent cryptocurrency by the same name. OneCoin began operating in the United States in or around 2015. Between the fourth quarter of 2014 and the fourth quarter

[10] https://www.justice.gov/usao-sdny/pr/co-founder-multibillion-dollar-cryptocurrency-scheme-onecoin-sentenced-20-years-prison

of 2016 alone, the scheme took in more than $4 billion from at least 3.5 million victims.

OneCoin marketed its fake cryptocurrency through a global MLM network of OneCoin members. GREENWOOD conceived of OneCoin's use of an MLM structure and was OneCoin's global master distributor and the leader of the MLM network through which the fraudulent cryptocurrency was marketed and sold. Through the MLM structure, OneCoin members received commissions for recruiting others to purchase cryptocurrency packages. As the top MLM distributor of OneCoin, GREENWOOD earned 5% of monthly OneCoin sales from anywhere in the world, which totaled more than $200 million from the fourth quarter of 2014 through the fourth quarter of 2016 alone and exceeded approximately $300 million in total. GREENWOOD's mastery as a salesman and the use of the MLM structure helped contribute to OneCoin's rapid growth and incredible success.

From OneCoin's inception, GREENWOOD and IGNATOVA used the notoriety of Bitcoin to convince investors that OneCoin was the next "can't miss" investment opportunity. GREENWOOD and IGNATOVA wanted investors to believe that OneCoin was a legitimate cryptocurrency like Bitcoin and deliberately drew the comparison between the two cryptocurrencies through their representations to investors and their marketing materials. For example, in a OneCoin PowerPoint presentation prepared by GREENWOOD, OneCoin described itself as "a unique and innovative cryptocurrency, that is born on the success of the pioneering and famous cryptocoin, Bitcoin." In another slide, OneCoin highlighted the explosive growth of Bitcoin, stating that "Bitcoins increased their value 75 times in 2013," and including the following quote from The Guardian newspaper, "Man buys $27 of bitcoin, forgets that he had bought and finds that they're now worth $886,000."

In reality, unlike legitimate cryptocurrencies, OneCoin had no actual value and was conceived of by GREENWOOD and IGNATOVA as a fraud from day one. The misrepresentations made by GREENWOOD and others to OneCoin investors were legion, and the cryptocurrency was worthless. Among other things, OneCoin lied to its members about how its cryptocurrency was valued, claiming that the price of OneCoin was based on market supply and demand, when in fact OneCoin itself arbitrarily set the value of the coin without regard to market forces. The purported value of a OneCoin grew steadily from 0.50 € to approximately 29.95 € per coin, as of in or about January 2019. The purported price of OneCoins never decreased in value.

GREENWOOD also lied to investors about the utility of the tokens included in trader packages, claiming that they could be used to secure positions in OneCoin's "mining pools," depicted in promotional materials as computer hardware used to "mine" OneCoins. But there were no mining pools and no computers to mine OneCoin either. GREENWOOD knew that this lie was essential to convincing investors that OneCoin was a legitimate cryptocurrency. As he wrote in an email to IGNATOVA, "[t]he concept of converting tokens into OneCoin is an important phase for validity and truth behind the OneCoin. The so called 'mining' of coins is a concept that is very familiar in the industry and a story we can sell to the members." However, as GREENWOOD and IGNATOVA both knew, OneCoin was "not mining actually—but telling people shit." In the same email exchange, GREENWOOD asked IGNATOVA, "how can this be investigated and found out?" and "Can any member (trying to be clever) find out that we actually are not investing in machines to mine but it is merely a piece of software doing this for us?"

OneCoin also claimed to have a private "blockchain," or a digital ledger identifying OneCoins and recording historical transactions. But, in reality, OneCoin lacked a true blockchain—that is, a public and verifiable blockchain. Indeed, by approximately March 2015, GREENWOOD and IGNATOVA had started allocating to members OneCoins that did not even exist in OneCoin's purported private blockchain, referring to these coins as "fake coins." By at least June 2015, GREENWOOD and IGNATOVA began emailing one another models tabulating current and projected future trader package sales volumes along with outstanding tokens and OneCoins. The spreadsheets identified separate lines for "mined coins," "mined coins (real)," and "fake coins." The references to "fake coins" in those records referred to OneCoins that had been distributed to members but did not exist on the OneCoin "blockchain." Two months later, in August 2015, IGNATOVA wrote to GREENWOOD, in an email with the subject line, "I am afraid this is an issue," "This is the implication from the big sales 4 weeks ago. 1.3 [billion] fake coins. We are fucked, this came unexpected and now needs serious, serious thinking."

On July 4, 2015, IGNATOVA announced the official opening of the United States market for OneCoin during an online webinar. During the webinar, IGNATOVA said, among other things: "[I]f we want to go and catch Bitcoin, we never can do this without being strong in the U.S. and without being part of the community. So, um, this is actually why I am so excited about the U.S. as the market. It's something that is about prestige. It's a huge market. And, um, it is, I think, a place of innovation, of Wall Street, a place where we have to be if we want to be big."

Many victims in the United States invested in fraudulent OneCoin cryptocurrency packages, including residents of the Southern District of New York. In total, more than 3.5 million victims invested in OneCoin and lost more than $4 billion dollars from the scheme —money that GREENWOOD, IGNATOVA, and others used to fund extravagant lifestyles. As the top MLM distributor of OneCoin, GREENWOOD earned more than $300 million during the scheme, much of which he spent on his own lavish lifestyle. For example, in or around December 2015, GREENWOOD used approximately $10,000 of fraud proceeds to stay at an exclusive five-star resort in Brazil. Later that month, GREENWOOD used an additional $21,000 of fraud proceeds to stay at a luxury villa with a beach view in Koh Samui, Thailand. Later, when GREENWOOD traveled to Barcelona in May 2016, he used investor funds to stay at another luxury five-star hotel and rented a Range Rover for the duration of his trip.

GREENWOOD also used proceeds from the scheme to purchase luxury designer clothes, footwear, and watches totaling approximately $2 million; pay a down payment of approximately 475,000 British Pound Sterling for a Sunseeker yacht; and to purchase real estate properties in various countries, including in Spain, Dubai, and Thailand. Finally, GREENWOOD used investor funds to travel around the world on a private "OneCoin" airplane and posted promotional videos of his travel online.

GREENWOOD was arrested at his residence on the island of Koh Samui, Thailand, in July 2018 and was extradited to the United States to face fraud and money laundering charges in October 2018. GREENWOOD has been detained since his arrest in July 2018.

On October 12, 2017, IGNATOVA was charged with OneCoin-related fraud and money laundering charges in the U.S. District Court for the Southern District of New York, and a federal warrant was issued for her arrest. On October 25, 2017, IGNATOVA traveled on a commercial flight from Sofia, Bulgaria, to Athens, Greece, and has not been seen publicly since. IGNATOVA was added to the FBI's Top Ten Most Wanted List in June 2022. The FBI is offering a $100,000 reward for information leading to IGNATOVA's arrest.

* * *

In addition to his prison term, GREENWOOD, 46, a citizen of Sweden and the United Kingdom, was ordered to pay approximately $300 million in forfeiture . . .

If you have any information about IGNATOVA's whereabouts, please contact your local FBI office or the nearest American Embassy or Consulate. Tips can be reported anonymously and can also be reported online at tips.fbi.gov. . .

AND

Co-founder of multibillion-dollar cryptocurrency pyramid scheme "OneCoin" pleads guilty (US IRS press notice)[11]

OneCoin was a fraudulent cryptocurrency marketed and sold to millions of victims around the world, resulting in billions of dollars in losses (December 16, 2022)

Damian Williams, the United States Attorney for the Southern District of New York, announced today that Karl Sebastian Greenwood, who co-founded OneCoin with Ruja Ignatova, aka "the Cryptoqueen," pled guilty today in Manhattan federal court to wire fraud and money laundering charges in connection with his participation in the massive OneCoin fraud scheme. OneCoin, which began operations in 2014 and was based in Sofia, Bulgaria, marketed and sold a fraudulent cryptocurrency by the same name through a global multi-level-marketing ("MLM") network. As a result of misrepresentations that Greenwood, Ignatova, and others made about OneCoin, victims invested over four billion dollars worldwide in the fraudulent cryptocurrency. Today, District Judge Edgardo Ramos accepted Greenwood's guilty plea Ignatova, who was added to the Federal Bureau of Investigation's Top Ten Most Wanted List in June 2022, remains at large.

U.S. Attorney Damian Williams said: "As a founder and leader of OneCoin, Karl Sebastian Greenwood operated one of the largest international fraud schemes ever perpetrated. Greenwood and his co-conspirators, including fugitive Ruja Ignatova, conned unsuspecting victims out of billions of dollars, claiming that OneCoin would

[11] https://www.irs.gov/compliance/criminal-investigation/co-founder-of-multibillion-dollar-cryptocurrency-pyramid-scheme-onecoin-pleads-guilty

be the 'Bitcoin killer.' In fact, OneCoins were entirely worthless. Greenwood's lies were designed with one goal, to get everyday people all over the world to part with their hard-earned money—real money—and to line his own pockets to the tune of hundreds of millions of dollars. This guilty plea by the co-founder of OneCoin caps a week at SDNY that sends a clear message that we are coming after all those who seek to exploit the cryptocurrency ecosystem through fraud, no matter how big or sophisticated you are."

According to the allegations in the superseding information and other filings and statements made in court:

In 2014, Greenwood and Ignatova co-founded OneCoin, a company based in Sofia, Bulgaria, that marketed a purported cryptocurrency by the same name, which was in fact a fraudulent pyramid scheme. OneCoin has operated using several corporate entities and d/b/a names, including "OneCoin Ltd," "OnePayments Ltd," "OneNetwork Services Ltd," "OneAcademy," and "OneLife." These entities and d/b/a names are referred to collectively here as "OneCoin." OneCoin operated as a MLM network through which members received commissions for recruiting others to purchase cryptocurrency packages. This MLM structure influenced rapid growth of the OneCoin member network. Indeed, according to OneCoin's promotional materials, over three million people invested in fraudulent cryptocurrency packages. OneCoin records show that, between the fourth quarter of 2014 and the fourth quarter of 2016 alone, OneCoin generated 4.037 billion euros in sales revenue and earned "profits" of 2.735 billion euros.

Ignatova served as OneCoin's top leader until her disappearance from public view, in October 2017. Greenwood was OneCoin's "global master distributor" and the leader of the MLM network through which the fraudulent cryptocurrency was marketed and sold. In a video posted online, Ignatova attributed to Greenwood the idea of marketing and selling OneCoin through an MLM network structure. Greenwood earned approximately 20 million euros a month in his role as the top MLM distributor of OneCoin.

Greenwood and Ignatova conceived of and built the OneCoin business fully intending to use it to defraud investors. For example, in the summer of 2014, when Greenwood and Ignatova were developing the concept for OneCoin, they referred to the cryptocurrency in email correspondence as "trashy coin." On June 11, 2014, Ignatova wrote to Greenwood concerning the OneCoin business plan, stating in part:

It might not be [something] really clean or that I normally work on or even can be proud of (except with you in private when we make the money)—but... I am especially good in this very borderline cases [sic], where the things become gray—and you as the magic sales machine—and me as someone who really can work with numbers, legal and back you up in a good and professional way—we could really make it big—like MLM meets bitch of wall street;-)

In an August 9, 2014, email between Greenwood and Ignatova, Ignatova described her thoughts on the "exit strategy" for OneCoin. The first option that Ignatova listed was, "Take the money and run and blame someone else for this . . ." And in a September 11, 2016, exchange with Ignatova's brother, Konstantin

Ignatov, Greenwood referred to OneCoin investors stating, "These ppl are idiots," to which Ignatov responded, "as you told me, the network would not work with intelligent people ;)"

As a result of misrepresentations made by Greenwood, Ignatova, and other OneCoin representatives, victims throughout the world wired investment funds to OneCoin-controlled bank accounts in order to purchase OneCoin packages. OneCoin falsely claimed that the value of OneCoin was based on market supply and demand, when in fact, the value of the cryptocurrency was simply set by OneCoin itself. For example, on June 9, 2014, in an email sent by Ignatova to a representative of a blockchain development company, copying Greenwood, Ignatova stated, "we are building our own cryptocurrency—and would like to set up an internal exchange service for them. We would like to be able to set the price manually and automatically and also control the traded volume." On March 21, 2015, Ignatova wrote an email to Greenwood, in which Ignatova stated, "We can manipulate the exchange by simulating some volatility and intraday pricing." (bold in original). And in an August 1, 2015, email, Ignatova wrote to Greenwood, and included as part of a section of the email entitled "Goals": "6. Trading coin, stable exchange, always close on a high price end of day open day with high price, build confidence - better manipulation so they are happy." The purported value of a OneCoin grew steadily from 0.50 € to approximately 29.95 € per coin. The purported price of OneCoins never decreased in value.

Greenwood and other OneCoin leaders also claimed that the OneCoin cryptocurrency was "mined" using mining servers maintained and operated by the company. In fact, OneCoins were never mined using computer resources. For example, in an email to Ignatova dated August 11, 2014, Greenwood proposed, "Get members to think that they are mining their OneCoin via crunching (exchanging) tokens for OneCoin. This storey [sic] is good as ppl will then not go super crazy and just try and sell tokens all the time." Greenwood emailed Ignatova the following day, writing, "The concept of converting tokens into OneCoin is an important phase for validity and truth behind the OneCoin. The so called 'mining' of coins is a concept that is very familiar in the industry and a story we can sell to the members." Ignatova then wrote to Greenwood, "We are not mining actually - but telling people shit," to which Greenwood responded, "how can this be investigated and found out?" and "Can any member (trying to be clever) find out that we actually are not investing in machines to mine but it is merely a piece of software doing this for us?"

Greenwood and other OneCoin leaders further claimed that OneCoin maintained a private "blockchain," or a digital ledger identifying OneCoins and recording historical transactions. But OneCoin lacked a true blockchain, that is, a public and verifiable blockchain. Indeed, by approximately March 2015, Ignatova and Greenwood had started allocating to OneCoin members coins that did not even exist in OneCoin's purported private blockchain, referring to those coins as "fake coins."

Greenwood and Ignatova promoted OneCoin, including at official OneCoin events all over the globe. One such event, called "Coin Rush," was held at Wembley Arena in London on June 11, 2016. Thousands of OneCoin members attended Coin

Rush. During the event, Greenwood introduced Ignatova to the crowd, stating in part: “This is the creator, the mastermind, the founder of cryptocurrency, of OneCoin ... Now, this will be the biggest welcoming on stage that we’ve ever done in history.” Then, to the tune of Alicia Keys’s “Girl on Fire,” and surrounded by actual onstage fireworks, Ignatova strode onto the Wembley Arena stage wearing a red ball gown. She proceeded to repeatedly and favorably compare her fraudulent cryptocurrency to Bitcoin, stating, among other things, “OneCoin ... is supposed to be the Bitcoin killer” and “In two years, nobody will speak about Bitcoin anymore.”

On July 4, 2015, a federal holiday commemorating the independence of the United States, Ignatova announced the official opening of the United States market for OneCoin. In early July 2015, Greenwood sent Ignatova an email stating in part, “I thought this could go out tonight, problem is I don’t have the access to send out to the members,” and attaching a document which announced a July 4, 2015, online webinar hosted by Ignatova and others to mark the official opening of the United States market for OneCoin. Thereafter, on July 4, 2015, Ignatova participated in an online webinar, later posted to YouTube.com, in which Ignatova announced the official opening of the United States market for OneCoin. During the webinar, Ignatova said, among other things, “[I]f we want to go and catch Bitcoin, we never can do this without being strong in the U.S. and without being part of the community. So, um, this is actually why I am so excited about the U.S. as the market. It’s something that is about prestige. It’s a huge market. And, um, it is, I think, a place of innovation, of Wall Street, a place where we have to be if we want to be big.” Many victims in the United States invested in fraudulent OneCoin cryptocurrency packages, including residents of the Southern District of New York.

Greenwood was arrested at his residence on the island of Koh Samui, Thailand, in July 2018, and was extradited to the United States to face fraud and money laundering charges in October 2018. Greenwood has been detained since his arrest in July 2018.

On October 12, 2017, Ignatova was charged with OneCoin-related fraud and money laundering charges in the United States District Court for the Southern District of New York and a federal warrant was issued for her arrest. On October 25, 2017, Ignatova traveled on a commercial flight from Sofia, Bulgaria, to Athens, Greece, and has not been seen publicly since. Ignatova was added to the FBI’s Top Ten Most Wanted List in June 2022. The FBI is offering a $100,000 reward for information leading to Ignatova’s arrest.

Greenwood, a citizen of Sweden and the United Kingdom, pled guilty to one count of conspiracy to commit wire fraud, which carries a maximum potential sentence of 20 years in prison, one count of wire fraud, which carries a maximum potential sentence of 20 years in prison, and one count of conspiracy to commit money laundering, which carries a maximum potential sentence of 20 years in prison ...

FBI Top Ten Most Wanted Fugitive RUJA IGNATOVA[12]

[12] https://www.fbi.gov/wanted/topten/ruja-ignatova/@@download.pdf

Ruja IgnatovaI is wanted for her participation in the large scale fraud scheme. Beginning in approximately 2014, Ignatova and others are alleged to have defrauded billions of dollars from investors all over the world. Ignatova was the founder of OneCoin Ltd, a Bulgarian-based company that marketed a purported cryptocurrency. In order to execute the scheme, Ignatova allehedly made false statements and representations to individuals in order to solicit investments in OneCoin. She allegedly instructed victims to transmit investment funds to OneCoin accounts in order to purchase OneCoin packages, causing victims to send wire transfers representing these investments. Throughout the scheme, OneCoin is believed to have defrauded victims out of more than $4 billion...

On October 12, 2017, Ignatova was charged in the United States District Court, Southern District of New York and a federal warrant was issued for her arrest. On February 6, 2018, a superseding indictment was issued charging Ignatova with one count each of Conspiracy to Commit Wire Fraud; Wire Fraud; Conspiracy to Money Laundering; Conspiracy to Commit Securities Fraud; and Securities Fraud...

AND

A **BBC News report** (dated June 9, 2023) noted:[13]

An FBI-wanted former spy and trusted adviser to the fugitive "Missing Cryptoqueen" has disappeared. Frank Schneider, 53, was under house arrest in France awaiting extradition to the US. But like his former boss Ruja Ignatova, he has gone missing before facing US justice.

He faces a maximum of 40 years in prison on fraud and money laundering charges for his alleged role in a $4bn (£3.2bn) cryptocurrency scam...

He worked as a troubleshooter for Miss Ignatova, architect of the OneCoin crypto scam. As investigators closed in on her, she boarded a Ryanair flight from Sofia to Athens in 2017, never to be seen again. The FBI is offering a $250,000 (£200,000) reward for information leading to her arrest ...

AND

Former Law Firm Partner Sentenced To 10 Years In Prison For Laundering $400 Million Of OneCoin Fraud Proceeds (DoJ report dated January 25, 2024)[14]

Damian Williams, the United States Attorney for the Southern District of New York, announced today that MARK SCOTT was sentenced to 10 years in prison by U.S. District Judge Edgardo Ramos for laundering approximately $400 million of proceeds from the massive international fraud scheme known as "OneCoin." Today's sentencing followed SCOTT's conviction on all counts at trial on November 21, 2019.

U.S. Attorney Damian Williams said: "Mark Scott, previously convicted at trial of laundering over $400 million of OneCoin proceeds for 'Crypto Queen,' Ruja Ignatova, used his law license as a means to participate in a massive money

---

[13] https://www.bbc.com/news/world-europe-65861495

[14] https://www.justice.gov/usao-sdny/pr/former-law-firm-partner-sentenced-10-years-prison-laundering-400-million-onecoin-fraud

laundering scheme for a cryptocurrency that had no value since its inception. Scott, an equity partner at a prominent international law firm, had boasted of earning '50 by 50.' Indeed, Scott accomplished his goal, but by fraud and deception, and will now spend a decade in prison and has been ordered to forfeit all of his illegal proceeds."

According to the Indictment, documents filed in the case, and evidence introduced at trial:

OneCoin, which began operations in 2014 and was based in Sofia, Bulgaria, marketed and sold a fraudulent cryptocurrency by the same name through a global multi-level-marketing ("MLM") network. OneCoin began operating in the U.S. in or around 2015. The OneCoin scheme was one of the largest fraud schemes ever perpetrated. Between the fourth quarter of 2014 and the fourth quarter of 2016 alone, the scheme took in more than $4 billion from at least 3.5 million victims.

OneCoin marketed its fake cryptocurrency through a global MLM network of OneCoin members. Unlike legitimate cryptocurrencies, OneCoin had no actual value and was conceived of as a fraud from day one. The misrepresentations made to OneCoin investors were legion, and the cryptocurrency was worthless. Among other things, OneCoin lied to its members about how its cryptocurrency was valued, claiming that the price of OneCoin was based on market supply and demand, when in fact OneCoin itself arbitrarily set the value of the coin without regard to market forces. The purported value of a OneCoin grew steadily from 0.50 € to approximately 29.95 € per coin, as of in or about January 2019. The purported price of OneCoins never decreased in value.

SCOTT, who was employed between June 2015 and September 2016 as an equity partner at Locke Lord LLP, a prominent international law firm, was first introduced to OneCoin's co-founder, RUJA IGNATOVA, in September 2015. Beginning in early 2016, SCOTT formed a series of fake private equity investment funds in the British Virgin Islands known as the "Fenero Funds." SCOTT then disguised incoming transfers of approximately $400 million into the Fenero Funds as investments from "wealthy European families," when in fact the money represented proceeds of the OneCoin fraud scheme. SCOTT layered the money through various Fenero Fund bank accounts in the Cayman Islands and the Republic of Ireland. SCOTT subsequently transferred the funds back to IGNATOVA and other OneCoin associated entities, this time disguising the transfers as outbound investments from the Fenero Funds. As part of the scheme, SCOTT and his co-conspirators lied to banks and other financial institutions all over the world, including to banks in the U.S., to cause those institutions to make transfers of OneCoin proceeds and evade anti-money laundering procedures.

SCOTT, who boasted about earning "50 by 50," was paid more than $50 million for his money laundering services. He used that money to purchase, among other things, a collection of luxury watches worth hundreds of thousands of dollars, a Ferrari and several Porsches, a 57-foot Sunseeker yacht, and three multimillion-dollar seaside homes in Cape Cod, Massachusetts.

* * *

In addition to the prison term, SCOTT, 55, of Coral Gables, Florida, was sentenced to three years of supervised release. SCOTT was also ordered to forfeit a money judgment in the amount of $392,940,000, several bank accounts, a yacht, two Porsche automobiles, and four real-estate properties . . .

Part III
Materials

Chapter 14
International Materials

i) **Excerpt from UN Convention Against Illicit Traffic In Narcotic Drugs and Psychotropic Substances (the Vienna Convention 1988)—Articles 2–7**[1]

Article 2
SCOPE OF THE CONVENTION

1. The purpose of this Convention is to promote co-operation among the Parties so that they may address more effectively the various aspects of illicit traffic in narcotic drugs and psychotropic substances having an international dimension. In carrying out their obligations under the Convention, the Parties shall take necessary measures, including legislative and administrative measures, in conformity with the fundamental provisions of their respective domestic legislative systems.
2. The Parties shall carry out their obligations under this Convention in a manner consistent with the principles of sovereign equality and territorial integrity of States and that of non-intervention in the domestic affairs of other States.
3. A Party shall not undertake in the territory of another Party the exercise of jurisdiction and performance of functions which are exclusively reserved for the authorities of that other Party by its domestic law.

Article 3
OFFENCES AND SANCTIONS

1. Each Party shall adopt such measures as may be necessary to establish as criminal offences under its domestic law, when committed intentionally:

   a) i) The production, manufacture, extraction; preparation, offering, offering for sale, distribution, sale, delivery on any terms whatsoever, brokerage, dispatch, dispatch in transit, transport, importation or exportation of any narcotic drug or any psychotropic substance contrary to the provisions of

[1] https://www.unodc.org/pdf/convention_1988_en.pdf

D. Smith, *Money Laundering, Terrorist Financing and Virtual Assets*, Contributions to Finance and Accounting, https://doi.org/10.1007/978-3-031-59842-5_14

the 1961 Convention, the 1961 Convention as amended or the 1971 Convention;

ii) The cultivation of opium poppy, coca bush or cannabis plant for the purpose of the production of narcotic drugs contrary to the provisions of the 1961 Convention and the 1961 Convention as amended;

iii) The possession or purchase of any narcotic drug or psychotropic substance for the purpose of any of the activities enumerated in i) above;

iv) The manufacture, transport or distribution of equipment, materials or of substances [listed in Table I and Table II], knowing that they are to be used in or for the illicit cultivation, production or manufacture of narcotic drugs or psychotropic substances;

v) The organization, management or financing of any of the offences enumerated in i), ii), iii) or iv) above;

b) i) The conversion or transfer of property, knowing that such property is derived from any offence or offences established in accordance with subparagraph *a)* of this paragraph, or from an act of participation in such offence or offences, for the purpose of concealing or disguising the illicit origin of the property or of assisting any person who is involved in the commission of such an offence or offences to evade the legal consequences of his actions;

ii) The concealment or disguise of the true nature, source, location, disposition, movement, rights with respect to, or ownership of property, knowing that such property is derived from an offence or offences established in accordance with subparagraph *a)* of this paragraph or from an act of participation in such an offence or offences;

c) Subject to its constitutional principles and the basic concepts of its legal system:

i) The acquisition, possession or use of property, knowing, at the time of receipt, that such property was derived from an offence or offences established in accordance with subparagraph a) of this paragraph or from an act of participation in such offence or offences;

ii) The possession of equipment or materials or substances [listed in Table I and Table II], knowing that they are being or are to be used in or for the illicit cultivation, production or

iii) Publicly inciting or inducing others, by any means, to commit any of the offences established in accordance with this article or to use narcotic drugs or psychotropic substances illicitly;

iv) Participation in, association or conspiracy to commit, attempts to commit and aiding, abetting, facilitating and counselling the commission of any of the offences established in accordance with this article.

2. Subject to its constitutional principles and the basic concepts of its legal system, each Party shall adopt such measures as may be necessary to establish as a criminal offence under its domestic law, when committed intentionally, the possession, purchase or cultivation of narcotic drugs or psychotropic substances

for personal consumption contrary to the provisions of the 1961 Convention, the 1961 Convention as amended or the 1971 Convention.

3. Knowledge, intent or purpose required as an element of an offence set forth in paragraph 1 of this article may be inferred from objective factual circumstances.
4. a) Each Party shall make the commission of the offences established in accordance with paragraph 1 of this article liable to sanctions which take into account the grave nature of these offences, such as imprisonment or other forms of deprivation of liberty, pecuniary sanctions and confiscation.
   b) The Parties may provide, in addition to conviction or punishment, for an offence established in accordance with paragraph 1 of this article, that the offender shall undergo measures such as treatment, education, aftercare, rehabilitation or social reintegration.
   c) Notwithstanding the preceding subparagraphs, in appropriate cases of a minor nature, the Parties may provide, as alternatives to conviction or punishment, measures such as education, rehabilitation or social reintegration, as well as, when the offender is a drug abuser, treatment and aftercare.
   d) The Parties may provide, either as an alternative to conviction or punishment, or in addition to conviction or punishment of an offence established in accordance with paragraph 2 of this article, measures for the treatment, education, aftercare, rehabilitation or social reintegration of the offender.
5. The Parties shall ensure that their courts and other competent authorities having jurisdiction can take into account factual circumstances which make the commission of the offences established in accordance with paragraph 1 of this article particularly serious, such as:

   a) The involvement in the offence of an organized criminal group to which the offender belongs;
   b) The involvement of the offender in other international organized criminal activities;
   c) The involvement of the offender in other illegal activities facilitated by commission of the offence;
   d) The use of violence or arms by the offender;
   e) The fact that the offender holds a public office and that the offence is connected with the office in question;
   f) The victimization or use of minors;
   g) The fact that the offence is committed in a penal institution or in an educational institution or social service facility or in their immediate vicinity or in other places to which school children and students resort for educational, sports and social activities;
   h) Prior conviction, particularly for similar offences, whether foreign or domestic, to the extent permitted under the domestic law of a Party.

6. The Parties shall endeavour to ensure that any discretionary legal powers under their domestic law relating to the prosecution of persons for offences established in accordance with this article are exercised to maximize the effectiveness of law

enforcement measures in respect of those offences, and with due regard to the need to deter the commission of such offences.

7. The Parties shall, ensure that their courts or other competent authorities bear in mind the serious nature of the offences enumerated in paragraph l of this article and the circumstances enumerated in paragraph 5 of this article when considering the eventuality of early release or parole of persons convicted of such offences.
8. Each Party shall, where appropriate, establish under its domestic law a long statute of limitations period in which to commence proceedings for any offence established in accordance with paragraph 1 of this article, and a longer period where the alleged offender has evaded the administration of justice.
9. Each Party shall take appropriate measures, consistent with its legal system, to ensure that a person charged with or convicted of an offence established in accordance with paragraph 1 of this article, who is found within its territory, is present at the necessary criminal proceedings.
10. For the purpose of co-operation among the Parties under this Convention, including, in particular, co-operation under articles 5, 6, 7 and 9, offences established in accordance with this article shall not be considered as fiscal offences or as political offences or regarded as politically motivated, without prejudice to the constitutional limitations and the fundamental domestic law of the Parties.
11. Nothing contained in this article shall affect the principle that the description of the offences to which it refers and of legal defences thereto is reserved to the domestic law of a Party and that such offences shall be prosecuted and punished in conformity with that law.

Article 4
JURISDICTION

1. Each Party:

   a) Shall take such measures as may be necessary to establish its jurisdiction over the offences it has established in accordance with article 3, paragraph 1, when:

      i) The offence is committed in its territory;
      ii) The offence is committed on board a vessel flying its flag or an aircraft which is registered under its laws at the time the offence is committed;

   b) May take such measures as maybe necessary to establish its jurisdiction over the offences it has established in accordance with article 3, paragraph 1, when:

      i) The offence is committed by one of its nationals or by a person who has his habitual residence in its territory;
      ii) The offence is committed on board a vessel concerning which that Party has been authorized to take appropriate action pursuant to article 17, provided that such jurisdiction shall be exercised only on the basis of

agreements or arrangements referred to in paragraphs 4 and 9 of that article;

iii) The offence is one of those established in accordance with article 3, paragraph 1, subparagraph c) iv), and is committed outside its territory with a view to the commission, within its territory, of an offence established in accordance with article 3, paragraph 1.

2. Each Party:

a) Shall also take such measures as may be necessary to establish its jurisdiction over the offences it has established in accordance with article 3, paragraph 1, when the alleged offender is present in its territory and it does not extradite him to another Party on the ground:

i) That the offence has been committed in its territory or on board a vessel flying its flag or an aircraft which was registered under its law at the time the offence was committed; or

ii) That the offence has been committed by one of its nationals;

b) May also take such measures as may be necessary to establish its jurisdiction over the offences it has established in accordance with article 3, paragraph 1, when the alleged offender is present in its territory and it does not extradite him to another Party.

3. This Convention does not exclude the exercise of any criminal jurisdiction established by a Party in accordance with its domestic law.

Article 5

CONFISCATION

1. Each Party shall adopt such measures as may be necessary to enable confiscation of:

a) Proceeds derived from offences established in accordance with article 3, paragraph 1, or property the value of which corresponds to that of such proceeds;

b) Narcotic drugs and psychotropic substances, materials and equipment or other instrumentalities used in or intended for use in any manner in offences established in accordance with article 3, paragraph 1.

2. Each Party shall also adopt such measures as may be necessary to enable its competent authorities to identify, trace, and freeze or seize proceeds, property, instrumentalities or any other things referred to in paragraph 1 of this article, for the purpose of eventual confiscation.

3. In order to carry out the measures referred to in this article, each Party shall empower its courts or other competent authorities to order that bank, financial or commercial records be made available or be seized. A Party shall not decline to act under the provisions of this paragraph on the ground of bank secrecy.

4. a) Following a request made pursuant to this article by another Party having jurisdiction over an offence established in accordance with article 3, paragraph

1, the Party in whose territory proceeds, property, instrumentalities or any other things referred to in paragraph 1 of this article are situated shall:

i) Submit the request to its competent authorities for the purpose of obtaining an order of confiscation and, if such order is granted, give effect to it; or
ii) Submit to its competent authorities, with a view to giving effect to it to the extent requested, an order of confiscation issued by the requesting Party in accordance with paragraph 1 of this article, in so far as it relates to proceeds, property, instrumentalities or any other things referred to in paragraph 1 situated in the territory of the requested Party.

b) Following a request made pursuant to this article by another Party having jurisdiction over an offence established in accordance with article 3, paragraph 1, the requested Party shall take measures to identify, trace, and freeze or seize proceeds, property, instrumentalities or any other things referred to in paragraph 1 of this article for the purpose of eventual confiscation to be ordered either by the requesting Party or, pursuant to a request under subparagraph a) of this paragraph, by the requested Party.
c) The decisions or actions provided for in subparagraphs a) and b) of this paragraph shall be taken by the requested Party, in accordance with and subject to the provisions of its domestic law and its procedural rules or any bilateral or multilateral treaty, agreement or arrangement to which it may be bound in relation to the requesting Party.
d) The provisions of article 7, paragraphs 6 to 19 are applicable mutatis mutandis. In addition to the information specified in article 7, paragraph 10, requests made pursuant to this article shall contain the following:

i) In the case of a request pertaining to subparagraph a) i) of this paragraph, a description of the property to be confiscated and a statement of the facts relied upon by the requesting Party sufficient to enable the requested Party to seek the order under its domestic law;
ii) In the case of a request pertaining to subparagraph a) ii), a legally admissible copy of an order of confiscation issued by the requesting Party upon which the request is based, a statement of the facts and information as to the extent to which the execution of the order is requested;
iii) In the case of a request pertaining to subparagraph b), a statement of the facts relied upon by the requesting Party and a description of the actions requested.

e) Each Party shall furnish to the Secretary-General the text of any of its laws and regulations which give effect to this paragraph and the text of any subsequent changes to such laws and regulations.
f) If a Party elects to make the taking of the measures referred to in subparagraphs a) and b) of this paragraph conditional on the existence of a relevant treaty, that Party shall consider this Convention as the necessary and sufficient treaty basis.

g) The Parties shall seek to conclude bilateral and multilateral treaties, agreements or arrangements to enhance the effectiveness of international co-operation pursuant to this article.

5. a) Proceeds or property confiscated by a Party pursuant to paragraph 1 or paragraph 4 of this article shall be disposed of by that Party according to its domestic law and administrative procedures.
   b) When acting on the request of another Party in accordance with this article, a Party may give special consideration to concluding agreements on:
   i) Contributing the value of such proceeds and property, or funds derived from the sale of such proceeds or property, or a substantial part thereof, to intergovernmental bodies specializing in the fight against illicit traffic in and abuse of narcotic drugs and psychotropic substances;
   ii) Sharing with other Parties, on a regular or case-by-case basis, such proceeds or property, or funds derived from the sale of such proceeds or property, in accordance with its domestic law, administrative procedures or bilateral or multilateral agreements entered into for this purpose.

6. a) If proceeds have been transformed or converted into other property, such property shall be liable to the measures referred to in this article instead of the proceeds.
   b) If proceeds have been intermingled with property acquired from legitimate sources, such property shall, without prejudice to any powers relating to seizure or freezing, be liable to confiscation up to the assessed value of the intermingled proceeds.
   c) Income or other benefits derived from:
   i) Proceeds;
   ii) Property into which proceeds have been transformed or converted; or
   iii) Property with which proceeds have been intermingled shall also be liable to the measures referred to in this article, in the same manner and to the same extent as proceeds.

7. Each Party may consider ensuring that the onus of proof be reversed regarding the lawful origin of alleged proceeds or other property liable to confiscation, to the extent that such action is consistent with the principles of its domestic law and with the nature of the judicial and other proceedings.
8. The provisions of this article shall not be construed as prejudicing the rights of bona fide third parties.
9. Nothing contained in this article shall affect the principle that the measures to which it refers shall be defined and implemented in accordance with and subject to the provisions of the domestic law of a Party.

Article 6
EXTRADITION

1. This article shall apply to the offences established by the Parties in accordance with article 3, paragraph 1.
2. Each of the offences to which this article applies shall be deemed to be included as an extraditable offence in any extradition treaty existing between Parties. The Parties undertake to include such offences as extraditable offences in every extradition treaty to be concluded between them.
3. If a Party which makes extradition conditional on the existence of a treaty receives a request for extradition from another Party with which it has no extradition treaty, it may consider this Convention as the legal basis for extradition in respect of any offence to which this article applies. The Parties which require detailed legislation in order to use this Convention as a legal basis for extradition shall consider enacting such legislation as may be necessary.
4. The Parties which do not make extradition conditional on the existence of a treaty shall recognize offences to which this article applies as extraditable offences between themselves.
5. Extradition shall be subject to the conditions provided for by the law of the requested Party or by applicable extradition treaties, including the grounds upon which the requested Party may refuse extradition.
6. In considering requests received pursuant to this article, the requested State may refuse to comply with such requests where there are substantial grounds leading its judicial or other competent authorities to believe that compliance would facilitate the prosecution or punishment of any person on account of his race, religion, nationality or political opinions, or would cause prejudice for any of those reasons to any person affected by the request.
7. The Parties shall endeavour to expedite extradition procedures and to simplify evidentiary requirements relating thereto in respect of any offence to which this article applies.
8. Subject to the provisions of its domestic law and its extradition treaties, the requested Party may, upon being satisfied that the circumstances so warrant and are urgent, and at the request of the requesting Party, take a person whose extradition is sought and who is present in its territory into custody or take other appropriate measures to ensure his presence at extradition proceedings.
9. Without prejudice to the exercise of any criminal jurisdiction established in accordance with its domestic law, a Party in whose territory an alleged offender is found shall:

   a) If it does not extradite him in respect of an offence established in accordance with article 3, paragraph l, on the grounds set forth in article 4, paragraph 2, subparagraph a), submit the case to its competent authorities for the purpose of prosecution, unless otherwise agreed with the requesting Party;
   b) If it does not extradite him in respect of such an offence and has established its jurisdiction in relation to that offence in accordance with article 4, paragraph 2, subparagraph b), submit the case to its competent authorities for the

purpose of prosecution, unless otherwise requested by the requesting Party for the purposes of preserving its legitimate jurisdiction.

10. If extradition, sought for purposes of enforcing a sentence, is refused because the person sought is a national of the requested Party, the requested Party shall, if its law so permits and in conformity with the requirements of such law, upon application of the requesting Party, consider, the enforcement of the sentence which has been imposed under the law of the requesting Party, or the remainder thereof.
11. The Parties shall seek to conclude bilateral and multilateral agreements to carry out or to enhance the effectiveness of extradition.
12. The Parties may consider entering into bilateral or multilateral agreements, whether *ad hoc* or general, on the transfer to their country of persons sentenced to imprisonment and other forms of deprivation of liberty for offences to which this article applies, in order that they may complete their sentences there.

Article 7
MUTUAL LEGAL ASSISTANCE

1. The Parties shall afford one another, pursuant to this article, the widest measure of mutual legal assistance in investigations, prosecutions and judicial proceedings in relation to criminal offences established in accordance with article 3, paragraph 1.
2. Mutual legal assistance to be afforded in accordance with this article may be requested for any of the following purposes:

   a) Taking evidence or statements from persons;
   b) Effecting service of judicial documents;
   c) Executing searches and seizures;
   d) Examining objects and sites;
   e) Providing information and evidentiary items;
   f) Providing originals or certified copies of relevant documents and records, including bank, financial, corporate or business records;
   g) Identifying or tracing proceeds, property, instrumentalities or other things for evidentiary purposes.

3. The Parties may afford one another any other forms of mutual legal assistance allowed by the domestic law of the requested Party.
4. Upon request, the Parties shall facilitate or encourage, to the extent consistent with their domestic law and practice, the presence or availability of persons, including persons in custody, who consent to assist in investigations or participate in proceedings.
5. A Party shall not decline to render mutual legal assistance under this article on the ground of bank secrecy.
6. The provisions of this article shall not affect the obligations under any other treaty, bilateral or multilateral, which governs or will govern, in whole or in part, mutual legal assistance in criminal matters.

7. Paragraphs 8 to 19 of this article shall apply to requests made pursuant to this article if the Parties in question are not bound by a treaty of mutual legal assistance. If these Parties are bound by such a treaty, the corresponding provisions of that treaty shall apply unless the Parties agree to apply paragraphs 8 to 19 of this article in lieu thereof.
8. Parties shall designate an authority, or when necessary authorities, which shall have the responsibility and power to execute requests for mutual legal assistance or to transmit them to the competent authorities for execution. The authority or the authorities designated for this purpose shall be notified to the Secretary-General. Transmission of requests for mutual legal assistance and any communication related thereto shall be effected between the authorities designated by the Parties; this requirement shall be without prejudice to the right of a Party to require that such requests and communications be addressed to it through the diplomatic channel and, in urgent circumstances, where the Parties agree, through channels of the International Criminal Police Organization, if possible.
9. Requests shall be made in writing in a language acceptable to the requested Party. The language or languages acceptable to each Party shall be notified to the Secretary-General. In urgent circumstances, and where agreed by the Parties, requests may be made orally, but shall be confirmed in writing forthwith.
10. A request for mutual legal assistance shall contain:

    a) The identity of the authority making the request;
    b) The subject matter and nature of the investigation, prosecution or proceeding to which the request relates, and the name and the functions of the authority conducting such investigation, prosecution or proceeding;
    c) A summary of the relevant facts, except in respect of requests for the purpose of service of judicial documents;
    d) A description of the assistance sought and details of any particular procedure the requesting Party wishes to be followed;
    e) Where possible, the identity, location and nationality of any person concerned;
    f) The purpose for which the evidence, information or action is sought.

11. The requested Party may request additional information when it appears necessary for the execution of the request in accordance with its domestic law or when it can facilitate such execution.
12. A request shall be executed in accordance with the domestic law of the requested Party and, to the extent not contrary to the domestic law of the requested Party and where possible, in accordance with the procedures specified in the request.
13. The requesting Party shall not transmit nor use information or evidence furnished by the requested Party for investigations, prosecutions or proceedings other than those stated in the request without the prior consent of the requested Party.
14. The requesting Party may require that the requested Party keep confidential the fact and substance of the request, except to the extent necessary to execute the

request. If the requested Party cannot comply with the requirement of confidentiality, it shall promptly inform the requesting Party.

15. Mutual legal assistance may be refused:
    a) If the request is not made in conformity with the provisions of this article;
    b) If the requested Party considers that execution of the request is likely to prejudice its sovereignty, security, ordre public or other essential interests;
    c) If the authorities of the requested Party would be prohibited by its domestic law from carrying out the action requested with regard to any similar offence, had it been subject to investigation, prosecution or proceedings under their own jurisdiction;
    d) If it would be contrary to the legal system of the requested Party relating to mutual legal assistance for the request to be granted.
16. Reasons shall be given for any refusal of mutual legal assistance.
17. Mutual legal assistance may be postponed by the requested Party on the ground that it interferes with an ongoing investigation, prosecution or proceeding. In such a case, the requested Party shall consult with the requesting Party to determine if the assistance can still be given subject to such terms and conditions as the requested Party deems necessary.
18. A witness, expert or other person who consents to give evidence in a proceeding or to assist in an investigation, prosecution or judicial proceeding in the territory of the requesting Party, shall not be prosecuted, detained, punished or subjected to any other restriction of his personal liberty in that territory in respect of acts, omissions or convictions prior to his departure from the territory of the requested Party. Such safe conduct shall cease when the witness, expert or other person having had, for a period of 15 consecutive days, or for any period agreed upon by the Parties, from the date on which he has been officially informed that his presence is no longer required by the judicial authorities, an opportunity of leaving, has nevertheless remained voluntarily in the territory or, having left it, has returned of his own free will.
19. The ordinary costs of executing a request shall be borne by the requested Party, unless otherwise agreed by the Parties concerned. If expenses of a substantial or extraordinary nature are or will be required to fulfil the request, the Parties shall consult to determine the terms and conditions under which the request will be executed as well as the manner in which the costs shall be borne.
20. The Parties shall consider, as may be necessary, the possibility of concluding bilateral or multilateral agreements or arrangements that would serve the purposes of, give practical effect to, or enhance the provisions of this article.

ii) **The Council of Europe Convention on Laundering, Search, Seizure and Confiscation of the Proceeds from Crime (Strasbourg Convention 1990)**

The **Convention**[2], also known as the **Strasbourg Convention** (or CETS 141), is a Council of Europe convention which aims to facilitate international co-operation and mutual assistance in investigating crime and tracking down, seizing and confiscating the proceeds thereof. The Convention is intended to assist States in attaining a similar degree of efficiency even in the absence of full legislative harmony.

Parties undertake in particular to criminalise the laundering of the proceeds of crime and to confiscate instrumentalities and proceeds (or property the value of which corresponds to such proceeds):[3]

Chapter I—Use of terms

Article 1—Use of terms

For the purposes of this Convention:

a. "proceeds" means any economic advantage from criminal offences. It may consist of any property as defined in sub-paragraph b of this article;
b. "property" includes property of any description, whether corporeal or incorporeal, movable or immovable, and legal documents or instruments evidencing title to, or interest in such property;
c. "instrumentalities" means any property used or intended to be used, in any manner, wholly or in part, to commit a criminal offence or criminal offences;
d. "confiscation" means a penalty or a measure, ordered by a court following proceedings in relation to a criminal offence or criminal offences resulting in the final deprivation of property;
e. "predicate offence" means any criminal offence as a result of which proceeds were generated that may become the subject of an offence as defined in Article 6 of this Convention.

Chapter II—Measures to be taken at national level

Article 2—Confiscation measures

1. Each Party shall adopt such legislative and other measures as may be necessary to enable it to confiscate instrumentalities and proceeds or property the value of which corresponds to such proceeds.
2. Each Party may, at the time of signature or when depositing its instrument of ratification, acceptance, approval or accession, by a declaration addressed to the Secretary General of the Council of Europe, declare that paragraph 1 of this article applies only to offences or categories of offences specified in such declaration.

Article 3—Investigative and provisional measures

Each Party shall adopt such legislative and other measures as may be necessary to enable it to identify and trace property which is liable to confiscation pursuant to Article 2, paragraph 1, and to prevent any dealing in, transfer or disposal of such property.

[2] https://rm.coe.int/168007bd23

[3] https://en.wikipedia.org/wiki/CETS141

Article 4—Special investigative powers and techniques

1. Each Party shall adopt such legislative and other measures as may be necessary to empower its courts or other competent authorities to order that bank, financial or commercial records be made available or be seized in order to carry out the actions referred to in Articles 2 and 3. A Party shall not decline to act under the provisions of this article on grounds of bank secrecy.
2. Each Party shall consider adopting such legislative and other measures as may be necessary to enable it to use special investigative techniques facilitating the identification and tracing of proceeds and the gathering of evidence related thereto. Such techniques may include monitoring orders, observation, interception of telecommunications, access to computer systems and orders to produce specific documents.

Article 5—Legal remedies

Each Party shall adopt such legislative and other measures as may be necessary to ensure that interested parties affected by measures under Articles 2 and 3 shall have effective legal remedies in order to preserve their rights.

Article 6—Laundering offences

1. Each Party shall adopt such legislative and other measures as may be necessary to establish as offences under its domestic law, when committed intentionally:
   a. the conversion or transfer of property, knowing that such property is proceeds, for the purpose of concealing or disguising the illicit origin of the property or of assisting any person who is involved in the commission of the predicate offence to evade the legal consequences of his actions;
   b. the concealment or disguise of the true nature, source, location, disposition, movement, rights with respect to, or ownership of, property, knowing that such property is proceeds;

and, subject to its constitutional principles and the basic concepts of its legal system;

   c. the acquisition, possession or use of property, knowing, at the time of receipt, that such property was proceeds;
   d. participation in, association or conspiracy to commit, attempts to commit and aiding, abetting, facilitating and counselling the commission of any of the offences established in accordance with this article.

2. For the purposes of implementing or applying paragraph 1 of this article:
   a. it shall not matter whether the predicate offence was subject to the criminal jurisdiction of the Party;
   b. it may be provided that the offences set forth in that paragraph do not apply to the persons who committed the predicate offence;
   c. knowledge, intent or purpose required as an element of an offence set forth in that paragraph may be inferred from objective, factual circumstances.

3. Each Party may adopt such measures as it considers necessary to establish also as offences under its domestic law all or some of the acts referred to in paragraph 1 of this article, in any or all of the following cases where the offender:

   a. ought to have assumed that the property was proceeds;
   b. acted for the purpose of making profit;
   c. acted for the purpose of promoting the carrying on of further criminal activity.

4. Each Party may, at the time of signature or when depositing its instrument of ratification, acceptance, approval or accession, by declaration addressed to the Secretary General of the Council of Europe declare that paragraph 1 of this article applies only to predicate offences or categories of such offences specified in such declaration.

Chapter III—International co-operation

Section 1—Principles of international co-operation

Article 7—General principles and measures for international co-operation

1. The Parties shall co-operate with each other to the widest extent possible for the purposes of investigations and proceedings aiming at the confiscation of instrumentalities and proceeds.
2. Each Party shall adopt such legislative or other measures as may be necessary to enable it to comply, under the conditions provided for in this chapter, with requests:

   a. for confiscation of specific items of property representing proceeds or instrumentalities, as well as for confiscation of proceeds consisting in a requirement to pay a sum of money corresponding to the value of proceeds;
   b. for investigative assistance and provisional measures with a view to either form of confiscation referred to under a above.

Section 2—Investigative assistance

Article 8—Obligation to assist

The Parties shall afford each other, upon request, the widest possible measure of assistance in the identification and tracing of instrumentalities, proceeds and other property liable to confiscation. Such assistance shall include any measure providing and securing evidence as to the existence, location or movement, nature, legal status or value of the aforementioned property.

Article 9—Execution of assistance

The assistance pursuant to Article 8 shall be carried out as permitted by and in accordance with the domestic law of the requested Party and, to the extent not incompatible with such law, in accordance with the procedures specified in the request.

Article 10—Spontaneous information

Without prejudice to its own investigations or proceedings, a Party may without prior request forward to another Party information on instrumentalities and proceeds, when it considers that the disclosure of such information might assist the receiving

Party in initiating or carrying out investigations or proceedings or might lead to a request by that Party under this chapter.

Section 3—Provisional measures

Article 11—Obligation to take provisional measures

1. At the request of another Party which has instituted criminal proceedings or proceedings for the purpose of confiscation, a Party shall take the necessary provisional measures, such as freezing or seizing, to prevent any dealing in, transfer or disposal of property which, at a later stage, may be the subject of a request for confiscation or which might be such as to satisfy the request.
2. A Party which has received a request for confiscation pursuant to Article 13 shall, if so requested, take the measures mentioned in paragraph 1 of this article in respect of any property which is the subject of the request or which might be such as to satisfy the request.

Article 12—Execution of provisional measures

1. The provisional measures mentioned in Article 11 shall be carried out as permitted by and in accordance with the domestic law of the requested Party and, to the extent not incompatible with such law, in accordance with the procedures specified in the request.
2. Before lifting any provisional measure taken pursuant to this article, the requested Party shall, wherever possible, give the requesting Party an opportunity to present its reasons in favour of continuing the measure.

Section 4—Confiscation

Article 13—Obligation to confiscate

1. A Party, which has received a request made by another Party for confiscation concerning instrumentalities or proceeds, situated in its territory, shall:
   a. enforce a confiscation order made by a court of a requesting Party in relation to such instrumentalities or proceeds; or
   b. submit the request to its competent authorities for the purpose of obtaining an order of confiscation and, if such order is granted, enforce it.
2. For the purposes of applying paragraph 1.b of this article, any Party shall whenever necessary have competence to institute confiscation proceedings under its own law.
3. The provisions of paragraph 1 of this article shall also apply to confiscation consisting in a requirement to pay a sum of money corresponding to the value of proceeds, if property on which the confiscation can be enforced is located in the requested Party. In such cases, when enforcing confiscation pursuant to paragraph 1, the requested Party shall, if payment is not obtained, realise the claim on any property available for that purpose.
4. If a request for confiscation concerns a specific item of property, the Parties may agree that the requested Party may enforce the confiscation in the form of a requirement to pay a sum of money corresponding to the value of the property.

Article 14—Execution of confiscation

1. The procedures for obtaining and enforcing the confiscation under Article 13 shall be governed by the law of the requested Party.
2. The requested Party shall be bound by the findings as to the facts in so far as they are stated in a conviction or judicial decision of the requesting Party or in so far as such conviction or judicial decision is implicitly based on them.
3. Each Party may, at the time of signature or when depositing its instrument of ratification, acceptance, approval or accession, by a declaration addressed to the Secretary General of the Council of Europe, declare that paragraph 2 of this article applies only subject to its constitutional principles and the basic concepts of its legal system.
4. If the confiscation consists in the requirement to pay a sum of money, the competent authority of the requested Party shall convert the amount thereof into the currency of that Party at the rate of exchange ruling at the time when the decision to enforce the confiscation is taken.
5. In the case of Article 13, paragraph 1.a, the requesting Party alone shall have the right to decide on any application for review of the confiscation order.

Article 15—Confiscated property

Any property confiscated by the requested Party shall be disposed of by that Party in accordance with its domestic law, unless otherwise agreed by the Parties concerned.

Article 16—Right of enforcement and maximum amount of confiscation

1. A request for confiscation made under Article 13 does not affect the right of the requesting Party to enforce itself the confiscation order.
2. Nothing in this Convention shall be so interpreted as to permit the total value of the confiscation to exceed the amount of the sum of money specified in the confiscation order. If a Party finds that this might occur, the Parties concerned shall enter into consultations to avoid such an effect.

Article 17—Imprisonment in default

The requested Party shall not impose imprisonment in default or any other measure restricting the liberty of a person as a result of a request under Article 13, if the requesting Party has so specified in the request.

Section 5—Refusal and postponement of co-operation

Article 18—Grounds for refusal

1. Co-operation under this chapter may be refused if:

   a. the action sought would be contrary to the fundamental principles of the legal system of the requested Party; or
   b. the execution of the request is likely to prejudice the sovereignty, security, ordre public or other essential interests of the requested Party; or
   c. in the opinion of the requested Party, the importance of the case to which the request relates does not justify the taking of the action sought; or
   d. the offence to which the request relates is a political or fiscal offence; or

e. the requested Party considers that compliance with the action sought would be contrary to the principle of ne bis in idem; or
f. the offence to which the request relates would not be an offence under the law of the requested Party if committed within its jurisdiction. However, this ground for refusal applies to co-operation under Section 2 only in so far as the assistance sought involves coercive action.

2. Co-operation under Section 2, in so far as the assistance sought involves coercive action, and under Section 3 of this chapter, may also be refused if the measures sought could not be taken under the domestic law of the requested Party for the purposes of investigations or proceedings, had it been a similar domestic case.
3. Where the law of the requested Party so requires, co-operation under Section 2, in so far as the assistance sought involves coercive action, and under Section 3 of this chapter may also be refused if the measures sought or any other measures having similar effects would not be permitted under the law of the requesting Party, or, as regards the competent authorities of the requesting Party, if the request is not authorised by either a judge or another judicial authority, including public prosecutors, any of these authorities acting in relation to criminal offences.
4. Co-operation under Section 4 of this chapter may also be refused if:

a. under the law of the requested Party confiscation is not provided for in respect of the type of offence to which the request relates; or
b. without prejudice to the obligation pursuant to Article 13, paragraph 3, it would be contrary to the principles of the domestic laws of the requested Party concerning the limits of confiscation in respect of the relationship between an offence and:

1. i an economic advantage that might be qualified as its proceeds; or
2. ii property that might be qualified as its instrumentalities; or

c. under the law of the requested Party confiscation may no longer be imposed or enforced because of the lapse of time; or
d. the request does not relate to a previous conviction, or a decision of a judicial nature or a statement in such a decision that an offence or several offences have been committed, on the basis of which the confiscation has been ordered or is sought; or
e. confiscation is either not enforceable in the requesting Party, or it is still subject to ordinary means of appeal; or
f. the request relates to a confiscation order resulting from a decision rendered in absentia of the person against whom the order was issued and, in the opinion of the requested Party, the proceedings conducted by the requesting Party leading to such decision did not satisfy the minimum rights of defence recognised as due to everyone against whom a criminal charge is made.

5. For the purpose of paragraph 4.f of this article a decision is not considered to have been rendered in absentia if:

a. it has been confirmed or pronounced after opposition by the person concerned; or
b. it has been rendered on appeal, provided that the appeal was lodged by the person concerned.

6. When considering, for the purposes of paragraph 4.f of this article if the minimum rights of defence have been satisfied, the requested Party shall take into account the fact that the person concerned has deliberately sought to evade justice or the fact that that person, having had the possibility of lodging a legal remedy against the decision made in absentia, elected not to do so. The same will apply when the person concerned, having been duly served with the summons to appear, elected not to do so nor to ask for adjournment.
7. A Party shall not invoke bank secrecy as a ground to refuse any co-operation under this chapter. Where its domestic law so requires, a Party may require that a request for co- operation which would involve the lifting of bank secrecy be authorised by either a judge or another judicial authority, including public prosecutors, any of these authorities acting in relation to criminal offences.
8. Without prejudice to the ground for refusal provided for in paragraph 1.a of this article:

a. the fact that the person under investigation or subjected to a confiscation order by the authorities of the requesting Party is a legal person shall not be invoked by the requested Party as an obstacle to affording any co-operation under this chapter;
b. the fact that the natural person against whom an order of confiscation of proceeds has been issued has subsequently died or the fact that a legal person against whom an order of confiscation of proceeds has been issued has subsequently been dissolved shall not be invoked as an obstacle to render assistance in accordance with Article 13, paragraph 1.a.

Article 19—Postponement

The requested Party may postpone action on a request if such action would prejudice investigations or proceedings by its authorities.

Article 20—Partial or conditional granting of a request

Before refusing or postponing co-operation under this chapter, the requested Party shall, where appropriate after having consulted the requesting Party, consider whether the request may be granted partially or subject to such conditions as it deems necessary.

Section 6—Notification and protection of third parties' rights

Article 21—Notification of documents

1. The Parties shall afford each other the widest measure of mutual assistance in the serving of judicial documents to persons affected by provisional measures and confiscation.
2. Nothing in this article is intended to interfere with:

a. the possibility of sending judicial documents, by postal channels, directly to persons abroad;
b. the possibility for judicial officers, officials or other competent authorities of the Party of origin to effect service of judicial documents directly through the consular authorities of that Party or through judicial officers, officials or other competent authorities of the Party of destination,

unless the Party of destination makes a declaration to the contrary to the Secretary General of the Council of Europe at the time of signature or when depositing its instrument of ratification, acceptance, approval or accession.

3. When serving judicial documents to persons abroad affected by provisional measures or confiscation orders issued in the sending Party, this Party shall indicate what legal remedies are available under its law to such persons.

Article 22—Recognition of foreign decisions

1. When dealing with a request for co-operation under Sections 3 and 4, the requested Party shall recognise any judicial decision taken in the requesting Party regarding rights claimed by third parties.
2. Recognition may be refused if:

a. third parties did not have adequate opportunity to assert their rights; or
b. the decision is incompatible with a decision already taken in the requested Party on the same matter; or
c. it is incompatible with the ordre public of the requested Party; or
d. the decision was taken contrary to provisions on exclusive jurisdiction provided for by the law of the requested Party.

Section 7—Procedural and other general rules

Article 23—Central authority

1. The Parties shall designate a central authority or, if necessary, authorities, which shall be responsible for sending and answering requests made under this chapter, the execution of such requests or the transmission of them to the authorities competent for their execution.
2. Each Party shall, at the time of signature or when depositing its instrument of ratification, acceptance, approval or accession, communicate to the Secretary General of the Council of Europe the names and addresses of the authorities designated in pursuance of paragraph 1 of this article.

Article 24—Direct communication

1. The central authorities shall communicate directly with one another.
2. In the event of urgency, requests or communications under this chapter may be sent directly by the judicial authorities, including public prosecutors, of the requesting Party to such authorities of the requested Party. In such cases a copy shall be sent at the same time to the central authority of the requested Party through the central authority of the requesting Party.

3. Any request or communication under paragraphs 1 and 2 of this article may be made through the International Criminal Police Organisation (Interpol).
4. Where a request is made pursuant to paragraph 2 of this article and the authority is not competent to deal with the request, it shall refer the request to the competent national authority and inform directly the requesting Party that it has done so.
5. Requests or communications under Section 2 of this chapter, which do not involve coercive action, may be directly transmitted by the competent authorities of the requesting Party to the competent authorities of the requested Party.

Article 25—Form of request and languages

1. All requests under this chapter shall be made in writing. Modern means of telecommunications, such as telefax, may be used.
2. Subject to the provisions of paragraph 3 of this article, translations of the requests or supporting documents shall not be required.
3. At the time of signature or when depositing its instrument of ratification, acceptance, approval or accession, any Party may communicate to the Secretary General of the Council of Europe a declaration that it reserves the right to require that requests made to it and documents supporting such requests be accompanied by a translation into its own language or into one of the official languages of the Council of Europe or into such one of these languages as it shall indicate. It may on that occasion declare its readiness to accept translations in any other language as it may specify. The other Parties may apply the reciprocity rule.

Article 26—Legalisation

Documents transmitted in application of this chapter shall be exempt from all legalisation formalities.

Article 27—Content of request

1. Any request for co-operation under this chapter shall specify:
   a. the authority making the request and the authority carrying out the investigations or proceedings;
   b. the object of and the reason for the request;
   c. the matters, including the relevant facts (such as date, place and circumstances of the offence) to which the investigations or proceedings relate, except in the case of a request for notification;
   d. in so far as the co-operation involves coercive action:
      i. the text of the statutory provisions or, where this is not possible, a statement of the relevant law applicable; and
      ii. an indication that the measure sought or any other measures having similar effects could be taken in the territory of the requesting Party under its own law;
   e. where necessary and in so far as possible:
      i. details of the person or persons concerned, including name, date and place of birth, nationality and location, and, in the case of a legal person, its seat; and

ii. the property in relation to which co-operation is sought, its location, its connection with the person or persons concerned, any connection with the offence, as well as any available information about other persons, interests in the property; and

f. any particular procedure the requesting Party wishes to be followed.

2. A request for provisional measures under Section 3 in relation to seizure of property on which a confiscation order consisting in the requirement to pay a sum of money may be realised shall also indicate a maximum amount for which recovery is sought in that property.
3. In addition to the indications mentioned in paragraph 1, any request under Section 4 shall contain:

a. in the case of Article 13, paragraph 1.a:

i. a certified true copy of the confiscation order made by the court in the requesting Party and a statement of the grounds on the basis of which the order was made, if they are not indicated in the order itself;
ii. an attestation by the competent authority of the requesting Party that the confiscation order is enforceable and not subject to ordinary means of appeal;
iii. information as to the extent to which the enforcement of the order is requested; and
iv. information as to the necessity of taking any provisional measures;

b. in the case of Article 13, paragraph 1.b, a statement of the facts relied upon by the requesting Party sufficient to enable the requested Party to seek the order under its domestic law;
c. when third parties have had the opportunity to claim rights, documents demonstrating that this has been the case.

Article 28—Defective requests

1. If a request does not comply with the provisions of this chapter or the information supplied is not sufficient to enable the requested Party to deal with the request, that Party may ask the requesting Party to amend the request or to complete it with additional information.
2. The requested Party may set a time-limit for the receipt of such amendments or information.
3. Pending receipt of the requested amendments or information in relation to a request under Section 4 of this chapter, the requested Party may take any of the measures referred to in Sections 2 or 3 of this chapter.

Article 29—Plurality of requests

1. Where the requested Party receives more than one request under Sections 3 or 4 of this chapter in respect of the same person or property, the plurality of requests shall not prevent that Party from dealing with the requests involving the taking of provisional measures.

2. In the case of plurality of requests under Section 4 of this chapter, the requested Party shall consider consulting the requesting Parties.

Article 30—Obligation to give reasons

The requested Party shall give reasons for any decision to refuse, postpone or make conditional any co-operation under this chapter.

Article 31—Information

1. The requested Party shall promptly inform the requesting Party of:

   a. the action initiated on a request under this chapter;
   b. the final result of the action carried out on the basis of the request;
   c. a decision to refuse, postpone or make conditional, in whole or in part, any co-operation under this chapter;
   d. any circumstances which render impossible the carrying out of the action sought or are likely to delay it significantly; and
   e. in the event of provisional measures taken pursuant to a request under Sections 2 or 3 of this chapter, such provisions of its domestic law as would automatically lead to the lifting of the provisional measure.

2. The requesting Party shall promptly inform the requested Party of:

   a. any review, decision or any other fact by reason of which the confiscation order ceases to be wholly or partially enforceable; and
   b. any development, factual or legal, by reason of which any action under this chapter is no longer justified.

3. Where a Party, on the basis of the same confiscation order, requests confiscation in more than one Party, it shall inform all Parties which are affected by an enforcement of the order about the request.

Article 32—Restriction of use

1. The requested Party may make the execution of a request dependent on the condition that the information or evidence obtained will not, without its prior consent, be used or transmitted by the authorities of the requesting Party for investigations or proceedings other than those specified in the request.
2. Each Party may, at the time of signature or when depositing its instrument of ratification, acceptance, approval or accession, by declaration addressed to the Secretary General of the Council of Europe, declare that, without its prior consent, information or evidence provided by it under this chapter may not be used or transmitted by the authorities of the requesting Party in investigations or proceedings other than those specified in the request.

Article 33—Confidentiality

1. The requesting Party may require that the requested Party keep confidential the facts and substance of the request, except to the extent necessary to execute the request. If the requested Party cannot comply with the requirement of confidentiality, it shall promptly inform the requesting Party.

2. The requesting Party shall, if not contrary to basic principles of its national law and if so requested, keep confidential any evidence and information provided by the requested Party, except to the extent that its disclosure is necessary for the investigations or proceedings described in the request.
3. Subject to the provisions of its domestic law, a Party which has received spontaneous information under Article 10 shall comply with any requirement of confidentiality as required by the Party which supplies the information. If the other Party cannot comply with such requirement, it shall promptly inform the transmitting Party.

Article 34—Costs

The ordinary costs of complying with a request shall be borne by the requested Party. Where costs of a substantial or extraordinary nature are necessary to comply with a request, the Parties shall consult in order to agree the conditions on which the request is to be executed and how the costs shall be borne.

Article 35—Damages

1. When legal action on liability for damages resulting from an act or omission in relation to co- operation under this chapter has been initiated by a person, the Parties concerned shall consider consulting each other, where appropriate, to determine how to apportion any sum of damages due.
2. A Party which has become subject of a litigation for damages shall endeavour to inform the other Party of such litigation if that Party might have an interest in the case.

Chapter IV—Final provisions

Article 36—Signature and entry into force

1. This Convention shall be open for signature by the member States of the Council of Europe and non-member States which have participated in its elaboration. Such States may express their consent to be bound by:

   a. signature without reservation as to ratification, acceptance or approval; or
   b. signature subject to ratification, acceptance or approval, followed by ratification, acceptance or approval.

2. Instruments of ratification, acceptance or approval shall be deposited with the Secretary General of the Council of Europe.
3. This Convention shall enter into force on the first day of the month following the expiration of a period of 3 months after the date on which three States, of which at least two are member States of the Council of Europe, have expressed their consent to be bound by the Convention in accordance with the provisions of paragraph 1.
4. In respect of any signatory State which subsequently expresses its consent to be bound by it, the Convention shall enter into force on the first day of the month following the expiration of a period of 3 months after the date of the expression of its consent to be bound by the Convention in accordance with the provisions of paragraph 1.

Article 37—Accession to the Convention

1. After the entry into force of this Convention, the Committee of Ministers of the Council of Europe, after consulting the Contracting States to the Convention, may invite any State not a member of the Council and not having participated in its elaboration to accede to this Convention, by a decision taken by the majority provided for in Article 20.d. of the Statute of the Council of Europe and by the unanimous vote of the representatives of the Contracting States entitled to sit on the Committee.
2. In respect of any acceding State the Convention shall enter into force on the first day of the month following the expiration of a period of 3 months after the date of deposit of the instrument of accession with the Secretary General of the Council of Europe.

Article 38—Territorial application

1. Any State may, at the time of signature or when depositing its instrument of ratification, acceptance, approval or accession, specify the territory or territories to which this Convention shall apply.
2. Any State may, at any later date, by a declaration addressed to the Secretary General of the Council of Europe, extend the application of this Convention to any other territory specified in the declaration. In respect of such territory the Convention shall enter into force on the first day of the month following the expiration of a period of 3 months after the date of receipt of such declaration by the Secretary General.
3. Any declaration made under the two preceding paragraphs may, in respect of any territory specified in such declaration, be withdrawn by a notification addressed to the Secretary General. The withdrawal shall become effective on the first day of the month following the expiration of a period of 3 months after the date of receipt of such notification by the Secretary General.

Article 39—Relationship to other conventions and agreements

1. This Convention does not affect the rights and undertakings derived from international multilateral conventions concerning special matters.
2. The Parties to the Convention may conclude bilateral or multilateral agreements with one another on the matters dealt with in this Convention, for purposes of supplementing or strengthening its provisions or facilitating the application of the principles embodied in it.
3. If two or more Parties have already concluded an agreement or treaty in respect of a subject which is dealt with in this Convention or otherwise have established their relations in respect of that subject, they shall be entitled to apply that agreement or treaty or to regulate those relations accordingly, in lieu of the present Convention, if it facilitates international co-operation.

Article 40—Reservations

1. Any State may, at the time of signature or when depositing its instrument of ratification, acceptance, approval or accession, declare that it avails itself of one or more of the reservations provided for in Article 2, paragraph 2, Article 6, paragraph 4, Article 14, paragraph 3, Article 21, paragraph 2, Article 25, paragraph 3 and Article 32, paragraph 2. No other reservation may be made.
2. Any State which has made a reservation under the preceding paragraph may wholly or partly withdraw it by means of a notification addressed to the Secretary General of the Council of Europe. The withdrawal shall take effect on the date of receipt of such notification by the Secretary General.
3. A Party which has made a reservation in respect of a provision of this Convention may not claim the application of that provision by any other Party; it may, however, if its reservation is partial or conditional, claim the application of that provision in so far as it has itself accepted it.

Article 41—Amendments

1. Amendments to this Convention may be proposed by any Party, and shall be communicated by the Secretary General of the Council of Europe to the member States of the Council of Europe and to every non-member State which has acceded to or has been invited to accede to this Convention in accordance with the provisions of Article 37.
2. Any amendment proposed by a Party shall be communicated to the European Committee on Crime Problems which shall submit to the Committee of Ministers its opinion on that proposed amendment.
3. The Committee of Ministers shall consider the proposed amendment and the opinion submitted by the European Committee on Crime Problems and may adopt the amendment.
4. The text of any amendment adopted by the Committee of Ministers in accordance with paragraph 3 of this article shall be forwarded to the Parties for acceptance.
5. Any amendment adopted in accordance with paragraph 3 of this article shall come into force on the thirtieth day after all Parties have informed the Secretary General of their acceptance thereof.

Article 42—Settlement of disputes

1. The European Committee on Crime Problems of the Council of Europe shall be kept informed regarding the interpretation and application of this Convention.
2. In case of a dispute between Parties as to the interpretation or application of this Convention, they shall seek a settlement of the dispute through negotiation or any other peaceful means of their choice, including submission of the dispute to the European Committee on Crime Problems, to an arbitral tribunal whose decisions shall be binding upon the Parties, or to the International Court of Justice, as agreed upon by the Parties concerned.

Article 43—Denunciation

1. Any Party may, at any time, denounce this Convention by means of a notification addressed to the Secretary General of the Council of Europe.
2. Such denunciation shall become effective on the first day of the month following the expiration of a period of 3 months after the date of receipt of the notification by the Secretary General.
3. The present Convention shall, however, continue to apply to the enforcement under Article 14 of confiscation for which a request has been made in conformity with the provisions of this Convention before the date on which such a denunciation takes effect.

Article 44—Notifications

The Secretary General of the Council of Europe shall notify the member States of the Council and any State which has acceded to this Convention of:

a. any signature;
b. the deposit of any instrument of ratification, acceptance, approval or accession;
c. any date of entry into force of this Convention in accordance with Articles 36 and 37;
d. any reservation made under Article 40, paragraph 1;
e. any other act, notification or communication relating to this Convention.

In witness whereof the undersigned, being duly authorised thereto, have signed this Convention.

Done at Strasbourg, the 8th day of November 1990, in English and in French, both texts being equally authentic, in a single copy which shall be deposited in the archives of the Council of Europe. The Secretary General of the Council of Europe shall transmit certified copies to each member State of the Council of Europe, to the non-member States which have participated in the elaboration of this Convention, and to any State invited to accede to it.

iii) International Convention for the Suppression of the Financing of Terrorism (New York, 9 December 1999)[4]

The objective of the International Convention for the Suppression of the Financing of Terrorism (the Convention) is to enhance international cooperation among States in devising and adopting effective measures for the prevention of the financing of terrorism, as well as for its suppression through the prosecution and punishment of its perpetrators.

The **Terrorist Financing Convention** is a 1999 United Nations treaty designed to criminalize acts of financing acts of terrorism. The convention also seeks to promote police and judicial co-operation to prevent, investigate and punish the financing of such acts. As of October 2018, the treaty has been ratified by 188 states;

[4] https://treaties.un.org/doc/Treaties/1999/12/19991209%2009-59%20AM/Ch_XVIII_11p.pdf and https://treaties.un.org/doc/db/Terrorism/english-18-11.pdf

in terms of universality, it is therefore one of the most successful anti-terrorism treaties in history.[5]

Article 1

For the purposes of this Convention:

1. "Funds" means assets of every kind, whether tangible or intangible, movable or immovable, however acquired, and legal documents or instruments in any form, including electronic or digital, evidencing title to, or interest in, such assets, including, but not limited to, bank credits, travellers cheques, bank cheques, money orders, shares, securities, bonds, drafts, letters of credit.
2. "A State or governmental facility" means any permanent or temporary facility or conveyance that is used or occupied by representatives of a State, members of Government, the legislature or the judiciary or by officials or employees of a State or any other public authority or entity or by employees or officials of an intergovernmental organization in connection with their official duties.
3. "Proceeds" means any funds derived from or obtained, directly or indirectly, through the commission of an offence set forth in article 2.

Article 2

1. Any person commits an offence within the meaning of this Convention if that person by any means, directly or indirectly, unlawfully and wilfully, provides or collects funds with the intention that they should be used or in the knowledge that they are to be used, in full or in part, in order to carry out:
   (a) An act which constitutes an offence within the scope of and as defined in one of the treaties listed in the annex; or
   (b) Any other act intended to cause death or serious bodily injury to a civilian, or to any other person not taking an active part in the hostilities in a situation of armed conflict, when the purpose of such act, by its nature or context, is to intimidate a population, or to compel a government or an international organization to do or to abstain from doing any act.
2. (a) On depositing its instrument of ratification, acceptance, approval or accession, a State Party which is not a party to a treaty listed in the annex may declare that, in the application of this Convention to the State Party, the treaty shall be deemed not to be included in the annex referred to in paragraph 1, subparagraph (a). The declaration shall cease to have effect as soon as the treaty enters into force for the State Party, which shall notify the depositary of this fact;
   (b) When a State Party ceases to be a party to a treaty listed in the annex, it may make a declaration as provided for in this article, with respect to that treaty.
3. For an act to constitute an offence set forth in paragraph 1, it shall not be necessary that the funds were actually used to carry out an offence referred to in paragraph 1, subparagraphs (a) or (b).

[5] https://en.wikipedia.org/wiki/Terrorist_Financing_Convention

4. Any person also commits an offence if that person attempts to commit an offence as set forth in paragraph 1 of this article.
5. Any person also commits an offence if that person:

   (a) Participates as an accomplice in an offence as set forth in paragraph 1 or 4 of this article;
   (b) Organizes or directs others to commit an offence as set forth in paragraph1or 4 of this article;
   (c) Contributes to the commission of one or more offences as set forth in paragraphs 1 or 4 of this article by a group of persons acting with a common purpose. Such contribution shall be intentional and shall either:

      (i) Be made with the aim of furthering the criminal activity or criminal purpose of the group, where such activity or purpose involves the commission of an offence as set forth in paragraph 1 of this article; or
      (ii) Be made in the knowledge of the intention of the group to commit an offence as set forth in paragraph 1 of this article.

Article 3

This Convention shall not apply where the offence is committed within a single State, the alleged offender is a national of that State and is present in the territory of that State and no other State has a basis under article 7, paragraph 1, or article 7, paragraph 2, to exercise jurisdiction, except that the provisions of articles 12 to 18 shall, as appropriate, apply in those cases.

Article 4

Each State Party shall adopt such measures as may be necessary:

(a) To establish as criminal offences under its domestic law the offences set forth in article 2;
(b) To make those offences punishable by appropriate penalties which take into account the grave nature of the offences.

Article 5

1. Each State Party, in accordance with its domestic legal principles, shall take the necessary measures to enable a legal entity located in its territory or organized under its laws to be held liable when a person responsible for the management or control of that legal entity has, in that capacity, committed an offence set forth in article 2. Such liability may be criminal, civil or administrative.
2. Such liability is incurred without prejudice to the criminal liability of individuals having committed the offences.
3. Each State Party shall ensure, in particular, that legal entities liable in accordance with paragraph 1 above are subject to effective, proportionate and dissuasive criminal, civil or administrative sanctions. Such sanctions may include monetary sanctions.

Article 6

Each State Party shall adopt such measures as may be necessary, including, where appropriate, domestic legislation, to ensure that criminal acts within the scope of this Convention are under no circumstances justifiable by considerations of a political, philosophical, ideological, racial, ethnic, religious or other similar nature.

Article 7

1. Each State Party shall take such measures as may be necessary to establish its jurisdiction over the offences set forth in article 2 when:
   (a) The offence is committed in the territory of that State;
   (b) The offence is committed onboard a vessel flying the flag of that State or an aircraft registered under the laws of that State at the time the offence is committed;
   (c) The offence is committed by a national of that State.
2. A State Party may also establish its jurisdiction over any such offence when:
   (a) The offence was directed towards or resulted in the carrying out of an offence referred to in article 2, paragraph 1, subparagraph (a) or (b), in the territory of or against a national of that State;
   (b) The offence was directed towards or resulted in the carrying out of an offence referred to in article 2, paragraph 1, subparagraph (a) or (b), against a State or government facility of that State abroad, including diplomatic or consular premises of that State;
   (c) The offence was directed towards or resulted in an offence referred to in article 2, paragraph 1, subparagraph (a) or (b), committed in an attempt to compel that State to do or abstain from doing any act;
   (d) The offence is committed by a stateless person who has his or her habitual residence in the territory of that State;
   (e) The offence is committed on board an aircraft which is operated by the Government of that State.
3. Upon ratifying, accepting, approving or acceding to this Convention, each State Party shall notify the Secretary-General of the United Nations of the jurisdiction it has established in accordance with paragraph 2. Should any change take place, the State Party concerned shall immediately notify the Secretary-General.
4. Each State Party shall likewise take such measures as may be necessary to establish its jurisdiction over the offences set forth in article 2 in cases where the alleged offender is present in its territory and it does not extradite that person to any of the States Parties that have established their jurisdiction in accordance with paragraphs 1 or 2.
5. When more than one State Party claims jurisdiction over the offences set forth in article 2, the relevant States Parties shall strive to coordinate their actions appropriately, in particular concerning the conditions for prosecution and the modalities for mutual legal assistance.

6. Without prejudice to the norms of general international law, this Convention does not exclude the exercise of any criminal jurisdiction established by a State Party in accordance with its domestic law.

Article 8

1. Each State Party shall take appropriate measures, in accordance with its domestic legal principles, for the identification, detection and freezing or seizure of any funds used or allocated for the purpose of committing the offences set forth in article 2 as well as the proceeds derived from such offences, for purposes of possible forfeiture.
2. Each State Party shall take appropriate measures, in accordance with its domestic legal principles, for the forfeiture of funds used or allocated for the purpose of committing the offences set forth in article 2 and the proceeds derived from such offences.
3. Each State Party concerned may give consideration to concluding agreements on the sharing with other States Parties, on a regular or case-by-case basis, of the funds derived from the forfeitures referred to in this article.
4. Each State Party shall consider establishing mechanisms whereby the funds derived from the forfeitures referred to in this article are utilized to compensate the victims of offences referred to in article 2, paragraph 1, subparagraph (a) or (b), or their families.
5. The provisions of this article shall be implemented without prejudice to the rights of third parties acting in good faith.

Article 9

1. Upon receiving information that a person who has committed or who is alleged to have committed an offence set forth in article 2 may be present in its territory, the State Party concerned shall take such measures as may be necessary under its domestic law to investigate the facts contained in the information.
2. Upon being satisfied that the circumstances so warrant, the State Party in whose territory the offender or alleged offender is present shall take the appropriate measures under its domestic law so as to ensure that person's presence for the purpose of prosecution or extradition.
3. Any person regarding whom the measures referred to in paragraph 2 are being taken shall be entitled to:

   (a) Communicate without delay with the nearest appropriate representative of the State of which that person is a national or which is otherwise entitled to protect that person's rights or, if that person is a stateless person, the State in the territory of which that person habitually resides;
   (b) Be visited by a representative of that State;
   (c) Be informed of that person's rights under subparagraphs (a) and (b).

4. The rights referred to in paragraph 3 shall be exercised in conformity with the laws and regulations of the State in the territory of which the offender or alleged offender is present, subject to the provision that the said laws and regulations

must enable full effect to be given to the purposes for which the rights accorded under paragraph 3 are intended.

5. The provisions of paragraphs 3 and 4 shall be without prejudice to the right of any State Party having a claim to jurisdiction in accordance with article 7, paragraph 1, subparagraph (b), or paragraph 2, subparagraph (b), to invite the International Committee of the Red Cross to communicate with and visit the alleged offender.
6. When a State Party, pursuant to the present article, has taken a person into custody, it shall immediately notify, directly or through the Secretary-General of the United Nations, the States Parties which have established jurisdiction in accordance with article 7, paragraph 1 or 2, and, if it considers it advisable, any other interested States Parties, of the fact that such person is in custody and of the circumstances which warrant that person=s detention. The State which makes the investigation contemplated in paragraph 1 shall promptly inform the said States Parties of its findings and shall indicate whether it intends to exercise jurisdiction.

Article 10

1. The State Party in the territory of which the alleged offender is present shall, in cases to which article 7 applies, if it does not extradite that person, be obliged, without exception whatsoever and whether or not the offence was committed in its territory, to submit the case without undue delay to its competent authorities for the purpose of prosecution, through proceedings in accordance with the laws of that State. Those authorities shall take their decision in the same manner as in the case of any other offence of a grave nature under the law of that State.
2. Whenever a State Party is permitted under its domestic law to extradite or otherwise surrender one of its nationals only upon the condition that the person will be returned to that State to serve the sentence imposed as a result of the trial or proceeding for which the extradition or surrender of the person was sought, and this State and the State seeking the extradition of the person agree with this option and other terms they may deem appropriate, such a conditional extradition or surrender shall be sufficient to discharge the obligation set forth in paragraph 1.

Article 11

1. The offences set forth in article 2 shall be deemed to be included as extraditable offences in any extradition treaty existing between any of the States Parties before the entry into force of this Convention. States Parties undertake to include such offences as extraditable offences in every extradition treaty to be subsequently concluded between them.
2. When a State Party which makes extradition conditional on the existence of a treaty receives a request for extradition from another State Party with which it has no extradition treaty, the requested State Party may, at its option, consider this Convention as a legal basis for extradition in respect of the offences set forth in article 2. Extradition shall be subject to the other conditions provided by the law of the requested State.
3. States Parties which do not make extradition conditional on the existence of a treaty shall recognize the offences set forth in article 2 as extraditable offences

between themselves, subject to the conditions provided by the law of the requested State.

4. If necessary, the offences set forth in article 2 shall be treated, for the purposes of extradition between States Parties, as if they had been committed not only in the place in which they occurred but also in the territory of the States that have established jurisdiction in accordance with article 7, paragraphs 1 and 2.
5. The provisions of all extradition treaties and arrangements between States Parties with regard to offences set forth in article 2 shall be deemed to be modified as between States Parties to the extent that they are incompatible with this Convention.

Article 12

1. States Parties shall afford one another the greatest measure of assistance in connection with criminal investigations or criminal or extradition proceedings in respect of the offences set forth in article 2, including assistance in obtaining evidence in their possession necessary for the proceedings.
2. States Parties may not refuse a request for mutual legal assistance on the ground of bank secrecy.
3. The requesting Party shall not transmit nor use information or evidence furnished by the requested Party for investigations, prosecutions or proceedings other than those stated in the request without the prior consent of the requested Party.
4. Each State Party may give consideration to establishing mechanisms to share with other States Parties information or evidence needed to establish criminal, civil or administrative liability pursuant to article 5.
5. States Parties shall carry out their obligations under paragraphs 1 and 2 in conformity with any treaties or other arrangements on mutual legal assistance or information exchange that may exist between them. In the absence of such treaties or arrangements, States Parties shall afford one another assistance in accordance with their domestic law.

Article 13

None of the offences set forth in article 2 shall be regarded, for the purposes of extradition or mutual legal assistance, as a fiscal offence. Accordingly, States Parties may not refuse a request for extradition or for mutual legal assistance on the sole ground that it concerns a fiscal offence.

Article 14

None of the offences set forth in article 2 shall be regarded for the purposes of extradition or mutual legal assistance as a political offence or as an offence connected with a political offence or as an offence inspired by political motives. Accordingly, a request for extradition or for mutual legal assistance based on such an offence may not be refused on the sole ground that it concerns a political offence or an offence connected with a political offence or an offence inspired by political motives.

Article 15

Nothing in this Convention shall be interpreted as imposing an obligation to extradite or to afford mutual legal assistance, if the requested State Party has substantial grounds for believing that the request for extradition for offences set forth in article 2 or for mutual legal assistance with respect to such offences has been made for the purpose of prosecuting or punishing a person on account of that person's race, religion, nationality, ethnic origin or political opinion or that compliance with the request would cause prejudice to that person's position for any of these reasons.

Article 16

1. A person who is being detained or is serving a sentence in the territory of one State Party whose presence in another State Party is requested for purposes of identification, testimony or otherwise providing assistance in obtaining evidence for the investigation or prosecution of offences set forth in article 2 may be transferred if the following conditions are met:
   (a) The person freely gives his or her informed consent;
   (b) The competent authorities of both States agree, subject to such conditions as those States may deem appropriate.
2. For the purposes of the present article:
   (a) The State to which the person is transferred shall have the authority and obligation to keep the person transferred in custody, unless otherwise requested or authorized by the State from which the person was transferred;
   (b) The State to which the person is transferred shall without delay implement its obligation to return the person to the custody of the State from which the person was transferred as agreed beforehand, or as otherwise agreed, by the competent authorities of both States;
   (c) The State to which the person is transferred shall not require the State from which the person was transferred to initiate extradition proceedings for the return of the person;
   (d) The person transferred shall receive credit for service of the sentence being served in the State from which he or she was transferred for time spent in the custody of the State to which he or she was transferred.
3. Unless the State Party from which a person is to be transferred in accordance with the present article so agrees, that person, whatever his or her nationality, shall not be prosecuted or detained or subjected to any other restriction of his or her personal liberty in the territory of the State to which that person is transferred in respect of acts or convictions anterior to his or her departure from the territory of the State from which such person was transferred.

Article 17

Any person who is taken into custody or regarding whom any other measures are taken or proceedings are carried out pursuant to this Convention shall be guaranteed fair treatment, including enjoyment of all rights and guarantees in conformity with the law of the State in the territory of which that person is present and applicable provisions of international law, including international human rights law.

Article 18

1. States Parties shall cooperate in the prevention of the offences set forth in article 2 by taking all practicable measures, inter alia, by adapting their domestic legislation, if necessary, to prevent and counter preparations in their respective territories for the commission of those offences within or outside their territories, including:

   (a) Measures to prohibit in their territories illegal activities of persons and organizations that knowingly encourage, instigate, organize or engage in the commission of offences set forth in article 2;
   (b) Measures requiring financial institutions and other professions involved in financial transactions to utilize the most efficient measures available for the identification of their usual or occasional customers, as well as customers in whose interest accounts are opened, and to pay special attention to unusual or suspicious transactions and report transactions suspected of stemming from a criminal activity. For this purpose, States Parties shall consider:

      (i) Adopting regulations prohibiting the opening of accounts the holders or beneficiaries of which are unidentified or unidentifiable, and measures to ensure that such institutions verify the identity of the real owners of such transactions;
      (ii) With respect to the identification of legal entities, requiring financial institutions, when necessary, to take measures to verify the legal existence and the structure of the customer by obtaining, either from a public register or from the customer or both, proof of incorporation, including information concerning the customer's name, legal form, address, directors and provisions regulating the power to bind the entity;
      (iii) Adopting regulations imposing on financial institutions the obligation to report promptly to the competent authorities all complex, unusual large transactions and unusual patterns of transactions, which have no apparent economic or obviously lawful purpose, without fear of assuming criminal or civil liability for breach of any restriction on disclosure of information if they report their suspicions in good faith;
      (iv) Requiring financial institutions to maintain, for at least 5 years, all necessary records on transactions, both domestic or international.

2. States Parties shall further cooperate in the prevention of offences set forth in article 2 by considering:

   (a) Measures for the supervision, including, for example, the licensing, of all money- transmission agencies;
   (b) Feasible measures to detect or monitor the physical cross-border transportation of cash and bearer negotiable instruments, subject to strict safeguards to ensure proper use of information and without impeding in any way the freedom of capital movements.

3. States Parties shall further cooperate in the prevention of the offences set forth in article 2 by exchanging accurate and verified information in accordance with their domestic law and coordinating administrative and other measures taken, as appropriate, to prevent the commission of offences set forth in article 2, in particular by:
   (a) Establishing and maintaining channels of communication between their competent agencies and services to facilitate the secure and rapid exchange of information concerning all aspects of offences set forth in article 2;
   (b) Cooperating with one another in conducting inquiries, with respect to the offences set forth in article 2, concerning:
      (i) The identity, whereabouts and activities of persons in respect of whom reasonable suspicion exists that they are involved in such offences;
      (ii) The movement of funds relating to the commission of such offences.
4. States Parties may exchange information through the International Criminal Police Organization (Interpol).

Article 19

The State Party where the alleged offender is prosecuted shall, in accordance with its domestic law or applicable procedures, communicate the final outcome of the proceedings to the Secretary-General of the United Nations, who shall transmit the information to the other States Parties.

Article 20

The States Parties shall carry out their obligations under this Convention in a manner consistent with the principles of sovereign equality and territorial integrity of States and that of non-intervention in the domestic affairs of other States.

Article 21

Nothing in this Convention shall affect other rights, obligations and responsibilities of States and individuals under international law, in particular the purposes of the Charter of the United Nations, international humanitarian law and other relevant conventions.

Article 22

Nothing in this Convention entitles a State Party to undertake in the territory of another State Party the exercise of jurisdiction or performance of functions which are exclusively reserved for the authorities of that other State Party by its domestic law.

Article 23

1. The annex may be amended by the addition of relevant treaties that:
   a) Are open to the participation of all States;
   b) Have entered into force;
   c) Have been ratified, accepted, approved or acceded to by at least 22 States Parties to the present Convention.
2. After the entry into force of this Convention, any State Party may propose such an amendment. Any proposal for an amendment shall be communicated to the

depositary in written form. The depositary shall notify proposals that meet the requirements of paragraph 1 to all States Parties and seek their views on whether the proposed amendment should be adopted.

3. The proposed amendment shall be deemed adopted unless one third of the States Parties object to it by a written notification not later than 180 days after its circulation.
4. The adopted amendment to the annex shall enter into force 30 days after the deposit of the twenty-second instrument of ratification, acceptance or approval of such amendment for all those States Parties having deposited such an instrument. For each State Party ratifying, accepting or approving the amendment after the deposit of the 22 instrument, the amendment shall enter into force on the thirtieth day after deposit by such State Party of its instrument of ratification, acceptance or approval.

Article 24

1. Any dispute between two or more States Parties concerning the interpretation or application of this Convention which cannot be settled through negotiation within a reasonable time shall, at the request of one of them, be submitted to arbitration. If, within 6 months from the date of the request for arbitration, the parties are unable to agree on the organization of the arbitration, any one of those parties may refer the dispute to the International Court of Justice, by application, in conformity with the Statute of the Court.
2. Each State may at the time of signature, ratification, acceptance or approval of this Convention or accession thereto declare that it does not consider itself bound by paragraph 1. The other States Parties shall not be bound by paragraph 1 with respect to any State Party which has made such a reservation.
3. Any State which has made a reservation in accordance with paragraph 2 may at any time withdraw that reservation by notification to the Secretary-General of the United Nations.

Article 25

1. This Convention shall be open for signature by all States from 10 January 2000 to 31 December 2001 at United Nations Headquarters in New York.
2. This Convention is subject to ratification, acceptance or approval. The instruments of ratification, acceptance or approval shall be deposited with the Secretary-General of the United Nations.
3. This Convention shall be open to accession by any State. The instruments of accession shall be deposited with the Secretary-General of the United Nations.

Article 26

1. This Convention shall enter into force on the thirtieth day following the date of the deposit of the twenty-second instrument of ratification, acceptance, approval or accession with the Secretary-General of the United Nations.
2. For each State ratifying, accepting, approving or acceding to the Convention after the deposit of the twenty-second instrument of ratification, acceptance, approval

or accession, the Convention shall enter into force on the thirtieth day after deposit by such State of its instrument of ratification, acceptance, approval or accession.

Article 27

1. Any State Party may denounce this Convention by written notification to the Secretary- General of the United Nations.
2. Denunciation shall take effect 1 year following the date on which notification is received by the Secretary-General of the United Nations.

Article 28

The original of this Convention, of which the Arabic, Chinese, English, French, Russian and Spanish texts are equally authentic, shall be deposited with the Secretary-General of the United Nations who shall send certified copies thereof to all States.

IN WITNESS WHEREOF, the undersigned, being duly authorized thereto by their respective Governments, have signed this Convention, opened for signature at United Nations Headquarters in New York on 10 January 2000.

iv) **UN Palermo Convention 2000**[6]

The **United Nations Convention Against Transnational Organized Crime** (**UNTOC** or **Palermo Convention**) is a 2000 United Nations-sponsored multilateral treaty against transnational organized crime.

The convention was adopted by a resolution of the United Nations General Assembly on 15 November 2000 and came into force on 29 September 2003. There are three supplementary protocols (the Palermo Protocols) to UNTOC (which are not reproduced here):

- Protocol to Prevent, Suppress and Punish Trafficking in Persons, Especially Women and Children;
- Protocol Against the Smuggling of Migrants by Land, Sea and Air; and
- Protocol Against the Illicit Manufacturing of and Trafficking in Firearms.

All four instruments contain elements of the current international law on human trafficking, arms trafficking and money laundering. The United Nations Office on Drugs and Crime (UNODC) acts as custodian of the UNTOC and its protocols.[7]

[6] https://www.unodc.org/documents/middleeastandnorthafrica/organised-crime/UNITED_NATIONS_CONVENTION_AGAINST_TRANSNATIONAL_ORGANIZED_CRIME_AND_THE_PROTOCOLS_THERETO.pdf

[7] https://en.wikipedia.org/wiki/United_Nations_Convention_Against_Transnational_Organized_Crime#:~:text=The%20United%20Nations%20Convention%20Against,treaty%20against%20transnational%20organized%20crime.

United Nations Convention against Transnational Organized Crime

Article 1. Statement of purpose

The purpose of this Convention is to promote cooperation to prevent and combat transnational organized crime more effectively.

Article 2. Use of terms

For the purposes of this Convention:

(a) "Organized criminal group" shall mean a structured group of three or more persons, existing for a period of time and acting in concert with the aim of committing one or more serious crimes or offences established in accordance with this Convention, in order to obtain, directly or indirectly, a financial or other material benefit;
(b) "Serious crime" shall mean conduct constituting an offence punish- able by a maximum deprivation of liberty of at least 4 years or a more serious penalty;
(c) "Structured group" shall mean a group that is not randomly formed for the immediate commission of an offence and that does not need to have formally defined roles for its members, continuity of its membership or a developed structure;
(d) "Property" shall mean assets of every kind, whether corporeal or incorporeal, movable or immovable, tangible or intangible, and legal documents or instruments evidencing title to, or interest in, such assets;
(e) "Proceeds of crime" shall mean any property derived from or obtained, directly or indirectly, through the commission of an offence;
(f) "Freezing" or "seizure" shall mean temporarily prohibiting the transfer, conversion, disposition or movement of property or temporarily assuming custody or control of property on the basis of an order issued by a court or other competent authority;
(g) "Confiscation", which includes forfeiture where applicable, shall mean the permanent deprivation of property by order of a court or other competent authority;
(h) "Predicate offence" shall mean any offence as a result of which proceeds have been generated that may become the subject of an offence as defined in article 6 of this Convention;
(i) "Controlled delivery" shall mean the technique of allowing illicit or suspect consignments to pass out of, through or into the territory of one or more States, with the knowledge and under the supervision of their competent authorities, with a view to the investigation of an offence and the identification of persons involved in the commission of the offence;
(j) "Regional economic integration organization" shall mean an organization constituted by sovereign States of a given region, to which its member States have transferred competence in respect of matters governed by this Convention and which has been duly authorized, in accordance with its internal procedures, to sign, ratify, accept, approve or accede to it; references to "States Parties" under this Convention shall apply to such organizations within the limits of their competence.

Article 3. Scope of application

1. This Convention shall apply, except as otherwise stated herein, to the prevention, investigation and prosecution of:
   (a) The offences established in accordance with articles 5, 6, 8 and 23 of this Convention; and
   (b) Serious crime as defined in article 2 of this Convention;

where the offence is transnational in nature and involves an organized criminal group.

2. For the purpose of paragraph 1 of this article, an offence is transnational in nature if:
   (a) It is committed in more than one State;
   (b) It is committed in one State but a substantial part of its preparation, planning, direction or control takes place in another State;
   (c) It is committed in one State but involves an organized criminal group that engages in criminal activities in more than one State; or
   (d) It is committed in one State but has substantial effects in another State.

Article 4. Protection of sovereignty

1. States Parties shall carry out their obligations under this Convention in a manner consistent with the principles of sovereign equality and territorial integrity of States and that of non-intervention in the domestic affairs of other States.
2. Nothing in this Convention entitles a State Party to undertake in the territory of another State the exercise of jurisdiction and performance of functions that are reserved exclusively for the authorities of that other State by its domestic law.

Article 5. Criminalization of participation in an organized criminal group

1. Each State Party shall adopt such legislative and other measures as may be necessary to establish as criminal offences, when committed intentionally:
   a) Either or both of the following as criminal offences distinct from those involving the attempt or completion of the criminal activity:
      (i) Agreeing with one or more other persons to commit a serious crime for a purpose relating directly or indirectly to the obtaining of a financial or other material benefit and, where required by domestic law, involving an act undertaken by one of the participants in furtherance of the agreement or involving an organized criminal group;
      (ii) Conduct by a person who, with knowledge of either the aim and general criminal activity of an organized criminal group or its intention to commit the crimes in question, takes an active part in:
         a. Criminal activities of the organized criminal group;
         b. Other activities of the organized criminal group in the knowledge that his or her participation will contribute to the achievement of the above-described criminal aim;

b) Organizing, directing, aiding, abetting, facilitating or counselling the commission of serious crime involving an organized criminal group.

2. The knowledge, intent, aim, purpose or agreement referred to in paragraph 1 of this article may be inferred from objective factual circumstances.
3. States Parties whose domestic law requires involvement of an organized criminal group for purposes of the offences established in accordance with paragraph 1 *(a)* (i) of this article shall ensure that their domestic law covers all serious crimes involving organized criminal groups. Such States Parties, as well as States Parties whose domestic law requires an act in furtherance of the agreement for purposes of the offences established in accordance with paragraph 1 *(a)* (i) of this article, shall so inform the Secretary-General of the United Nations at the time of their signature or of deposit of their instrument of ratification, acceptance or approval of or accession to this Convention.

Article 6. Criminalization of the laundering of proceeds of crime

1. Each State Party shall adopt, in accordance with fundamental principles of its domestic law, such legislative and other measures as may be necessary to establish as criminal offences, when committed intentionally:

   (a) (i) The conversion or transfer of property, knowing that such property is the proceeds of crime, for the purpose of concealing or disguising the illicit origin of the property or of helping any person who is involved in the commission of the predicate offence to evade the legal consequences of his or her action;
   (ii) The concealment or disguise of the true nature, source, location, disposition, movement or ownership of or rights with respect to property, knowing that such property is the proceeds of crime;
   (b) Subject to the basic concepts of its legal system:

      (i) The acquisition, possession or use of property, knowing, at the time of receipt, that such property is the proceeds of crime;
      (ii) Participation in, association with or conspiracy to commit, attempts to commit and aiding, abetting, facilitating and counselling the commission of any of the offences established in accordance with this article.

2. For purposes of implementing or applying paragraph 1 of this article:

   (a) Each State Party shall seek to apply paragraph 1 of this article to the widest range of predicate offences;
   (b) Each State Party shall include as predicate offences all serious crime as defined in article 2 of this Convention and the offences established in accordance with articles 5, 8 and 23 of this Convention. In the case of States Parties whose legislation sets out a list of specific predicate offences, they shall, at a minimum, include in such list a comprehensive range of offences associated with organized criminal groups;
   (c) For the purposes of subparagraph *(b),* predicate offences shall include offences committed both within and outside the jurisdiction of the State

Party in question. However, offences committed outside the jurisdiction of a State Party shall constitute predicate offences only when the relevant conduct is a criminal offence under the domestic law of the State where it is committed and would be a criminal offence under the domestic law of the State Party imple- menting or applying this article had it been committed there;

(d) Each State Party shall furnish copies of its laws that give effect to this article and of any subsequent changes to such laws or a description thereof to the Secretary-General of the United Nations;

(e) If required by fundamental principles of the domestic law of a State Party, it may be provided that the offences set forth in paragraph 1 of this article do not apply to the persons who committed the predicate offence;

(f) Knowledge, intent or purpose required as an element of an offence set forth in paragraph 1 of this article may be inferred from objective factual circumstances.

Article 7. Measures to combat money-laundering

1. Each State Party:

   (a) Shall institute a comprehensive domestic regulatory and supervisory regime for banks and non-bank financial institutions and, where appropriate, other bodies particularly susceptible to money-laundering, within its competence, in order to deter and detect all forms of money-laundering, which regime shall emphasize requirements for customer identification, record-keeping and the reporting of suspicious transactions;

   (b) Shall, without prejudice to articles 18 and 27 of this Convention, ensure that administrative, regulatory, law enforcement and other authorities dedicated to combating money-laundering (including, where appropriate under domestic law, judicial authorities) have the ability to cooperate and exchange information at the national and international levels within the conditions prescribed by its domestic law and, to that end, shall consider the establishment of a financial intelligence unit to serve as a national centre for the collection, analysis and dissemination of information regarding potential money-laundering.

2. States Parties shall consider implementing feasible measures to detect and monitor the movement of cash and appropriate negotiable instruments across their borders, subject to safeguards to ensure proper use of information and without impeding in any way the movement of legitimate capital. Such measures may include a requirement that individuals and businesses report the cross-border transfer of substantial quantities of cash and appropriate negotiable instruments.
3. In establishing a domestic regulatory and supervisory regime under the terms of this article, and without prejudice to any other article of this Convention, States Parties are called upon to use as a guideline the relevant initiatives of regional, interregional and multilateral organizations against money-laundering.

4. States Parties shall endeavour to develop and promote global, regional, subregional and bilateral cooperation among judicial, law enforcement and financial regulatory authorities in order to combat money-laundering.

Article 8. Criminalization of corruption

1. Each State Party shall adopt such legislative and other measures as may be necessary to establish as criminal offences, when committed intentionally:
   (a) The promise, offering or giving to a public official, directly or indirectly, of an undue advantage, for the official himself or herself or another person or entity, in order that the official act or refrain from acting in the exercise of his or her official duties;
   (b) The solicitation or acceptance by a public official, directly or indirectly, of an undue advantage, for the official himself or herself or another person or entity, in order that the official act or refrain from acting in the exercise of his or her official duties.
2. Each State Party shall consider adopting such legislative and other measures as may be necessary to establish as criminal offences conduct referred to in paragraph 1 of this article involving a foreign public official or international civil servant. Likewise, each State Party shall consider establishing as criminal offences other forms of corruption.
3. Each State Party shall also adopt such measures as may be necessary to establish as a criminal offence participation as an accomplice in an offence established in accordance with this article.
4. For the purposes of paragraph 1 of this article and article 9 of this Convention, "public official" shall mean a public official or a person who provides a public service as defined in the domestic law and as applied in the criminal law of the State Party in which the person in question performs that function.

Article 9. Measures against corruption

1. In addition to the measures set forth in article 8 of this Convention, each State Party shall, to the extent appropriate and consistent with its legal system, adopt legislative, administrative or other effective measures to promote integrity and to prevent, detect and punish the corruption of public officials.
2. Each State Party shall take measures to ensure effective action by its authorities in the prevention, detection and punishment of the corruption of public officials, including providing such authorities with adequate independence to deter the exertion of inappropriate influence on their actions.

Article 10. Liability of legal persons

1. Each State Party shall adopt such measures as may be necessary, consistent with its legal principles, to establish the liability of legal persons for participation in serious crimes involving an organized criminal group and for the offences established in accordance with articles 5, 6, 8 and 23 of this Convention.

2. Subject to the legal principles of the State Party, the liability of legal persons may be criminal, civil or administrative.
3. Such liability shall be without prejudice to the criminal liability of the natural persons who have committed the offences.
4. Each State Party shall, in particular, ensure that legal persons held liable in accordance with this article are subject to effective, proportionate and dissuasive criminal or non-criminal sanctions, including monetary sanctions.

Article 11. Prosecution, adjudication and sanctions

1. Each State Party shall make the commission of an offence established in accordance with articles 5, 6, 8 and 23 of this Convention liable to sanctions that take into account the gravity of that offence.
2. Each State Party shall endeavour to ensure that any discretionary legal powers under its domestic law relating to the prosecution of persons for offences covered by this Convention are exercised to maximize the effectiveness of law enforcement measures in respect of those offences and with due regard to the need to deter the commission of such offences.
3. In the case of offences established in accordance with articles 5, 6, 8 and 23 of this Convention, each State Party shall take appropriate measures, in accordance with its domestic law and with due regard to the rights of the defence, to seek to ensure that conditions imposed in connection with decisions on release pending trial or appeal take into consideration the need to ensure the presence of the defendant at subsequent criminal proceedings.
4. Each State Party shall ensure that its courts or other competent authorities bear in mind the grave nature of the offences covered by this Convention when considering the eventuality of early release or parole of persons convicted of such offences.
5. Each State Party shall, where appropriate, establish under its domestic law a long statute of limitations period in which to commence proceedings for any offence covered by this Convention and a longer period where the alleged offender has evaded the administration of justice.
6. Nothing contained in this Convention shall affect the principle that the description of the offences established in accordance with this Convention and of the applicable legal defences or other legal principles controlling the lawfulness of conduct is reserved to the domestic law of a State Party and that such offences shall be prosecuted and punished in accordance with that law.

Article 12. Confiscation and seizure

1. States Parties shall adopt, to the greatest extent possible within their domestic legal systems, such measures as may be necessary to enable confiscation of:

    (a) Proceeds of crime derived from offences covered by this Convention or property the value of which corresponds to that of such proceeds;
    (b) Property, equipment or other instrumentalities used in or destined for use in offences covered by this Convention.

2. States Parties shall adopt such measures as may be necessary to enable the identification, tracing, freezing or seizure of any item referred to in paragraph 1 of this article for the purpose of eventual confiscation.
3. If proceeds of crime have been transformed or converted, in part or in full, into other property, such property shall be liable to the measures referred to in this article instead of the proceeds.
4. If proceeds of crime have been intermingled with property acquired from legitimate sources, such property shall, without prejudice to any powers relating to freezing or seizure, be liable to confiscation up to the assessed value of the intermingled proceeds.
5. Income or other benefits derived from proceeds of crime, from property into which proceeds of crime have been transformed or converted or from property with which proceeds of crime have been intermingled shall also be liable to the measures referred to in this article, in the same manner and to the same extent as proceeds of crime.
6. For the purposes of this article and article 13 of this Convention, each State Party shall empower its courts or other competent authorities to order that bank, financial or commercial records be made available or be seized. States Parties shall not decline to act under the provisions of this paragraph on the ground of bank secrecy.
7. States Parties may consider the possibility of requiring that an offender demonstrate the lawful origin of alleged proceeds of crime or other property liable to confiscation, to the extent that such a requirement is consistent with the principles of their domestic law and with the nature of the judicial and other proceedings.
8. The provisions of this article shall not be construed to prejudice the rights of bona fide third parties.
9. Nothing contained in this article shall affect the principle that the measures to which it refers shall be defined and implemented in accordance with and subject to the provisions of the domestic law of a State Party.

Article 13. International cooperation for purposes of confiscation

1. A State Party that has received a request from another State Party having jurisdiction over an offence covered by this Convention for confiscation of proceeds of crime, property, equipment or other instrumentalities referred to in article 12, paragraph 1, of this Convention situated in its territory shall, to the greatest extent possible within its domestic legal system:

   (a) Submit the request to its competent authorities for the purpose of obtaining an order of confiscation and, if such an order is granted, give effect to it; or
   (b) Submit to its competent authorities, with a view to giving effect to it to the extent requested, an order of confiscation issued by a court in the territory of the requesting State Party in accordance with article 12, paragraph 1, of this Convention insofar as it relates to proceeds of crime, property, equipment or other instrumentalities referred to in article 12, paragraph 1, situated in the territory of the requested State Party.

2. Following a request made by another State Party having jurisdiction over an offence covered by this Convention, the requested State Party shall take measures to identify, trace and freeze or seize proceeds of crime, property, equipment or other instrumentalities referred to in article 12, paragraph 1, of this Convention for the purpose of eventual confiscation to be ordered either by the requesting State Party or, pursuant to a request under paragraph 1 of this article, by the requested State Party.
3. The provisions of article 18 of this Convention are applicable, mutatis mutandis, to this article. In addition to the information specified in article 18, paragraph 15, requests made pursuant to this article shall contain:

   (a) In the case of a request pertaining to paragraph 1 *(a)* of this article, a description of the property to be confiscated and a statement of the facts relied upon by the requesting State Party sufficient to enable the requested State Party to seek the order under its domestic law;
   (b) In the case of a request pertaining to paragraph 1 *(b)* of this article, a legally admissible copy of an order of confiscation upon which the request is based issued by the requesting State Party, a statement of the facts and information as to the extent to which execution of the order is requested;
   (c) In the case of a request pertaining to paragraph 2 of this article, a statement of the facts relied upon by the requesting State Party and a description of the actions requested.

4. The decisions or actions provided for in paragraphs 1 and 2 of this article shall be taken by the requested State Party in accordance with and subject to the provisions of its domestic law and its procedural rules or any bilateral or multilateral treaty, agreement or arrangement to which it may be bound in relation to the requesting State Party.
5. Each State Party shall furnish copies of its laws and regulations that give effect to this article and of any subsequent changes to such laws and regulations or a description thereof to the Secretary-General of the United Nations.
6. If a State Party elects to make the taking of the measures referred to in paragraphs 1 and 2 of this article conditional on the existence of a relevant treaty, that State Party shall consider this Convention the necessary and sufficient treaty basis.
7. Cooperation under this article may be refused by a State Party if the offence to which the request relates is not an offence covered by this Convention.
8. The provisions of this article shall not be construed to prejudice the rights of bona fide third parties.
9. States Parties shall consider concluding bilateral or multilateral treaties, agreements or arrangements to enhance the effectiveness of international cooperation undertaken pursuant to this article.

Article 14. Disposal of confiscated proceeds of crime or property

1. Proceeds of crime or property confiscated by a State Party pursuant to articles 12 or 13, paragraph 1, of this Convention shall be disposed of by that State Party in accordance with its domestic law and administrative procedures.

2. When acting on the request made by another State Party in accordance with article 13 of this Convention, States Parties shall, to the extent permitted by domestic law and if so requested, give priority consideration to returning the confiscated proceeds of crime or property to the requesting State Party so that it can give compensation to the victims of the crime or return such proceeds of crime or property to their legitimate owners.
3. When acting on the request made by another State Party in accordance with articles 12 and 13 of this Convention, a State Party may give special consideration to concluding agreements or arrangements on:

    (a) Contributing the value of such proceeds of crime or property or funds derived from the sale of such proceeds of crime or property or a part thereof to the account designated in accordance with article 30, paragraph 2 *(c),* of this Convention and to intergovernmental bodies specializing in the fight against organized crime;
    (b) Sharing with other States Parties, on a regular or case-by-case basis, such proceeds of crime or property, or funds derived from the sale of such proceeds of crime or property, in accordance with its domestic law or administrative procedures.

Article 15. Jurisdiction

1. Each State Party shall adopt such measures as may be necessary to establish its jurisdiction over the offences established in accordance with articles 5, 6, 8 and 23 of this Convention when:

    (a) The offence is committed in the territory of that State Party; or
    (b) The offence is committed on board a vessel that is flying the flag of that State Party or an aircraft that is registered under the laws of that State Party at the time that the offence is committed.

2. Subject to article 4 of this Convention, a State Party may also establish its jurisdiction over any such offence when:

    (a) The offence is committed against a national of that State Party;
    (b) The offence is committed by a national of that State Party or a stateless person who has his or her habitual residence in its territory; or
    (c) The offence is:

        (i) One of those established in accordance with article 5, paragraph 1, of this Convention and is committed outside its territory with a view to the commission of a serious crime within its territory;
        (ii) One of those established in accordance with article 6, paragraph 1 *(b)* (ii), of this Convention and is committed outside its territory with a view to the commission of an offence established in accordance with article 6, paragraph 1 *(a)* (i) or (ii) or *(b)* (i), of this Convention within its territory.

3. For the purposes of article 16, paragraph 10, of this Convention, each State Party shall adopt such measures as may be necessary to establish its jurisdiction over the offences covered by this Convention when the alleged offender is present in its territory and it does not extradite such person solely on the ground that he or she is one of its nationals.
4. Each State Party may also adopt such measures as may be necessary to establish its jurisdiction over the offences covered by this Convention when the alleged offender is present in its territory and it does not extradite him or her.
5. If a State Party exercising its jurisdiction under paragraph 1 or 2 of this article has been notified, or has otherwise learned, that one or more other States Parties are conducting an investigation, prosecution or judicial proceeding in respect of the same conduct, the competent authorities of those States Parties shall, as appropriate, consult one another with a view to coordinating their actions.
6. Without prejudice to norms of general international law, this Convention does not exclude the exercise of any criminal jurisdiction established by a State Party in accordance with its domestic law.

Article 16. Extradition

1. This article shall apply to the offences covered by this Convention or in cases where an offence referred to in article 3, paragraph 1 *(a)* or *(b),* involves an organized criminal group and the person who is the subject of the request for extradition is located in the territory of the requested State Party, provided that the offence for which extradition is sought is punishable under the domestic law of both the requesting State Party and the requested State Party.
2. If the request for extradition includes several separate serious crimes, some of which are not covered by this article, the requested State Party may apply this article also in respect of the latter offences.
3. Each of the offences to which this article applies shall be deemed to be included as an extraditable offence in any extradition treaty existing between States Parties. States Parties undertake to include such offences as extraditable offences in every extradition treaty to be concluded between them.
4. If a State Party that makes extradition conditional on the existence of a treaty receives a request for extradition from another State Party with which it has no extradition treaty, it may consider this Convention the legal basis for extradition in respect of any offence to which this article applies.
5. States Parties that make extradition conditional on the existence of a treaty shall:

   (a) At the time of deposit of their instrument of ratification, acceptance, approval of or accession to this Convention, inform the Secretary-General of the United Nations whether they will take this Convention as the legal basis for cooperation on extradition with other States Parties to this Convention; and

   (b) If they do not take this Convention as the legal basis for cooperation on extradition, seek, where appropriate, to conclude treaties on extradition with other States Parties to this Convention in order to implement this article.

6. States Parties that do not make extradition conditional on the existence of a treaty shall recognize offences to which this article applies as extraditable offences between themselves.
7. Extradition shall be subject to the conditions provided for by the domestic law of the requested State Party or by applicable extradition treaties, including, inter alia, conditions in relation to the minimum penalty requirement for extradition and the grounds upon which the requested State Party may refuse extradition.
8. States Parties shall, subject to their domestic law, endeavour to expedite extradition procedures and to simplify evidentiary requirements relating thereto in respect of any offence to which this article applies.
9. Subject to the provisions of its domestic law and its extradition treaties, the requested State Party may, upon being satisfied that the circumstances so warrant and are urgent and at the request of the requesting State Party, take a person whose extradition is sought and who is present in its territory into custody or take other appropriate measures to ensure his or her presence at extradition proceedings.
10. A State Party in whose territory an alleged offender is found, if it does not extradite such person in respect of an offence to which this article applies solely on the ground that he or she is one of its nationals, shall, at the request of the State Party seeking extradition, be obliged to submit the case without undue delay to its competent authorities for the purpose of prosecution. Those authorities shall take their decision and conduct their proceedings in the same manner as in the case of any other offence of a grave nature under the domestic law of that State Party. The States Parties concerned shall cooperate with each other, in particular on procedural and evidentiary aspects, to ensure the efficiency of such prosecution.
11. Whenever a State Party is permitted under its domestic law to extradite or otherwise surrender one of its nationals only upon the condition that the person will be returned to that State Party to serve the sentence imposed as a result of the trial or proceedings for which the extradition or surrender of the person was sought and that State Party and the State Party seeking the extradition of the person agree with this option and other terms that they may deem appropriate, such conditional extradition or surrender shall be sufficient to discharge the obligation set forth in paragraph 10 of this article.
12. If extradition, sought for purposes of enforcing a sentence, is refused because the person sought is a national of the requested State Party, the requested Party shall, if its domestic law so permits and in conformity with the requirements of such law, upon application of the requesting Party, consider the enforcement of the sentence that has been imposed under the domestic law of the requesting Party or the remainder thereof.
13. Any person regarding whom proceedings are being carried out in connection with any of the offences to which this article applies shall be guaranteed fair treatment at all stages of the proceedings, including enjoyment of all the rights and guarantees provided by the domestic law of the State Party in the territory of which that person is present.

14. Nothing in this Convention shall be interpreted as imposing an obligation to extradite if the requested State Party has substantial grounds for believing that the request has been made for the purpose of prosecuting or punishing a person on account of that person's sex, race, religion, nationality, ethnic origin or political opinions or that compliance with the request would cause prejudice to that person's position for any one of these reasons.
15. States Parties may not refuse a request for extradition on the sole ground that the offence is also considered to involve fiscal matters.
16. Before refusing extradition, the requested State Party shall, where appropriate, consult with the requesting State Party to provide it with ample opportunity to present its opinions and to provide information relevant to its allegation.
17. States Parties shall seek to conclude bilateral and multilateral agreements or arrangements to carry out or to enhance the effectiveness of extradition.

Article 17. Transfer of sentenced persons

States Parties may consider entering into bilateral or multilateral agreements or arrangements on the transfer to their territory of persons sentenced to imprisonment or other forms of deprivation of liberty for offences covered by this Convention, in order that they may complete their sentences there.

Article 18. Mutual legal assistance

1. States Parties shall afford one another the widest measure of mutual legal assistance in investigations, prosecutions and judicial proceedings in relation to the offences covered by this Convention as provided for in article 3 and shall reciprocally extend to one another similar assistance where the requesting State Party has reasonable grounds to suspect that the offence referred to in article 3, paragraph 1 *(a)* or *(b),* is transnational in nature, including that victims, witnesses, proceeds, instrumentalities or evidence of such offences are located in the requested State Party and that the offence involves an organized criminal group.
2. Mutual legal assistance shall be afforded to the fullest extent possible under relevant laws, treaties, agreements and arrangements of the requested State Party with respect to investigations, prosecutions and judicial proceedings in relation to the offences for which a legal person may be held liable in accordance with article 10 of this Convention in the requesting State Party.
3. Mutual legal assistance to be afforded in accordance with this article may be requested for any of the following purposes:

   (a) Taking evidence or statements from persons;
   (b) Effecting service of judicial documents;
   (c) Executing searches and seizures, and freezing;
   (d) Examining objects and sites;
   (e) Providing information, evidentiary items and expert evaluations;
   (f) Providing originals or certified copies of relevant documents and records, including government, bank, financial, corporate or business records;

(g) Identifying or tracing proceeds of crime, property, instrumentalities or other things for evidentiary purposes;
(h) Facilitating the voluntary appearance of persons in the requesting State Party;
(i) Any other type of assistance that is not contrary to the domestic law of the requested State Party.

4. Without prejudice to domestic law, the competent authorities of a State Party may, without prior request, transmit information relating to criminal matters to a competent authority in another State Party where they believe that such information could assist the authority in undertaking or successfully concluding inquiries and criminal proceedings or could result in a request formulated by the latter State Party pursuant to this Convention.
5. The transmission of information pursuant to paragraph 4 of this article shall be without prejudice to inquiries and criminal proceedings in the State of the competent authorities providing the information. The competent authorities receiving the information shall comply with a request that said information remain confidential, even temporarily, or with restrictions on its use. However, this shall not prevent the receiving State Party from disclosing in its proceedings information that is exculpatory to an accused person. In such a case, the receiving State Party shall notify the transmitting State Party prior to the disclosure and, if so requested, consult with the transmitting State Party. If, in an exceptional case, advance notice is not possible, the receiving State Party shall inform the transmitting State Party of the disclosure without delay.
6. The provisions of this article shall not affect the obligations under any other treaty, bilateral or multilateral, that governs or will govern, in whole or in part, mutual legal assistance.
7. Paragraphs 9 to 29 of this article shall apply to requests made pursuant to this article if the States Parties in question are not bound by a treaty of mutual legal assistance. If those States Parties are bound by such a treaty, the corresponding provisions of that treaty shall apply unless the States Parties agree to apply paragraphs 9 to 29 of this article in lieu thereof. States Parties are strongly encouraged to apply these paragraphs if they facilitate cooperation.
8. States Parties shall not decline to render mutual legal assistance pursuant to this article on the ground of bank secrecy.
9. States Parties may decline to render mutual legal assistance pursuant to this article on the ground of absence of dual criminality. However, the requested State Party may, when it deems appropriate, provide assistance, to the extent it decides at its discretion, irrespective of whether the conduct would constitute an offence under the domestic law of the requested State Party.
10. A person who is being detained or is serving a sentence in the territory of one State Party whose presence in another State Party is requested for purposes of identification, testimony or otherwise providing assistance in obtaining evidence for investigations, prosecutions or judicial proceedings in relation to offences

covered by this Convention may be transferred if the following conditions are met:

(a) The person freely gives his or her informed consent;
(b) The competent authorities of both States Parties agree, subject to such conditions as those States Parties may deem appropriate.

11. For the purposes of paragraph 10 of this article:

(a) The State Party to which the person is transferred shall have the authority and obligation to keep the person transferred in custody, unless otherwise requested or authorized by the State Party from which the person was transferred;
(b) The State Party to which the person is transferred shall without delay implement its obligation to return the person to the custody of the State Party from which the person was transferred as agreed beforehand, or as otherwise agreed, by the competent authorities of both States Parties;
(c) The State Party to which the person is transferred shall not require the State Party from which the person was transferred to initiate extradition proceedings for the return of the person;
(d) The person transferred shall receive credit for service of the sentence being served in the State from which he or she was transferred for time spent in the custody of the State Party to which he or she was transferred.

12. Unless the State Party from which a person is to be transferred in accordance with paragraphs 10 and 11 of this article so agrees, that person, whatever his or her nationality, shall not be prosecuted, detained, punished or subjected to any other restriction of his or her personal liberty in the territory of the State to which that person is transferred in respect of acts, omissions or convictions prior to his or her departure from the territory of the State from which he or she was transferred.
13. Each State Party shall designate a central authority that shall have the responsibility and power to receive requests for mutual legal assistance and either to execute them or to transmit them to the competent authorities for execution. Where a State Party has a special region or territory with a separate system of mutual legal assistance, it may designate a distinct central authority that shall have the same function for that region or territory. Central authorities shall ensure the speedy and proper execution or transmission of the requests received. Where the central authority transmits the request to a competent authority for execution, it shall encourage the speedy and proper execution of the request by the competent authority. The Secretary-General of the United Nations shall be notified of the central authority designated for this purpose at the time each State Party deposits its instrument of ratification, acceptance or approval of or accession to this Convention. Requests for mutual legal assistance and any communication related thereto shall be transmitted to the central authorities designated by the States Parties. This requirement shall be without prejudice to the right of a State Party to require that such requests and communications be addressed to it

through diplomatic channels and, in urgent circumstances, where the States Parties agree, through the International Criminal Police Organization, if possible.

14. Requests shall be made in writing or, where possible, by any means capable of producing a written record, in a language acceptable to the requested State Party, under conditions allowing that State Party to establish authenticity. The Secretary-General of the United Nations shall be notified of the language or languages acceptable to each State Party at the time it deposits its instrument of ratification, acceptance or approval of or accession to this Convention. In urgent circumstances and where agreed by the States Parties, requests may be made orally, but shall be confirmed in writing forthwith.
15. A request for mutual legal assistance shall contain:
    (a) The identity of the authority making the request;
    (b) The subject matter and nature of the investigation, prosecution or judicial proceeding to which the request relates and the name and functions of the authority conducting the investigation, prosecution or judicial proceeding;
    (c) A summary of the relevant facts, except in relation to requests for the purpose of service of judicial documents;
    (d) A description of the assistance sought and details of any particular procedure that the requesting State Party wishes to be followed;
    (e) Where possible, the identity, location and nationality of any person concerned; and
    (f) The purpose for which the evidence, information or action is sought.
16. The requested State Party may request additional information when it appears necessary for the execution of the request in accordance with its domestic law or when it can facilitate such execution.
17. A request shall be executed in accordance with the domestic law of the requested State Party and, to the extent not contrary to the domestic law of the requested State Party and where possible, in accordance with the procedures specified in the request.
18. Wherever possible and consistent with fundamental principles of domestic law, when an individual is in the territory of a State Party and has to be heard as a witness or expert by the judicial authorities of another State Party, the first State Party may, at the request of the other, permit the hearing to take place by video conference if it is not possible or desirable for the individual in question to appear in person in the territory of the requesting State Party. States Parties may agree that the hearing shall be conducted by a judicial authority of the requesting State Party and attended by a judicial authority of the requested State Party.
19. The requesting State Party shall not transmit or use information or evidence furnished by the requested State Party for investigations, prosecutions or judicial proceedings other than those stated in the request without the prior consent of the requested State Party. Nothing in this paragraph shall prevent the requesting State Party from disclosing in its proceedings information or evidence that is exculpatory to an accused person. In the latter case, the requesting State Party

shall notify the requested State Party prior to the disclosure and, if so requested, consult with the requested State Party. If, in an exceptional case, advance notice is not possible, the requesting State Party shall inform the requested State Party of the disclosure without delay.

20. The requesting State Party may require that the requested State Party keep confidential the fact and substance of the request, except to the extent necessary to execute the request. If the requested State Party cannot comply with the requirement of confidentiality, it shall promptly inform the requesting State Party.
21. Mutual legal assistance may be refused:

    (a) If the request is not made in conformity with the provisions of this article;
    (b) If the requested State Party considers that execution of the request is likely to prejudice its sovereignty, security, *ordre public* or other essential interests;
    (c) If the authorities of the requested State Party would be prohibited by its domestic law from carrying out the action requested with regard to any similar offence, had it been subject to investigation, prosecution or judicial proceedings under their own jurisdiction;
    (d) If it would be contrary to the legal system of the requested State Party relating to mutual legal assistance for the request to be granted.

22. States Parties may not refuse a request for mutual legal assistance on the sole ground that the offence is also considered to involve fiscal matters.
23. Reasons shall be given for any refusal of mutual legal assistance.
24. The requested State Party shall execute the request for mutual legal assistance as soon as possible and shall take as full account as possible of any deadlines suggested by the requesting State Party and for which reasons are given, preferably in the request. The requested State Party shall respond to reasonable requests by the requesting State Party on progress of its handling of the request. The requesting State Party shall promptly inform the requested State Party when the assistance sought is no longer required.
25. Mutual legal assistance may be postponed by the requested State Party on the ground that it interferes with an ongoing investigation, prosecution or judicial proceeding.
26. Before refusing a request pursuant to paragraph 21 of this article or postponing its execution pursuant to paragraph 25 of this article, the requested State Party shall consult with the requesting State Party to consider whether assistance may be granted subject to such terms and conditions as it deems necessary. If the requesting State Party accepts assistance subject to those conditions, it shall comply with the conditions.
27. Without prejudice to the application of paragraph 12 of this article, a witness, expert or other person who, at the request of the requesting State Party, consents to give evidence in a proceeding or to assist in an investigation, prosecution or judicial proceeding in the territory of the requesting State Party shall not be prosecuted, detained, punished or subjected to any other restriction of his or her personal liberty in that territory in respect of acts, omissions or convictions prior

to his or her departure from the territory of the requested State Party. Such safe conduct shall cease when the witness, expert or other person having had, for a period of 15 consecutive days or for any period agreed upon by the States Parties from the date on which he or she has been officially informed that his or her presence is no longer required by the judicial authorities, an opportunity of leaving, has nevertheless remained voluntarily in the territory of the requesting State Party or, having left it, has returned of his or her own free will.

28. The ordinary costs of executing a request shall be borne by the requested State Party, unless otherwise agreed by the States Parties concerned. If expenses of a substantial or extraordinary nature are or will be required to fulfil the request, the States Parties shall consult to determine the terms and conditions under which the request will be executed, as well as the manner in which the costs shall be borne.
29. The requested State Party:

    (a) Shall provide to the requesting State Party copies of government records, documents or information in its possession that under its domestic law are available to the general public;
    (b) May, at its discretion, provide to the requesting State Party in whole, in part or subject to such conditions as it deems appropriate, copies of any government records, documents or information in its possession that under its domestic law are not available to the general public.

30. States Parties shall consider, as may be necessary, the possibility of concluding bilateral or multilateral agreements or arrangements that would serve the purposes of, give practical effect to or enhance the provisions of this article.

Article 19. Joint investigations

States Parties shall consider concluding bilateral or multilateral agreements or arrangements whereby, in relation to matters that are the subject of investigations, prosecutions or judicial proceedings in one or more States, the competent authorities concerned may establish joint investigative bodies. In the absence of such agreements or arrangements, joint investigations may be undertaken by agreement on a case-by-case basis. The States Parties involved shall ensure that the sovereignty of the State Party in whose territory such investigation is to take place is fully respected.

Article 20. Special investigative techniques

1. If permitted by the basic principles of its domestic legal system, each State Party shall, within its possibilities and under the conditions prescribed by its domestic law, take the necessary measures to allow for the appropriate use of controlled delivery and, where it deems appropriate, for the use of other special investigative techniques, such as electronic or other forms of surveillance and undercover operations, by its competent authorities in its territory for the purpose of effectively combating organized crime.
2. For the purpose of investigating the offences covered by this Convention, States Parties are encouraged to conclude, when necessary, appropriate bilateral or multilateral agreements or arrangements for using such special inves- tigative

techniques in the context of cooperation at the international level. Such agreements or arrangements shall be concluded and implemented in full compliance with the principle of sovereign equality of States and shall be carried out strictly in accordance with the terms of those agreements or arrangements.

3. In the absence of an agreement or arrangement as set forth in paragraph 2 of this article, decisions to use such special investigative techniques at the international level shall be made on a case-by-case basis and may, when necessary, take into consideration financial arrangements and understandings with respect to the exercise of jurisdiction by the States Parties concerned.
4. Decisions to use controlled delivery at the international level may, with the consent of the States Parties concerned, include methods such as intercepting and allowing the goods to continue intact or be removed or replaced in whole or in part.

Article 21. Transfer of criminal proceedings

States Parties shall consider the possibility of transferring to one another proceedings for the prosecution of an offence covered by this Convention in cases where such transfer is considered to be in the interests of the proper administration of justice, in particular in cases where several jurisdictions are involved, with a view to concentrating the prosecution.

Article 22. Establishment of criminal record

Each State Party may adopt such legislative or other measures as may be necessary to take into consideration, under such terms as and for the purpose that it deems appropriate, any previous conviction in another State of an alleged offender for the purpose of using such information in criminal proceedings relating to an offence covered by this Convention.

Article 23. Criminalization of obstruction of justice

Each State Party shall adopt such legislative and other measures as may be necessary to establish as criminal offences, when committed intentionally:

(a) The use of physical force, threats or intimidation or the promise, offering or giving of an undue advantage to induce false testimony or to interfere in the giving of testimony or the production of evidence in a proceeding in relation to the commission of offences covered by this Convention;
(b) The use of physical force, threats or intimidation to interfere with the exercise of official duties by a justice or law enforcement official in relation to the commission of offences covered by this Convention. Nothing in this subparagraph shall prejudice the right of States Parties to have legislation that protects other categories of public officials.

Article 24. Protection of witnesses

1. Each State Party shall take appropriate measures within its means to provide effective protection from potential retaliation or intimidation for witnesses in criminal proceedings who give testimony concerning offences covered by this Convention and, as appropriate, for their relatives and other persons close to them.

2. The measures envisaged in paragraph 1 of this article may include, inter alia, without prejudice to the rights of the defendant, including the right to due process:

   (a) Establishing procedures for the physical protection of such persons, such as, to the extent necessary and feasible, relocating them and permitting, where appropriate, non-disclosure or limitations on the disclosure of information concerning the identity and whereabouts of such persons;
   (b) Providing evidentiary rules to permit witness testimony to be given in a manner that ensures the safety of the witness, such as permitting testimony to be given through the use of communications technology such as video links or other adequate means.

3. States Parties shall consider entering into agreements or arrangements with other States for the relocation of persons referred to in paragraph 1 of this article.
4. The provisions of this article shall also apply to victims insofar as they are witnesses.

Article 25. Assistance to and protection of victims

1. Each State Party shall take appropriate measures within its means to provide assistance and protection to victims of offences covered by this Convention, in particular in cases of threat of retaliation or intimidation.
2. Each State Party shall establish appropriate procedures to provide access to compensation and restitution for victims of offences covered by this Convention.
3. Each State Party shall, subject to its domestic law, enable views and concerns of victims to be presented and considered at appropriate stages of criminal proceedings against offenders in a manner not prejudicial to the rights of the defence.

Article 26. Measures to enhance cooperation with law enforcement authorities

1. Each State Party shall take appropriate measures to encourage persons who participate or who have participated in organized criminal groups:

   (a) To supply information useful to competent authorities for investigative and evidentiary purposes on such matters as:

      (i) The identity, nature, composition, structure, location or activities of organized criminal groups;
      (ii) Links, including international links, with other organized criminal groups;
      (iii) Offences that organized criminal groups have committed or may commit;

   (b) To provide factual, concrete help to competent authorities that may contribute to depriving organized criminal groups of their resources or of the proceeds of crime.

2. Each State Party shall consider providing for the possibility, in appropriate cases, of mitigating punishment of an accused person who provides substantial

cooperation in the investigation or prosecution of an offence covered by this Convention.

3. Each State Party shall consider providing for the possibility, in accordance with fundamental principles of its domestic law, of granting immunity from prosecution to a person who provides substantial cooperation in the investigation or prosecution of an offence covered by this Convention.
4. Protection of such persons shall be as provided for in article 24 of this Convention.
5. Where a person referred to in paragraph 1 of this article located in one State Party can provide substantial cooperation to the competent authorities of another State Party, the States Parties concerned may consider entering into agreements or arrangements, in accordance with their domestic law, concerning the potential provision by the other State Party of the treatment set forth in paragraphs 2 and 3 of this article.

Article 27. Law enforcement cooperation

1. States Parties shall cooperate closely with one another, consistent with their respective domestic legal and administrative systems, to enhance the effectiveness of law enforcement action to combat the offences covered by this Convention. Each State Party shall, in particular, adopt effective measures:

   (a) To enhance and, where necessary, to establish channels of communication between their competent authorities, agencies and services in order to facilitate the secure and rapid exchange of information concerning all aspects of the offences covered by this Convention, including, if the States Parties concerned deem it appropriate, links with other criminal activities;
   (b) To cooperate with other States Parties in conducting inquiries with respect to offences covered by this Convention concerning:

      (i) The identity, whereabouts and activities of persons suspected of involvement in such offences or the location of other persons concerned;
      (ii) The movement of proceeds of crime or property derived from the commission of such offences;
      (iii) The movement of property, equipment or other instrumentalities used or intended for use in the commission of such offences;

   (c) To provide, when appropriate, necessary items or quantities of sub- stances for analytical or investigative purposes;
   (d) To facilitate effective coordination between their competent authorities, agencies and services and to promote the exchange of personnel and other experts, including, subject to bilateral agreements or arrangements between the States Parties concerned, the posting of liaison officers;
   (e) To exchange information with other States Parties on specific means and methods used by organized criminal groups, including, where applicable, routes and conveyances and the use of false identities, altered or false documents or other means of concealing their activities;

(f) To exchange information and coordinate administrative and other measures taken as appropriate for the purpose of early identification of the offences covered by this Convention.

2. With a view to giving effect to this Convention, States Parties shall consider entering into bilateral or multilateral agreements or arrangements on direct cooperation between their law enforcement agencies and, where such agreements or arrangements already exist, amending them. In the absence of such agreements or arrangements between the States Parties concerned, the Parties may consider this Convention as the basis for mutual law enforcement cooperation in respect of the offences covered by this Convention. Whenever appropriate, States Parties shall make full use of agreements or arrangements, including international or regional organizations, to enhance the cooperation between their law enforcement agencies.
3. States Parties shall endeavour to cooperate within their means to respond to transnational organized crime committed through the use of modern technology.

Article 28. Collection, exchange and analysis of information on the nature of organized crime

1. Each State Party shall consider analysing, in consultation with the scientific and academic communities, trends in organized crime in its territory, the circumstances in which organized crime operates, as well as the professional groups and technologies involved.
2. States Parties shall consider developing and sharing analytical expertise concerning organized criminal activities with each other and through international and regional organizations. For that purpose, common definitions, standards and methodologies should be developed and applied as appropriate.
3. Each State Party shall consider monitoring its policies and actual measures to combat organized crime and making assessments of their effectiveness and efficiency.

Article 29. Training and technical assistance

1. Each State Party shall, to the extent necessary, initiate, develop or improve specific training programmes for its law enforcement personnel, including prosecutors, investigating magistrates and customs personnel, and other personnel charged with the prevention, detection and control of the offences covered by this Convention. Such programmes may include secondments and exchanges of staff. Such programmes shall deal, in particular and to the extent permitted by domestic law, with the following:

(a) Methods used in the prevention, detection and control of the offences covered by this Convention;
(b) Routes and techniques used by persons suspected of involvement in offences covered by this Convention, including in transit States, and appropriate countermeasures;
(c) Monitoring of the movement of contraband;

(d) Detection and monitoring of the movements of proceeds of crime, property, equipment or other instrumentalities and methods used for the transfer, concealment or disguise of such proceeds, property, equipment or other instrumentalities, as well as methods used in combating money-laundering and other financial crimes;
(e) Collection of evidence;
(f) Control techniques in free trade zones and free ports;
(g) Modern law enforcement equipment and techniques, including electronic surveillance, controlled deliveries and undercover operations;
(h) Methods used in combating transnational organized crime committed through the use of computers, telecommunications networks or other forms of modern technology; and
(i) Methods used in the protection of victims and witnesses.

2. States Parties shall assist one another in planning and implementing research and training programmes designed to share expertise in the areas referred to in paragraph 1 of this article and to that end shall also, when appropriate, use regional and international conferences and seminars to promote cooperation and to stimulate discussion on problems of mutual concern, including the special problems and needs of transit States.
3. States Parties shall promote training and technical assistance that will facilitate extradition and mutual legal assistance. Such training and technical assistance may include language training, secondments and exchanges between personnel in central authorities or agencies with relevant responsibilities.
4. In the case of existing bilateral and multilateral agreements or arrangements, States Parties shall strengthen, to the extent necessary, efforts to maximize operational and training activities within international and regional organizations and within other relevant bilateral and multilateral agreements or arrangements.

Article 30. Other measures: implementation of the Convention through economic development and technical assistance

1. States Parties shall take measures conducive to the optimal implementation of this Convention to the extent possible, through international cooperation, taking into account the negative effects of organized crime on society in general, in particular on sustainable development.
2. States Parties shall make concrete efforts to the extent possible and in coordination with each other, as well as with international and regional organizations:

(a) To enhance their cooperation at various levels with developing countries, with a view to strengthening the capacity of the latter to prevent and combat transnational organized crime;
(b) To enhance financial and material assistance to support the efforts of developing countries to fight transnational organized crime effectively and to help them implement this Convention successfully;
(c) To provide technical assistance to developing countries and countries with economies in transition to assist them in meeting their needs for the

implementation of this Convention. To that end, States Parties shall endeavour to make adequate and regular voluntary contributions to an account specifically designated for that purpose in a United Nations funding mechanism. States Parties may also give special consideration, in accordance with their domestic law and the provisions of this Convention, to contributing to the aforementioned account a percentage of the money or of the corresponding value of proceeds of crime or property confiscated in accordance with the provisions of this Convention;

(d) To encourage and persuade other States and financial institutions as appropriate to join them in efforts in accordance with this article, in particular by providing more training programmes and modern equipment to developing countries in order to assist them in achieving the objectives of this Convention.

3. To the extent possible, these measures shall be without prejudice to existing foreign assistance commitments or to other financial cooperation arrangements at the bilateral, regional or international level.
4. States Parties may conclude bilateral or multilateral agreements or arrangements on material and logistical assistance, taking into consideration the financial arrangements necessary for the means of international cooperation provided for by this Convention to be effective and for the prevention, detection and control of transnational organized crime.

Article 31. Prevention

1. States Parties shall endeavour to develop and evaluate national projects and to establish and promote best practices and policies aimed at the prevention of transnational organized crime.
2. States Parties shall endeavour, in accordance with fundamental principles of their domestic law, to reduce existing or future opportunities for organized criminal groups to participate in lawful markets with proceeds of crime, through appropriate legislative, administrative or other measures. These measures should focus on:

(a) The strengthening of cooperation between law enforcement agencies or prosecutors and relevant private entities, including industry;
(b) The promotion of the development of standards and procedures designed to safeguard the integrity of public and relevant private entities, as well as codes of conduct for relevant professions, in particular lawyers, notaries public, tax consultants and accountants;
(c) The prevention of the misuse by organized criminal groups of tender procedures conducted by public authorities and of subsidies and licences granted by public authorities for commercial activity;
(d) The prevention of the misuse of legal persons by organized criminal groups; such measures could include:

(i) The establishment of public records on legal and natural persons involved in the establishment, management and funding of legal persons;
(ii) The introduction of the possibility of disqualifying by court order or any appropriate means for a reasonable period of time persons convicted of offences covered by this Convention from acting as directors of legal persons incorporated within their jurisdiction;
(iii) The establishment of national records of persons disqualified from acting as directors of legal persons; and
(iv) The exchange of information contained in the records referred to in subparagraphs *(d)* (i) and (iii) of this paragraph with the competent authorities of other States Parties.

3. States Parties shall endeavour to promote the reintegration into society of persons convicted of offences covered by this Convention.
4. States Parties shall endeavour to evaluate periodically existing relevant legal instruments and administrative practices with a view to detecting their vulnerability to misuse by organized criminal groups.
5. States Parties shall endeavour to promote public awareness regarding the existence, causes and gravity of and the threat posed by transnational organized crime. Information may be disseminated where appropriate through the mass media and shall include measures to promote public participation in preventing and combating such crime.
6. Each State Party shall inform the Secretary-General of the United Nations of the name and address of the authority or authorities that can assist other States Parties in developing measures to prevent transnational organized crime.
7. States Parties shall, as appropriate, collaborate with each other and relevant international and regional organizations in promoting and developing the measures referred to in this article. This includes participation in international projects aimed at the prevention of transnational organized crime, for example by alleviating the circumstances that render socially marginalized groups vulnerable to the action of transnational organized crime.

Article 32. Conference of the Parties to the Convention

1. A Conference of the Parties to the Convention is hereby established to improve the capacity of States Parties to combat transnational organized crime and to promote and review the implementation of this Convention.
2. The Secretary-General of the United Nations shall convene the Conference of the Parties not later than 1 year following the entry into force of this Convention. The Conference of the Parties shall adopt rules of procedure and rules governing the activities set forth in paragraphs 3 and 4 of this article (including rules concerning payment of expenses incurred in carrying out those activities).
3. The Conference of the Parties shall agree upon mechanisms for achieving the objectives mentioned in paragraph 1 of this article, including:

(a) Facilitating activities by States Parties under articles 29, 30 and 31 of this Convention, including by encouraging the mobilization of voluntary contributions;
(b) Facilitating the exchange of information among States Parties on patterns and trends in transnational organized crime and on successful practices for combating it;
(c) Cooperating with relevant international and regional organizations and non-governmental organizations;
(d) Reviewing periodically the implementation of this Convention;
(e) Making recommendations to improve this Convention and its implementation.

4. For the purpose of paragraphs 3 *(d)* and *(e)* of this article, the Conference of the Parties shall acquire the necessary knowledge of the measures taken by States Parties in implementing this Convention and the difficulties encountered by them in doing so through information provided by them and through such supplemental review mechanisms as may be established by the Conference of the Parties.
5. Each State Party shall provide the Conference of the Parties with information on its programmes, plans and practices, as well as legislative and administrative measures to implement this Convention, as required by the Conference of the Parties.

Article 33. Secretariat

1. The Secretary-General of the United Nations shall provide the necessary secretariat services to the Conference of the Parties to the Convention.
2. The secretariat shall:

(a) Assist the Conference of the Parties in carrying out the activities set forth in article 32 of this Convention and make arrangements and provide the necessary services for the sessions of the Conference of the Parties;
(b) Upon request, assist States Parties in providing information to the Conference of the Parties as envisaged in article 32, paragraph5, of this Convention; and
(c) Ensure the necessary coordination with the secretariats of relevant international and regional organizations.

Article 34. Implementation of the Convention

1. Each State Party shall take the necessary measures, including legislative and administrative measures, in accordance with fundamental principles of its domestic law, to ensure the implementation of its obligations under this Convention.
2. The offences established in accordance with articles 5, 6, 8 and 23 of this Convention shall be established in the domestic law of each State Party independently of the transnational nature or the involvement of an organized criminal group as described in article 3, paragraph 1, of this Convention, except to the extent that article 5 of this Convention would require the involvement of an organized criminal group.

3. Each State Party may adopt more strict or severe measures than those provided for by this Convention for preventing and combating transnational organized crime.

Article 35. Settlement of disputes

1. States Parties shall endeavour to settle disputes concerning the interpretation or application of this Convention through negotiation.
2. Any dispute between two or more States Parties concerning the interpretation or application of this Convention that cannot be settled through negotiation within a reasonable time shall, at the request of one of those States Parties, be submitted to arbitration. If, 6 months after the date of the request for arbitration, those States Parties are unable to agree on the organization of the arbitration, any one of those States Parties may refer the dispute to the International Court of Justice by request in accordance with the Statute of the Court.
3. Each State Party may, at the time of signature, ratification, acceptance or approval of or accession to this Convention, declare that it does not consider itself bound by paragraph 2 of this article. The other States Parties shall not be bound by paragraph 2 of this article with respect to any State Party that has made such a reservation.
4. Any State Party that has made a reservation in accordance with paragraph 3 of this article may at any time withdraw that reservation by notification to the Secretary-General of the United Nations.

Article 36. Signature, ratification, acceptance, approval and accession

1. This Convention shall be open to all States for signature from 12 to 15 December 2000 in Palermo, Italy, and thereafter at United Nations Headquarters in New York until 12 December 2002.
2. This Convention shall also be open for signature by regional economic integration organizations provided that at least one member State of such organization has signed this Convention in accordance with paragraph 1 of this article.
3. This Convention is subject to ratification, acceptance or approval. Instruments of ratification, acceptance or approval shall be deposited with the Secretary-General of the United Nations. A regional economic integration organization may deposit its instrument of ratification, acceptance or approval if at least one of its member States has done likewise. In that instrument of ratification, acceptance or approval, such organization shall declare the extent of its competence with respect to the matters governed by this Convention. Such organization shall also inform the depositary of any relevant modification in the extent of its competence.
4. This Convention is open for accession by any State or any regional economic integration organization of which at least one member State is a Party to this Convention. Instruments of accession shall be deposited with the Secretary-General of the United Nations. At the time of its accession, a regional economic integration organization shall declare the extent of its competence with respect to

matters governed by this Convention. Such organization shall also inform the depositary of any relevant modification in the extent of its competence.

Article 37. Relation with protocols

1. This Convention may be supplemented by one or more protocols.
2. In order to become a Party to a protocol, a State or a regional economic integration organization must also be a Party to this Convention.
3. A State Party to this Convention is not bound by a protocol unless it becomes a Party to the protocol in accordance with the provisions thereof.
4. Any protocol to this Convention shall be interpreted together with this Convention, taking into account the purpose of that protocol.

Article 38. Entry into force

1. This Convention shall enter into force on the ninetieth day after the date of deposit of the fortieth instrument of ratification, acceptance, approval or accession. For the purpose of this paragraph, any instrument deposited by a regional economic integration organization shall not be counted as additional to those deposited by member States of such organization.
2. For each State or regional economic integration organization ratifying, accepting, approving or acceding to this Convention after the deposit of the fortieth instrument of such action, this Convention shall enter into force on the thirtieth day after the date of deposit by such State or organization of the relevant instrument.

Article 39. Amendment

1. After the expiry of 5 years from the entry into force of this Convention, a State Party may propose an amendment and file it with the Secretary-General of the United Nations, who shall thereupon communicate the proposed amendment to the States Parties and to the Conference of the Parties to the Convention for the purpose of considering and deciding on the proposal. The Conference of the Parties shall make every effort to achieve consensus on each amendment. If all efforts at consensus have been exhausted and no agreement has been reached, the amendment shall, as a last resort, require for its adoption a two-thirds majority vote of the States Parties present and voting at the meeting of the Conference of the Parties.
2. Regional economic integration organizations, in matters within their competence, shall exercise their right to vote under this article with a number of votes equal to the number of their member States that are Parties to this Convention. Such organizations shall not exercise their right to vote if their member States exercise theirs and vice versa.
3. An amendment adopted in accordance with paragraph 1 of this article is subject to ratification, acceptance or approval by States Parties.
4. An amendment adopted in accordance with paragraph 1 of this article shall enter into force in respect of a State Party 90 days after the date of the deposit with the Secretary-General of the United Nations of an instrument of ratification, acceptance or approval of such amendment.

5. When an amendment enters into force, it shall be binding on those States Parties which have expressed their consent to be bound by it. Other States Parties shall still be bound by the provisions of this Convention and any earlier amendments that they have ratified, accepted or approved.

Article 40. Denunciation

1. A State Party may denounce this Convention by written notification to the Secretary-General of the United Nations. Such denunciation shall become effective 1 year after the date of receipt of the notification by the Secretary-General.
2. A regional economic integration organization shall cease to be a Party to this Convention when all of its member States have denounced it.
3. Denunciation of this Convention in accordance with paragraph 1 of this article shall entail the denunciation of any protocols thereto.

Article 41. Depositary and languages

1. The Secretary-General of the United Nations is designated depositary of this Convention.
2. The original of this Convention, of which the Arabic, Chinese, English, French, Russian and Spanish texts are equally authentic, shall be deposited with the Secretary-General of the United Nations.

v) **EU's 6th Directive on Money Laundering**

On 20 July 2021, the European Commission presented an ambitious package of legislative proposals to strengthen the EU's anti-money laundering and countering the financing of terrorism. The package also included a proposal for the creation of a new EU authority to fight money laundering. The Commission's aim is to protect EU citizens and the EU's financial system from money laundering and terrorist financing by the detection of suspicious transactions and activities, and close loopholes used by criminals to launder illicit proceeds or finance terrorist activities through the financial system . . .[8]

However, the previous framework had been poorly implemented with money laundering scandals showing that the EU remained an attractive destination for illicit funds and that European banks and other intermediaries were indispensable in helping—either knowingly or negligently—design and run such illegal schemes.

Consequently, there was considerable pressure for the EU to get its house in order, resulting in the approval of the 6th Directive and, in particular, the creation of a new EU supervisory body, Anti-Money Laundering Authority (AMLA), to conduct independent investigations and sanction non-compliant firms or Member States.[9]

[8] See also summaries of the EU's 4th, 5th and 6th AML Directives below and the EU Factsheet at: https://finance.ec europa.eu/system/files/2021-07/210720-anti-money-laundering-countering-financing-terrorism-factsheet_en.pdf

[9] https://transparency.eu/priority/financial-flows-crime/#anti-money-laundering

As seen below, the 6th Directive is lengthy (60 articles, each article having many sub-paragraphs[10]) and came into effect on 3 December 2020 to be implemented by regulated entities by 3 June 2021.

One of the key aspects of the Directive is the harmonisation of the definition of what constitutes a money laundering offence. With this harmonisation, the EU closes loopholes of interpretation between the different legislation of Member States, making the fight against money laundering more homogeneous and consistent. Also, the Directive introduces 22 predicate offences, including notably, cybercrime and environmental crimes.[11]

CHAPTER I—GENERAL PROVISIONS

Section 1: Subject matter, scope and definitions

Article 1

Subject matter

This Directive lays down rules concerning:

(a) measures applicable to sectors exposed to money laundering and terrorist financing at national level;
(b) the identification of money laundering and terrorist financing risks at Union and Member States level;
(c) the set-up and access to beneficial ownership, bank account and real estate registers;
(d) the responsibilities and tasks of Financial Intelligence Units (FIUs);
(e) the responsibilities and tasks of bodies involved in the supervision of obliged entities,
(f) cooperation between competent authorities and cooperation with authorities covered by other Union acts.

Article 2

Definitions

For the purposes of this Directive, the definitions set out in Article 2 of Regulation [please insert reference—proposal for Anti-Money Laundering Regulation—COM/2021/420 final] apply.

The following definitions also apply:

(1) 'financial supervisor' means a supervisor in charge of credit and financial institutions;
(2) 'obliged entities' means the natural or legal persons listed in Article 3 of Regulation [please insert reference—proposal for Anti-Money Laundering Regulation—COM/2021/420 final] that are not exempted in accordance with article 4,5,6 of that Regulation;

[10] https://eur-lex.europa.eu/legal-content/EN/TXT/?uri=celex%3A52021PC0423

[11] https://www.pwc.com/mt/en/publications/financial-crime-news/highlights-of-the-6th-anti-money-laundering-directive.html

(3) 'home Member State' means the Member State where the registered office of the obliged entity is situated or, if the obliged entity has no registered office, the Member State in which its head office is situated;
(4) 'host Member State' means the Member State other than the home Member State in which the obliged entity has a subsidiary or a branch or provides services;
(5) 'customs authorities' means the customs authorities as defined in Article 5(1) of Regulation (EU) 952/2013 of the European Parliament and of the Council 42 and the competent authorities as defined in Article 2(1), point (g), of Regulation (EU) 2018/1672 of the European Parliament and of the Council 43;
(6) 'anti-money laundering/counter-terrorist financing supervisory college' or 'AML/CFT supervisory college' means a permanent structure for cooperation and information sharing for the purposes of supervising a group or an entity operating on a cross-border basis;
(7) 'entity operating on a cross-border basis' means an obliged entity having at least one establishment in another Member State or in a third country;
(8) 'establishment' means a branch or any other form of establishment of an obliged entity that operates in a Member State or third country other than the country where its head office is established, or the subsidiary of a parent undertaking established in a country other than the country where that parent undertaking has been established.

Section 2: National measures in sectors exposed to money laundering and terrorist financing

Article 3

Identification of exposed sectors at national level

1. Where the national risk assessment carried out by Member States pursuant to Article 8 identifies that, in addition to obliged entities, entities in other sectors are exposed to money laundering and terrorist financing risks, Member States may decide to apply the requirements of Regulation [please insert reference—proposal for Anti-Money Laundering Regulation—COM/2021/420 final] to those additional entities.
2. For the purposes of paragraph 1, Member States shall notify to the Commission their intention to apply of requirements of Regulation [please insert reference—proposal for Anti-Money Laundering Regulation—COM/2021/420 final] to entities in additional sectors, accompanied by:

   (a) a justification of the money laundering and terrorist financing risks underpinning such intention;
   (b) an assessment of the impact that such extension will have on the provision of services within the internal market;
   (c) the text of the national measures that the Member State intends to adopt.

3. Member States shall suspend the adoption of national measures referred to in paragraph 2, point (c), for 6 months from the date of the notification referred to in paragraph 2.
4. Before the end of the period referred to in paragraph 3, the Commission, having consulted the Authority for anti-money laundering and countering the financing of terrorism established by Regulation [please insert reference—proposal for establishment of an Anti-Money Laundering Authority—COM/2021/421 final] (AMLA), shall issue a detailed opinion regarding whether the measure envisaged:
   (a) is adequate to address the risks identified, in particular as regards whether the risks identified by the Member State concern the internal market;
   (b) may create obstacles to the free movement of services or capital or to the freedom of establishment of service operators within the internal market which are not proportionate to the money laundering and terrorist financing risks the measure aims to mitigate.

The detailed opinion shall also indicate whether the Commission intends to propose action at Union level.

5. Where the Commission does not consider it appropriate to propose action at Union level, the Member State concerned shall, within 2 months of receiving the detailed opinion referred to in paragraph 4, report to the Commission on the action it proposes to take on that detailed opinion. The Commission shall comment on the action proposed by the Member State.
6. Where the Commission indicates its intention to propose action at Union level, the Member State concerned shall abstain from adopting the national measures referred to in paragraph 2, point (c).
7. Where, on [please insert the date of entry into force of this Directive], Member States have already applied national provisions transposing Directive (EU) 2015/849 to other sectors than obliged entities, they may apply the requirements of Regulation [please insert reference—proposal for Anti-Money Laundering Regulation—COM/2021/420 final] to those sectors.

   By [6 months after the date of transposition of this Directive], Member States shall notify the Commission the sectors identified at national level pursuant to the first sub-paragraph to which the requirements of Regulation [please insert reference—proposal for Anti-Money Laundering Regulation—COM/2021/420 final] shall apply, accompanied by a justification of the exposure of those sectors to money laundering and terrorist financing risks. Within 6 months of such notification, the Commission having consulted AMLA, shall issue a detailed opinion covering paragraph 4, points (a) and (b), and indicating whether it intends to propose action at Union level. Where the Commission does not consider it appropriate to propose action at Union level, paragraph 5 shall apply.
8. By [1 years after the date of transposition of this Directive] and every year thereafter, the Commission shall publish a consolidated list of the sectors to which Member States have decided to apply the requirements of Regulation

[please insert reference—proposal for Anti-Money Laundering Regulation—COM/2021/420 final] in the Official Journal of the European Union.

Article 4
Requirements relating to certain service providers

1. Member States shall ensure that currency exchange and cheque cashing offices, and trust or company service providers are either licensed or registered.
2. Member States shall ensure that all providers of gambling services are regulated.

Article 5
Contact points

1. Member States may require electronic money issuers as defined in Article 2(3) of Directive 2009/110/EC 44, payment service providers as defined in Article 4(11) of Directive (EU) 2015/2366 and crypto-assets service providers operating through agents located in the host Member State and operating under either the right of establishment or the freedom to provide services, and whose head office is situated in another Member State, to appoint a central contact point in their territory. That central contact point shall ensure, on behalf of the entity operating on a cross-border basis, compliance with AML/CFT rules and shall facilitate supervision by supervisors, including by providing supervisors with documents and information on request.
2. By [2 years after the date of entry into force of this Directive], AMLA shall develop draft regulatory technical standards and submit them to the Commission for adoption. Those draft regulatory technical standards shall set out the criteria for determining the circumstances in which the appointment of a central contact point pursuant to paragraph 1 is appropriate, and the functions of the central contact points.
3. The Commission is empowered to supplement this Directive by adopting the regulatory technical standards referred to in paragraph 2 of this Article in accordance with Articles 38 to 41 of Regulation [please insert reference—proposal for establishment of an Anti-Money Laundering Authority—COM/2021/421 final].

Article 6
Checks on the senior management and beneficial owners of certain obliged entities

1. Member States shall require supervisors to verify that the members of the senior management in the obliged entities referred to in Article 4, and the beneficial owners of such entities, act with honesty and integrity. Senior management of such entities should also possess knowledge and expertise necessary to carry out their functions.
2. With respect to the obliged entities referred to in Article 3, points (3)(a), (b), (d), (e) and (h) to (l), of Regulation [please insert reference—proposal for Anti-Money Laundering Regulation—COM/2021/420 final], Member States shall ensure that supervisors take the necessary measures to prevent persons convicted

of money laundering, any of its predicate offences or terrorist financing or their associates from being professionally accredited, holding a management function in or being the beneficial owners of those obliged entities.

3. Member States shall ensure that supervisors verify at regular intervals and on a risk-sensitive basis whether the requirements of paragraphs 1 and 2 continue to be met. In particular, they shall verify whether the senior management acts with honesty and integrity and possesses knowledge and expertise necessary to carry out their functions in cases where there are reasonable grounds to suspect that money laundering or terrorist financing is being or has been committed or attempted, or there is increased risk thereof in an obliged entity.
4. Supervisors shall have the power to request the removal of any person convicted of money laundering, any of its predicate offences or terrorist financing from the management role of the obliged entities referred to in paragraphs 1 and 2. Supervisors shall have the power to remove members of the senior management that are not deemed to act with honesty and integrity and possess knowledge and expertise necessary to carry out their functions.
5. Where the person convicted of money laundering, any of its predicate offences or terrorist financing is the beneficial owner of an obliged entity referred to in paragraph 2, Member States shall ensure that such persons can be disassociated from any obliged entity, including by granting supervisors the power to request the divestment of the holding by the beneficial owner in an obliged entity.
6. For the purposes of this Article, Member States shall ensure that, in accordance with their national law, supervisors or any other authority competent at national level for assessing the appropriateness of persons referred to in paragraphs 1 and 2, check the existence of a relevant conviction in the criminal record of the person concerned. Any exchange of information for those purposes shall be carried out in accordance with Framework Decision 2009/315/JHA and Decision 2009/316/JHA as implemented in national law.

Section 2: Risk assessments

Article 7

Supra-national risk assessment

1. The Commission shall conduct an assessment of the risks of money laundering and terrorist financing affecting the internal market and relating to cross-border activities.

   To that end, the Commission shall, at the latest by [4 years after the date of transposition of this Directive], draw up a report identifying, analysing and evaluating those risks at Union level. Thereafter, the Commission shall update its report every 4 years. The Commission may update parts of the report more frequently, if appropriate.
2. The report referred to in paragraph 1 shall cover at least the following:
   (a) the areas and sectors of the internal market that are exposed to money laundering and terrorist financing risks;
   (b) the nature and level of the risks associated with each area and sector;

(c) the most widespread means used to launder illicit proceeds, including, where available, those particularly used in transactions between Member States and third countries, independently of the identification of a third country pursuant to Section 2 of Chapter III of Regulation [please insert reference—proposal for Anti-Money Laundering Regulation—COM/2021/420 final];
(d) the risks of non-implementation and evasion of proliferation financing-related targeted financial sanctions.

3. The Commission shall make recommendations to Member States on the measures suitable for addressing the identified risks. In the event that Member States decide not to apply any of the recommendations in their national AML/CFT regimes, they shall notify the Commission thereof and provide a justification for such a decision.
4. By [3 years after the date of transposition of this Directive], AMLA shall issue an opinion addressed to the Commission on the risks of money laundering and terrorist financing affecting the Union. Thereafter, AMLA shall issue an opinion every 2 years.
5. In conducting the assessment referred to in paragraph 1, the Commission shall organise the work at Union level, shall take into account the opinions referred to in paragraph 4 and shall involve the Member States' experts in the area of AML/CFT, representatives from national supervisory authorities and FIUs, as well as AMLA and other Union level bodies where appropriate.
6. Within 2 years of the adoption of the report referred to in paragraph 1, and every 4 years thereafter, the Commission shall submit a report to the European Parliament and to the Council on the actions taken based on the findings of that report.

Article 8
National risk assessment

1. Each Member State shall carry out a national risk assessment to identify, assess, understand and mitigate the risks of money laundering and terrorist financing affecting it. It shall keep that risk assessment up to date and review it at least every 4 years.
   Each Member State shall also take appropriate steps to identify, assess, understand and mitigate the risks of non-implementation and evasion of proliferation financing-related targeted financial sanctions.
2. Each Member State shall designate an authority or establish a mechanism to coordinate the national response to the risks referred to in paragraph 1. The identity of that authority or the description of the mechanism shall be notified to the Commission, AMLA, and other Member States.
3. In carrying out the national risk assessments referred to in paragraph 1 of this Article, Member States shall take into account the report referred to in Article 7(1).
4. Each Member State shall use the national risk assessment to:

(a) improve its AML/CFT regime, in particular by identifying any areas where obliged entities are to apply enhanced measures and, where appropriate, specifying the measures to be taken;
(b) identify, where appropriate, sectors or areas of lower or greater risk of money laundering and terrorist financing;
(c) assess the risks of money laundering and terrorist financing associated with each type of legal person and legal arrangement in their territory and have an understanding of the exposure to risks deriving from foreign legal persons and legal arrangements;
(d) decide on the allocation and prioritisation of resources to combat money laundering and terrorist financing as well as non-implementation and evasion of proliferation financing-related targeted financial sanctions;
(e) ensure that appropriate rules are drawn up for each sector or area, in accordance with the risks of money laundering and terrorist financing;
(f) make appropriate information available promptly to competent authorities and to obliged entities to facilitate the carrying out of their own money laundering and terrorist financing risk assessments as well as the assessment of risks of evasion of proliferation financing-related targeted financial sanctions referred to in Article 8 of Regulation [please insert reference—proposal for Anti-Money Laundering Regulation—COM/2021/420 final].

In the national risk assessment, Member States shall describe the institutional structure and broad procedures of their AML/CFT regime, including, inter alia, the FIU, tax authorities and prosecutors, as well as the allocated human and financial resources to the extent that this information is available.

5. Member States shall make the results of their national risk assessments, including their updates, available to the Commission, to AMLA and to the other Member States. Any Member State may provide relevant additional information, where appropriate, to the Member State carrying out the national risk assessment. A summary of the assessment shall be made publicly available. That summary shall not contain classified information. The information contained therein shall not permit the identification of any natural or legal person.

Article 9
Statistics

1. Member States shall maintain comprehensive statistics on matters relevant to the effectiveness of their AML/CFT frameworks in order to review the effectiveness of those frameworks.
2. The statistics referred to in paragraph 1 shall include:

(a) data measuring the size and importance of the different sectors which fall within the scope of this Directive, including the number of natural persons and entities and the economic importance of each sector;

(b) data measuring the reporting, investigation and judicial phases of the national AML/CFT regime, including the number of suspicious transaction reports made to the FIU, the follow-up given to those reports, the information on cross-border physical transfers of cash submitted to the FIU in accordance with Article 9 of Regulation (EU) 2018/1672 together with the follow-up given to the information submitted and, on an annual basis, the number of cases investigated, the number of persons prosecuted, the number of persons convicted for money laundering or terrorist financing offences, the types of predicate offences identified in accordance with Article 2 of Directive (EU) 2018/1673 of the European Parliament and of the Council 45 where such information is available, and the value in euro of property that has been frozen, seized or confiscated;
(c) if available, data identifying the number and percentage of reports resulting in further investigation, together with the annual report drawn up by FIUs pursuant to Article 21;
(d) data regarding the number of cross-border requests for information that were made, received, refused and partially or fully answered by the FIU, broken down by counterpart country;
(e) the number of mutual legal assistance or other international requests for information relating to beneficial ownership and bank account information as referred to in Chapter IV of Regulation [please insert reference—proposal for Anti-Money Laundering Regulation—COM/2021/420 final]and Sections 1 and 2 of Chapter II of this Directive received from or made to counterparts outside the Union, broken down by competent authority and counterpart country;
(f) human resources allocated to supervisors as well as human resources allocated to the FIU to fulfil the tasks specified in Article 17;
(g) the number of on-site and off-site supervisory actions, the number of breaches identified on the basis of supervisory actions and sanctions or administrative measures applied by supervisory authorities and self-regulatory bodies pursuant to Section 4 of Chapter IV;
(h) the number and type of breaches identified in relation to the obligations of Chapter IV of Regulation [please insert reference—proposal for Anti-Money Laundering Regulation—COM/2021/420 final] and sanctions or administrative measures applied in relation to those breaches, as well as the number of inspections carried out by the entity in charge of the central register pursuant to Article 10(8) of this Directive.

3. Member States shall ensure that the statistics referred to in paragraph 2 are collected and transmitted to the Commission on an annual basis. The statistics referred to in paragraph 2, points (a), (c), (d) and (f), shall also be transmitted to AMLA.

AMLA shall store those statistics in its database in accordance with Article 11 of Regulation [please insert reference—proposal for establishment of an Anti-Money Laundering Authority—COM/2021/421 final].

4. By [3 years after the date of transposition of this Directive], AMLA shall adopt an opinion addressed to the Commission on the methodology for the collection of the statistics referred to in paragraph 2, points (a), (c), (d) and (f).
5. The Commission is empowered to adopt implementing acts laying down the methodology for the collection of the statistics referred to in paragraph 2 and the arrangements for their transmission to the Commission and AMLA. Those implementing acts shall be adopted in accordance with the examination procedure referred to in Article 54(2).
6. The Commission shall publish a biennial report summarising and explaining the statistics referred to in paragraph 2, which shall be made available on its website.

CHAPTER II—REGISTERS

Section I: Beneficial ownership registers

Article 10

Beneficial ownership registers

1. Member States shall ensure that beneficial ownership information referred to in Article 44 of Regulation [please insert reference—proposal for Anti-Money Laundering Regulation—COM/2021/420 final] and information on nominee arrangements referred to in Article 47 of that Regulation is held in a central register in the Member State where the legal entity is incorporated or where the trustee or person holding an equivalent position in a similar legal arrangement is established or resides. Such requirement shall not apply to companies listed on a regulated market that are subject to disclosure requirements equivalent to the requirements laid down in this Directive or subject to equivalent international standards.

   The beneficial ownership information contained in the central registers may be collected in accordance with national systems.
2. Where there are reasons to doubt the accuracy of the beneficial ownership information held by the central registers, Member States shall ensure that legal entities and legal arrangements are required to provide additional information on a risk-sensitive basis, including resolutions of the board of directors and minutes of their meetings, partnership agreements, trust deeds, power of attorney or other contractual agreements and documentation.
3. Where no person is identified as beneficial owner pursuant to Article 45(2) and (3) of Regulation [please insert reference—proposal for Anti-Money Laundering Regulation—COM/2021/420 final], the central register shall include:

   (a) a statement accompanied by a justification, that there is no beneficial owner or that the beneficial owner(s) could not be identified and verified;
   (b) the details of the natural person(s) who hold the position of senior managing official(s) in the corporate or legal entity equivalent to the information required under Article 44(1), point (a), of Regulation [please insert reference—proposal for Anti-Money Laundering Regulation—COM/2021/420 final].

4. The Commission is empowered to adopt, by means of implementing acts, the format for the submission of beneficial ownership information to the central register. Those implementing acts shall be adopted in accordance with the examination procedure referred to in Article 54(2).
5. Member States shall require that the beneficial ownership information held in the central registers is adequate, accurate and up-to-date. For that purpose, Member State shall apply at least the following requirements:

   (a) obliged entities shall report to the entity in charge of the central registers any discrepancies they find between the beneficial ownership information available in the central registers and the beneficial ownership information available to them pursuant to Article 18 of Regulation [please insert reference—proposal for Anti-Money Laundering Regulation].
   (b) competent authorities, if appropriate and to the extent that this requirement does not interfere unnecessarily with their functions, shall report to the entity in charge of the central registers any discrepancies they find between beneficial ownership information available in the central registers and the beneficial ownership information available to them.

6. Member States shall require that the reporting of discrepancies referred to in paragraph 5 takes place within 14 calendar days after detecting the discrepancy. In cases of lower risk to which measures under Section 3 of Chapter III of Regulation [please insert reference—proposal for Anti-Money Laundering Regulation] apply, Member States may allow obliged entities to request the customer to rectify discrepancies of a technical nature that do not hinder the identification of the beneficial owner(s) directly with the entity in charge of the central registers.
7. Member States shall ensure that the entity in charge of the central registers takes appropriate actions to cease the discrepancies, including amending the information included in the central registers where the entity is able to identify and verify the beneficial ownership information. A specific mention of the fact that there are discrepancies reported shall be included in the central registers and visible at least to competent authorities and obliged entities.
8. In the case of corporate and other legal entities, Member States shall ensure that the entity in charge of the central beneficial ownership register is empowered to carry out checks, including on-site investigations at the premises or registered office of the legal entity, in order to establish the current beneficial ownership of the entity and to verify that the information submitted to the central register is accurate, adequate and up-to-date. The right of the central register to verify such information shall not be restricted, obstructed or precluded in any manner.
9. Member States shall ensure that the entity in charge of the central register is empowered to impose effective, proportionate and dissuasive measures or sanctions for failures to provide the register with accurate, adequate and up-to-date information about their beneficial ownership.

10. Member States shall ensure that if, in the course of the checks carried out pursuant to this Article, or in any other way, the entities in charge of the beneficial ownership registers discover facts that could be related to money laundering or to terrorist financing, they shall promptly inform the FIU.
11. The central registers shall be interconnected via the European Central Platform established by Article 22(1) of Directive (EU) 2017/1132.
12. The information referred to in paragraph 1 shall be available through the national registers and through the system of interconnection of central beneficial ownership registers for at least 5 years and no more than 10 years after the corporate or other legal entity has been struck off from the register.

Article 11

General rules regarding access to beneficial ownership registers by competent authorities, self-regulatory bodies and obliged entities

1. Member States shall ensure that competent authorities have timely, unrestricted and free access to the information held in the interconnected central registers referred to in Article 10, without alerting the entity or arrangement concerned.
2. Access to the central registers referred to in Article 10 shall be granted to FIUs, supervisory authorities, public authorities with designated responsibilities for combating money laundering or terrorist financing, as well as tax authorities and authorities that have the function of investigating or prosecuting money laundering, its predicate offences and terrorist financing, tracing and seizing or freezing and confiscating criminal assets. Self-regulatory bodies shall be granted access to the registers when performing supervisory functions.
3. Member States shall ensure that, when taking customer due diligence measures in accordance with Chapter III of Regulation [please insert reference—proposal for Anti-Money Laundering Regulation], obliged entities have timely access to the information held in the interconnected central registers referred to in Article 10.
4. By [3 months after the date of transposition of this Directive], Member States shall notify to the Commission the list of competent authorities and self-regulatory bodies and the categories of obliged entities that were granted access to the registers and the type of information available to obliged entities, as well as the beneficial ownership information that can be accessed by the public pursuant to Article 12. Member States shall update such notification when changes to the list of competent authorities or categories of obliged entities or to the extent of access granted to obliged entities or the public occur. The Commission shall make the information on the access by competent authorities and obliged entities, including any change to it, available to the other Member States.

Article 12

Specific access rules to beneficial ownership registers for the public

1. Member States shall ensure that any member of the general public has access to the following information held in the interconnected central registers referred to in Article 10:

   (a) in the case of legal entities, at least the name, the month and year of birth and the country of residence and nationality of the beneficial owner as well as the nature and extent of the beneficial interest held;
   (b) in case of express trusts or similar legal arrangements, the name, the month and year of birth and the country of residence and nationality of the beneficial owner as well as the nature and extent of the beneficial interest held, provided that a legitimate interest can be demonstrated.

In addition to the information listed in the first subparagraph, point (a), Member States may, under conditions to be determined in national law, provide for access to additional information necessary for the identification of the beneficial owner. That additional information shall include at least the date of birth or contact details in accordance with Union and Member State data protection rules.

2. Member States may choose to make beneficial ownership information held in their central registers available to the public on the condition of authentication using electronic identification means and relevant trust services as set out in Regulation (EU) 910/2014 of the European Parliament and of the Council 46 and the payment of a fee, which shall not exceed the administrative costs of making the information available, including costs of maintenance and developments of the register.

Article 13

Exceptions to the access rules to beneficial ownership registers

In exceptional circumstances to be laid down in national law, where the access referred to in Articles 11(3) and 12(1) would expose the beneficial owner to disproportionate risk of fraud, kidnapping, blackmail, extortion, harassment, violence or intimidation, or where the beneficial owner is a minor or otherwise legally incapable, Member States may provide for an exemption from such access to all or part of the personal information on the beneficial owner on a case-by-case basis. Member States shall ensure that those exemptions are granted upon a detailed evaluation of the exceptional nature of the circumstances. Rights to an administrative review of the decision granting an exemption and to an effective judicial remedy shall be guaranteed. A Member State that has granted exemptions shall publish annual statistical data on the number of exemptions granted and reasons stated and report the data to the Commission.

Exemptions granted pursuant to this Article shall not apply to the obliged entities referred to in Article 3, point (3)(b), of Regulation [please insert reference—proposal for Anti-Money Laundering Regulation] that are public officials.

Section 2: Bank account information
Article 14
Bank account registers and electronic data retrieval systems

1. Member States shall put in place centralised automated mechanisms, such as a central registers or central electronic data retrieval systems, which allow the identification, in a timely manner, of any natural or legal persons holding or controlling payment accounts and bank accounts identified by IBAN, as defined by Regulation (EU) No 260/2012 of the European Parliament and of the Council4 7 , and safe-deposit boxes held by a credit institution within their territory.
   Member States shall notify the Commission of the characteristics of those national mechanisms as well as the criteria pursuant to which information is included in those national mechanisms.
2. Member States shall ensure that the information held in the centralised mechanisms referred to in paragraph 1 is directly accessible in an immediate and unfiltered manner to national FIUs. The information shall also be accessible to national competent authorities for fulfilling their obligations under this Directive.
3. The following information shall be accessible and searchable through the centralised mechanisms referred to in paragraph 1:
   (a) for the customer-account holder and any person purporting to act on behalf of the customer: the name, complemented by either the other identification data required under Article 18(1) of Regulation [please insert reference—proposal for Anti-Money Laundering Regulation] or a unique identification number;
   (b) for the beneficial owner of the customer-account holder: the name, complemented by either the other identification data required under Article 18(1) of Regulation [please insert reference—proposal for Anti-Money Laundering Regulation] or a unique identification number;
   (c) for the bank or payment account: the IBAN number and the date of account opening and closing;
   (d) for the safe-deposit box: name of the lessee complemented by either the other identification data required under Article 18(1) of Regulation [please insert reference—proposal for Anti-Money Laundering Regulation] or a unique identification number and the duration of the lease period.
4. Member States may require other information deemed essential for FIUs and other competent authorities for fulfilling their obligations under this Directive to be accessible and searchable through the centralised mechanisms.
5. The centralised automated mechanisms referred to in paragraph 1 shall be interconnected via the bank account registers (BAR) single access point to be developed and operated by the Commission.
   The Commission is empowered to adopt, by means of implementing acts, the technical specifications and procedures for the connection of the Member States' centralised automated mechanisms to the single access point. Those implementing acts shall be adopted in accordance with the examination procedure referred to in Article 54(2).

6. Member States shall ensure that the information referred to in paragraph 3 is available through the single access point interconnecting the centralised automated mechanisms. Member States shall take adequate measures to ensure that only the information referred to in paragraph 3 that is up to date and corresponds to the actual bank account information is made available through their national centralised automated mechanisms and through the single access point interconnecting the centralised automated mechanisms referred to in this paragraph. The access to that information shall be granted in accordance with data protection rules.

   The other information that Member States consider essential for FIUs and other competent authorities pursuant to paragraph 4 shall not be accessible and searchable through the single access point interconnecting the centralised automated mechanisms.
7. National FIUs shall be granted immediate and unfiltered access to the information on payment and bank accounts and safe-deposit boxes in other Member States available through the single access point interconnecting the centralised automated mechanisms. Member States shall cooperate among themselves and with the Commission in order to implement this paragraph.

   Member States shall ensure that the staff of the national FIUs maintain high professional standards of confidentiality and data protection, are of high integrity and are appropriately skilled.
8. Member States shall ensure that technical and organisational measures are put in place to ensure the security of the data to high technological standards for the purposes of the exercise by FIUs of the power to access and search the information available through the single access point interconnecting the centralised automated mechanisms in accordance with paragraphs 5 and 6.

Article 15
Implementing acts for the interconnection of registers

1. Where necessary, the Commission is empowered to adopt, by means of implementing acts, technical specifications and procedures necessary to provide for the interconnection of Member States' central registers in accordance with Article 10(11) with regard to:

   (a) the technical specification defining the set of the technical data necessary for the platform to perform its functions as well as the method of storage, use and protection of such data;
   (b) the common criteria according to which beneficial ownership information is available through the system of interconnection of registers, depending on the level of access granted by Member States;
   (c) the technical details on how the information on beneficial owners is to be made available;
   (d) the technical conditions of availability of services provided by the system of interconnection of registers;

(e) the technical modalities to implement the different types of access to information on beneficial ownership in accordance with Articles 11 and 12 of this Directive, including the authentication of users through the use of electronic identification means and relevant trust services as set out in Regulation (EU) 910/2014;
(f) the payment modalities where access to beneficial ownership information is subject to the payment of a fee according to Article 12(2) taking into account available payment facilities such as remote payment transactions.

Those implementing acts shall be adopted in accordance with the examination procedure referred to in Article 54(2).

2. Where necessary, the Commission is empowered to adopt, by means of implementing acts, technical specifications and procedures necessary to provide for the interconnection of Member States' centralised mechanisms as referred to in Article 14(5), with regard to:

   (a) the technical specification defining the methods of communication by electronic means for the purposes of the bank account registers (BAR) single access point;
   (b) the technical specification of the communication protocols;
   (c) the technical specifications defining the data security, data protection safeguards, use and protection of the information which is searchable and accessible by means of the bank account registers (BAR) single access point interconnecting the centralised automated mechanisms;
   (d) the common criteria according to which bank account information is searchable through the single access point interconnecting the centralised automated mechanisms;
   (e) the technical details on how the information is made available by means of the single access point interconnecting the centralised automated mechanisms, including the authentication of users through the use of electronic identification means and relevant trust services as set out in Regulation (EU) 910/2014;
   (f) the technical conditions of availability of services provided by the single access point interconnecting the centralised automated mechanisms.

Those implementing acts shall be adopted in accordance with the examination procedure referred to in Article 54(2).

3. When adopting the implementing acts referred to in paragraphs 1 and 2, the Commission shall take into account proven technology and existing practices. The Commission shall ensure that the single access point to be developed and operated does not incur costs above what is absolutely necessary in order to implement this Directive.

Section 3: Real estate registers

Article 16

Real estate registers

1. Member States shall provide competent authorities with access to information which allows the identification in a timely manner of any natural or legal person owning real estate, including through registers or electronic data retrieval systems where such registers or systems are available. Competent authorities shall also have access to information allowing the identification and analysis of transactions involving real estate, including their economic value and details of the natural or legal persons involved in those transactions including, where available, whether the natural or legal person owns, sells or acquires real estate on behalf of a legal arrangement.

   FIUs shall be granted direct and immediate access to the information referred to in the first subparagraph.
2. By [3 months after the date of transposition of this Directive], Member States shall notify to the Commission the list of competent authorities that were granted access to the registers or systems referred to in paragraph 1 and the type of information available to them. Member States shall update such notification when changes to the list of competent authorities or to the extent of access to information granted occurs. The Commission shall make that information, including any change to it, available to the other Member States.

CHAPTER III—FIUs

Article 17

Establishment of FIUs

1. Each Member State shall establish an FIU in order to prevent, detect and effectively combat money laundering and terrorist financing.
2. The FIU shall be the single central national unit responsible for receiving and analysing suspicious transactions and other information relevant to money laundering, its predicate offences or terrorist financing submitted by obliged entities in accordance with Article 50 or reports submitted by obliged entities in accordance with Article 59(4), point (b), of Regulation [please insert reference—proposal for Anti-Money Laundering Regulation—COM/2021/420 final] and by customs authorities pursuant to Article 9 of Regulation (EU) 2018/1672.
3. The FIU shall be responsible for disseminating the results of its analyses and any additional relevant information to other competent authorities where there are grounds to suspect money laundering, its predicate offences or terrorist financing. It shall be able to obtain additional information from obliged entities.

   The FIU's financial analysis function shall consist of the following:

   (a) an operational analysis which focuses on individual cases and specific targets or on appropriate selected information, depending on the type and volume of the disclosures received and the expected use of the information after dissemination;

(b) a strategic analysis addressing money laundering and terrorist financing trends and patterns.

By [1 year after the date of transposition of this Directive], AMLA shall issue guidelines addressed to FIUs on the nature, features and objectives of operational and of strategic analysis.

4. Each FIU shall be operationally independent and autonomous, which means that it shall have the authority and capacity to carry out its functions freely, including the ability to take autonomous decisions to analyse, request and disseminate specific information. It shall be free from any undue political, government or industry influence or interference.

   When a FIU is located within the existing structure of another authority, the FIU's core functions shall be independent and operationally separated from the other functions of the host authority.
5. Member States shall provide their FIUs with adequate financial, human and technical resources in order to fulfil their tasks. FIUs shall be able to obtain and deploy the resources needed to carry out their functions. Their staff shall be of high integrity and appropriately skilled, and maintain high professional standards.
6. Member States shall ensure that FIUs have rules in place governing the security and confidentiality of information.
7. Each Member States shall ensure that its FIU is able to make arrangements or engage independently with other domestic competent authorities pursuant to Article 45 on the exchange of information.

Article 18

Access to information

1. Member States shall ensure that their FIUs have:

   (a) immediate and, with the exception of point (ii), direct access to at least the following financial information:

      (i) information contained in the national centralised automated mechanisms in accordance with Article 14;
      (ii) information on wire transfers;
      (iii) information from obliged entities;
      (iv) information on mortgages and loans;
      (v) information contained in the national currency and currency exchange databases;
      (vi) information on securities;

   (b) immediate and, with the exception of point (xiv), direct access to at least the following administrative information:

      (i) fiscal data, including data held by tax and revenue authorities;
      (ii) national real estate registers or electronic data retrieval systems and land and cadastral registers;

(iii) national citizenship and population registers of natural persons;
(iv) national passports and visas registers;
(v) cross-border travel databases;
(vi) commercial databases, including business and company registers and PEP databases;
(vii) national motor vehicles, aircraft and watercraft registers;
(viii) national social security registers;
(ix) customs data, including cross-border physical transfers of cash;
(x) national weapons and arms registers;
(xi) national beneficial ownership registers;
(xii) data available through the interconnection of beneficial ownership registers in accordance with Article 10(11).
(xiii) registers on non-profit organisations;
(xiv) information held by national financial supervisors and regulators, in accordance with Article 45 and Article 50(2);
(xv) databases storing data on CO2 emission trading established pursuant to Commission Regulation (EU) 389/2013 48.
(xvi) information on annual financial statements by companies;
(xvii) national migration/immigration registers;
(xviii) information held by commercial courts;
(xix) information held in insolvency databases and by insolvency practitioners;

(c) direct or indirect access to the following law enforcement information:

(i) any type of information or data which is already held by competent authorities in the context of preventing, detecting, investigating or prosecuting criminal offences;
(ii) any type of information or data which is held by public authorities or by private entities in the context of preventing, detecting, investigating or prosecuting criminal offences and which is available to competent authorities without the taking of coercive measures under national law.

The information referred to in point (c) may include criminal records, information on investigations, information on the freezing or seizure of assets or on other investigative or provisional measures and information on convictions and on confiscations.

2. Where the information referred to in paragraph 1, points (a), (b) and (c), is not stored in databases or registers, Member States shall take the necessary measures to ensure that FIUs can obtain that information by other means.
3. In the cases where the FIUs are provided with indirect access to information, the requested authority shall respond to the request in a timely manner.
4. In the context of its functions, each FIU shall be able to request, obtain and use information from any obliged entity to perform its functions pursuant to Article 17(3), even if no prior report is filed pursuant to Article 50(1), point (a), or Article 51(1) of Regulation [please insert reference—proposal for Anti-Money

Laundering Regulation—COM/2021/420 final]. Obliged entities shall not be obliged to comply with requests for information made pursuant to this paragraph when they concern information obtained in the situations referred to in Article 51(2) of Regulation [please insert reference—proposal for Anti-Money Laundering Regulation—COM/2021/420 final].

Article 19

Responses to requests for information

1. Member States shall ensure that FIUs respond in a timely manner to reasoned requests for information by other competent authorities in their respective Member State or Union authorities competent for investigating or prosecuting criminal activities when such requests for information are motivated by concerns relating to money laundering, its predicate offences or terrorist financing or when this information is necessary for the competent authority to perform its tasks under this Directive. The decision on conducting the dissemination of information shall remain with the FIU.

   Where there are objective grounds for assuming that the provision of such information would have a negative impact on ongoing investigations or analyses, or, in exceptional circumstances, where disclosure of the information would be clearly disproportionate to the legitimate interests of a natural or legal person or irrelevant with regard to the purposes for which it has been requested, the FIU shall be under no obligation to comply with the request for information.
2. Competent authorities shall provide feedback to the FIU about the use made of the information provided in accordance with this Article. Such feedback shall be provided as soon as possible and in any case, at least on an annual basis, in such a way as to inform the FIU about the actions taken by the competent authorities on the basis of the information provided by the FIU and allow the FIU to execute its operational analysis function.

Article 20

Suspension or withholding of consent to a transaction and suspension of an account

1. Member States shall ensure that FIUs are empowered to take urgent action, directly or indirectly, where there is a suspicion that a transaction is related to money laundering or terrorist financing, to suspend or withhold consent to a transaction that is proceeding. Such suspension shall be imposed on the obliged entity within 48 hours of receiving the suspicious transaction report in order to analyse the transaction, confirm the suspicion and disseminate the results of the analysis to the competent authorities. Member States shall ensure that subject to national procedural safeguards, the transaction is suspended for a period of a maximum of 15 calendar days from the day of the imposition of such suspension to the obliged entity.

   The FIU shall be empowered to impose such suspension, directly or indirectly, at the request of an FIU from another Member State for the periods and under the conditions specified in the national law of the FIU receiving the request.

2. Where there is a suspicion that several transactions involving a bank or payment account are related to money laundering or terrorist financing, Member States shall ensure that the FIU is empowered to take urgent action, directly or indirectly, to suspend the use of a bank or payment account in order to analyse the transactions performed through the account, confirm the suspicion and disseminate the results of the analysis to the competent authorities.

   Such suspension shall be imposed on the obliged entity within 48 h of receiving the suspicious transaction report and immediately notified to the competent judicial authority. Member States shall ensure that the use of that bank or payment account is suspended for a period of a maximum of 5 days from the day of the imposition of the suspension. Member States shall ensure that any extension of such suspension shall be authorized by the competent judicial authority.
3. Member States shall provide for the effective possibility for the person whose bank or payment account is affected to challenge the suspension before a court in accordance with procedures provided for in national law.
4. FIUs shall be empowered to impose the suspensions referred to in paragraphs 1 and 2, directly or indirectly, at the request of an FIU from another Member State under the conditions specified in the national law of the FIU receiving the request.

Article 21
Feedback by FIU

1. Each Member State shall ensure that its FIU issues a yearly report on its activities. The report shall contain statistics on:

   (a) suspicious transaction reports submitted by obliged entities;
   (b) disclosures by supervisors and beneficial ownership registers;
   (c) disseminations to competent authorities;
   (d) requests submitted to and received from other FIUs;
   (e) data on cross-border physical transfers of cash submitted by customs authorities.

The report referred to in the first subparagraph shall also contain information on the trends and typologies identified in the files disseminated to other competent authorities.

FIUs shall disseminate the report to obliged entities. Such report shall be made public within 4 months of its dissemination, except for the elements of the report which contain classified information. The information contained therein shall not permit the identification of any natural or legal person.

2. Member States shall ensure that FIUs provide obliged entities with feedback on the reports of suspected money laundering or terrorist financing. Such feedback shall cover at least the quality of the information provided, the timeliness of reporting, the description of the suspicion and the documentation provided at submission stage.

   The FIU shall provide such feedback at least once per year, whether provided to the individual obliged entity or to groups of obliged entities, taking into consideration the overall number of suspicious transactions reported by the obliged entities.

Such feedback shall also be made available to supervisors to allow them to perform risk-based supervision in accordance with Article 31.

The obligation to provide feedback shall not jeopardise any ongoing analytical work carried out by the FIU or any investigation or administrative action subsequent to the dissemination by the FIU, and shall not affect the applicability of data protection and confidentiality requirements.

3. Member States shall ensure that FIUs provide customs authorities with timely feedback on the effectiveness of and follow-up to the information submitted pursuant to Article 9 of Regulation (EU) 2018/1672.

Article 22

Cooperation between FIUs

Member States shall ensure that FIUs cooperate with each other and with their counterparts in third countries to the greatest extent possible, regardless of their organisational status.

Article 23

Protected channels of communication

1. A system for the exchange of information between FIUs of the Member States shall be set up ('FIU.net'). The system shall ensure the secure communication and shall be capable of producing a written record under conditions that allow ascertaining authenticity. That system may also be used for communications with FIUs counterparts in third countries and with other authorities and Union bodies. FIU.net shall be managed by AMLA.
2. Member States shall ensure that any exchange of information pursuant to Article 24 is transmitted using the FIU.net. In the event of technical failure of the FIU.net, the information shall be transmitted by any other appropriate means ensuring a high level of data security.

   Exchanges of information between FIUs and their counterparts in third countries shall also take place through protected channels of communication.
3. Member States shall ensure that, in order to fulfil their tasks as laid down in this Directive, their FIUs cooperate in the application of state-of-the-art technologies in accordance with their national law.

Article 24

Exchange of information between FIUs

1. Member States shall ensure that FIUs exchange, spontaneously or upon request, any information that may be relevant for the processing or analysis of information by the FIU related to money laundering, its predicate offences, or terrorist financing, and the natural or legal person involved, even if the type of predicate offences that may be involved is not identified at the time of the exchange.

   A request shall contain the relevant facts, background information, reasons for the request and how the information sought will be used.

When an FIU receives a report pursuant to Article 50(1), the first subparagraph, point (a), of Regulation [please insert reference—proposal for Anti-Money Laundering Regulation—COM/2021/420 final] which concerns another Member State, it shall promptly forward the report, or all the relevant information obtained from it, to the FIU of that Member State.

2. By [2 years after the date of entry into force of this Directive], AMLA shall develop draft implementing technical standards and submit them to the Commission for adoption. Those draft implementing technical standards shall specify the format to be used for the exchange of the information referred to in paragraph 1.
3. The Commission is empowered to adopt the implementing technical standards referred to in paragraph 2 of this Article in accordance with Article 42 of Regulation [please insert reference—proposal for establishment of an Anti-Money Laundering Authority—COM/2021/421 final].
4. By [1 year after the date of transposition of this Directive], AMLA shall issue guidelines addressed to FIUs on the relevant factors to be taken into consideration when determining whether a report pursuant to Article 50(1), the first subparagraph, point (a), of Regulation [please insert reference—proposal for Anti-Money Laundering Regulation—COM/2021/420 final] concerns another Member State, the procedures to be put in place when forwarding and receiving that report, and the follow-up to be given.
5. Member States shall ensure that the FIU to whom the request is made is required to use the whole range of its available powers which it would normally use domestically for receiving and analysing information when it replies to a request for information referred to in paragraph 1 from another FIU.

   When an FIU seeks to obtain additional information from an obliged entity established in another Member State which operates on the territory of its Member State, the request shall be addressed to the FIU of the Member State in whose territory the obliged entity is established. That FIU shall obtain information in accordance with Article 50(1) of Regulation [please insert reference—proposal for Anti-Money Laundering Regulation—COM/2021/420 final] and transfer the answers promptly.
6. Member States shall ensure that where an FIU is requested to provide information pursuant to paragraph 1, it shall respond to the request as soon as possible and in any case no later than 7 days after the receipt of the request. In exceptional, duly justified cases, this time limit may be extended to a maximum of 14 calendar days. Where the requested FIU is unable to obtain the requested information, it shall inform the requesting FIU thereof.
7. Member States shall ensure that in exceptional, justified and urgent cases and, by way of derogation from paragraph 6, where pursuant to paragraph 1 an FIU is requested to provide information which is either held in a database or registry directly accessible by the requested FIU or which is already in its possession, the requested FIU shall provide that information no later than 24 h after the receipt of the request.

   If the requested FIU is unable to respond within 24 hours or cannot access the information directly, it shall provide a justification. Where the provision of the information requested within the period of 24 hours would put a disproportionate burden on the requested FIU, it may postpone the provision of the information. In that case the requested FIU shall immediately inform the requesting FIU of this postponement and shall provide the requested information as soon as possible, but not later than within 3 calendar days.

8. An FIU may refuse to exchange information only in exceptional circumstances where the exchange could be contrary to fundamental principles of its national law. Those exceptional circumstances shall be specified in a way which prevents misuse of, and undue limitations on, the free exchange of information for analytical purposes.

   By [1 year after the date of transposition of this Directive], Member States shall notify to the Commission the exceptional circumstances referred to in the first subparagraph. Member States shall update such notifications where changes to the exceptional circumstances identified at national level occur.

Article 25
Joint analyses

1. Member States shall ensure that their FIUs are able to carry out joint analyses of suspicious transactions and activities.
2. For the purpose of paragraph 1, the relevant FIUs, assisted by AMLA in accordance with Article 33 of Regulation [please insert reference—proposal for establishment of an Anti-Money Laundering Authority—COM/2021/421 final], shall set up a joint analysis team for a specific purpose and limited period, which may be extended by mutual consent, to carry out operational analyses of suspicious transactions or activities involving one or more of the FIUs setting up the team.
3. A joint analysis team may be set up where:

   (a) an FIU's operational analyses require difficult and demanding analyses having links with other Member States;
   (b) a number of FIUs are conducting operational analyses in which the circumstances of the case necessitate coordinated, concerted action in the Member States involved.

A request for the setting up of a joint analysis team may be made by any of the FIUs concerned.

4. Member States shall ensure that the member of their FIU allocated to the joint analysis team is able, in accordance with his or her national law and within the limits of his or her competence, to provide the team with information available to its FIU for the purpose of the analysis conducted by the team.
5. Where the joint analysis team needs assistance from an FIU other than those which are part of the team, it might request that other FIU to:

   (a) join the joint analysis team;
   (b) submit financial intelligence and financial information to the joint analysis team.

Article 26

Use by FIUs of information exchanged between them

Information and documents received pursuant to Articles 22 and 24 shall be used for the accomplishment of the FIU's tasks as laid down in this Directive. When exchanging information and documents pursuant to Articles 22 and 24, the transmitting FIU may impose restrictions and conditions for the use of that information. The receiving FIU shall comply with those restrictions and conditions.

Member States shall ensure that FIUs designate at least one contact person or point to be responsible for receiving requests for information from FIUs in other Member States.

Article 27

Consent to further dissemination of information exchanged between FIUs

1. Member States shall ensure that the information exchanged pursuant to Articles 22 and 24 is used only for the purpose for which it was sought or provided and that any dissemination of that information by the receiving FIU to any other authority, agency or department, or any use of this information for purposes beyond those originally approved, is made subject to the prior consent by the FIU providing the information.
2. Member States shall ensure that the requested FIU's prior consent to disseminate the information to competent authorities is granted promptly and to the largest extent possible, regardless of the type of predicate offences. The requested FIU shall not refuse its consent to such dissemination unless this would fall beyond the scope of application of its AML/CFT provisions or could lead to impairment of an investigation, or would otherwise not be in accordance with fundamental principles of national law of that Member State. Any such refusal to grant consent shall be appropriately explained. The cases where FIUs may refuse to grant consent shall be specified in a way which prevents misuse of, and undue limitations to, the dissemination of information to competent authorities.

Article 28

Effect of criminal law provisions

Differences between national law definitions of predicate offences shall not impede the ability of FIUs to provide assistance to another FIU and shall not limit the exchange, dissemination and use of information pursuant to Articles 24, 26 and 27.

CHAPTER IV—ANTI-MONEY LAUNDERING SUPERVISION

Section 1: General provisions

Article 29

Powers and resources of national supervisors

1. Member States shall ensure that all obliged entities are subject to adequate supervision. To that end, Member States shall appoint supervisors to monitor effectively, and to take the measures necessary to ensure, compliance by the obliged entities with the requirements set out in Regulation [please insert

reference—proposal for Anti-Money Laundering Regulation—COM/2021/420 final] and with the requirement to implement targeted financial sanctions.

2. Member States shall ensure that supervisors have adequate financial, human and technical resources to perform their tasks as listed in paragraph 4. Member States shall ensure that staff of those authorities are of high integrity and appropriately skilled, and maintain high professional standards, including standards of confidentiality, data protection and standards addressing conflicts of interest.
3. In the case of the obliged entities referred to in Article 3, points (3)(a), (b) and (d), of Regulation [please insert reference—proposal for Anti-Money Laundering Regulation—COM/2021/420 final], Member States may allow the function referred to in paragraph 1 of this Article to be performed by self-regulatory bodies, provided that those self-regulatory bodies have the powers referred to in paragraph 5 of this Article and have adequate financial, human and technical resources to perform their functions. Member States shall ensure that staff of those bodies are of high integrity and appropriately skilled, and that they maintain high professional standards, including standards of confidentiality, data protection and standards addressing conflicts of interest.
4. For the purposes of paragraph 1, Member States shall ensure that the national supervisors perform the following tasks:

   (a) to disseminate relevant information to obliged entities pursuant to Article 30;
   (b) to decide of those cases where the specific risks inherent in a sector are clear and understood and individual documented risk assessments pursuant to Article 8 of Regulation [please insert reference—proposal for Anti-Money Laundering Regulation—COM/2021/420 final] are not required;
   (c) to verify the adequacy and implementation of the internal policies, controls and procedures of obliged entities pursuant to Chapter II of Regulation [please insert reference—proposal for Anti-Money Laundering Regulation—COM/2021/420 final] and of the human resources allocated to the performance of the tasks required under that Regulation;
   (d) to regularly assess and monitor the money laundering and terrorist financing risks the obliged entities are exposed to;
   (e) to monitor compliance by obliged entities with regard to their obligations in relation to targeted financial sanctions;
   (f) to conduct all the necessary off-site, on-site and thematic investigations and any other inquiries, assessments and analyses necessary to verify that obliged entities comply with the requirements of Regulation [please insert reference—proposal for Anti-Money Laundering Regulation—COM/2021/420 final], with the requirement to implement targeted financial sanctions, and with any administrative measures taken pursuant to Article 41;
   (g) to take appropriate supervisory measures to address any breaches of applicable requirements by the obliged entities identified in the process of supervisory assessments and follow up on the implementation of such measures.

5. Member States shall ensure that supervisors have adequate powers to perform their tasks as provided in paragraph 4, including the power to:

(a) compel the production of any information from obliged entities which is relevant for monitoring and verifying compliance with the requirements of Regulation [please insert reference—proposal for Anti-Money Laundering Regulation—COM/2021/420 final] and to perform checks, including from agents or external service providers to whom the obliged entity has outsourced part of its tasks to meet the requirements of Regulation [please insert reference—proposal for Anti-Money Laundering Regulation—COM/ 2021/420 final];
(b) impose appropriate and proportionate administrative measures to remedy the situation in the case of breaches, including through the imposition of administrative sanctions in accordance with Section 4 of this Chapter.

6. Member States shall ensure that financial supervisors and supervisors in charge of gambling operators have powers additional to those referred to in paragraph 5, including the power to investigate the business premises of the obliged entity without prior announcement where the proper conduct and efficiency of inspection so require, and that they have all the necessary means to carry out such investigation.

   For the purposes of the first subparagraph, the supervisors shall at least be able to:

   (a) examine the books and records of the obliged entity and take copies or extracts from such books and records;
   (b) obtain access to any software, databases, IT tools or other electronic means of recording information used by the obliged entity;
   (c) obtain written or oral explanations from any person responsible for AML/CFT internal policies and controls or their representatives or staff, as well as any representative or staff of entities to which the obliged entity has outsourced tasks pursuant to Article 40 of Regulation [please insert reference—proposal for Anti-Money Laundering Regulation—COM/2021/ 420 final], and interview any other person who consents to be interviewed for the purpose of collecting information relating to the subject matter of an investigation.

Article 30
Provision of information to obliged entities

1. Member States shall ensure that supervisors make information on money laundering and terrorist financing available to the obliged entities under their supervision.
2. The information referred to in paragraph 1 shall include the following:

   (a) the supra-national risk assessment drawn up by the Commission pursuant to Article 7 and any relevant recommendation by the Commission on the basis of that Article;
   (b) national or sectoral risk assessments drawn up pursuant to Article 8;

(c) relevant guidelines, recommendations and opinions issued by AMLA in accordance with Articles 43 and 44 of Regulation [please insert reference—proposal for establishment of an Anti-Money Laundering Authority—COM/2021/421 final];
(d) information on third countries identified pursuant to Section 2 of Chapter III of Regulation [please insert reference—proposal for Anti-Money Laundering Regulation—COM/2021/420 final];
(e) any guidance and report produced by AMLA and other supervisors and, where relevant, the public authority overseeing self-regulatory bodies, the FIU or any other competent authority or international organisations and standard setters regarding money laundering and terrorist financing methods which might apply to a sector and indications which may facilitate the identification of transactions or activities at risk of being linked to money laundering and terrorist financing in that sector, as well as on obliged entities' obligations in relation to targeted financial sanctions.

3. Member States shall ensure that supervisors make information on persons or entities designated in relation to targeted financial sanctions available to the obliged entities under their supervision immediately.

Article 31
Risk-based supervision

1. Member States shall ensure that supervisors apply a risk-based approach to supervision. To that end, Member States shall ensure that they:

(a) have a clear understanding of the risks of money laundering and terrorist financing present in their Member State;
(b) assess all relevant information on the specific domestic and international risks associated with customers, products and services of the obliged entities;
(c) base the frequency and intensity of on-site, off-site and thematic supervision on the risk profile of obliged entities, and on the risks of money laundering and terrorist financing in that Member State. To that end, supervisors shall draw up annual supervisory programmes.

2. By [2 years after the date of entry into force of this Directive], AMLA shall develop draft regulatory technical standards and submit them to the Commission for adoption. Those draft regulatory technical standards shall set out the benchmarks and a methodology for assessing and classifying the inherent and residual risk profile of obliged entities, as well as the frequency at which such risk profile shall be reviewed. Such frequency shall take into account any major events or developments in the management and operations of the obliged entity, as well as the nature and size of the business.
3. The Commission is empowered to supplement this Directive by adopting the regulatory technical standards referred to in paragraph 2 of this Article in accordance with Articles 38 to 41 of Regulation [please insert reference—

proposal for establishment of an Anti-Money Laundering Authority—COM/2021/421 final].

4. By [1 year after the date of transposition of this Directive], AMLA shall issue guidelines addressed to supervisors on the characteristics of a risk-based approach to supervision and the steps to be taken when conducting supervision on a risk-sensitive basis.
5. Member States shall ensure that supervisors take into account the degree of discretion allowed to the obliged entity, and appropriately review the risk assessments underlying this discretion, and the adequacy of its policies, internal controls and procedures.
6. Member States shall ensure that the results of the risk assessments performed by supervisors pursuant to this Article are made available in aggregated form to the FIU.

Article 32

Disclosure to FIUs

1. Member States shall ensure that if, in the course of the checks carried out on the obliged entities, or in any other way, supervisors discover facts that could be related to money laundering or to terrorist financing, they shall promptly inform the FIU.
2. Member States shall ensure that supervisors empowered to oversee the stock, foreign exchange and financial derivatives markets, inform the FIU if they discover facts that could be related to money laundering or terrorist financing.

Article 33

Supervision of obliged entities operating under the freedom of establishment and freedom to provide services

1. Member States shall ensure that supervisors cooperate with each other to the greatest extent possible, regardless of their respective nature or status. Such cooperation may include conducting, within the powers of the requested supervisor, inquiries on behalf of a requesting supervisor, and the subsequent exchange of the information obtained through such inquiries.
2. In addition to Article 5, obliged entities wishing to exercise the freedom to provide services by carrying out activities within the territory of another Member State for the first time shall notify the supervisors of the home Member State of the activities which they intend to carry out. Such notification shall also be required where provision of cross-border services is carried out by agents of the obliged entity.
3. The supervisors of the home Member State shall, within 1 month of receipt of the notification provided for in paragraph 2, transmit that notification to the supervisors of the host Member State.
4. In the cases covered by paragraph 2 of this Article and Article 5, supervisors of the host Member State shall cooperate with supervisors of the home Member State and lend assistance to ensure the verification of compliance by the obliged entity with the requirements of Regulation [please insert reference—proposal for

Anti-Money Laundering Regulation—COM/2021/420 final] and of Regulation [please insert reference—proposal for a recast of Regulation (EU) 2015/847-COM/2021/422 final] and to take appropriate and proportionate measures to address breaches.

In the cases covered by Article 5, the supervisors of the host Member State shall be allowed at their own initiative to take appropriate and proportionate measures to address serious failings that require immediate remedies. Those measures shall be temporary and be terminated when the failings identified are addressed, including with the assistance of or in cooperation with the supervisors of the home Member State of the obliged entity.

5. Where the supervisors of the home and host Member State disagree on the measures to be taken in relation to an obliged entity, they may refer the matter to AMLA and request its assistance in accordance with Articles 5 and 10 of Regulation [please insert reference—proposal for establishment of an Anti-Money Laundering Authority—COM/2021/421 final]. AMLA shall provide its advice on the matter of disagreement within 1 month.

Article 34

Provisions related to cooperation in the context of group supervision

1. In the case of credit and financial institutions that are part of a group, Member States shall ensure that, for the purposes laid down in Article 29(1), financial supervisors of the home Member State and those of the host Member State cooperate with each other to the greatest extent possible, regardless of their respective nature or status. They shall also cooperate with AMLA when it exercises supervisory functions in accordance with Article 5(2) of Regulation [please insert reference—proposal for establishment of an Anti-Money Laundering Authority—COM/2021/421 final].
2. Except where AMLA exercises supervisory functions in accordance with Article 5(2) of Regulation [please insert reference—proposal for establishment of an Anti-Money Laundering Authority—COM/2021/421 final], Member States shall ensure that the financial supervisors of the home Member State supervise the effective implementation of the group-wide policies, controls and procedures referred to in Article 13 of Regulation [please insert reference—proposal for Anti-Money Laundering Regulation—COM/2021/420 final]. Member States shall also ensure that financial supervisors of the host Member State supervise the compliance of the establishments located in the territory of its Member State with the requirements of Regulation [please insert reference—proposal for Anti-Money Laundering Regulation—COM/2021/420 final].
3. For the purposes of this Article, and except in cases where AML/CFT supervisory colleges are established in accordance with Article 36, Member States shall ensure that financial supervisors provide one another with any information they require for the exercise of their supervisory tasks, whether on request or on their own initiative. In particular, financial supervisors shall exchange any information that could significantly influence the assessment of the inherent or residual risk exposure of a credit or financial institution in another Member State, including:

(a) identification of the group's legal, governance and organisational structure, covering all subsidiaries and branches;
(b) internal controls, policies and procedures in place within the group;
(c) adverse developments in relation to the parent undertaking, subsidiaries or branches, which could seriously affect other parts of the group;
(d) administrative measures and sanctions taken by financial supervisors in accordance with Section 4 of this chapter.

Member States shall also ensure that financial supervisors are able to conduct, within their powers, inquiries on behalf of a requesting supervisor, and to share the information obtained through such inquiries.

4. By [2 years after the date of entry into force of this Directive], AMLA shall develop draft regulatory technical standards and submit them to the Commission for adoption. Those draft regulatory technical standards shall detail the respective duties of the home and host supervisors, and the modalities of cooperation between them.

   The Commission is empowered to supplement this Directive by adopting the regulatory technical standards referred to in the first sub-paragraph in accordance with Articles 38 to 41 of Regulation [please insert reference—proposal for establishment of an Anti-Money Laundering Authority—COM/2021/421 final].
5. Financial supervisors may refer to AMLA any of the following situations:

   (a) where a financial supervisor has not communicated the information referred to in paragraph 3;
   (b) where a request for cooperation has been rejected or has not been acted upon within a reasonable time.

AMLA may act in accordance with the powers conferred on it under Articles 5 and 10 of Regulation [please insert reference—proposal for establishment of an Anti-Money Laundering Authority—COM/2021/421 final]. When doing so, AMLA shall provide its opinion on the subject-matter of the request within 1 month.

6. Member States shall ensure that the provisions of this Article also apply to the supervision of groups of obliged entities other than credit or financial institutions. Member States shall also ensure that in cases where obliged entities other than credit and financial institutions are part of structures which share common ownership, management or compliance control, including networks or partnerships, cooperation and exchange of information between supervisors is facilitated.

Article 35

Exchange of information in relation to implementation of group policies in third countries

Supervisors, including AMLA, shall inform each other of instances in which the law of a third country does not permit the implementation of the policies, controls and procedures required under Article 13 of Regulation [please insert reference—

proposal for Anti-Money Laundering Regulation—COM/2021/420 final]. In such cases, coordinated actions may be taken by supervisors to pursue a solution. In assessing which third countries do not permit the implementation of the policies, controls and procedures required under Article 13 of Regulation [please insert reference—proposal for Anti-Money Laundering Regulation—COM/2021/420 final], supervisors shall take into account any legal constraints that may hinder proper implementation of those policies and procedures, including professional secrecy, an insufficient level of data protection and other constraints limiting the exchange of information that may be relevant for that purpose.

Section 2: Specific provisions applicable to the financial sector

Article 36

AML/CFT supervisory colleges

1. Member States shall ensure that dedicated AML/CFT supervisory colleges are established in any of the following situations:
   (a) where a credit or financial institution has set up establishments in at least two different Member States other than the Member State where its head office is situated;
   (b) where a third-country credit or financial institution has set up establishments in at least three Member States.
2. For the purposes of paragraph 1, Member States shall ensure that financial supervisors identify:
   (a) all credit and financial institutions operating on a cross-border basis that have been authorised in their Member State;
   (b) all establishments set up by those institutions in other jurisdictions;
   (c) establishments set up in their territory by credit and financial institutions from other Member States or third countries.
3. Members States may allow the establishment of AML/CFT supervisory colleges when a credit or financial institution established in the Union has set up establishments in at least two third countries. Financial supervisors may invite their counterparts in those third countries to set up such college. The financial supervisors participating in the college shall establish a written agreement detailing the conditions and procedures of the cooperation and exchange of information.
4. Such colleges may be used for exchanging information, providing mutual assistance or coordinating the supervisory approach to the institution, including, where relevant, the taking of appropriate and proportionate measures to address serious breaches of the requirements of Regulation [please insert reference—proposal for Anti-Money Laundering Regulation—COM/2021/420 final] that are detected across the establishments set up by the institution in the jurisdiction of a supervisor participating in the college.
5. AMLA shall attend the meetings of the AML/CFT supervisory colleges and shall facilitate their work in accordance with Article 29 of Regulation [please insert

reference—proposal for establishment of an Anti-Money Laundering Authority—COM/2021/421 final].

6. By [2 year after the date of entry into force of this Directive], AMLA shall develop draft regulatory technical standards and submit them to the Commission for adoption. Those draft regulatory technical standards shall specify the general conditions for the functioning of the AML/CFT supervisory colleges, including the terms of cooperation between participants, and the operational functioning of such colleges.

   The Commission is empowered to supplement this Directive by adopting the regulatory technical standards referred to in the first subparagraph in accordance with Articles 38 to 41 of Regulation [please insert reference—proposal for establishment of an Anti-Money Laundering Authority—COM/2021/421 final].

Article 37

Cooperation with financial supervisors in third countries

1. Member States may authorise financial supervisors to conclude cooperation agreements providing for collaboration and exchanges of confidential information with their counterparts in third countries. Such cooperation agreements shall comply with applicable data protection rules for data transfers and be concluded on the basis of reciprocity and only if the information disclosed is subject to a guarantee of professional secrecy requirements at least equivalent to that referred to in Article 50(1). Confidential information exchanged in accordance with those cooperation agreements shall be used for the purpose of performing the supervisory tasks of those authorities only.

   Where the information exchanged originates in another Member State, it shall only be disclosed with the explicit consent of the financial supervisor which shared it and, where appropriate, solely for the purposes for which that supervisor gave its consent.

2. For the purposes of paragraph 1, AMLA may lend such assistance as may be necessary to assess the equivalence of professional secrecy requirements applicable to the third country counterpart.
3. Member States shall ensure that financial supervisors notify any agreement signed pursuant to this Article to AMLA within 1 month of its signature.

Section 3: Specific provisions relating to self-regulatory bodies

Article 38

Oversight of self-regulatory bodies

1. Where Member States decide, pursuant to Article 29(3), to allow self-regulatory bodies to perform supervision of the entities referred to in Article 3, points (3)(a), (b) and (d), of Regulation [please insert reference—proposal for Anti-Money Laundering Regulation—COM/2021/420 final], they shall ensure that the activities of such self-regulatory bodies in the performance of such functions are subject to oversight by a public authority.

2. The authority overseeing self-regulatory bodies shall be responsible for:

   (a) verifying that any self-regulatory body performing the functions or aspiring to perform the functions referred to in Article 29(1) satisfies the requirements of paragraph 3 of that Article;
   (b) issuing guidance as regards the performance of the functions referred to in Article 29(1);
   (c) ensuring that self-regulatory bodies perform their functions under Section 1 of this chapter to the highest standards;
   (d) reviewing the exemptions granted by self-regulatory bodies from the obligation to draw up an individual documented risk assessment pursuant to Article 29(4), point (b).

3. Member States shall ensure that the authority overseeing self-regulatory bodies is granted adequate powers to discharge its responsibilities under paragraph 2. As a minimum, Member States shall ensure that the authority has the power to:

   (a) compel the production of any information that is relevant to monitoring compliance and performing checks, except for any information collected by obliged entities referred to in Article 3, points (3)(a), (b) and (d), of Regulation [please insert reference—proposal for Anti-Money Laundering Regulation—COM/2021/420 final] in the course of ascertaining the legal position of their client, or for performing the task of defending or representing that client in, or concerning, judicial proceedings, including providing advice on instituting or avoiding such proceedings; whether such information was collected before, during or after such proceedings;
   (b) issue instructions to a self-regulatory body for the purpose of remedying a failure to perform its functions under Article 29(1) or to comply with the requirements of paragraph 6 of that Article, or to prevent any such failures. When issuing such instructions, the authority shall consider any relevant guidance it provided or that has been provided by AMLA.

4. Member States shall ensure that the authority overseeing self-regulatory bodies informs the authorities competent for investigating and prosecuting criminal activities timely, directly or through the FIU, of any breaches which are subject to criminal sanctions that it detects in the performance of its tasks.
5. The authority overseeing self-regulatory bodies shall publish an annual report containing information about:

   (a) the number and nature of breaches detected by each self-regulatory body and the administrative measures or sanctions imposed on obliged entities;
   (b) the number of suspicious transactions reported by the entities subject to supervision by each self-regulatory body to the FIU, whether submitted directly pursuant to Article 50(1) of Regulation [please insert reference—proposal for Anti-Money Laundering Regulation—COM/2021/420 final], or forwarded by each self-regulatory body to the FIU pursuant to Article 51(1) of that Regulation;

(c) the number and description of measures taken under Article 40 by each self-regulatory body to monitor compliance by obliged entities with the requirements of Regulation [please insert reference—proposal for Anti-Money Laundering Regulation—COM/2021/420 final] referred to in Article 40(1);
(d) the number and description of measures taken by the authority overseeing self-regulatory bodies under this Article and the number of instructions issued to self-regulatory bodies.

Such report shall be made available on the website of the authority overseeing self-regulatory bodies and submitted to the Commission and AMLA.

Section 4: Administrative sanctions and measures
Article 39
General provisions

1. Member States shall ensure that obliged entities can be held liable for breaches of the Regulation [please insert reference—proposal for Anti-Money Laundering Regulation—COM/2021/420 final] in accordance with this Section.
2. Without prejudice to the right of Member States to provide for and impose criminal sanctions, Member States shall lay down rules on administrative sanctions and measures and ensure that supervisors may impose such sanctions and measures with respect to breaches of this Directive, and shall ensure that they are applied. Any resulting sanction or measure imposed pursuant to this Section shall be effective, proportionate and dissuasive.
3. In the event of a breach of Regulation [please insert reference—proposal for Anti-Money Laundering Regulation—COM/2021/420 final], Member States shall ensure that where obligations apply to legal persons, administrative sanctions and measures can be applied to the senior management and to other natural persons who under national law are responsible for the breach.

   Member States shall ensure that where supervisors identify breaches which are subject to criminal sanctions, they inform the authorities competent for investigating and prosecuting criminal activities in a timely manner.
4. Supervisors shall exercise their powers to impose administrative sanctions and measures in accordance with this Directive and with national law, in any of the following ways:

   (a) directly;
   (b) in collaboration with other authorities;
   (c) under their responsibility by delegation to such other authorities;
   (d) by application to the competent judicial authorities.

By [3 months after the deadline for transposition of this Directive], Member States shall notify to the Commission and AMLA the information as regards the arrangements relating to the imposition of administrative sanctions or measures pursuant to this paragraph, including, where relevant, information whether certain sanctions or measures require the recourse to a specific procedure.

5. Member States shall ensure that, when determining the type and level of administrative sanctions or measures, supervisors take into account all relevant circumstances, including where applicable:
   (a) the gravity and the duration of the breach;
   (b) the degree of responsibility of the natural or legal person held responsible;
   (c) the financial strength of the natural or legal person held responsible, including in light of its total turnover or annual income;
   (d) the benefit derived from the breach by the natural or legal person held responsible, insofar as it can be determined;
   (e) the losses to third parties caused by the breach, insofar as they can be determined;
   (f) the level of cooperation of the natural or legal person held responsible with the competent authority;
   (g) previous breaches by the natural or legal person held responsible.
6. In the exercise of their powers to impose administrative sanctions and measures, supervisors shall cooperate closely in order to ensure that those administrative sanctions or measures produce the desired results and coordinate their action when dealing with cross-border cases.
7. By [2 years after the date of entry into force of this Directive], AMLA shall develop draft regulatory technical standards and submit them to the Commission for adoption. Those draft regulatory technical standards shall define indicators to classify the level of gravity of breaches and criteria to be taken into account when setting the level of administrative sanctions or taking administrative measures pursuant to this Section.

   The Commission is empowered to supplement this Directive by adopting the regulatory technical standards referred to in the first subparagraph in accordance with Articles 38 to 41 of Regulation [please insert reference—proposal for establishment of an Anti-Money Laundering Authority—COM/2021/421 final].

Article 40
Administrative sanctions

1. Member States shall ensure that administrative sanctions are applied to obliged entities for serious, repeated or systematic breaches of the requirements laid down in the following provisions of Regulation [please insert reference—proposal for Anti-Money Laundering Regulation—COM/2021/420 final]:
   (a) Chapter III (customer due diligence);
   (b) Chapter V (reporting obligations);
   (c) Article 56 (record-retention);
   (d) Section 1 of Chapter II (internal controls).
2. Member States shall ensure that in the cases referred to in paragraph 1, the maximum pecuniary sanctions that can be applied amount at least to twice the amount of the benefit derived from the breach where that benefit can be determined, or at least EUR 1,000,000.

3. Member States shall ensure that, by way of derogation from paragraph 2, where the obliged entity concerned is a credit institution or financial institution, the following sanctions can also be applied:

   (a) in the case of a legal person, maximum administrative pecuniary sanctions of at least EUR 10,000,000 or 10% of the total annual turnover according to the latest available accounts approved by the management body; where the obliged entity is a parent undertaking or a subsidiary of a parent undertaking which is required to prepare consolidated financial accounts in accordance with Article 22 of Directive 2013/34/EU of the European Parliament and of the Council 49, the relevant total annual turnover shall be the total annual turnover or the corresponding type of income in accordance with the relevant accounting regime according to the last available consolidated accounts approved by the management body of the ultimate parent undertaking;
   (b) in the case of a natural person, maximum administrative pecuniary sanctions of at least EUR 5,000,000 or, in the Member States whose currency is not the euro, the corresponding value in the national currency on [please insert the date of entry into force of this Directive].

4. Member States may empower competent authorities to impose administrative pecuniary sanctions exceeding the amounts referred to in paragraphs 2 and 3.

Article 41
Administrative measures other than sanctions

1. When supervisors identify breaches of requirements of the Regulation [please insert reference—proposal for Anti-Money Laundering Regulation—COM/2021/420 final] which are not deemed sufficiently serious to be punished with an administrative sanction, they may decide to impose administrative measures on the obliged entity. Member States shall ensure that the supervisors are able at least to:

   (a) issue recommendations;
   (b) order obliged entities to comply, including to implement specific corrective measures;
   (c) issue a public statement which identifies the natural or legal person and the nature of the breach;
   (d) issue an order requiring the natural or legal person to cease the conduct and to desist from repetition of that conduct;
   (e) where an obliged entity is subject to an authorisation, withdraw or suspend the authorisation;
   (f) impose a temporary ban against any person discharging managerial responsibilities in an obliged entity, or any other natural person, held responsible for the breach, from exercising managerial functions in obliged entities.

2. When taking the administrative measures referred to in paragraph 1, supervisors shall be able to:

(a) request an ad-hoc or regular submission of any document necessary for the performance of their tasks, including those to justify the process of implementation of the requested administrative measures;
(b) require the reinforcement of the arrangements, processes, mechanisms and strategies;
(c) require the obliged entity to apply a specific policy or requirements relating to individual clients, transactions or activities that pose high risks;
(d) require the implementation of measures to bring about the reduction of the money laundering or terrorist financing risks inherent in the activities and products of the obliged entity.

3. The administrative measures referred to in paragraph 1 shall be accompanied by a binding deadline for their effective implementation. Member States shall ensure that supervisors follow up and assess the effective implementation by the obliged entity of the actions requested.
4. Member States may empower supervisors to impose additional types of administrative measures to those referred to in paragraph 1.

Article 42

Publication of administrative sanctions and measures

1. Member States shall ensure that a decision imposing an administrative sanction or measure for breach of Regulation [please insert reference—proposal for Anti-Money Laundering Regulation—COM/2021/420 final] against which there is no appeal shall be published by the supervisors on their official website immediately after the person sanctioned is informed of that decision. The publication shall include at least information on the type and nature of the breach and the identity of the persons responsible. Member States shall not be obliged to apply this subparagraph to decisions imposing measures that are of an investigatory nature.

   Where the publication of the identity of the persons responsible as referred to in the first subparagraph or the personal data of such persons is considered by the supervisors to be disproportionate following a case-by-case assessment, or where publication jeopardises the stability of financial markets or an on-going investigation, supervisors shall:

   (a) delay the publication of the decision to impose an administrative sanction or measure until the moment at which the reasons for not publishing it cease to exist;
   (b) publish the decision to impose an administrative sanction or measure on an anonymous basis in a manner in accordance with national law, if such anonymous publication ensures an effective protection of the personal data concerned; in that case, the publication of the relevant data may be postponed for a reasonable period of time if it is provided that within that period the reasons for anonymous publication shall cease to exist;
   (c) not publish the decision to impose an administrative sanction or measure at all in the event that the options set out in points (a) and (b) are considered insufficient to ensure one of the following:

(i) that the stability of financial markets would not be put in jeopardy;
(ii) the proportionality of the publication of the decision with regard to measures which are deemed to be of a minor nature.

2. Where Member States permit publication of decisions against which there is an appeal, supervisors shall also publish, immediately, on their official website such information and any subsequent information on the outcome of such appeal. Moreover, any decision annulling a previous decision to impose an administrative sanction or a measure shall also be published.
3. Supervisors shall ensure that any publication in accordance with this Article shall remain on their official website for a period of 5 years after its publication. However, personal data contained in the publication shall only be kept on the official website of the competent authority for the period which is necessary in accordance with the applicable data protection rules and in any case for no more than 5 years.
4. Member States shall ensure that legal persons can be held liable for the breaches referred to in Article 40(1) committed for their benefit by any person, acting individually or as part of an organ of that legal person, and having a leading position within the legal person based on any of the following:

(a) power to represent the legal person;
(b) authority to take decisions on behalf of the legal person;
(c) authority to exercise control within the legal person.

5. Member States shall ensure that legal persons can be held liable where the lack of supervision or control by the persons referred to in paragraph 4 of this Article has made possible the commission, by a person under their authority, of the breaches referred to in Article 40(1) for the benefit of that legal person.

Article 43
Whistle-blower protection

1. Member States shall ensure that supervisory authorities, as well as, where applicable, self-regulatory bodies, establish effective and reliable mechanisms to encourage the reporting of potential and actual breaches of Regulation [please insert reference—proposal for Anti-Money Laundering Regulation—COM/2021/420 final].

   For that purpose, they shall provide one or more secure communication channels for the reporting referred to in the first subparagraph. Such channels shall ensure that the identity of persons providing information is known only to the supervisory authority, or, where applicable, self-regulatory body.
2. The mechanisms referred to in paragraph 1 shall include at least:

(a) specific procedures for the receipt of reports on breaches and their follow-up;
(b) appropriate protection for employees or persons in a comparable position, of obliged entities who report breaches committed within the obliged entity;
(c) appropriate protection for the accused person;

(d) protection of personal data concerning both the person who reports the breaches and the natural person who is allegedly responsible for a breach, in compliance with the principles laid down in Regulation (EU) 2016/679;
(e) clear rules that ensure that confidentiality is guaranteed in all cases in relation to the person who reports the breaches committed within the obliged entity, unless disclosure is required by national law in the context of further investigations or subsequent judicial proceedings.

3. Member States shall ensure that individuals, including employees and representatives of the obliged entity who report potential or actual breaches of Regulation [please insert reference—proposal for Anti-Money Laundering Regulation—COM/2021/420 final] internally or to the FIU, are legally protected from being exposed to threats, retaliatory or hostile action, and in particular from adverse or discriminatory employment actions.
   Member States shall ensure that individuals who are exposed to threats, hostile actions, or adverse or discriminatory employment actions for reporting potential or actual breaches of Regulation [please insert reference—proposal for Anti-Money Laundering Regulation—COM/2021/420 final] internally or to the FIU are entitled to present a complaint in a safe manner to the respective competent authorities. Without prejudice to the confidentiality of information gathered by the FIU, Member States shall also ensure that such individuals have the right to effective remedy to safeguard their rights under this paragraph.

Article 44
Exchange of information on sanctions

1. Member States shall ensure that their supervisors and, where relevant, the national authority overseeing self-regulatory bodies in their performance of supervisory functions inform AMLA of all administrative sanctions and measures imposed in accordance with this Section, including of any appeal in relation thereto and the outcome thereof. Such information shall also be shared with other supervisors when the administrative sanction or measure concerns an entity operating in two or more Member States.
2. AMLA shall maintain on its website links to each supervisor's publication of administrative sanctions and measures imposed in accordance with Article 42, and shall show the time period for which each Member State publishes administrative sanctions and measures.

CHAPTER V—COOPERATION
Section 1: AML/CFT cooperation
Article 45
General provisions

1. Member States shall ensure that policy makers, the FIUs, supervisors, including AMLA, and other competent authorities, as well as tax authorities have effective mechanisms to enable them to cooperate and coordinate domestically concerning the development and implementation of policies and activities to combat money

laundering and terrorist financing and to prevent the non-implementation and evasion of proliferation financing-related targeted financial sanctions, including with a view to fulfilling their obligations under Article 8.

2. With regard to beneficial ownership information obtained by competent authorities pursuant to Chapter IV of Regulation [please insert reference—proposal for Anti-Money Laundering Regulation—COM/2021/420 final] and Section I of Chapter II of this Directive, Member States shall ensure that competent authorities are able to provide such information to the competent authorities of other Member States or third countries in a timely manner and free of charge.
3. Member States shall not prohibit or place unreasonable or unduly restrictive conditions on the exchange of information or assistance between competent authorities for the purposes of this Directive. Member States shall ensure that competent authorities do not refuse a request for assistance on the grounds that:

   (a) the request is also considered to involve tax matters;
   (b) national law requires obliged entities to maintain secrecy or confidentiality, except in those cases where the relevant information that is sought is protected by legal privilege or where legal professional secrecy applies, as provided for in Article 51(2) of Regulation [please insert reference—proposal for Anti-Money Laundering Regulation—COM/2021/420 final];
   (c) there is an inquiry, investigation or proceeding underway in the requested Member State, unless the assistance would impede that inquiry, investigation or proceeding;
   (d) the nature or status of the requesting counterpart competent authority is different from that of requested competent authority.

Article 46

Communication of the list of the competent authorities

1. In order to facilitate and promote effective cooperation, and in particular the exchange of information, Member States shall communicate to the Commission and AMLA:

   (a) the list of supervisors responsible for overseeing the compliance of the obliged entities with the requirements of Regulation [please insert reference—proposal for Anti-Money Laundering Regulation—COM/2021/420 final], as well as, where relevant, name of the public authority overseeing self-regulatory bodies in their performance of supervisory functions under this Directive, and their contact details;
   (b) the contact details of their FIU;
   (c) the list of other competent national authorities.

2. For the purposes of paragraph 1, the following contact details shall be provided:

   (a) the name and role of the contact person;
   (b) the professional email address and phone number of the contact person.

3. Member States shall ensure that the information provided to the Commission and AMLA pursuant to paragraph 1 is updated as soon as a change takes place.
4. AMLA shall publish a register of the authorities referred to in paragraph 1 on its website and facilitate the exchange of information referred to in paragraph 2 between competent authorities. The authorities in the register shall, within the scope of their powers, serve as a contact point for the counterpart competent authorities. FIUs and supervisory authorities shall also serve as a contact point for AMLA.

Article 47

Cooperation with AMLA

FIU and supervisory authorities shall cooperate with AMLA and shall provide it with all the information necessary to allow it to carry out its duties under this Directive, under Regulation [please insert reference—proposal for Anti-Money Laundering Regulation—COM/2021/420 final] and under Regulation [please insert reference—proposal for establishment of an Anti-Money Laundering Authority—COM/2021/421 final].

Section 2: Cooperation with other authorities and exchange of confidential information

Article 48

Cooperation in relation to credit institutions

1. Member States shall ensure that financial supervisors, FIUs and authorities competent for the supervision of credit institutions under other legal acts cooperate closely with each other within their respective competences and provide each other with information relevant for the performance of their respective tasks. Such cooperation and information exchange shall not impinge on an ongoing inquiry, investigation or proceedings in accordance with the criminal or administrative law of the Member State where the financial supervisor or authority entrusted with competences for the supervision of credit institutions under other legal acts is located and shall not affect obligations of professional secrecy as provided in Article 50(1).
2. Member States shall ensure that, where financial supervisors identify weaknesses in the AML/CFT internal control system and application of the requirements of Regulation [please insert reference—proposal for Anti-Money Laundering Regulation—COM/2021/420 final] of a credit institution which materially increase the risks to which the institution is or might be exposed, the financial supervisor immediately notifies the European Banking Authority (EBA) and the authority or body that supervises the credit institution in accordance with Directive (EU) 2013/36, including the ECB acting in accordance with Council Regulation (EU) 1024/2013 50.

   In the event of potential increased risk, financial supervisors shall be able to liaise with the authorities supervising the institution in accordance with Directive (EU) 2013/36 and draw up a common assessment to be notified to EBA. AMLA shall be kept informed of any such notifications.

3. Member States shall ensure that, where financial supervisors find that a credit institution has refused to enter into a business relationship but the documented customer due diligence pursuant to Article 17(2) does not justify such refusal, they shall inform the authority responsible for ensuring compliance by that institution with Directive (EU) 2014/92 or Directive (EU) 2015/2366.
4. Member States shall ensure that financial supervisors cooperate with resolution authorities as defined in Article 3(18) of Directive 2014/59/EU or designated authorities as defined in Article 2(1)(18) of Directive 2014/49/EU. Financial supervisors shall inform such authorities of the outcome of the customer due diligence measures applied pursuant to Chapter III of Regulation [please insert reference—proposal for Anti-Money Laundering Regulation—COM/2021/420 final] and of any account that has been suspended by the FIU pursuant to Article 20.
5. Financial supervisors and FIUs shall report on a yearly basis to AMLA on their cooperation with other authorities pursuant to this Article.
6. By [2 years after the date of transposition of this Directive], AMLA shall, in consultation with EBA, issue guidelines on cooperation between financial supervisors and the authorities referred to in paragraphs 2, 3 and 4, including on the level of involvement of FIUs in such cooperation.

Article 49
Cooperation in relation to auditors

1. Member States shall ensure that supervisors in charge of auditors and, where relevant, public authorities overseeing self-regulatory bodies pursuant to Chapter IV of this Directive, their FIU and the public authorities competent for overseeing statutory auditors and audit firms pursuant to Article 32 of Directive 2006/43/EC of the European Parliament and of the Council 51 and Article 20 of Regulation (EU) 537/2014 of the European Parliament and of the Council 52 cooperate closely with each other within their respective competences and provide each other with information relevant for the performance of their respective tasks.

   Confidential information exchanged pursuant to this Article shall be used by the authorities referred to in the first subparagraph solely for the exercise of their functions within the scope of this Directive or the other Union acts referred to in the first subparagraph and in the context of administrative or judicial proceedings specifically related to the exercise of those functions.
2. Member States may prohibit the authorities referred to in paragraph 1 from cooperating when such cooperation, including the exchange of information, would impinge on an ongoing inquiry, investigation or proceedings in accordance with the criminal or administrative law of the Member State where the authorities are located.

Article 50

Exchange of information in relation to credit and financial institutions among entities bound by professional secrecy

1. Member States shall require that all persons working for or who have worked for financial supervisors and auditors or experts acting on behalf of financial supervisors be bound by the obligation of professional secrecy.

   Without prejudice to cases covered by criminal investigations and prosecutions under Member States and Union law and information provided to the FIU pursuant to Article 32, confidential information which the persons referred to in the first subparagraph receive in the course of their duties under this Directive may be disclosed only in summary or aggregate form, in such a way that individual credit and financial institutions cannot be identified.
2. Paragraph 1 shall not prevent the exchange of information between:

   (a) financial supervisors, whether within a Member State or in different Member States, including AMLA when acting in accordance with Article 5(2) of Regulation [please insert reference—proposal for establishment of an Anti-Money Laundering Authority—COM/2021/421 final];
   (b) financial supervisors and FIUs;
   (c) financial supervisors and competent authorities in charge of credit and financial institutions in accordance with other legislative acts relating to the supervision of credit and financial institutions, including the ECB acting in accordance with Regulation (EU) 1024/2013, whether within a Member State or in different Member States.

For the purposes of the first subparagraph, point (c), the exchange of information shall be subject to the professional secrecy requirements provided for in paragraph 1.

3. Any authority that receives confidential information pursuant to paragraph 2 shall only use this information:

   (a) in the discharge of its duties under this Directive or under other legislative acts in the field of AML/CFT, of prudential regulation and supervision of credit and financial institutions, including sanctioning;
   (b) in an appeal against a decision of the authority, including court proceedings;
   (c) in court proceedings initiated pursuant to special provisions provided for in Union law adopted in the field of this Directive or in the field of prudential regulation and supervision of credit and financial institutions.

Article 51

Exchange of information among supervisors and with other authorities

1. With the exception of cases covered by Article 51(2) of Regulation [please insert reference—proposal for Anti-Money Laundering Regulation—COM/2021/420 final], Member States shall authorise the exchange of information between:
   (a) supervisors and the public authorities overseeing self-regulatory bodies pursuant to Chapter IV of this Directive, whether in the same Member State or in different Member States;
   (b) supervisors and the authorities responsible by law for the supervision of financial markets in the discharge of their respective supervisory functions;
   (c) supervisors in charge of auditors and, where relevant, public authorities overseeing self-regulatory bodies pursuant to Chapter IV of this Directive, and the public authorities competent for overseeing statutory auditors and audit firms pursuant to Article 32 of Directive 2006/43/EC and Article 20 of Regulation (EU) 537/2014, including authorities in different Member States.

The professional secrecy requirements laid down in Article 50(1) and (3) shall not prevent such exchange of information.

Confidential information exchanged pursuant to this paragraph shall only be used in the discharge of the duties of the authorities concerned, and in the context of administrative or judicial proceedings specifically related to the exercise of those functions. The information received shall in any event be subject to professional secrecy requirements at least equivalent to those referred to in Article 50(1).

2. Member States may authorise the disclosure of certain information to other national authorities responsible by law for the supervision of the financial markets, or with designated responsibilities in the field of combating or investigating money laundering, its predicate offences or terrorist financing. The professional secrecy requirements laid down Article 50(1) and (3) shall not prevent such disclosure.

   However, confidential information exchanged pursuant to this paragraph shall only be used for the purpose of performing the legal tasks of the authorities concerned. Persons having access to such information shall be subject to professional secrecy requirements at least equivalent to those referred to in Article 50(1).
3. Member States may authorise the disclosure of certain information relating to the supervision of obliged entities for compliance with the requirements of Regulation [please insert reference—proposal for Anti-Money Laundering Regulation—COM/2021/420 final] to parliamentary inquiry committees, courts of auditors and other entities in charge of enquiries in their Member State, under the following conditions:

(a) the entities have a precise mandate under national law to investigate or scrutinise the actions of supervisors or authorities responsible for laws on such supervision;
(b) the information is strictly necessary for fulfilling the mandate referred to in point (a);
(c) the persons with access to the information are subject to professional secrecy requirements under national law at least equivalent to those referred to in paragraph 1;
(d) where the information originates in another Member State, it shall not be disclosed without the express consent of the supervisor which disclosed it and solely for the purposes for which that supervisor gave its consent.

Section 3: Guidelines on cooperation

Article 52

AML/CFT cooperation guidelines

By [2 years after the date of transposition of this Directive], AMLA shall, in cooperation with the ECB, the European Supervisory Authorities, Europol, Eurojust, and the European Public Prosecutor's Office, issue guidelines on:

(a) the cooperation between competent authorities under Section 1 of this chapter, as well as with the authorities referred to under Section 2 of this chapter and the authorities in charge of the registers referred to in Section 1 of Chapter II of this Directive, to prevent money laundering and terrorist financing;
(b) the procedures to be used by authorities competent for the supervision or oversight of obliged entities under other Union acts to take into account money laundering and terrorist financing concerns in the performance of their duties under their respective Union acts.

CHAPTER VI—DATA PROTECTION

Article 53

Processing of certain categories of personal data

1. To the extent that it is strictly necessary for the purposes of this Directive, competent authorities may process special categories of personal data referred to in Article 9(1) of Regulation (EU) 2016/679 and personal data relating to criminal convictions and offences referred to in Article 10 of that Regulation subject to appropriate safeguards for the rights and freedoms of the data subject and the following additional safeguards:

   (a) processing of such data shall be performed only on a case-by-case basis by the staff of each competent authority that have been specifically designated and authorised to perform those tasks;
   (b) staff of the competent authorities shall maintain high professional standards of confidentiality and data protection, they shall be of high integrity and are appropriately skilled;
   (c) technical and organisational measures shall be in place to ensure the security of the data to high technological standards.

2. The safeguards referred to in paragraph 1 shall also apply to the processing for the purposes of this Directive of special categories of data referred to in Article 10(1) of Regulation (EU) 2018/1725 and personal data relating to criminal convictions and offences referred to in Article 11 of that regulation by Union institutions, agencies or bodies.

CHAPTER VII—FINAL PROVISIONS

Article 54

Committee

1. The Commission shall be assisted by the Committee on the Prevention of Money Laundering and Terrorist Financing established by Article 28 of Regulation [please insert reference—proposal for a recast of Regulation (EU) 2015/847—COM/2021/422 final]. That committee shall be a committee within the meaning of Regulation (EU) No 182/2011.
2. Where reference is made to this paragraph, Article 5 of Regulation (EU) No 182/2011 shall apply.

Article 55

Transitional management of FIU.net

At the latest by [3 years after the date of entry into force of this Directive], the Commission shall transfer to AMLA the management of FIU.net.

Until such transfer is completed, the Commission shall lend the necessary assistance for the operation of FIU.net and the exchange of information between FIUs within the Union. To this end, the Commission shall regularly convene meetings of the EU FIU's Platform composed of representatives from Member States' FIUs in order to oversee the functioning of FIU.net.

Article 56

Review

By [5 years from the date of transposition of this Directive], and every 3 years thereafter, the Commission shall present a report to the European Parliament and to the Council on the implementation of this Directive.

Article 57

Repeal

Directive (EU) 2015/849 is repealed with effect from [date of transposition].

References to the repealed Directive shall be construed as references to this Directive and to Regulation [please insert reference—proposal for Anti-Money Laundering Regulation] in accordance with the correlation table set out in the Annex.

Article 58

Transposition

1. Member States shall bring into force the laws, regulations and administrative provisions necessary to comply with this Directive by [please insert date—3 years after the date of entry into force] at the latest. They shall forthwith communicate to the Commission the text of those provisions.

When Member States adopt those measures, they shall contain a reference to this Directive or be accompanied by such a reference on the occasion of their official publication. Member States shall determine how such reference is to be made.

2. Member States shall communicate to the Commission the text of the main provisions of national law which they adopt in the field covered by this Directive.

Article 59

Entry into force

This Directive shall enter into force on the twentieth day following that of its publication in the Official Journal of the European Union.

Article 60

Addressees

This Directive is addressed to the Member States.

vi) **The Council of Europe Convention on Laundering, Search, Seizure and Confiscation of the Proceeds from Crime and on the Financing of Terrorism** (Warsaw Convention 2005)[12]

The **Council of Europe Convention on Laundering, Search, Seizure and Confiscation of the Proceeds from Crime and on the Financing of Terrorism**, also known as the **Warsaw Convention** or **CETS 198** aims to facilitate international co-operation and mutual assistance in investigating crime and tracking down, seizing and confiscating the proceeds thereof.

This Convention is the first international treaty covering both the prevention and the control of money laundering and the financing of terrorism. This instrument recognises that quick access to financial information or information on assets held by criminal organisations, including terrorist groups, is the key to successful preventive and repressive measures, and, ultimately, is the best way to stop them.

It builds on and updates the 1990 Strasbourg Convention; it takes into account the fact that terrorism can be financed not only through money laundering from criminal activity, but also through legitimate activities. The Convention also includes a mechanism to ensure the proper implementation by Parties of its provisions. The Convention opened for signature in Warsaw on 16 May 2005 and entered into force on 1 May 2008.[13]

Chapter I—Use of terms

Article 1—Use of terms

For the purposes of this Convention:

a. "proceeds" means any economic advantage, derived from or obtained, directly or indirectly, from criminal offences. It may consist of any property as defined in sub-paragraph b of this article;

[12] https://rm.coe.int/168008371f

[13] https://en.wikipedia.org/wiki/2005_Warsaw_Convention

b. "property" includes property of any description, whether corporeal or incorporeal, movable or immovable, and legal documents or instruments evidencing title to or interest in such property;
c. "instrumentalities" means any property used or intended to be used, in any manner, wholly or in part, to commit a criminal offence or criminal offences;
d. "confiscation" means a penalty or a measure, ordered by a court following proceedings in relation to a criminal offence or criminal offences resulting in the final deprivation of property;
e. "predicate offence" means any criminal offence as a result of which proceeds were generated that may become the subject of an offence as defined in Article 9 of this Convention.
f. "financial intelligence unit" (hereinafter referred to as "FIU") means a central, national agency responsible for receiving (and, as permitted, requesting), analysing and disseminating to the competent authorities, disclosures of financial information

    i. concerning suspected proceeds and potential financing of terrorism, or
    ii. required by national legislation or regulation, in order to combat money laundering and financing of terrorism;

g. "freezing" or "seizure" means temporarily prohibiting the transfer, destruction, conversion, disposition or movement of property or temporarily assuming custody or control of property on the basis of an order issued by a court or other competent authority;
h. "financing of terrorism" means the acts set out in Article 2 of the International Convention for the Suppression of the Financing of Terrorism, cited above.

Chapter II—Financing of terrorism Article 2—Application of the Convention to the financing of terrorism

1. Each Party shall adopt such legislative and other measures as may be necessary to enable it to apply the provisions contained in Chapters III, IV and V of this Convention to the financing of terrorism.
2. In particular, each Party shall ensure that it is able to search, trace, identify, freeze, seize and confiscate property, of a licit or illicit origin, used or allocated to be used by any means, in whole or in part, for the financing of terrorism, or the proceeds of this offence, and to provide co-operation to this end to the widest possible extent.

Chapter III—Measures to be taken at national level
Section 1—General provisions Article 3—Confiscation measures

1. Each Party shall adopt such legislative and other measures as may be necessary to enable it to confiscate instrumentalities and proceeds or property the value of which corresponds to such proceeds and laundered property.
2. Provided that paragraph 1 of this article applies to money laundering and to the categories of offences in the appendix to the Convention, each Party may, at the time of signature or when depositing its instrument of ratification, acceptance,

approval or accession, by a declaration addressed to the Secretary General of the Council of Europe, declare that paragraph 1 of this article applies

a. only in so far as the offence is punishable by deprivation of liberty or a detention order for a maximum of more than 1 year. However, each Party may make a declaration on this provision in respect of the confiscation of the proceeds from tax offences for the sole purpose of being able to confiscate such proceeds, both nationally and through international cooperation, under national and international tax-debt recovery legislation; and/or
b. only to a list of specified offences.

3. Parties may provide for mandatory confiscation in respect of offences which are subject to the confiscation regime. Parties may in particular include in this provision the offences of money laundering, drug trafficking, trafficking in human beings and any other serious offence.
4. Each Party shall adopt such legislative or other measures as may be necessary to require that, in respect of a serious offence or offences as defined by national law, an offender demonstrates the origin of alleged proceeds or other property liable to confiscation to the extent that such a requirement is consistent with the principles of its domestic law.

Article 4—Investigative and provisional measures

Each Party shall adopt such legislative and other measures as may be necessary to enable it to identify, trace, freeze or seize rapidly property which is liable to confiscation pursuant to Article 3, in order in particular to facilitate the enforcement of a later confiscation.

Article 5—Freezing, seizure and confiscation

Each Party shall adopt such legislative and other measures as may be necessary to ensure that the measures to freeze, seize and confiscate also encompass:

a. the property into which the proceeds have been transformed or converted;
b. property acquired from legitimate sources, if proceeds have been intermingled, in whole or in part, with such property, up to the assessed value of the intermingled proceeds;
c. income or other benefits derived from proceeds, from property into which proceeds of crime have been transformed or converted or from property with which proceeds of crime have been intermingled, up to the assessed value of the intermingled proceeds, in the same manner and to the same extent as proceeds.

Article 6—Management of frozen or seized property

Each Party shall adopt such legislative or other measures as may be necessary to ensure proper management of frozen or seized property in accordance with Articles 4 and 5 of this Convention.

Article 7—Investigative powers and techniques

1. Each Party shall adopt such legislative and other measures as may be necessary to empower its courts or other competent authorities to order that bank, financial or commercial records be made available or be seized in order to carry out the

actions referred to in Articles 3, 4 and 5. A Party shall not decline to act under the provisions of this article on grounds of bank secrecy.

2. Without prejudice to paragraph 1, each Party shall adopt such legislative and other measures as may be necessary to enable it to:

   a. determine whether a natural or legal person is a holder or beneficial owner of one or more accounts, of whatever nature, in any bank located in its territory and, if so obtain all of the details of the identified accounts;
   b. obtain the particulars of specified bank accounts and of banking operations which have been carried out during a specified period through one or more specified accounts, including the particulars of any sending or recipient account;
   c. monitor, during a specified period, the banking operations that are being carried out through one or more identified accounts; and,
   d. ensure that banks do not disclose to the bank customer concerned or to other third persons that information has been sought or obtained in accordance with sub- paragraphs a, b, or c, or that an investigation is being carried out.

Parties shall consider extending this provision to accounts held in non-bank financial institutions.

3. Each Party shall consider adopting such legislative and other measures as may be necessary to enable it to use special investigative techniques facilitating the identification and tracing of proceeds and the gathering of evidence related thereto, such as observation, interception of telecommunications, access to computer systems and order to produce specific documents.

Article 8—Legal remedies

Each Party shall adopt such legislative and other measures as may be necessary to ensure that interested parties affected by measures under Articles 3, 4 and 5 and such other provisions in this Section as are relevant, shall have effective legal remedies in order to preserve their rights.

Article 9—Laundering offences

Each Party shall adopt such legislative and other measures as may be necessary to establish as offences under its domestic law, when committed intentionally:

a. the conversion or transfer of property, knowing that such property is proceeds, for the purpose of concealing or disguising the illicit origin of the property or of assisting any person who is involved in the commission of the predicate offence to evade the legal consequences of his actions;
b. the concealment or disguise of the true nature, source, location, disposition, movement, rights with respect to, or ownership of, property, knowing that such property is proceeds;

and, subject to its constitutional principles and the basic concepts of its legal system;

c. the acquisition, possession or use of property, knowing, at the time of receipt, that such property was proceeds;

d. participation in, association or conspiracy to commit, attempts to commit and aiding, abetting, facilitating and counselling the commission of any of the offences established in accordance with this article.

2. For the purposes of implementing or applying paragraph 1 of this article:

   a. it shall not matter whether the predicate offence was subject to the criminal jurisdiction of the Party;
   b. it may be provided that the offences set forth in that paragraph do not apply to the persons who committed the predicate offence;
   c. knowledge, intent or purpose required as an element of an offence set forth in that paragraph may be inferred from objective, factual circumstances.

3. Each Party may adopt such legislative and other measures as may be necessary to establish as an offence under its domestic law all or some of the acts referred to in paragraph 1 of this article, in either or both of the following cases where the offender

   a. suspected that the property was proceeds,
   b. ought to have assumed that the property was proceeds.

4. Provided that paragraph 1 of this article applies to the categories of predicate offences in the appendix to the Convention, each State or the European Community may, at the time of signature or when depositing its instrument of ratification, acceptance, approval or accession, by a declaration addressed to the Secretary General of the Council of Europe, declare that paragraph 1 of this article applies:

   a. only in so far as the predicate offence is punishable by deprivation of liberty or a detention order for a maximum of more than 1 year, or for those Parties that have a minimum threshold for offences in their legal system, in so far as the offence is punishable by deprivation of liberty or a detention order for a minimum of more than 6 months; and/or
   b. only to a list of specified predicate offences; and/or
   c. to a category of serious offences in the national law of the Party.

5. Each Party shall ensure that a prior or simultaneous conviction for the predicate offence is not a prerequisite for a conviction for money laundering.
6. Each Party shall ensure that a conviction for money laundering under this Article is possible where it is proved that the property, the object of paragraph 1.a or b of this article, originated from a predicate offence, without it being necessary to establish precisely which offence.
7. Each Party shall ensure that predicate offences for money laundering extend to conduct that occurred in another State, which constitutes an offence in that State, and which would have constituted a predicate offence had it occurred domestically. Each Party may provide that the only prerequisite is that the conduct would have constituted a predicate offence had it occurred domestically.

Article 10—Corporate liability

1. Each Party shall adopt such legislative and other measures as may be necessary to ensure that legal persons can be held liable for the criminal offences of money laundering established in accordance with this Convention, committed for their benefit by any natural person, acting either individually or as part of an organ of the legal person, who has a leading position within the legal person, based on:

   d. a power of representation of the legal person; or
   e. an authority to take decisions on behalf of the legal person; or
   f. an authority to exercise control within the legal person,

as well as for involvement of such a natural person as accessory or instigator in the above- mentioned offences.

2. Apart from the cases already provided for in paragraph 1, each Party shall take the necessary measures to ensure that a legal person can be held liable where the lack of supervision or control by a natural person referred to in paragraph 1 has made possible the commission of the criminal offences mentioned in paragraph 1 for the benefit of that legal person by a natural person under its authority.
3. Liability of a legal person under this Article shall not exclude criminal proceedings against natural persons who are perpetrators, instigators of, or accessories to, the criminal offences mentioned in paragraph 1.
4. Each Party shall ensure that legal persons held liable in accordance with this Article, shall be subject to effective, proportionate and dissuasive criminal or non-criminal sanctions, including monetary sanctions.

Article 11—Previous decisions

Each Party shall adopt such legislative and other measures as may be necessary to provide for the possibility of taking into account, when determining the penalty, final decisions against a natural or legal person taken in another Party in relation to offences established in accordance with this Convention.

Section 2—Financial intelligence unit (FIU) and prevention

Article 12—Financial intelligence unit (FIU)

1. Each Party shall adopt such legislative and other measures as may be necessary to establish an FIU as defined in this Convention.
2. Each Party shall adopt such legislative and other measures as may be necessary to ensure that its FIU has access, directly or indirectly, on a timely basis to the financial, administrative and law enforcement information that it requires to properly undertake its functions, including the analysis of suspicious transaction reports.

Article 13—Measures to prevent money laundering

1. Each Party shall adopt such legislative and other measures as may be necessary to institute a comprehensive domestic regulatory and supervisory or monitoring regime to prevent money laundering and shall take due account of applicable

international standards, including in particular the recommendations adopted by the Financial Action Task Force on Money Laundering (FATF).

2. In that respect, each Party shall adopt, in particular, such legislative and other measures as may be necessary to:

   a. require legal and natural persons which engage in activities which are particularly likely to be used for money laundering purposes, and as far as these activities are concerned, to:

      i. identify and verify the identity of their customers and, where applicable, their ultimate beneficial owners, and to conduct ongoing due diligence on the business relationship, while taking into account a risk based approach;
      ii. report suspicions on money laundering subject to safeguard;
      iii. take supporting measures, such as record keeping on customer identification and transactions, training of personnel and the establishment of internal policies and procedures, and if appropriate, adapted to their size and nature of business;

   b. prohibit, as appropriate, the persons referred to in sub-paragraph a from disclosing the fact that a suspicious transaction report or related information has been transmitted or that a money laundering investigation is being or may be carried out;
   c. ensure that the persons referred to in sub-paragraph a are subject to effective systems for monitoring, and where applicable supervision, with a view to ensure their compliance with the requirements to combat money laundering, where appropriate on a risk sensitive basis.

3. In that respect, each Party shall adopt such legislative or other measures as may be necessary to detect the significant physical cross border transportation of cash and appropriate bearer negotiable instruments.

Article 14—Postponement of domestic suspicious transactions

Each Party shall adopt such legislative and other measures as may be necessary to permit urgent action to be taken by the FIU or, as appropriate, by any other competent authorities or body, when there is a suspicion that a transaction is related to money laundering, to suspend or withhold consent to a transaction going ahead in order to analyse the transaction and confirm the suspicion. Each party may restrict such a measure to cases where a suspicious transaction report has been submitted. The maximum duration of any suspension or withholding of consent to a transaction shall be subject to any relevant provisions in national law.

Chapter IV—International co-operationSection 1—Principles of international co-operation

Article 15—General principles and measures for international co-operation

1. The Parties shall mutually co-operate with each other to the widest extent possible for the purposes of investigations and proceedings aiming at the confiscation of instrumentalities and proceeds.

2. Each Party shall adopt such legislative or other measures as may be necessary to enable it to comply, under the conditions provided for in this chapter, with requests:

   a. for confiscation of specific items of property representing proceeds or instrumentalities, as well as for confiscation of proceeds consisting in a requirement to pay a sum of money corresponding to the value of proceeds;
   b. for investigative assistance and provisional measures with a view to either form of confiscation referred to under a above.

3. Investigative assistance and provisional measures sought in paragraph 2.b shall be carried out as permitted by and in accordance with the internal law of the requested Party. Where the request concerning one of these measures specifies formalities or procedures which are necessary under the law of the requesting Party, even if unfamiliar to the requested Party, the latter shall comply with such requests to the extent that the action sought is not contrary to the fundamental principles of its law.
4. Each Party shall adopt such legislative or other measures as may be necessary to ensure that the requests coming from other Parties in order to identify, trace, freeze or seize the proceeds and instrumentalities, receive the same priority as those made in the framework of internal procedures.

Section 2—Investigative assistance

Article 16—Obligation to assist

The Parties shall afford each other, upon request, the widest possible measure of assistance in the identification and tracing of instrumentalities, proceeds and other property liable to confiscation. Such assistance shall include any measure providing and securing evidence as to the existence, location or movement, nature, legal status or value of the aforementioned property.

Article 17—Requests for information on bank accounts

1. Each Party shall, under the conditions set out in this article, take the measures necessary to determine, in answer to a request sent by another Party, whether a natural or legal person that is the subject of a criminal investigation holds or controls one or more accounts, of whatever nature, in any bank located in its territory and, if so, provide the particulars of the identified accounts.
2. The obligation set out in this article shall apply only to the extent that the information is in the possession of the bank keeping the account.
3. In addition to the requirements of Article 37, the requesting party shall, in the request:

   a. state why it considers that the requested information is likely to be of substantial value for the purpose of the criminal investigation into the offence;
   b. state on what grounds it presumes that banks in the requested Party hold the account and specify, to the widest extent possible, which banks and/or accounts may be involved; and
   c. include any additional information available which may facilitate the execution of the request.

4. The requested Party may make the execution of such a request dependant on the same conditions as it applies in respect of requests for search and seizure.
5. Each State or the European Community may, at the time of signature or when depositing its instrument of ratification, acceptance, approval or accession, by a declaration addressed to the Secretary General of the Council of Europe, declare that this article applies only to the categories of offences specified in the list contained in the appendix to this Convention.
6. Parties may extend this provision to accounts held in non-bank financial institutions. Such extension may be made subject to the principle of reciprocity.

Article 18—Requests for information on banking transactions

1. On request by another Party, the requested Party shall provide the particulars of specified bank accounts and of banking operations which have been carried out during a specified period through one or more accounts specified in the request, including the particulars of any sending or recipient account.
2. The obligation set out in this article shall apply only to the extent that the information is in the possession of the bank holding the account.
3. In addition to the requirements of Article 37, the requesting Party shall in its request indicate why it considers the requested information relevant for the purpose of the criminal investigation into the offence.
4. The requested Party may make the execution of such a request dependant on the same conditions as it applies in respect of requests for search and seizure.
5. Parties may extend this provision to accounts held in non-bank financial institutions. Such extension may be made subject to the principle of reciprocity.

Article 19—Requests for the monitoring of banking transactions

1. Each Party shall ensure that, at the request of another Party, it is able to monitor, during a specified period, the banking operations that are being carried out through one or more accounts specified in the request and communicate the results thereof to the requesting Party.
2. In addition to the requirements of Article 37, the requesting Party shall in its request indicate why it considers the requested information relevant for the purpose of the criminal investigation into the offence.
3. The decision to monitor shall be taken in each individual case by the competent authorities of the requested Party, with due regard for the national law of that Party.
4. The practical details regarding the monitoring shall be agreed between the competent authorities of the requesting and requested Parties.
5. Parties may extend this provision to accounts held in non-bank financial institutions.

Article 20—Spontaneous information

Without prejudice to its own investigations or proceedings, a Party may without prior request forward to another Party information on instrumentalities and proceeds, when it considers that the disclosure of such information might assist the receiving

Party in initiating or carrying out investigations or proceedings or might lead to a request by that Party under this chapter.

Section 3—Provisional measures

Article 21—Obligation to take provisional measures

1. At the request of another Party which has instituted criminal proceedings or proceedings for the purpose of confiscation, a Party shall take the necessary provisional measures, such as freezing or seizing, to prevent any dealing in, transfer or disposal of property which, at a later stage, may be the subject of a request for confiscation or which might be such as to satisfy the request.
2. A Party which has received a request for confiscation pursuant to Article 23 shall, if so requested, take the measures mentioned in paragraph 1 of this article in respect of any property which is the subject of the request or which might be such as to satisfy the request.

Article 22—Execution of provisional measures

1. After the execution of the provisional measures requested in conformity with paragraph 1 of Article 21, the requesting Party shall provide spontaneously and as soon as possible to the requested Party all information which may question or modify the extent of these measures. The requesting Party shall also provide without delays all complementary information requested by the requested Party and which is necessary for the implementation of and the follow up to the provisional measures.
2. Before lifting any provisional measure taken pursuant to this article, the requested Party shall, wherever possible, give the requesting Party an opportunity to present its reasons in favour of continuing the measure.

Section 4—Confiscation

Article 23—Obligation to confiscate

1. A Party, which has received a request made by another Party for confiscation concerning instrumentalities or proceeds, situated in its territory, shall:

   a. enforce a confiscation order made by a court of a requesting Party in relation to such instrumentalities or proceeds; or
   b. submit the request to its competent authorities for the purpose of obtaining an order of confiscation and, if such order is granted, enforce it.

2. For the purposes of applying paragraph 1.b of this article, any Party shall whenever necessary have competence to institute confiscation proceedings under its own law.
3. The provisions of paragraph 1 of this article shall also apply to confiscation consisting in a requirement to pay a sum of money corresponding to the value of proceeds, if property on which the confiscation can be enforced is located in the requested Party. In such cases, when enforcing confiscation pursuant to paragraph 1, the requested Party shall, if payment is not obtained, realise the claim on any property available for that purpose.

4. If a request for confiscation concerns a specific item of property, the Parties may agree that the requested Party may enforce the confiscation in the form of a requirement to pay a sum of money corresponding to the value of the property.
5. The Parties shall co-operate to the widest extent possible under their domestic law with those Parties which request the execution of measures equivalent to confiscation leading to the deprivation of property, which are not criminal sanctions, in so far as such measures are ordered by a judicial authority of the requesting Party in relation to a criminal offence, provided that it has been established that the property constitutes proceeds or other property in the meaning of Article 5 of this Convention.

Article 24—Execution of confiscation

1. The procedures for obtaining and enforcing the confiscation under Article 23 shall be governed by the law of the requested Party.
2. The requested Party shall be bound by the findings as to the facts in so far as they are stated in a conviction or judicial decision of the requesting Party or in so far as such conviction or judicial decision is implicitly based on them.
3. Each State or the European Community may, at the time of signature or when depositing its instrument of ratification, acceptance, approval or accession, by a declaration addressed to the Secretary General of the Council of Europe, declare that paragraph 2 of this article applies only subject to its constitutional principles and the basic concepts of its legal system.
4. If the confiscation consists in the requirement to pay a sum of money, the competent authority of the requested Party shall convert the amount thereof into the currency of that Party at the rate of exchange ruling at the time when the decision to enforce the confiscation is taken.
5. In the case of Article 23, paragraph 1.a, the requesting Party alone shall have the right to decide on any application for review of the confiscation order.

Article 25—Confiscated property

1. Property confiscated by a Party pursuant to Articles 23 and 24 of this Convention, shall be disposed of by that Party in accordance with its domestic law and administrative procedures.
2. When acting on the request made by another Party in accordance with Articles 23 and 24 of this Convention, Parties shall, to the extent permitted by domestic law and if so requested, give priority consideration to returning the confiscated property to the requesting Party so that it can give compensation to the victims of the crime or return such property to their legitimate owners.
3. When acting on the request made by another Party in accordance with Articles 23 and 24 of this Convention, a Party may give special consideration to concluding agreements or arrangements on sharing with other Parties, on a regular or case-by-case basis, such property, in accordance with its domestic law or administrative procedures.

Article 26—Right of enforcement and maximum amount of confiscation

1. A request for confiscation made under Articles 23 and 24 does not affect the right of the requesting Party to enforce itself the confiscation order.
2. Nothing in this Convention shall be so interpreted as to permit the total value of the confiscation to exceed the amount of the sum of money specified in the confiscation order. If a Party finds that this might occur, the Parties concerned shall enter into consultations to avoid such an effect.

Article 27—Imprisonment in default

The requested Party shall not impose imprisonment in default or any other measure restricting the liberty of a person as a result of a request under Article 23, if the requesting Party has so specified in the request.

Section 5—Refusal and postponement of co-operation

Article 28—Grounds for refusal

1. Co-operation under this chapter may be refused if:
   a. the action sought would be contrary to the fundamental principles of the legal system of the requested Party; or
   b. the execution of the request is likely to prejudice the sovereignty, security, ordre public or other essential interests of the requested Party; or
   c. in the opinion of the requested Party, the importance of the case to which the request relates does not justify the taking of the action sought; or
   d. the offence to which the request relates is a fiscal offence, with the exception of the financing of terrorism;
   e. the offence to which the request relates is a political offence, with the exception of the financing of terrorism; or
   f. the requested Party considers that compliance with the action sought would be contrary to the principle of "ne bis in idem"; or
   g. the offence to which the request relates would not be an offence under the law of the requested Party if committed within its jurisdiction. However, this ground for refusal applies to co-operation under Section 2 only in so far as the assistance sought involves coercive action. Where dual criminality is required for co-operation under this chapter, that requirement shall be deemed to be satisfied regardless of whether both Parties place the offence within the same category of offences or denominate the offence by the same terminology, provided that both Parties criminalise the conduct underlying the offence.
2. Co-operation under Section 2, in so far as the assistance sought involves coercive action, and under Section 3 of this chapter, may also be refused if the measures sought could not be taken under the domestic law of the requested Party for the purposes of investigations or proceedings, had it been a similar domestic case.
3. Where the law of the requested Party so requires, co-operation under Section 2, in so far as the assistance sought involves coercive action, and under Section 3 of this chapter may also be refused if the measures sought or any other measures having similar effects would not be permitted under the law of the requesting

Party, or, as regards the competent authorities of the requesting Party, if the request is not authorised by either a judge or another judicial authority, including public prosecutors, any of these authorities acting in relation to criminal offences.

4. Co-operation under Section 4 of this chapter may also be refused if:
   a. under the law of the requested Party confiscation is not provided for in respect of the type of offence to which the request relates; or
   b. without prejudice to the obligation pursuant to Article 23, paragraph 3, it would be contrary to the principles of the domestic law of the requested Party concerning the limits of confiscation in respect of the relationship between an offence and:
      i. an economic advantage that might be qualified as its proceeds; or
      ii. property that might be qualified as its instrumentalities; or
   c. under the law of the requested Party confiscation may no longer be imposed or enforced because of the lapse of time; or
   d. without prejudice to Article 23, paragraph 5, the request does not relate to a previous conviction, or a decision of a judicial nature or a statement in such a decision that an offence or several offences have been committed, on the basis of which the confiscation has been ordered or is sought; or
   e. confiscation is either not enforceable in the requesting Party, or it is still subject to ordinary means of appeal; or
   f. the request relates to a confiscation order resulting from a decision rendered in absentia of the person against whom the order was issued and, in the opinion of the requested Party, the proceedings conducted by the requesting Party leading to such decision did not satisfy the minimum rights of defence recognised as due to everyone against whom a criminal charge is made.
5. For the purpose of paragraph 4.f of this article a decision is not considered to have been rendered in absentia if:
   a. it has been confirmed or pronounced after opposition by the person concerned; or
   b. it has been rendered on appeal, provided that the appeal was lodged by the person concerned.
6. When considering, for the purposes of paragraph 4.f of this article if the minimum rights of defence have been satisfied, the requested Party shall take into account the fact that the person concerned has deliberately sought to evade justice or the fact that that person, having had the possibility of lodging a legal remedy against the decision made in absentia, elected not to do so. The same will apply when the person concerned, having been duly served with the summons to appear, elected not to do so nor to ask for adjournment.
7. A Party shall not invoke bank secrecy as a ground to refuse any co-operation under this chapter. Where its domestic law so requires, a Party may require that a request for co- operation which would involve the lifting of bank secrecy be

authorised by either a judge or another judicial authority, including public prosecutors, any of these authorities acting in relation to criminal offences.
8. Without prejudice to the ground for refusal provided for in paragraph 1.a of this article:

   a. the fact that the person under investigation or subjected to a confiscation order by the authorities of the requesting Party is a legal person shall not be invoked by the requested Party as an obstacle to affording any co-operation under this chapter;
   b. the fact that the natural person against whom an order of confiscation of proceeds has been issued has died or the fact that a legal person against whom an order of confiscation of proceeds has been issued has subsequently been dissolved shall not be invoked as an obstacle to render assistance in accordance with Article 23, paragraph 1.a;
   c. the fact that the person under investigation or subjected to a confiscation order by the authorities of the requesting Party is mentioned in the request both as the author of the underlying criminal offence and of the offence of money laundering, in accordance with Article 9.2.b of this Convention, shall not be invoked by the requested Party as an obstacle to affording any co-operation under this chapter.

Article 29—Postponement

The requested Party may postpone action on a request if such action would prejudice investigations or proceedings by its authorities.

Article 30—Partial or conditional granting of a request

Before refusing or postponing co-operation under this chapter, the requested Party shall, where appropriate after having consulted the requesting Party, consider whether the request may be granted partially or subject to such conditions as it deems necessary.

Section 6—Notification and protection of third parties' rights

Article 31—Notification of documents

1. The Parties shall afford each other the widest measure of mutual assistance in the serving of judicial documents to persons affected by provisional measures and confiscation.
2. Nothing in this article is intended to interfere with:

   a. the possibility of sending judicial documents, by postal channels, directly to persons abroad;
   b. the possibility for judicial officers, officials or other competent authorities of the Party of origin to effect service of judicial documents directly through the consular authorities of that Party or through judicial officers, officials or other competent authorities of the Party of destination,

unless the Party of destination makes a declaration to the contrary to the Secretary General of the Council of Europe at the time of signature or when depositing its instrument of ratification, acceptance, approval or accession.

3. When serving judicial documents to persons abroad affected by provisional measures or confiscation orders issued in the sending Party, this Party shall indicate what legal remedies are available under its law to such persons.

Article 32—Recognition of foreign decisions

1. When dealing with a request for co-operation under Sections 3 and 4, the requested Party shall recognise any judicial decision taken in the requesting Party regarding rights claimed by third parties.
2. Recognition may be refused if:

   a. third parties did not have adequate opportunity to assert their rights; or
   b. the decision is incompatible with a decision already taken in the requested Party on the same matter; or
   c. it is incompatible with the ordre public of the requested Party; or
   d. the decision was taken contrary to provisions on exclusive jurisdiction provided for by the law of the requested Party.

Section 7—Procedural and other general rules

Article 33—Central authority

1. The Parties shall designate a central authority or, if necessary, authorities, which shall be responsible for sending and answering requests made under this chapter, the execution of such requests or the transmission of them to the authorities competent for their execution.
2. Each Party shall, at the time of signature or when depositing its instrument of ratification, acceptance, approval or accession, communicate to the Secretary General of the Council of Europe the names and addresses of the authorities designated in pursuance of paragraph 1 of this article.

Article 34—Direct communication

1. The central authorities shall communicate directly with one another.
2. In the event of urgency, requests or communications under this chapter may be sent directly by the judicial authorities, including public prosecutors, of the requesting Party to such authorities of the requested Party. In such cases a copy shall be sent at the same time to the central authority of the requested Party through the central authority of the requesting Party.
3. Any request or communication under paragraphs 1 and 2 of this article may be made through the International Criminal Police Organisation (Interpol).
4. Where a request is made pursuant to paragraph 2 of this article and the authority is not competent to deal with the request, it shall refer the request to the competent national authority and inform directly the requesting Party that it has done so.
5. Requests or communications under Section 2 of this chapter, which do not involve coercive action, may be directly transmitted by the competent authorities of the requesting Party to the competent authorities of the requested Party.
6. Draft requests or communications under this chapter may be sent directly by the judicial authorities of the requesting Party to such authorities of the requested

Party prior to a formal request to ensure that it can be dealt with efficiently upon receipt and contains sufficient information and supporting documentation for it to meet the requirements of the legislation of the requested Party.

Article 35—Form of request and languages

1. All requests under this chapter shall be made in writing. They may be transmitted electronically, or by any other means of telecommunication, provided that the requesting Party is prepared, upon request, to produce at any time a written record of such communication and the original. However each Party may, at any time, by a declaration addressed to the Secretary General of the Council of Europe, indicate the conditions in which it is ready to accept and execute requests received electronically or by any other means of communication.
2. Subject to the provisions of paragraph 3 of this article, translations of the requests or supporting documents shall not be required.
3. At the time of signature or when depositing its instrument of ratification, acceptance, approval or accession, any State or the European Community may communicate to the Secretary General of the Council of Europe a declaration that it reserves the right to require that requests made to it and documents supporting such requests be accompanied by a translation into its own language or into one of the official languages of the Council of Europe or into such one of these languages as it shall indicate. It may on that occasion declare its readiness to accept translations in any other language as it may specify. The other Parties may apply the reciprocity rule.

Article 36—Legalisation

Documents transmitted in application of this chapter shall be exempt from all legalisation formalities.

Article 37—Content of request

1. Any request for co-operation under this chapter shall specify:
   a. the authority making the request and the authority carrying out the investigations or proceedings;
   b. the object of and the reason for the request;
   c. the matters, including the relevant facts (such as date, place and circumstances of the offence) to which the investigations or proceedings relate, except in the case of a request for notification;
   d. insofar as the co-operation involves coercive action:
      i. the text of the statutory provisions or, where this is not possible, a statement of the relevant law applicable; and
      ii. an indication that the measure sought or any other measures having similar effects could be taken in the territory of the requesting Party under its own law;
   e. where necessary and in so far as possible:

   i. details of the person or persons concerned, including name, date and place of birth, nationality and location, and, in the case of a legal person, its seat; and
   ii. the property in relation to which co-operation is sought, its location, its connection with the person or persons concerned, any connection with the offence, as well as any available information about other persons, interests in the property; and

f. any particular procedure the requesting Party wishes to be followed.

2. A request for provisional measures under Section 3 in relation to seizure of property on which a confiscation order consisting in the requirement to pay a sum of money may be realised shall also indicate a maximum amount for which recovery is sought in that property.
3. In addition to the indications mentioned in paragraph 1, any request under Section 4 shall contain:

   a. in the case of Article 23, paragraph 1.a:

      i. a certified true copy of the confiscation order made by the court in the requesting Party and a statement of the grounds on the basis of which the order was made, if they are not indicated in the order itself;
      ii. an attestation by the competent authority of the requesting Party that the confiscation order is enforceable and not subject to ordinary means of appeal;
      iii. information as to the extent to which the enforcement of the order is requested; and
      iv. information as to the necessity of taking any provisional measures;

   b. in the case of Article 23, paragraph 1.b, a statement of the facts relied upon by the requesting Party sufficient to enable the requested Party to seek the order under its domestic law;
   c. when third parties have had the opportunity to claim rights, documents demonstrating that this has been the case.

Article 38—Defective requests

1. If a request does not comply with the provisions of this chapter or the information supplied is not sufficient to enable the requested Party to deal with the request, that Party may ask the requesting Party to amend the request or to complete it with additional information.
2. The requested Party may set a time-limit for the receipt of such amendments or information.
3. Pending receipt of the requested amendments or information in relation to a request under Section 4 of this chapter, the requested Party may take any of the measures referred to in Sections 2 or 3 of this chapter.

Article 39—Plurality of requests

1. Where the requested Party receives more than one request under Sections 3 or 4 of this chapter in respect of the same person or property, the plurality of requests shall not prevent that Party from dealing with the requests involving the taking of provisional measures.
2. In the case of plurality of requests under Section 4 of this chapter, the requested Party shall consider consulting the requesting Parties.

Article 40—Obligation to give reasons

The requested Party shall give reasons for any decision to refuse, postpone or make conditional any co-operation under this chapter.

Article 41—Information

1. The requested Party shall promptly inform the requesting Party of:

    a. the action initiated on a request under this chapter;
    b. the final result of the action carried out on the basis of the request;
    c. a decision to refuse, postpone or make conditional, in whole or in part, any co-operation under this chapter;
    d. any circumstances which render impossible the carrying out of the action sought or are likely to delay it significantly; and
    e. in the event of provisional measures taken pursuant to a request under Sections 2 or 3 of this chapter, such provisions of its domestic law as would automatically lead to the lifting of the provisional measure.

2. The requesting Party shall promptly inform the requested Party of:

    a. any review, decision or any other fact by reason of which the confiscation order ceases to be wholly or partially enforceable; and
    b. any development, factual or legal, by reason of which any action under this chapter is no longer justified.

3. Where a Party, on the basis of the same confiscation order, requests confiscation in more than one Party, it shall inform all Parties which are affected by an enforcement of the order about the request.

Article 42—Restriction of use

1. The requested Party may make the execution of a request dependent on the condition that the information or evidence obtained will not, without its prior consent, be used or transmitted by the authorities of the requesting Party for investigations or proceedings other than those specified in the request.
2. Each State or the European Community may, at the time of signature or when depositing its instrument of ratification, acceptance, approval or accession, by declaration addressed to the Secretary General of the Council of Europe, declare that, without its prior consent, information or evidence provided by it under this chapter may not be used or transmitted by the authorities of the requesting Party in investigations or proceedings other than those specified in the request.

Article 43—Confidentiality

1. The requesting Party may require that the requested Party keep confidential the facts and substance of the request, except to the extent necessary to execute the request. If the requested Party cannot comply with the requirement of confidentiality, it shall promptly inform the requesting Party.
2. The requesting Party shall, if not contrary to basic principles of its national law and if so requested, keep confidential any evidence and information provided by the requested Party, except to the extent that its disclosure is necessary for the investigations or proceedings described in the request.
3. Subject to the provisions of its domestic law, a Party which has received spontaneous information under Article 20 shall comply with any requirement of confidentiality as required by the Party which supplies the information. If the other Party cannot comply with such requirement, it shall promptly inform the transmitting Party.

Article 44—Costs

The ordinary costs of complying with a request shall be borne by the requested Party. Where costs of a substantial or extraordinary nature are necessary to comply with a request, the Parties shall consult in order to agree the conditions on which the request is to be executed and how the costs shall be borne.

Article 45—Damages

1. When legal action on liability for damages resulting from an act or omission in relation to co-operation under this chapter has been initiated by a person, the Parties concerned shall consider consulting each other, where appropriate, to determine how to apportion any sum of damages due.
2. A Party which has become subject of a litigation for damages shall endeavour to inform the other Party of such litigation if that Party might have an interest in the case.

Chapter V—Co-operation between FIUs

Article 46—Co-operation between FIUs

1. Parties shall ensure that FIUs, as defined in this Convention, shall cooperate for the purpose of combating money laundering, to assemble and analyse, or, if appropriate, investigate within the FIU relevant information on any fact which might be an indication of money laundering in accordance with their national powers.
2. For the purposes of paragraph 1, each Party shall ensure that FIUs exchange, spontaneously or on request and either in accordance with this Convention or in accordance with existing or future memoranda of understanding compatible with this Convention, any accessible information that may be relevant to the processing or analysis of information or, if appropriate, to investigation by the FIU regarding financial transactions related to money laundering and the natural or legal persons involved.

3. Each Party shall ensure that the performance of the functions of the FIUs under this article shall not be affected by their internal status, regardless of whether they are administrative, law enforcement or judicial authorities.
4. Each request made under this article shall be accompanied by a brief statement of the relevant facts known to the requesting FIU. The FIU shall specify in the request how the information sought will be used.
5. When a request is made in accordance with this article, the requested FIU shall provide all relevant information, including accessible financial information and requested law enforcement data, sought in the request, without the need for a formal letter of request under applicable conventions or agreements between the Parties.
6. An FIU may refuse to divulge information which could lead to impairment of a criminal investigation being conducted in the requested Party or, in exceptional circumstances, where divulging the information would be clearly disproportionate to the legitimate interests of a natural or legal person or the Party concerned or would otherwise not be in accordance with fundamental principles of national law of the requested Party. Any such refusal shall be appropriately explained to the FIU requesting the information.
7. Information or documents obtained under this article shall only be used for the purposes laid down in paragraph 1. Information supplied by a counterpart FIU shall not be disseminated to a third party, nor be used by the receiving FIU for purposes other than analysis, without prior consent of the supplying FIU.
8. When transmitting information or documents pursuant to this article, the transmitting FIU may impose restrictions and conditions on the use of information for purposes other than those stipulated in paragraph 7. The receiving FIU shall comply with any such restrictions and conditions.
9. Where a Party wishes to use transmitted information or documents for criminal investigations or prosecutions for the purposes laid down in paragraph 7, the transmitting FIU may not refuse its consent to such use unless it does so on the basis of restrictions under its national law or conditions referred to in paragraph 6. Any refusal to grant consent shall be appropriately explained.
10. FIUs shall undertake all necessary measures, including security measures, to ensure that information submitted under this article is not accessible by any other authorities, agencies or departments.
11. The information submitted shall be protected, in conformity with the Council of Europe Convention of 28 January 1981 for the Protection of Individuals with regard to Automatic Processing of Personal Data (ETS No. 108) and taking account of Recommendation No R(87)15 of 15 September 1987 of the Committee of Ministers of the Council of Europe Regulating the Use of Personal Data in the Police Sector, by at least the same rules of confidentiality and protection of personal data as those that apply under the national legislation applicable to the requesting FIU.

12. The transmitting FIU may make reasonable enquiries as to the use made of information provided and the receiving FIU shall, whenever practicable, provide such feedback.
13. Parties shall indicate the unit which is an FIU within the meaning of this article.

Article 47—International co-operation for postponement of suspicious transactions

1. Each Party shall adopt such legislative or other measures as may be necessary to permit urgent action to be initiated by a FIU, at the request of a foreign FIU, to suspend or withhold consent to a transaction going ahead for such periods and depending on the same conditions as apply in its domestic law in respect of the postponement of transactions.
2. The action referred to in paragraph 1 shall be taken where the requested FIU is satisfied, upon justification by the requesting FIU, that:
   a. the transaction is related to money laundering; and
   b. the transaction would have been suspended, or consent to the transaction going ahead would have been withheld, if the transaction had been the subject of a domestic suspicious transaction report.

Chapter VI—Monitoring mechanism and settlement of disputes

Article 48—Monitoring mechanism and settlement of disputes

1. The Conference of the Parties (COP) shall be responsible for following the implementation of the Convention. The COP:
   a. shall monitor the proper implementation of the Convention by the Parties;
   b. shall, at the request of a Party, express an opinion on any question concerning the interpretation and application of the Convention.
2. The COP shall carry out the functions under paragraph 1.a above by using any available Select Committee of Experts on the Evaluation of Anti-Money Laundering Measures (Moneyval) public summaries (for Moneyval countries) and any available FATF public summaries (for FATF countries), supplemented by periodic self assessment questionnaires, as appropriate. The monitoring procedure will deal with areas covered by this Convention only in respect of those areas which are not covered by other relevant international standards on which mutual evaluations are carried out by the FATF and Moneyval.
3. If the COP concludes that it requires further information in the discharge of its functions, it shall liaise with the Party concerned, taking advantage, if so required by the COP, of the procedure and mechanism of Moneyval. The Party concerned shall then report back to the COP. The COP shall on this basis decide whether or not to carry out a more in-depth assessment of the position of the Party concerned. This may, but need not necessarily, involve, a country visit by an evaluation team.
4. In case of a dispute between Parties as to the interpretation or application of the Convention, they shall seek a settlement of the dispute through negotiation or any other peaceful means of their choice, including submission of the dispute to the

COP, to an arbitral tribunal whose decisions shall be binding upon the Parties, or to the International Court of Justice, as agreed upon by the Parties concerned.
5. The COP shall adopt its own rules of procedure.
6. The Secretary General of the Council of Europe shall convene the COP not later than 1 year following the entry into force of this Convention. Thereafter, regular meetings of the COP shall be held in accordance with the rules of procedure adopted by the COP.

Chapter VII—Final Provisions

Article 49—Signature and entry into force

1. The Convention shall be open for signature by the member States of the Council of Europe, the European Community and non-member States which have participated in its elaboration. Such States or the European Community may express their consent to be bound by:

   a. signature without reservation as to ratification, acceptance or approval; or
   b. signature subject to ratification, acceptance or approval, followed by ratification, acceptance or approval.

2. Instruments of ratification, acceptance or approval shall be deposited with the Secretary General of the Council of Europe.
3. This Convention shall enter into force on the first day of the month following the expiration of a period of 3 months after the date on which 6 signatories, of which at least four are member States of the Council of Europe, have expressed their consent to be bound by the Convention in accordance with the provisions of paragraph 1.
4. In respect of any Signatory which subsequently expresses its consent to be bound by it, the Convention shall enter into force on the first day of the month following the expiration of a period of 3 months after the date of the expression of its consent to be bound by the Convention in accordance with the provisions of paragraph 1.
5. No Party to the 1990 Convention may ratify, accept or approve this Convention without considering itself bound by at least the provisions corresponding to the provisions of the 1990 Convention to which it is bound.
6. As from its entry into force, Parties to this Convention, which are at the same time Parties to the 1990 Convention:

   a. shall apply the provisions of this Convention in their mutual relationships;
   b. shall continue to apply the provisions of the 1990 Convention in their relations with other Parties to the said Convention, but not to the present Convention.

Article 50—Accession to the Convention

1. After the entry into force of this Convention, the Committee of Ministers of the Council of Europe, after consulting the Parties to the Convention, may invite any State not a member of the Council and not having participated in its elaboration to accede to this Convention, by a decision taken by the majority provided for in

Article 20.d. of the Statute of the Council of Europe and by the unanimous vote of the representatives of the Parties entitled to sit on the Committee.

2. In respect of any acceding State, the Convention shall enter into force on the first day of the month following the expiration of a period of 3 months after the date of deposit of the instrument of accession with the Secretary General of the Council of Europe.

Article 51—Territorial application

1. Any State or the European Community may, at the time of signature or when depositing its instrument of ratification, acceptance, approval or accession, specify the territory or territories to which the Convention shall apply.
2. Any Party may, at any later date, by a declaration addressed to the Secretary General of the Council of Europe, extend the application of the Convention to any other territory specified in the declaration. In respect of such territory the Convention shall enter into force on the first day of the month following the expiration of a period of 3 months after the date of receipt of such declaration by the Secretary General.
3. Any declaration made under the two preceding paragraphs may, in respect of any territory specified in such declaration, be withdrawn by a notification addressed to the Secretary General. The withdrawal shall become effective on the first day of the month following the expiration of a period of 3 months after the date of receipt of such notification by the Secretary General.

Article 52—Relationship to other conventions and agreements

1. This Convention does not affect the rights and undertakings of Parties derived from international multilateral instruments concerning special matters.
2. The Parties to this Convention may conclude bilateral or multilateral agreements with one another on the matters dealt with in this Convention, for the purposes of supplementing or strengthening its provisions or facilitating the application of the principles embodied in it.
3. If two or more Parties have already concluded an agreement or treaty in respect of a subject which is dealt with in this Convention or otherwise have established their relations in respect of that subject, they shall be entitled to apply that agreement or treaty or to regulate these relations accordingly, in lieu of the Convention, if it facilitates international co-operation.
4. Parties which are members of the European Union shall, in their mutual relations, apply Community and European Union rules in so far as there are Community or European Union rules governing the particular subject concerned and applicable to the specific case, without prejudice to the object and purpose of the present Convention and without prejudice to its full application with other Parties.(1)

(1) Note by the Secretariat: See the Declaration formulated by the European Community and the Member States of the European Union upon the adoption of the Convention by the Committee of Ministers of the Council of Europe, on 3 May 2005:

"The European Community/European Union and its Member States reaffirm that their objective in requesting the inclusion of a "disconnection clause" is to take account of the institutional structure of the Union when acceding to international conventions, in particular in case of transfer of sovereign powers from the Member States to the Community.

This clause is not aimed at reducing the rights or increasing the obligations of a non-European Union Party vis-à-vis the European Community/European Union and its Member States, inasmuch as the latter are also parties to this Convention.

The disconnection clause is necessary for those parts of the Convention which fall within the competence of the Community/Union, in order to indicate that European Union Member States cannot invoke and apply the rights and obligations deriving from the Convention directly among themselves (or between themselves and the European Community/Union). This does not detract from the fact that the Convention applies fully between the European Community/European Union and its Member States on the one hand, and the other Parties to the Convention, on the other; the Community and the European Union Members States will be bound by the Convention and will apply it like any Party to the Convention, if necessary, through Community/Union legislation. They will thus guarantee the full respect of the Convention's provisions vis-à-vis non-European Union Parties."

Article 53—Declarations and reservations

1. Any State or the European Community may, at the time of signature or when depositing its instrument of ratification, acceptance, approval or accession, make one or more of the declaration provided for in Article 3, paragraph 2, Article 9, paragraph 4, Article 17, paragraph 5, Article 24, paragraph 3, Article 31, paragraph 2, Article 35, paragraphs 1 and 3 and Article 42, paragraph 2.
2. Any State or the European Community may also, at the time of signature or when depositing its instrument of ratification, acceptance, approval or accession, by a declaration addressed to the Secretary General, reserve its right not to apply, in part or in whole, the provisions of Article 7, paragraph 2, sub-paragraph c; Article 9, paragraph 6; Article 46, paragraph 5; and Article 47.
3. Any State or the European Community may, at the time of signature or when depositing its instrument of ratification, acceptance, approval or accession, declare the manner in which it intends to apply Articles 17 and 19 of this Convention, particularly taking into account applicable international agreements in the field of international co-operation in criminal matters. It shall notify any changes in this information to the Secretary General of the Council of Europe.
4. Any State or the European Community may, at the time of signature or when depositing its instrument of ratification, acceptance, approval or accession, declare:

   a. that it will not apply Article 3, paragraph 4 of this Convention; or
   b. that it will apply Article 3, paragraph 4 of this Convention only partly; or
   c. the manner in which it intends to apply Article 3, paragraph 4 of this Convention.

It shall notify any changes in this information to the Secretary General of the Council of Europe.

5. No other reservation may be made.
6. Any Party which has made a reservation under this article may wholly or partly withdraw it by means of a notification addressed to the Secretary General of the Council of Europe. The withdrawal shall take effect on the date of receipt of such notification by the Secretary General.
7. A Party which has made a reservation in respect of a provision of the Convention may not claim the application of that provision by any other Party; it may, however, if its reservation is partial or conditional, claim the application of that provision in so far as it has itself accepted it.

Article 54—Amendments

1. Amendments to the Convention may be proposed by any Party, and shall be communicated by the Secretary General of the Council of Europe to the member States of the Council of Europe, to the European Community and to every non-member State which has acceded to or has been invited to accede to this Convention in accordance with the provisions of Article 50.
2. Any amendment proposed by a Party shall be communicated to the European Committee on Crime Problems (CDPC) which shall submit to the Committee of Ministers its opinion on that proposed amendment.
3. The Committee of Ministers shall consider the proposed amendment and the opinion submitted by the CDPC and may adopt the amendment by the majority provided for in Article 20.d of the Statute of the Council of Europe.
4. The text of any amendment adopted by the Committee of Ministers in accordance with paragraph 3 of this article shall be forwarded to the Parties for acceptance.
5. Any amendment adopted in accordance with paragraph 3 of this article shall come into force on the thirtieth day after all Parties have informed the Secretary General of their acceptance thereof.
6. In order to update the categories of offences contained in the appendix, as well as amend Article 13, amendments may be proposed by any Party or by the Committee of Ministers. They shall be communicated by the Secretary General of the Council of Europe to the Parties.
7. After having consulted the Parties which are not members of the Council of Europe and, if necessary the CDPC, the Committee of Ministers may adopt an amendment proposed in accordance with paragraph 6 by the majority provided for in Article 20.d of the Statute of the Council of Europe. The amendment shall enter into force following the expiry of a period of 1 year after the date on which it has been forwarded to the Parties. During this period, any Party may notify the Secretary General of any objection to the entry into force of the amendment in its respect.
8. If one-third of the Parties notifies the Secretary General of an objection to the entry into force of the amendment, the amendment shall not enter into force.

9. If less than one-third of the Parties notifies an objection, the amendment shall enter into force for those Parties which have not notified an objection.
10. Once an amendment has entered into force in accordance with paragraphs 6 to 9 of this article and a Party has notified an objection to it, this amendment shall come into force in respect of the Party concerned on the first day of the month following the date on which it has notified the Secretary General of the Council of Europe of its acceptance. A Party which has made an objection may withdraw it at any time by notifying it to the Secretary General of the Council of Europe.
11. If an amendment has been adopted by the Committee of Ministers, a State or the European Community may not express their consent to be bound by the Convention, without accepting at the same time the amendment.

Article 55—Denunciation

1. Any Party may, at any time, denounce the Convention by means of a notification addressed to the Secretary General of the Council of Europe.
2. Such denunciation shall become effective on the first day of the month following the expiration of a period of 3 months after the date of receipt of the notification by the Secretary General.
3. The present Convention shall, however, continue to apply to the enforcement under Article 23 of confiscation for which a request has been made in conformity with the provisions of the Convention before the date on which such a denunciation takes effect.

Article 56—Notifications

The Secretary General of the Council of Europe shall notify the member States of the Council of Europe, the European Community, the non-member States which have participated in the elaboration of the Convention, any State invited to accede to it and any other Party to the Convention of:

a. any signature;
b. the deposit of any instrument of ratification, acceptance, approval or accession;
c. any date of entry into force of the Convention in accordance with Articles 49 and 50;
d. any declaration or reservation made under Article 53;
e. any other act, notification or communication relating to the Convention.

In witness whereof the undersigned, being duly authorised thereto, have signed this Convention.

Done at Warsaw, this 16th day of May 2005, in English and in French, both texts being equally authentic, in a single copy which shall be deposited in the archives of the Council of Europe. The Secretary General of the Council of Europe shall transmit certified copies to each member State of the Council of Europe, to the European Community, to the non-member States which have participated in the elaboration of the Convention and to any State invited to accede to it.

vii) **United Nations** Global Programme Against Money Laundering[14]

The Global Programme against Money Laundering, Proceeds of Crime and the Financing of Terrorism (GPML) is a global programme providing in-depth assistance to countries to build and strengthen their anti-money laundering and countering financing of terrorism (AML/CFT) capacity.

GPML is mandated to assist Member States—via their legal, financial, law enforcement and judicial authorities—to develop effective and comprehensive domestic AML/CFT legal and regulatory frameworks, as well as the institutional infrastructures and practitioner skills needed to implement them, in accordance with UN instruments and international standards. GPML is committed to promoting national coordination and regional and international cooperation on issues concerning money laundering and terrorism financing.

GPML has specifically been tasked by the United Nations General Assembly, most recently in resolutions 74/177 (2019), 73/186 (2018), 72/196 (2017), and 71/20 9 (2016) to:

"... continue providing technical assistance to Member States to combat money laundering and the financing of terrorism in accordance with United Nations related instruments and internationally accepted standards, including, where applicable, recommendations of relevant intergovernmental bodies, inter alia, the Financial Action Task Force on Money Laundering, and relevant initiatives of regional, interregional and multilateral organizations against money laundering."

viii) **UNODC** Global Programme on Cybercrime[15]

The UNODC Global Programme on Cybercrime ,according to General Assembly resolution 65/230, provides technical assistance and training to Member States to prevent and respond to cybercrime and technology-enabled crimes, including combating online sexual exploitation of children, responding to ransomware attacks and other cybercrimes, and collecting and preserving digital evidence. The Global Programme on Cybercrime is designed to respond flexibly to the needs identified in Member States to prevent and combat cybercrime in a holistic manner. It does so by providing technical support in crime prevention and criminal justice, based on UNODC's assessment protocols and technical assistance tools. The programme utilizes an integrated approach to assist member states. It focuses on policy development and technical assistance, including capacity building activities, normative assistance, strengthening international and national cooperation within countries and with the private sector, and prevention and sensitization on the threats of cybercrime.

ix) **FATF** International Standards on Combatting Money Laundering and the Financing of Terrorism & Proliferation: The FATF 40 Recommendations[16]

---

[14] https://www.unodc.org/unodc/es/money-laundering/global-programme-against-money-laundering/.html

[15] https://www.unodc.org/westandcentralafrica/en/Cyber-Crime.html

[16] https://www.fatf-gafi.org/content/dam/fatf-gafi/recommendations/FATF%20Recommendations%202012.pdf.coredownload.inline.pdf

The FATF Recommendations (as amended in November 2023) set out a comprehensive and consistent framework of measures which countries should implement in order to combat money laundering and terrorist financing, as well as the financing of proliferation of weapons of mass destruction. Countries have diverse legal, administrative and operational frameworks and different financial systems, and so cannot all take identical measures to counter these threats.

The FATF Recommendations, therefore, set an international standard, which countries should implement through measures adapted to their particular circumstances. The FATF Standards comprise the Recommendations themselves and their Interpretive Notes, together with the applicable definitions in the Glossary:

A. AML/CFT Policies and Coordination

1. Assessing risks and applying a risk-based approach *

Countries should identify, assess, and understand the money laundering and terrorist financing risks for the country, and should take action, including designating an authority or mechanism to coordinate actions to assess risks, and apply resources, aimed at ensuring the risks are mitigated effectively. Based on that assessment, countries should apply a risk-based approach (RBA) to ensure that measures to prevent or mitigate money laundering and terrorist financing are commensurate with the risks identified. This approach should be an essential foundation to efficient allocation of resources across the anti-money laundering and countering the financing of terrorism (AML/CFT) regime and the implementation of risk-based measures throughout the FATF Recommendations. Where countries identify higher risks, they should ensure that their AML/CFT regime adequately addresses such risks. Where countries identify lower risks, they may decide to allow simplified measures for some of the FATF Recommendations under certain conditions.Countries should also identify, assess, and understand the proliferation financing risks for the country. In the context of Recommendation 1, "proliferation financing risk" refers strictly and only to the potential breach, non-implementation or evasion of the targeted financial sanctions obligations referred to in Recommendation 7. Countries should take commensurate action aimed at ensuring that these risks are mitigated effectively, including designating an authority or mechanism to coordinate actions to assess risks, and allocate resources efficiently for this purpose. Where countries identify higher risks, they should ensure that they adequately address such risks. Where countries identify lower risks, they should ensure that the measures applied are commensurate with the level of proliferation financing risk, while still ensuring full implementation of the targeted financial sanctions as required in Recommendation 7.Countries should require financial institutions and designated non-financial businesses and professions (DNFBPs) to identify, assess and take effective action to mitigate their money laundering, terrorist financing and proliferation financing risks.

2. National cooperation and coordinationCountries should have national AML/CFT/CPF policies, informed by the risks 1 identified, which should be regularly reviewed, and should designate an authority or have a coordination or other mechanism that is responsible for such policies.Countries should ensure that policy-makers, the financial intelligence unit (FIU), law enforcement authorities, supervisors and other relevant competent authorities, at the policymaking and operational

levels, have effective mechanisms in place which enable them to cooperate, and, where appropriate, coordinate and exchange information domestically with each other concerning the development and implementation of policies and activities to combat money laundering, terrorist financing and the financing of proliferation of weapons of mass destruction. This should include cooperation and coordination between relevant authorities to ensure the compatibility of AML/CFT/CPF requirements with Data Protection and Privacy rules and other similar provisions (e.g. data security/localisation).

1 Proliferation financing risk refers strictly and only to the potential breach, non-implementation or evasion of the targeted financial sanctions obligations referred to in Recommendation 7.

B. Money Laundering and Confiscation

3. Money laundering offence *

Countries should criminalise money laundering on the basis of the Vienna Convention and the Palermo Convention. Countries should apply the crime of money laundering to all serious offences, with a view to including the widest range of predicate offences.

4. Confiscation and provisional measures *

Countries should ensure that they have policies and operational frameworks that prioritise asset recovery in both the domestic and international context.

Taking into account the Vienna Convention, the Palermo Convention, the United Nations Convention against Corruption, and the Terrorist Financing Convention, countries should have measures, including legislative measures, to enable their competent authorities to:

a) identify, trace and evaluate criminal property and property of corresponding value;
b) suspend or withhold consent to a transaction;
c) take any appropriate investigative measures;
d) expeditiously carry out provisional measures, such as freezing and seizing, to prevent any dealing, transfer or disposal of criminal property and property of corresponding value;
e) confiscate criminal property and property of corresponding value through conviction-based confiscation;
f) confiscate criminal property through non-conviction based confiscation;
g) enforce a resulting confiscation order; and
h) ensure effective management of property that is frozen, seized or confiscated.

C. Terrorist Financing and Financing of Proliferation

5. Terrorist financing offence *

Countries should criminalise terrorist financing on the basis of the Terrorist Financing Convention, and should criminalise not only the financing of terrorist acts but also the financing of terrorist organisations and individual terrorists even in the absence of a link to a specific terrorist act or acts. Countries should ensure that such offences are designated as money laundering predicate offences.

6. Targeted financial sanctions related to terrorism and terrorist financing *

Countries should implement targeted financial sanctions regimes to comply with United Nations Security Council resolutions relating to the prevention and suppression of terrorism and terrorist financing. The resolutions require countries to freeze without delay the funds or other assets of, and to ensure that no funds or other assets are made available, directly or indirectly, to or for the benefit of, any person or entity either (i) designated by, or under the

authority of, the United Nations Security Council under Chapter VII of the Charter of the United Nations, including in accordance with resolution 1267 (1999) and its successor resolutions; or (ii) designated by that country pursuant to resolution 1373 (2001).

7. Targeted financial sanctions related to proliferation *

Countries should implement targeted financial sanctions to comply with United Nations Security Council resolutions relating to the prevention, suppression and disruption of proliferation of weapons of mass destruction and its financing. These resolutions require countries to freeze without delay the funds or other assets of, and to ensure that no funds and other assets are made available, directly or indirectly, to or for the benefit of, any person or entity designated by, or under the authority of, the United Nations Security Council under

Chapter VII of the Charter of the United Nations.

8. Non-profit organisations *

Countries should identify the organisations which fall within the FATF definition of non-profit organisations (NPOs) and assess their terrorist financing risks. Countries should have in place focused, proportionate and risk-based measures, without unduly disrupting or discouraging legitimate NPO activities, in line with the risk-based approach. The purpose of these measures is to protect such NPOs from terrorist financing abuse, including:

(a) by terrorist organisations posing as legitimate entities;
(b) by exploiting legitimate entities as conduits for terrorist financing, including for the purpose of escaping asset-freezing measures; and
(c) by concealing or obscuring the clandestine diversion of funds intended for legitimate purposes to terrorist organisations.

D. Preventive Measures

9. Financial institution secrecy laws

Countries should ensure that financial institution secrecy laws do not inhibit implementation of the FATF Recommendations.

Customer due Diligence and Record-keeping

10. Customer due diligence *

Financial institutions should be prohibited from keeping anonymous accounts or accounts in obviously fictitious names.

Financial institutions should be required to undertake customer due diligence (CDD) measures when:

(i) establishing business relations;
(ii) carrying out occasional transactions: (i) above the applicable designated threshold
(USD/EUR 15,000); or (ii) that are wire transfers in the circumstances covered by the Interpretive Note to Recommendation 16;
(iii) there is a suspicion of money laundering or terrorist financing; or
(iv) the financial institution has doubts about the veracity or adequacy of previously obtained customer identification data.

The principle that financial institutions should conduct CDD should be set out in law. Each country may determine how it imposes specific CDD obligations, either through law or enforceable means.

The CDD measures to be taken are as follows:

(a) Identifying the customer and verifying that customer's identity using reliable, independent source documents, data or information.
(b) Identifying the beneficial owner, and taking reasonable measures to verify the identity of the beneficial owner, such that the financial institution is satisfied that it knows who the beneficial owner is. For legal persons and arrangements this should include financial institutions understanding the ownership and control structure of the customer.
(c) Understanding and, as appropriate, obtaining information on the purpose and intended nature of the business relationship.
(d) Conducting ongoing due diligence on the business relationship and scrutiny of transactions undertaken throughout the course of that relationship to ensure that the transactions being conducted are consistent with the institution's knowledge of the customer, their business and risk profile, including, where necessary, the source of funds.

Financial institutions should be required to apply each of the CDD measures under (a) to (d) above, but should determine the extent of such measures using a risk-based approach (RBA) in accordance with the Interpretive Notes to this Recommendation and to Recommendation 1.

Financial institutions should be required to verify the identity of the customer and beneficial owner before or during the course of establishing a business relationship or conducting transactions for occasional customers. Countries may permit financial institutions to complete the verification as soon as reasonably practicable following the establishment of the relationship, where the money laundering and terrorist financing risks are effectively managed and where this is essential not to interrupt the normal conduct of business.

Where the financial institution is unable to comply with the applicable requirements under paragraphs (a) to (d) above (subject to appropriate modification of the extent of the measures on a risk-based approach), it should be required not to open the account, commence business relations or perform the transaction; or should be required to terminate the business relationship; and should consider making a suspicious transactions report in relation to the customer.

These requirements should apply to all new customers, although financial institutions should also apply this Recommendation to existing customers on the basis of materiality and risk, and should conduct due diligence on such existing relationships at appropriate times.

11. Record-keeping

Financial institutions should be required to maintain, for at least 5 years, all necessary records on transactions, both domestic and international, to enable them to comply swiftly with information requests from the competent authorities. Such records must be sufficient to permit reconstruction of individual transactions (including the amounts and types of currency involved, if any) so as to provide, if necessary, evidence for prosecution of criminal activity.

Financial institutions should be required to keep all records obtained through CDD measures (e.g. copies or records of official identification documents like passports, identity cards, driving licences or similar documents), account files and business correspondence, including the results of any analysis undertaken (e.g. inquiries to establish the background and purpose of complex, unusual large transactions), for at least 5 years after the business relationship is ended, or after the date of the occasional transaction.

Financial institutions should be required by law to maintain records on transactions and information obtained through the CDD measures.

The CDD information and the transaction records should be available to domestic competent authorities upon appropriate authority.

Additional Measures for Specific Customers and Activities

12. Politically exposed persons *

Financial institutions should be required, in relation to foreign politically exposed persons (PEPs) (whether as customer or beneficial owner), in addition to performing normal customer due diligence measures, to:

(a) have appropriate risk-management systems to determine whether the customer or the beneficial owner is a politically exposed person;
(b) obtain senior management approval for establishing (or continuing, for existing customers) such business relationships;
(c) take reasonable measures to establish the source of wealth and source of funds; and
(d) conduct enhanced ongoing monitoring of the business relationship.

Financial institutions should be required to take reasonable measures to determine whether a customer or beneficial owner is a domestic PEP or a person who is or has been entrusted with a prominent function by an international organisation. In cases of a higher risk business relationship with such persons, financial institutions should be required to apply the measures referred to in paragraphs (b), (c) and (d).

The requirements for all types of PEP should also apply to family members or close associates of such PEPs.

13. Correspondent banking *

Financial institutions should be required, in relation to cross-border correspondent banking and other similar relationships, in addition to performing normal customer due diligence measures, to:

(a) gather sufficient information about a respondent institution to understand fully the nature of the respondent's business and to determine from publicly available information the reputation of the institution and the quality of supervision, including whether it has been subject to a money laundering or terrorist financing investigation or regulatory action;
(b) assess the respondent institution's AML/CFT controls;
(c) obtain approval from senior management before establishing new correspondent relationships;
(d) clearly understand the respective responsibilities of each institution; and
(e) with respect to "payable-through accounts", be satisfied that the respondent bank has conducted CDD on the customers having direct access to accounts of the correspondent bank, and that it is able to provide relevant CDD information upon request to the correspondent bank.

Financial institutions should be prohibited from entering into, or continuing, a correspondent banking relationship with shell banks. Financial institutions should be required to satisfy themselves that respondent institutions do not permit their accounts to be used by shell banks.

14. Money or value transfer services *

Countries should take measures to ensure that natural or legal persons that provide money or value transfer services (MVTS) are licensed or registered, and subject to effective systems for monitoring and ensuring compliance with the relevant measures called for in the FATF Recommendations. Countries should take action to identify natural or legal persons that carry out MVTS without a license or registration, and to apply appropriate sanctions.

Any natural or legal person working as an agent should also be licensed or registered by a competent authority, or the MVTS provider should maintain a current list of its agents accessible by competent authorities in the countries in which the MVTS provider and its agents operate. Countries should take measures to ensure that MVTS providers that use agents include them in their AML/CFT programmes and monitor them for compliance with these programmes.

15. New technologies

Countries and financial institutions should identify and assess the money laundering or terrorist financing risks that may arise in relation to (a) the development of new products and new business practices, including new delivery mechanisms, and (b) the use of new or developing technologies for both new and pre-existing products. In the case of financial institutions, such a risk assessment should take place prior to the launch of the new products, business practices or the use of new or developing technologies. They should take appropriate measures to manage and mitigate those risks.

To manage and mitigate the risks emerging from virtual assets, countries should ensure that virtual asset service providers are regulated for AML/CFT purposes, and licensed or registered and subject to effective systems for monitoring and ensuring compliance with the relevant measures called for in the FATF Recommendations.

16. Wire transfers *

Countries should ensure that financial institutions include required and accurate originator information, and required beneficiary information, on wire transfers and related messages, and that the information remains with the wire transfer or related message throughout the payment chain.

Countries should ensure that financial institutions monitor wire transfers for the purpose of detecting those which lack required originator and/or beneficiary information, and take appropriate measures.

Countries should ensure that, in the context of processing wire transfers, financial institutions take freezing action and should prohibit conducting transactions with designated persons and entities, as per the obligations set out in the relevant United Nations Security resolutions, such as resolution 1267 (1999) and its successor resolutions, and resolution 1373(2001), relating to the prevention and suppression of terrorism and terrorist financing.

Reliance, Controls and Financial Groups

17. Reliance on third parties *

Countries may permit financial institutions to rely on third parties to perform elements (a)-(c) of the CDD measures set out in Recommendation 10 or to introduce business, provided that the criteria set out below are met. Where such reliance is permitted, the ultimate responsibility for CDD measures remains with the financial institution relying on the third party.

The criteria that should be met are as follows:

(a) A financial institution relying upon a third party should immediately obtain the necessary information concerning elements (a)-(c) of the CDD measures set out in Recommendation 10.
(b) Financial institutions should take adequate steps to satisfy themselves that copies of identification data and other relevant documentation relating to the CDD requirements will be made available from the third party upon request without delay.
(c) The financial institution should satisfy itself that the third party is regulated, supervised or monitored for, and has measures in place for compliance with, CDD and record-keeping requirements in line with Recommendations 10 and 11.
(d) When determining in which countries the third party that meets the conditions can be based, countries should have regard to information available on the level of country risk.

When a financial institution relies on a third party that is part of the same financial group, and (i) that group applies CDD and record-keeping requirements, in line with Recommendations 10, 11 and 12, and programmes against money laundering and terrorist financing, in accordance with Recommendation 18; and (ii) where the effective implementation of those CDD and record-keeping requirements and AML/CFT programmes is supervised at a group level by a competent authority, then relevant competent authorities may consider that the financial institution applies measures under (b) and (c) above through its group programme, and may decide that (d) is not a necessary precondition to reliance when higher country risk is adequately mitigated by the group AML/CFT policies.

18. Internal controls and foreign branches and subsidiaries *

Financial institutions should be required to implement programmes against money laundering and terrorist financing. Financial groups should be required to implement group-wide programmes against money laundering and terrorist financing, including policies and procedures for sharing information within the group for AML/CFT purposes.

Financial institutions should be required to ensure that their foreign branches and majority-owned subsidiaries apply AML/CFT measures consistent with the home country implementing the FATF Recommendations through the financial groups' programmes against money laundering and terrorist financing.

19. Higher-risk countries *

Financial institutions should be required to apply enhanced due diligence measures to business relationships and transactions with natural and legal persons, and financial institutions, from countries for which this is called for by the FATF. The type of enhanced due diligence measures applied should be effective and proportionate to the risks.

Countries should be able to apply appropriate countermeasures when called upon to do so by the FATF. Countries should also be able to apply countermeasures independently of any call by the FATF to do so. Such countermeasures should be effective and proportionate to the risks.

Reporting of Suspicious Transactions

20. Reporting of suspicious transactions *

If a financial institution suspects or has reasonable grounds to suspect that funds are the proceeds of a criminal activity, or are related to terrorist financing, it should be required, by law, to report promptly its suspicions to the financial intelligence unit (FIU).

21. Tipping-off and confidentiality

Financial institutions, their directors, officers and employees should be:

(a) protected by law from criminal and civil liability for breach of any restriction on disclosure of information imposed by contract or by any legislative, regulatory or administrative provision, if they report their suspicions in good faith to the FIU, even if they did not know precisely what the underlying criminal activity was, and regardless of whether illegal activity actually occurred; and
(b) prohibited by law from disclosing ("tipping-off") the fact that a suspicious transaction report (STR) or related information is being filed with the FIU. These provisions are not intended to inhibit information sharing under Recommendation 18.

Designated Non-financial Businesses and Professions

22. DNFBPs: customer due diligence *

The customer due diligence and record-keeping requirements set out in Recommendations 10, 11, 12, 15, and 17, apply to designated non-financial businesses and professions (DNFBPs) in the following situations:

(a) Casinos—when customers engage in financial transactions equal to or above the applicable designated threshold.
(b) Real estate agents—when they are involved in transactions for their client concerning the buying and selling of real estate.
(c) Dealers in precious metals and dealers in precious stones—when they engage in any cash transaction with a customer equal to or above the applicable designated threshold.
(d) Lawyers, notaries, other independent legal professionals and accountants—when they prepare for or carry out transactions for their client concerning the following activities:

- buying and selling of real estate;
- managing of client money, securities or other assets;
- management of bank, savings or securities accounts;
- organisation of contributions for the creation, operation or management of companies;
- creation, operation or management of legal persons or arrangements, and buying and selling of business entities.

(e) Trust and company service providers—when they prepare for or carry out transactions for a client concerning the following activities:

- acting as a formation agent of legal persons;
- acting as (or arranging for another person to act as) a director or secretary of a company, a partner of a partnership, or a similar position in relation to other legal persons;
- providing a registered office, business address or accommodation, correspondence or administrative address for a company, a partnership or any other legal person or arrangement;
- acting as (or arranging for another person to act as) a trustee of an express trust or performing the equivalent function for another form of legal arrangement;
- acting as (or arranging for another person to act as) a nominee shareholder for another person.

23. DNFBPs: Other measures *

The requirements set out in Recommendations 18 to 21 apply to all designated non-financial businesses and professions, subject to the following qualifications:

(a) Lawyers, notaries, other independent legal professionals and accountants should be required to report suspicious transactions when, on behalf of or for a client, they engage in a financial transaction in relation to the activities described in paragraph (d) of Recommendation 22. Countries are strongly encouraged to extend the reporting requirement to the rest of the professional activities of accountants, including auditing.

(b) Dealers in precious metals and dealers in precious stones should be required to report suspicious transactions when they engage in any cash transaction with a customer equal to or above the applicable designated threshold.

(c) Trust and company service providers should be required to report suspicious

(d) transactions for a client when, on behalf of or for a client, they engage in a transaction in relation to the activities referred to in paragraph (e) of Recommendation 22.

E. Transparency and Beneficial Ownership of Legal Persons and Arrangements

24. Transparency and beneficial ownership of legal persons *

Countries should assess the risks of misuse of legal persons for money laundering or terrorist financing, and take measures to prevent their misuse. Countries should ensure that there is adequate, accurate and up-to-date information on the beneficial ownership and control of legal persons that can be obtained or accessed rapidly and efficiently by competent authorities, through either a register of beneficial ownership or an alternative mechanism. Countries should not permit legal persons to issue new bearer shares or bearer share warrants, and take measures to prevent the misuse of existing bearer shares and bearer share warrants. Countries should take effective measures to ensure that nominee shareholders and directors are not misused for money laundering or terrorist financing.

Countries should consider facilitating access to beneficial ownership and control information by financial institutions and DNFBPs undertaking the requirements set out in Recommendations 10 and 22.

25. Transparency and beneficial ownership of legal arrangements *

Countries should assess the risks of the misuse of legal arrangements for money laundering or terrorist financing and take measures to prevent their misuse. In particular, countries should ensure that there is adequate, accurate and up-to-date information on express trusts and other similar legal arrangements including information on the settlor(s), trustee(s) and beneficiary(ies), that can be obtained or accessed efficiently and in a timely manner by competent authorities. Countries should consider facilitating access to beneficial ownership

and control information by financial institutions and DNFBPs undertaking the requirements set out in Recommendations 10 and 22.

F. Powers and Responsibilities of Competent Authorities, and Other Institutional Measures

REGULATION AND SUPERVISION

26. Regulation and supervision of financial institutions *

Countries should ensure that financial institutions are subject to adequate regulation and supervision and are effectively implementing the FATF Recommendations. Competent authorities or financial supervisors should take the necessary legal or regulatory measures to prevent criminals or their associates from holding, or being the beneficial owner of, a significant or controlling interest, or holding a management function in, a financial institution. Countries should not approve the establishment, or continued operation, of shell banks.

For financial institutions subject to the Core Principles, the regulatory and supervisory measures that apply for prudential purposes, and which are also relevant to money laundering and terrorist financing, should apply in a similar manner for AML/CFT purposes. This should include applying consolidated group supervision for AML/CFT purposes.

Other financial institutions should be licensed or registered and adequately regulated, and subject to supervision or monitoring for AML/CFT purposes, having regard to the risk of money laundering or terrorist financing in that sector. At a minimum, where financial institutions provide a service of money or value transfer, or of money or currency changing, they should be licensed or registered, and subject to effective systems for monitoring and ensuring compliance with national AML/CFT requirements.

27. Powers of supervisors

Supervisors should have adequate powers to supervise or monitor, and ensure compliance by, financial institutions with requirements to combat money laundering and terrorist financing, including the authority to conduct inspections. They should be authorised to compel production of any information from financial institutions that is relevant to monitoring such compliance, and to impose sanctions, in line with Recommendation 35, for failure to comply with such requirements. Supervisors should have powers to impose a range of disciplinary and financial sanctions, including the power to withdraw, restrict or suspend the financial institution's license, where applicable.

28. Regulation and supervision of DNFBPs *

Designated non-financial businesses and professions should be subject to regulatory and supervisory measures as set out below.

(a) Casinos should be subject to a comprehensive regulatory and supervisory regime that ensures that they have effectively implemented the necessary AML/CFT measures. At a minimum:

- casinos should be licensed;
- competent authorities should take the necessary legal or regulatory measures to prevent criminals or their associates from holding, or being the beneficial owner of, a significant or controlling interest, holding a management function in, or being an operator of, a casino; and
- competent authorities should ensure that casinos are effectively supervised for compliance with AML/CFT requirements.

(b) Countries should ensure that the other categories of DNFBPs are subject to effective systems for monitoring and ensuring compliance with AML/CFT requirements. This should be performed on a risk-sensitive basis. This may be performed by (a) a supervisor or (b) by an appropriate self-regulatory body (SRB), provided that such a body can ensure that its members comply with their obligations to combat money laundering and terrorist financing.

The supervisor or SRB should also (a) take the necessary measures to prevent criminals or their associates from being professionally accredited, or holding or being the beneficial owner of a significant or controlling interest or holding a management function, e.g. through evaluating persons on the basis of a "fit and proper" test; and (b) have effective, proportionate, and dissuasive sanctions in line with Recommendation 35 available to deal with failure to comply with AML/CFT requirements.

Operational and Law Enforcement

29. Financial intelligence units *

Countries should establish a financial intelligence unit (FIU) that serves as a national centre for the receipt and analysis of: (a) suspicious transaction reports; and (b) other information relevant to money laundering, associated predicate offences and terrorist financing, and for the dissemination of the results of that analysis. The FIU should be able to obtain additional information from reporting entities, and should have access on a timely basis to the financial, administrative and law enforcement information that it requires to undertake its functions properly.

30. Responsibilities of law enforcement and investigative authorities *

Countries should ensure that designated law enforcement authorities have responsibility for money laundering and terrorist financing investigations within the framework of national AML/CFT policies. At least in all cases related to major proceeds-generating offences, these designated law enforcement authorities should develop a pro-active parallel financial investigation when pursuing money laundering, predicate offences and terrorist financing. This should include cases where the associated predicate offence occurs outside their jurisdictions.

Countries should ensure that competent authorities have responsibility for expeditiously identifying, tracing and initiating actions to freeze and seize criminal property and property of corresponding value. Countries should also make use, when necessary, of permanent temporary multi-disciplinary groups specialised in financial or asset investigations. Countries should ensure that, when necessary, cooperative investigations with appropriate competent authorities in other countries take place.

31. Powers of law enforcement and investigative authorities

When conducting investigations of money laundering, associated predicate offences and terrorist financing, competent authorities should be able to obtain access to all necessary documents and information for use in those investigations, and in prosecutions and related actions. This should include powers to use compulsory measures for the production of records held by financial institutions, DNFBPs and other natural or legal persons, for the search of persons and premises, for taking witness statements, and for the seizure and obtaining of evidence. Countries should ensure that competent authorities conducting investigations are able to use a wide range of investigative techniques suitable for the investigation of money laundering, associated predicate offences and terrorist financing. These investigative techniques include: undercover operations, intercepting communications, accessing computer systems and controlled delivery.

Countries should ensure that competent authorities have timely access to a wide range of information, particularly to support the identification and tracing of criminal property and property of corresponding value. This may include, but is not limited to, basic and beneficial ownership information, information held by tax authorities, information held in asset registries (such as for land, property, vehicles, shares, or other assets), and information held in citizenship, residency, or social benefit registries.

In addition, countries should have effective mechanisms in place to identify, in a timely manner, whether natural or legal persons hold or control accounts. They should also have mechanisms to ensure that competent authorities have a process to identify assets without prior notification to the owner. When conducting investigations of money laundering, associated predicate offences and terrorist financing, competent authorities should be able to ask for all relevant information held by the FIU.

32. Cash couriers *

Countries should have measures in place to detect the physical cross-border transportation of currency and bearer negotiable instruments, including through a declaration system and/or disclosure system.

Countries should ensure that their competent authorities have the legal authority to stop or restrain currency or bearer negotiable instruments that are suspected to be related to terrorist financing, money laundering or predicate offences, or that are falsely declared or disclosed.

Countries should ensure that effective, proportionate and dissuasive sanctions are available to deal with persons who make false declaration(s) or disclosure(s). In cases where the currency or bearer negotiable instruments are related to terrorist financing, money laundering or predicate offences, countries should also adopt measures, including legislative ones consistent with Recommendation 4, which would enable the confiscation of such currency or instruments.

General Requirements

33. Statistics

Countries should maintain comprehensive statistics on matters relevant to the effectiveness and efficiency of their AML/CFT systems. This should include statistics on the STRs received and disseminated; on money laundering and terrorist financing investigations, prosecutions and convictions; on property frozen, seized and confiscated; and on mutual legal assistance or other international requests for cooperation.

34. Guidance and feedback

The competent authorities, supervisors and SRBs should establish guidelines, and provide feedback, which will assist financial institutions and designated non-financial businesses and professions in applying national measures to combat money laundering and terrorist financing, and, in particular, in detecting and reporting suspicious transactions.

Sanctions

35. Sanctions

Countries should ensure that there is a range of effective, proportionate and dissuasive sanctions, whether criminal, civil or administrative, available to deal with natural or legal persons covered by Recommendations 6, and 8 to 23, that fail to comply with AML/CFT requirements. Sanctions should be applicable not only to financial institutions and DNFBPs, but also to their directors and senior management.

G. International Cooperation

36. International instruments

Countries should take immediate steps to become party to and implement fully the Vienna Convention, 1988; the Palermo Convention, 2000; the United Nations Convention against Corruption, 2003; and the Terrorist Financing Convention, 1999. Where applicable, countries are also encouraged to ratify and implement other relevant international conventions, such as the Council of Europe Convention on Cybercrime, 2001; the Inter-American Convention against Terrorism, 2002; and the Council of Europe Convention on Laundering, Search, Seizure and Confiscation of the Proceeds from Crime and on the Financing of Terrorism, 2005.

37. Mutual legal assistance

Countries should rapidly, constructively and effectively provide the widest possible range of mutual legal assistance in relation to money laundering, associated predicate offences and terrorist financing investigations, prosecutions, and related proceedings. Countries should have an adequate legal basis for providing assistance and, where appropriate, should have in place treaties, arrangements or other mechanisms to enhance cooperation. In particular, countries should:

(a) Not prohibit, or place unreasonable or unduly restrictive conditions on, the provision of mutual legal assistance.
(b) Ensure that they have clear and efficient processes for the timely prioritisation and execution of mutual legal assistance requests. Countries should use a central authority, or another established official mechanism, for effective transmission and execution of requests. To monitor progress on requests, a case management system should be maintained.
(c) Not refuse to execute a request for mutual legal assistance on the sole ground that the offence is also considered to involve fiscal matters.
(d) Not refuse to execute a request for mutual legal assistance on the grounds that laws require financial institutions or DNFBPs to maintain secrecy or confidentiality (except where the relevant information that is sought is held in circumstances where legal professional privilege or legal professional secrecy applies).
(e) Maintain the confidentiality of mutual legal assistance requests they receive and the information contained in them, subject to fundamental principles of domestic law, in order to protect the integrity of the investigation or inquiry. If the requested country cannot comply with the requirement of confidentiality, it should promptly inform the requesting country.

Countries should render mutual legal assistance, notwithstanding the absence of dual criminality, if the assistance does not involve coercive actions. Countries should consider adopting such measures as may be necessary to enable them to provide a wide scope of assistance in the absence of dual criminality.

Where dual criminality is required for mutual legal assistance, that requirement should be deemed to be satisfied regardless of whether both countries place the offence within the same category of offence, or denominate the offence by the same terminology, provided that both countries criminalise the conduct underlying the offence.

Countries should ensure that, of the powers and investigative techniques required under Recommendation 31, and any other powers and investigative techniques available to their competent authorities:

(a) all those relating to the production, search and seizure of information, documents or evidence (including financial records) from financial institutions or other persons, and the taking of witness statements; and
(b) a broad range of other powers and investigative techniques; are also available for use in response to requests for mutual legal assistance, and, if consistent with their domestic framework, in response to direct requests from foreign judicial or law enforcement authorities to domestic counterparts.

To avoid conflicts of jurisdiction, consideration should be given to devising and applying mechanisms for determining the best venue for prosecution of defendants in the interests of justice in cases that are subject to prosecution in more than one country.

Countries should, when making mutual legal assistance requests, make best efforts to provide complete factual and legal information that will allow for timely and efficient execution of requests, including any need for urgency, and should send requests using expeditious means.

Countries should, before sending requests, make best efforts to ascertain the legal requirements and formalities to obtain assistance.

The authorities responsible for mutual legal assistance (e.g. a Central Authority) should be provided with adequate financial, human and technical resources. Countries should have in place processes to ensure that the staff of such authorities maintain high professional standards, including standards concerning confidentiality, and should be of high integrity and be appropriately skilled.

38. Mutual legal assistance: freezing and confiscation *

Countries should have measures, including legislative measures, to take expeditious action in response to requests by foreign countries seeking assistance to identify, trace, evaluate investigate, freeze, seize and confiscate criminal property and property of corresponding value.

These measures should also enable countries to recognise and enforce foreign freezing, seizing. or confiscation orders. Further, countries should be able to manage property subject to confiscation at all stages of the asset recovery process and share or return confiscated property.

Countries should have in place the widest possible range of treaties, arrangements, or other mechanisms to enhance cooperation in asset recovery.

39. Extradition

Countries should constructively and effectively execute extradition requests in relation to money laundering and terrorist financing, without undue delay. Countries should also take all possible measures to ensure that they do not provide safe havens for individuals charged with the financing of terrorism, terrorist acts or terrorist organisations. In particular, countries should:

(a) ensure money laundering and terrorist financing are extraditable offences;
(b) ensure that they have clear and efficient processes for the timely execution of extradition requests including prioritisation where appropriate. To monitor progress of requests a case management system should be maintained;
(c) not place unreasonable or unduly restrictive conditions on the execution of requests; and
(d) ensure they have an adequate legal framework for extradition.

Each country should either extradite its own nationals, or, where a country does not do so solely on the grounds of nationality, that country should, at the request of the country seeking extradition, submit the case, without undue delay, to its competent authorities for the purpose of prosecution of the offences set forth in the request. Those authorities should take their decision and conduct their proceedings in the same manner as in the case of any other offence of a serious nature under the domestic law of that country. The countries concerned should cooperate with each other, in particular on procedural and evidentiary aspects, to ensure the efficiency of such prosecutions.

Where dual criminality is required for extradition, that requirement should be deemed to be satisfied regardless of whether both countries place the offence within the same category of offence, or denominate the offence by the same terminology, provided that both countries criminalise the conduct underlying the offence.

Consistent with fundamental principles of domestic law, countries should have simplified extradition mechanisms, such as allowing direct transmission of requests for provisional arrests between appropriate authorities, extraditing persons based only on warrants of arrests or judgments, or introducing a simplified extradition of consenting persons who waive formal extradition proceedings. The authorities responsible for extradition should be provided with adequate financial, human and technical resources. Countries should have in place processes to ensure that the staff of such authorities maintain high professional standards, including standards concerning confidentiality, and should be of high integrity and be appropriately skilled.

40. Other forms of international cooperation *

Countries should ensure that their competent authorities can rapidly, constructively and effectively provide the widest range of international cooperation in relation to money laundering, associated predicate offences and terrorist financing. Countries should do so both spontaneously and upon request, and there should be a lawful basis for providing cooperation.

Countries should authorise their competent authorities to use the most efficient means to cooperate. Should a competent authority need bilateral or multilateral agreements or arrangements, such as a Memorandum of Understanding (MOU), these should be negotiated and signed in a timely way with the widest range of foreign counterparts. Competent authorities should use clear channels or mechanisms for the effective transmission and execution of requests for information or other types of assistance. Competent authorities. should have clear and efficient processes for the prioritisation and timely execution of requests, and for safeguarding the information received.

N.B. There are a number of interpretative notes and the two annexes (listed below) that are not reproduced here.

- Annex I: FATF Guidance Documents (listed at: https://www.fatf-gafi.org/en/publications/Fatfrecommendations/Fatf-recommendations.html);
- Annex II: Information on Updates Made to the FATF Recommendations

x) **FATF:** IX Special Recommendations on Terrorist Financing[17]

Recognising the vital importance of taking action to combat the financing of terrorism, the FATF has agreed these Recommendations, which, when combined with the FATF Forty Recommendations on money laundering, set out the basic framework to detect, prevent and suppress the financing of terrorism and terrorist acts.

I. Ratification and implementation of UN instruments

Each country should take immediate steps to ratify and to implement fully the 1999 United Nations International Convention for the Suppression of the Financing of Terrorism.

Countries should also immediately implement the United Nations resolutions relating to the prevention and suppression of the financing of terrorist acts, particularly United Nations Security Council Resolution 1373.

II. Criminalising the financing of terrorism and associated money laundering

Each country should criminalise the financing of terrorism, terrorist acts and terrorist organisations. Countries should ensure that such offences are designated as money laundering predicate offences.

III. Freezing and confiscating terrorist assets

Each country should implement measures to freeze without delay funds or other assets of terrorists, those who finance terrorism and terrorist organisations in accordance with the United Nations resolutions relating to the prevention and suppression of the financing of terrorist acts.

Each country should also adopt and implement measures, including legislative ones, which would enable the competent authorities to seize and confiscate property that is the proceeds of, or used in, or intended or allocated for use in, the financing of terrorism, terrorist acts or terrorist organisations.

[17] https://www.fatf-gafi.org/en/publications/Fatfrecommendations/Ixspecialrecommendations.html

IV. Reporting suspicious transactions related to terrorism

If financial institutions, or other businesses or entities subject to anti-money laundering obligations, suspect or have reasonable grounds to suspect that funds are linked or related to, or are to be used for terrorism, terrorist acts or by terrorist organisations, they should be required to report promptly their suspicions to the competent authorities.

V. International Co-operation

Each country should afford another country, on the basis of a treaty, arrangement or other mechanism for mutual legal assistance or information exchange, the greatest possible measure of assistance in connection with criminal, civil enforcement, and administrative investigations, inquiries and proceedings relating to the financing of terrorism, terrorist acts and terrorist organisations.

Countries should also take all possible measures to ensure that they do not provide safe havens for individuals charged with the financing of terrorism, terrorist acts or terrorist organisations, and should have procedures in place to extradite, where possible, such individuals.

VI. Alternative Remittance

Each country should take measures to ensure that persons or legal entities, including agents, that provide a service for the transmission of money or value, including transmission through an informal money or value transfer system or network, should be licensed or registered and subject to all the FATF Recommendations that apply to banks and non-bank financial institutions. Each country should ensure that persons or legal entities that carry out this service illegally are subject to administrative, civil or criminal sanctions.

VII. Wire transfers

Countries should take measures to require financial institutions, including money remitters, to include accurate and meaningful originator information (name, address and account number) on funds transfers and related messages that are sent, and the information should remain with the transfer or related message through the payment chain.

Countries should take measures to ensure that financial institutions, including money remitters, conduct enhanced scrutiny of and monitor for suspicious activity funds transfers which do not contain complete originator information (name, address and account number).

VIII. Non-profitorganisations

Countries should review the adequacy of laws and regulations that relate to entities that can be abused for the financing of terrorism. Non-profit organisations are particularly vulnerable, and countries should ensure that they cannot be misused:

(i) by terrorist organisations posing as legitimate entities;
(ii) to exploit legitimate entities as conduits for terrorist financing, including for the purpose of escaping asset freezing measures; and
(iii) to conceal or obscure the clandestine diversion of funds intended for legitimate purposes to terrorist organisations.

IX. Cash Couriers

Countries should have measures in place to detect the physical cross-border transportation of currency and bearer negotiable instruments, including a declaration system or other disclosure obligation.

Countries should ensure that their competent authorities have the legal authority to stop or restrain currency or bearer negotiable instruments that are suspected to be related to terrorist financing or money laundering, or that are falsely declared or disclosed.

Countries should ensure that effective, proportionate and dissuasive sanctions are available to deal with persons who make false declaration(s) or disclosure(s). In cases where the currency or bearer negotiable instruments are related to terrorist financing or money laundering, countries should also adopt measures, including legislative ones consistent with Recommendation 3 and Special Recommendation III, which would enable the confiscation of such currency or instruments.

N.B.: as with the FATF 40 Recommendations, there are Interpretative Notes which have not been reproduced here.

xi) **FATF:** High-risk and other monitored jurisdictions[18]

Global safeguards to combat money laundering and terrorist financing (AML/CFT) are only as strong as the jurisdiction with the weakest measures. Criminals can circumvent weak AML/CFT controls to successfully launder money or to move assets to finance terrorism through the financial system. A key objective of the FATF is to continually identify jurisdictions with significant weaknesses in their AML/CFT regimes, and to work with them to address those weaknesses. The FATF's process helps protect the integrity of the international financial system by issuing a public warning about the risks emanating from the identified jurisdictions. These public warnings also put pressure on the identified jurisdictions to address their deficiencies in order to maintain their position in the global economy. Public identification, and the prospect of public identification, encourages countries to swiftly make significant improvements.

Review Process

The FATF continually identifies and reviews jurisdictions with strategic AML/CFT deficiencies that present a risk to the international financial system and closely monitors their progress. The FATF's International Co-operation Review Group (ICRG) oversees the process. The process began in 2007 and was enhanced in 2009. It was further updated in 2015 to take into account revisions to FATF standards and mutual evaluation process, which assess the effective implementation of AML/CFT measures.

The FATF reviews jurisdictions based on threats, vulnerabilities, or particular risks arising from the jurisdiction. Specifically, a jurisdiction will be reviewed when:

[18] https://www.fatf-gafi.org/en/topics/high-risk-and-other-monitored-jurisdictions.html

1. It does not participate in a FATF-style regional body (FSRB) or does not allow mutual evaluation results to be published in a timely manner; or
2. It is nominated by a FATF member or an FSRB. The nomination is based on specific money laundering, terrorist financing, or proliferation financing risks or threats coming to the attention of delegations; or
3. It has achieved poor results on its mutual evaluation, specifically:

   - it has 20 or more non-Compliant (NC) or Partially Compliance (PC) ratings for technical compliance; or
   - it is rated NC/PC on 3 or more of the following Recommendations: 3, 5, 6, 10, 11, and 20; or
   - it has a low or moderate level of effectiveness for 9 or more of the 11 Immediate Outcomes, with a minimum of two lows; or
   - it has a low level of effectiveness for 6 or more of the 11 Immediate Outcomes.

A jurisdiction that enters the ICRG review process as a result of its mutual evaluation results has a 1-year Observation Period to work with the FATF or its FATF-style regional body (FSRB) to address deficiencies before possible public identification and formal review by the FATF. The FATF then prioritises the review of those countries with more significant financial sectors—e.g. USD 5 billion or more in financial sector assets.

During the review process the FATF considers the strategic AML/CFT deficiencies identified both in terms of technical compliance and effectiveness of measures in place, and any relevant progress made by the jurisdiction. If the FATF deems the progress insufficient to address its strategic deficiencies, the FATF develops an action plan with the jurisdiction to address the remaining strategic deficiencies.

For all countries under ICRG review, the FATF requires a high-level political commitment that the jurisdiction will implement the legal, regulatory, and operational reforms required by the action plan.

Four regional Joint Groups of the ICRG carry out the reviews, covering: Africa/Middle East, the Americas, Asia/Pacific, and Europe/Eurasia. Each jurisdiction under review has the opportunity to participate in a face-to-face meeting to discuss the analysis of the Joint Group in advance of FATF plenary meetings.

Public Identification

The FATF publishes two statements at the end of each plenary meeting, in February, June, and October. These statements provide a short summary of the recent actions taken in accordance with each jurisdiction's action plan, as well as a list of the strategic deficiencies remaining to be addressed. The two statements reflect the different levels of risk posed at any given time by the deficiencies in the jurisdictions under review.

Removal from FATF Review

In order to be removed from FATF monitoring, a jurisdiction must address all or nearly all the components of its action plan. Once the FATF has determined that a jurisdiction has done so, it will organise an on-site visit to confirm that the implementation of the necessary legal, regulatory, and/or operational reforms is underway and there is the necessary political commitment and institutional capacity to sustain implementation. If the on-site visit has a positive outcome, the FATF will decide on removing the jurisdiction from public identification at the next FATF plenary. The concerned jurisdiction will then continue to work within the FATF or the relevant FSRB, through its normal follow-up process, to improve its AML/CFT regime.

xii) **FATF**: Updated Guidance for a Risk-Based Approach—Virtual Assets and Virtual Asset Service Providers (2021)[19]

Executive Summary

In October 2018, the Financial Action Task Force (FATF) adopted changes to its Recommendations to explicitly clarify that they apply to financial activities involving virtual assets; FATF also added two new definitions to the Glossary: "virtual asset" (VA) and "virtual asset service provider" (VASP). The amended FATF Recommendation 15 requires that VASPs be regulated for anti-money laundering and countering the financing of terrorism (AML/CFT) purposes, that they be licensed or registered, and subject to effective systems for monitoring or supervision.

In June 2019, the FATF adopted an Interpretive Note to Recommendation 15 to further clarify how the FATF requirements should apply in relation to VAs and VASPs, in particular with regard to the application of the risk-based approach to VA activities or operations and VASPs; supervision or monitoring of VASPs for AML/CFT purposes; licensing or registration; preventive measures, such as customer due diligence, recordkeeping, and suspicious transaction reporting, among others; sanctions and other enforcement measures; and international co-operation.

The FATF also adopted a first version of this Guidance1 on the application of the risk-based approach to VAs and VASPs in June 2019; the Guidance was updated in October 2021. It is intended to both help national authorities in understanding and developing regulatory and supervisory responses to VA activities and VASPs, and to help private sector entities seeking to engage in VA activities, in understanding their AML/CFT obligations and how they can effectively comply with these requirements.

This Guidance outlines the need for countries and VASPs, and other entities involved in VA activities, to understand the money laundering and terrorist financing (ML/TF) risks associated with VA activities and to take appropriate mitigating measures to address those risks. In particular, the Guidance provides examples of risk indicators that should specifically be considered in a VA context, with an emphasis on factors that would further obfuscate transactions or inhibit VASPs' ability to identify customers.

The Guidance examines how VA activities and VASPs fall within the scope of the FATF Standards. It discusses the five types of activities covered by the VASP definition and provides examples of VA-related activities that would fall within the

[19]The report is 109 pages. This is the Executive Summary to provide an outline of the document which can be accessed at: https://www.fatf-gafi.org/content/dam/fatf-gafi/guidance/Updated-Guidance-VA-VASP.pdf.coredownload.inline.pdf

definition and also those that would potentially be excluded from the FATF scope. In that respect, it highlights the key elements required to qualify as a VASP, namely acting as a business for or on behalf of another person and providing or actively facilitating VA-related activities.

The Guidance describes the application of the FATF Recommendations to countries and competent authorities; as well as to VASPs and other obliged entities that engage in VA activities, including financial institutions such as banks and securities broker-dealers, among others. Almost all of the FATF Recommendations are directly relevant to address the ML/TF risks associated with VAs and VASPs, while other Recommendations are less directly or explicitly linked to VAs or VASPs, though they are still relevant and applicable. VASPs therefore have the same full set of obligations as financial institutions and designated non-financial businesses and professions.

The Guidance details the full range of obligations applicable to VASPs as well as to VAs under the FATF Recommendations, following a Recommendation-by-Recommendation approach. This includes clarifying that all of the funds or value-based terms in the FATF Recommendations (e.g., "property," "proceeds," "funds," "funds or other assets," and other "corresponding value") include VAs. Consequently, countries should apply all of the relevant measures under the FATF Recommendations to VAs, VA activities, and VASPs.

The Guidance explains the VASP registration or licensing requirements, in particular how to determine in which country/ies VASPs should be registered or licensed—at a minimum where they were created; or in the jurisdiction where their business is located in cases where they are a natural person. However, jurisdictions can also choose to require VASPs to be licensed or registered before conducting business in their jurisdiction or from their jurisdiction. The Guidance further underlines that national authorities are required to take action to identify natural or legal persons that carry out VA activities without the requisite license or registration. This would be equally applicable to countries that have chosen to prohibit VAs and VA activities at the national level.

Regarding VASP supervision, the Guidance makes clear that only competent authorities, and not self-regulatory bodies, can act as VASP supervisory or monitoring bodies. They should conduct risk-based supervision or monitoring, and have adequate powers, including to conduct inspections, compel the production of information and impose sanctions. There is a specific focus on the importance of international co-operation between supervisors, given the cross-border nature of VASPs' activities and provision of services.

The Guidance makes clear that VASPs, and other entities involved in VA activities, need to apply all the preventive measures described in FATF Recommendations 10 to 21. The Guidance explains how these obligations should be fulfilled in a VA context and provides clarifications regarding the specific requirements applicable to the USD/EUR 1000 threshold for occasional transactions, above which VASPs must conduct customer due diligence (Recommendation 10); and the obligation to obtain, hold, and transmit required originator and beneficiary information, immediately and securely, when conducting VA transfers (Recommendation 16) (the 'travel rule'). As the guidance makes clear, relevant authorities should co-ordinate to ensure this can be done in a way that is compatible with national data protection and privacy rules.

Finally, the Guidance provides examples of jurisdictional approaches to regulating, supervising, and enforcing VA activities, VASPs, and other obliged entities for AML/CFT.

In October 2021, this Guidance was updated to provide the public and private sectors with revised guidance. These revisions focused on six key areas where greater guidance from the FATF was sought. These are to (1) clarify the definitions of VA and VASP to make clear that these definitions are expansive and there should not be a case where a relevant financial asset is not covered by the FATF Standards (either as a VA or as another financial asset), (2) provide guidance on how the FATF Standards apply to stablecoins and clarify that a range of entities involved in stablecoin arrangements could qualify as VASPs under the FATF Standards, (3) provide additional guidance on the risks and the tools available to countries to address the ML/TF risks for peer-to-peer transactions, which are transactions that do not involve any obliged entities, (4) provide updated guidance on the licensing and registration of VASPs, (5) provide additional guidance for the public and private sectors on the implementation of the 'travel rule', and (6) include Principles of Information-Sharing and Co-operation Amongst VASP Supervisors.

This document incorporates and supersedes the 2019 Guidance.

xiii) **THE OECD OSLO DIALOGUE**[20]

The OECD Task Force on Tax Crimes and Other Crimes (TFTC) supports global efforts to stamp out illicit financial flows through implementation of the "Oslo Dialogue", a strategy launched in 2011 to promote 'whole of government' approaches to fighting tax crime and other financial crimes through standard setting, sharing of best practices, and capacity building.

Countries around the globe are facing a common threat posed by increasingly complex and innovative forms of financial crime. Tax evasion, fraud, corruption, money laundering, and other financial crimes threaten the strategic, political, and economic interests of all countries and undermine public trust in government and the financial system. Combatting these closely related crimes requires financial transparency, robust legal and institutional frameworks, and effective co-operation between tax administrations and other law enforcement authorities.

Underpinned by the OECD's Ten Global Principles for Fighting Tax Crime, the TFTC delivers a range of practical tools, guidance, training, and other capacity building initiatives that provide critical support to jurisdictions in their fight against tax and other financial crimes both domestically and internationally.

[20] https://www.oecd.org/tax/crime/

Governance
As a subsidiary body of the OECD's Committee on Fiscal Affairs (CFA), the OECD Task Force on Tax Crimes and Other Crimes (TFTC) comprises all 38 OECD Member countries and Argentina. In keeping with OECD standard-setting in other areas of taxation, participation in TFTC meetings is also open to non-OECD Member countries and is regularly attended by a diverse range of developed and developing jurisdictions from around the globe.*

In line with its mandate to promote whole of government approaches to combatting tax and other financial crimes, broad-ranging government authorities make up the TFTC, including civil and criminal tax examiners and other financial crimes authorities (e.g. police, prosecutors, and authorities working on anti-corruption, financial intelligence, anti-money laundering, asset recovery, etc.).

The TFTC's mission to crack down on illicit financial flows is more important than ever with a new wave of threats and vulnerabilities arising from the COVID-19 crisis, the continued growth of cybercrime spurred on by new technologies, and the increasingly sophisticated use of professional enablers for criminal enterprise. To keep pace with these ever-evolving threats, the TFTC meets twice yearly in Paris for real-time exchange of experiences, case studies, best practices, and other tools and measures to counter this damaging conduct.

* For a full list of non-OECD Member jurisdictions eligible to participate in TFTC meetings and projects, please see the CFA's Participation Plan.

Capacity Building Activities
While illicit financial flows (IFFs) are a global concern, they are particularly damaging to developing countries, which struggle to mobilise domestic resources to finance their own development in a sustainable manner. In Africa alone, a 2020 UNCTAD report estimates annual losses in excess of USD 88 billion due to IFFs—close half of the USD 200 billion financing gap the continent faces to achieve the United Nations Sustainable Development Goals. This lost revenue could otherwise have been invested in sustainable development, for example, by improving healthcare, education, infrastructure, and other public services. Helping governments to tackle this issue more effectively will not only bolster domestic resource mobilisation but also help build trust and confidence in the fairness of the tax system and in government as a whole, which is critical given the central role that tax measures have played in providing relief throughout the pandemic.

xiv) **OECD** Ten Global Principles for Fighting Tax Crime[21]

In June 2022, the OECD strengthened its role as a leading standard setter on combatting illicit financial flows through the publication of the *Recommendation*

[21] https://www.oecd.org/tax/crime/tftc-standard-setting-best-practices/

of the Council on the Ten Global Principles for Fighting Tax Crime. This landmark OECD Recommendation offers the first comprehensive global standard on combatting tax crimes, by setting out the ten essential legal, institutional, administrative, and operational frameworks necessary to effectively prevent, detect, investigate, and prosecute tax crimes, and to recover the proceeds of those crimes.

This new Recommendation complements and strengthens the previously published Ten Global Principles guidance document by converting it into an official OECD standard, included in the Compendium of OECD Legal Instruments. The Recommendation is supported by a practical guide on implementation, designed to support jurisdictions' application of the Ten Global Principles to their domestic tax crime frameworks, including strategies for tackling professionals who enable tax and white-collar crimes and fostering international co-operation in the recovery of assets. The guide is supported by a compendium of "country chapters" which benchmark the domestic tax crime frameworks of 33 jurisdictions, including 27 Members, against the Ten Global Principles. These country chapters are available online, in English and French.

Furthermore, the OECD's Tax Crime Maturity Model serves as an important practical tool for jurisdictions to self-assess, monitor, and track their progress on implementation of the Ten Global Principles over time.

- See the Council Recommendation on Fighting Tax Crime
- Practical Guide on the Implementation of the Ten Global Principles for Fighting Tax Crime (EN/FR/ES)
- Read more about the OECD Tax Crime Maturity Model
- E-Learning module: Fighting tax crime: the Ten Global Principles (EN/FR/ES)

xv) **OECD**: Money Laundering and Terrorist Financing Awareness Handbook for Tax Examiners and Tax Auditors[22]

First launched in 2009 as a practical tool to assist tax authorities in identifying money laundering during the course of regular tax audits, this revised handbook includes updated money laundering indicators and new material to increase the detection and reporting of terrorist financing. This edition of the report was published in June 2019 (the original version was published in October 2009).

Executive Summary

Financial crimes, including tax crimes, money laundering, and terrorist financing, undermine jurisdictions' political and economic interests and pose a serious threat to national security. Law enforcement authorities working to combat these crimes operate in an environment with limited resources, and advances in technology mean that criminals are using ever more sophisticated methods to avoid detection. Combatting these crimes therefore necessitates a "whole of government approach"

[22]Reproduced here is only the executive summary - the full text is at: https://www.oecd.org/ctp/exchange-of-tax-information/money-laundering-awareness-handbook.htm

where different financial crime authorities can pool their knowledge and skills to collectively prevent, detect, and enforce these crimes.

By their very nature, tax crimes are closely linked to other financial crimes and it is well recognised that tax authorities have a central role to play in identifying and reporting money laundering and terrorist financing. While the benefits of reporting and information sharing between tax authorities and anti-money laundering authorities are well recognised, both developed and developing jurisdictions alike face ongoing challenges when it comes to applying this cross-government co-operation in practice.

The OECD originally developed this Handbook in 2009 as a practical tool to enhance co-operation between tax authorities and anti-money laundering authorities. This revised Handbook updates the 2009 version with respect to money laundering indicators, and includes, for the first time, material to raise the awareness of tax examiners, auditors, and investigators of issues concerning terrorism financing.

There are substantial gains to be made by developing strong legal, institutional, operational, and cultural frameworks for tax authorities to report and share information with authorities responsible for combatting money laundering and terrorist financing. Efforts to frustrate these criminal activities start with a firm commitment from political leaders but ultimately end with government officials implementing these policies on the ground.

Authorities around the globe are encouraged to make use of this Handbook and adapt it to their jurisdiction's particular circumstances, taking into account the varying roles that tax administrations have in terms of reporting unusual or suspicious transactions, receiving suspicious transaction reports, and investigating money laundering and terrorist financing offences. Doing so can strengthen the ability of tax examiners and auditors to identify and report money laundering and terrorist financing, thus enhancing the whole-of-government efforts to detect, deter and prevent these illegal and destructive activities.

The handbook includes lists of money laundering red flags for:

- *Individuals*
- *Business*
- *Charities and Foreign Legal Entities*
- *Real Estate*
- *Cash*
- *Cryptocurrencies*
- *International Trade*
- *Loans*
- *Professional Service Providers*

And terrorist financing indicators for:

- *Individuals*
- *Businesses*
- *Charities and Non-Profit Organisations and*
- *Cryptocurrencies*

xvi) **Egmont Group of Financial Intelligence Units**: Communiqué dated February 1, 2016[23]

Egmont Group of Financial Intelligence Units Reinforces Its Efforts in Combatting Money Laundering

MONACO—The increasing actions of terrorists and terrorist organizations such as ISIL, al-Qaida and their respective affiliates, as demonstrated by recent terrorist acts in Indonesia, Egypt, France, Lebanon, Mali, Saudi Arabia, Turkey and the United States, and the proliferation of Foreign Terrorist Fighters (FTFs), poses serious threats to security and international financial stability.

In response, the Egmont Group members have cooperated to produce an operational analysis of the financing for ISIL FTFs. The project identified challenges and highlighted successes to information sharing in combating terrorist financing (TF).

Recognizing its important role, on 1 February 2016, the Heads, or their designated representatives, of 102 Financial Intelligence Units, convened an extraordinary meeting of its governing body to discuss how the Egmont Group could positively respond to this increasing threat. As the international group that unites its members to exchange financial intelligence and expertise, the Egmont Group is committed to capitalising on its unique global network.

During this extraordinary intersessional meeting, the Heads of FIUs, within the context of each jurisdictions TF risk assessment, adopted the following recommendations and initiatives to:

- provide indicators of terrorism financing to industry partners to assist the identification of suspicious financial activity;
- engage with domestic intelligence agencies to strive to improve the flow of TF-related information;
- examine the utility of cross-border wire transfer information in the context of combating TF;
- consider the reporting of couriers transporting cash or non-cash instruments across borders;
- identify the need to expand the range of reporting entities subject to Suspicious Transaction Reports (STR) reporting regime;
- update the Egmont foundational documents to enable spontaneous and multilateral information exchange;
- implement solutions for appropriate access to more sources of information necessary to share actionable financial intelligence to counter TF threats; continue cooperation with the Financial Action Task Force (FATF)—which sets the international AML/CTF standards—to overcome information access and sharing challenges and ensure the international standards enable effective combating of terrorist financing; and,

[23] https://egmontgroup.org/wp-content/uploads/2021/09/2016_Monte_Carlo_Monaco_-_Working_Group_Meetings_Communique.pdf

- commit to improve FIU capability leveraging expertise and technology to better capitalise on data, exchange intelligence and enable cooperation.

By undertaking these initiatives and taking on-board these recommendations, the Egmont Group demonstrates that it recognizes its important role in combating terrorist financing. Continuously improving the flow of financial intelligence through its unique global network is a priority of the Egmont Group. The Egmont Group is committed to support its members and further cooperate with its international partners in combating terrorist financing.

Background

The Egmont Group is a united body of FIUs from 151 jurisdictions. It provides a platform for the secure exchange of expertise and financial intelligence on combating money laundering and terrorist financing. FIUs are uniquely positioned to cooperate and support national and international efforts to counter terrorist financing and are the trusted gateway for sharing financial information domestically and internationally in accordance with global AML/CTF standards.

The Egmont Group continues to support the efforts of its international partners and other stakeholders to give effect to the resolutions and statements by the United Nations Security Council, the G20 Finance Ministers, and the FATF calls for greater international cooperation and exchange of operational and strategic information to combat ISIL, its affiliates and FTFs.

Chair, Egmont Group of Financial Intelligence Units.

1. February 2016

xvii) **Egmont Group of Financial Intelligence Units**: Report on Abuse of Virtual Assets for Terrorist Financing Purposes[24] (dated June 2023)

1. Introduction

As an organization of FIUs, the Egmont Group (EG) is conscious that Virtual Assets (VAs) abused in terrorism financing is a current focal point of discussions at fora. Understanding trends in emerging technologies will aid in the identification of potential vulnerabilities associated with new technologies, specifically virtual assets (VAs). They can be instantly traded through peer2peer platforms, for example, and transferred on the Internet, which is generally characterized by non-face-to-face customer relationships and may permit anonymous funding. In addition, it is well-known that terrorist organizations and individual terrorists are trying to work in full conspiracy, which makes VAs a natural target for facilitating their financial activities.

The Information Exchange Working Group (IEWG) project on the Abuse of Virtual Assets for Terrorist Financing Purposes was designed to assess the exposure

[24] https://egmontgroup.org/wp-content/uploads/2023/12/2023-July-HoFIU-06-IEWG-Project-Abuse-of-VA-for-TF-Summary-1.pdf

to possible abuse, as well as to record the best practices that are used by EG member FIUs to prevent the abuse of virtual assets for terrorist financing purposes.

The project's key objectives were to explore the abuse of VAs for TF, by:

- Understanding the regulation of VAs in different countries,
- Identify how VAs are defined in different countries,
- Determine VA usage and detection,
- Develop a framework, standard or best practices document for the use by FIUs, and
- Sharing of case studies.

EG member FIUs are well-positioned to identify and trace suspicious transactions, activities, individuals, and entities. However, as previously identified in other Egmont Group reports (Lone Actors and Small Cells), FIUs usually face difficulties with TF cases, especially when they are excluded from the domestic (CFT) apparatus, when they are not appropriately empowered or provided with the necessary technical and analytical capacity to produce financial intelligence effectively, or when information is generally missing for specific financial or other services. This could be the case with VAs, where although jurisdictions are obliged by the Financial Action Task Force (FATF) Standards to collect and possess information regarding Virtual Asset Service Providers (VASPs') activities on their territory and apply the FATF "travel rule," (https://www.fatf-gafi.org/content/fatf-gafi/en/publications/Fatfrecommendations/Targeted-update-virtual-%20assets-vasps.html) many remain under the radar of the competent domestic authorities engaged with the registration and/or licensing of VASPs.

2. Literature Review

Several research papers reflect on how VA presents a huge AML/CFT risk to the integrity of the financial system. The Egmont Group itself has previously dedicated resources to examine the topics of TF through the ISIL Project and Vas through the development of the e-Catalogue on regulated VASPs. In addition, the FATF and the IMF have produced public reports that examine the abuse of VAs.

FATF work:

2020 FATF Report Virtual Assets Red Flag Indicators

In October 2018, the FATF updated its Standards to clarify the application of the FATF Standards to VA activities and VASPs. The updates assisted jurisdictions in mitigating the money laundering and terrorist financing (ML/TF) risks associated with VA activities and in protecting the integrity of the global financial system. In June 2019, the FATF adopted an Interpretative Note to Recommendation 15 to further clarify the application of FATF requirements to VA activities or operations and VASPs, including with respect to suspicious transaction reporting.

The 2020 FATF Virtual Assets Red Flag Indicators Report (https://www.fatf-gafi.org/publications/methodsandtrends/documents/virtual-assets-red-flag-indicators.html) provided a practical tool for both the public and private sectors in identifying, detecting, and ultimately preventing criminal, ML, and TF activities involving VAs. The report provided ML/TF red flag indicators associated with VAs to assist reporting entities, including financial institutions (FIs), designated non-financial businesses and professions (DNFBPs), and VASPs. The indications (or any single sign) should not be considered in isolation because they are frequently just one of many components that go into a larger overall picture of possible ML or TF risk. Therefore, it is recommended that competent authorities distribute this study to reporting entities and hold engagement and awareness-raising workshops with them to help them better comprehend it. Competent authorities may also provide private sectors with the indicators and information most relevant for that jurisdiction.

IMF Work:

2021 Virtual Assets and Anti-Money Laundering and Combating the Financing of Terrorism (2) Effective Anti-Money Laundering and Combating the Financing of Terrorism Regulatory and Supervisory Framework—Some Legal and Practical Considerations

The 2018 and 2019 revisions to the standards provided much-needed clarification on how VASP regulation and supervision should be carried out. This has been crucial for establishing greater uniformity among jurisdictions' strategies for reducing the risks to VAs' financial integrity and preventing regulatory arbitrage. The FATF has ensured that the new actors in the virtual environment are treated properly and that comparable risks are addressed equitably by subjecting VASPs to measures identical to those already applicable to FIs and DNFBPs.

The likelihood of the VASPs Interacting with the traditional financial sector, including the banking sector, has also increased. Several VASPs have stated that the advantages of implementing reliable AML/CFT systems outweigh the drawbacks, particularly because it has given banks confidence that the ML/TF/PF risks were sufficiently mitigated to allow them to conduct banking activities.

The 2021 paper (https://www.imf.org/en/Publications/fintech-notes/Issues/2021/10/14/Virtual-Assets-and-Anti-Money-Laundering-and-Combating-the-Financing-of-Terrorism-1-463654) offered recommendations to make it possible to comprehend and reduce the financial integrity issues that VAs pose. The first Fintech note clarified which assets and service providers should be subject to AML/CFT measures, the steps that all jurisdictions should take, the kind of action required in cases of criminal misuse of VAs, and the reasons why VAs are vulnerable to misuse for ML/TF/financing the proliferation of weapons of mass destruction (PF).

The second Fintech note focused on the AML/CFT regulation and supervision of VASPs. It expanded on Fintech Note 1 and aimed to give competent authorities and policymakers a high-level overview of the AML/CFT regulatory and supervisory frameworks planned for VA and VASPs, as well as some of the practical and legal concerns they bring.

3. Methodology

To achieve the project objectives, the project team relied on existing literature and new information collection through a tailor-made questionnaire. The survey/

questionnaire was circulated, and FIUs provided their respective responses. From the responses received, a report was drafted that included several case studies on the abuse of VAs for TF, which highlights several key risks and best practices on the abuse of VAs for TF purposes. However, these case studies are not included in this sanitized version of the report.

It is the understanding of the project team that the collected data represents a sufficient level of regional diversity and generally reflects the amount of information collected within other CFT-related projects.

This IEWG report serves as a guide to understanding new trends and the sharing of best practices in emerging technologies that will aid towards the identification of potential vulnerabilities associated with VAs.

In that sense, the conclusions provided in the last chapter of the report could be instrumental for FIUs' attempts to tackle TF through VAs.

4. Technology and Compliance

4.1 Regulatory Requirements in Terms of Virtual Asset Transactions

In this section of the document, the necessary regulatory requirements concerning virtual asset transactions in their respective jurisdictions were analyzed.

Of the total FIUs that replied to this question, our analysis shows that:

- 55% of FIUs state that their jurisdictions have regulatory requirements in terms of VA transactions.
- 45% of FIUs state that their jurisdictions do not have regulatory requirements in terms of VA transactions.

Although the FATF amendments in R.15, introducing requirements regarding transactions and services with VAs, were adopted back in October 2018, around 45% of the responding FIUs are still not regulating them. This shows the need for such regulation, which would allow competent authorities to collect relevant data and apply direct risk-mitigation measures.

4.1.1 Restrictions, Disclosures, or Regulatory Compliance Requirements

Out of the 55% FIUs that stated that their jurisdictions have regulatory requirements in terms of VA transactions, all of them answered this question and shared some restrictions, disclosures, or regulatory compliance requirements applicable to virtual asset transactions to their jurisdiction, such as:

- Complying with AML/CFT laws and measures set by their jurisdictions.
- Following regulatory standards comparable to those applicable to licensed FIs.
- Proceeding to a proper assessment of Know Your Customer (KYC) procedures.
- Identifying the origin of funds and the beneficiary of transactions.
- Understanding and monitoring business relationships.
- Gathering information on whether a person is a politically exposed person.
- Reporting suspicious transactions (STR).

4.1.2 Virtual Assets Defined

Amongst the participating FIUs, our analysis shows that:

- 36% of FIUs have a clear definition of VA.
- 26% of FIUs do not have any definitions regarding VA.
- 6% of FIUs unfortunately did not provide a reply to the question.
- 32% of FIUs gave alternative definitions of VA.

The results of this question show that there might be a gap in the proper understanding of what VAs are and which of them should be precisely regulated. This may lead to gaps in the overall reporting.

5. Encrypted Networks (Dark Web)
5.1 Use of Virtual Assets in Illicit Markets

Most FIUs who provided an answer to this specific question have significant experience in identifying the use of virtual assets in illicit markets (dark web). 16% of FIUs indicated not having information on the widespread use of virtual assets in illicit markets in their jurisdiction. However, the potential use of VAs as a tool to finance illicit activities is acknowledged well. One FIU noted that virtual assets as such are illegal in their corresponding jurisdiction.

In general, most FIUs have experience in identified use of virtual assets in illicit markets. Several FIUs regularly receive suspicious transaction reports related to the activity involving the use of virtual assets in the darknet. Investigations have led to particular darknet platforms where the common payment method includes cryptocurrency, the most popular being Bitcoin.

6. Virtual Currency Usage and Terrorist Financing Detection
6.1 Detecting and Analyzing Financial Transactions

Under the challenges related to the investigation process, there is a noted difficulty in identifying VASPs and obtaining KYC information.

In 2015, FATF expanded the risk-based approach to include operations involving virtual assets in its guidance. In 2018, the FATF amended Recommendation 15, extending AML standards to crypto businesses, including exchanges and wallet providers.

In 2019, the FATF updated its recommendations on virtual assets and issued an Interpretive Note to Recommendation 15. The documents addressed the definition of virtual assets service providers and their AML requirements, including customer due diligence, KYC, recordkeeping, transaction monitoring, suspicious transaction reporting, and applying the risk-based approach.

There is a need for strong international cooperation with partner FIUs, as mentioned by some of the FIUs, especially in cases where the VASP is registered in another jurisdiction. Cooperation with the INTERPOL and with the overseas LEAs was also noted for a better understanding of the asset recovery system and of legal frameworks in different jurisdictions.

Some of the FIUs indicated the need to enhance the legal framework to include the VAs. A small group of FIUs noted the plan to introduce a licencing regime for VASPs and subject them to a fit-and-proper test similar to that of other financial sectors.

7. Virtual Currency Usage and TF Detection

7.1 Challenges, Lessons Learned and Best Practices for FIUs

7.1.1 Use of Commercial Subscription Services to Gather Blockchain Intelligence

Many tools are available on the market to collect information on blockchain and to link wallets, virtual assets, and other technical data with a potential criminal user.

These various tools can be used by FIUs to improve their analyses as they provide tracing possibilities of transactions with VAs.

7.1.2 Determining Red Flag Indicators

As is the case in the traditional financial system, it is possible to observe certain potentially suspicious behaviour in the context of transactions that take place with Virtual Assets. Each suspicion concerning a transaction, an attempted transaction or knowledge of a fact in the customer's domain, must prompt the obliged entity to send an STR/SAR to the FIU.

To detect a potentially suspicious transaction, red flags can be used to cover many possible scenarios. These indicators can be used within transaction monitoring tools to automatically highlight any potential suspicious transactions.

However, to avoid having too much information to analyze that would turn out to be irrelevant, it is necessary to have red flag indicators that are as precise as possible and adapted to different scenarios. The idea is to have the lowest possible number of false positives. The red flag indicators must therefore act as a first filter to select certain potentially suspicious transactions.

The potentially suspicious transactions highlighted by the indicators combined with facts or additional elements obtained during the analysis of the client make it possible to determine whether there are sufficiently reasonable grounds to suspect that the transaction was carried out to commit or attempt to commit an ML/FT offence. A red flag indicator may not, on its own, be sufficient to determine whether an operation or transaction is truly suspicious.

In the context of cryptocurrencies, indicators relating to the financing of terrorism can be established. However, the difficulty lies in the fact that these indicators can sometimes be the same as those used to detect suspicious transactions in the context of money laundering.

Some red flag indicators can be more oriented in cases of terrorist financing, and some are part of a much broader context and can be linked to suspicions of money laundering as well as terrorist financing. The contribution of additional elements, in particular related to knowing the customer (KYC), is, therefore, all the more important to determine the suspicious nature of the transaction in the context of the financing of terrorism.

Geographical risks associated with exchange transactions usually take place via digital asset exchanges or brokers. The choice of digital asset exchanges and brokers for an exchange transaction should not be underestimated.

It was also noted from recent statements by a jihadist group that they have discontinued using VAs for fundraising purposes due to the "successful government efforts to identify and prosecute donors".

7.1.3 Modus Operandi Linked to Groups or Individuals

In general, in the context of terrorist financing, the difficulty of detection lies in the fact that the amounts transferred are often small and that this financing is not often directly linked to an individual or group involved in terrorism.

Due to this indirect nature of funding, the funds transferred through Virtual Assets can therefore move from one virtual address to another without being detected.

7.2 Identified Cases by the FIU Over the Past Five Years (2018–2022)

Of the FIUs that took part in the survey:

- 29% of the respondents have identified cases in which Virtual Assets were linked to terrorism financing.
- 71% of the respondents did not report any cases.

7.3 Identified Terrorist Organizations

Among the various FIUs that have been able to identify cases where Virtual Assets were used to conduct terrorist financing activities, different types of organisations (domestic or international) were found to be involved.

Most of the time, donors or supporters were identified as sending funds to individual or group addresses linked to terrorist organizations present in conflict zones, such as ISIL, Al-Qaeda, and other extremist groups, such as Hamas and the Al-Qassam Brigades.

Other cases concerned the sending of funds directly to cryptocurrency exchange platforms located in the Middle East having links to TF.

FIUs also observed the abuse of VA by individuals who support right-wing organizations and individuals known to be rooted in radical religious behaviour.

All the aforementioned information suggests that terrorist organizations and groups deliberately misuse VAs for their purposes.

8. Conclusion

Based on the above study, it is clear that VAs pose a potential threat for ML/TF. Understanding trends and sharing of best practices in emerging technologies will aid in the identification of potential vulnerabilities associated with new technologies.

While a limited number of FIUs submitted replies and case studies, the collected data represents a sufficient level of regional diversity. A majority of responding FIUs indicated that they have regulatory requirements regarding VA transactions, and it is compulsory to comply with the anti-money laundering and countering the financing of terrorism laws and measures set by their jurisdictions. Although the FATF amendments in R.15 introduced requirements regarding transactions and services with VAs in October 2018, a significant portion of the responding FIUs are still not regulating it.

Due to the nature of the VAs, they currently cannot be widely used for purchasing goods or services and, therefore, cannot provide an optimal capacity to serve as a medium of exchange. This is also important in TF cases because most terrorists are deprived of using their assets due to sanctions regimes or of keeping their criminal conspiracy. Therefore, for terrorists and their financiers, it would be of profound importance to be able to transform VAs into fiat currency anonymously and vice versa.

In general, most FIUs have experience in identifying the use of VA in illicit markets. Several FIUs regularly receive suspicious transaction reports related to the activity involving the use of Virtual Assets in the darknet.

Challenges include raising awareness of obliged entities and receiving STRs on VAs. In addition, FIUs mentioned that none of the STRs they have received involving VAs incorporate a TF aspect. There is a need for strong international cooperation with partner FIUs, especially in cases where the VASP is registered in another jurisdiction.

xviii) **Wolfsburg Group:** The Wolfsberg Group and the private initiative for developing develop frameworks and guidance for the management of financial crime risks.[25]

The Wolfsberg Group is an association of 12 global banks aiming to develop frameworks and guidance for the management of financial crime risks. The members are senior financial crime compliance leaders from member banks. They work jointly through various Working Groups to develop new documents or update existing ones, including the Correspondent Banking Due Diligence Questionnaire (CBDDQ)[26] which seeks to help Financial Institutions to conduct due diligence on Correspondent Banking relationships, as per regulatory requirements and to adopt internal policies and procedures.

Also, they note: the financial crime compliance sphere continues to evolve rapidly. Professionals in (the finance) industry can use our various user-friendly guidance documents and other resources to deepen their understanding of the issues and to meet both internal objectives and regulatory requirements.

Our materials provide you with an industry perspective on effective financial crime risk management. You will need to adapt them to your needs, considering the risks described, the applicable regulatory standards, your business profile and your institution's defined risk management strategy.[27]

---

[25] https://wolfsberg-group.org/about/

[26] https://db.wolfsberg-group.org/assets/3964cedf-a462-4e55-a1e7-ca7c70dfa7ec/CBDDQ%20v1.4.pdf

[27] https://wolfsberg-group.org/about/

xix) Wolfsberg Group: Statement on the Suppression of the Financing of Terrorism (2002)[28]

1 Preamble

The Wolfsberg Group of financial institutions (the "Wolfsberg Group")[29] is committed to contributing to the fight against terrorism and is making the following statement to describe the role of financial institutions in preventing the flow of terrorist funds through the worldís financial system.

This fight presents new challenges. Funds used in the financing of terrorism do not necessarily derive from criminal activity, which is a requisite element of most existing money laundering offences. Successful participation in this fight by the financial sector requires global cooperation by governments with the financial institutions to an unprecedented degree.

2. Role of Financial Institutions in the Fight Against Terrorism

Financial institutions can assist governments and their agencies in the fight against terrorism. They can help this effort through prevention, detection and information sharing. They should seek to prevent terrorist organizations from accessing their financial services, assist governments in their efforts to detect suspected terrorist financing and promptly respond to governmental enquiries.

3. Rights of the Individual

The Wolfsberg Group is committed to participating in the fight against terrorism in a manner which is non-discriminatory and is respectful of the rights of individuals.

4 Know Your Customer

The Wolfsberg Group recognises that adherence to existing ìKnow Your Customerî policies and procedures is important to the fight against terrorism. Specifically the proper identification of customers by financial institutions can improve the efficacy of searches against lists of known or suspected terrorists issued by competent authorities having jurisdiction over the relevant financial institution ("applicable lists").

In addition to the continued application of existing customer identification, acceptance and due diligence procedures, the Wolfsberg Group is committed to:

- Implementing procedures for consulting applicable lists and taking reasonable and practicable steps to determine whether a person involved in a prospective or existing business relationship appears on such a list.

---

[28] https://db.wolfsberg-group.org/assets/223bfb8c-6536-41e1-8f3c-6c9f7bebae8a

[29] The Wolfsberg Group consists of the following leading international banks ABN Amro N.V., Banco Santander Central Hispano, S.A., Bank of Tokyo-Mitsubishi, Ltd., Barclays Bank, Citigroup, Credit Suisse Group, Deutsche Bank AG, Goldman Sachs, HSBC, J.P. Morgan Chase, SociÈtÈ GÈnÈrale, UBS AG and became known when they, together with Transparency International and Mark Pieth, agreed to a set of global anti-money-laundering guidelines for international private banks in October 2000. Wolfsberg is the location in Switzerland where an important working session to formulate the guidelines was held.

- Reporting to the relevant authorities matches from lists of known or suspected terrorists or terrorist organisations consistent with applicable laws and regulations regarding the disclosure of customer information.
- Exploring with governmental agencies ways of improving information exchange within and between jurisdictions.
- Exploring ways of improving the maintenance of customer information to facilitate the timely retrieval of such information.

5 High Risk Sectors and Activities

The Wolfsberg Group is committed to applying enhanced and appropriate due diligence in relation to those of their customers engaged in sectors and activities which have been identified by competent authorities as being widely used for the financing of terrorism, such as underground banking businesses or alternative remittance systems. This will include the adoption, to the extent not already in place, of specific policies and procedures on acceptance of business from customers engaged in such sectors or activities, and increased monitoring of activity of customers who meet the relevant acceptance criteria.

In particular the Wolfsberg Group is committed to restricting their business relationships with remittance businesses, exchange houses, casas de cambio, bureaux de change and money transfer agents to those which are subject to appropriate regulation aimed at preventing such activities and businesses from being used as a conduit to launder the proceeds of crime and/or finance terrorism.

The Wolfsberg Group recognises that many jurisdictions are currently in the process of developing and implementing regulations with regard to these businesses and that appropriate time needs to be given for these regulations to take effect.

6 Monitoring

Recognising the difficulties inherent in identifying financial transactions linked to the financing of terrorism (many of which appear routine in relation to information known at the time) the Wolfsberg Group is committed to the continued application of existing monitoring procedures for identifying unusual or suspicious transactions. The Wolfsberg Group recognises that while the motive for such transactions may be unclear, monitoring and then identifying and reporting unusual or suspicious transactions may assist government agencies by linking seemingly unrelated activity to the financing of terrorism.

In addition, the Wolfsberg Group is committed to:

- Exercising heightened scrutiny in respect of customers engaged in sectors identified by competent authorities as being widely used for the financing of terrorism.
- Monitoring account and transactional activity (to the extent meaningful information is available to financial institutions) against lists generated by competent authorities of known or suspected terrorists or terrorist organisations.
- Working with governments and agencies in order to recognise patterns and trends identified as related to the financing of terrorism.
- Considering the modification of existing monitoring procedures as necessary to assist in the identification of such patterns and trends.

7 Need for Enhanced Global Co-operation

The Wolfsberg Group is committed to co-operating with and assisting law enforcement and government agencies in their efforts to combat the financing of terrorism. The Wolfsberg Group has identified the following areas for discussion with governmental agencies, with a view to enhancing the contribution financial institutions are able to make:

- The provision of official lists of suspected terrorists and terrorist organisations on a globally co-ordinated basis by the relevant competent authority in each jurisdiction.
- The inclusion of appropriate details and information in official lists to assist financial institutions in efficient and timely searches of their customer bases. This information should ideally include (where known) in the case of individuals: date of birth; place of birth; passport or identity card number; in the case of corporations; place of incorporation or establishment; details of principals; to the extent possible, reason for inclusion on the list; and geographic information, such as the location, date and time of the transaction.
- Providing prompt feedback to financial institutions on reports made following circulation of such official lists.
- The provision of meaningful information in relation to patterns, techniques and mechanisms used in the financing of terrorism to assist with monitoring procedures.
- The provision of meaningful information about corporate and other types of vehicles used to facilitate terrorist financing.
- The development of guidelines on appropriate levels of heightened scrutiny in relation to sectors or activities identified by competent authorities as being widely used for terrorist financing.
- The development by governments and clearing agencies of uniform global formats for funds transfers that require information which may assist their efforts to prevent and detect the financing of terrorism.
- Ensuring that national legislation:
- Permits financial institutions to maintain information derived from official lists within their own databases and to share such information within their own groups.
- Affords financial institutions protection from civil liability for relying on such lists.
- Permits financial institutions to report unusual or suspicious transactions that may relate to terrorism to the relevant authorities without breaching any duty of customer confidentiality or privacy legislation.
- Permits the prompt exchange of information between governmental agencies of different nation states.

The Wolfsberg Group supports the FATF Special Recommendations on Terrorist Financing as measures conducive to the suppression of the financing of terrorism.

xx) Wolfsberg Group Anti-Money Laundering Principles for Private Banking (2012)[30]

Preamble

The following Principles are understood to be appropriate for private banking relationships. Principles for other market segments may differ.

The Principles were initially formulated in 2000 (and revised in 2002) to take into account certain perceived risks associated with private banking. Such risks continue to warrant appropriate levels of attention, no less today than 10 years ago. Regulators continue to expect strong anti-money laundering ("AML") standards, robust controls, enhanced client due diligence and suitable AML policies and procedures. The Wolfsberg Group1 takes this opportunity to provide a further revision of the Principles.

The objectives of suitable AML policies and procedures are to prevent the use of the bank's worldwide operations for criminal purposes and to protect the firm's reputation. Such policies and procedures are designed to mitigate

the risk of money laundering and to cooperate with governments and their agencies in the detection of money laundering.

The bank will periodically assess the risk of its private banking business and the bank's Senior/Executive Management will be made aware of these risks. It is the responsibility of Senior/Executive Management of the bank to approve written policies and procedures to address these risks, reflecting a risk based approach and to oversee the implementation of these policies, procedures and relevant controls. Such policies and procedures will adhere to these Principles and will be periodically updated in light of relevant developments.

1 Client Acceptance: General Principles

1.1 General

The bank will endeavour to accept only those clients whose source of wealth and funds can be reasonably established to be legitimate. The primary responsibility for this lies with the private banker who sponsors the client for acceptance. Mere fulfilment of internal review procedures does not relieve the private banker of this basic responsibility. Bank policy will specify what such responsibility and sponsorship entail.

1.2 Identification and Verification of Identity

1.2.1 Client Identity

The bank will establish the identity of its clients and beneficial owners prior to establishing business relationships with such persons. Identity is generally established by obtaining the name, date of birth (in the case of individuals), address and such further information that may be required by the laws of the relevant jurisdictions.

---

[30] https://db.wolfsberg-group.org/assets/7d384fb4-8c82-4669-acb8-621aed03e928/Wolfsberg%20Private%20Banking%20Principles.pdf

1.2.2 Verification of Identity

The bank will take reasonable measures to verify identity when establishing a business relationship as noted below, subject to applicable local requirements.

- Natural persons: identity will be verified to the bank's satisfaction on the basis of official identity papers or other reliable, independent source documents, data, or information as may be appropriate under the circumstances.
- Corporations, partnerships, foundations: identity will be verified on the basis of documentary evidence of due organisation and existence.
- Trusts: identity will be verified on the basis of appropriate evidence of formation and existence or similar documentation. The identity of the trustees will be established and verified.

Identification documents, if used for verification purposes, must be current at the time of opening and copies of such documents will be obtained.

1.2.3 Beneficial Owner

Beneficial ownership, for AML purposes, must be established for all accounts. Beneficial owners will ordinarily include the individuals (i) who generally have ultimate control through ownership or other means over the funds in the account and/or (ii) who are the ultimate source of funds for the account and whose source of wealth should be subject to due diligence. Mere signature authority does not necessarily constitute control for these purposes. The meaning of beneficial ownership for purposes of determining who should be subject to due diligence is dependent on the circumstances and due diligence must be done on all beneficial owners identified in applying the following principles:

- Natural persons: when the account is in the name of an individual, the private banker must establish whether the client is acting on his/her own behalf. If doubt exists, the bank will establish the capacity in which and on whose behalf the accountholder is acting.
- Legal entities: where the client is a private investment company, the private banker will understand the structure of the company sufficiently to determine the provider of funds, the beneficial owner(s) of the assets held by the company and those with the power to give direction to the directors of the company. This principle applies regardless of whether the share capital is in registered or bearer form.[31]
- Trusts: where the client is a trust, the private banker will understand the structure of the trust sufficiently to determine (i) the provider of funds (e.g. settlor), (ii) those who have control over the funds (e.g. trustees), (iii) any persons or entities who have the power to remove the trustees and (iv) the persons for whose benefit the trust is established.
- Partnerships: where the client is a partnership, the private banker will understand the structure of the partnership sufficiently to determine the provider of funds and the general partners.

[31] Legal entities that are operating companies are not addressed in these Principles.

- Foundations: where the client is a foundation, the private banker will understand the structure of the foundation sufficiently to determine the provider(s) of funds and how the foundation is managed.
- Unincorporated associations: the above principles apply to unincorporated associations.

In each of the above cases, the private banker will make a reasonable judgment as to the need for further due diligence.

Local law may characterise beneficial owners by reference to specific minimum levels of ownership.

The identity of each beneficial owner will be established and, as appropriate, verified unless the identity is previously verified in accordance with the beneficial owner's role as a client. Identity will be verified to the bank's satisfaction on the basis of official identity papers or other reliable, independent source documents, data, or information as may be appropriate under the circumstances. In the event verification is based on identity papers, copies of such identity papers should be obtained.

"Beneficial ownership," as that term may be used for other purposes, may have different meanings.

1.2.4 Intermediaries

The nature of the relationship of the bank with an intermediary depends on the type of intermediary involved:

Introducing Intermediary: an introducing intermediary introduces clients to the bank, whereupon the introducing intermediary's clients become clients of the bank. The bank will generally obtain the same type of information with respect to an introduced client that would otherwise be obtained by the bank, absent the involvement of an introducing intermediary. The bank's policies will address the circumstances in, and the extent to, which, the bank may rely on the introducing intermediary in obtaining this information.

Managing Intermediary: a managing intermediary acts as a professional asset manager for another person and either (i) is authorised to act in connection with an account that such person has with the bank (in which case the considerations noted above with respect to introducing intermediaries would apply); or (ii) is itself the accountholder with the bank, to be treated as the client of the bank.

The private banker will perform due diligence on the introducing or managing intermediary and establish, as appropriate, that the intermediary has relevant due diligence procedures for its clients, or a regulatory obligation to conduct such due diligence, that is satisfactory to the bank.

1.2.5 Powers of Attorney/Authorised Signers

The relationship between the holder of a power of attorney or another authorised signer, the accountholder and if different, the beneficial owner of the account, must be understood.

The identity of a holder of general powers over an account (such as the power to act as a signatory for the account) will be established and, as appropriate, verified.

1.2.6 Practices for Walk-In Clients and Electronic Banking Relationships

A bank will determine whether walk-in clients or relationships initiated through electronic channels require a higher degree of due diligence prior to account opening. The bank will specifically address measures to satisfactorily establish and verify the identity of non-face-to-face customers.

1.3 Due Diligence

In addition to the information contemplated in 1.2, it is essential to collect and record information covering the client profile categories outlined in Appendix I.

Applying a risk based approach, the bank will corroborate the information set forth in Appendix I on the basis of documentary evidence or reliable sources. Unless other measures reasonably suffice to conduct the due diligence on a client (e.g. favourable and reliable references), a client will be met prior to account opening, at which time, if identity is verified on the basis of official identity documents, such documents will be reviewed.

1.4 Numbered or Alternate Name Accounts

Numbered or alternate name accounts will only be accepted if the bank has established the identity of the client and the beneficial owner. These accounts must be open to a level of scrutiny by the bank's appropriate control layers equal to the level of scrutiny applicable to other client accounts. Wire transfers from these accounts must reflect the true name of the accountholder.

1.5 Concentration Accounts

The bank will not permit the use of its internal non-client accounts (sometimes referred to as "concentration" accounts) to prevent association of the identity of a client with the movement of funds on the client's behalf, i.e., the bank will not permit the use of such internal accounts in a manner that would prevent the bank from appropriately monitoring the client's account activity.

1.6 Oversight Responsibility

There will be a requirement that new clients, subject to a risk based approach, be approved by at least one person other than the private banker.

2 Client Acceptance: Situations requiring Additional Diligence/Attention; Prohibited Customers

2.1 Prohibited Customers

The bank will specify categories of customers that it will not accept or maintain.

2.2 General

In its internal policies, the bank must define categories of persons whose circumstances warrant enhanced due diligence. This will typically be the case where the circumstances are likely to pose a higher than average risk to a bank.

2.3 Indicators

The circumstances of the following categories of persons are indicators for defining them as requiring Enhanced Due Diligence:

- Persons residing in and/or having funds sourced from countries identified by credible sources as having inadequate AML standards or representing high risk for crime and corruption.
- Persons engaged in types of economic or business activities or sectors known to be susceptible to money laundering.
- "Politically Exposed Persons," frequently abbreviated as "PEPs" referring to individuals holding or, as appropriate, having held, senior, prominent, or important public positions with substantial authority over policy, operations or the use or allocation of government-owned resources, such as senior government officials, senior executives of government corporations, senior politicians, important political party officials, etc., as well as their close family and close associates. PEPs from different jurisdictions may be subject to different levels of diligence.[32]

Clients who are not deemed to warrant enhanced due diligence may be subjected to greater scrutiny as a result of (i) monitoring of their activities, (ii) external inquiries, (iii) derogatory information (e.g. negative media reports) or (iv) other factors which may expose the bank to reputational risk.

2.4 Senior Management Approval

The bank's internal policies should indicate whether, for any one or more among these categories, Senior Management must approve entering into new relationships. Relationships with Politically Exposed Persons may only be entered into with the approval of Senior Management.

2.5 Cash Handling

The bank's policies and procedures will address client cash transactions, including specifically the receipt and withdrawal of large amounts of cash.

3 Updating Client Files

The private banker is responsible for updating the client file on a defined basis and/or when there are major changes. The private banker's supervisor or an independent control person will review relevant portions of client files on a regular basis to ensure consistency and completeness. The frequency of the reviews depends on the size, complexity and risk posed by the relationship.

With respect to clients classified under any category of persons mentioned in 2, the bank's internal policies will indicate whether Senior Management must be involved in these reviews and what management information must be provided to

[32]For more information regarding Politically Exposed Persons, please see the Wolfsberg Group's "Wolfsberg Frequently Asked Questions ("FAQs") on Politically Exposed Persons ("PEPs")" available at http://www.wolfsberg-principles.com/pdf/PEP-FAQ-052008.pdf.

management and/or other control layers. The policies and/or procedures should also address the frequency of these information flows.

Reviews of PEPs must require Senior Management's involvement.

4 Practices when identifying Unusual or Suspicious Activities
4.1 Definition of Unusual or Suspicious Activities

The bank will have a written policy on the identification of, and follow-up on, unusual or suspicious activities. This policy and/or related procedures will include a definition of what is considered to be suspicious or unusual and give examples thereof.

Unusual or suspicious activities may include:

- Account transactions or other activities which are not consistent with the due diligence file
- Cash transactions over a certain amount
- Pass-through / in-and-out-transactions.

4.2 Identification of Unusual or Suspicious Activities

Unusual or suspicious activities can be identified through:

- Monitoring of transactions
- Client contacts (meetings, discussions, in-country visits etc.)
- Third party information (e.g. newspapers, other media sources, internet)
- Private banker's internal knowledge of the client's environment (e.g. political situation in his/her country).

4.3 Follow-up on Unusual or Suspicious Activities

The private banker, management and/or the control function will carry out an analysis of the background of any unusual or suspicious activity. If there is no plausible explanation a decision involving the control function will be made to:

- continue the business relationship with increased monitoring
- cancel the business relationship
- report the business relationship to the Authorities.

The report to the Authorities is made by the control function and Senior Management may need to be notified (e.g. Senior Compliance Officer, CEO, Chief Auditor, General Counsel). As required by local laws and regulations, the assets may be blocked and transactions may be subject to approval by the control function.

5 Monitoring and Screening
5.1 Monitoring Programme

The primary responsibility for reviewing account activities lies with the private banker. The private banker will be familiar with significant transactions and increased activity in the account and will be especially aware of unusual or suspicious activities (see 4.1). In addition, a sufficient monitoring programme must be in place. The bank will decide to what extent fulfilment of this responsibility will need to be supported through the use of automated systems or other means.

5.2 Ongoing Monitoring

With respect to clients classified under any category of persons mentioned in 2, the bank's internal policies will indicate how the account activities will be subject to monitoring.

5.3 Sanctions Screening

A sufficient Sanctions Programme must be in place. Prospective clients must be screened on the basis of applicable sanctions and existing clients must be screened as applicable sanctions are updated. Transactions must be screened on the basis of applicable sanctions.

6 No Inappropriate Assistance

Neither the private banker, nor any other bank employee, will provide clients with any assistance with the knowledge that such assistance will be used to deceive Authorities, including Tax Authorities.

7 Control Responsibilities

The bank's policies and procedures will include standard controls to be undertaken by the various "control layers" (private banker, line management, independent operations unit, Compliance, Internal Audit). These controls will cover issues of frequency, degree of control, areas to be controlled, responsibilities and follow-up, compliance testing, etc.

An independent audit function (which may be internal to the bank) will test the programmes contemplated by these controls.

8 Reporting

There will be regular management reporting established on money laundering issues (e.g. number of reports to authorities, monitoring tools, changes in applicable laws and regulations, the number and scope of training sessions provided to employees).

9 Education, Training and Information

The bank will establish a training programme on the identification and prevention of money laundering for employees who have client contact and for Compliance personnel. Regular training (e.g. annually) will also include

how to identify and follow-up on unusual or suspicious activities. In addition, employees will be informed about any major changes in AML laws and regulations.

All new employees will be provided with guidelines on the AML procedures.

10 Record Retention Requirements

The bank will establish record retention requirements for all AML related documents. The documents must be kept for a minimum of 5 years, or longer, as may be required by local law and regulation.

11 Exceptions and Deviations

The bank will establish an exception and deviation procedure that requires risk assessment and approval by an independent unit.

12 AML Organisation

The bank will establish an adequately staffed and independent department responsible for the prevention of money laundering (e.g. Compliance, independent control unit, Legal).

Appendix I Due Diligence of New Clients and Principal Beneficial Owners

Using a risk-based approach, the bank must ensure that it collects and records a sufficient amount of pertinent information when establishing a business relationship and must update the client profile with additional information as the relationship develops. The information should enable an independent reviewer (whether internal or external to the bank) to understand the client and the relationship on the basis of the information recorded. In the event the client is not the beneficial owner, not all of the information contemplated by this Appendix will be obtained with respect to the client; however, in these circumstances, the relevant information will be obtained with respect to the beneficial owner(s).

Source of Wealth

In order to evaluate the source of a client's (or beneficial owner's) wealth, the bank should gather information relevant to the manner in which the wealth was obtained. For example, the information collected by the bank will differ depending on whether the wealth was acquired through ownership of a business, employment or professional practice, inheritance, investments or otherwise.

Net Worth

Source of Initial Funding of Account

The financial institution and jurisdiction from which the assets funding the account will be transmitted (e.g. a transfer from the client's account at another financial institution). This is distinct from an explanation of the source of wealth.

Account Information

- Purpose for Account
- Expected Account Size
- Expected Account Activity

Occupation

Nature of Client's (or Beneficial Owner's) Business

Role/Relationship of Powers of Attorney or Authorised Third Parties

Other Pertinent Information (e.g. Source of Referral)

xxi) **Basel Committee on Banking Supervision (BCBS) Guidelines:** Sound management of risks related to money laundering and financing of terrorism

BCBS have published the following updated (in 2020) Guidelines for Sound Management of Risks related to Money Laundering and Financing of Terrorism[33]:

[33] https://www.bis.org/bcbs/publ/d505.pdf

1. Introduction

1. Being aware of the risks incurred by banks of being used, intentionally or unintentionally, for criminal activities, the Basel Committee on Banking Supervision is issuing these guidelines to describe how banks should include money laundering (ML) and financing of terrorism (FT) risks within their overall risk management.
2. The Committee has a long-standing commitment to promote the implementation of sound Anti-Money Laundering and Countering Financing of Terrorism (AML/CFT) policies and procedures that are critical in protecting the safety and soundness of banks and the integrity of the international financial system. Following an initial statement in 1988,[34] it has published several documents in support of this commitment. In September 2012, the Committee reaffirmed its stance by publishing the revised version of the Core principles for effective banking supervision, in which a dedicated principle (BCP 29) deals with the abuse of financial services.
3. The Committee supports the adoption of the standards issued by the Financial Action Task Force (FATF).[35] In February 2012, the FATF released a revised version of the International Standards on Combating Money Laundering and the Financing of Terrorism and Proliferation (the FATF standards), to which the Committee provided input.[36] In March 2013, the FATF also issued Financial Inclusion Guidance, which has also been considered by the Committee in drafting these guidelines. The Committee's intention in issuing this paper is to support national implementation of the FATF standards by exploring complementary areas and leveraging the expertise of both organisations. These guidelines embody both the FATF standards and the Basel Core Principles for banks operating across borders and fits into the overall framework of banking supervision. Therefore, these guidelines are intended to be consistent with and to supplement the goals and objectives of the FATF standards, and in no way should they be interpreted as modifying the FATF standards, either by strengthening or weakening them.

[34] See BCBS, Prevention of criminal use of the banking system for the purpose of money-laundering, December 1988, accessible at www.bis.org/publ/bcbsc137.pdf

[35] The FATF is an intergovernmental body that develops international standards and promotes policies to protect the global financial system against money laundering, terrorist financing and the financing of proliferation of weapons of mass destruction. The FATF defines money laundering as the processing of criminal proceeds in order to disguise their illegal origin. The FATF works in close cooperation with other entities involved in this area, and in particular FATF associate members and observers. The Committee has observer status within the FATF.

[36] Annex 3 contains an excerpt of the most relevant FATF Recommendations that banks and supervisors should comply with when implementing their AML/CFT measures. This is not exhaustive and other FATF Recommendations, including the Interpretive Notes, may be relevant. The full document is accessible at www.fatf-gafi.org/recommendations.

4. In some instances, the Committee has included cross-references to FATF standards in this document in order to assist banks in complying with national requirements based on the implementation of those standards. However, as the Committee's intention is not to simply duplicate the existing FATF standards, cross-references are not included as a matter of routine.
5. The Committee's commitment to combating money laundering and the financing of terrorism is fully aligned with its mandate "to strengthen the regulation, supervision and practices of banks worldwidewith the purpose of enhancing financial stability".[37] Sound ML/FT risk management has particular relevance to the overall safety and soundness of banks and of the banking system, the primary objective for banking supervision, in that:

   - it helps protect the reputation of both banks and national banking systems by preventing and deterring the use of banks to launder illicit proceeds or to raise or move funds in support of terrorism; and
   - it preserves the integrity of the international financial system as well as the work of governments in addressing corruption and in combating the financing of terrorism.

6. The inadequacy or absence of sound ML/FT risk management exposes banks to serious risks, especially reputational, operational, compliance and concentration risks. Recent developments, including robust enforcement actions taken by regulators and the corresponding direct and indirect costs incurred by banks due to their lack of diligence in applying appropriate risk management policies, procedures and controls, have highlighted those risks. These costs and damage could probably have been avoided had the banks maintained effective risk-based AML/CFT policies and procedures.
7. It is worth noting that all these risks are interrelated. However, in addition to incurring fines and sanctions by regulators, any one of them could result in significant financial costs to banks (eg through the termination of wholesale funding and facilities, claims against the bank, investigation costs, asset seizures and freezes, and loan losses), as well as the diversion of limited and valuable management time and operational resources to resolve problems.
8. Consequently, this paper should be read in conjunction with a number of related Committee papers, including the following:

   - Core principles for effective banking supervision, September 2012[38]
   - The internal audit function in banks, June 2012[39]
   - Principles for the sound management of operational risk, June 2011[40]

[37] See Basel Committee on Banking Supervision, Charter, June 2018, accessible at www.bis.org/bcbs/charter.htm

[38] Accessible at: www.bis.org/publ/bcbs230.pdf

[39] Accessible at: www.bis.org/publ/bcbs223.pdf

[40] Accessible at: www.bis.org/publ/bcbs195.pdf

- Corporate governance principles for banks, July 2015[41]
- Due diligence and transparency regarding cover payment messages related to cross-border wire transfers, May 2009[42]
- Compliance and the compliance function in banks, April 2005[43]
- Principles for effective supervisory colleges, June 2014[44]

9. In an effort to rationalise the Committee's publications on AML/CFT guidance, this document merges and supersedes two of the Committee's previous publications dealing with related topics: *Customer due diligence for banks*, October 2001 and Consolidated KYC risk management, October 2004. In updating these papers, the Committee has also increased its focus on risks associated with the usage by banks of third parties to introduce business (see Annex 1) and the provision of correspondent banking services (see Annex 2). Despite their importance and relevance, other specific risk areas such as politically exposed persons (PEPs), private banking and specific legal structures that were addressed in the previous papers have not been specifically developed in this guidance, since they are the subject of existing FATF publications.[45] In February 2016, this document was revised with a general guide to account opening (see Annex 4). Revisions to Annexes 2 (Correspondent banking) and 4 (General guide to account opening) issued in June 2017 guide the banks in the application of the risk-based approach for correspondent banking relationships, recognising that not all correspondent banking relationships bear the same level of risk and including an updated list of risk indicators that correspondent banks should consider in their risk assessment.
10. With respect to the scope of application, these guidelines should be read in conjunction with other standards and guidelines produced by the Committee that promote supervision of banking groups on a consolidated level.[46] This is particularly relevant in the context of AML/CFT since customers frequently have multiple relationships and/or accounts with the same banking group, but in offices located in different countries.

xxii) **International Organisation for Standardisation (ISO) 20022**[47]

ISO 2022 provides a "single standardisation approach (methodology, process, repository) to be used by all financial standards initiatives" which makes it easier for organisations to screen for sanctioned, embargoed entities or politically exposed persons (PEPs):

---

[41] Accessible at: https://www.bis.org/bcbs/publ/d328.pdf

[42] Accessible at: www.bis.org/publ/bcbs154.pdf

[43] Accessible at: www.bis.org/publ/bcbs113.pdf

[44] Accessible at: https://www.bis.org/publ/bcbs287.pdf

[45] See in particular the *FATF Guidance on Politically Exposed Persons* (recommendations 12 and 22), accessible at www.fatf-gafi.org/fr/documents/documents/peps-r12-r22.html

[46] See for example BCP 12 in *Core principles for effective banking supervision*, September 2012.

[47] https://www.iso20022.org

When financial institutions exchange payments, they must also exchange essential data associated with them—for example, the payment amount, currency, sender and receiver, intermediary institution details, and other important information. This information needs to be structured to be usable by a firm. Unfortunately, the standards used to structure this data—and even to determine what data to include in the first place—have historically varied among firms, creating inconsistencies and introducing friction in the payment lifecycle. Financial institutions must often translate the data exchanged into a format that matches their standard in order to perform transactions. The lack of a central standard can lead to inefficiencies—and even misinterpreted information...

ISO 20022 is a standard ... that helps financial institutions more reliably structure the data they exchange with each other during a transaction. It seeks to improve these data exchanges by creating a shared global standard between financial institutions to make the process clearer, faster, and more data-rich.

With this in mind, what benefits might these efficiency gains offer to firms—both at a business level and, more particularly, at the level of anti-money laundering and countering of terrorist financing (AML/CFT)?

The Benefits of ISO 20022

Although ISO 20022 can be used as a common standard, it also helps firms using different standards communicate better...

Key Benefits to AML/CFT and Financial Crime Risk Management

Economist Dave Ramsden, Bank of England Deputy Director for Markets and Banking, situated ISO 20022's benefits in the context of the "G20/FSB Roadmap on cross-border payments," which focuses "on how a more effective use of and greater standardization of data could help to streamline AML/CFT and sanctions compliance." Indeed, the new open data standard's benefits have several specific applications to AML/CFT. Three key compliance areas especially stand to benefit from the standard:

The Travel Rule (FATF R.16): ISO 20022 can potentially enhance firms' compliance with this Financial Action Task Force (FATF) rule by enriching the available data and structuring it in a more accessible and standardized manner. The rule requires countries to collect identifying information from the originators and beneficiaries of domestic and cross-border wire transfers to ensure a reliable AML/CFT audit trail.

Transaction monitoring: As the new messaging standard becomes more widespread, transaction monitoring systems will have access to richer and more standardized data. This will help fight money laundering and other predicate crimes, such as fraud, while also reducing false positives caused by misread or missing data fields, resulting in more reliable transaction monitoring alerts...

xxiii) **Basel Institute on Governance AML Index**[48]

For the last decade, Basel Institute has produced an AML Index which ranks the money laundering and terrorist financing risks of countries around the world.[49]

The Basel AML Index ranks global jurisdictions according to their risks of ML/TF based on a composite index of 18 indicators of ML/TF risk in five domains:

1. Quality of AML / CFT Framework
2. Bribery and Corruption
3. Financial Transparency and Standards
4. Public Transparency and Accountability
5. Legal and Political Risks

xxiv) **Transparency International Knowledge Hub/U4 Helpdesk article** by S. Elsayed (March 2023): Cryptocurrencies, corruption and organised crime—Implications of the growing use of cryptocurrencies in enabling illicit finance and corruption[50]

Cryptocurrency is becoming an increasingly popular tool for organised crime groups (OCGs) to conduct illicit activities. OCGs can exploit the inherent pseudonymity and decentralised nature of cryptocurrencies to conduct money laundering and other crimes related to corruption. Criminals can use cryptocurrencies instead of the formal banking system to move large sums of money which entails a potentially lower risk of being detected by law enforcement or the traditional financial institutions which are required to submit suspicious transaction reports.

The development sector can play an important role in mitigating the risks associated with the criminal use of cryptocurrency. Relevant actions include coordinating the development and implementation of regulatory and legislative frameworks, educating the public about the risks of cryptocurrency use and strengthening law enforcement agencies' capacity to dismantle criminal networks . . .

Main points

- Cryptocurrency is not only restricted to cybercrime but is used for all types of crimes that involve the transmission of monetary value. This includes money laundering, financial sanctions evasions and other corruption related crimes such as bribery and embezzlement.
- There are constraints associated with the use of cryptocurrencies in criminal activities, such as the volatile value fluctuations, which contribute to the reluctance of criminals to use cryptocurrencies for long-term investments.

---

[48] https://index.baselgovernance.org

[49] The Index for 2023 is at: https://index.baselgovernance.org/api/uploads/Basel_AML_Index_2023_12th_Edition_879b07b7b2.pdf

[50] This is an excerpt; the full article is at: https://knowledgehub.transparency.org/helpdesk/cryptocurrencies-corruption-and-organised-crime-implications-of-the-growing-use-of-cryptocurrencies-in-enabling-illicit-finance-and-corruption

- International development agencies can play a role in mitigating the criminal use of cryptocurrencies. This includes coordinating the development and implementation of regulatory and legislative frameworks, encouraging bilateral and multilateral coordination to establish networks for experience sharing, and supporting platforms for public-private collaboration.
- However, resources spent by donors to curb crypto-related corruption imply an opportunity cost. Donors will need to determine whether the same resources would be better spent on improving traditional law enforcement practices or other development priorities.
- This is a pertinent consideration given that although the use of cryptocurrency in criminal activities is increasing, cryptocurrency transactions related to criminal activities represent only a limited share of the criminal economy compared to cash.

xiv) **Blockchain**—virtual currencies[51]

Blockchain technology records and confirms cryptocurrency trades, much like a digital ledger. A blockchain collects and stores the information when you buy, sell, or exchange cryptocurrency. This information stays in a secure location that's not under a centralized government overseeing or controlling the cryptocurrency market. Many professionals consider crypto coins a "global currency" because they hold the same value worldwide.

With blockchain technology, each transaction or piece of data is stored as a "block." You then add this block to the existing chain of blocks to create a chronological picture of all activity. The blockchain is secure and transparent, so each block is irreversible and viewable by everyone.

Blockchain in Cryptocurrency

Bitcoin, Ethereum, and other wide-scale cryptocurrency coins use blockchain to process and record transactions securely. This remains the primary use of the technology. However, it is making its way into projects outside of cryptocurrency. Understanding how these blocks are coded and how different industries may benefit from this application can help you market yourself to new roles in this field.

xxv) **World Bank article**: Money Laundering and International Efforts to Fight It In Public Policy for the Financial Sector, Note 48[52]

Although money laundering is impossible to measure with precision, it is estimated that US$300 billion to US$500 billion in proceeds from serious crime (not tax evasion) is laundered each year.

---

[51] https://www.blockchain.com . This is an excerpt from a note at: https://www.coursera.org/articles/blockchain-cryptocurrency#. See also the FCPA Blog article by Selva Ozelli dated February 12 2020 entitled: Qatar bans cryptocurrencies after updating its AML laws

[52] This article (dated May 1995) by David Scott provides a historical perspective on early attempts to combat money laundering and terrorist financing. The full article is at: https://documents1.worldbank.org/curated/en/900151468762300572/pdf/16907-Replacement-file-048SCOTT.pdf

Measures in major financial markets to detect and prosecute laundering are driving it toward less developed markets linked to the global financial system. If left unchecked, money laundering could criminalize the financial system and undermine development efforts in emerging markets. This Note surveys efforts by international bodies to combat money laundering. It looks in particular at the Financial Action Task Force based at the OECD, which has made the most continuous effort.

How Money is Laundered

In money laundering, the proceeds of crime are run through the financial system to disguise their illegal origins and make them appear to be legitimate funds. Most often associated with organized crime, money laundering can be linked to any crime that generates significant proceeds, such as extortion, drug trafficking, arms smuggling, and white collar crime. Although money laundering often involves a complex series of transactions, it generally includes three basic steps.

The first step is the physical disposal of cash.

This placement might be accomplished by depositing the cash in domestic banks or, increasingly, in other types of formal or informal financial institutions. Or the cash might be shipped across borders for deposit in foreign financial institutions, or used to buy high-value goods, such as artwork, airplanes, and precious metals and stones, that can then be resold for payment by check or bank transfer.

The second step in money laundering is known as layering, carrying out complex layers of financial transactions to separate the illicit proceeds from their source and disguise the audit trail. This phase can involve such transactions as the wire transfer of deposited cash, the conversion of deposited cash into monetary instruments (bonds, stocks, traveler's checks), the resale of high-value goods and monetary instruments, and investment in real estate and legitimate businesses, particularly in the leisure and tourism industries. Shell companies, typically registered in offshore havens, are a common tool in the layering phase.

These companies, whose directors often are local attorneys acting as nominees, obscure the beneficial owners through restrictive bank secrecy laws and attorney-client privilege.

The last step is to make the wealth derived from the illicit proceeds appear legitimate. This integration might involve any number of techniques, such as using front companies to "lend" the proceeds back to the owner or using funds on deposit in foreign financial institutions as security for domestic loans. Another common technique is over invoicing or producing false invoices for goods sold—or supposedly sold—across borders.

Exposed Emerging Markets

Money laundering is a problem not only in the world's major financial markets and offshore centers. Any country integrated into the international financial system is at risk. As emerging markets open their economies and financial sectors, they become increasingly viable targets for money laundering activity. Increased efforts by authorities in the major financial markets and in many offshore financial centers to combat this activity provide further incentive for launderers to shift activities to emerging markets. There is evidence, for example, of increasing cross-border cash shipments to markets with loose arrangements for detecting and recording the placement of cash in the financial system and of growing investment by organized crime groups in real estate and businesses in emerging markets.

International Accords

Concerted efforts by governments to fight money laundering have been going on for the past 15 years. The main international agreements addressing money laundering are the United Nations Vienna Convention against Illicit Traffic in Narcotic Drugs and Psychotropic Substances (the Vienna Convention) and the 1990 Council of Europe Convention on Laundering, Search, Seizure and Confiscation of the Proceeds of Crime. And the role of financial institutions in preventing and detecting money laundering has been the subject of pronouncements by the Basle Committee on Banking Supervision, the European Union, and the International Organization of Securities Commissions.

The Vienna Convention

The Vienna Convention, adopted in December 1988, lays the groundwork for efforts to combat money laundering by creating an obligation for signatory states to criminalize the laundering of money from drug trafficking. It promotes international cooperation in investigations and makes extradition between signatory states applicable to money laundering. And it establishes the principle that domestic bank secrecy provisions should not interfere with international criminal investigations.

The 1990 Council of Europe Convention

Adopted in November 1990, the Council of Europe Convention establishes a common criminal policy on money laundering. It sets out a common definition of money laundering and common measures for dealing with it. The convention lays down the principles for international cooperation among the contracting parties, which may include states outside the Council of Europe. Its scope is not limited to money from drug trafficking.

Basle Committee Statement of Principles

In December 1988, the G-10's Basle Committee on Banking Supervision issued a "statement of principles" with which the international banks of member states are expected to comply. These principles cover identifying customers, avoiding suspicious transactions, and cooperating with law enforcement agencies. In issuing these principles, the committee noted the risk to public confidence in banks, and thus to their stability, that can arise if they inadvertently become associated with money laundering.

European Union Directive

In June 1991, the Council of the European Communities adopted a directive on the "Prevention of the Use of the Financial System for the Purpose of Money Laundering." This directive was issued in response to the new opportunities for money laundering opened up by the liberalization of capital movements and cross border financial services in the European Union. The directive obligates member states to outlaw money laundering. They must require financial institutions to establish and maintain internal systems to prevent laundering, to obtain the identification of customers with whom they enter into transactions of more than ECU 15,000, and to keep proper records for at least 5 years. Member states must also require financial institutions to report suspicious transactions and must ensure that such reporting does not result in liability for the institution or its employees.

Resolution of the International Organization of Securities Commissions

The International Organization of Securities Commissions (IOSCO) adopted, in October 1992, a report and resolution encouraging its members to take necessary steps to combat money laundering in securities and futures markets. A working group of IOSCO's Consultative Committee has been set up to collect information from IOSCO members' self-regulatory organizations and exchanges on their efforts to encourage their own members to fight money laundering.

The Financial Action Task Force

The main international body engaged in continuous, comprehensive efforts both to definepolicy and to promote the adoption of countermeasures against money laundering is the Financial Action Task Force (FATF). The FATF, set up by the governments of the G-7 countries at their 1989 Economic Summit, has representatives from twenty-four OECD countries, Hong Kong, Singapore, the Gulf Cooperation Council, and the European Commission. Participants include representatives from members' financial regulatory authorities, law enforcement agencies, and ministries of finance, justice, and external affairs. Representatives of international and regional organizations concerned with combating money laundering also attend FATF meetings as observers.

The FATF has pursued three main tasks:

- Monitoring members' progress in applying measures to counter money laundering.
- Reviewing money laundering techniques and countermeasures.
- Promoting the adoption and implementation of appropriate measures by nonmember countries.

A cornerstone of the FATF's efforts is its detailed definition of appropriate countermeasures for countries to use. These measures are set out in the "Forty Recommendations" formulated and adopted by the group in 1990.

The Forty Recommendations

The Forty Recommendations address four general themes:

- The overall context, in which the recommendations urge member countries to ratify the Vienna Convention, to ensure that financial institution secrecy laws do not inhibit implementation of the recommendations, and to promote multilateral cooperation and mutual assistance in investigations, prosecutions, and extraditions.
- The legal framework, in which the recommendations require the criminalization of laundering the proceeds of drug-related crimes, encourage the coverage of all serious crimes or all crimes that generate large proceeds, and promote provisions

allowing the freezing, seizing, and confiscation of property related to laundered funds.

- The role of the financial system, in which the recommendations define roles for banks, life insurance companies, and other nonbank financial institutions, as well as financial regulatory authorities. The role envisioned for financial institutions is identifying their customers, maintaining records sufficient to allow the reconstruction of transactions, and making these records available to the right authorities for criminal investigations and prosecutions. The recommendations thus imply that financial institutions should not keep anonymous accounts. The recommendations encourage institutions to make a serious effort to identify and report suspicious activities and to adopt good internal policies, procedures, and controls. And they encourage states to adopt legal provisions protecting institutions and their employees from legal liability for reporting suspicious activity in good faith. The authorities are supposed to ensure that financial institutions have put in place adequate internal safeguards against money laundering. And states are to take legal or regulatory measures to prevent criminals from getting control of financial institutions.
- The strengthening of international cooperation, in which the recommendations encourage authorities to exchange information on currency flows and money laundering techniques and on suspicious transactions or operations. International cooperation should be supported by bilateral and multilateral agreements based on generally shared legal concepts. Cooperation and mutual assistance should include the production of records by financial institutions, the identification, freezing, seizure, and confiscation of criminal proceeds, and extraditions and prosecutions.

The Discipline of Self-assessment and Peer Review

The FATF has two mechanisms for promoting effective action by member states. The first is a self-assessment by authorities in each state to evaluate the state's progress in implementing the Forty Recommendations. The second is a peer review. Both have proved highly effective in highlighting weaknesses in states' legal frameworks and procedures and in generating support for needed improvements.

Self-assessment. The self-assessment is based on a detailed questionnaire developed by the FATF in 1991 and periodically revised to take account of developments in laundering techniques. The questionnaire is designed to elicit objective indicators of whether recommendations have been implemented and how they have been implemented. Each member completes the questionnaire once a year.

Peer evaluation. In the peer evaluation, a team of representatives from at least three member governments reviews the performance of another member government. The evaluation team, reviews information submitted by the government and verifies and supplements that information through on-site visits and interviews. Under the guidance of the evaluation team, the FATF secretariat writes a draft confidential report, which is discussed with the member in meetings with other FATF members.

The final report gives a confidential assessment of how well the member is adhering to the recommendations and identifies areas needing further work.

Training and Support Network
The goals of the FATF are, first, to persuade all countries with important financial centers to endorse and implement its recommendations and, second, to support those countries' efforts.

The FATF runs international seminars on combating money laundering and sends missions to countries to encourage the adoption of its recommendations. The FATF also acts as a clearinghouse for requests from nonmember countries for training and technical assistance. With the help of the FATF, a separate task force has been established for governments of the Caribbean and the Caribbean rim. The FATF has also recently set up an Asian secretariat to work with governments in that region.

World Bank Operations
Emerging markets are increasingly becoming the venue for large-scale money laundering operations. If left unchecked, this activity eventually will undermine the credibility of the formal financial sector. In its financial sector operations, the World Bank can promote measures to counter the flow of illicit funds into the financial systems of countries and arrange for external assistance. In doing so, the Bank needs to recognize that measures to prevent and detect money laundering activities cannot focus only on banks. Effective measures must also address the formal securities, insurance, and money changing sectors.

xxvi) **EIB Group's Policy on Anti-Money Laundering and Combatting the Financing of Terrorism** (dated July 2021)[53]

1 Introduction

ML, TF, and tax crimes undermine, among others, the stability and integrity of financial systems, the efforts by governments to ensure sustainable development of their economies and their ability to collect adequate public revenues. The EU, its institutions, and its bodies are strongly committed to the fight against ML/TF both within the EU and globally. Since the first AMLD in 1990, the EU has developed a solid and continually evolving regulatory framework for countering and combatting ML/TF.

The EIB Group, consisting of the EIB and the EIF, places great emphasis on integrity and good governance and is committed to the highest standards of AML-CFT.

The nature of the EIB, the nature of its members, the non-profit making basis of its operations and its strategy driven also by public policy objectives are important features that distinguish the EIB from commercial banks. In fulfilling its public policy mission, the EIB applies BBP principles[54], as contemplated in the EIB Statute and the EIB Rules of Procedure. Although the EIB is generally not subject to EU Legislative Acts and Guidelines, it has voluntarily decided to comply with these EU

[53] https://www.eib.org/attachments/strategies/eib_group_aml_cft_policy_en.pdf

[54] The EIF applies Best Market Practice (BMP).

Legislative Acts and Guidelines to the extent determined by the BBP Guiding Principles. This applies on an individual and on a basis of the consolidated situation, which means the situation as if the EIB formed a single entity together with its subsidiaries (entities controlled by the EIB, such as the EIF).

Accordingly, EIB Group applies as BBP the general principles and standards set out in EU law, notably the AMLD[55] and for interpretation purposes, takes into account international standards such as the FATF recommendations. The EIB Group hence requires its counterparties (those receiving financial support from the EIB Group) to comply with applicable laws in the field of AML-CFT.

Against this background, the EIB Group continuously monitors and enhances the effectiveness of its compliance standards and controls. It hence aims to mitigate the risk of misuse of funds from EIB Group or from other sources for the purpose of activities that are illegal or abusive in relation to applicable laws.

The EIB Group AML-CFT Policy establishes the key principles governing AML-CFT and related integrity aspects in relevant EIB Group professional activities. It is applied through respective EIB and EIF implementing procedures.

The EIB Group AML-CFT Policy supersedes the "EIB Group Anti-Money Laundering and Combating the Financing of Terrorism Framework" and applies when establishing a business relationship, as well as to all new or renewed operations where EIB Group entities provide professional activities, as detailed in the implementing procedures.

All Persons subject to this Policy are responsible for adhering to the EIB Group AML-CFT Policy and its implementing procedures, as applicable.

2. Scope
2.1 Objectives

The EIB Group AML-CFT Policy and its implementing procedures establish principles and measures designed to prevent the EIB Group and Persons subject to this Policy from being used for or connected with ML, TF or other criminal activities.[56]

Adherence to the EIB Group AML-CFT Policy also aims, among others, at preventing the EIB Group from being exposed to reputational damage and financial loss as a result of non-compliance with applicable AML-CFT standards.

2.2 Applicability

This Policy is applicable to the professional activities of EIB Group entities, as detailed in the applicable implementing procedures.

[55] Directive (EU) 2018/843 of the European Parliament and of the Council of 30 May 2018 amending Directive (EU) 2015/849 on the prevention of the use of the financial system for the purposes of money laundering or terrorist financing, and amending Directives 2009/138/EC and 2013/36/EU (5th AMLD) and Directive (EU) 2015/849 of the European Parliament and of the Council of 20 May 2015 on the prevention of the use of the financial system for the purposes of money laundering or terrorist financing, amending Regulation (EU) No 648/2012 of the European Parliament and of the Council, and repealing Directive 2005/60/EC of the European Parliament and of the Council and Commission Directive 2006/70/EC (4th AMLD).

[56] See definition in Art. 3 (4) AMLD.

This Policy shall apply to all Persons subject to this Policy.

The responsibilities of EIB Group entities' Management Bodies include, setting, approving, and overseeing the implementation of adequate and effective internal governance and internal control frameworks such as this Policy, to ensure compliance with applicable requirements. In the context of countering ML/TF, this also includes setting the risk appetite, monitoring against risk exposures and taking decisions in respect of granting finance and establishing business relationships.

2.3 Definition of Money Laundering

ML[57] is intentionally engaging in:

a) the conversion or transfer of property, knowing that such property is derived from criminal activity or from an act of participation in such activity, for the purpose of concealing or disguising the illicit origin of the property or of assisting any person who is involved in the commission of such an activity to evade the legal consequences of that person's action;
b) the concealment or disguise of the true nature, source, location, disposition, movement, rights with respect to, or ownership of, property, knowing that such property is derived from criminal activity or from an act of participation in such an activity;
c) the acquisition, possession or use of property, knowing, at the time of receipt, that such property was derived from criminal activity or from an act of participation in such an activity;
d) the participation in, association to commit, attempts to commit and aiding, abetting, facilitating and counselling the commission of any of the actions referred to in foregoing points.

ML shall be regarded as such even where the activities which generated the property to be laundered were carried out in any country / jurisdiction.[58]

2.4 Definition of Terrorist Financing

TF is the provision or collection of funds, by any means, directly or indirectly, with the intention that they be used, or in the knowledge that they are to be used (in full or in part) to commit or to contribute to the commission of any of the offences referred to in Articles 3 to 10 of Directive (EU) 2017/541 of 15 March 2017 on combatting terrorism.

Where TF concerns any of the offences laid down in articles 3, 4 and 9 of Directive (EU) 2017/541, it shall not be necessary that the funds be in fact used, in full or in part, to commit or to contribute to the commission of any of those offences, nor shall it be required that the offender knows for which specific offence or offences the funds are to be used.[59]

[57] See definitions in Art. 1 (3) and (4) AMLD.

[58] See definition in Art. 1 (3) AML Directive.

[59] See definition in Art. 1 (5) AMLD, together with Art. 11 of Directive (EU) 2017/541 on combating terrorism and replacing Council Framework Decision 2002/475/JHA and amending Council Decision 2005/671/JHA.

3 Three Lines of Defence Framework

The internal management of ML/TF risks and controls of the EIB Group entities follows the three lines of defence model for addressing and managing risk.

Business lines, as the first line of defence, take risks and are responsible for their operational management directly and on a permanent basis, as detailed in the implementing procedures.

In the AML-CFT context, the EIB Group compliance functions constitute the second line of defence and performs, among others, risk-based monitoring of first line of defence controls, set standards and provide guidance, support and counsel on ML/TF risk tolerances. The involvement of the compliance functions shall be commensurate to identified ML/TF risk factors.

Internal Audit represents the third line of defence. It independently reviews the first two lines of defence, assesses the adequacy and effectiveness of AML-CFT controls, and provides assurance to the EIB and EIF Boards of Directors on the sound management of AML-CFT risks.

4 Risk Management

4.1 Risk Appetite

Under the EIB Group Risk Management Charter , the Group Risk Appetite Framework includes a risk appetite statement incorporating among other limits to the exposure to ML/TF risks, and an outline of the roles and responsibilities of those overseeing the implementation and monitoring of the relevant Risk Appetite Framework aspects.

4.2 Compliance Risk Assessment

For the management of ML/TF risks, the EIB and the EIF conduct Compliance Risk Assessments, as applicable to the EIB Group. Their standards and principles follow the AMLD and best industry practice with regard to the risk dimensions and factors used to assess the ML/TF risk exposure, and are adapted to the nature and size of each entity. These results are also consolidated on a Group level. To this end, the EIB Group entities may also incorporate input from relevant EU-wide risk assessments.

4.3 Risk-Based Approach

While its entities do not open or manage accounts or accept deposits and are driven by public policy objectives, the EIB Group has adopted this Policy and its implementing procedures with the aim of applying AML-CFT measures to proportionally respond to the AML-CFT risks that it may be exposed to.

The EIB Group applies a risk-based approach to AML-CFT when mitigating the ML/TF risk of its professional activities, taking into account, among others, factors such as the type of counterparty (including sector), business relationship, product or transaction and country of operation. The ML/TF risk associated with new products and significant changes applied to existing ones are identified, assessed and approved.

5 Counterparty Due Diligence

The EIB Group has in place a counterparty due diligence process which takes into account, among others, factors including the type of counterparty (including sector), business relationship, product, service or transaction and country(ies) of operation.[60] Through the EIB Group NCJ Policy and its implementing procedures, the EIB Group takes into consideration jurisdictions classified by one or more Lead Organisations for not having made sufficient progress towards satisfactory implementation of EU and/or internationally agreed standards in connection with AML-CFT and/or tax transparency/tax good governance standards. The EIB Group entities also apply the following counterparty due diligence measures to an extent determined on a risk-sensitive basis.

5.1 Identification and Verification of Identity of Counterparties benefiting from EIB Group professional activities

The EIB Group identifies and verifies the identity of the counterparties benefiting from its professional activities, on the basis of documents, data or information obtained from a reliable and independent source.

5.2 Identification and Verification of Identity of Beneficial Owner(s)

The EIB Group takes reasonable measures to verify and record the identity of the beneficial owner(s) i.e. the individual(s) of counterparties benefiting from EIB professional activities:

- who (ultimately) own(s) or control(s) the counterparty or its assets; or
- on whose behalf a transaction is carried out, or the business relationship with the EIB Group is established.

For relevant entities which do not have a beneficial owner or if there is any doubt that the person(s) identified are the beneficial owner(s), equivalent controls are applied to the senior managing official(s).

That is, the natural person(s) who exercise(s) (executive) control over the management of the relevant entity.

5.3 Establishment of Purpose of Business Relationship

Within the context of its professional activities, the EIB Group takes reasonable measures to duly assess the purpose and intended nature of its business relationships and the overall ML/TF risk. This includes related integrity aspects of its business relationships in order to avoid being involved in professional activities and /or business relationships structured for the purposes of criminal activities or co-financed through funds of possibly illicit origin.

[60] See Art. 13 of the AMLD.

5.4 On-going Monitoring

On-going monitoring (including monitoring of transactions) is implemented in order to detect possible ML/TF or related integrity risks which may arise throughout the life of business relationships. The intensity and extent of the ongoing monitoring is calibrated following a risk-based approach.

6 Reporting Obligations

6.1 Persons Subject to Reporting Obligations

Persons subject to this Policy are required to report, in line with the reporting channels set out therein, any alleged misconduct, breaches or any suspicions of ML/TF.

Unlawfully informing prospective or existing EIB counterparty(ies) or other third persons, that compliance concerns may be, or have been raised in relation to an operation and/or counterparty, and/or that an investigation has been, is being, or may be, carried out, including its outcome is prohibited (Tipping off). Tipping off a prospective or existing counterparty is a breach of professional duties and may constitute a criminal offence, therefore allegations of Tipping off may trigger the opening of an investigation/inquiry against the person who has tipped off the prospective or existing counterparty, which may result in disciplinary proceedings and sanctions and possible referral to national authorities for criminal prosecution. Suspicions that funds, regardless of amount, may be the proceeds of criminal activities or related to ML or TF in the professional activities of the EIB Group, must be reported for assessment and, if appropriate, investigation, to the Inspectorate General.

Results of relevant assessments and investigations are shared with the EIB and EIF Heads of Compliance in their capacity as MLROs reporting ML/TF suspicions to the Luxembourg FIU, as appropriate (please see 6.2 below).

The applicable EIB and EIF Codes of Conduct and the EIB Group Whistleblowing Policy stipulate the conditions under which the EIB Group provides assistance and ensures confidentiality of the identity and protection against retaliation for Persons subject to this Policy who report suspicions of ML or TF.

6.2 Compliance Functions

The EIB Group has in place Memoranda of Understandings, for EIB and EIF with the FIU of the Grand Duchy of Luxembourg for the reporting of suspicious transactions or activities. The Heads of Compliance act as designated MLROs for EIB and EIF, respectively. In their capacity, the Heads of Compliance or their delegates report suspicions of ML/TF to the Luxembourg FIU.

6.3 Inspectorate General

The Inspectorate General assesses, and if appropriate investigates, allegations of prohibited conduct, including ML/TF related to EIB Group professional activities. It cooperates directly with and reports to the EPPO and OLAF. It may also refer suspected prohibited conduct to other competent authorities per the EIB and EIF Anti-Fraud Policies.

7 Sanctions Compliance

The EIB Group entities are committed to comply with applicable sanctions provisions/regulations relating to its professional activities (EU, UN, and as determined by the EIB Group, Sanctions Authorities outside the EU) as per the EIB Group Sanctions Compliance Policy as periodically amended.

8 Data Management

8.1 Data Protection

Personal data processed by the EIB Group entities under this Policy and its implementing procedures are subject to the provisions of the Data Protection Regulation[61]. The processing of personal data for the purposes of AML-CFT is considered by the AMLD to be a matter of public interest and as such, the processing is lawful for the purposes of the Data Protection Regulation[62]. The Regulation is applicable to any potential exchange of KYC personal data of common counterparties benefiting from EIB professional activities.

Data subjects are entitled to request an access, rectification and, for duly justified reasons, blockage and erasing of the data (Rights of the Data Subject), and may exercise their rights by contacting the Data Controller. Data subjects also have the right of recourse to the European Data Protection Supervisor at any time.

Detailed provisions relating to the application of the Data Protection Regulation for AML-CFT purposes are available in the related EIB and EIF Privacy statements available on the respective public website.

8.2 Record Retention

Records of all transaction data and data obtained for the purposes of identification, as well as of all documents related to AML-CFT will be kept for a 5-year retention period after the end of the business relationship.

9 Training

The EIB Group entities provide compulsory training on AML-CFT, including on the protection of personal data, to all staff and, as appropriate, to members of its governing bodies. The training is updated regularly and held on recurrent basis to help recipients recognise operations or activities which may be related to ML/TF and to instruct them as how to proceed in such cases. In addition, specific ad-hoc training or other awareness-raising initiatives may be provided to staff regarding responsibilities with respect to their line of defence.

---

[61] See Regulation (EU) 2018/1725 of the European Parliament and of the Council of 23 October 2018 on the protection of natural persons with regard to the processing of personal data by the Union institutions, bodies, offices and agencies and on the free movement of such data, and repealing Regulation (EC) No 45/2001 and Decision No 1247/2002/EC.

[62] See Art. 43 AMLD as well as Art. 5 (1)(a) Data Protection Regulation.

10 Review

In respect of international standards and relevant EU Legislative Acts and Guidelines to the extent determined by the BBP Guiding Principles, this document remains in effect unless replaced by an updated version approved by the EIB and EIF Boards of Directors.

The EIB Head of Compliance maintains the EIB Group AML-CFT Policy in cooperation with the EIF Head of Compliance and with the EIB Group services concerned. The Heads of Compliance propose for approval by the relevant decision-making bodies any appropriate updating, taking into account international standards and relevant EU Legislative Acts and Guidelines to the extent determined by the BBP Guiding Principles

xxvii) **UNODC Initiative: Sharing Electronic Resources and Laws on Crime (SHERLOC)**[63]

The SHERLOC portal is an initiative to facilitate the dissemination of information regarding the implementation of the United Nations Convention against Transnational Organized Crime, the three Protocols thereto and the international legal framework against terrorism.[64]

- **LEGISLATION DATABASE**

Legislation implementing the Organized Crime Convention, the Protocols thereto and the international legal framework against terrorism and addressing specific forms of organized crime and relevant "cross cutting" issues

- **CASE LAW DATABASE**
  Case Summaries of judicial decisions relating to organised crime and terrorism
- **CAN DIRECTORY**
  Directory of Central and competent national authorities designated for international cooperation in criminal matters
- **TREATIES DATABASE**
  Bilateral and multilateral treaties concerning organized crime and terrorism, including information on the adherence status of each instrument
- **STRATEGIES DATABASE**
  National and Regional strategies to prevent and combat organised crime and terrorism
- **REV MOD**
  Access to the secure module used for the Mechanism for the Review of Implementation of the Organised Crime Convention and the protocols thereto
- **BIBLIOGRAPHY DATABASE**
  Bibliographic data of publications relating to organized crime and terrorism
- **LEGISLATIVE GUIDE**
  A web version of UNODC's Legislative Guide for the Implementation of the United Nations Convention Against Transnational Organised Crime 2017

[63] https://sherloc.unodc.org/cld/st/home.html

[64] https://sherloc.unodc.org/cld/en/st/home.html

Chapter 15
National Materials

There are a number of cities around the world where finance plays a major role[1] including:

- London;
- New York;
- Singapore; and
- Sydney.

Hence, the focus previously and in this chapter on those nations, along with some European Member States (France, Germany and Italy also included). However there are, of course, others including Hong Kong in China, Geneva and Zurich in Switzerland, jurisdictions in the Caribbean, Tokyo in Japan, and many of those impacted by the Panama,[2] Paradise,[3] Pandora[4] and Luanda[5] papers disclosures.

With any large financial hub, there are significant risks of money laundering being used to clean funds, from a national or international source, that have been obtained by criminal activity; not only from drugs but the proceeds of fraud, corruption, tax evasion, evading sanctions and organised crime. Indeed, a UK Conservative Member of Parliament (MP) was noted[6] (in the discussion aboutcontext of the disclosure of the Panama Papers in 2016 to have said that "London is the money laundering capital of the world."

---

[1] https://en.wikipedia.org/wiki/Financial_centre#:~:text=Sydney%27s%20northern%20CBD%20serves%20as,for%2C the%20Asia%2DPacific%20region

[2] https://www.icij.org/investigations/panama-papers/pages/panama-papers-about-the-investigation/ ; https://en.wikipedia.org/wiki/Panama_Papers

[3] https://www.icij.org/investigations/paradise-papers/; https://en.wikipedia.org/wiki/Paradise_Papers

[4] https://www.icij.org/investigations/pandora-papers/

[5] https://www.icij.org/investigations/luanda-leaks/luanda-leaks-isabel-dos-santos-loses-fight-against-733-million-asset-freeze/

[6] On the BBC TV programme: Have I Got News For You in 2021.

D. Smith, *Money Laundering, Terrorist Financing and Virtual Assets*, Contributions to Finance and Accounting, https://doi.org/10.1007/978-3-031-59842-5_15

15.1 UK

i. Freezing Orders

A freezing order or freezing injunction (formerly known as a Mareva injunction) is a court order specifically designed to prevent the disposal or removal of property, money or other assets by the respondent (often called "the Defendant" or "the Respondent") beyond the reach of the person or company applying for the order until judgment can be obtained or satisfied.[7]

The UK Government publishes the list of designated persons currently subject to an asset freeze under the Anti-Terrorism, Crime and Security Act 2001.[8]

ii. Unexplained Wealth Orders (UWOs)

A Factsheet on UWOs states:[9]

An unexplained wealth order (UWO) is an investigatory order placed on a respondent whose assets appear disproportionate to their income to explain the origins of their wealth.

An Unexplained Wealth Order (UWO) requires a person who is a Politically Exposed Person (PEP) or reasonably suspected of involvement in, or of being connected to a person involved in, serious crime to explain the origin of assets (minimum combined value of £50,000) that appear to be disproportionate to their known lawfully obtained income.

As noted in the joint Home Office and HM Treasury National Risk Assessment of money laundering and terrorist financing 2020, property in the UK is attractive to both foreign and domestic criminals seeking to conceal large amounts of illicit funds, disguise their ownership, and realise the proceeds of their criminal activities.

A UWO is not (by itself) a power to recover assets. However, any response from a UWO can be used in subsequent civil recovery proceeding.

A failure to respond will mean that the assets can be made subject to civil recovery action under the Proceeds of Crime Act 2002.

A person can also be found guilty of an offence if they provide false or misleading information in response to an UWO.

The desired outcome of these [proposed] (in October 2023) amendments is to strengthen the UWO regimes to enable law enforcement to take more effective action against kleptocrats, corrupt elites and serious and organised criminals who launder their funds in the UK. In turn, this will lead to greater prospects of the recovery of assets bought with the proceeds of serious and organised crime, particularly corruption.

Key Facts

---

[7] E.g. https://uk.practicallaw.thomsonreuters.com/0-107-6602?transitionType=Default&contextData=(sc.Default)&firstPage=true

[8] https://www.gov.uk/government/publications/financial-sanctions-uk-freezing-orders

[9] The Factsheet is published by the government at: https://www.gov.uk/government/publications/economic-crime-transparency-and-enforcement-bill-2022-overarching-documents/factsheet-unexplained-wealth-order-reforms-web-accessible

1. Serious and organised crimes (SOC), for example, corruption, money laundering, ransomware attacks and terrorism-financing, are estimated to cost the UK economy £37 billion per year.
2. The Proceeds of Crime Act 2002 (POCA 2002) provides the statutory framework and broad powers to trace, investigate and recover illicit finance gained through unlawful conduct. In 2020/21, just under £219 million of the proceeds of crime were recovered within England, Wales, and Northern Ireland. This continues the general trend of improved performance since 2016 to 2017. Overall, just under £1.3 billion has been recovered from criminals using these powers, significantly curtailing corrupt actors' ability to further criminality.
3. The Financial Action Task Force found that the UK has one of the strongest systems in the world for combatting money laundering.
4. UWOs have been granted in four cases since their introduction in relation to assets with a combined value of £143 million. In October 2020, property worth an estimated £ten million was recovered following the use of an UWO.

iii. OFSI: The UK's **Office of Financial Sanctions Implementation** (OFSI) is part of the UK's Treasury and is responsible for monitoring compliance with financial sanctions and for assessing suspected breaches. It also has the power to impose monetary penalties for breaches of financial sanctions and to refer cases to law enforcement agencies for investigation and potential prosecution.[10]

OFSI helps ensure financial sanctions are properly understood, implemented and enforced in the United Kingdom. This includes the Oil Price Cap on Russian oil.

OFSI's assessment of breaches is informed by their approach to financial sanctions enforcement: promote, enable, respond, change. For more information on OFSI's enforcement approach, see Enforcement and Monetary Penalty Guidance.

Details of actions OFSI has taken as part of its enforcement of financial sanctions can also be found on their website.

iv. NCA's "Flag It Up Campaign" News release (3 January, 2018).[11]

Serious and organised crime costs the UK an estimated £24bn a year and money laundering not only allows criminals to hide the proceeds of their crimes, but helps fund further criminal activity. In its latest report, the Government has set out the threats posed by money laundering and is relaunching the Flag it Up campaign to raise awareness and show how you can help stamp it out.

Headed by the National Crime Agency, *Flag it Up* is a joint campaign, between the Government, the legal and accountancy sectors that aims to raise awareness of the tell-tale signs of money laundering and the risks for firms and professionals from being caught in this financial crime.

Elizabeth Baker, Head of Proceeds of Crime at the Serious Fraud Office, spoke to *Flag it Up* about . . . how you can help catch criminals . . . through using Suspicious Activity Reports (SARs).

---

[10] https://www.gov.uk/government/collections/enforcement-of-financial-sanctions

[11] https://www.sfo.gov.uk/2018/01/03/tell-tale-signs-role-preventing-money-laundering-flagging/

v. Joint Statement on Sanctions and the Cryptoasset Sector[12]

The UK, in partnership with our allies across the globe, has imposed an unprecedented package of economic sanctions on Russia and Belarus, in response to Russia's invasion of Ukraine on 24 February.

The UK financial regulatory authorities reiterate that all UK financial services firms, including the cryptoasset sector, are expected to play their part in ensuring that sanctions are complied with.

We are working closely with partners in government and law enforcement both here and abroad, including regulatory authorities, to share intelligence and act to prevent sanctions evasion, including through cryptoassets. We also remain ready to act in the event of sanctions breaches.

Legal and regulatory requirements on firms

Financial sanctions regulations do not differentiate between cryptoassets and other forms of assets. The use of cryptoassets to circumvent economic sanctions is a criminal offence under the Money Laundering Regulations 2017 and regulations made under the Sanctions and Anti-Money Laundering Act 2018.

The FCA has already written to all registered cryptoasset firms and those holding temporary registration status to highlight the application of sanctions on various entities and individuals.

Where transactions give rise to concerns about sanctions evasion or money laundering firms should also consider their obligations to report to the UK Financial Intelligence Unit (UKFIU) at the National Crime Agency under the Proceeds of Crime Act 2002. The UKFIU has published guidance and a Suspicious Activity Reports (SARs) glossary code that should be used when reporting any suspicions.

We remind all other authorised financial institutions to check the FCA register to identify whether any cryptoasset firms they do business with are registered, or to

---

[12] The joint statement by the UK Financial Regulation Authorities is at: https://www.fca.org.uk/news/statements/uk-financial-regulatory-authorities-sanctions-cryptoasset-sector . The regulatory authorities are:

- The Office of Financial Sanctions Implementation (OFSI), part of HM Treasury, ensures financial sanctions are properly understood, enforced and implemented in the UK. If you have information to report regarding financial sanctions, this must be sent to OFSI (ofsi@hmtreasury.gov.uk).
- The Financial Conduct Authority (FCA) is the anti-money laundering and counter-terrorist financing supervisor for cryptoasset businesses and other financial institutions in the UK. It is also the conduct regulator for financial institutions which carry out activities within scope of the Regulated Activities Order. If a person you are dealing with, directly or indirectly, is a designated person; if you hold any frozen assets; or if knowledge or suspicion of these come to you while conducting your business, you must also notify the FCA (firm.queries@fca.org.uk).
- The Bank of England prudentially regulates and supervises financial services firms through the PRA. The PRA is responsible for the prudential regulation and supervision of banks, building societies, credit unions, insurers and major investment firms.

Please also see a note by Oraz Kereibayev dated August 9, 2023, at: https://sumsub.com/blog/all-you-need-to-know-about-uk-crypto-regulations-2023-guide/

check the equivalent register of the jurisdiction in which the cryptoasset firm is based. Both the FCA and the PRA will act if they see authorised financial institutions supporting cryptoasset firms operating in the UK illegally.

The Office of Financial Sanctions Implementation (OFSI), part of HM Treasury, ensures financial sanctions are properly understood, enforced and implemented in the UK. If you know, or have 'reasonable cause to suspect' that you are in possession or control of, or are otherwise dealing with, the funds or economic resources of a designated person you must:

- freeze them
- not deal with them or make them available to, or for the benefit of, the designated person, unless:
  - there is an exception in the legislation that you can rely on; or
  - you have a license from OFSI
- report them to OFSI (ofsi@hmtreasury.gov.uk)

Full guidance can be found on OFSI's website.

Steps to reduce the risk of sanctions evasion via cryptoassets

As set out in communications from the FCA, cryptoasset firms must take steps to ensure they are compliant with their legal obligations in relation to sanctions.

Controls developed to identify customers and monitor their transactions under the Money Laundering Regulations 2017 can help with compliance, but firms will need to implement additional sanctions specific controls as appropriate. In particular, firms should consider:

- updating business-wide and customer risk assessments to account for changes in the nature and type of sanctions measures
- ensuring that customer onboarding and due diligence processes identify customers who make use of corporate vehicles to obscure ownership or source of funds
- ensuring that customers and their transactions are screened against relevant updated sanctions lists and that effective re-screening is in place to identify activity that may indicate sanctions breaches
- identifying activity that is not in line with the customer profile or is otherwise suspicious and ensuring that these are reported quickly to the nominated officer for timely consideration
- where blockchain analytics solutions are deployed, ensuring that compliance teams understand how these capabilities can be best used to identify transactions linked to higher risk wallet addresses
- engage with public-private partnerships and private-private partnerships to gather insights on the latest typologies and additional controls that might be relevant and share their own best practice examples

Firms should also look for red flag indicators that suggest an increased risk of sanctions evasion. These may include, but are not limited to:

- a customer who is resident in or conducting transactions to or from a jurisdiction which is subject to sanctions, or which is on the UK's High Risk Third Countries list for anti-money laundering and counter-terrorist financing purposes, or any jurisdiction you have identified as posing an increased risk of illicit financial activity
- transactions to or from a wallet address associated with a sanctioned entity, or a wallet address otherwise deemed to be high-risk, based on its transaction history or that of associated addresses, or other factors
- transactions involving a cryptoasset exchange or custodian wallet provider known to have poor customer due diligence procedures or which is otherwise deemed high-risk
- the use of tools designed to obfuscate the location of the customer (e.g. an IP address associated with a virtual private network or proxy) or the source of cryptoassets (e.g. mixers and tumblers)
- other red flag indicators that are normally associated with money laundering more broadly. In both situations, the aim of the illicit actor is to make an illegal transaction seem legitimate

Red flag indicators should be considered in context. What may appear innocent in isolation may be indicative of sanctions evasion when considered alongside other red flag indicators or contextual information.

vi. Bank of England Statement on digital currency[13]

The digital pound would be a new type of money issued by the Bank of England for everyone to use for day-to-day spending. You would be able to use it in-store or online to make payments.

This type of money is known as a central bank digital currency (CBDC). You may also hear it being called 'digital sterling' or even 'Britcoin'. We call the UK version of CBDC **the digital pound**.

The digital pound would be denominated in sterling and its value would be stable, just like banknotes. £10 in digital pounds would always have the same value as a £10 banknote.

If we introduced it, it would not replace cash. We know being able to use cash is important for many people. That's why we will continue to issue it for as long as people want to keep using it.

The digital pound would not be a cryptocurrency or cryptoasset. As opposed to cryptocurrencies, which are issued privately, the digital pound would be issued by the Bank of England and be backed by the Government.

We have published a **Consultation Paper**, which explores the need for the digital pound and proposes a set of design choices for it.

[13] Currently undated (website last updated December 2023): https://www.bankofengland.co.uk/the-digital-pound#:~:text=The%20digital%20pound%20would%20be,bank%20digital%20currency%20(CBDC).

15.2 United States of America

i. Laundering of monetary instruments

18 U.S. Code § 1956

(a)

(1) Whoever, knowing that the property involved in a financial transaction represents the proceeds of some form of unlawful activity, conducts or attempts to conduct such a financial transaction which in fact involves the proceeds of specified unlawful activity—.

(A)

(i) with the intent to promote the carrying on of specified unlawful activity; or.

(ii) with intent to engage in conduct constituting a violation of section 7201 or 7206 of the Internal Revenue Code of 1986; or.

(B) knowing that the transaction is designed in whole or in part—

(i) to conceal or disguise the nature, the location, the source, the ownership, or the control of the proceeds of specified unlawful activity; or

(ii) to avoid a transaction reporting requirement under State or Federal law,

shall be sentenced to a fine of not more than $500,000 or twice the value of the property involved in the transaction, whichever is greater, or imprisonment for not more than twenty years, or both. For purposes of this paragraph, a financial transaction shall be considered to be one involving the proceeds of specified unlawful activity if it is part of a set of parallel or dependent transactions, any one of which involves the proceeds of specified unlawful activity, and all of which are part of a single plan or arrangement.

(2) Whoever transports, transmits, or transfers, or attempts to transport, transmit, or transfer a monetary instrument or funds from a place in the United States to or through a place outside the United States or to a place in the United States from or through a place outside the United States—

(A) with the intent to promote the carrying on of specified unlawful activity; or

(B) knowing that the monetary instrument or funds involved in the transportation, transmission, or transfer represent the proceeds of some form of unlawful activity and knowing that such transportation, transmission, or transfer is designed in whole or in part—

(i) to conceal or disguise the nature, the location, the source, the ownership, or the control of the proceeds of specified unlawful activity; or

(ii) to avoid a transaction reporting requirement under State or Federal law,

shall be sentenced to a fine of not more than $500,000 or twice the value of the monetary instrument or funds involved in the transportation, transmission, or transfer, whichever is greater, or imprisonment for not more than twenty years, or both. For the purpose of the offense described in subparagraph (B), the defendant's knowledge may be established by proof that a law enforcement officer represented the matter specified in subparagraph (B) as true, and the defendant's subsequent statements or actions indicate that the defendant believed such representations to be true.

(3) Whoever, with the intent—

(A) to promote the carrying on of specified unlawful activity;

(B) to conceal or disguise the nature, location, source, ownership, or control of property believed to be the proceeds of specified unlawful activity; or

(C) to avoid a transaction reporting requirement under State or Federal law,

conducts or attempts to conduct a financial transaction involving property represented to be the proceeds of specified unlawful activity, or property used to conduct or facilitate specified unlawful activity, shall be fined under this title or imprisoned for not more than 20 years, or both. For purposes of this paragraph and paragraph (2), the term "represented" means any representation made by a law enforcement officer or by another person at the direction of, or with the approval of, a Federal official authorized to investigate or prosecute violations of this section.

(b) Penalties.—

(1) In general.—Whoever conducts or attempts to conduct a transaction described in subsection (a) (1) or (a)(3), or section 1957, or a transportation, transmission, or transfer described in subsection (a)(2), is liable to the United States for a civil penalty of not more than the greater of—

(A) the value of the property, funds, or monetary instruments involved in the transaction; or

(B) $10,000.

(2) Jurisdiction over foreign persons.—For purposes of adjudicating an action filed or enforcing a penalty ordered under this section, the district courts shall have jurisdiction over any foreign person, including any financial institution authorized under the laws of a foreign country, against whom the action is brought, if service of process upon the foreign person is made under the Federal Rules of Civil Procedure or the laws of the country in which the foreign person is found, and—

(A) the foreign person commits an offense under subsection (a) involving a financial transaction that occurs in whole or in part in the United States;

(B) the foreign person converts, to his or her own use, property in which the United States has an ownership interest by virtue of the entry of an order of forfeiture by a court of the United States; or

(C) the foreign person is a financial institution that maintains a bank account at a financial institution in the United States.

(3) Court authority over assets.—

A court may issue a pretrial restraining order or take any other action necessary to ensure that any bank account or other property held by the defendant in the United States is available to satisfy a judgment under this section...[14]

ii. Securities and Exchange Commission (SEC)

As the securities sector is one of the main industries through which persons and entities can access the financial system, thus providing opportunities for criminals to misuse the financial system, the SEC has developed and published this guide:

[14] https://www.law.cornell.edu/uscode/text/18/1956

Anti-Money Laundering (AML) Source Tool for Broker-Dealers (updated May 16, 2022)[15]

This research guide, or "source tool," is a compilation of key AML laws, rules, orders, and guidance applicable to broker-dealers. Several statutory and regulatory provisions, and related rules of the securities self-regulatory organizations (SROs), impose AML obligations on broker-dealers. A wealth of related AML guidance materials is also available. To aid research efforts into AML requirements and to assist broker-dealers with AML compliance, this source tool organizes key AML compliance materials and provides related source information.

When using this research tool, you should keep the following in mind:

First, broker-dealers are responsible for complying with all AML requirements to which they are subject. Although this research guide summarizes some of the key AML obligations that are applicable to broker-dealers, it is not comprehensive. You should not rely on the summary information provided, but should refer to the relevant statutes, rules, orders, and interpretations.

Second, AML laws, rules, and orders are subject to change and may change quickly. Statutes that include AML-related provisions may be amended from time to time, and new statutes may be enacted which include AML-related provisions. The Anti-Money Laundering Act of 2020 (AMLA) tasked the Secretary of the Treasury, in consultation with specified regulators and law enforcement, with undertaking a review of BSA regulations and guidance and directed the Secretary to make appropriate changes to improve the efficiency of the regulations and guidance.[1] Other provisions of AMLA and the Corporate Transparency Act require the Secretary to revise the AML program rules and beneficial ownership rule.[2]

Finally, you will find a list of telephone numbers and useful websites at the end of this guide. If you have questions concerning the meaning, application, or status of a particular law, rule, order, or guidance, you should consult with an attorney experienced in the areas covered by this guide.

This source tool represents the views of the staff of the Division of Examinations. It is not a rule, regulation, or statement of the Securities and Exchange Commission ("Commission"). The Commission has neither approved nor disapproved its content. This source tool, like all staff guidance, has no legal force or effect: it does not alter or amend applicable law, and it creates no new or additional obligations for any person.

The Division of Examinations regularly publishes Risk Alerts on its webpage, www.sec.gov/exams, some of which deal with AML topics, and also maintains a source tool regarding the AML obligations of mutual funds ...

The following topics are addressed in this guide:

1. The Bank Secrecy Act
2. The USA PATRIOT Act
3. AML Programs

[15] https://www.sec.gov/about/offices/ocie/amlsourcetool

4. Customer Identification Programs
5. Beneficial Ownership
6. Correspondent Accounts: Prohibition on Foreign Shell Banks and Due Diligence Programs
7. Due Diligence Programs for Private Banking Accounts
8. Suspicious Activity Monitoring and Reporting
9. Other BSA Reports
10. Records of Funds Transfers
11. Information Sharing With Law Enforcement and Financial Institutions
12. Special Measures Imposed by the Secretary of the Treasury
13. Office of Foreign Asset Control (OFAC) Sanctions Programs and Other Lists
14. Selected Additional AML Resources
15. Useful Contact Information

iii. Financial Crimes Enforcement Network (FINCEN)[16]

In its mission to "safeguard the financial system from the abuses of financial crime, including terrorist financing, money laundering and other illicit activity," the FINCEN[17] acts as the designated administrator of the Bank Secrecy Act (BSA). The BSA was established in 1970 and has become one of the most important tools in the fight against money laundering. Since then, numerous other laws have enhanced and amended the BSA to provide law enforcement and regulatory agencies with the most effective tools to combat money laundering.[18] An index of anti-money laundering laws since 1970 with their respective requirements and goals are listed below in chronological order:

- Money Laundering Control Act (1986)
- Anti-Drug Abuse Act of 1988
- Annunzio-Wylie Anti-Money Laundering Act (1992)
- Money Laundering Suppression Act (1994)
- Money Laundering and Financial Crimes Strategy Act (1998)
- Uniting and Strengthening America by Providing Appropriate Tools Required to Intercept and Obstruct Terrorism Act of 2001 (USA PATRIOT Act)
- Intelligence Reform & Terrorism Prevention Act of 2004

The FINCEN Factsheet on money laundering[19] states:

On January 1, 2021, Congress enacted the FY2021 National Defense Authorization Act (NDAA),which included significant reforms to the U.S. anti-money laundering (AML) regime. The NDAA includes the Anti-Money Laundering Act of 2020 (AML Act) and, within the AML Act, the Corporate Transparency Act (CTA).

[16] https://www.fincen.gov/about/mission

[17] https://www.fincen.gov

[18] https://www.fincen.gov/bsa-e-filing-system

[19] https://www.fincen.gov/sites/default/files/shared/20210615%20AMLA%20FinCEN%20One%20Pager_FINAL.pdf

The AML Act seeks to strengthen, modernize, and streamline the existing AML regime by promoting innovation, regulatory reform, and industry engagement through forums, such as the Bank Secrecy Act.

Advisory Group (BSAAG) and FinCEN Exchange. The Act also calls for FinCEN to work closely with our regulatory, national security, and law enforcement partners to identify risks and priorities and provide valuable feedback to our industry partners.

The CTA establishes uniform beneficial ownership reporting requirements for corporations, limited liability companies, and other similar entities formed or registered to do business in the United States.

The CTA authorizes FinCEN to collect that information and share it with authorized government authorities and financial institutions, subject to effective safeguards and controls.

Many provisions of the AML Act and the CTA require rulemaking or periodic reporting to Congress on implementation efforts, assessments, and findings. Some key requirements include:

1. Establishing standards for the reporting of information on beneficial ownership, building an IT system to collect and secure the data, and creating access protocols;
2. Establishing national anti-money laundering and countering the financing of terrorism priorities;
3. Enhancing the whistleblower provisions to provide for a robust whistleblower program and new anti-retaliation protections;
4. Reviewing, and revising as appropriate, Currency Transaction Report (CTR) and Suspicious Activity Report (SAR) reporting requirements, and other existing Bank Secrecy Act (BSA) regulations and guidance;
5. Expanding BSA requirements and obligations to persons engaged in the trade of antiquities, and mandating a study on the potential expansion of BSA requirements to persons engaged in the art trade;
6. Codifying the FinCEN Exchange program;
7. Hosting a Financial Crimes Tech Symposium, and establishing new BSAAG subcommittees and a supervisory committee to address public-private partnerships;
8. Establishing a BSA Analytical Hub;
9. Law enforcement reporting to FinCEN on the use of BSA data, procedures for additional feedback between FinCEN and financial institutions on the usefulness of SARs, and semi-annual publication of review of SAR activity and other BSA reports, including threat patterns, trends, and typologies; and
10. Codifying a pilot program to allow financial institutions to share SARs with their foreign branches, subsidiaries, and affiliates.

Timely and effective AML Act implementation will be challenging and is FinCEN's top priority, and we are working diligently with our domestic and international industry partners and law enforcement and regulatory stakeholders to further the national security of the United States and protect the American people.

iv. Office of Foreign Assets Control (OFAC)

This office is part of the US Treasury's Office of Terrorism and Financial Intelligence.[20] It administers and enforces economic sanctions programs primarily against countries and groups of individuals, such as terrorists and narcotics traffickers. The sanctions can be either comprehensive or selective, using the blocking of assets and trade restrictions to accomplish foreign policy and national security goals. They publish sanctions lists of Specially Designated Nationals and Blocked Persons, as well as maintaining other sanctions lists[21] for example on cyber-related activities.[22]

v. Federal Reserve: considerations on a Central Bank Digital Currency[23]

Money is a social and legal construct underpinned by trust. Conceptions of money have evolved and money has taken many forms over the years. In North America, pre-colonial trade was often conducted in wampum, corn, and fur pelts. In fact, wampum, which are decorative beads made from shells, were recognized as official currency by the Massachusetts Bay Colony in 1650.[2] The Federal Reserve note, which was first issued in 1914, is a relatively recent development by historical standards. Today, there are ongoing discussions on a new form of central bank money distinct from physical cash and limited-access central bank deposits. This report focuses on the potential for a general-purpose CBDC that can be used by the public for day-to-day payments.

Crucial to whether "money" is successful is whether it is seen as a safe, stable and reliable instrument. Cash, central bank deposits, and a potential CBDC are all liabilities of the central bank; funds in a bank account are the liability of a commercial bank; and honoring balances on a retail stored value card is an obligation of issuer—but most people do not think of money in terms of their status as a liability and obligation of banks or other entities. What people care about is not the nuances of how money is recorded on a ledger somewhere, but whether the "money" in question can be safely and reliably used to make a purchase today, as well as in the future. Most people take for granted that cash maintains its full value, funds at a bank are secure, and businesses will honor store credit. Seen in this light, a CBDC could offer another form of safe and reliable money . . . .

[20] https://ofac.treasury.gov/about-ofac

[21] https://ofac.treasury.gov/other-ofac-sanctions-lists

[22] https://ofac.treasury.gov/sanctions-programs-and-country-information/sanctions-related-to-significant-malicious-cyber-enabled-activities

[23] The full note is at: https://www.federalreserve.gov/econres/notes/feds-notes/preconditions-for-a-general-purpose-central-bank-digital-currency-20210224.html

15.3 European Union Member States

a. National Situation in an EU Member State: Italy/Banca d'Italia[24]

Anti-money laundering Supervision and Regulation

Money laundering and terrorism financing are a serious threat to the economy and to people's security, and can have destabilizing effects on the financial system.

The transnational nature of these phenomena is the foundation for a significant process of international harmonization of the rules on and the supervision of these issues. This is in order to prevent those who transfer funds of illegal origin from exploiting loopholes in the safeguards set up by various countries.

THE FATF AND EUROPE

At international level, the guiding role taken on by the Financial Action Task Force (FATF) is fundamental. It is an organization that draws up and promotes standards for the fight against money laundering and terrorism financing, analyses the techniques of and changes in these phenomena, and assesses and monitors national systems, thereby making a decisive contribution to the coordination between countries. The FATF comprises 37 member countries and two regional organizations—which represent most important financial centres at global level—and several important international and sectoral financial organizations have observer status. The FATF has drawn up a set of standards, known as the 40 Recommendations, adopted in February 2012 and regularly updated.

As regards the European Union, several initiatives have been taken or are underway to increase the effectiveness of actions to combat money laundering and terrorism financing.

On the regulatory front, the rules have been increasingly harmonized over the years. They are currently constituted by the fourth anti-money laundering directive (2015/849, as amended by the fifth directive, 2018/843), by the delegated regulations of the European Commission and by the Guidelines of the European Banking Authority (EBA). However, an important review process is underway, which will transfer the main anti-money laundering directives, currently contained in the directive, to a European regulation.

In order to ensure more robust and uniform supervisory practices, the role of the EBA has been strengthened in the last few years. It has been entrusted with certain coordination and monitoring powers over national authorities. Further measures are expected in the near future: the review process currently underway in Europe includes setting up a new European authority, the Anti Money-Laundering Authority, (AMLA), which will directly supervise European intermediaries with the riskiest profiles in terms of money laundering and terrorism financing. For the remaining intermediaries and other entities that, like intermediaries, contribute to the fight against these phenomena (for example, lawyers, accountants, notaries, gaming

[24] https://www.bancaditalia.it/compiti/supervisione-normativa-antiriciclaggio/index.html?com.dotmarketing.htmlpage.language=1&dotcache=refresh

sector operators, auditing firms and estate agents), it is envisaged that the European authority is tasked with indirect supervision, coordination and assistance for national authorities. This is to ensure uniform standards for supervision and common methodologies for assessing the risks of money laundering and terrorism financing.

NATIONAL LEGISLATION AND THE ROLE OF THE BANK OF ITALY

In Italy, the anti-money laundering rules are contained in Legislative Decree 231/2007 (amended over time, in part to reflect the changes in European legislation). The same legislative decree tasks the Bank of Italy with the regulation and supervision of intermediaries for anti-money laundering purposes and to combat the financing of terrorism. It also established the Financial Intelligence Unit (UIF), which operates autonomously and independently within the Bank of Italy.

In order to implement this legislative decree, the Bank of Italy has issued a series of secondary provisions, addressed to the intermediaries it supervises, on the following aspects:

1. organization, procedures and internal controls;
2. customer due diligence;
3. record keeping and sharing of documents, data and information
4. sanctions and the administrative sanction procedure.

The Bank of Italy's supervision of money laundering is directed at all banks, investment firms (SIM), intermediaries for managed assets, financial intermediaries, some trust companies, payment institutions and electronic money institutions operating in Italy. Its purpose is to verify the compliance of these intermediaries with the obligations provided for by the legislation and the adequacy of their organizational and procedural safeguards, which are required to combat money laundering and terrorism financing. Supervision is conducted by means of analyses and interventions designed to swiftly identify signs of weakness in the technical and organizational anti-money laundering set-ups and to prompt their removal by adopting appropriate corrective measures. The work consists of off-site checks - based on analysis of the intelligence gathered, including from financial intermediaries - and inspections, mainly intended to verify the adequacy of the anti-money laundering organization and of the procedures followed by intermediaries.

SANCTION MEASURES AND INTERVENTIONS

Specific measures are adopted in the event of criticalities involving operators. They include convening the administrative, management and supervisory bodies of the intermediaries as well as prohibiting new transactions.

In the event of management irregularities or of serious, repeated, systematic and multiple regulatory violations, sanctions procedures are undertaken against intermediaries and/or executives, which may end with the application of financial and non-financial sanctions. The latter can be imposed on natural persons (such as a temporary ban on the activities performed by intermediaries) or on the entity (such as a 'cease and desist' order).

b. **EU AML package for the new regulatory framework (AMLA)**

EU Council and Parliament agree on procedure to select seat for new authority[25]

In December 2023, the EU Council and the European Parliament representatives reached a common understanding on the process for selecting the seat of the future European authority for countering money laundering and terrorist financing (AMLA).

The new authority is the centrepiece of the reform of the EU's anti-money laundering framework. The authority will have direct and indirect supervisory powers over obliged entities and the power to impose sanctions and measures . . .

c. **The EU 4th, 5th & 6th AML Directives**

A) EU's 6th AML Directive[26]

The EU's 6th AML Directive, which came into effect 3 December 2020 and was implemented by regulated entities by 3 June 2021, aims to strengthen anti-money laundering (AML) rules in the EU and place higher responsibility on regulated entities to fight financial crime.

i. **Harmonised definition and predicate offences**

The 6th AML Directive aims to harmonise the definition of predicate offences against money laundering by all Member States. The 22 predicate offences for money laundering now includes cybercrime and environmental crime.

ii. **Expanded regulatory scope**

The new Directive defines initiators, facilitators and inciters of crimes as accomplices, "aiding and abetting" and self-laundering now also constitute criminal acts.

iii. **Extended criminal liability**

6AMLD will extend criminal liability to allow for the punishment of legal persons, such as companies or partnerships. Companies may be criminally liable for the actions of employees who engage in criminal activity.

iv. **Tougher punishment**

The sentence for money laundering crimes increased to minimum of 4 year imprisonment.

[25] https://www.consilium.europa.eu/en/press/press-releases/2023/12/18/anti-money-laundering-council-and-parliament-agree-on-procedure-to-select-seat-for-new-authority/

[26] https://www.lseg.com/en/risk-intelligence/financial-crime-risk-management/eu-anti-money-laundering-directive#:~:text=Directives%20(AMLDs)%3A-,6th%20AML%20Directive,entities%20to%20fight%20financial%20crime

v. **Member States' cooperation**

6AMLD addresses the issue of dual criminality, requiring EU Member States to criminalise certain predicate offences whether they are illegal in that jurisdiction or not.

B) EU's 5th AML Directive[27]

The EU's 5th Anti-Money Laundering Directive, which took effect on 10 January 2020, is designed to bring more transparency to improve the fight against money laundering and terrorist financing and tightens regulatory controls across more sectors. The scope of the Directive is extended to include virtual currency exchanges, estate agents and rental intermediaries, art dealers, customers who are applying for Citizenship or Residency by Investment, and more:

i) **Crypto currencies**

Crypto currencies face more stringent controls, with exchanges being required to register with the relevant authorities in their jurisdictions, conduct customer due diligence, and prepare suspicious activity reports where necessary. Financial Intelligence Units (FIUs) will be required to keep records of those purchasing virtual currency.

ii) **Beneficial owners**

Greater emphasis on transparency around ultimate beneficial ownership (UBO) as part of a targeted attempt to fight back against financial criminals who hide behind often complex and opaque corporate structures. Member States will be required to maintain publicly available national UBO registries.

iii) **Politically Exposed Persons (PEPs)**

Member States are required to create and publicly release functional PEP lists that include all titles, roles or functions that are deemed to be politically exposed.

iv) **High-value goods**

The Directive extends the range of high-value goods that will be subject to reporting requirements and regulatory enforcement, including art, oil, arms, precious metals, tobacco, historical, cultural and archaeological artefacts.

v) **High risk countries**

When dealing with high risk countries — specifically those identified by the EU as having sub-standard AML regulations — companies will be required to perform enhanced due diligence, which may also include Source of Wealth investigations.

---

[27] https://www.lseg.com/en/risk-intelligence/financial-crime-risk-management/eu-anti-money-laundering-directive#:~:text=Directives%20(AMLDs)%3A-,6th%20AML%20Directive,entities%20to%20fight%20financial%20crime. See also Thomas Wahl's EUCRIM article entitled: New Directive on the Criminalising of Money Laundering at: https://eucrim.eu/news/new-directive-criminalisation-money-laundering/

vi) **Prepaid cards**

The limit of prepaid cards is lowered from €250 to €150, with a €50 online/remote limit applicable. Only cards issued within the EU are allowed, unless they were issued in a country with legislation that is deemed on par with EU AML standards.

C) EU's 4th AML Directive

The EU's 4th AMLD was designed to strengthen the EU's defences against money laundering and terrorist financing, while also ensuring that the EU framework is aligned with the Financial Action Task Force's (FATF) international anti-money laundering (AML) and counter-terrorist financing (CTF) standards. Key modifications included:

- Emphasis on ultimate beneficial ownership and enhanced customer due diligence
- Expanded definition of a politically exposed person (PEPs) to domestic PEPs
- Cash payment threshold lowered to €10,000 (US$11,250)
- Expanded to include the entire gambling sector beyond just casinos
- Enhanced risk-based approach, requiring evidence-based measures

d. **Proposal by the European Commission for a Regulation on Markets in Crypto-assets**, and amending Directive (EU) 2019/1937[28]

This proposal is part of the Digital Finance package, a package of measures to further enable and support the potential of digital finance in terms of innovation and competition while mitigating the risks. It is in line with the Commission priorities to make Europe fit for the digital age and to build a future-ready economy that works for the people. The digital finance package includes a new Strategy on digital finance for the EU financial 1 sector with the aim to ensure that the EU embraces the digital revolution and drives it with innovative European firms in the lead, making the benefits of digital finance available to European consumers and businesses. In addition to this proposal, the package also includes a proposal for a pilot regime on distributed ledger technology (DLT) market infrastructures 2, a proposal for digital operational resilience 3, and a proposal to clarify or amend certain related EU financial services rules 4.

One of the strategy's identified priority areas is ensuring that the EU financial services regulatory framework is innovation-friendly and does not pose obstacles to the application of new technologies. This proposal, together with the proposal on a DLT pilot regime, represents the first concrete action within this area.

Crypto-assets are one of the major applications of blockchain technology in finance. Since the publication of the Commission's Fintech Action plan 5, in March 2018, the Commission has been examining the opportunities and challenges raised by crypto-assets. Following a big surge in the market capitalisation of crypto-assets during 2017, in December 2017, Executive Vice-President Dombrovskis, in a letter addressed to the European Banking Authority (EBA) and the European

[28] The full text is available at: https://eur-lex.europa.eu/legal-content/EN/TXT/?uri=CELEX%3A52020PC0593

Securities and Markets Authority (ESMA), urged them to reiterate their warnings to investors. In the 2018 FinTech Action plan, the Commission mandated the EBA and ESMA to assess the applicability and suitability of the existing EU financial services regulatory framework to crypto-assets. The advice 6, issued in January 2019, argued that while some crypto-assets could fall within the scope of EU legislation, effectively applying it to these assets is not always straightforward. Moreover, the advice noted that provisions in existing EU legislation may inhibit the use of DLT. At the same time, the EBA and ESMA underlined that—beyond EU legislation aimed at combating money laundering and terrorism financing—most crypto-assets fall outside the scope of EU financial services legislation and therefore are not subject to provisions on consumer and investor protection and market integrity, among others, although they give rise to these risks. In addition, a number of Member States have recently legislated on issues related to crypto-assets leading to market fragmentation.

A relatively new subset of crypto-assets – the so-called 'stablecoins'—has recently emerged and attracted the attention of both the public and regulators around the world. While the crypto-asset market remains modest in size and does not currently pose a threat to financial stability 7, this may change with the advent of 'global stablecoins', which seek wider adoption by incorporating features aimed at stabilising their value and by exploiting the network effects stemming from the firms promoting these assets 8 .

Given these developments and as part of the Commission's broader digital agenda, President Ursula von der Leyen has stressed the need for "a common approach with Member States on cryptocurrencies to ensure we understand how to make the most of the opportunities they create and address the new risks they may pose" 9. While acknowledging the risks they may present, the Commission and the Council also jointly declared in December 2019 that they "are committed to put in place a framework that will harness the potential opportunities that some crypto-assets may offer" 10. More recently, the European Parliament is working on a report on digital finance, which has a particular focus on crypto assets.11

To respond to all of these issues and create an EU framework that both enables markets in crypto-assets as well as the tokenisation of traditional financial assets and wider use of DLT in financial services, this Regulation will be accompanied by other legislative proposals: the Commission is also proposing a clarification that the existing definition of 'financial instruments' - which defines the scope of the Markets in Financial Instruments Directive (MiFID II) 12 - includes financial instruments based on DLT, 13 as well as a pilot regime on DLT market infrastructures for these instruments 14. The pilot regime will allow for experimentation within a safe environment and provide evidence for possible further amendments.

This proposal, which covers crypto-assets falling outside existing EU financial services legislation, as well as e-money tokens, has four general and related objectives. The first objective is one of legal certainty. For crypto-asset markets to develop within the EU, there is a need for a sound legal framework, clearly defining the regulatory treatment of all crypto-assets that are not covered by existing financial services legislation. The second objective is to support innovation. To promote the development of crypto-assets and the wider use of DLT, it is necessary to put in place a safe and proportionate framework to support innovation and fair competition. The third objective is to instil appropriate levels of consumer and investor protection and market integrity given that crypto-assets not covered by existing financial services legislation present many of the same risks as more familiar financial instruments. The fourth objective is to ensure financial stability. Crypto-assets are continuously evolving. While some have a quite limited scope and use, others, such as the emerging category of 'stablecoins', have the potential to become widely accepted and potentially systemic. This proposal includes safeguards to address potential risks to financial stability and orderly monetary policy that could arise from 'stablecoins'. . . .

As stated by President von der Leyen in her Political Guidelines, 17 and set out in the Communication 'Shaping Europe's digital future', 18 it is crucial for Europe to reap all the benefits of the digital age and to strengthen its industrial and innovation capacity within safe and ethical boundaries. In addition, the mission letter provided to Executive Vice-President Dombrovskis calls for a common approach with Member States on cryptocurrencies to ensure Europe can make the most of the opportunities they create and address the new risks they may pose.19

This proposal is closely linked with wider Commission policies on blockchain technology, since crypto-assets, as the main application of blockchain technologies, are inextricably linked to the promotion of blockchain technology throughout Europe. This proposal supports a holistic approach to blockchain and DLT, which aims at positioning Europe at the forefront of blockchain innovation and uptake. Policy work in this area has included the creation of the European Blockchain Observatory and Forum, and the European Blockchain Partnership, which unites all Member States at political level, as well as the public-private partnerships envisaged with the International Association for Trusted Blockchain Applications.20

This proposal is also consistent with the Union policies aimed at creating a Capital Markets Union (CMU). It notably responds to the High-level Forum's final report, which stressed the underused potential of crypto-assets and called on the Commission to bring legal certainty and establish clear rules for the use of crypto-assets. 21 This proposal is consistent with the SME strategy adopted on 10 March 2020, which also highlights DLT and crypto-assets as innovations that can enable SMEs to engage directly with investors. . . .22

e. **EU Sanctions Whistleblower's Tool**[29]

EU sanctions support the objectives of the EU's common foreign and security policy, such as conflict resolution, the fight against terrorism, non-proliferation of weapons of mass destruction, and the promotion of democracy, rule of law and

[29] See: https://finance.ec.europa.eu/eu-and-world/sanctions-restrictive-measures/overview-sanctions-and-related-resources/eu-sanctions-whistleblower-tool_en and https://eusanctions.integrityline.com/frontpage

human rights. EU sanctions create legal obligations for all EU citizens, operators and business conducted within the EU.

While EU sanctions are adopted by the Council of the EU, Member States are responsible for their enforcement, including through the application of penalties in case of violations. The European Commission monitors the implementation and enforcement of EU sanctions across Member States.

Proper implementation is essential for the effectiveness of EU sanctions. Sharing first-hand information can be a powerful tool to help uncover cases of sanctions violations, including evasion and circumvention. By voluntarily providing us with information about EU sanctions violations of which you might be aware, you can help us investigate such practices and ensure sanctions compliance in the EU.

The EU Sanctions Whistleblower Tool protects your identity and allows you to contact us anonymously to report violations of EU sanctions.

15.4 Council of Europe Monitoring of National Systems by MONEYVAL[30]

The Committee of Experts on the Evaluation of Anti-Money Laundering Measures and the Financing of Terrorism - MONEYVAL is a permanent monitoring body of the Council of Europe entrusted with the task of assessing compliance with the principal international standards to counter money laundering and the financing of terrorism and the effectiveness of their implementation, as well as with the task of making recommendations to national authorities in respect of necessary improvements to their systems. Through a dynamic process of mutual evaluations, peer review and regular follow-up of its reports, MONEYVAL aims to improve the capacities of national authorities to fight money laundering and the financing of terrorism more effectively.

MONEYVAL (formerly PC-R-EV) was established in 1997... At their meeting on 13 October 2010, the Committee of Ministers adopted the Resolution CM/Res (2010)12 on the Statute of the Committee of Experts on the Evaluation of Anti-Money Laundering Measures and the Financing of Terrorism (MONEYVAL). The statute elevates MONEYVAL as from 1 January 2011 to an independent monitoring mechanism within the Council of Europe answerable directly to the Committee of Ministers. MONEYVAL Statute was further amended in 2013 by the Resolution CM/Res(2013)13 and in 2017 by the Resolution CM/Res(2017)19. . .

[30] https://www.coe.int/en/web/moneyval

15.5 Australia

i) The Battle against Money Laundering[31]

The *Anti-Money Laundering and Counter-Terrorism Financing Act 2006* (AML/CTF Act), and the Anti-Money Laundering and Counter-Terrorism Financing Rules (AML/CTF Rules) aim to prevent money laundering and the financing of terrorism by imposing a number of obligations on the financial sector, gambling sector, remittance (money transfer) services, bullion dealers and other professionals or businesses (known as 'reporting entities') that provide particular services (known as 'designated services'). These obligations include collecting and verifying certain 'know your customer' (KYC) information about a customer's identity when providing those services.

Businesses that are required to comply with the AML/CTF Act are also required to comply with the *Privacy Act 1988* when handling personal information collected for the purposes of compliance with their AML/CTF Act obligations.

The Australian Transaction Reports and Analysis Centre (AUSTRAC) is the Australian Government agency responsible for ensuring compliance with the AML/CTF Act.

ii) AUSTRAC

From their website[32]: AUSTRAC performs a dual role as Australia's anti-money laundering and counter-terrorism financing (AML/CTF) regulator and financial intelligence unit. This dual role helps to build resilience in the financial system and enables AUSTRAC to use financial intelligence and regulation to disrupt money laundering, terrorism financing and other serious crime.

As Australia's AML/CTF regulator, we regulate more than 17,000 businesses that provide financial, gambling, bullion, remittance and digital currency exchange services. We ensure regulated businesses comply with their obligations to have systems and controls in place to manage their risks and protect them and the community from criminal abuse.

As a financial intelligence unit, we collect and analyse financial reports and information to generate financial intelligence that contributes to law enforcement and national security investigations. Our specialist analysts generate targeted, actionable intelligence and work closely with industry, government and law enforcement partners to deliver tangible investigative and operational outcomes…

New and emerging technologies are changing the way financial services are delivered. As criminals become more sophisticated and develop new ways to exploit vulnerabilities in the Australian financial system, we will continue to evolve how we

---

[31] https://www.oaic.gov.au/privacy/privacy-legislation/related-legislation/anti-money-laundering#:~:text=The%20Anti%2DMoney%20Laundering%20and,sector%2C%20gambling%20sector%2C%20remittance%20(

[32] https://www.austrac.gov.au/about-us/what-we-do

work with industry and our partners. Key to this is our highly collaborative approach and investment in our specialist workforce.

AUSTRAC also supported the ASEAN-Australia 32 hour Codeathon to develop innovative digital solutions to combat terrorism financing and cyber security risks.[33]

iii) **Department of Foreign Affairs and Trade**

The department notes: Australia's international counter-terrorism efforts are focused on law enforcement, intelligence, border and transport security, diplomacy, defence, terrorist financing, building counter-terrorism capacity in the region and countering violent extremism.[34]

Also that:[35] Australia has enacted legislation to ensure it meets its international obligations under United Nations Security Council Resolutions 1267 (and successor resolutions) and 1373 to freeze the assets of terrorists. The Government has passed laws to prohibit a person who is holding assets that are owned or controlled by a designated terrorist individual or entity from using or dealing with those assets (in other words, the person holding those assets must freeze them) and to prohibit any person from making any assets available to designated terrorist individuals or entities. The Department of Foreign Affairs and Trade maintains a Consolidated List of all individuals and entities to which this terrorist asset freezing regime applies. For additional information on Australia's international obligations, please see: Australia's terrorist asset freezing regime

The Department of Foreign Affairs and Trade maintains close contacts with Australia's financial sector to ensure asset freezing arrangements take account of the sector's legitimate interests. Australian businesses, in particular exporters, should also be aware of their responsibility to ensure that they do not do business with an individual or entity listed on the Consolidated List.

In addition to the Consolidated List, the Australian Government also maintains information about groups that are proscribed as terrorist organisations under the Australian Criminal Code.

iv) **Digital Currency**

As elsewhere, the development and use of a digital currency would change how people use and think about money in Australia. For example, decentralised digital currencies, like Bitcoin (BTC) and Ethereum(ETH) that only exist in electronically, have received worldwide interest, leading central banks in a number of countries (according to the IMF, more than 100) to explore how central bank digital currencies

[33] https://www.austrac.gov.au/news-and-media/media-release/minister-law-enforcement-and-cyber-security-media-release-asean-australias-most-innovative-solutions-combat-cybercrime

[34] https://www.dfat.gov.au/international-relations/security/counter-terrorism/Pages/counter-terrorism

[35] https://www.dfat.gov.au/international-relations/security/counter-terrorism/Pages/dealings-with-terrorists-information-for-australians-and-australian-businesses

(CBDCs) could work.[36] A CBDC is a digital currency that would be issued and overseen by the country's central bank, as if Bitcoin were managed by the Reserve Bank of Australia (RBA) and had the full backing of the Australian government. This is something that is being explored in Australia.

v) **Cryptocurrency regulation**

There has been growth in innovative financial services as a result of Australia's approach to blockchain and cryptocurrency, although progress with policy and legislation has been slower. Digital currencies are included in Australia's anti-money laundering and counter-terrorism financing (AML/CTF) regime with the increased recognition of the associated risks of digital currencies.[37]

In 2021, Australia's Securities and Investments Commission (ASIC), the financial services regulator, clarified its guidance on crypto assets that form part of underlying assets of exchange-traded products and other investment products.[38]

Also, digital currency exchange (DCE) providers have to register with the Australian Transaction Reports and Analysis Centre (AUSTRAC) as a reporting entity under Australia's AML/CTF framework. Registered exchanges should undertake KYC to verify the identity of customers, in addition to regular reporting obligations like annual compliance reporting and the requirement to monitor and report suspicious and large transactions.

Cybersecurity is a very important issue that accompanies the rise of interest in virtual assets in Australia. ASIC have stated that the enhancement of cyber resilience is a key priority in the light of recent high-profile cyber attacks on Australian and international businesses.[39]

In terms of border restrictions, there are no restrictions or requirements to declare cryptocurrency holdings when entering or leaving Australia, although Australia's Anti-Money Laundering and Counter-Terrorism Financing Act 2006 requires both individuals and businesses to report when physical currency of more than A$10, 000 (or the equivalent in foreign currency) is brought in or taken out of the country. The virtual nature of cryptocurrency means it is not captured by current declaration

[36] See note entitled: Central Bank Digital Currency: The Future Of Your Money by David Rodeck, Michael Adams and Patrick McGimpsey (July 28, 2023) at: https://www.forbes.com/advisor/au/investing/cryptocurrency/digital-currency/

[37] For more detail, see note dated November 6, 2023 published by Gilbert & Tobin entitled "Global Legal Insights: Blockchain & Cryptocurrency Regulation 2024" by Peter Reeves and Emily Shen at: https://www.gtlaw.com.au/knowledge/global-legal-insights-blockchain-cryptocurrency-regulation#:~:text=The%20sale%20of%20cryptocurrency%20and,existing%20financial%20services%20regulatory%20regime

[38] This is set out in ASIC Information Sheet 230: https://asic.gov.au/regulatory-resources/markets/market-supervision/exchange-traded-products-admission-guidelines/. This ASIC Sheet is in addition to setting out the regulatory status of certain crypto assets in Information Sheet 225: https://asic.gov.au/regulatory-resources/digital-transformation/crypto-assets/

[39] See https://asic.gov.au/regulatory-resources/find-a-document/reports/rep-716-cyber-resilience-of-firms-in-australia-s-financial-markets-2020-21/ and https://download.asic.gov.au/media/fmfdhegw/rep716-published-6-december-2021.pdf

obligations under the AML/CTF Act. Although the Act was amended to address aspects of cryptocurrency transfer in 2017, border restrictions were unchanged.

15.6 Singapore

i. **Extension of Money Laundering rules to virtual assets**

As noted above, FATF extended its anti-money laundering and counter-terrorist financing (AML/CFT) measures to virtual assets (VA) and virtual asset service providers (VASPs). FATF Recommendation 16 (also known as the Travel Rule) requires that VASPs obtain and disclose details pertaining to the sender and recipient of a virtual asset transfer to counterpart VASPs or financial institutions, either during the transaction or prior to it.[40]

The financial regulatory body, the Monetary Authority of Singapore (MAS), monitors risks associated with crypto-related transactions.[41] In particular, MAS's Travel Rule regulations (PSN02 on AML/CFT, para 13) require additional counter-party information for deposits or withdrawals.[42]

ii. **MAS: Use of Digital Money in Singapore**[43]

The MAS unveiled ... three initiatives to ensure the safe and innovative use of digital money in Singapore, namely:

---

[40] See also the note at: https://help.coinbase.com/en/exchange/managing-my-account/travel-rule

[41] See article by Murtuza Merchant entitled: "An overview of the cryptocurrency regulations in Singapore and Thailand" at: https://cointelegraph.com/learn/an-overview-of-the-cryptocurrency-regulations-in-singapore-and-thailand which notes that Singapore has "a balanced regulatory and legal framework for cryptocurrencies and entities dealing with them" and that "MAS introduced the Payment Services Act (PSA) in January 2020 as an overarching regulatory structure for traditional and cryptocurrency exchanges ... (which) brought all payment-related services under a single legislation and detailed license and money laundering compliance requirements for cryptocurrency business operators". It also notes that the PSA refers to digital currencies as digital payments tokens (DPTs), with Bitcoin and Ether recognized as cryptocurrencies by the MAS, making "approved cryptocurrencies legal assets in Singapore, allowing them to be treated similarly to other asset classes."

[42] Merchant's article notes that the MAS issued Notice PSN02 (or Crypto Travel Rule) that detailed Anti-Money Laundering (AML) and Combating the Financing of Terrorism (CFT) guidelines for DPT service providers and that "(t)his notice (and subsequent amendments) have necessitated that DPT service providers perform customer due diligence, report suspicious customer transactions, and have a detailed transactions monitoring process for signs of misuse ... Singapore's detailed cryptocurrency regulations are often used to draft cryptocurrency-related contracts across the globe, largely due to advanced dispute resolution clauses and clarity of the wording of the law. In addition to the PSA and SFA, the Singapore parliament passed the Financial Services and Markets Bill 2022 (FSM Bill) in April 2022 with the intent of enhancing the MAS' powers and controls over the country's financial sector."

[43] Press release dated 16 November 2023: https://www.mas.gov.sg/news/media-releases/2023/mas-lays-foundation-for-safe-and-innovative-use-of-digital-money-in-singapore

- a blueprint outlining the infrastructure required for a digital Singapore dollar;
- expanding digital money trials; and
- a plan to issue a "live" central bank digital currency (CBDC) for wholesale settlement.

The three forms of digital money that MAS is promoting are wholesale CBDCs, tokenised bank liabilities, and regulated stablecoins[1].

15.7 Generally

A recent article entitled "22 Crypto-Friendly Countries in 2023: Regulations, Taxes, and Adoption" by Anndy Lian[44] lists 22 of the most crypto-friendly countries in 2023 (based on their regulatory environment, taxation, and adoption), including 11 from Europe (Switzerland, Malta, Estonia, Lithuania, Portugal, Germany, Slovenia, Netherlands, Georgia, Luxembourg and Cyprus) and 7 from Asia (Singapore, Japan, South Korea, Indonesia, Taiwan, Philippines and Hong Kong):

1. **Switzerland** Switzerland is a global leader in finance and innovation, and it has also become a hub for blockchain and crypto companies. The Swiss city of Zug, nicknamed "Crypto Valley", hosts many prominent crypto firms, such as **Ethereum** Foundation, **Cardano** Foundation, Tezos Foundation, and more. Switzerland has a favorable regulatory environment for cryptocurrencies, with clear and supportive guidelines for initial coin offerings (ICOs) and token classifications. The country also offers low or no taxes on crypto profits for individuals and businesses.
2. **Malta** Malta is another small European nation that has earned the reputation of being a "Blockchain Island". The island nation has attracted some of the biggest names in the crypto industry, such as Binance, OKX, BitBay, and more, due to its progressive and comprehensive crypto regulations. Malta has enacted three laws that provide legal certainty and protection for crypto businesses and investors: the Virtual Financial Assets Act, the Innovative Technology Arrangements and Services Act, and the Malta Digital Innovation Authority Act. Malta also does not impose any capital gains tax on crypto transactions.
3. **Estonia** Estonia is a Baltic country that has embraced technology and innovation. The country is known for its e-government services, such as e-residency, e-voting, e-health, and more. Estonia is also applying its digital-first approach to the cryptocurrency sector, by offering a licensing system for crypto exchanges and wallet service providers. Estonia has a low corporate tax rate of 20%, which

[44] Lian's article is dated 3 October 2023 and is at: https://www.linkedin.com/pulse/22-crypto-friendly-countries-2023-regulations-taxes-adoption-lian#:~:text=4.,supportive%20and%20pragmatic%20regulatory%20framework

is only payable on distributed profits. Additionally, Estonia does not levy any capital gains tax on the sale of digital assets.

4. **Singapore** Singapore is a global financial center and a leading fintech hub in Asia. The city-state has also become a hotspot for crypto businesses and investors, due to its supportive and pragmatic regulatory framework. Singapore has introduced the Payment Services Act, which regulates crypto service providers under the supervision of the Monetary Authority of Singapore (MAS). The act also provides a clear distinction between payment tokens (such as **Bitcoin**), utility tokens (such as Ether), and security tokens (such as tokenized shares). Singapore also does not tax crypto profits for individuals, unless they are derived from trading activities.
5. **Japan** Japan is one of the most advanced and mature markets for cryptocurrencies in the world. The country has recognized Bitcoin as a legal form of payment since 2017, and has implemented strict but clear regulations for crypto exchanges under the Financial Services Agency (FSA). Japan has also established a self-regulatory body called the Japan Virtual Currency Exchange Association (JVCEA), which sets standards and best practices for the industry. Japan imposes income tax on crypto profits for individuals, ranging from 15% to 55%, depending on the amount.
6. **Canada** Canada is another North American country that has a friendly attitude towards cryptocurrencies. The country has a well-developed crypto ecosystem, with many local exchanges, start-ups, and communities. Canada has also introduced regulations for crypto businesses under the Proceeds of Crime (Money Laundering) and Terrorist Financing Act (PCMLTFA), which requires them to register with the Financial Transactions and Reports Analysis Centre of Canada (FINTRAC) and comply with anti-money laundering (AML) and counter-terrorism financing (CTF) rules. Canada taxes crypto profits as either income or capital gains, depending on the nature and frequency of the transactions.
7. **South Korea** South Korea is one of the most active and enthusiastic countries for cryptocurrency trading and adoption in the world. The country has a large number of crypto exchanges, users, and merchants that accept digital currencies as payment. South Korea has also legalized and regulated crypto activities under the Act on Reporting and Use of Specific Financial Transaction Information, which requires crypto service providers to register with the Financial Services Commission (FSC) and partner with local banks to offer real-name accounts to their customers. South Korea taxes crypto profits as income at a flat rate of 20%.
8. **Lithuania** Lithuania is a small Baltic country that has emerged as a leading fintech hub in Europe. The country has attracted many foreign crypto companies, such as Revolut, Wirex, Bitstamp, and more, due to its favorable regulatory environment and incentives. Lithuania has issued guidelines for ICOs and token classifications under the Bank of Lithuania (BoL), which oversees the crypto sector. The country also offers tax exemptions for crypto transactions that do not involve fiat currencies.
9. **Portugal** Portugal is another European country that has a positive stance on cryptocurrencies. The country has created a welcoming environment for crypto

users and investors, by exempting them from paying any taxes on crypto profits. Portugal's tax authority, the Autoridade Tributária e Aduaneira (AT), has clarified that crypto transactions are not subject to value-added tax (VAT) or personal income tax. However, crypto businesses are still subject to corporate tax and VAT on their services.

10. **The Bahamas** The Bahamas is a Caribbean island nation that has become a pioneer in launching its own central bank digital currency (CBDC), called the Sand Dollar. The Sand Dollar is a digital version of the Bahamian dollar, which can be used for peer-to-peer transactions, online payments, and cross-border remittances. The Bahamas has also introduced regulations for crypto service providers under the Payment Systems and Services Act, which requires them to obtain a license from the Central Bank of The Bahamas (CBOB) and comply with AML and CTF rules. The Bahamas does not impose any income tax or capital gains tax on individuals or businesses.
11. **Germany** Germany is one of the largest and most influential economies in Europe and the world. The country has also shown a progressive and supportive attitude towards cryptocurrencies and blockchain technology. Germany has recognized Bitcoin as a legal form of payment since 2013, and has regulated crypto service providers under the Banking Act, which requires them to obtain a license from the Federal Financial Supervisory Authority (BaFin) and comply with AML and CTF rules. Germany also offers a tax exemption for crypto transactions that are held for more than one year.
12. **Slovenia** Slovenia is a small Central European country that has a vibrant and innovative crypto community. The country hosts many crypto events, projects, and initiatives, such as the Bitcoin City, which is a shopping mall that accepts Bitcoin as payment. Slovenia has also adopted a friendly and flexible regulatory approach for cryptocurrencies, by allowing them to operate without any specific licenses or permits. However, crypto profits are subject to income tax or capital gains tax, depending on the type and frequency of the transactions.
13. **Netherlands** The Netherlands is another European country that has a strong and active crypto scene. The country has many crypto exchanges, start-ups, and organizations, such as Bitonic, BitPay, Bitfury, and the Bitcoin Foundation. The Netherlands has also adopted a self-regulatory model for crypto service providers, by requiring them to register with the Dutch Central Bank (DNB) and adhere to AML and CTF rules. The Netherlands does not tax crypto profits for individuals, unless they are derived from trading activities.
14. **Georgia** Georgia is a former Soviet republic that has become one of the leading countries in cryptocurrency mining in the world. The country has abundant and cheap electricity, which attracts many local and foreign miners to set up their operations there. Georgia has also introduced favorable regulations for crypto businesses, by exempting them from paying any taxes on their income or profits. However, individuals are still subject to income tax on their crypto earnings.
15. **Luxembourg** Luxembourg is a small landlocked country in Western Europe that has a high standard of living and a strong financial sector. The country has also been supportive of cryptocurrencies and blockchain technology, by

granting legal status to Bitcoin as a form of payment in 2016, and by regulating crypto service providers under the Law on Payment Services Providers, which requires them to obtain a license from the Commission de Surveillance du Secteur Financier (CSSF) and comply with AML and CTF rules. Luxembourg also taxes crypto profits as income at progressive rates.

16. **Argentina** Argentina is a South American country that has experienced economic instability and currency devaluation for many years. As a result, many Argentinians have turned to cryptocurrencies as a hedge against inflation and capital controls. Argentina has also become a hotspot for crypto innovation and adoption, with many local exchanges, start-ups, and projects, such as Ripio, Bitso, RSK, Decentraland, and more. Argentina does not have any specific regulations for cryptocurrencies, but they are subject to income tax or capital gains tax depending on the nature of the transactions.
17. **Cyprus** Cyprus is an island nation in the Mediterranean Sea that has a history of financial crises and bailouts. The country has also been one of the early adopters of cryptocurrencies in Europe, with many local businesses accepting Bitcoin as payment since 2013. Cyprus has also established itself as a hub for blockchain education and research, by hosting the University of Nicosia (UNIC), which offers the world's first master's degree in digital currency. Cyprus does not have any specific regulations for cryptocurrencies, but they are subject to income tax or capital gains tax depending on the type of transaction.
18. **Taiwan** Taiwan is another crypto-friendly country in Asia, as it has a progressive and open-minded approach to crypto regulation and innovation. Taiwan does not impose any specific taxes or restrictions on crypto transactions, making it a favorable environment for traders and investors. Crypto businesses are also allowed to operate freely in Taiwan, as long as they comply with existing laws on AML/CTF and consumer protection. Taiwan is also home to many crypto influencers, such as Justin Sun of Tron, Changpeng Zhao of Binance and Arthur Hayes of BitMEX, as well as projects such as IOTA, VeChain and Kusama.
19. **Indonesia** Indonesia is the largest economy and the most populous country in Southeast Asia, with more than 270 million people. Indonesia has a young and tech-savvy population, who are increasingly adopting crypto as a way to access the global digital economy. Indonesia has legalized crypto as a commodity that can be traded on licensed platforms, but has banned its use as a payment method. Indonesia also imposes a 10% VAT on crypto transactions, which could deter some users and investors.
20. **Philippines** The Philippines is an archipelagic country with more than 7000 islands and 110 million people. The Philippines has a large remittance market, as many of its citizens work overseas and send money back home. Crypto offers a cheaper and faster way to transfer money across borders, which has attracted many Filipinos to use it. The Philippines has a progressive and pragmatic approach to crypto regulation, allowing its use as a payment method and issuing licenses to crypto exchanges and service providers. The Philippines also has a vibrant crypto community, with many events, meetups and initiatives taking place there.

21. **Hong Kong** Hong Kong is a major financial hub and a gateway to mainland China. The city has a relatively liberal and open attitude towards crypto, allowing its residents to freely trade and use digital assets without imposing taxes or restrictions. Hong Kong also has a thriving crypto scene, with many exchanges, funds, media outlets and events based there. The Hong Kong Monetary Authority (HKMA) is currently approaching the crypto industry from three dimensions: stablecoins that can be used for payments, investor protection, and how authorized institutions deal with digital assets. The HKMA plans to adopt a so-called "same risk, same regulation" approach to crypto.[45]
22. **Turkey** Turkey is another country that has shown a high level of interest and adoption of crypto in recent years. Turkey has one of the highest rates of inflation in the world, which has eroded the value and trust in its national currency, the lira. As a result, many Turks have turned to crypto as an alternative store of value and medium of exchange. Turkey does not have any specific laws or regulations for crypto, but treats it as an asset that is subject to capital gains tax. Turkey also has a growing number of crypto service providers and platforms that cater to its local market.

Summing up In conclusion, the cryptocurrency landscape in 2023 is a dynamic and rapidly evolving space, with various countries positioning themselves as crypto-friendly destinations. From the innovative and regulation-savvy Switzerland to the progressive Malta and Estonia, and the bustling crypto scenes in Singapore, Japan, Canada, and South Korea, the global crypto map is expanding.

Each of these 22 crypto-friendly countries offers unique advantages for cryptocurrency enthusiasts, investors, and businesses. Whether it's clear regulatory frameworks, low taxation on crypto profits, or a supportive ecosystem for blockchain technology, these nations are paving the way for the future of finance.

As the world continues to adapt to the ever-changing crypto landscape, it's essential for individuals and businesses to stay informed about the latest developments and opportunities in these crypto-friendly jurisdictions. The choices made today can significantly impact the future of digital assets and financial innovation worldwide.

[45] Note that Lian also has concerns. While he includes Hong Kong in this list of favourable jurisdictions, he separately says that HK is a jurisdiction prone to fraud. See: https://anndy.com/op-ed/is-hong-kongs-reputation-at-the-mercy-of-crypto-scammers/

Part IV
Conclusion

Chapter 16
Conclusion

Currently, the processes that are used by financial and other businesses to try to combat money laundering and terrorist financing are significant. They may have been boosted in Europe, America and elsewhere in response to recent events but, given the amount of money involved, seem not to be particularly effective. This may be through a combination of:

(i) criminals constantly looking for a gap and then exploiting it (which can take regulators a while to recognise and propose a solution);
(ii) a lack of appreciation that other financial tools (such as venture capital and equity investment funds) can also be used to launder the funds;
(iii) national governments and regulators have their own (domestic) issues/interests and their solutions may not be internationally consistent; and
(iv) complacent business leaders not realising the full implications of ethical laxity.

This raises a number of questions such as:

- What could we do differently?
- How can we make the system and processes more effective and/or efficient?
- What other alternative approaches, systems or processes could be used?
- Indeed, whilst the current situation could have been much worse without any of the controls and processes we currently use, ultimately is the use of resources efficient and effective?

As noted by Tim Parkman:[1]

> . . . we need to look . . . to see how we can make a better impact *(to combat money laundering and terrorist financing).* As ever, technology offers a chance of making a real difference and the developments in the application of Artificial Intelligence (AI), machine-learning and blockchain . . . can perhaps help to turn

[1] Tim Parkman in Mastering Anti-Money Laundering and Counter-Terrorist Financing (second edition).

D. Smith, *Money Laundering, Terrorist Financing and Virtual Assets*, Contributions to Finance and Accounting, https://doi.org/10.1007/978-3-031-59842-5_16

> the tide in a more positive direction. But it is unlikely to provide the entire answer and anyone thinking that we will ever be able to let machines get on with fighting financial crime ... is likely to be disappointed.

The increasing use of AI and other technology is one option.[2] However, current money laundering laws may only become effective if law enforcement investigate and prosecute sufficient breaches and violations for there to be a change in the perception of bankers (and their corporations) of a real risk of prosecution.[3] However, the few convictions for Danske Bank's failings[4] and the acquittal of former Swedbank CEO Birgitte Bonneson[5] for the handling of the bank's anti-money laundering protocols in Estonia demonstrate how difficult it can be to hold senior management to account to a criminal standard for compliance-related failures.[6]

Decentralised digital currencies, like Bitcoin and Ethereum, have resulted in significant interest across the globe from investors, institutions, regulators and governments, leading in particular to central banks in many countries exploring how central bank digital currencies (CBDCs) might work. However, so far as virtual assets and cryptocurrencies are concerned, the rapid technological developments need to be monitored and considered carefully, as the landscape is ever-changing, making it essential for individuals and businesses to be well informed about and understand the latest developments, so they can use new opportunities where appropriate, and for law enforcement and regulators to seek to prevent misuse of them. Unfortunately, criminals adapt to new technology faster than the authorities, a recent report says.[7]

A general rise in cybercrime, especially related to hacking, ransomware and the spreading of disinformation, has caused global concern. Consequently, financial

[2] Rick Messick in the Global Anticorruption Blog on January 19, 2024 wrote an article entitled: Breakthrough in the Use of Artificial Intelligence to Fight Corruption, at: https://globalanticorruptionblog.com/2024/01/19/breakthrough-in-the-use-of-artificial-intelligence-to-fight-corruption/

[3] See Allison Haugen's article in International Affairs Review: https://www.iar-gwu.org/blog/2015/05/19/more-than-sanctions-criminally-prosecute-big-banks-for-money-laundering

[4] See LuxTimes article entitled Danish court jails two people for laundering $4.2bn—case connected to one of Europe's biggest money laundering scams, linked to Danske Bank in Estonia at: https://www.luxtimes.lu/businessandfinance/danish-court-jails-two-people-for-laundering-4.2bn/7976302.html

[5] See article entitled Swedbank Ex-CEO Cleared of Money-Laundering Cover-Up published by OCCRP at: https://www.occrp.org/en/daily/17272-swedbank-ex-ceo-cleared-of-money-laundering-cover-up

[6] See also the article by Koos Couvée dated January 25, 2023 at: https://www.moneylaundering.com/news/former-swedbank-chief-acquitted-over-aml-disclosures/

[7] The article by Eve Sampson dated September 26, 2023 says that a new Europol report has found that 70% of criminal enterprises are utilizing money laundering techniques to hide wealth and garner assets, outpacing authorities who are struggling to uncover their crimes. The full article is at: https://www.icij.org/investigations/fincen-files/money-laundering-criminals-are-adapting-to-new-technology-faster-than-authorities-can-keep-up-eu-report-says/

crime compliance has had to adapt, in particular to the development and use of virtual assets, digital currency and dark web marketplaces by criminals.

In recent times the geopolitical conflicts involving Ukraine-Russia and Israel-Palestine have made financial crime compliance even more important; there is concern about the use of money laundering and other financial crimes to fund them.[8] However one of the problems that it is particularly difficult to resolve is when precisely a supporter's financial donations to assist a political campaign (e.g. by the separatist Basques in Spain or Republicans in Northern Ireland) becomes more than just sympathy for a political cause and extends to the intent to assist financing of a specific, terrorist operation. Similar concerns could apply also for social care undertaken in Palestine and elsewhere.

Also, questions frequently arise in economic crime cases about how to make auditors and their regular reviews of and for listed companies: (i) stronger and more efficient; and (ii) more independent (and therefore not as favorable to or overlooking problems caused by the company that will paying the auditor's bill).[9]

The use of big data can assist decision-making. In addition, greater real-time monitoring of transactions can reduce the 'fraud window' but with increasing focus on the environment, a company's Environmental Social and Governance (ESG) will become increasingly valuable, with the attendant risk of green-washing and that cutting corners can lead to misrepresentative or fraudulent statements replacing fact.

In any event, positive developments like improved regulation can only be effective with better international cooperation, primarily due to (i) the cross-border nature of virtual assets (VA) and their service providers (VASP) and (ii) importance of national regulators and law enforcement.[10]

Indeed, jurisdictions will need to consider whether to:

- Clearly identify supervisor(s) of VASPs for AML/CFT purposes and publish a list of VASPs licensed or regulated in their jurisdiction;
- Share information on risk to support VA/VASP risk assessments (both jurisdiction and supervisory).
- Share information to support fit and proper assessments (beneficial owner information, background/criminal history, supervisory findings).
- Share information to support market entry/registration applications (LEA, intelligence, supervisory).
- Share information on blockchain surveillance and analytical tools.

---

[8] https://www.euronews.com/business/2024/01/03/financial-crime-compliance-trends-to-watch-in-2024

[9] See for an example ENRON and Arthur Andersen: https://en.wikipedia.org/wiki/Enron_scandal or Madoff: https://en.wikipedia.org/wiki/Madoff_investment_scandal

[10] Indeed, according to Eurojust: . . . the Belgian Presidency of the Council of the European Union will put a particular focus on tackling serious organised drug-related crime [in 2024]. Special attention will be paid to the use of logistic hubs for this type of cross-border crime and, more specifically, how to combat drug trafficking via major ports: https://www.eurojust.europa.eu/news/tackling-major-organised-drug-crime-top-priority-belgian-eu-presidency

- Conduct joint supervision (notification and consultation between home and foreign supervisors in relation to entities under supervision or where a foreign VASP is conducting unregulated or illegal activity in a jurisdiction).[11]

It will become increasingly important that we can identify, recognise and act on suspicions of money laundering and that we can do so quickly given the speed of change in the virtual assets sector. Ultimately the due diligence/KYC question "why?" can be extremely helpful when used by financial entities and others to gain an understanding of a client's purpose and reason to move funds.

[11] https://www.un.org/securitycouncil/ctc/sites/www.un.org.securitycouncil.ctc/files/apg.pdf

Appendix A: Further Reading/Information

(a) **Books**

(1) Mastering Anti-Money Laundering and Counter-Terrorist Financing (second edition) by Parkman
(2) Understanding Terrorist Finance by Wittig
(3) Countering Terrorist Financing by Pieth, Thelesklaf and Ivory

(b) **Other**

1. UK NCA: https://www.nationalcrimeagency.gov.uk
   FCA: https://www.fca.org.uk
   SFO: https://www.sfo.gov.uk
2. US SEC: https://www.sec.gov
   FINCEN: https://www.fincen.gov
3. EU: https://finance.ec.europa.eu/financial-crime/eu-context-anti-money-laundering-and-countering-financing-terrorism_en#:~:text=The%20joint%20committee%20of%20the,to%20understand%20the%20regulatory%20expectations.&text=The%20new%20Regulation%20on%20the,new%20EU%20authority%20(AMLA).
   Europol: https://www.europol.europa.eu
   Transparency International: https://transparency.eu
   Basel Institute on Governance: https://baselgovernance.org/about-us
4. Australia AUSTRAC: https://www.austrac.gov.au
   ASIC: https://asic.gov.au/about-asic/
5. Singapore MAS: https://www.mas.gov.sg
6. Generally: https://en.wikipedia.org/wiki/Money_laundering
   https://en.wikipedia.org/wiki/Cryptocurrency
   https://www.investopedia.com/terms/c/cryptocurrency.asp
   https://www.blockchain.com
   https://bitcoin.org/en/
   https://ethereum.org

D. Smith, *Money Laundering, Terrorist Financing and Virtual Assets*, Contributions to Finance and Accounting, https://doi.org/10.1007/978-3-031-59842-5

https://www.coinbase.com/en-gb/learn/crypto-basics/what-is-cryptocurrency
https://www.vara.ae/en/

AML Specialist training/certification, e.g. from ACAMS (https://www.acams.org/en), IMF (https://www.imf.org/en/Capacity-Development/Training/ICDTC/Courses/AMLCFTX) or ICA (https://www.int-comp.org/learn-and-develop/subject-areas/anti-money-laundering/)

Appendix B: UN Instruments

UN https://www.imolin.org/pdf/imolin/UNres03e.pdf

MONEY LAUNDERING AND THE FINANCING OF TERRORISM: THE UNITED NATIONS RESPONSE

INSTRUMENTS AGAINST MONEY LAUNDERING

- 1988 UNITED NATIONS CONVENTION AGAINST ILLICIT TRAFFIC IN NARCOTIC DRUGS AND PSYCHOTROPIC SUBSTANCES
- 2000 UNITED NATIONS CONVENTION AGAINST TRANSNATIONAL ORGANIZED CRIME
- 1988 POLITICAL DECLARATION AND ACTION PLAN AGAINST MONEY LAUNDERING
- NAPLES POLITICAL DECLARATION AND GLOBAL ACTION PLAN AGAINST ORGANIZED TRANSNATIONAL CRIME

INSTRUMENTS AGAINST THE FINANCING OF TERRORISM

- 1999 INTERNATIONAL CONVENTION FOR THE SUPPRESSION OF THE FINANCING OF TERRORISM
- RESOLUTION 1373 (2001): ADOPTED BY THE SECURITY COUNCIL AT ITS 4385TH MEETING, ON SEPTEMBER 2001
- RESOLUTION 1377 (2001): ADOPTED BY THE SECURITY COUNCIL AT ITS 4413TH MEETING, ON 12 NOVEMBER 2001

D. Smith, *Money Laundering, Terrorist Financing and Virtual Assets*, Contributions to Finance and Accounting, https://doi.org/10.1007/978-3-031-59842-5

www.ingramcontent.com/pod-product-compliance
Lightning Source LLC
Chambersburg PA
CBHW070105150926
51510CB00003B/58
* 9 7 8 3 0 3 1 5 9 8 4 1 8 *